EYEWITNESS TRAVEL
NEW ENGLAND

DK

LONDON, NEW YORK,
MELBOURNE, MUNICH AND DELHI
www.dk.com

PRODUCED BY St. Remy Media Inc.,
Montréal, Canada
PRESIDENT Pierre Léveillé
VICE PRESIDENT, FINANCE Natalie Watanabe
MANAGING EDITOR Carolyn Jackson
MANAGING ART DIRECTOR Diane Denoncourt
PRODUCTION MANAGER Michelle Turbide
DIRECTOR, BUSINESS DEVELOPMENT Christopher Jackson
EDITOR Neale McDevitt
ART DIRECTORS Michel Giguère, Anne-Marie Lemay
SENIOR RESEARCH EDITOR Heather Mills
RESEARCHERS Tal Ashkenazi, Jessica Braun, Genevieve Ring
PICTURE RESEARCHER Linda Castle
MAP COORDINATOR Peter Alec Fedun
SENIOR EDITOR, PRODUCTION Brian Parsons
INDEXER Linda Cardella Cournoyer
PREPRESS PRODUCTION Martin Francoeur, Jean Sirois
MAIN CONTRIBUTORS
Eleanor Berman, Patricia Brooks, Tom Bross, Patricia Harris, Pierre
Home-Douglas, Helga Loverseed, David Lyon
PHOTOGRAPHERS
Alan Briere, Ed Homonylo, David Lyon
ILLUSTRATORS
Gilles Beauchemin, Martin Gagnon, Vincent Gagnon, Stéphane Jorisch,
Patrick Jougla, Luc Normandin, Jean-François Vachon
MAPS
Dimension DPR

Filmwork by Colourscan, Singapore
Printed and bound by South China Printing Co. Ltd., China
First published in Great Britain in 2001
by Dorling Kindersley Limited
80 Strand, London WC2R 0RL
Reprinted with revisions 2003, 2004, 2005, 2006, 2007, 2009, 2010
Copyright 2001, 2010 © Dorling Kindersley Limited, London
A Penguin Company

A CIP CATALOGUE RECORD IS AVAILABLE FROM THE BRITISH LIBRARY
ISBN 978-1-40535-326-7

Floors are referred to throughout in accordance with American
usage; ie the "first floor" is the floor on street level

Front cover main image: Autumn foliage, Tunbridge, Vermont

MIX
From responsible
sources
FSC
www.fsc.org FSC™C018179

◁ **Permiquid Point, Maine**

CONTENTS

HOW TO USE
THIS GUIDE **6**

Sailboat off the Cape Cod coast

INTRODUCING
NEW ENGLAND

DISCOVERING NEW
ENGLAND **10**

PUTTING NEW
ENGLAND ON THE MAP
12

A PORTRAIT OF
NEW ENGLAND **14**

NEW ENGLAND
THROUGH THE YEAR **32**

THE HISTORY OF NEW
ENGLAND **36**

Vermont's dazzling fall foliage

West Quoddy Head Light, Maine

Mansion in Waterbury, Vermont

Costumed interpreter at
Plimoth Plantation,
Plymouth, Massachusetts

Mark Twain House
in Hartford,
Connecticut

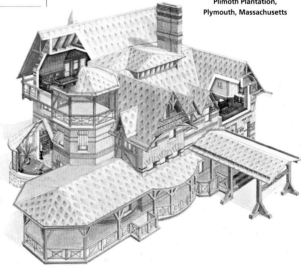

HOW TO USE THIS GUIDE

This guide helps you to get the most from your visit to New England. *Introducing New England* maps the region and sets it in its historical and cultural context. Each of the six states, along with the city of Boston, has its own chapter describing the important sights using maps, pictures, and detailed illustrations. Suggestions on restaurants, accommodations, shopping, entertainment and outdoor activities are covered in *Travelers' Needs*. The *Survival Guide* has tips on everything from changing currency in New England to getting around in Boston.

BOSTON

Boston has been divided into five sightseeing areas, each one opening with a list of the sights described. All the sights are numbered and plotted on an *Area Map*. The detailed information for each sight is presented in numerical order, making it easy to locate within the chapter.

Sights at a Glance lists the chapter's sights by category: Historic Streets and Squares; Historic Buildings, Churches, Museums, and Theaters; Waterfront Sights; Gardens and Zoos; and Parks and Cemeteries.

1 Area Map
For easy reference, the sights are numbered and located on a map. The sights are also shown on the Boston Street Finder on pages 122–7.

A locator map shows where you are in relation to other areas of the city center.

2 Street-by-Street Map
This gives a bird's-eye view of the heart of each sightseeing area.

A suggested route for a walk covers the more interesting streets in the area.

All pages relating to Boston have yellow thumb tabs.

Stars indicate the sights that no visitor should miss.

3 Detailed Information on Each Sight
All the sights in Boston are described individually. Addresses, telephone numbers, opening hours, and information on admission charges and wheelchair access are also provided. The key to all the symbols used in the information block is shown on the back flap.

1 Introduction
The landscape, history, and character of each state is described here, showing how the area has developed over the centuries and what it has to offer the visitor today.

NEW ENGLAND REGION BY REGION
In this book, New England has been divided into the six states, each of which has a separate chapter. The most interesting sights to visit have been numbered on the *Regional Map.*

Each state of New England can be quickly identified by its color coding, which is shown on the inside front cover.

2 Regional Map
This shows the road network and gives an illustrated overview of the whole state. All the sights are numbered, and there are also useful tips on getting around the state.

Story boxes explore specific subjects further.

3 Detailed Information
All the important towns and other places to visit are described individually. They are listed in order, following the numbering on the Regional Map. Within each town or city, there is detailed information on important buildings and other sights.

For all the top sights, a Visitors' Checklist provides the practical information you will need to plan your visit.

4 The Top Sights
These are given two or more pages. Historic buildings are dissected to reveal their interiors; museums and galleries have color-coded floor plans; national parks have maps showing facilities and trails.

Stars indicate the best features and works of art.

INTRODUCING
NEW ENGLAND

DISCOVERING NEW ENGLAND

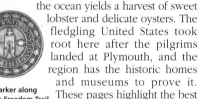

With snowy winters for skiing, temperate summers of blue skies and gentle breezes, and an autumn set ablaze by the vibrant foliage, New England is both a land for all seasons and for all senses. Rolling waves crash on its craggy northern shores or break as surf on its sandy southern beaches. The scent of pine forest permeates mountain trails, and the ocean yields a harvest of sweet lobster and delicate oysters. The fledgling United States took root here after the pilgrims landed at Plymouth, and the region has the historic homes and museums to prove it. These pages highlight the best that each region has to offer to help you make the most of your trip.

A marker along Boston's Freedom Trail

BOSTON

- **Fascinating Revolutionary history**
- **World-class culture**
- **Harvard University**

New England's largest city rings with history and teems with contemporary culture. Follow the path of Boston's patriots along the **Freedom Trail** *(see pp54–7)* that stretches from **Boston Common** *(see pp64–5)* to the waterfront, where new cafés, restaurants, and parks line the harbor.

Stop to marvel at Monet's haystacks and Van Gogh's landscapes at the **Museum of Fine Arts** *(see pp106–9)*, at the Old Masters in the **Isabella Stewart Gardner Museum** *(see p105)*, or at video installations in the **Institute of Contemporary Art** *(see p101)*. Catch a world premiere by the Boston Symphony Orchestra or a new play

in the historic halls of the **Theater District** *(see pp58–71)*.

Bostonians prize learning, and you can sample the intellectual vibe (and street musicians) of lively **Harvard Square** *(see p110)* or take a tour of **Harvard University** *(see pp112–17)*, the country's oldest university and one of its most prestigious.

MASSACHUSETTS

- **Sweeping Cape Cod beaches**
- **Opulent estates in the Berkshires**
- **Historic Salem**
- **Plymouth's Pilgrim heritage**

Summer playgrounds adorn the Bay State. In the east, the **Cape Cod National Seashore** is known for its 40-mile (64-km) stretch of beaches, lively arts scene, and delectable shellfish *(see pp154–5)*. Hop a ferry to the salty and historic islands of **Martha's Vineyard** *(see p152)* and **Nantucket** *(see p153)*. In the west, the rolling hills of the **Berkshires** *(see pp166–7)* are home to Gilded Age estates and the country's top summer arts, including Tanglewood Music Festival and Jacob's Pillow Dance Festival *(see p33)*.

The dark past of 17th-century witch trials still haunts **Salem** *(see pp136–8)*, a city also rich in literary connections and maritime history. In **Plymouth** *(see pp148–51)*, the **Plimoth Plantation** and *Mayflower II* recount the arrival in 1620 of the Pilgrim Fathers, the first English settlers in the US.

The lighthouse at Race Point on Massachusetts' Cape Cod

RHODE ISLAND

- **Revitalized Providence**
- **Nautical Newport**
- **Quaint Block Island**

The thriving capital of the country's smallest state, **Providence** *(see pp174–7)*, has reinvented itself in recent years with a riverside park that complements the historic homes and churches of Benefit Street. The city has one of the region's liveliest restaurant scenes, including the Old World Italian neighborhood of Federal Hill.

Be sure to get out on the water in **Newport** *(see pp182–7)*, famous for its racing yachts. Hop a trolley to Bellevue Avenue to tour its lavish mansions and gardens. Or enjoy both sea and mansions alike from the 3.5-mile (5.5-km) Cliff Walk.

Out at sea, **Block Island** *(see pp192–3)* beckons with long sandy beaches, comfy Victorian hotels, and a natural landscape ideal for touring by bicycle.

Elegant, historic brownstones in the center of Boston

◁ Boston Harbor circa 1750

CONNECTICUT

- Connecticut River landscapes
- Antiques-hunting in the Litchfield Hills
- Glittering casinos
- Mystic Seaport

American Impressionist painters from New York sought inspiration a century ago in the idyllic landscape of the lower Connecticut River, which feeds the interior woodlands and is ideal for canoeists. Today the region enchants bird- and wildlife-watchers and informs with the lessons of the **Connecticut River Museum** in Essex *(see p216)* and the spectacle of **Gillette Castle** *(see pp218–19)*.

New Yorkers still flock to the **Litchfield Hills** *(see pp208–9)*, in part to forage for antiques in the villages of this rolling green country-side. True riches remain a tantalizing prospect if you try your luck at the glamorous Native American casinos in the woods. **Foxwoods Resort Casino** *(see p212)* and **Mohegan Sun** are among the largest gaming operations in the country.

Let maritime history come to life at **Mystic Seaport** *(see pp214–15)* – the world's largest maritime museum – as you board the last wooden whaling vessel in the world or cruise the coastline on a coal-fueled steamship.

Typical Colonial church in Litchfield, Connecticut

Vivid fall foliage at Franconia Notch State Park, New Hampshire

VERMONT

- Green Mountain trails
- Glorious Lake Champlain
- Historic Bennington

In the **Green Mountain National Forest** *(see p244)* you can hike ridgeline trails to alpine valleys or ski down challenging pistes. At summer's end, the maples, birches, and beeches in the lower hills glow red, orange, and gold. Vermont's biggest city, **Burlington** *(see pp232–5)*, enjoys the spectacle from the shore of **Lake Champlain** *(see p236)*. After sight-seeing on a modern cruiser, visit the steam-boat in the **Shelburne Museum** *(see pp238–9)*. In **Bennington** *(see p244)*, the revolutionary era comes alive in the town's historic district.

New England Maple Syrup

NEW HAMPSHIRE

- Blazing foliage in the White Mountains
- Grand resorts
- Seafaring Portsmouth

The majestic **White Mountains** *(see p265)* are a prime fall foliage destination, whether you want to hike into the hidden recesses of **Franconia Notch State Park** *(see pp272–3)* or drive the exhilarating twists and turns of the **Kancamagus Highway** *(see p270)*, one of America's most scenic routes. New Hampshire's high country has been a prized getaway since the mid-19th century. Indulge in pampered luxury amid breathtaking views by staying in a historic mountain hotel, such as the Mt. Washington in **Bretton Woods** *(see pp267)*. Mountain streams flow to the sea in **Portsmouth**, with its bountiful local history at **Strawbery Banke** *(see pp252–5)*.

MAINE

- Lighthouses on the rocky coast
- Hip shopping in Portland
- Spectacular Acadia National Park

Maine's sweeping coast is dotted with lighthouses and punctuated by museums that recount the experience of life at sea. Learn about local shipbuilding at the **Maine Maritime Museum** in Bath *(see p285)* and marvel at the adventures of the China Trade at the **Penobscot Marine Museum** in Searsport *(see p286)*. Follow the coast from lighthouse to light-house, but be sure to stop in the state's largest city, **Portland** *(see pp280–83)*, where hip boutiques, fine restau-rants, and art galleries line the brick and stone side-walks of the Old Port.

You can detour down to **Mount Desert Island**, which is home to rugged **Acadia National Park** *(see pp288–9)* where there are panoramic views atop Cadillac Mountain. From the bustling waterfront at **Bar Harbor** *(see p290)* there are whale-watching and sightseeing schooner cruises.

Putting New England on the Map

Northern New England shows the region at its most
rural. Vermont is famous for its rolling farmland, and
New Hampshire for its White Mountains and the
spectacular passes between the peaks. Sparsely populated Maine is covered in dense forest and an intricate
network of lakes, streams, and rivers, with a rugged
coastline. Southern New England has traditionally been
the industrial and cultural hub of the region, with Boston
its capital. Massachusetts is the historical center of the
New England colonies. Tiny Rhode Island contains
some of New England's most extravagant mansions, and
Connecticut's proximity to New York City has graced
many of its towns and cities with a cosmopolitan flavor.

KEY

═══ Interstate

═══ Major road

═══ Minor road

─── Railroad

✈ International airport

KEY TO COLOR CODING

New England

▮ Vermont

▮ New Hampshire

▯ Maine

▯ Massachussetts

▯ Connecticut

▮ Rhode Island

▯ Boston

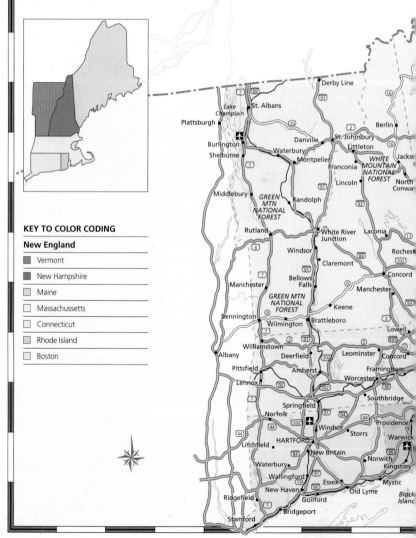

For additional map symbols *see back flap*

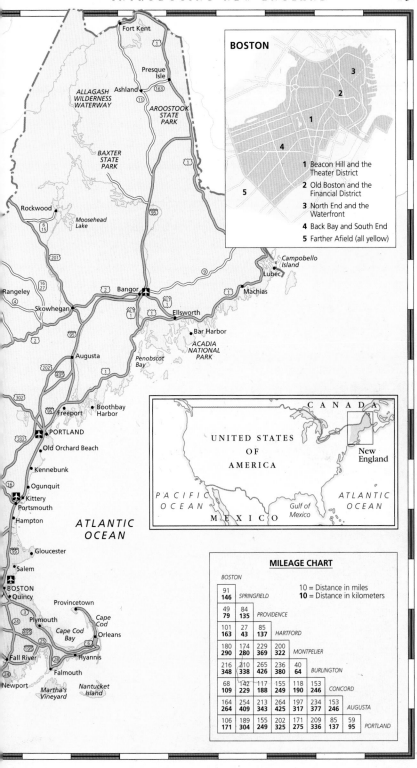

BOSTON

3

2

1

4

5

1 Beacon Hill and the Theater District

2 Old Boston and the Financial District

3 North End and the Waterfront

4 Back Bay and South End

5 Farther Afield (all yellow)

Fort Kent

Presque Isle

Ashland

ALLAGASH WILDERNESS WATERWAY

AROOSTOOK STATE PARK

BAXTER STATE PARK

Rockwood

Moosehead Lake

Campobello Island

Lubec

Rangeley

Bangor

Machias

Skowhegan

Ellsworth

Augusta

Bar Harbor

ACADIA NATIONAL PARK

Penobscot Bay

Freeport

Boothbay Harbor

PORTLAND

Old Orchard Beach

Kennebunk

Ogunquit

Kittery

Portsmouth

Hampton

ATLANTIC OCEAN

Gloucester

Salem

BOSTON

Quincy

Provincetown

Plymouth

Cape Cod

Cape Cod Bay

Orleans

Fall River

Hyannis

Falmouth

Newport

Martha's Vineyard

Nantucket Island

CANADA

UNITED STATES OF AMERICA

New England

PACIFIC OCEAN

ATLANTIC OCEAN

Gulf of Mexico

MEXICO

MILEAGE CHART

BOSTON								
91 / **146**	SPRINGFIELD							
49 / **79**	84 / **135**	PROVIDENCE						
101 / **163**	27 / **43**	85 / **137**	HARTFORD					
180 / **290**	174 / **280**	229 / **369**	200 / **322**	MONTPELIER				
216 / **348**	210 / **338**	265 / **426**	236 / **380**	40 / **64**	BURLINGTON			
68 / **109**	142 / **229**	117 / **188**	155 / **249**	118 / **190**	153 / **246**	CONCORD		
164 / **264**	254 / **409**	213 / **343**	264 / **425**	197 / **317**	234 / **377**	153 / **246**	AUGUSTA	
106 / **171**	189 / **304**	155 / **249**	202 / **325**	171 / **275**	209 / **336**	85 / **137**	59 / **95**	PORTLAND

10 = Distance in miles
10 = Distance in kilometers

A PORTRAIT OF NEW ENGLAND

For many people, New England is white-steepled churches, craggy coastlines, and immaculate village greens. However, the region is also home to the opulence of Newport, Rhode Island, the beautiful suburban communities of Connecticut, and the self-assured sophistication of Boston – as well as the picture-postcard villages, covered bridges, timeless landscapes, and back-road gems.

From its beginning, the region has been shaped by both geography and climate. Early explorers charted its coastline, and communities soon sprang up by the sea, where goods and people could be ferried more easily from the Old World to the New. Much of the area's early commerce depended heavily on the ocean, from shipping and whaling to fishing and boat-building. Inland the virgin forests and hilly terrain of areas such as New Hampshire, Vermont, and Maine created communities that survived and thrived on independence. The slogan "Live free or die" on today's New Hampshire license plates is a reminder that the same spirit still lives on. New England

Uncle Sam puppet

winters are long and harsh, and spring can bring unpredictable weather. As the 19th-century author Harriet Martineau (1802–76) declared, "I believe no one attempts to praise the climate of New England." Combined with the relatively poor growing conditions of the region – glaciers during the last Ice Age scoured away much of New England's precious soil – this has meant that farming has always been a struggle against the capricious forces of nature. To survive in these northeastern states required toughness, ingenuity, and resourcefulness, all traits that became ingrained in the New England psyche. Indeed, the area today is as much a state of mind as it is a physical space.

Victorian cottage in the Trinity Park district in Oak Bluffs, Massachusetts

◁ White steeple of the Town Hall in Fitzwilliam, New Hampshire

Former frontier outpost, Old Fort Western in Augusta, Maine – a view into New England's past

and the Ivy League universities and other institutions of higher learning continue to draw some of America's best and brightest to the region.

MOUNTAINS AND SEASHORE

From the heights of the White Mountains – the highest terrain in the northeastern US – to the windswept seashore of Cape Cod, New England offers a stunning range of landscapes. And while industrialization and urbanization have left their stamp, there is plenty of the wild past still in the present. The woods of Maine, for example, look much as they did when American writer and naturalist Henry David Thoreau visited them more than 150 years ago. Vermont's Green Mountains would be instantly recognizable by the explorer Samuel de Champlain (1567–1635) who first saw them almost 400 years ago. But it is not only the countryside that has endured; there are homes scattered throughout New England that preserve an array of early American architectural styles, from Colonial to Greek Revival. Just as the terrain is varied, so, too, is New England's population. The earliest settlers to the region were mostly of English and Scottish stock. Even by the early 19th century New England was still a relatively homogenous society, but this changed dramatically during the mid-1800s as waves of Irish immigrants arrived, driven from their homeland by the potato famines.

Few places in America – if any – are richer in historical connections. This is where European civilization first gained a toehold in America. And even long after the American Revolution (1776–83), New England continued to play an important role in the life of the developing nation, supplying many of its political and intellectual leaders. That spirit endures. An intellectual confidence, some may call it smugness, persists; some people would say it is with good reason since it was New England that produced the first flowering of American culture. Writers such as Henry David Thoreau (1817–62), Ralph Waldo Emerson (1803–82), Louisa May Alcott (1832–88), and Herman Melville (1819–91) became the first American writers of an international caliber. Even today, New England still figures prominently in the arts and letters, and its famous preparatory schools

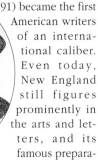

Statue of Samuel de Champlain

New England-born Louisa May Alcott

This altered the political balance of the area. Whereas the earliest leaders tended to be of British ancestry – men such as President John Adams (1735–1826) and John Hancock

Machine Shed inside the Boott Cotton Mill Museum in Lowell, Massachusetts

people who can trace their ancestry directly to the Pilgrims who first came here aboard the *Mayflower.*

OUTDOOR ACTIVITIES

Despite the area's proximity to some of America's most populated areas – a mere 40-mile (64-km) commute separates Stamford, Connecticut, and New York City – it offers a wealth of outdoor activities. There is something here to keep just about any sports enthusiast satisfied. For canoeists and white-water rafters, there are the beautiful Allagash and Connecticut rivers and a captivating collection of lakes.

Rafting on the Kennebec River

(1737–93), signatories of the Declaration of Independence – now Irish-born politicians came to the fore. In 1884 one such man, Hugh O'Brien (1827–95), won the mayoral race in Boston. Meanwhile immigrants from Italy, Portugal, and eastern Europe also arrived, as well as an influx of French-Canadians, who flocked to the mill towns looking for employment. Still, the Irish represented a sizable part of the New England community and their impact on New England society and politics continued to grow, culminating in the election of John F. Kennedy (1917–63) in 1960 as America's first Roman Catholic president. Today some of the fourth-, fifth-, and sixth-generation Irish Americans have ascended to the top of New England's social hierarchy, although there remains a special cachet for

For skiers, resorts such as Killington, Stowe, and Sugarloaf offer some of the best skiing in the eastern US. The region's heavy snowfalls provide a wonderful base for cross-country skiers and snowshoers as well. There's biking on the back roads of New Hampshire and excellent hiking on the Appalachian Trail and Vermont's Long Trail, considered by many as one of the best hiking trails in the world.

Of course, many popular outdoor activities center around the ocean. There's kayaking among the islands and inlets of the Maine shoreline, wind surfing off Cape Cod, and ample opportunities for sailing, fishing, swimming, and scuba diving up and down the entire New England coast.

Fisherman with a large striped bass

The Landscape and Wildlife of New England

Considering its proximity to major cities, rural New England boasts a surprisingly diverse collection of wildlife, including many species of birds, moose, bears, beavers, and, rarely, bobcats. The topography of the region includes rolling hills, dense woodlands, rugged mountains, and a coastline that is jagged and rocky in some areas and sandy and serene in others. Northern Maine has the closest thing to wilderness found in the eastern United States, with hundreds of square miles of trackless land and a vast network of clear streams, rivers, and lakes. New England is also home to the White, Green, and Appalachian mountain ranges.

Bald eagles *are found around water, making Maine their favorite New England state.*

COASTLINE
From the crenelated coastline of Maine, which measures almost 3,500 miles (5,630 km) in length, to the sandy beaches of Connecticut, the New England shoreline is richly varied. Here visitors find various sea and shore birds, many attracted by the food provided by the expansive salt marshes that have been created by barrier beaches. A few miles offshore, there is excellent whale-watching.

MOUNTAIN LANDSCAPE
The western and northern parts of New England are dominated by the Appalachian Mountains, a range that extends from Georgia to Canada. The highest point is 6,288-ft (1,917-m) Mount Washington, also known for drastic weather changes at its summit. Birch and beech trees are plentiful at elevations up to 2,000 ft (610 m). At the higher elevations, pine, spruce, and fir trees are most common.

The great blue heron *is the largest of the North American herons. This elegant bird is easily spotted in wetlands and on lakeshores.*

White-tailed deer *can be found in a range of habitats, from forest edges to open woodland. They are frequently spotted on mountainsides up to 2,000 ft (610 m).*

Whales *are plentiful off the coast, particularly in the Gulf of Maine from early spring to mid-October. Finbacks, minke and right whales are most common, but humpbacks generally put on the best show, often leaping out of the water.*

Coyotes *were once all but extinct in the region, but in recent years their numbers have exploded. They tend to live in forested and mountainous areas, but might be seen in urban areas.*

NATIONAL WILDLIFE REFUGE

With 150 million acres (61 million ha) under its control, the National Wildlife Refuge (NWR) offers protection for some of the country's most ecologically rich areas. The NWR system began in 1903 when President Theodore Roosevelt (1858–1919) established Pelican Island in Florida as a refuge for birds. Thirty-five refuges are located in New England, including 11 in Massachusetts, 6 in Rhode Island, 4 in New Hampshire, 11 in Maine, 1 in Connecticut, and 2 in Vermont. They offer some of the best bird-watching in the region. See www.fws.gov/refuges for more information.

Rachel Carson National Wildlife Refuge, a vast wetland stop for migratory birds

LAKES AND RIVERS

The rivers and lakes of New England provide fishermen, canoeists, and vacationers in general with a world of outdoor pleasures. The network of waterways is particularly extensive in Maine, which has more lakes than any state in the northeastern United States. Among the rivers, the Connecticut is New England's longest, at more than 400 miles (644 km) in length. It runs from the Canadian border along the Vermont-New Hampshire border and through Massachusetts and Connecticut.

FORESTS

The logging industry and the switch to agricultural and grazing land – especially for sheep – decimated many of the forests of New England in the 19th and early 20th centuries, but the tide has turned. Vermont, for example, has far more forests today than it did 100 years ago. In the lower elevations, the trees are mostly deciduous, such as ash, maple, and birch, but higher up in the mountains coniferous trees such as balsam fir predominate.

Mallard ducks *are a frequent sight throughout New England wetlands. The birds can be seen from April to October, when they migrate to warmer climes.*

The pigeon hawk, *also known as the merlin, can be found throughout New England, even in urban areas.*

Chipmunks *are seen virtually throughout rural New England, especially in the forests.*

Moose *are common in Maine, northern Vermont, and New Hampshire. Although they can be spotted in the woods, they are most often seen along the shores of lakes. Drivers should be wary of moose, especially at dawn and dusk.*

Raccoons *are commonly seen in wooded areas. They often pay visits to campsites, brazenly foraging for food with dexterous paws.*

Fall Foliage

The cool weather in the fall signals more than back-to-school time in New England. It also sounds a clarion call to hundreds of thousands of visitors to head outdoors to gaze in wonder at one of Nature's most splendid offerings: the annual changing of leaf colors. Planning foliage tours is an inexact science, however. Generally, leaves start to change earliest in more northern areas and higher up mountainsides. On some mountains in northern New England, for example, the leaves will begin changing color as early as August. In general, the peak period varies from early October in the northern part of the region to late October in the southern section. But this can differ, depending on the weather. Cooler temperatures than normal tend to speed up the leaf-changing timetable and vice versa.

Young boy during fall's pumpkin harvest

Blue sky
The rich palette created by the foliage is made even more dramatic by a backdrop of a deep blue fall sky.

VERMONT'S FALL COLORS

While each of the New England states offers something for "leaf peepers," none can top Vermont. With its rich mix of deciduous trees, the Green Mountain State is anything but just green in late September and October. Inns and hotels tend to be booked up months in advance on the key weekends as the Vermont countryside swells with one of its biggest influxes of out-of-state visitors.

Forest floor
Fallen leaves are more than just beautiful to the eye. They will eventually decay and replenish the humus layer.

Nature's paint box
One of the most remarkable features of the fall foliage season is how it transforms the scenery. Here Quechee Gorge, Vermont's Grand Canyon, has changed its verdant green cloak for one of many colors.

Maple leaf
The maple tree is one of the most common trees in New England. Its leaves change to yellow, red, or orange.

WHY LEAVES TURN

The changing of leaf colors is not just a capricious act of Nature. It is a direct response to the changing realities of the seasons. As daylight hours diminish, the leaves of deciduous trees stop producing the green pigment chlorophyll. With the disappearance of chlorophyll, other pigments that had been hidden behind the chlorophyll's color now burst into view. More pigments are produced by sugars that remain trapped in the leaves. The result is a riotous display that makes this the high point of the year for many visitors. Two of the most spectacular areas for color are Litchfield Hills, Connecticut *(see pp208–209)*, and Penobscot Bay, Maine *(see pp286–7)*. Foliage hotlines give updates and are listed on page 395.

Fall hiking
Hikers should wear bright clothing and stick to well-marked trails and paths in the fall as this is also hunting season in the area.

A single crimson leaf aglow on the forest floor

The Appalachian Trail

The Appalachian Trail is one of the longest footpaths in the world at 2,175 miles (3,500 km). From its southern terminus at Springer Mountain in the state of Georgia to its northernmost point on the summit of Mount Katahdin, Maine, the trail crosses 14 states and two national

A common squirrel parks as it wends its way through forests, meadows, and mountains. The trail travels through five of the six New England states, missing only Rhode Island, and reaches its highest point in the northeast on windswept Mount Washington (*see p267*) in New Hampshire. Each year about 400 intrepid souls, called "thru hikers," complete the journey in a single trip. The vast majority of people, however, choose to walk the trail in smaller, more manageable sections. The trail is usually marked by rectangular white blazes painted on trees and rocks, and overnight hikers can take advantage of primitive shelters that are situated roughly every 10 miles (16 km).

LOCATOR MAP

☐ New England

···· Appalachian Trail

Hanover, New Hampshire
Home of Dartmouth College, Hanover is located on the Appalachian Trail. This stretch of the trail, called the Dartmouth Outing Club section, runs through a series of scenic valleys and mountain passes.

Vermont's lush *green cloak becomes a brilliant patchwork in the fall, a popular time to hike this section of the trail.*

Mount Greylock is one of the highlights of the Massachusetts section.

The Connecticut section runs through the Housatonic Highlands and the valley along the Taconic Range.

Burlington
St. Johnsbur
Montpelier
Hanover
Rutland
Lebanon
Concor
Brattleboro
Bennington
Pittsfield
Worcester
Springfield
Hartford
Waterbury
New Haven
Housatonic River
Connecticut River
Thames River

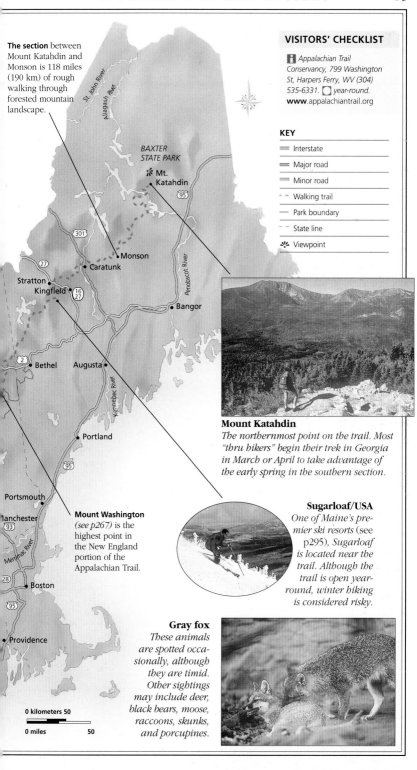

The section between Mount Katahdin and Monson is 118 miles (190 km) of rough walking through forested mountain landscape.

BAXTER STATE PARK

Mt. Katahdin

Monson

Caratunk

Stratton

Kingfield

Bangor

Bethel

Augusta

Portland

Portsmouth

Manchester

Boston

Providence

St. John River

Allagash River

Penobscot River

Kennebec River

Merrimac River

VISITORS' CHECKLIST

Appalachian Trail Conservancy, 799 Washington St, Harpers Ferry, WV (304) 535-6331. ☐ year-round. www.appalachiantrail.org

KEY

═══ Interstate

━━━ Major road

─── Minor road

- - - Walking trail

─── Park boundary

- - State line

☀ Viewpoint

Mount Katahdin
The northernmost point on the trail. Most "thru hikers" begin their trek in Georgia in March or April to take advantage of the early spring in the southern section.

Mount Washington *(see p267)* is the highest point in the New England portion of the Appalachian Trail.

Sugarloaf/USA
One of Maine's premier ski resorts (see p295), Sugarloaf is located near the trail. Although the trail is open year-round, winter hiking is considered risky.

Gray fox
These animals are spotted occasionally, although they are timid. Other sightings may include deer, black bears, moose, raccoons, skunks, and porcupines.

0 kilometers 50

0 miles   50

Maritime New England

It was the sea that helped open up the region to settlement in the 17th century. The sea also provided New Englanders with a way of life. In the early years, ships worked the fertile waters off Cape Cod for whales, fish, and lobster. Whaling reached its zenith in the 19th century, when hundreds of whaleboats fanned out to the uttermost ends of the Earth. Today the best places to explore the area's rich maritime history are the New Bedford Whaling

Whaleboat figurehead

National Historical Park and the New Bedford Whaling Museum in New Bedford, Massachusetts *(see p121)*, Mystic Seaport *(see pp214–15)*, Connecticut, and the Penobscot Marine Museum in Searsport, Maine *(see p286)*.

Ropes and pulleys *were important for hoisting sails and lowering the whaleboats.*

Antique whaling harpoons
Harpoons and lances were hand-forged in New Bedford. Harpoons were thrown to attach a line to the whale. When the leviathan tired of pulling boat and men, the lance was used for the kill.

NEW ENGLAND'S WHALERS
Competition in 19th-century whaling was fierce. In 1857 some 330 whalers sailed out of New Bedford, Massachusetts, alone. The *Catalpa*, portrayed by C.S. Raleigh in his late-1800s painting, is an example of a well-outfitted whaler.

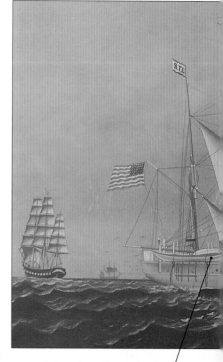

Whaleboats were lowered into the water to hunt and harpoon whales. Whale oil was used for illumination and was a valuable commodity.

Maritime art
Maritime influences still appear throughout New England. This contemporary chest by Harriet Scudder depicts an early whaling scene.

THE ICE TRADE

The cold winters of northern New England provided the source of a valuable export in the 19th century. In the days before mechanical refrigeration, ice from the region's frozen rivers, lakes, and ponds was cut up into large blocks, packed in sawdust, and shipped as far away as India. To keep the ice from melting, engineers designed ships with special airtight hulls. The ice trade finally collapsed in the late 1800s when mechanical methods for keeping perishables cool began to make ice obsolete for refrigeration in an increasing number of places in the world.

Harvesting ice

Barks were popular whaling vessels in the 19th century because they were maneuverable and could undertake long voyages.

Scrimshaw
New England sailors killed long periods of inactivity on the sea making etchings on whale teeth or jawbones. Ink and tobacco juice added color.

Whale carcasses were secured to the sides of the ship so that the blubber could be stripped and boiled onboard for its oil.

Lobster industry
In colonial times, lobster was so common it was used as fertilizer. Today it is considered a delicacy.

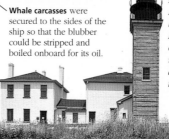

Lighthouses
Nearly 200 lighthouses dot New England's coast, testimony to the area's maritime ties.

New England Architecture

Scrolled door pediment

New England architecture encompasses a variety of styles. In the early years of colonization, the influences of England predominated. But after the Revolutionary War (1775–83), the new republic wanted to distance itself from its colonial past. Drawing on French Neo-Classicism, the newest European style of the late 18th century, American architects brought into being a distinctive American version known as Federal. In its efforts to define itself, New England did not reject foreign ideas, however, as evidenced by the Greek Revival style of the early 19th century and the adaptation of English and French Revival styles for the next 100 years.

First Church of Christ in West Hartford, Connecticut

COLONIAL STYLE

Colonial style, the style of the period when America was still a British colony, has two aspects: the homes of ordinary people and the more elaborate architecture of public buildings, mansions, and churches. The large wooden houses built in towns and rural areas in New England between 1607 and 1780 constitute one of the area's architectural treasures. Numerous examples survive, and the style has many regional variations. The famous Connecticut "saltbox" houses are an example. They featured distinctive close-cropped eaves and a long back roof that projected over a kitchen lean-to.

Eleazer Arnold House chimney, Providence, Rhode Island

Roof
Shingles became the main roofing material and were frequently used for walls as well.

Chimney
The large chimney provided a vital outlet for smoke.

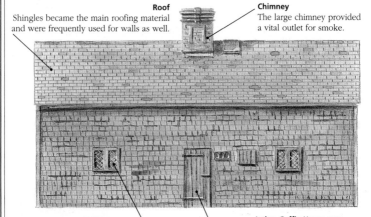

Jethro Coffin House *was built in 1686 and is the oldest surviving structure in Nantucket, Massachusetts. A slot beside the front door allowed inhabitants to see who was standing outside.*

Windows
Small casement windows were fitted with diamond-shaped panes of glass imported from England.

Casement window

Door
In keeping with the practical Colonial aesthetics, doors featured a simple, vertical-board design.

GEORGIAN STYLE

The term Georgian, or Palladian, refers to the mainstream Classical architecture of 18th-century England, which drew on designs of 16th-century Italian architect Andrea Palladio (1508–80). In the colonies and England, these elegant buildings marked the presence of the British ruling class.

Pedimented dormers, Ladd Gilman House, in Exeter, New Hampshire

Roof
Roofs were less steeply pitched than earlier Colonial-era designs. A delicate balustrade crowns the roof.

Windows
Georgian windows were usually double-hung sash with 6 panes.

Doors
Doors featured a raised-panel design with six or more panels and Classical moldings.

Vassall/Craigie/ Longfellow House *in Cambridge, Massachusetts, built in 1759. Its facade has Classical columns and a triangular pediment.*

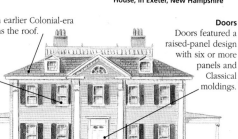

FEDERAL STYLE

American architects viewed the Federal style as a distinctive national statement. Some Federal buildings drew on both Greek and Roman architecture, representing the tenets of democracy and republicanism. Federal style is more restrained than Georgian, with less intricate woodwork.

The Colony House in Newport (see pp182–7), Rhode Island

Fanlights
Fanlights, frequent in Georgian archi-tecture, were also found in Neo-Classical design.

Roof
Neo-Classical roofs were often flat.

Facade
Neo-Classical facades were less decorated than Georgian. Often stories were separated by bands of stone called string courses.

Gardner-Pingree House *in Salem, Massachusetts, is known for its graceful proportions.*

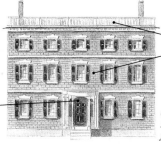

GREEK REVIVAL STYLE

Popular between 1820 and 1845, this style is a more literal version of Classical architecture than the Federal style. Greek Revival buildings typically borrowed the façades of ancient Greek temples, often sensitively re-creating them in wood.

Samuel Russell House *in Middletown, Connecticut, features a white exterior common in Greek Revival structures.*

Facade
The "temple fronts" of Greek Revival buildings were inspired by the archaeological discoveries in Greece and Turkey in the 18th century.

Providence, Rhode Island, church door

Columns
These Corinthian columns faithfully follow conventions of ancient Greek architecture.

Colleges and Universities

New England is not only the cradle of American civilization, it is also the birthplace of higher education in the New World. Harvard University *(see pp112–17)* was founded in 1636, only 16 years after the Pilgrims arrived at Plymouth Rock *(see pp148–9)*. Four of the country's eight renowned Ivy League colleges are located in New England: Harvard, Brown *(see p175)*, Dartmouth *(see p263)*, and Yale *(see pp222–5)*. Here higher learning goes hand in hand with tradition and culture. Many of America's most famous art collections and natural history museums are found on campus grounds. As well, many of the top-ranked liberal arts colleges are found here, including Bowdoin and all-women Smith and Wellesley Colleges.

1764 Rhode Island College, later Brown University, is founded in Providence, Rhode Island

1852 The Harvard crew wins inaugural Harvard-Yale Regatta – beginning one of the longest rivalries in US college sports

1778 Phillips Academy is founded by educator Samuel Phillips in Andover, Massachusetts

1781 John Phillips, uncle of Samuel, founds Phillips Exeter Academy in Exeter, New Hampshire

1801 Daniel Webster graduates from Dartmouth and goes on to an illustrious career as US statesman and orator

1636 Harvard University is founded in Cambridge, Massachusetts; 12 students enroll in the inaugural year

1701 Puritan clergymen found Collegiate School in Saybrook, Connecticut

1640	1680	1720	1760	1800	1840

1640	1680	1720	1760	1800	1840

1642 Physics becomes a mandatory subject at Harvard, using text by Aristotle

1777 Brown's University Hall building is used as barracks for Colonial troops during War of Independence

1817 Harvard Law School is established

1832 Yale Art Gallery is founded after US artist John Trumbull donates some 100 pieces of art from his personal collection

1717 Collegiate School is moved to New Haven, Connecticut, and is renamed Yale in 1718 in honor of benefactor Elihu Yale

1844 Yale graduate Samuel Morse sends world's first telegraphic message in Morse code

1853 Franklin Pierce, graduate of Bowdoin College in Brunswick, Maine, is elected 14th president of the United States

1919 Philanthropist and Brown University graduate John D. Rockefeller, Jr. donates 5,000 acres (2,025 ha) of Maine's Mount Desert Island for use as a preserve. His further gifts would form almost one-third of Acadia National Park *(see pp288–9)*

1992 Yale graduate Bill Clinton is elected 42nd president of the United States

1861 Massachusetts Institute of Technology (MIT) is founded

1925 S.J. Perelman graduates from Brown; goes on to win Academy Award for screenplay of *Around the World in 80 Days* (1956)

2004 M.I.T. completes Stata Center, designed by Frank Gehry, to house computer science and artificial Intelligence laboratories

1868 William Dubois is born. Dubois would go on to become the first black person to earn a Ph.D. from Harvard

2008 Harvard Law School graduate Barack Obama is elected as the first African-American president of the United States

1957 Theodor Geisel (Dr. Seuss), Dartmouth alumnus, publishes *The Cat in the Hat*

1880	1920	1960	2000	2040

1880	1920	1960	2000	2040

1946 Percy Bridgman becomes first Harvard physicist to receive Nobel Prize in Physics

1969 Women are admitted to Yale's undergraduate program

2000 Yale graduate George W. Bush is elected 43rd president, following in the footsteps of his father George H.W. Bush – Yale graduate and 41st president

NEW ENGLAND BOARDING SCHOOLS

New England boasts the most prestigious collection of college preparatory, or "prep," schools in the US. The two preeminent institutions are Phillips Academy in Andover, Massachusetts, and Phillips Exeter Academy *(see p256)* in Exeter, New Hampshire. Both are private, coeducational schools and attract the sons and daughters of some of the country's wealthiest and most influential families. Other prominent prep schools include Choate Rosemary Hall in Wallingford, Connecticut, and Groton in Groton, Massachusetts.

1877 Former slave Inman Page becomes first African-American to graduate from Brown

1861 Yale awards country's first Ph.D. degrees

Campus of Phillips Exeter Academy

Literary New England

Writing in his seminal work *Democracy in America* (1835), French historian Alexis de Tocqueville (1805–1859) declared, "The inhabitants of the United States have, then, at present, no literature." Less than two decades later that scenario had changed radically. By then, writers such as Ralph Waldo Emerson (1803–82), Henry David Thoreau (1817–62), and Nathaniel Hawthorne (1804–64) were creating works that would take their place among the classics of 19th-century literature – and that was just in one town, Concord *(see pp144–5)*, Massachusetts. Since that first flowering, New England writers have been taking their place among the best in the world.

Author Nathaniel Hawthorne (1804–64)

Ralph Waldo Emerson, speaking to Transcendentalists in Concord

FATHER OF TRANSCENDENTALISM

Born in Boston, Ralph Waldo Emerson graduated from Harvard University in 1821 and became the pastor of the Second Church (Unitarian) in Boston in 1829. In many ways Emerson turned his back on his formal religious education in the 1830s when he founded the Transcendentalism movement. Among other things, Emerson's writings espoused a system of spiritual independence in which each individual was responsible for his or her own moral judgments.

Moving to Concord in 1834, the popular essayist and lecturer soon became known as the "Sage of Concord" for his insightful teachings.

Concord was also the birthplace of Emerson's most famous disciple, Henry David Thoreau. A one-time school teacher, Thoreau worked as a pencil maker before quitting to undertake his lifelong study of nature. Deeply influenced by the Transcendentalist belief that total unity with nature was achievable, Thoreau built a small cabin at Walden Pond *(see p145)* in 1845, living as a recluse for the next two years.

Henry David Thoreau's simple grave in Concord, Massachusetts

In 1854 he published *Walden; or, Life in the Woods,* in which he outlined how people could escape a life of "quiet desperation" by paring away the extraneous, anxiety-inducing trappings of the industrial age and living in harmony with the natural world.

19TH-CENTURY LITERARY FLOWERING

It was also in Concord that Nathaniel Hawthorne penned *Mosses from an Old Manse* in 1846. Hawthorne later returned to his hometown, Salem *(see pp136–7)*, Massachusetts, where he wrote his best-known work, *The Scarlet Letter* (1850). Moving to Lenox in western Massachusetts, Hawthorne became friends with Herman Melville (1819–91), who wrote his allegorical masterpiece *Moby-Dick* (1851) in

Illustration from Herman Melville's *Moby-Dick*

Visitor on the porch of the Robert Frost house in New Hampshire

neighboring Pittsfield. The book drew its inspiration from the voyage that Melville made from New Bedford, Massachusetts, to the South Seas aboard the New England whaler *Acushnet*.

Like Melville, Mark Twain (1835–1910) was not a New Englander by birth. However, it was during his long stay in Hartford *(see pp198–201)*, Connecticut, that he penned the novels that would vault him into worldwide prominence, including *The Adventures of Tom Sawyer* (1876), *The Adventures of Huckleberry Finn* (1885), and *A Connecticut Yankee in King Arthur's Court* (1889).

19TH-CENTURY WOMEN AUTHORS

Although opportunities for women were limited in 19th-century America, several New England female writers still managed to leave their mark on literature. One of the region's most famous – and mysterious – literary figures was Emily Dickinson (1830–86). Born in Amherst *(see p162–3)*, Massachusetts, she was educated at the Mount Holyoke Female Seminary *(see p162)* before withdrawing from society in her early 20s. Living the rest of her life in her family's home, Dickinson wrote more than 1,000 poems – the vast majority of which remained unpublished until after her death. Today her finely crafted poems are

Cover of sheet music for Harriet Beecher Stowe's *Uncle Tom's Cabin*

admired for their complex rhythms and intensely personal lyrics.

The greatest single indictment of the slavery that would catapult America into civil war came from the pen of Harriet Beecher Stowe (1811–96), who would later become Mark Twain's next door neighbor in Hartford. *Uncle Tom's Cabin; or, Life Among the Lowly* (1852) told the story of a slave family's desperate flight for freedom to a rapt, largely sympathetic audience worldwide. Louisa May Alcott (1832–88) – yet another Concord resident – left a lasting and loving portrait of domestic life in the United States during the Civil War in *Little Women* (1868), a perennial favorite of children.

20TH CENTURY

In the 20th century, New England continued to play a defining role in American literature, spawning native writers as diverse as "Beat" chronicler Jack Kerouac *(see p142)* and the "Chekhov of the suburbs," John Cheever (1912–82). The region has also provided a fertile base for transplanted New Englanders. The poet Robert Frost (1874–1963), a native of San Francisco, lived most of his life in Vermont and New Hampshire, and the mountains, meadows, and people of the region figure prominently in his poetry, which won the Pulitzer Prize an unprecedented four times. Poet and novelist John Updike (1932–2009) lived much of his life in Ipswich, Massachusetts, and set both *Couples* (1968) and *The Witches of Eastwick* (1984) in the northeast. Novelist John Irving was born in Exeter, New Hampshire, in 1942. Much of his later fiction is set in New England, including *The World According to Garp* (1978) and *Cider House Rules* (1985). Perhaps the area's best-known living writer is horror master Stephen King (b.1947), a longtime resident of Bangor, Maine. Boston-based mystery writer Dennis Lehane (b. 1966) sets his novels in gritty working-class neighborhoods.

Fright master and longtime Bangor resident Stephen King

NEW ENGLAND
THROUGH THE YEAR

New England is really a year-round tourist destination – depending on what it is people are looking to do. Generally, spring is the shortest season. Occurring sometime between April and June, spring in New England can be short-lived but glorious; wildflowers bursting forth in colorful bloom provide a feast for the eyes. Summer is the busiest period for tourism. With the good weather stretching from mid-June into early September, this part of

Colorful hot-air balloon

the year is characterized by warm temperatures that have people flocking to lakes and the ocean. Fall is when New England is at its most beautiful, with its lush forests changing from green to a riot of gold, red, and orange. The peak period for fall foliage generally occurs from mid-September to late October. Winter, which usually lasts from December through to mid-April, is often marked by heavy snowfalls – a boon for winter sport enthusiasts.

Cars decorated with flowers in Nantucket's Daffodil Festival

SPRING

New England's shortest season is sometimes little more than a three-week interval between winter and summer. As well as being the prime time for maple syrup tapping, spring brings with it a host of festivals.

APRIL

Boston Marathon *(third Monday, April)*, Boston, MA. America's oldest and most prestigious marathon.
Patriot's Day *(third Monday, April)*, Lexington and Concord, MA. Costumed reenactments of the pivotal battles that were waged at the outset of the Revolutionary War.
Daffodil Festival *(late April)*, Nantucket, MA. The town is decked out in millions of yellow daffodils.

MAY

Lilac Sunday *(early May)*, Boston, MA. This beloved rite of spring features picnics and folk dances throughout the city in celebration of the seasonal lilac blossom.
Cape Cod Maritime Days *(mid-May)*, Cape Cod, MA. Celebration of seaside life with lectures, boat rides, kayaking, and kite-flying.
Gaspee Days *(mid-May–mid-June)*, Cranston and Warwick, RI. Reenactment of the burning of a British schooner.
Brimfield Antique Show *(May, July, and September)*, Brimfield, MA. Dealers from across the US gather at this show to sell their wares.
Lobster Days *(late May)*, Mystic, CT. A lobsterbake popular with locals and visitors.

Patriot Days celebration in Lexington, Massachusetts

Delicious lobsters served up during Mystic's Lobster Days

Waterfire *(May–Oct)*, Providence, RI. This dazzling art event features 100 bonfires, which are lit on the city's three rivers.

EARLY JUNE

Discover Jazz Festival *(early June)*, Burlington, VT. Jazz, blues, and gospel are the highlights of this popular festival.
Circus Smirkus *(early June–mid-August)*. This international youth circus performs around New England.
Cambridge River Festival *(mid-June)*, Cambridge, MA. This community festival features food and arts.

SUMMER

New England summers can be hot and humid. This is vacation time for students and families, making the region a very busy place, especially the coastline and beaches.

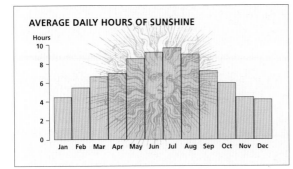

AVERAGE DAILY HOURS OF SUNSHINE

Hours

Jan Feb Mar Apr May Jun Jul Aug Sep Oct Nov Dec

Sunshine Chart
New England's weather can vary greatly from year to year. Generally, the short spring is cloudy and wet, giving way to better weather in June. July and August are usually the sunniest months. Bright fall days out among the colorful foliage are spectacular.

LATE JUNE

Secret Garden Tour *(mid-June)*, Newport, RI. Private gardens open to the public for self-guided walking tour.
International Festival of Art and Ideas *(mid-June–July)*, New Haven, Hartford, Stamford, and New London, CT. A showcase of performance and visual arts.
Jacob's Pillow Dance Festival *(mid-June–late August)*, Becket, MA. Ballet, jazz, and modern dance feature in the country's oldest dance festival.
Windjammer Days *(late June)*, Boothbay Harbor, ME. Shoreside events complement parade of graceful sailboats.
Stowe Garden Festival *(late June)*, Stowe, VT. Seminars and tours of formal gardens.
Antique Tractor Festival *(late June)*, Farmington, ME. Antique machinery demonstrations, crafts, tractor pulls, and a flea market.
Block Island Race Week *(late June in odd-numbered years)*, Block Island, RI. The largest sailing event on the coast.
Williamstown Theater Festival *(late June–August)*, Williamstown, MA. Featuring classical and new theater productions.

JULY

Independence Day Celebrations *(July 4th)*, throughout New England. Parades, fireworks, and concerts.
Tanglewood Music Festival *(early July–late August)*, Lenox, MA. Boston Symphony and Boston Pops orchestras give concerts on this grand estate *(see p167)*.

Riverfest *(July)*, Hartford, CT. Fireworks and free concerts along the Connecticut River.
Vermont Quilt Festival *(late June–early July)*, Essex Junction, VT. A quilting celebration.
Mozart Festival *(July, August, and October–December)*, Burlington, VT. A celebration of the music of Wolfgang Amadeus Mozart.
American Independence Festival *(mid-July)*, Exeter, NH. Beer festival, fireworks and reenactments.
Newport Regatta *(mid-July)*, Newport, RI. This huge regatta attracts some 300 boats.
Guilford Handcrafts Exposition *(mid-July)*, Guilford, CT. This event features pottery, glass, jewelry, folk art, and quilts.
Lowell Folk Festival *(late July)*, Lowell, MA. Dance troupes, musicians, and ethnic food are served up here.

AUGUST

Maine Lobster Festival *(early August)*, Rockland, ME. Lobster and live entertainment are on the menu at this event.
Newport Folk Festival *(early August)*, Newport, RI. One of the country's top folk festivals, held at Fort Adams State Park.
League of New Hampshire Craftsmen Annual Fair *(early August)* Newbury, NH. The oldest crafts fair in the US features craft demonstrations, workshops, performing arts, and 200 booths selling high-quality crafts.
Addison County Fair *(early August)*, New Haven, VT. This is one of the state's largest agricultural fairs.

July 4th road markings

One of many festivals celebrating New England's nautical past

Mystic Outdoor Arts Festival *(mid-August)*, Mystic, CT. This art show attracts 300 artists.
Newport JVC Jazz Festival *(mid-August)*, Newport, RI. International jazz stars gather to perform at this festival.
Wild Blueberry Festival *(mid–late August)*, Machias, ME. Foot races, pie-eating contests, and musical comedy celebrate the berry harvest.
Brooklyn Fair *(late August)*, Brooklyn, CT. The country's oldest continuously running agricultural fair has ox pulls and livestock shows.
Champlain Valley Fair *(late August–early September)*, Essex Junction, VT. Horse shows and midway rides are part of this huge fair.
Classic Yacht Regatta *(late August–early September)*, Newport, RI. More than 100 vintage wooden yachts are on parade in this regatta.
Thomas Point Beach Bluegrass Festival *(late August–early September)*, Brunswick, ME. World-class lineup of musicians.

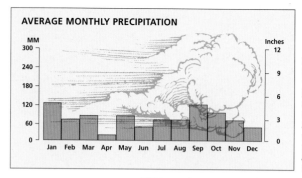

AVERAGE MONTHLY PRECIPITATION

Precipitation Chart
Spring is called "mud season" by locals, thanks to rainy skies and melting snow. Summer can be unpredictable, but is generally dry. Snow usually starts in December.

AUTUMN

Many people consider the fall to be New England's most beautiful season. Bright, crisp autumn days are made more glorious by the brilliant fall foliage *(see p20–21)*.

SEPTEMBER

Pawtucket Arts Festival *(early September)*, Pawtucket, RI. Music and food for all tastes and colorful dragon boat races are some of the highlights of this festival.
International Seaplane Fly-In *(early September)*, Greenville, ME. Spectators gather on the shores of Moosehead Lake to observe floatplane competitions and sample local food.
Windjammer Weekend *(early September)*, Camden, ME. A celebration of Maine's fleet of classic sailing ships.
Vermont State Fair *(early September)*, Rutland, VT. One of the most popular agricultural fairs in the state.
Woodstock Fair *(early September)*, South Woodstock, CT. The state's second-oldest agricultural fair includes crafts, go-cart races, livestock shows, and petting zoos for children.
Norwalk Oyster Festival *(early September)*, East Norwalk, CT. This nationally acclaimed celebration includes fireworks, antique boats, and lots of oyster sampling.
The Big "E" *(last two weeks of September)*, Eastern States Exhibition Ground, West Springfield, MA. One of New England's biggest fairs, with rodeos, rides, and a circus.
Harvest Festivals *(late September)*, throughout New England.

A Harvest Festival, this one in Keene, New Hampshire

Parades, apple picking, and hay rides are just some of the events held around the region to celebrate the fall harvest.
Sugar Hill Antique Show *(late September)*, Sugar Hill, NH. A popular, long-running antique show that attracts numerous dealers and their wares.
Fryeburg Fair *(late September–early October)*, Fryeburg, ME. Maine's oldest county fair emphasizes its agricultural roots, but also offers midway rides and live entertainment.
Northeast Kingdom Fall Foliage Festival *(late September–early October)*, throughout northern Vermont. Different towns hold foliage-

related bus tours, hiking parties, and family events.

OCTOBER

Mount Greylock Ramble *(Columbus Day)*, Adams, MA. The whole community climbs the state's highest mountain.
Woonsocket Autumnfest *(early October)*, Woonsocket, RI. Live music, craft displays, a midway, and a Columbus Day parade are top events.
Haunted Happenings *(October)*, Salem, MA. A month-long festival celebrating the city's witch-related past *(see pp136–9)* and Halloween.
Wellfleet Oyster Festival *(mid-October)*, Wellfleet, MA. Local cuisine, road race, oyster shuck-off, and music.
Keene Pumpkin Festival *(late Oct)*, Keene, NH. Celebration featuring more than 25,000 lit jack-o'-lanterns.

NOVEMBER

Dinner in a Country Village *(Nov–Mar)*, Old Sturbridge Village, Sturbridge, MA. Dinners cooked on open hearths relieve the winter chill.
Holiday Craft Exhibition and Sale *(mid-Nov–Dec 31)*,

Brilliant colors, heralding Northeast Kingdom Fall Foliage Festival

AVERAGE MONTHLY TEMPERATURE

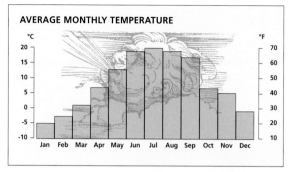

Temperature Chart
New England temperatures vary greatly through the year. In the summer, temperatures of 90° F (32° C) are quite frequent, while the thermometer can dip to 0° F (-18° C) or lower in winter. In general, it is warmer along the coast and in the southern section of New England.

Brookfield, CT. Craft artists put unique wares up for sale.
Thanksgiving Celebration *(mid–late November)*, Plymouth, MA. Thanksgiving traditions of the past are celebrated in historic homes. Visitors can also enjoy a Thanksgiving dinner at Plimoth Plantation *(see pp150–51)*.
Festival of Light *(late November–early January)*, Hartford, CT. Constitution Plaza is transformed into a spectacular world of more than 200,000 white lights.

WINTER

New England winters are often marked by heavy snowfalls, particularly in the mountainous areas farther inland. Temperatures can also plunge drastically overnight and from one day to the next. This, of course, is a boon for people who enjoy winter sports, as New England has some of the most popular ski centers in the eastern US.

DECEMBER

Christmas at Blithewold *(late November–December)*, Bristol, RI. Traditional Christmas celebrations are celebrated in this beautiful mansion.
Festival of Trees and Traditions *(early December)*, Hartford, CT. Hundreds of beautiful trees and wreaths are on display at Wadsworth Athenaeum.
Festival of Lights *(early December)*, Wickford Village, RI. This family-oriented festival includes tree- and window-decorating competitions, hayrides, and live music.

Wolfgang Amadeus Mozart, feted in Burlington, Vermont

Christmas Tree Lighting *(early December)*, Boston, MA. The huge tree in front of the Prudential Center is lit up with thousands of bright lights.
Candlelight Stroll *(mid-December)*, Portsmouth, NH. The town's historic Strawbery Banke district *(see pp254–5)* is resplendent with antique Christmas decorations.
Boston Tea Party Reenactment *(mid-December)*, Boston, MA. Costumed interpreters bring to life the famous protest that precipitated the Revolutionary War.
First Night Celebrations *(December 31st)*, throughout New England. Family-oriented festivities that started in Boston in 1976 and are now celebrated around the world.

JANUARY

Vermont Farm Show *(late January)*, Barre, VT. Vermont's premier winter show includes a variety of agricultural displays and livestock exhibits.

Chinese New Year *(late January–early March)*, Boston, MA. The location for this colorful festival is Boston's Chinatown.

FEBRUARY

National Toboggan Championships *(February)*, Camden, ME. Daredevils of all sizes and ages come to compete in this high-speed, often hilarious, event.
Stowe Derby *(late February)*, Stowe, VT. This is one of the oldest downhill and cross-country skiing races in the country.

MARCH

New England Spring Flower Show *(March)*, Boston, MA. Meticulous landscaped gardens and thousands of new blooms announce the end of winter.
St. Patrick's Day Parades *(mid-March)*, Boston and Holyoke, MA. Two of New England's oldest and largest celebrations.
Maple Season *(late March)*, throughout New England. Visitors can see how maple sap is collected and made into syrup.

Musicians in Boston's St. Patrick's Day Parade

THE HISTORY OF NEW ENGLAND

The early history of New England is the history of the United States itself, for it is here that Europeans first gained a toe-hold in America and where much of the drama of forming a new country was played out. But even after the rest of the country had been populated, New England continued to exert influence on the political, economic, and intellectual life of the country.

No one can say for sure which Europeans first made landfall in New England. Some historians claim that the Vikings, after first reaching Newfoundland around AD 1000, eventually ventured as far south as Massachusetts. Others suggest that Spanish, Portuguese, or Irish explorers were the first Old World visitors. But one thing is sure: none of these peoples actually discovered the area. Native Americans already had called the region home for several thousand years. They were descendants of nomads from central Asia who had journeyed to what is now Alaska via the then-dry Bering Strait between 20,000 and 12,000 years ago. Slowly they migrated east.

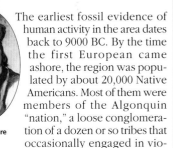

Paul Revere

The earliest fossil evidence of human activity in the area dates back to 9000 BC. By the time the first European came ashore, the region was populated by about 20,000 Native Americans. Most of them were members of the Algonquin "nation," a loose conglomeration of a dozen or so tribes that occasionally engaged in violent internecine struggles. Their inability to unite would later prove a fatal flaw when confronted by a common foe – white settlers. Unlike their Asian ancestors, the Algonquins, also known as Abenakis ("people of the dawn"), had given up nomadic life. They ate moose, deer, birds, and fish, but grew crops, too – maize, called Indian corn, beans, and pumpkins.

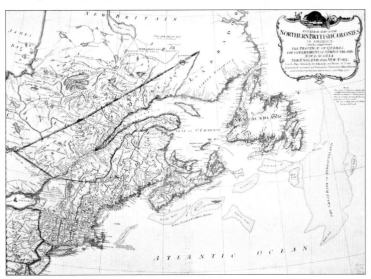

Map of the Northeast, printed in England a month after the Declaration of Independence was signed

◁ *Native American Indians Cooking and Preparing Food c.1850 by J. Fumagalli*

Embarkation and Departure of Columbus from the Port of Palos, undated painting by Ricardo Balaca

THE AGE OF DISCOVERY

The voyage of Christopher Columbus (1451–1506) to the New World in 1492 fired the imagination of maritime nations in Europe. Soon seafarers from England, France, and Spain were setting forth to explore the New World on behalf of their respective kings and queens. In 1497 the Italian explorer John Cabot (c.1425–1499) reached New England from Bristol, England, and claimed the land, along with all the territory north of Florida and east of the Rocky Mountains, for his English patron, Henry VII (1457–1509). By the end of the 16th century, helped largely by the 1588 defeat of the Spanish Armada, England was beginning to achieve mastery of the seas.

In 1606 England's King James I (1566–1625) granted a charter to two ventures to establish settlements in America. The Virginia Company was assigned an area near present-day Virginia; the Plymouth Company was granted rights to a more northern colony. This second group ran into

King James I (1566–1625)

trouble early on. One of its ships strayed off course and was captured by the Spanish near Florida. Another ship made it to New England, but had to turn back to England before winter arrived. In May 1607 two ships left Plymouth, England, with approximately 100 colonists. Three months later they made landfall at the mouth of the Kennebec River, where the settlers constructed Fort St. George. Their first winter proved to be an especially cold and snowy one, and the furs and mineral wealth fell far short of what the colonists expected. After just a year, the so-called Popham Colony was abandoned.

Despite this inauspicious beginning, the Plymouth Company hired surveyor John Smith (1580–1631) to conduct a more extensive evaluation of the territory. In 1614 Smith sailed along the Massachusetts coast, observing the region. His findings, published in *A Description of New England*, not only coined the name of the region, but also painted a glowing picture of this new land and its "greatnessse" of fish

TIMELINE

25,000-12,000 BC Central Asian nomads cross Bering Strait to become first North Americans	**7,000-1,000 BC** Warming temperatures lead to development of New England's forests	

25,000 BC	10,000 BC	AD 1000	1500
	10,000 BC Humans move into New England area after deglaciation	**AD 1000** Vikings sail to Newfoundland, Canada, and move south along the coast	

Leif Eriksson in Viking boat

and timber. Of all the places in the world, concluded Smith, this would be the best to support a new colony.

COLONIAL NEW ENGLAND

While the explorers of the early 17th century probed the shoreline of New England, events were taking place in Europe that would have a far-reaching impact on the settlement of the New World. The Reformation of the 16th century and the birth of the Protestant faith had created an upheaval in religious beliefs – particularly in England, where Henry VIII (1491–1547) had severed ties with Rome and had made sure that parliament declared him head of the Church of England.

Protestant Puritans believed that the Church of England, despite its claim to represent a reformed Christianity, was still rife with Catholic practices and that their faith was being debased in England, especially after James I, who was suspected of having Catholic sympathies, succeeded Elizabeth I in 1603. Puritans were persecuted for their beliefs and found themselves facing a stark choice: stay at home to fight against overwhelming odds or start anew somewhere else.

A small, radical faction of Puritans, known as Separatists, emigrated to Holland. The lifestyle of the Dutch did not live up to the demanding standards

Puritan governor addresses Colonists in 1621

of the Separatists' stern orthodoxy. As a result, they negotiated a deal with the Plymouth Company to finance a "pilgrimage" to America. In September 1620 they set sail. After a grueling 66-day voyage, their ship, the *Mayflower*, landed at what is now Provincetown (see p156), Massachusetts.

It was a short-lived stay. The barren, sandy coast seemed a forbidding place, so the ship sailed on to Plymouth Rock (see pp148–9), where the fatigued Pilgrims disembarked on December 26, 1620. During the winter of 1620–21, half of the Pilgrims succumbed to scurvy and the rigors of a harsh New England winter. But with the arrival of spring, the worst seemed to be behind them. The settlers found an ally among the indigenous people in Squanto (d.1622), a member of the Pawtuxet tribe who had been taken to England in 1605. Squanto had returned to the New World in 1615, and when word reached him that the English had arrived, he soon helped negotiate a 50-year peace treaty between the Pilgrims and the chief of the local Wampanoag tribe. Squanto also taught the newcomers how to live in their adopted home. He showed them how to shoot and trap, and told them which crops to grow. The first harvest was celebrated in the fall of 1621 with a three-day feast of thanksgiving.

Pilgrims board the *Mayflower* in 1620

1497 John Cabot explores North American coast	**1607** First North American colony founded at Jamestown	**1614** John Smith names territory New England	**1620** Pilgrims land at Plymouth, Massachusetts, aboard the *Mayflower*	
1500	1600		1615	1620
1492 Christopher Columbus discovers the New World	**1602** Captain Bartholomew Gosnold lands on Massachusetts coast	*John Smith*	**1616** Smallpox epidemic kills large number of New England Indians	*First feast of thanksgiving* **1621** Pilgrims celebrate feast of thanksgiving

The Battle of Bunker Hill

George III of England

The first major battle of the Revolutionary War took place in Boston on June 17, 1775, and actually was fought on Breed's Hill. The Americans had captured heavy British cannon on Breed's and Bunker hills overlooking Boston Harbor, which gave them a commanding position. Britain's first two attacks on Breed's Hill were repelled by the outnumbered defenders. The Colonial soldiers were running low on ammunition, however, which gave rise to commander Colonel William Prescott's orders, "Don't fire until you can see the whites of their eyes!" Reinforced with 400 fresh troops, British forces made a bayonet charge and seized the hill, forcing the Americans to retreat to nearby Bunker Hill. The British suffered more than 1,000 casualties to approximately 150 for the Americans. The battle reinforced the confidence of the American troops that had first been kindled by their successes at Lexington and Concord.

Bunker Hill Monument, *a granite obelisk, honors Colonial casualties.*

IN THE HEAT OF THE BATTLE

John Trumbull's 1786 painting Battle of Bunker Hill *depicts the hand-to-hand combat of the skirmish, fought mainly with bayonets and muskets. Victory came at a price. As one British soldier commented, "It was such a dear victory, another such would have ruined us."*

Colonial General Joseph Warren dies in final moments of battle after being shot in the head.

Declaration of Independence
Less than a year after the battle, the Second Continental Congress adopted the Declaration of Independence, which outlined the framework for democracy in the United States.

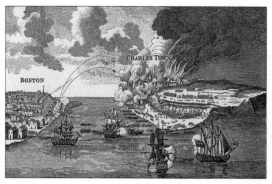

Attack on Breed's Hill
Prior to the infantry assault on the Colonial position, British men-of-war bombarded Breed's Hill with cannonade. Portions of nearby Charlestown caught fire and burned during the bombing.

A British officer prevents grenadier's coup de grâce.

British Firelocks
Loading a musket involved shaking gun-powder into a pan just above the trigger as well as into the barrel itself. The powder in the barrel was then tamped down with a small rod. This time-consuming process meant that soldiers stood unprotected on the battle-field as they reloaded.

British troops storm Colonial positions with renewed vigor after having suffered massive casualties on first two attempts.

British Major John Pitcairn collapses into his son's arms after being shot in chest, only to die while receiving medical treatment for his wounds.

COLONEL WILLIAM PRESCOTT

Born in Groton, Massachusetts, William Prescott (1726–95) led the Colonial forces during the battle of Bunker Hill. In the initial stages of the fight, British warships bombarded the Americans' fortified position with heavy cannon. The untested Colonial troops were taken aback, especially when a private was decapitated by a cannonball. Sensing his men were dis-heartened, Prescott, covered in the slain soldier's blood, leapt atop the redoubt wall and paced back and forth in defiance of the bombs bursting around him. His brave gesture galva-nized the troops, who went on to make one of the most courageous stands of the Revolutionary War.

Death of Metacomet (King Philip) in 1676

the Natives' loss. Initial cooperation between both groups gave way to competition and outright hostility as land-hungry settlers moved into Indian territory. War first erupted with the Pequot tribe in 1637, which resulted in their near annihilation as a people. The hostility reached its peak at the outset of the King Philip's War (1775–6), when several hundred members of the Narragansett tribe were killed by white settlers near South Kingston, Rhode Island.

WEAKENING TIES

The sheer distance dividing England and New England and the fact that communication could move no faster than wind-borne ships meant that there was very little contact between Old World and New. The colonists were largely self-governing, and there was no representation from them in the British parliament. Efforts by London to tighten control over the colonies were sporadic and in most cases successfully resisted until the Seven Years War between Britain and France (1756–1763) assured British domination of North America.

COLONIAL NEW ENGLAND

From this modest beginning, the settlement began slowly to prosper and expand. Within five years the group was self-sufficient. Nine years later the Massachusetts Bay Company was founded, which sent 350 people to Salem *(see pp136–9)*.

A second, much larger group joined the newly appointed governor, John Winthrop (c.1587–1649), and established a settlement at the mouth of the Charles River. They first called their new home Trimountain, but renamed it Boston in honor of the town some of the settlers had left in England.

During the 1630s immigrants started spreading farther afield, creating settlements along the coast of Massachusetts and New Hampshire, and even venturing inland. However, the colonists' gain proved to be

England's George III
(1738–1820)

Ironically, British success created the conditions that lessened the colonists' dependence on the mother country and also led to their growing estrangement. The colonies, especially New England, would come to feel that they no longer had to rely on British protection against the French in Canada and their Indian allies. Moreover, Britain's efforts after 1763 to derive a revenue from the colonies to help cover the debt incurred by the war and to contribute to imperial defense

TIMELINE

Harvard booster

Salem gravestone

1636 Harvard is founded, becoming America's first college

1656 Puritans of Massachusetts Bay Colony begin systematic persecution of newly arrived Quakers with imprisonment, banishment, and hanging

1676 King Philip's War ends when Wampanoag chief Metacomet is betrayed and killed

| 1630 | 1660 | 1675 | 1690 |

1630 Puritans led by John Winthrop found Boston

1636 Murder of two colonists, supposedly by Pequot Indians, sparks the beginning of Pequot War

1692 Salem witch trials begin, leading to the execution of 20 people

met growing resistance. The cry of "No taxation without representation" would become a rallying call to arms for the independence movement, with the most vocal protests coming from New England.

The taxation issue came to a head under the reign of King George III (1738–1820), who ascended the throne of Great Britain in 1760. The Hanoverian

Paul Revere's 1770 engraving of the Boston Massacre

king believed that the American colonists should remain under the control of Britain, and enacted a series of heavy taxes on various commodities, such as silk and sugar. In 1765 British parliament passed the Stamp Act, which placed a tax on commercial and legal documents, newspapers, agendas, and even playing cards and dice. The act had a galvanizing effect throughout New England as its incensed inhabitants banded together and refused to use the stamps. They even went so far as to hold stamp-burning ceremonies.

Parliament eventually repealed the act in 1766, but this did not end the issue. In fact, at the same time that the Stamp Act was rescinded, it was replaced by the Declaratory Act, which stated that every part of the British Empire would continue to be taxed however the parliament saw fit. To make sure that the colonists would not flout the law, the British sent two regiments to Boston to

British stamp for American colony goods

enforce its control. The troops, called Redcoats for their distinctive uniforms, proved decidedly unpopular. A series of small skirmishes between them and local sailors and workers culminated in the Boston Massacre (March 5, 1770), in which the British soldiers opened fire on an unruly crowd, killing five, including a free black man, Crispus Attucks.

REVOLUTIONARY SPIRIT

After the massacre an uneasy truce ensued. A simmering distrust remained between the two sides, and it only needed a suitable provocation to boil over again. That provocation came in the form of yet another proclamation – this one giving the East India Company the right to market tea directly in America, thus bypassing American merchants. When three ships arrived in Boston Harbor in 1773 with a shipment to unload, a group of about 60 men, including local politicians Samuel Adams (1722–1803) and John Hancock (1737–93), disguised themselves with Indian headdresses and then boarded the ships. They dumped 342 tea chests, valued at £18,000, into the harbor. The Boston Tea Party (see p89) was celebrated by the colonists as a

Protesters during the 1773 Boston Tea Party

1704 The *Boston News Letter*, America's first newspaper, is published

1737 John Hancock, an original signatory of the Declaration of Independence, is born

John Hancock's signature

1773 New taxes spur Boston Tea Party

1710	1725	1740	1750	1770

1713 Boatyard in Gloucester, Massachusetts, produces America's first schooner

1770 British soldiers kill five in Boston Massacre

Crowd in Philadelphia celebrating the signing of the Declaration of Independence on July 4, 1776

justifiable act of defiance against an oppressive regime. Parliament responded by passing the Intolerable Acts of 1774. These included the closing of the port of Boston by naval blockade until payment was made for the tea that had been destroyed.

On September 5, 1774, 56 representatives from the various American colonies, including New England, met in Philadelphia to establish the First Continental Congress to consider how to deal with grievances against Britain. The first concrete step toward nationhood had been taken.

Although the British troops garrisoned in Boston in the mid-1770s represented a formidable force, a large part of New England lay beyond their control. In the countryside, locals stockpiled arms. In 1775 the royal governor of Massachusetts, General Thomas Gage (1721–87), learned about such a cache at Concord (see pp144–5), 20 miles (32 km) west of Boston. He ordered 700 British soldiers to travel there under cover of darkness and destroy the arms.

The Americans were tipped off by dramatic horseback rides from Boston by Paul Revere and William Dawes. By the time the troops arrived at Lexington a few miles to the east of Concord, 77 colonial soldiers had set up a defensive formation, slowing the British advance. The Redcoats pressed onward to Concord, where close to 400 American patriots, called Minutemen for their ability to muster at a moment's notice, repelled the British attack. By the end of that day, April 19, 1775, 70 British had been killed and the casualty toll was 273. American losses were 95.

Minutemen repelling the British, who were trying to march through to Concord

TIMELINE

1774 British navy imposes blockade of Boston Harbor

1775 Battles at Concord and Lexington mark beginning of Revolutionary War

1783 Treaty of Paris signals end to Revolutionary War

1789 George Washington becomes first president of the United States

George Washingt

1775	1780	1785	1790	1795

1774 First Continental Congress held in Philadelphia

1776 Second Continental Congress ratifies the Declaration of Independence

1781 Colonial forces win decisive battle over British at Yorktown, Virginia

1791 First mechanical cotton mill of Samuel Slater at Pawtucket, Rhode Island

Slater Mill

Boston shipbuilding c.1850

The days of discussion were now clearly over. Colonial leaders signed the Declaration of Independence on July 4, 1776, and the American Revolution had begun. For the next six years the war would be waged first on New England soil, but then mostly beyond its borders at such key places as the Valley Forge encampment, Pennsylvania, and Yorktown, Virginia. Although the fighting ceased in 1781, the war officially came to an end with the signing of the 1783 Treaty of Paris.

A NEW INDUSTRIAL POWER

The fledgling United States of America was rich in natural resources, especially in New England. The region had excellent harbors that gave it access to the West Indies, Europe, and farther afield, where a developing maritime trade *(see pp24–5)* with the spices, teas, and other riches of the Far East proved increasingly lucrative. Indeed, New England ships became a familiar sight at docks from Nantucket *(see p153)* to New Guinea and from Portsmouth *(see pp252–3)* to Port-au-Prince, Haiti. New England also became a world center for the whaling

Antique harpoon

industry, as local ships plied the Seven Seas in search of the leviathans of the deep, which were killed for their oil, baleen, and blubber. The burgeoning shipbuilding industry that had sprung up along the coast also supplied a fleet of fishing boats that trolled the Grand Banks and the waters off Cape Cod, returning with their holds full of cod and halibut.

Ultimately it was an invention of the Industrial Revolution that transformed New England into an economic powerhouse. In the late 18th century, the first of Richard Arkwright's (1732–92) cotton spinning machines was imported to North America from England and installed on the Blackstone River at Pawtucket *(see pp172–3)*, Rhode Island. Previously cotton had been processed on individual looms in homes. Arkwright's device permitted cotton spinning to be carried out on factory-sized machines, which increased productivity a thousandfold. Soon mills sprang up, mainly in Massachusetts, in towns such as Lowell *(see pp142–3)*, Waltham, and Lawrence.

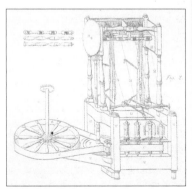
Richard Arkwright's sketch for his revolutionary cotton spinning machine

1800 National census results: 5.3 million people

Noah Webster

1805	1810	1815	1820	1825

1806 New Haven's Noah Webster publishes *Compendious Dictionary of the English Language*

1820 Maine gains independence from Massachusetts and becomes 20th state in the Union

By the mid-19th century, New England held two-thirds of America's cotton mills. The region offered two main advantages: a ready supply of rivers to power the mills' machinery and an increasing flow of cheap labor. Escaping the Potato Famine in the 1840s, numerous Irish immigrants fled to Massachusetts, where the mill towns beckoned with dormitory housing for their employees. Despite their numbers, however, this group faced discrimination.

Irish peasant contemplating failed crop

In Boston many such newcomers settled in squalid tenements along the city's waterfront. Eventually the Irish would come to dominate Boston politics, but for much of the 19th century they faced a daily struggle just to survive.

The extent of industrialization was felt in a relatively small area of New England, mostly Massachusetts, Rhode Island, and Connecticut. In the hinterland of Vermont, New Hampshire, and Maine, farming and logging remained the key industries well into the 20th century. These far-flung regions provided some of the manpower for the heartland's factories, as people left the hardscrabble life of subsistence farming for new lives farther south. Northern New England also helped supply the factories with some of their raw materials. The forests of Vermont, for example, were hacked down to make grazing land for sheep, which supplied wool for the textile mills.

ABOLITIONIST NEW ENGLAND

New England's role in 19th-century America was not merely one of economic powerhouse. The region also dominated the fields of education, science, politics, and architecture, as well as serving as the cultural heart of the nation, with Boston and its environs producing some of the nation's most influential writers and thinkers. The Massachusetts capital was also the center of a prominent protest against slavery, which was firmly entrenched in the southern states and reviled in much of the North.

William Lloyd Garrison (1805–79) began publishing a newspaper called *The Liberator* in 1831. In Garrison's view, "There is only one theme which should be dwelt upon till our whole country is free from the curse – SLAVERY." His polemics in *The Liberator* drew the wrath of pro-slavery forces. The House of Representatives of the southern state of Georgia offered $5,000 for his arrest. But Garrison continued publishing his newspaper, never missing an issue until it ceased publication at the end of the Civil War (1861–65), when slavery had been expunged from American society.

Some residents of New England towns went beyond merely reading and writing about the injustices of slavery. Stirred by Garrison and the so-called abolitionist movement, some antislavery exponents offered safe houses for what came to be known as the Underground Railroad. This loosely

Abolitionist William Lloyd Garrison

TIMELINE

Colt six-shooters

1835 Connecticut's Samuel Colt invents the six-shooter handgun

1851–2 *Uncle Tom's Cabin* appears in serial form in *The National Era* newspaper

1861 Civil War begins

| 1830 | 1845 | 1860 |

1831 Abolitionist William Lloyd Garrison publishes first edition of anti-slavery newspaper *The Liberator*

1840 Ireland's first Potato Famine devastates country

1851 Herman Melville publishes *Moby-Dick*, written in the southern Berkshires

1865 Civil War ends, leaving some 620,000 Americans dead

connected network of escape routes helped slaves fleeing the South make their way to freedom in the North and in Canada, beyond the reach of slave hunters. Towns such as New Bedford *(see p121)*, Massachusetts, Portland *(see pp280–83)*, Maine, and Burlington *(see pp232–5)*, Vermont, served as key "stations" on the slaves' road to freedom. The Underground Railroad was immortalized in Harriet Beecher Stowe's novel *Uncle Tom's Cabin; or, Life Among the Lowly* (1852).

DECLINING POWER

In the latter part of the 19th century there were signs that the days of New England's industrial preeminence were over. The transcontinental railroad had opened up the West to an army of new immigrants, which flooded in after the Civil War. The New World was a far, far bigger place than it had been when the Pilgrims landed, and the opportunities were boundless. The Great Plains encompassed thousands of square miles of arable land that New England farmers could only dream about. And for those looking for a more temperate climate, many other areas of the US now beckoned.

Meanwhile, the exploitation of natural resources and the development of new technologies were changing the face of industry. The discovery of petroleum meant that whale oil lost its economic importance, while steam engines offered a way of powering mills that no longer required river waterpower – one of the natural advantages upon which the region had relied.

Cover of sheet music based on Harriet Beecher Stowe's *Uncle Tom's Cabin* by artist Louisa Corbauy

Child laborer in cotton spinning plant

These problems were compounded by the fact that local labor was organizing to fight for better pay and working conditions, driving some factories to move to the South where labor costs were cheaper. Between 1880 and 1923, the South's share of the cotton-weaving industry rose from 6 percent to almost 50 percent.

The call for unionization even reached into the ranks of the police force, sparking one of America's most bitter labor confrontations. In 1919 Boston's men in blue sought to affiliate themselves with the American Federation of Labor. The city's police commissioner refused the request, and the entire force went on strike. Boston was beset by a

Modern Red Sox fan

1884 Mark Twain publishes *The Adventures of Huckleberry Finn*, a novel he wrote at his home in Hartford, Connecticut

1875	1890	1910

1882 Massachusetts-born poet/philosopher Ralph Waldo Emerson dies

1897 Country's first subway is opened in Boston

1903 Boston Red Sox win first World Series baseball championship

Ralph Waldo Emerson

wave of crime and riots, prompting the governor to send in the militia. By the time order was restored, at least five people had been killed and dozens had been wounded.

The loss of New England's economic importance was accompanied by a wave of change in the social makeup of the region. What had long been a homogeneous society – largely Protestant and of English or Scottish descent – was transformed by a rapid influx of immigrants. By the turn of the 20th century more than two-thirds of the residents of Massachusetts had at least one parent born outside the country.

The Depression of the 1930s hit the inhabitants of New England particularly hard. Unemployment in some towns topped 40 percent and wages plunged dramatically. World War II provided a temporary boost to the economy as shipyards and munition factories worked overtime to provide the military with the tools of their trade. However, with the return of peace, New England struggled to find its way in the new post-war era, and its economy continued to have its difficulties. The glory

Women making shell casings in a munitions plant during World War II

days, at least economically speaking, seemed to be irretrievable.

NEW ENGLAND REBIRTH

Even in its worse decline, as factories crumbled and residents headed for greener pastures, New England still possessed advantages that set the stage for recovery. One important factor was its concentration of higher educational institutions *(see pp28–9)*. As the Manufacturing Age gave way to the Information Age beginning in the 1960s, knowledge and adaptability became increasingly valuable commodities. With their well-endowed

Unknown artist's depiction of Harvard University campus c.1857

TIMELINE

	1914–1918 World War I		1929 Stock market crash marks beginning of Great Depression *Depression soup kitchen*		
	1915	**1925**	**1935**	**1945**	**1955**
Calvin Coolidge	1923 Vermont's Calvin Coolidge is sworn in as country's 30th president by his father		1939–45 World War II: US enters conflict in 1941	1954 World's first nuclear submarine is built in Groton, Connecticut	

Falmouth Heights Beach in Cape Cod

England's stunning physical beauty: the craggy coastline of Maine, the beaches of Cape Cod *(see pp156–9)*, the picturesque Vermont villages, and the coiled-up mountains of New Hampshire. As America became more prosperous and its workers had more free time in which to spend their mounting disposable income, tourism became an even bigger business than manufacturing had once been. The skiers, fishermen, beachcombers, antique hunters, campers, and others who flocked to the Northeast year-round pumped billions of dollars into the states' economies. By the 1990s tourism ranked alongside manufacturing as one of New England's most profitable industries.

research facilities, venerable institutions such as Harvard University *(see pp112–17)* and the Massachusetts Institute of Technology *(see p111)* attracted a new generation of young entrepreneurs looking to cash in on this newest opportunity. Meanwhile a son of one of Boston's most prominent families was proving that New England's impact on the national political scene was not over yet. John F. Kennedy *(see pp104–5)*, the great-grandson of an Irish potato-famine immigrant, became America's first Catholic president in 1960.

John Fitzgerald Kennedy

Starting in the mid-1980s, companies producing computer software and biomedical technology set up shop in the Boston suburbs and southern New Hampshire. The meteoric growth of high-tech industries represented a second revolution of sorts – proving far more valuable than the Industrial Revolution of the previous century. Meanwhile certain businesses, such as the insurance trade, weathered the shifts in the economy better than traditional manufacturing ventures, with Hartford *(see pp198–201)*, Connecticut, continuing to serve as the insurance capital of the nation.

One thing that all the economic upheavals did not change was New

Somehow, it seems fitting. After all, it was the beauty of the area that had helped convince people such as John Smith, close to four centuries ago, that New England had a viable future. And now, that same natural beauty is proving to be both timeless and lucrative, helping to bring about a renaissance in the prosperity of the place where American society had begun so tenuously so many years before.

Vermont's trademark rural landscape

1960	1970	1980	1990	2000	2010	2020

1961 Massachusetts-born John F. Kennedy becomes first Catholic president

1990 Thieves make off with artwork valued at $100 million from Boston's Isabella Stewart Gardner Museum

2004 Red Sox "reverse the curse" and win Baseball World Series

2005 New England Patriots win the Super Bowl

2009 NE states (except Rhode Island) legalize gay marriage

1968 Senator Robert Kennedy is assassinated in Los Angeles

1999 John F. Kennedy, Jr. dies in plane crash off Martha's Vineyard

2008 Boston Celtics win their 17th NBA championship

1963 President Kennedy is assassinated in Dallas

Robert F. Kennedy

2004 Massachusetts legally recognizes gay marriage

BOSTON

Boston's Best

The city of Boston's Athenian self-image is
manifested in dozens of museums, galleries,
and archives, paramount of which is the Museum
of Fine Arts. The city's importance in America's
history has left it with a unique legacy of old
buildings, with much fine religious and civic
architecture, including Trinity Church and Massachusetts State House. This strong architectural
heritage continues to the present day, and includes
modern structures such as the John Hancock Tower.
Boston's wealth of sights, along with its many parks
and gardens, make it a fascinating city to explore.

**Boston Common
and Public Garden**
*At the heart of the city,
the spacious common,
and smaller, more
formal Public Garden,
provide open space
for both sport
and relaxation.*

Trinity Church
*Perhaps Boston's finest
building, this Romanesque
Revival masterpiece by
Henry Hobson Richardson
was completed in 1877.*

John Hancock Tower
*Dominating the Back
Bay skyline, with its
mirrored façade reflecting
the surroundings, the John
Hancock Tower is New
England's tallest building.*

Museum of Fine Arts
*One of the largest museums
in North America, the M.F.A.
is famous for its Egyptian,
Greek, and Roman art, and
French Impressionist paintings.*

◁ **Aerial view Boston and waterfront**

Old State House

The seat of British colonial government until independence, the building later undertook many different uses. It now houses a museum.

Old North Church

Dating from 1723, this is Boston's oldest surviving church. Due to its role in the Revolution, it is also one of the city's most important historical sites.

0 kilometers   0.5

0 miles   0.5

New England Aquarium

This aquarium displays a huge array of creatures from the world's oceans. Researchers here are also involved in key international fish and whale conservation programs.

Massachusetts State House

Built in the 1790s as the new center of state government, the Charles Bulfinch-designed State House sits imposingly at the top of Beacon Hill.

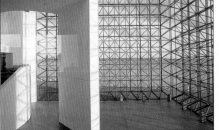

John F. Kennedy Library and Museum

The nation's 35th president is celebrated here in words and images – video clips of the first president to fully use the media make this a compelling museum.

The Freedom Trail

From Boston Common to Paul Revere House

Boston has more sites directly related to the American Revolution than any other city. The most important of these sites, as well as some relating to other freedoms gained by Bostonians, have been linked together as "The Freedom Trail." This 2.5-mile (4-km) walking route, marked in red on the sidewalks, starts at Boston Common and eventually ends at Bunker Hill in Charlestown. This first section weaves its way through the central city and Old Boston.

Elegant Georgian steeple of Park Street Church

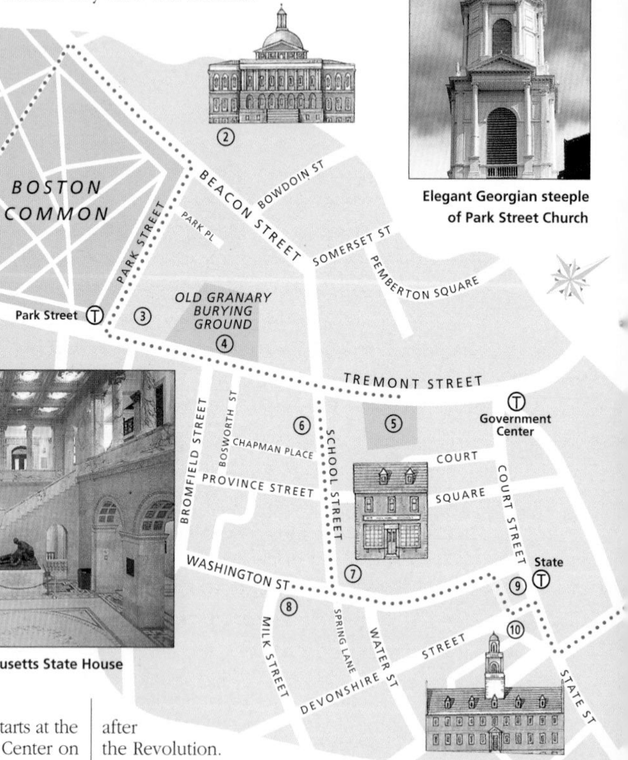

Nurses Hall in Massachusetts State House

Central City

The Freedom Trail starts at the Visitor Information Center on Boston Common ① *(see pp64–5)*. This is where angry colonials rallied against their British masters and where the British forces were encamped during the 1775–76 military occupation. Political speakers still expound from their soapboxes here, and the Common remains a center of activity.

Walking toward the northwest corner of the Common gives a great view of the Massachusetts State House ② *(see p68–9)* on Beacon Street, designed by Charles Bulfinch as the new center of state governance shortly after the Revolution.

Along Park Street, at the end of the Common, you will come to Park Street Church ③ *(see p66)*, built in 1810 and a bulwark of the antislavery movement. The church took the place of an old grain storage facility, which gave its name to the adjacent Granary Burying Ground ④, one of Boston's earliest cemeteries and the final resting place of patriots John Hancock and Paul Revere *(see p120)*. Continuing along Tremont Street you will come to King's Chapel and Burying Ground ⑤ *(see p76)*. The tiny cemetery is Boston's oldest, containing, among others, the grave of city founder John Winthrop. As the name suggests, King's Chapel was the principal Anglican church in Puritan Boston, and more than half of its congregation fled to Nova Scotia at the outbreak of the Revolution. The box pew on the right just inside the front entrance was reserved for condemned prisoners to hear their last sermons before going to the gallows on Boston Common.

Heart of Old Boston

Head back along Tremont Street and turn down School Street, where a hopscotch-like mosaic embedded in the sidewalk commemorates the site of the First Public School ⑥, established in 1635. At the bottom of the street is the Old Corner Bookstore ⑦ *(see p77)*, a landmark more associated with Boston's literary emergence of 1845–65 than with the Revolution.

The Old South Meeting House ⑧, a short way to the south on Washington Street, is a graceful, white-spired brick church, modeled on Sir Christopher Wren's English country churches. As one of the largest meeting halls in Revolutionary Boston, "Old South's" rafters rang with many a fiery speech urging revolt against the British. A few blocks along, the Old State House ⑨ presides over the head of State Street. The colonial government building, it also served as the first state legislature, and the merchants' exchange in the basement was where Boston's colonial shipping fortunes were made. The square in front of the Old State House is the Boston Massacre Site ⑩, where British soldiers opened fire on a taunting mob in 1770, killing five and providing ideal propaganda for revolutionary agitators.

Follow State Street down to Congress Street and turn left to reach Faneuil Hall ⑪, called the "Cradle of Liberty" for the history of patriotic speeches made in its public meeting hall. Donated to the city by Huguenot merchant Peter Faneuil, the building was Boston's first marketplace.

The red stripe of the Freedom Trail comes in handy when negotiating the way to the North End and the Paul Revere House ⑫ on North Square. Boston's oldest house, it was home to the man known for his famous "midnight ride" *(see p120)*.

TIPS FOR WALKERS

Starting point: *Boston Common. Maps at Boston Common Visitor Center.* ***Length:*** *2.5 miles (4 km).* ***Getting there:*** *Park Street Station (T Green and Red lines) to start. Free guided tours leave from National Park Visitor Center, 15 State St. Follow red stripe on sidewalk for the full route.* **www**.thefreedomtrail.org

Faneuil Hall, popularly known as "the Cradle of Liberty"

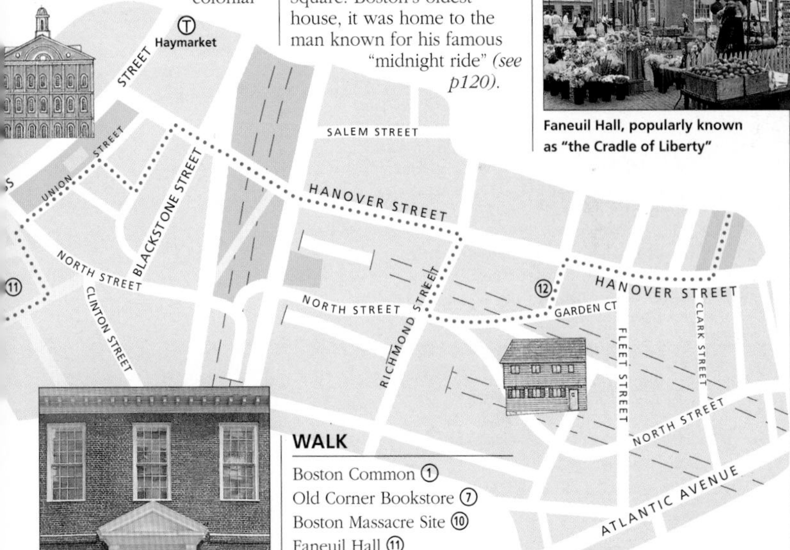

Old State House, the seat of colonial government

WALK

- Boston Common ①
- Old Corner Bookstore ⑦
- Boston Massacre Site ⑩
- Faneuil Hall ⑪
- First Public School Site ⑥
- Granary Burying Ground ④
- King's Chapel and Burying Ground ⑤
- Massachusetts State House ②
- Old South Meeting House ⑧
- Old State House ⑨
- Park Street Church ③
- Paul Revere House ⑫

0 meters 200

0 yards 200

KEY

- ••• Walk route
- [T] Subway
- [i] Tourist information

The Freedom Trail

From Old North Church to Bunker Hill Monument

Distances begin to stretch out on the second half of the Freedom Trail as it meanders through the narrow streets of the North End, then continues over the Charles River to Charlestown, where Boston's settlers first landed. The sites here embrace two wars – the War of Independence and the War of 1812.

View from Copp's Hill terrace, at the edge of Copp's Hill Burying Ground

The North End

Following the Freedom Trail through the North End, allow time to try some of the Italian cafés and bakeries along the neighborhood's main thoroughfare, Hanover Street. Cross through the Paul Revere Mall to reach Old North Church ⑬ (see p87), whose spire

Gravestone at Copp's Hill Burying Ground

is instantly visible over the shoulder of the statue of Paul Revere on horseback. Sexton Robert Newman hung two lanterns in the belfry here, signaling the advance of British troops on Lexington and Concord in 1775. The church retains its 18th-century interior, including the traditional box pews.

The crest of Copp's Hill lies close by on Hull Street. Some of Boston's earliest gallows stood here, and Bostonians would gather in boats below to watch the hangings of heretics and pirates. Much of the hilltop is covered by Copp's Hill

Burying Ground ⑭. This was established in 1660, and the cemetery holds the remains of several generations of the Mather family – Boston's influential 17th- and 18th-century theocrats – as well as the graves of many soldiers of the Revolution. Boston's first free African American community, "New Guinea," covered the west side of Copp's Hill. A broken column marks the grave of Prince Hall, head of the Black Masons, distinguished veteran of the Revolution, and prominent political leader in the early years of the Republic. The musketball-chipped tombstone of patriot Daniel Malcolm records that he asked to be buried "in a stone grave 10 feet deep" to rest beyond the reach of British gunfire.

Boston
Inner
Harbor

KEANY SQUARE

COMMERCIAL STREET

PRINCE STREET

HULL STREET

CHARLESTOWN BRIDGE

NORTH E.
PLAYGROU

SNOWHILL STREET

SHEAFE STREET

PRINCE STREET

HULL STREET

COPP'S HILL
⑭ BURYNG
GROUND

FOSTER ST

CHARTER STREET

ATLANTIC AVENUE

SALEM STREET

⑬

NORTH BENNETT STREET

TILESTON STREET

HANOVER STREET

Traditional box pews inside Old North Church

WALK

Bunker Hill Monument ⑯
Charlestown Navy Yard and
   the USS *Constitution* ⑮
Copp's Hill Burying Ground ⑭
Old North Church ⑬

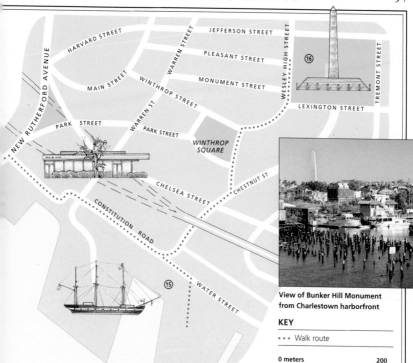

View of Bunker Hill Monument
from Charlestown harborfront

KEY

• • • Walk route

0 meters 200

0 yards 200

Charlestown

The iron bridge over the Charles River that links the North End in Boston with City Square in Charlestown dates from 1899. Across the bridge, turn right along Constitution Road, following signs to Charlestown Navy Yard ⑮. The National Park Service now operates the Visitor Center at Building 5, with a film and exhibits about the historic role of the Navy Yard and the history of the 18th- through to 20th-century warships that are berthed at its piers. The colonial navy had been no match for the might of Britain's naval forces during the Revolution, and building a more formidable naval force became a priority. This was one of several shipyards that were set up around 1800. Decommissioned in 1974, the yard is now maintained by the National Park Service.

Lion carving,
USS Constitution

Lying at her berth alongside Pier 1, the USS *Constitution* is probably the most famous ship in US history and still remains the flagship of the US Navy. Built at Hartt's shipyard in the North End, she was completed in 1797. In the War of 1812, she earned the nickname "Old Ironsides" for the resilience of her live oak hull against cannon fire. Fully restored for her bicentennial, the *Constitution* occasionally sails under her own power.

The granite obelisk that towers above the Charlestown waterfront is Bunker Hill Monument ⑯, commemorating the battle of June 17, 1775 that ended with a costly victory for British forces against an irregular colonial army, which finally ran out of ammunition. British losses were so heavy, however, that the battle would presage future success for the colonial forces. As a monument to the first large-scale battle of the Revolution, the obelisk, based on those of ancient Egypt, was a prototype for others across the US.

Defensive guns at Charlestown Navy Yard with view of the North End

BEACON HILL AND THE THEATER DISTRICT

By the 1790s, the south slope of Beacon Hill, facing Boston Common, had become the main seat of Boston's wealth and power. The north slope and the land up to the Charles River, known as the West End, was much poorer. Urban renewal has now cleared the slums of the West End, and the gentrification of Beacon Hill has made this one of Boston's most desirable neighborhoods. The area south of Boston Common is more down-to-earth, and home to the city's Theater District.

SIGHTS AT A GLANCE

Historic Streets and Squares

Bay Village 17
Beacon Street 6
Charles Street 1
Chinatown 16
Downtown Crossing 14
Louisburg Square 2
Mount Vernon Street 3

Historic Buildings, Museums, and Theaters

Boston Athenaeum 10
Colonial Theatre 15
Hepzibah Swan Houses 5
Massachusetts State House pp68–9 11
Museum of African American History 12
Museum of Science and Science Park 13
Nichols House Museum 4
Park Street Church 8
Shubert Theatre 18
Wang Theatre 19

Parks and Cemeteries

Boston Common and Public Garden 7
Granary Burying Ground 9

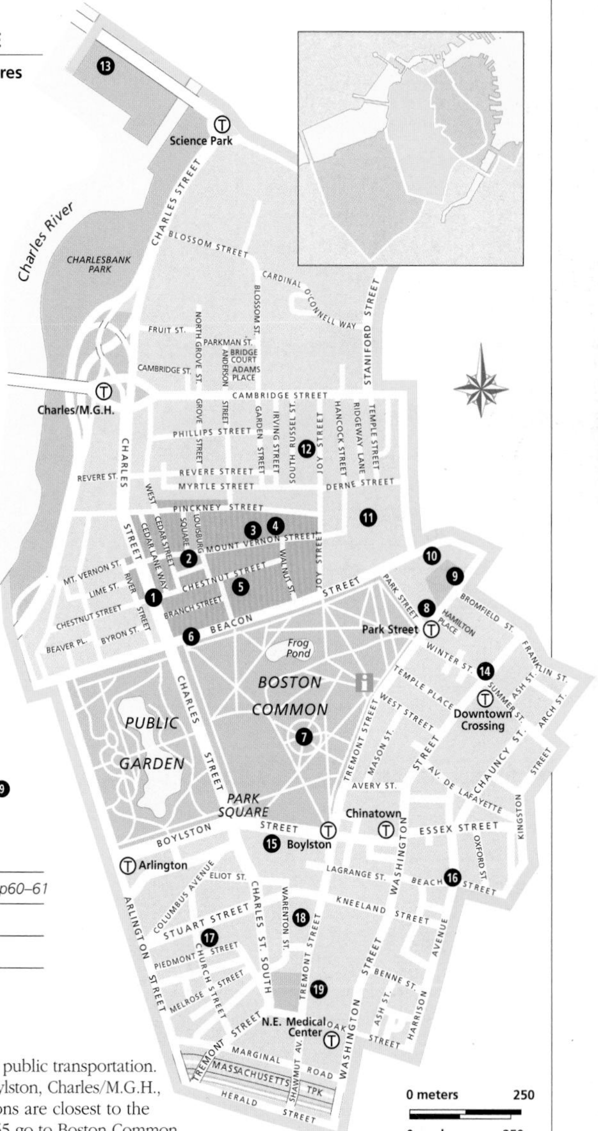

KEY

▒ Street-by-Street map *see pp60–61*

[T] "T" station

ℹ Tourist information

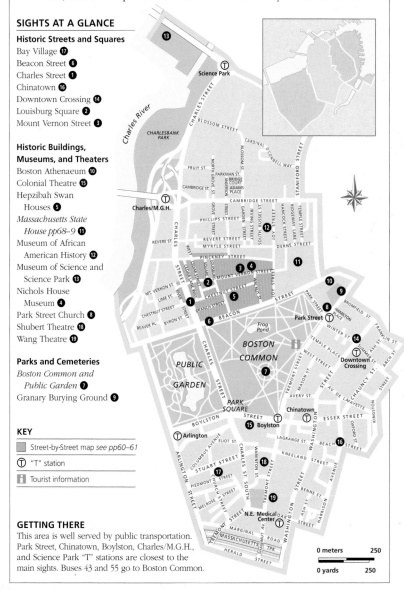

GETTING THERE

This area is well served by public transportation. Park Street, Chinatown, Boylston, Charles/M.G.H., and Science Park "T" stations are closest to the main sights. Buses 43 and 55 go to Boston Common.

◁ **Front view of the Massachusetts State House *(see pp68–9)*, seen from Boston Common**

Street-by-Street: Beacon Hill

Lion door
knocker,
Beacon St.

From the 1790s to the 1870s, the south slope of Beacon Hill was Boston's most sought-after neighborhood – its wealthy elite decamped only when the more exclusive Back Bay (see pp92–101) was built. Many of the district's houses were designed by Charles Bulfinch and his disciples, and the south slope evolved as a textbook example of Federal architecture. Elevation and view were all, and the finest homes are either on Boston Common or perched near the top of the hill. Early developers abided by a gentleman's agreement to set houses back from the street, but the economic depression of 1807–12 resulted in row houses being built right out to the street.

Cobblestone street, once typical of Beacon Hill

PINCKNEY STREET

LOUISBURG SQUARE

MOUNT VERNON STREET

CEDAR STREET

CHESTNUT STREET

CHARLES STREET

Louisburg Square
The crowning glory of the Beacon Hill district, this square was developed in the 1830s. Today, it is still Boston's most desirable address ❷

Charles Street Meeting House was built in the early 19th century to house a congregation of Baptists.

KEY

– – – Suggested route

Back Bay and South End

DE LUCA'S MARKET

"FRESHEST BY FAR SINCE 1905"

★ **Charles Street**
This elegant street is the main shopping area for Beacon Hill. Lined with upscale grocers and antique stores, it also has some fine restaurants ❶

For hotels and restaurants in this region see pp306–11 and pp332–9

STAR SIGHTS

★ Charles Street

★ Nichols House Museum

★ Nichols House Museum
This modest museum offers an insight into the life of Beacon Hill resident Rose Nichols, who lived here from 1885 to 1960 ❹

LOCATOR MAP
See Street Finder map 1

| 0 meters | 50 |
| 0 yards | 50 |

Mount Vernon Street
Described in the 19th century as the "most civilized street in America," this is where the developers of Beacon Hill (the Mount Vernon Proprietors) chose to build their own homes ❸

→ **Massachusetts State House**

WALNUT STREET

SPRUCE STREET

BEACON STREET

Boston Common

Hepzibah Swan Houses
Elegant in their simplicity, these three Bulfinch-designed houses were wedding gifts for the daughters of a wealthy Beacon Hill proprietress ❺

Beacon Street
The finest houses on Beacon Hill were invariably built on Beacon Street. Elegant, Federal-style mansions, some with ornate reliefs, overlook the city's most beautiful green space, Boston Common ❻

Charles Street, lined with shops catering to the residents of Beacon Hill

Charles Street ❶

Map 1 B4. ⓣ *Charles/MGH.*

This street originally ran along the bank of the Charles River, although subsequent landfill has removed it from the riverbank by several hundred feet. The main shopping and dining area of the Beacon Hill neighborhood, the curving line of Charles Street hugs the base of Beacon Hill, giving it a quaint, village-like air. Many of the houses remain residential on the upper stories, while street level and cellar levels were converted to commercial uses long ago. Though most of Charles Street dates from the 19th century, widening in the 1920s meant that some of the houses on the west side acquired new façades. The Charles Street Meeting House, designed by Asher Benjamin in 1807, was built for a Baptist congregation that practiced immersion in the then adjacent river. It is now a commercial building. Two groups of striking Greek Revival row houses are situated at the top of Charles

Street, between Revere and Cambridge Streets. Charles Street was one of the birthplaces of the antique trade in the US and now has some two dozen antique dealers.

Louisburg Square ❷

Map 1 B4. ⓣ *Charles/MGH, Park Street.*

Home to millionaire politicians, best-selling authors, and corporate moguls, Louisburg Square is perhaps Boston's most prestigious address. Developed in the 1830s as a shared private preserve on Beacon Hill, the square's tiny patch of greenery surrounded by a high iron fence sends a clear signal of the square's continued exclusivity. On the last private square in the city, the narrow, Greek

Revival bow-fronted town houses sell for a premium over comparable homes elsewhere on Beacon Hill. Even the on-street parking spaces are deeded. The traditions of Christmas Eve carol singing and candlelit windows are said to have begun on Louisburg Square. A statue of Christopher Columbus, presented by a wealthy Greek merchant in 1850, stands at its center.

Mount Vernon Street ❸

Map 1 B4. ⓣ *Charles/MGH, Park Street.*

In the 1890s the novelist Henry James called Mount Vernon Street "the most civilized street in America," and it still retains that air of urbane culture. Most of the developers of Beacon Hill, who called themselves the Mount Vernon Proprietors, chose to build their private homes along this street. Architect Charles Bulfinch envisioned Beacon Hill as a district of large freestanding mansions on spacious landscaped grounds, but building costs ultimately dictated much denser development. The sole remaining example of Bulfinch's vision is the second Harrison Gray Otis House, built in 1800 at No. 85 Mount Vernon Street. The current Greek Revival row houses next door (Nos. 59–83), graciously set back from the street by 30 ft (9 m), were built to replace the single mansion belonging to

Columbus Statue, Louisburg Square

Otis's chief development partner, Jonathan Mason. The original mansion was torn down after Mason's death in 1836. The three Bulfinch-designed houses at Nos. 55, 57, and 59 Mount Vernon Street were built by Mason for his daughters. No. 55 was ultimately passed on to the Nichols family in 1885.

OLIVER WENDELL HOLMES AND THE BOSTON BRAHMINS

In 1860, Oliver Wendell Holmes wrote that Boston's wealthy merchant class of the time constituted a Brahmin caste, a "harmless, inoffensive, untitled aristocracy" with "their houses by Bulfinch, their monopoly on Beacon Street, their ancestral portraits and Chinese porcelains, humanitarianism, Unitarian faith in the march of the mind, Yankee shrewdness, and New England exclusiveness." So keenly did he skewer the social class that the term has persisted. In casual usage today, a Brahmin is someone with an old family name, whose finances derive largely from trust funds, and whose politics blend conservatism with *noblesse oblige* toward those less fortunate. Boston's Brahmins founded most of the hospitals, performing arts bodies, and museums of the greater metropolitan area.

Oliver Wendell Holmes (1809–94)

Drawing room of the Bulfinch-designed Nichols House Museum

Nichols House Museum ❹

55 Mount Vernon St. **Map** 1 B4.
Tel (617) 227-6993. ⓣ Park Street.
◯ Apr–Oct: 11am–4pm Tue–Sat;
Nov–Mar: 11am–4pm Thu–Sat.

The Nichols House Museum was designed by Charles Bulfinch in 1804 and offers a rare glimpse into the tradition-bound lifestyle of Beacon Hill. Modernized in 1830 by the addition of a Greek Revival portico, the house is nevertheless a superb example of Bulfinch's domestic architecture. It also offers an insight into the life of a true Beacon Hill character. Rose Standish Nichols moved into the house at 13 when her father purchased it in 1885. She left it as a museum in her 1960 will. A woman ahead of her time,

strong-willed and famously hospitable, Nichols was, among other things, a self-styled landscape designer who traveled extensively around the world to write about gardens.

Hepzibah Swan Houses ❺

13, 15 & 17 Chestnut St. **Map** 1 B4.
ⓣ Park Street. ◉ to the public.

The only woman who was ever a member of the Mount Vernon Proprietors, Mrs. Swan had these houses built by Bulfinch as wedding presents for her daughters in 1806, 1807, and 1814. Some of the most elegant and distinguished houses on Chestnut Street, they are backed by Bulfinch-designed stables that face onto Mount Vernon Street. The deeds restrict the height of the stables to 13 ft (4 m) so that her daughters would still have a view over Mount Vernon Street. In 1863–65, No. 13 was home to Dr. Samuel Gridley Howe, abolitionist and educational pioneer who, in 1833, founded the first school for the blind in the US.

Beacon Street ❻

Map 1 B4. ⓣ Park Street.

Beacon Street is lined with urban mansions facing Boston Common. The 1808 William Hickling Prescott House at No. 55, designed by Asher Benjamin, offers tours of rooms in Federal, Victorian, and Colonial Revival styles on Wednesdays, Thursdays, and Saturdays between May and October. The American Meteorological Society in No. 45 was built as Harrison Gray Otis's last and finest house. It had 11 bedrooms and an elliptical room behind the front parlor, where the walls and even the doors are curved.

The elite Somerset Club stands at No. 42-43 Beacon Street. Between the 1920s and the 1940s, Irish Catholic mayor James Michael Curley would lead election night victory marches to the State House, pausing at the Somerset Club to taunt the Boston Brahmins inside.

The Parkman House at No. 33 Beacon Street is now a city-owned meeting center. It was the home of Dr. George Parkman, who was murdered by Harvard professor and fellow socialite Dr. John Webster in 1849. Boston society was torn apart when the presiding judge, a relative of Parkman, sentenced Webster to be hanged.

Elegant Federal-style houses on Beacon Street, overlooking Boston Common

Boston Common and Public Garden ➐

Acquired by Boston in 1634 from first settler William Blackstone, the 48-acre (19-ha) Boston Common served for two centuries as common pasture, military drill ground, and gallows site. British troops camped here during the 1775–76 military occupation. As Boston grew in the 19th century, the Boston Common became a center for open-air civic activity and remains so to this day. By contrast, the 24-acre (10-ha) Public Garden is more formal. When the Charles River mudflats were first filled in the 1830s, a succession of landscape plans were plotted for the Public Garden before the city chose the English-style garden scheme of George F. Meacham in 1869. The lagoon was added to the garden two years later.

The Public Garden, a popular green space in the heart of the city

Make Way for Ducklings
Based on the classic children's story by Robert McCloskey, this sculpture is of a duck and her brood of ducklings.

The Ether Monument memorializes the first use of anesthesia in 1846.

★ George Washington Statue
Cast by Thomas Ball from bronze, with a solid granite base, this is one the finest memorial statues in Boston. It was dedicated in 1869.

CHARLES STREET

Statue of Edward Everett Hale

Lagoon Bridge
This miniature, ornamental bridge over the Public Garden lagoon was designed by William G. Preston in 1869 in a moment of whimsy. The lagoon it "spans" was constructed in 1861.

Statue of Reverend William Ellery Channing

The Swan Boats, originally inspired by Wagner's *Löhengrin*, have been a feature of the Public Garden lake since 1877.

★ **Shaw Memorial**
This relief immortalizes the Civil War's 54th regiment of Massachusetts Infantry, the first free black regiment in the Union Army, and their white colonel Robert Shaw.

The Soldiers and Sailors Monument, erected in 1877, features prominent Bostonians from the time of the Civil War.

Blackstone Memorial Tablet recalls the purchase of the common in 1634 and is cited as proof that it belongs to the people.

Park Street subway

Brewer Fountain was purchased at the Paris expo of 1867.

Visitors' Center

Parkman Bandstand
This bandstand was built in 1912 to memorialize George F. Parkman, who bequeathed $5 million for the care of Boston Common and other parks in the city.

The Flagstaff

```
0 meters        100
0 yards         100
```

Central Burying Ground
This graveyard, which dates from 1756, holds the remains of many British and American casualties from the Battle of Bunker Hill (1775). The portraitist Gilbert Stuart is also buried here.

STAR FEATURES

★ George Washington Statue

★ Shaw Memorial

Park Street Church at the corner of Tremont and Park Streets

Park Street Church ❽

1 Park St. **Map** 1 C4. **Tel** (617) 523-3383. Ⓣ Park Street. ☐ Jul–Aug: 9am–3:30pm Tue–Sat; Sep–Jun: by appointment. ⛪ Jul–Aug: 10:45am, 5:30pm Sun; Sep–Jun: 8:30am, 11am, 4pm, 6pm Sun. Ⓖ ♿ www.parkstreet.org

Park Street Church's 217-ft (65-m) steeple has punctuated the intersection of Park and Tremont Streets since its dedication in 1810. Designed by English architect Peter Banner, who adapted a design by the earlier English architect Christopher Wren, the church was commissioned by parishioners wanting to establish a Congregational church in the heart of Boston. The church was, and still is, one of the city's most influential pulpits. Contrary to popular belief, the sermons of Park Street ministers did not earn the intersection the nickname of "Brimstone Corner." Rather, the name came about because

during the war of 1812 the US militia, based in Boston, stored its gunpowder in the church basement as safekeeping against bombardment from the British navy.

In 1829, William Lloyd Garrison (1805–79), fervently outspoken firebrand of the movement to abolish slavery, gave his first abolition speech from the Park Street pulpit.

In 1849 a speech entitled *The War System of Nations* was addressed to the American Peace Society by Senator Charles Sumner. Much later, in 1893, the anthem *America the Beautiful* by Katharine Lee Bates debuted at a Sunday service. Today the church continues, as always, to be involved in religious, political, cultural, and humanitarian activities.

Granary Burying Ground ❾

Tremont Street. **Map** 1 C4. Ⓣ Park Street. ☐ 9am–5pm daily.

Named after the early grain storage facility that once stood on the adjacent site of Park Street Church, the Granary Burying Ground dates from 1660. Buried here were three important signatories to the Declaration of Independence – Samuel Adams, John Hancock, and Robert Treat Paine, along with Paul Revere, Benjamin Franklin's parents, merchant-philanthropist Peter Faneuil, and victims of the Boston Massacre.

The orderly array of gravestones, often featured in films and television shows set in Boston, is the result of modern groundskeeping. Few stones, if any, mark the actual burial site of the person memorialized. In fact, John Hancock may not be here at all. On the night he was buried in 1793, grave robbers cut off the hand with which he had signed his name to the Declaration of Independence, and some believe that the rest of his body was removed during 19th-century construction work.

Boston Athenaeum ❿

10½ Beacon St. **Map** 1 C4. **Tel** (617) 227-0270. Ⓣ Park Street. ☐ 8:30am–8pm Mon, 8:30am–5:30pm Tue–Fri, 9am–4pm Sat. ● Jun–Aug: Sat. ⛯ www.bostonathenaeum.org

Organized in 1807, the collection of the Boston Athenaeum quickly became one of the country's leading private libraries. Sheep farmer Edward Clarke Cabot won the 1846 design competition to house the library, with plans for a gray sandstone building based on Palladio's Palazzo da Porta Festa in Vicenza, a building Cabot knew from a book in the Athenaeum's collection. Included in over half a million volumes are rare manuscripts, maps, and newspapers. Among the Athenaeum's major holdings are the personal

Granary Burying Ground, final resting place for Revolutionary heroes

For hotels and restaurants in this region see pp306–11 and pp332–9

Stone frieze decoration on the Renaissance Revival-style Athenaeum

Museum of Science and Science Park ⓭

Science Park. **Map** 1 B2.
Tel (617) 723-2500. Ⓣ *Science Park.* ◯ *9am–5pm Mon–Thu & Sat–Sun, (Jul–early Sep: 9am–7pm), 9am–9pm Fri.* ◉ *Thanksgiving, Dec 25.* ◪ ◖ ◗
www.mos.org

The Museum of Science straddles the Charles River atop the flood control dam that sits at the mouth of the Charles River. The Science Park that has developed around it includes a large-format cinema and planetarium.

With more than 550 inter-active exhibits covering natural history, medicine, astronomy, the physical sciences, and com-puting, the Science Museum is largely oriented to families. The Mugar Omni Theater contains a five-story domed screen with a multidimen-sional wrap-around sound system, and shows mostly films with a natural science theme. The Charles Hayden Planetarium offers laser shows as well as shows about stars, planets, and other celestial phenomena.

library that once belonged to George Washington and the theological library supplied by King William III of England to the King's Chapel *(see p76).* In its early years the Athenaeum was Boston's chief art museum, but when the Museum of Fine Arts was proposed, it gracious-ly donated much of its art, including unfinished portraits of George Washington pur-chased in 1831 from the widow of the painter Gilbert Stuart.

Massachusetts State House ⓫

See pp68–9.

Museum of African American History ⓬

46 Joy St. **Map** 1 C3. **Tel** *(617) 725-0022.* Ⓣ *Park Street.* ◯ *10am–4pm Mon–Sat.* ◉ *public hols.* ◪
www.afroammuseum.org

Built from town house plans designed by Asher Benjamin, the African Meeting House (the centerpiece of the museum) was dedicated in 1806. The oldest black church building in the United States, it was the political and reli-gious center of Boston's African American society. The interior is plain and simple but rang with the oratory of some of the 19th century's most fiery abolitionists: from Sojourner Truth and Frederick Douglass to William Lloyd Garrison, who founded the New England Anti-Slavery Society in 1832. The meeting house basement was Boston's

first school for African American children until the adjacent Abiel Smith School was built in 1831. When segregated education was barred in 1855, however, the Smith School closed. The meeting house became a Hasidic synagogue in the 1890s, as most of Boston's African American community moved to Roxbury and Dorchester. The synagogue closed in the 1960s, and in 1987 the African Meeting House reopened as the linchpin site on the Black Heritage Trail.

Holmes Alley, once an escape route for slaves on the run

BLACK HERITAGE TRAIL

In the first US census in 1790, Massachusetts was the only state to record no slaves. During the 19th century, Boston's substantial free African American community lived principally on the north slope of Beacon Hill and in the adjacent West End. The Black Heritage Trail links several key sites, ranging from the African Meeting House to several private homes, which are not open to visitors. Among them are the 1797 George Middleton House (Nos. 5–7 Pinckney Street), the oldest standing house built by African Americans on Beacon Hill, and the Lewis and Harriet Hayden House (No. 66 Phillips Street). Escaped slaves, the Haydens made their home a haven for runaways in the "Underground Railroad" of safe houses between the South and Canada. The walking tour also leads through mews and alleys, like Holmes Alley at the end of Smith Court, once used by fugitives to flee professional slave catchers.

Free tours of the Black Heritage Trail are led by National Park Service rangers – (617) 742-5415 – from Memorial Day weekend to Labor Day, 10am, noon, and 2pm Mon–Sat, departing from the Shaw Memorial. Tours are given at 2pm Mon–Sat or by appointment the rest of the year.

Massachusetts State House ⑪

The cornerstone of the Massachusetts State House was laid on July 4, 1795, by Samuel Adams and Paul Revere. Completed on January 11, 1798, the Charles Bulfinch-designed center of state government served as a model for the US Capitol Building in Washington and as an inspiration for many of the state capitols around the country. Later additions were made, but the original building remains the archetype of American government buildings. Its dome, sheathed in copper and gold, serves as the zero mile marker for Massachusetts, making it, as Oliver Wendell Holmes (*see p63*) remarked, "the hub of the universe."

The State House, from Boston Common

The Great Hall is the latest addition to the State House. Built in 1990, it is lined with marble and topped by a glass dome, and is used for state functions.

★ House of Representatives

This elegant oval chamber was built for the House of Representatives in 1895. The Sacred Cod, which now hangs over the gallery, came to the State House when it first opened in 1798, and it has since hung over any place where the representatives have met.

Main Staircase
Beautiful stained-glass windows decorate the main staircase. They illustrate the varied state seals of Massachusetts from its inception as a colony through to modern statehood.

STAR SIGHTS

★ House of Representatives

★ Nurses Hall

The Wings of the State House, thought by many to sit incongruously with the rest of the structure, were added in 1917.

Hall of Flags
Flags carried into battle by regiments from the state of Massachusetts are housed here. They are displayed beneath a stained-glass skylight depicting seals of the original 13 colonies.

VISITORS' CHECKLIST

Beacon Hill. **Map** 1 C4. *Tel (617) 727-3676.* Ⓣ *Park Street.* ◯ *10am–3:30pm Mon–Fri. Reservations recommended.* ♿ 🖳 www.sec.state.ma.us/trs

Administrative offices can be found on the upper floors of the building.

★ Nurses Hall
This marble hall is lined with murals depicting critical events leading up to the American Revolution. The name derives from the statue of an army nurse here, erected to honor all the nurses who took part in the Civil War.

The dome was sheathed in copper in 1802 to prevent water leakage, and, in 1872, gilded in 23-carat gold.

Entrance

Doric Hall
George Washington is among the historical figures represented here. The center doors of the hall are opened only for a state governor at the end of his term or for a visiting head of state.

Senate Chamber
Prior to 1895, this was the meeting chamber of the House of Representatives. Situated directly beneath the State House's magnificent dome, the chamber features a beautiful sunburst ceiling, also designed by Charles Bulfinch.

Brattle Book Shop, a Boston literary landmark

Downtown Crossing ⑭

Washington, Winter & Summer Sts. **Map** 4 F1. ⓣ *Downtown Crossing.*

As an antidote to heavy traffic congestion, this shopping-district crossroads, at the intersection of Washington, Winter, and Summer Streets, was laid out as a pedestrian zone between 1975 and 1978. Downtown's single remaining department store is Macy's, although the area also offers a range of other outlets, including bookstores, camera stores, and a jewelry district. Street vendors and summer lunchtime concerts create a lively scene.

The busy Macy's department store is one of a chain found throughout the US, with the most well-known store in New York. Across Summer Street, Filene's Basement occupies the lower levels of the Beaux-Arts building that housed Filene's Department Store until the marque disappeared in 2006. The Basement, as Bostonians call it, retains a powerful hold on residents eager for a bargain, as branches continue to offer discounts on merchandise, principally of clothing. The original Filene's Basement in Downtown Crossing is closed for redevelopment.

Another well-known store in the area is Brattle Book Shop, just off Washington Street on West Street. Founded in 1825, this bibliophiles' treasure-house is packed with more than 250,000 used, rare, and out-of-print books, as well as back issues of magazines, maps, prints, postcards, and manuscripts. Outside the store are bins of bargain books priced between $1 and $5.

Colonial Theatre ⑮

106 Boylston St. **Map** 4 E2. **Tel** *(617) 426-9366.* ⓣ *Boylston.* ⬭ *phone to check.* ♿ **www.** broadwayacrossamerica.com

Clarence H. Blackall designed 14 Boston theaters during his architectural career, among them the Colonial, which is the city's oldest theater in continuous operation under the same name. Although plain outside, the interior is impressively opulent. Designed by H.B. Pennell, the Rococo lobby has chandeliers, gilded trim, and lofty arched ceilings. The auditorium is decorated with figures, frescoes, and friezes.

Gilt cherub, the Colonial Theatre

The theater opened on December 20, 1900 with an extravagant performance of the melodrama *Ben Hur*. Today the theater is best remembered for premiering lavish musical productions, such as *Ziegfeld Follies*.

Chinatown ⑯

Bounded by Kingston, Kneeland, Washington & Essex Sts. **Map** 4 E2. ⓣ *Chinatown.*

This area is the third largest Chinatown in the US after those in San Francisco and New York. Pagoda-topped telephone booths, as well as a three-story gateway guarded by four marble lions, set the neighborhood's Asian tone.

The first 200 Chinese to settle in New England came by ship from San Francisco in 1870, recruited to break a labor strike at a shoe factory. Another wave of immigration from California in the 1880s was prompted by an economic boom that led to job openings in construction. Boston's Chinese colony was fully established by the turn of the 19th century.

Political turmoil in China immediately following World War II, and more recent arrivals from Vietnam, Laos, Korea, Thailand, and Cambodia, have swelled Chinatown's population. Along with the area's garment and textile industries, restaurants, bakeries, food markets, and dispensers of Chinese medicine are especially numerous along the main thoroughfare of Beach Street, as well as on Tyler, Oxford, and Harrison Streets.

Colorful August Moon Festival, held in Boston's Chinatown

For hotels and restaurants in this region see pp306–11 and pp332–9

Bay Village ⓱

Bounded by Tremont, Arlington & Charles Street South. **Map** 4 D2. Ⓣ *New England Medical Center, Boylston.*

Originally an expanse of mud flats, the Bay Village area was drained in the early 1800s and initially became habitable with the construction of a dam in 1825. Many carpenters, cabinetmakers, artisans, and house painters involved in the construction of Beacon Hill's pricier town houses built their own modest but well-crafted residences here. As a result there are many similarities between the two neighborhoods.

Fayette Street was laid out in 1824 to coincide with the visit of the Marquis de Lafayette, the French general who allied himself with George Washington. Bay Street, located just off Fayette Street, features a single dwelling and is generally regarded as the city's shortest street. In 1809, poet and short-story writer Edgar Allen Poe was born in a boarding house on Carver Street, where his thespian parents were staying while in Boston on tour with a traveling theatrical company.

In the 1920s, at the height of the Prohibition era, clandestine speakeasies gave Bay Village its still-prevalent bohemian ambience. More recently, the neighborhood has become a center for Boston's gay community.

Bay Village's Piedmont Street is well known for the W. S. Haynes Company at No. 12, which has been hand-crafting flutes and piccolos since 1888, and has acquired among musicians a world-wide reputation for its instruments.

Shubert Theatre ⓲

265 Tremont St. **Map** 4 E2. *Tel* (617) 482-9393. Ⓣ *Boylston, Tufts Medical Center.* ◻ *phone to check.* ♿ www.citicenter.org

The 1,650-seat Shubert Theatre rivals the Colonial Theatre for its long history of staging major pre-Broadway musical

The vast Grand Lobby of the Wang Theatre

productions. Designed by the architects Charles Bond and Thomas James, the theater features a white Neoclassical façade with a pair of Ionic columns flanking a monumental, Palladian-style window over the entrance. The theater first opened its doors in 1910, and during its heyday many stars walked the boards, including Sarah Bernhardt, W.C. Fields, Cary Grant, Mae West, Humphrey Bogart, Ingrid Bergman, Henry Ford, and Rex Harrison. Today, dance, theater, musicals, and opera are showcased here.

Wang Theatre ⓳

270 Tremont St. **Map** 4 E2. *Tel* (617) 482-9393. Ⓣ *Boylston, Tufts Medical Center.* ◻ *phone to check.* ♿ www.citicenter.org

Opened in 1925 as the Metropolitan Theatre and later named the Music Hall, New England's most ornate variety theater was inspired by the Paris Opera House, and was originally intended to be a movie theater. Designed by Clarence Blackall, the theater's auditorium was once one of the largest in the world. The theatre was restored and renamed as the Wang Center for the Performing Arts in 1983, but is now known simply as the Wang Theatre. The five-story Grand Lobby and seven-story auditorium are designed in Renaissance Revival style, with gold chandeliers, stained glass, ceiling murals, and jasper pillars.

Today the theater hosts Broadway road shows, visiting dance and opera companies, concerts, motion-picture revivals, and local productions. The Wang and Shubert theaters are now operated by the Citi Performing Arts Center.

THE HISTORY OF BOSTON'S THEATER DISTRICT

Boston's first theater opened in 1793 on Federal Street. Fifty years later, with patronage from the city's social elite, Boston had become a major tryout town and boasted a number of lavish theaters. The US premiere of Handel's *Messiah* opened in 1839, the US premiere of Gilbert and Sullivan's *H.M.S. Pinafore* in 1877, and the premiere of Tchaikovsky's *First Piano Concerto* in 1875. In the late 19th century theaters came under fire from the censorious Watch and Ward Society. Later, in the 20th century, dramas such as Tennessee Williams' *A Streetcar Named Desire* and Eugene O'Neill's *Long Day's Journey into Night* debuted here. Musicals included *Ziegfeld Follies*, Gershwin's *Porgy and Bess*, and works by Rodgers and Hammerstein.

***A Streetcar Named Desire*, starring a young Marlon Brando and Jessica Tandy**

OLD BOSTON AND THE FINANCIAL DISTRICT

This is an area of Boston where old and new sit one on top of the other. Some of its sights, situated in the older part of the district closest to Boston Common, predate the American Revolution. Much of what can be seen today, though, was built much more recently. The north of the district is home to Boston's late 20th-century, modernist-style City Hall and Government Center, while to the east is the city's bustling Financial District. This once formed part of Boston's harbor waterfront, a district built on mercantile wealth. Today, the wharves and warehouses have been replaced by skyscrapers belonging to banks, insurance companies, and high-tech industries.

British Lion, Old State House

SIGHTS AT A GLANCE

Historic Buildings and Churches

Custom House 10
Faneuil Hall 8
Government Center 7
King's Chapel and Burying Ground 2
New England Telephone Company Building 11
Old City Hall 3
Old Corner Bookstore 4
Old South Meeting House 5
Old State House pp78–9 6
Omni Parker House 1
Quincy Market 9

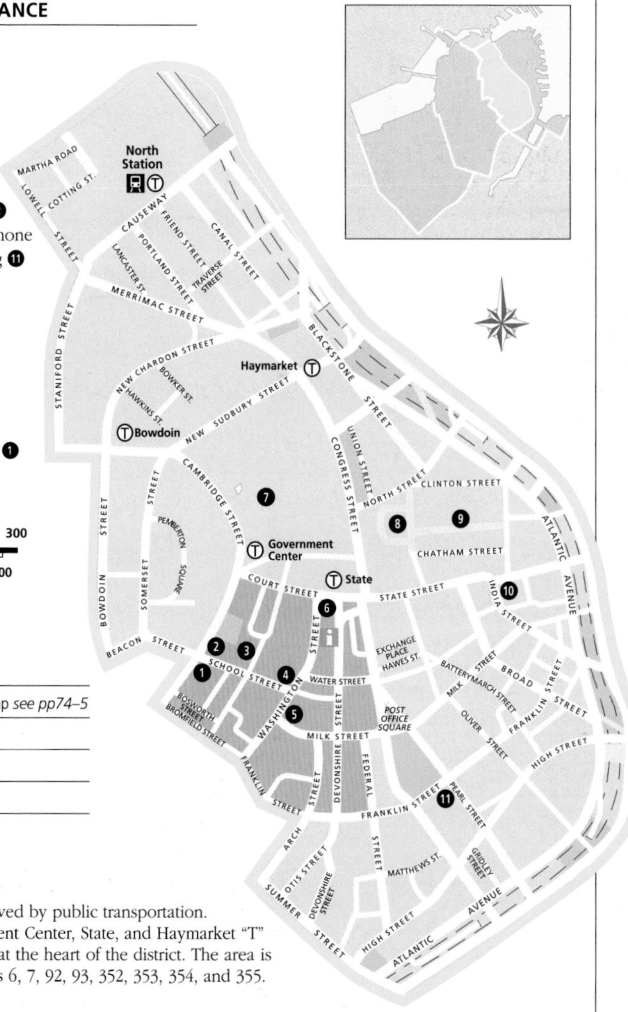

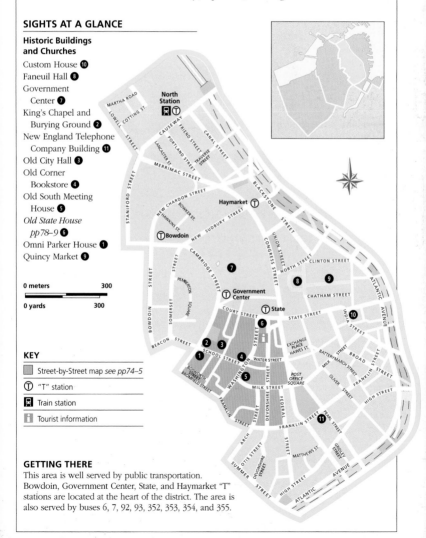

0 meters 300
0 yards 300

KEY

Street-by-Street map *see pp74–5*
Ⓣ "T" station
Train station
Tourist information

GETTING THERE

This area is well served by public transportation. Bowdoin, Government Center, State, and Haymarket "T" stations are located at the heart of the district. The area is also served by buses 6, 7, 92, 93, 352, 353, 354, and 355.

◁ **Custom House *(see p81)*, Boston's original skyscraper and one of its most distinctive buildings**

Street-by-Street: Colonial Boston

An important part of Boston's Freedom Trail *(see pp54–7)* runs through this historic core of the city, the site of which predates American Independence. Naturally, the area is now dominated by more recent 19th- and 20th-century development, but glimpses of a colonial past are prevalent here and there in the Old State House, King's Chapel and its adjacent burying ground, and the Old South Meeting House. Newer buildings of interest include the Omni Parker House, as well as the towering skyscrapers of Boston's financial district, located on the northwest edges of this area.

Irish Famine memorial, Washington Street

Government Center

SCHOOL STREET

PROVINCE STREET

★ **King's Chapel and Burying Ground**
A church has stood here since 1688, although the current building dates from 1749. The adjacent cemetery is the resting place of some of the most important figures in US history ②

Omni Parker House
This hotel (see p311) first opened its doors in 1855, then underwent many renovations. Famed for its opulence, the hotel also gained a reputation in the 19th century as a meeting place for Boston intellectuals. The current building was erected in 1927 ①

Old City Hall
This building served as Boston's City Hall from 1865 to 1969. Today it houses a steak house ③

0 meters	50
0 yards	50

STAR SIGHTS

★ King's Chapel and Burying Ground

★ Old South Meeting House

★ Old State House

For hotels and restaurants in this region see pp306–11 and pp332–9

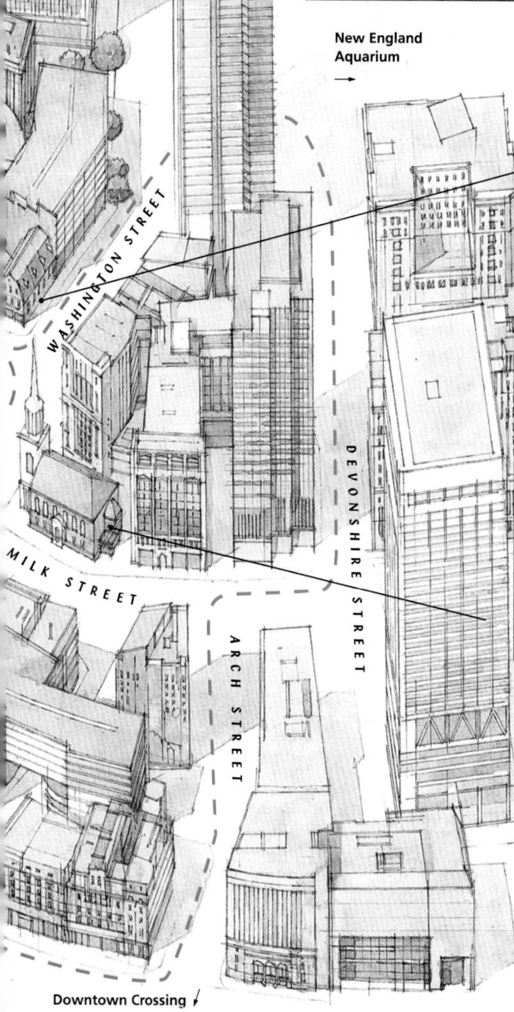
New England Aquarium
WASHINGTON STREET
DEVONSHIRE STREET
MILK STREET
ARCH STREET
Downtown Crossing

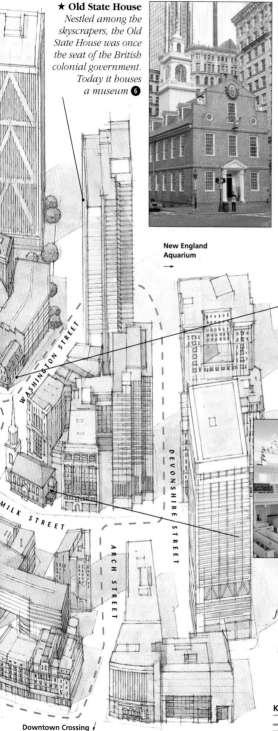

★ Old State House

Nestled among the skyscrapers, the Old State House was once the seat of the British colonial government. Today it houses a museum 6

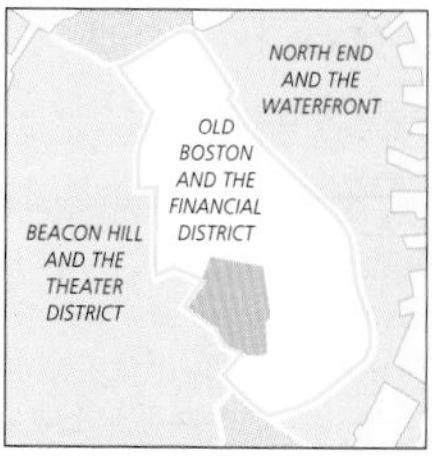
NORTH END AND THE WATERFRONT
OLD BOSTON AND THE FINANCIAL DISTRICT
BEACON HILL AND THE THEATER DISTRICT

LOCATOR MAP

See Street Finder maps 1 & 2.

Old Corner Bookstore

Built in 1718 as an apothecary, this building later became a literary gathering place as a bookstore and publishing company. It is now used as private offices 4

★ Old South Meeting House

Built in 1729, this church later became a focal point for protest in the days before the American Revolution. Today, visitors can hear reenactments of the debates that once raged here 5

KEY

– – – Suggested route

Omni Parker House ❶

60 School St. **Map** 1 C4.
***Tel** (617) 227-8600.* Ⓣ *Park Street, State, Government Center.*
www.omnihotels.com

Harvey D. Parker, raised on a farm in Maine, became so successful as the proprietor of his Boston restaurant that he achieved his ambition of expanding the property into a first-class, grand hotel. His Parker House opened in 1855, with a façade clad in white marble, standing five stories high, and featuring the first passenger elevator ever seen in Boston. It underwent several, rapid transformations during its early years, with additions made to the main structure in the 1860s and a 10-story, French chateau-style annex completed later that century. The building saw many successive transformations, and its latest 14-story incarnation has stood across from King's Chapel on School Street since 1927.

This hotel attained an instant reputation for luxurious accommodations and fine, even lavish, dining, typified by 11-course menus prepared by a French chef.

Among Parker House's many claims to fame are its Boston Cream Pie, which was first created here, and the word "scrod," a uniquely Bostonian term for the day's freshest seafood, still in common usage. Two former Parker House employees later became recognized for quite different careers. Vietnamese revolutionary leader Ho Chi Minh worked in the hotel's kitchens around 1915, while black activist Malcolm X was a busboy in Parker's Restaurant in the 1940s.

Simply decorated, pure white interior of King's Chapel on Tremont Street

PARKER HOUSE GUESTS

Boston's reputation as the "Athens of America" was widely acknowledged when members of a distinguished social club began meeting for lengthy dinners and lively intellectual exchanges in 1857. Their get-togethers took place on the last Saturday of every month at Harvey Parker's fancy new hotel. Regular participants included New England's literary elite *(see pp30–31)*: Henry Wadsworth Longfellow, Ralph Waldo Emerson, Nathaniel Hawthorne, and Henry David Thoreau, to name a few. Charles

John Wilkes Booth, infamous Parker House guest

Dickens participated while staying at the Parker House during his American speaking tours, and used his sitting-room mirror to rehearse the public readings he gave at Tremont Temple next door. The mirror now hangs on a mezzanine wall. In 1865, actor John Wilkes Booth, in town to see his brother, a fellow thespian, stayed at the hotel and took target practice at a nearby shooting gallery. Ten days later, at Ford's Theatre in Washington, he pulled a pistol and shot Abraham Lincoln.

King's Chapel and Burying Ground ❷

58 Tremont St. **Map** 1 C4. **Tel** *(617) 523-1749.* Ⓣ *Park Street, State, Government Center.* ☐ *late May–mid-Sep: 10am–4pm Mon, Thu–Sat, 10–11:15am & 1:30–4pm Tue–Wed, 1:30–4pm Sun; mid-Sep–May: call for hours.* ⬆ *11am Sun, 12:15pm Wed.* **Music Recitals:** *12:15pm Tue.*
www.kings-chapel.org

British Crown officials were among those who attended Anglican services at the first chapel on this site, which was built in 1688. When New England's governor decided a larger church was needed, the present granite edifice – begun in 1749 – was constructed around the original wooden chapel, which was dismantled and heaved out the windows of its replacement. After the Revolution, the congregation's religious allegiance switched from Anglican to Unitarian. The sanctuary's raised pulpit – dating from 1717 and shaped like a wine glass – is one of the oldest in the US. High ceilings and clear glass windows enhance the sense of spaciousness. The bell inside the King's Chapel is the largest ever cast by Paul Revere *(see p120).*

Among those interred in the adjacent cemetery, Boston's oldest, are John Winthrop and Elizabeth Pain, the inspiration for adultress Hester Prynne in Nathaniel Hawthorne's moralistic novel *The Scarlet Letter.*

Old City Hall ❸

45 School St. **Map** 2 D4. Ⓣ *Park Street, State, Government Center.*

This building is a wonderful example of French Second Empire architectural gaudiness and served as Boston's City Hall for over a century from 1865 to 1969. It was eventually superseded by the rakishly modern New City Hall structure at nearby Government Center *(see p80)*. Now the renovated 19th-century building features a steak house.

Previous occupants of the Old City Hall have included such flamboyant mayors as John "Honey Fitz" Fitzgerald and James Michael Curley. There are also statues here which memorialize Josiah Quincy, the second mayor of Boston, after whom Quincy market is named, as well as Benjamin Franklin, who was born on nearby Milk Street in 1706.

19th-century French-style façade of Boston's Old City Hall

Old Corner Bookstore ❹

1 School St. **Map** 2 D4. Ⓣ *Park Street, State, Government Center.* ◑ *to the public.*

A dormered gambrel roof crowns this brick landmark, which opened as Thomas Crease's apothecary shop in 1718 and was reestablished as the Old Corner Bookstore in 1829. Moving in 16 years later, the Ticknor & Fields publishing company became a gathering place for a notable roster of authors: Emerson, Hawthorne, Longfellow, Thoreau, early feminist writer Margaret Fuller, and *Uncle Tom's Cabin* novelist Harriet Beecher Stowe. The firm is often credited with carving out the first distinctively American literature. The earliest editions of the erudite *Atlantic Monthly* periodical were also printed here under editor James Russell Lowell before he handed the reins over to William Dean Howells. Julia Ward Howe's rousing tribute to American Civil War bravado, *The Battle Hymn of the Republic*, first appeared in the *Atlantic's* February 1862 issue. No publishing activities take place at the Old Corner Bookstore anymore.

Many consider the Old Corner Bookstore the cradle of American literature

Old South Meeting House ❺

310 Washington St. **Map** 2 D4. **Tel** *(617) 482-6439.* Ⓣ *Park Street, State, Government Center.* ◻ *Apr–Oct: 9:30am–5pm daily; Nov–Mar: 10am–4pm daily.* 🎧 📷 ♿ 🏪 **www**.oldsouthmeetinghouse.org

Built in 1729 for Puritan religious services, this edifice, with a tall octagonal steeple, had colonial Boston's biggest capacity for town meetings – a fact capitalized upon by a group of rebellious rabble-rousers calling themselves the Sons of Liberty *(see p43)*. Their outbursts against British taxation and other royal annoyances drew increasingly large and vociferous crowds to the pews and upstairs galleries.

During a candlelit protest rally on December 16, 1773, fiery speechmaker Samuel Adams flashed the signal that led to the Boston Tea Party *(see p89)* down at Griffin's Wharf several hours later. The British retaliated by turning Old South Meeting House into an officers' tavern and stable for General John Burgoyne's 17th Lighthorse Regiment of Dragoons. It was saved from destruction and became a museum in 1877. Displays and a multimedia presentation entitled *If These Walls Could Speak* relive those raucous days as well as more recent occurrences well into the 20th century. The Meeting House offers a series of lectures covering a wide range of New England topics and also holds chamber music concerts and other musical performances. The downstairs shop has a broad selection of merchandise, including books and the ubiquitous tins of "Boston Tea Party" tea.

Directly across Washington Street, sculptor Robert Shure's memorial to the victims of the 1845–49 Irish Potato Famine was added to the small plaza here in 1998.

Old South Meeting House, in stark contrast to the modern city

Old State House ❻

Dwarfed by the towers of the Financial District, this was the seat of British colonial government between 1713 and 1776. The royal lion and unicorn still decorate each corner of the eastern façade. After independence, the Massachusetts legislature took possession of the building, and it has had many uses since, including produce market, merchants' exchange, Masonic lodge, and Boston City Hall. Its wine cellars now function as a downtown subway station. The Old State House houses two floors of Bostonian Society memorabilia and a multimedia show about the Boston Massacre.

Old State House amid the sky-scrapers of the Financial District

A gold sculpture of an eagle, symbol of America, can be seen on the west façade.

West Façade
A Latin inscription, relating to the first Massachusetts Bay colony, runs around the outside of this crest. The relief in the center depicts a local Native American.

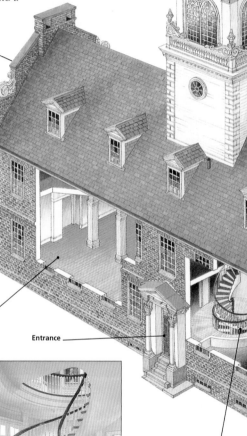

Entrance

Keayne Hall
This is named after Robert Keayne who, in 1658, gave £300 to the city so that the Town House, predating the Old State House, could be built. Exhibits in the room depict events from the Revolution.

★ Central Staircase
A fine example of 18th-century workmanship, the central spiral staircase has two beautifully crafted wooden handrails. It is one of the few such staircases still in existence in the US.

SITE OF THE BOSTON MASSACRE

Cobbled circle: site of the Boston Massacre

A circle of cobblestones below the balcony on the eastern façade of the Old State House marks the site of the Boston Massacre. After the Boston Tea Party, this was one of the most inflammatory events leading up to the American Revolution. On March 5, 1770, an angry mob of colonists taunted British guardsmen with insults, rocks, and snowballs. The soldiers opened fire, killing five colonists. A number of articles relating to the Boston Massacre are exhibited inside the Old State House, including a musket found near the site and a coroner's report detailing the incident.

VISITORS' CHECKLIST

Washington & State Sts. **Map** 2 D4. **Tel** (617) 720-1713. ⓣ State. ⬛ 9am–5pm daily (reduced hours Jan, extended hours Jul–Aug). ▧ ∅ ♿ ❑ www.bostonhistory.org

The tower is a classic example of Colonial style. In 18th-century paintings and engravings it can be seen clearly above the Boston skyline.

British Unicorn and Lion
A royal symbol of Britain, the original lion and unicorn were torn down when news of the Declaration of Independence reached Boston in 1776.

★ **East Façade**
This façade has seen many changes. An earlier clock from the 1820s was removed in 1957 and replaced with an 18th-century replica of the sundial that once hung here. The clock has now been reinstated.

Council Chamber
Once the chambers for the royal governors, and from 1780 chambers for the first governor of Massachusetts (John Hancock), this room has seen many key events. Among them were numerous impassioned speeches made by Boston patriots.

The Declaration of Independence was read from this balcony in 1776. In the 1830s, when the building was City Hall, the balcony was enlarged to two tiers.

STAR FEATURES

★ Central Staircase

★ East Façade

New City Hall and Government Center, a main city focal point

Government Center ❼

Cambridge, Court, New Sudbury & Congress Sts. **Map** 2 D3. Ⓣ *Government Center.*

This city center development was built on the site of what was once Scollay Square, demolished as part of the trend for local urban-renewal that began in the early 1960s. This trend had already seen the building of the strikingly Modernist concrete and brick New City Hall, which stands on the eastern side of the square and houses government offices.

Some viewed the development as controversial; others did not lament what was essentially a disreputable cluster of saloons, burlesque theaters, tattoo parlors, and scruffy hotels. The overall master plan for Government Center was inspired by the outdoors vitality and spaciousness of Italian piazzas. Architects I.M. Pei & Partners re-created some of this feeling by surrounding Boston's new City Hall with a vast terraced plaza covering 56 acres (23 ha), paved with 1,800,000 bricks. Its spaciousness makes it an ideal place for events such as skateboard contests, political and sports rallies, food fairs, patriotic military marches, and concerts.

Faneuil Hall ❽

Dock Sq. **Map** 2 D3. Ⓣ *Government Center, Haymarket, State.* **Great Hall** ⧖ *9am–5pm daily (closed for events).* ♿ 📷 🎧 www.nps.gov/bost

A gift to Boston from the wealthy merchant Peter Faneuil in 1742, this Georgian, brick landmark has always functioned simultaneously as a public market and town meeting place. Master tinsmith Shem Drowne modeled the building's grasshopper weathervane after the one on top of the Royal Exchange in the City of London, England. Revolutionary gatherings packed the hall, and as early as 1763 Samuel Adams used the hall as a platform to suggest that the American colonies should unite against British oppression and fight to establish their independence; hence the building's nickname "Cradle of Liberty" and the bold posture of the statue of Sam Adams at the front of the building. Toward the end of the 18th century it became apparent that the existing Faneuil Hall could no longer house the capacity crowds that it regularly attracted. The commission to expand the building was undertaken by Charles Bulfinch, who completed the work from 1805 to 1806. The building then remained unchanged until 1898, when

Sam Adams statue, in front of Faneuil Hall

it was expanded even more according to long-standing Bulfinch stipulations. Faneuil Hall was restored in the 1970s as part of the wider redevelopment of Quincy Market.

Quincy Market ❾

Between Chatham & Clinton Sts. **Map** 2 D3. **Tel** *(617) 523-1300.* Ⓣ *Government Center, State.* ⧖ *10am–9pm Mon–Sat, noon–6pm Sun.* ♿ www.faneuilhallmarketplace.com

This immensely popular shopping and dining complex attracts nearly 14 million people every year. It was developed from the buildings of the old Quincy Market, which was the city's meat, fish, and produce market. These buildings had fallen into disrepair before they underwent a widely acclaimed restoration in the 1970s. The 535-ft (163-m) long Greek Revival-style colonnaded market hall is now filled with a selection of fast food stands and a restaurant-nightclub, located in the spectacular central Rotunda. Completing the ensemble are twin North and South Market buildings – these individual warehouses have also been refurbished to accommodate numerous boutiques, stores, restaurants, and pubs, as well as upstairs business offices.

Gallery of the Greek Revival main dome in Quincy Market's central hall

For hotels and restaurants in this region see pp306–11 and pp332–9

Custom House ⑩

3 McKinley Square. **Map** 2 E3.
Tel (617) 310-6300. ⓣ *Aquarium.*
Museum ☐ *8am–9pm daily.* **Tower**
☐ *2pm Sat–Thu.* **www**.marriott.
com/vacationclub

Before landfill altered downtown topography, early
Boston's Custom House
perched at the water's edge.
A temple-like Greek Revival
structure with fluted Doric
columns, the granite building
had a skylit dome upon completion in 1847. Since 1915,
however, it has supported a
495 ft (150 m) tower with a
four-sided clock. For the best
part of the 20th century, the
Custom House was Boston's
only bona fide skyscraper.
The public has free access
to a small museum of maritime
history, with objects on loan
from the Peabody Museum in
Salem, and to the observatory.

Art Deco façade of the New England Telephone Company Building

**Greek Revival Custom House tower,
one of Boston's most striking sights**

New England Telephone Company Building ⑪

185 Franklin St. **Map** 2 D4.
Tel (617) 743-9340. ⓣ *State,
Aquarium.* **Museum** ☐ *call for
opening hours.* ♿

Dating from 1947 and overlooking the south side of Post
Office Square, this Art Deco
building is still in use today.
Dean Cornwell's monumental
160-ft (49-m) long *Telephone
Men and Women at Work*
mural – populated by 197 life-
size figures – has circled the
lobby since 1951 and is a
truly remarkable work of
art. It is possible to visit the
lobby but access may be
limited so call ahead. The
small museum at street level
features an accurate restoration of Alexander Graham
Bell's Court Street laboratory,
complete with his tools,
books, workbench, and one
of his garret windowframes
overlooking a diorama of
Scollay Square. The exhibit
was constructed from parts of
Bell's original workshop,
preserved when the house
where he lived was demo-
lished in the 1920s. It was
opened on June 3, 1959,
coincidentally the 84th
anniversary of the invention
of the telephone. The world's
first commercial telephone
and first telephone switch-
board are also displayed here.
The beautifully landscaped
Post Office Square, on the
northern side of the Telephone Company Building, is
a small island of green
situated amid the soaring
skyscrapers of the financial
district. Vines climb a 143-ft
(44-m) long trellis along one
side of the park, and a
fountain made of green glass
cascades on the square's Pearl
Street side. A focal point for
the whole district, the grassy
square comes into its own
in summer, when office
workers sprawl across its
well-kept lawns. The
square is also over-
looked by downtown's
former main post office,
housed in the John W.
McCormack courthouse
building, and Langham
Boston hotel *(see p311)*,
a classic Renaissance
Revival showpiece
completed in 1922.

ALEXANDER GRAHAM BELL (1847–1922)

A native of Edinburgh, Scotland, and son of a deaf
mother, Bell moved to Boston in 1871 to start a
career teaching speech to the deaf. Two years
later he was appointed as professor of vocal
physiology at Boston University. Bell worked
in his spare time on an apparatus for trans-
mitting sound by electrical current. History
was made on March 17, 1876, when Bell
called to his assistant in another room: "Mr.
Watson, come here. I want you." The first
demonstration of the "telephone" took place
in Boston on May 10, 1876, at the Academy
of Arts and Sciences. By 1878, he had set up
the first public telephone exchange in New
Haven, Connecticut.

NORTH END AND THE WATERFRONT

This was Boston's first neighborhood, and one that has been key to the city's fortunes. Fringed by numerous wharves, the area prospered initially through shipping and shipbuilding, with much of America's early trade passing through its warehouses. The more recent importance of finance and high-tech industries, however, has seen the waterfront evolve, its

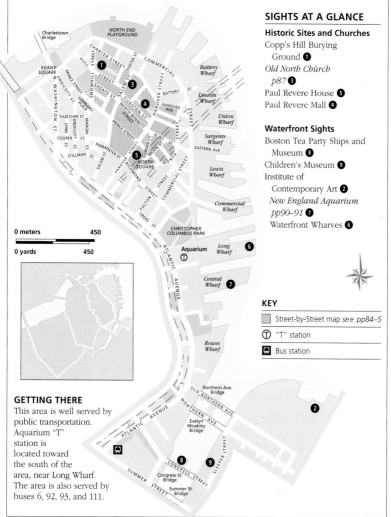

Statue in Old North Church garden

old warehouses transformed into luxury apartment blocks and offices. Away from the waterfront, the narrow streets of the North End have historically been home to European immigrants, drawn by the availability of work. The area today is populated largely by those of Italian descent, whose many cafés, delis, and restaurants make it one of the city's most distinct communities.

SIGHTS AT A GLANCE

Historic Sites and Churches

Copp's Hill Burying Ground ❶
Old North Church p87 ❸
Paul Revere House ❺
Paul Revere Mall ❹

Waterfront Sights

Boston Tea Party Ships and Museum ❽
Children's Museum ❾
Institute of Contemporary Art ❷
New England Aquarium pp90–91 ❼
Waterfront Wharves ❻

KEY

▨	Street-by-Street map *see pp84–5*
Ⓣ	"T" station
🚌	Bus station

GETTING THERE

This area is well served by public transportation. Aquarium "T" station is located toward the south of the area, near Long Wharf. The area is also served by buses 6, 92, 93, and 111.

◁ **The Institute of Contemporary Art, with the Financial District in the background**

Street-by-Street: North End

Old North Church clock

The main arteries of this area are Hanover and Salem Streets. Topped by the Old North Church, Salem Street is indicative of this area's historical connections – indeed the Old North Church is one of Boston's premier Revolutionary sights. In general the area consists of narrow streets and alleys, with four- and five-story tenements, many of which are now expensive condominiums. Hanover Street, like much of the area, has a distinctly Italian feel, while just south of here is North Square, site of the famous Paul Revere House (*see p88*).

Clough House was built by Ebenezer Clough who helped build the Old North Church. Benjamin Franklin's family home was just next door.

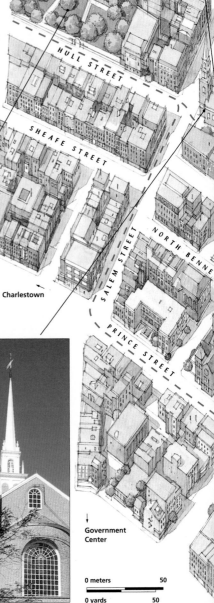

Charlestown →

Copp's Hill Burying Ground
During the American Revolution, the British used this low hilltop to fire cannon at American positions across Boston Harbor. Created in 1659 it is the city's second oldest graveyard ❶

★ Old North Church
Built in 1723 and famous for the part it played in Paul Revere's midnight ride (see p120), this is Boston's oldest religious building. On festive occasions, the North End still rings with the sound of its bells ❸

↓
Government Center

KEY

– – – Suggested route

STAR SIGHTS

★ Old North Church

★ Paul Revere House

★ Paul Revere Mall

| 0 meters | 50 |
| 0 yards | 50 |

★ Paul Revere Mall
*Linking the Old North Church to
Hanover Street, this tree-lined mall
dates only from 1933. Its antique feel
is enhanced by a statue of Paul Revere,
which was modeled in 1885* **4**

LOCATOR MAP
See Street Finder map 2

St. Stephen's Church echoes
the North End's Italian
theme, though only by
chance. Long before the
first Italians arrived, Charles
Bulfinch incorporated
Italian Renaissance features
and a bell tower into his
renovation of an earlier
church building.

Hanover Street is the most Italian of
all Boston's streets, brought to life by
restaurants and cafés, as well as the day-
to-day activities of its ethnic community.

↘ **The waterfront**

★ Paul Revere House
*This is the house where Paul Revere began
his midnight ride (see p120). Revere's home
from 1770 to 1800, it is now a museum* **5**

Slate tombstones of Boston's early settlers, Copp's Hill Burying Ground

Copp's Hill Burying Ground ❶

Entrances at Charter & Hull Sts. **Map** 2 D2. Ⓣ *Government Center, North Station.* ◯ *9am–5pm daily.*

Existing since 1659, this is Boston's second-oldest cemetery after the one by King's Chapel *(see p76)*. Nicknamed "Corpse Hill," the real name of the hill occupied by the cemetery derives from a local man by the name of William Copp. He owned a farm on its southeastern slope from 1643, and much of the cemetery's land was purchased from him. His children are buried here. Other more famous people

interred here include Robert Newman, the sexton who hung Paul Revere's signal lanterns in the belfry of Old North Church *(see p87)*, and Edmund Hartt, builder of the USS *Constitution (see p119)*. Increase, Cotton, and Samuel Mather, three generations of a family of highly influential colonial period Puritan ministers, are also buried here. Hundreds of Boston's Colonial-era black slaves and freedmen are also buried here, including Prince Hall, a free black man who founded the African Freemasonry Order in Massachusetts.

During the British occupation of Boston, the site was used by British commanders who had an artillery position here. They would later exploit the prominent hilltop location during the Revolution, when they directed cannon fire from here across Boston harbor toward American positions in Charlestown. King George III's troops were said to have used the slate headstones for target practice, and pockmarks from their musket balls are still visible on some of them.

Copp's Hill Terrace, directly across Charter Street, is a prime observation point for

Decorative column, Copp's Hill

Quiet, leafy street, typical of the area around Copp's Hill

views over to Charlestown and Bunker Hill. It is also the site where, in 1919, a 2.3-million-gallon molasses tank exploded, creating a huge, syrupy tidal wave that killed 21 people.

Institute of Contemporary Art ❷

100 Northern Ave. **Map** 2 F5. *Tel* (617) 478-3100. Ⓣ *Courthouse.* ◯ *10am–5pm Tue, Wed, Sat, Sun (to 9pm Thu, Fri).* ♿ 📷 *www.icaboston.org*

Since 1936, when it introduced Americans to the then-radical work of German Expressionism, the Institute of Contemporary Art has made a point of championing cutting-edge innovation and avant-garde expression. Over the years, the ICA has pushed the envelope of the definition of art, showing creations often outside the usual art-world boundaries, such as an entire exhibition devoted to blow-torches. The ICA was also in the vanguard of showing and interpreting video art when the technology was still in its infancy.

For its first 70 years, the ICA was an exhibiting but not a collecting institution, in part on the theory that the definition of "contemporary" changes from minute to minute. That focus changed in 2006 when the ICA moved from its quaint Back Bay building to a dramatic new wood, steel, and glass structure cantilevered above the Harbor Walk on Fan Pier on the South Boston water-front. The 65,000 sq ft (6,040 sq m) museum is the creation of the design firm Diller Scofidio + Renfro, and includes a 325-seat performing arts theater with clear walls that allow the harbor to serve as a stage backdrop, as well as a media center and art lab for educational programs. The vastly expanded facilities also allow the ICA to focus on collecting 21st-century art.

Old North Church™ ❸

Christ Episcopal Church is the official name of
Boston's oldest surviving religious edifice, which
dates from 1723. It was built of brick in the Georgian
style similar to that of St. Andrew's-by-the-Wardrobe
in Blackfriars, London, designed
by Sir Christopher Wren. The
church was made famous on April
18, 1775, when sexton Robert
Newman, aiding Paul Revere
(see p120), hung a pair of signal
lanterns in the belfry. These were
to warn the patriots in Charlestown of the westward departure
of British troops, on their way
to engage the revolutionaries.

VISITORS' CHECKLIST

193 Salem St. **Map** 2 E2. **Tel**
(617) 523-6676. Ⓣ *Haymarket,*
Aquarium, North Station. ☐
9am–5pm daily (reduced hours
Jan–Feb; extended Jun–Oct). ☐
9am, 11am. 📷 📹 📵 ♿ *(call*
for tours). **www**.oldnorth.com

Tower
The tower of the
Old North Church
contains the first set of
church bells in North
America cast in 1745.

★ **Box Pews**
The traditional, high-sided box
pews in the church were designed
to enclose footwarmers, which
were filled with hot coals or bricks
during wintry weather.

Chandeliers
The church's distinctive
chandeliers were
brought from England
in January 1724 for the
first Christmas season.

Entrance

STAR FEATURES

★ Bust of George
Washington

★ Box Pews

★ **Bust of George Washington**
This marble bust of the first US
president, modeled on an earlier
one by Christian Gullager, was
presented to the church in 1815.

Paul Revere Mall

Hanover St. **Map** 2 E2.
Ⓣ *Haymarket, Aquarium.* ♿

This brick-paved plaza gives
the crowded neighborhood
of the North End a precious
stretch of open space
between Hanover and Unity
Streets. A well-utilized
municipal resource, the Mall
is always full of local people:
children, teenagers, young
mothers, and older residents
chatting in Italian and playing
cards or checkers. Laid out
in 1933, and originally called
the Prado, its focal point is
Cyrus Dallin's equestrian statue
of local hero Paul Revere,
which was originally modeled
in 1885. However, it was not
sculpted and placed here
until 1940. Bronze bas-relief
plaques on the mall's side
walls commemorate a number
of North End residents who
have played an important
role in the history of Boston.
Benches, a fountain, and twin
rows of linden trees complete
the space, which has a
distinctly European feel.

At the north end of the
Mall, across Unity Street, is
Old North Church *(see p87)*,
one of the city's most important historical sites. To the
south is busy Hanover Street,
which is lined with numerous
Italian cafés and restaurants.

**Paul Revere House kitchen, as
it was in the 18th century**

Paul Revere House ❺

19 North Sq. **Map** 2 E2.
Tel *(617) 523-2338.* Ⓣ *Haymarket,
Aquarium.* ☐ *mid-Apr–Oct:
9:30am–5:15pm daily; Nov–mid-Apr:
9:30am–4:15pm daily.* ● *Jan–Mar:
Mon.* 🏷 ♿ ⊘ 📷 🔲 *call for
hours.* **www**.paulreverehouse.org

The city's oldest surviving
clapboard frame house is
historically significant, for it
was here in 1775 that Paul
Revere began his legendary
horseback ride to warn his
compatriots in Lexington of
the impending arrival of
British troops. This historic
event was later immortalized
in a boldly patriotic, epic
poem by Henry Wadsworth
Longfellow *(see p110)*. It
begins "Listen, my children,
and you shall hear of the
midnight ride of Paul Revere."

Revere, a Huguenot descen-
dent, was by trade a versatile
gold- and silversmith, copper
engraver, and maker of church
bells and cannons. He and his
second wife, Rachel, mother of
eight of his 16 children,
owned the house from 1770
to 1800. Small leaded casement
windows, an overhanging
upper story, and nail-studded
front door all contribute to
make it a fine example of
18th-century Early American
architecture. In the courtyard
along one side of the house
is a large bronze bell, cast by
Paul Revere for a church in
1804 – Revere made nearly
200 church bells. Three rooms
in the house contain period
artifacts, including original
pieces of family furniture,
items made in Revere's
workshop, and colonial bank-
notes. The house, which by
the mid-19th century had
become a decrepit tenement
fronted by stores, was saved
from demolition by preserva-
tionists' efforts led by one
of Revere's great-grandsons.

Next door, the early 18th-
century Pierce-Hichborn
House is the earliest brick
town house remaining in
New England.

View toward the Custom House and the Financial District, across Christopher Columbus Park

Rowes Wharf development, typical of Boston's waterfront regeneration

Waterfront Wharves ⑥

Atlantic Avenue. **Map** 2 E4.
Ⓣ *Aquarium.*

Boston's waterfront is fringed by many wharves, reminders of the city's past as a key trading port. One of the largest of these is Long Wharf, established in 1710 to accommodate the boom in early maritime commerce. Once extending 2,000 ft (610 m) into Boston Harbor and lined with shops and warehouses, Long Wharf provided mooring for the largest ships of the time. Many sightseeing excursion boats depart from here.

Harbor Walk connects Long Wharf with other adjacent wharves, such as Union, Lewis, and Commercial wharves. Dating from the early 19th century most are now converted to fashionable harborside apartments. Rowes Wharf, to the south of the waterfront, is a particularly fine example of

such revitalization. Built of Bostonian red brick, this modern development features a large archway that links the city to the harbor. It comprises the luxury Boston Harbor Hotel, restaurants, and a marina.

New England Aquarium ⑦

See pp90–91.

Boston Tea Party Ships & Museum ⑧

Congress St. Bridge. **Map** 2 E5.
Tel *(617) 338-1773.* Ⓣ *South Station.* ◐ *until at least summer 2010; call to check before visiting.* 🖥 **www**.historictours.com/boston

Griffin's Wharf, where the Boston Tea Party took place on December 16, 1773, was buried beneath landfill many years ago. Beginning in 2010, replicas of three British East

India Company ships involved in the Tea Party will anchor on Fort Point Channel, a short distance south of the old Griffin's Wharf site. Today, modern-day patriots toss imitation bales of tea overboard, re-creating one of the acts of defiance that prompted Britain to put the Massachusetts Bay Colony under martial law.

Ship models and Tea Party memorabilia are displayed in a museum on a nearby pier.

Children's Museum ⑨

300 Congress St. **Map** 2 E5. **Tel** *(617) 426-6500.* Ⓣ *South Station.* ◯ *10am–5pm daily (to 9pm Fri).* 🖥 ♿ **www**.bostonchildrensmuseum.org

Overlooking Fort Point Channel, a pair of rejuvenated 19th-century wool warehouses contain one of the country's best children's museums. The museum was expanded in 2007 and offers a host of interesting exhibits. Youngsters play games, join learning activities, and hoist themselves up a 30-foot (9-m) climbing structure in the New Balance Center addition. The Art Studio provides a hands-on recycling area with materials for projects. Visits to a silk merchant's house transplanted from Kyoto (Boston's sister city) inject a multicultural dimension while careers can be sampled as children work on a mini-construction site.

A towering milk bottle in front of the museum serves as a summer ice-cream stand, and mazes, giant boulders, and performance spaces grace an outdoor park.

Playing on the mini-construction site at Boston's Children's Museum

New England Aquarium ❼

The waterfront's prime attraction dominates Central Wharf. Designed by a consortium of architects in 1969, the aquarium's core encloses a vast four-story ocean tank, which contains an innumerable array of marine animals. A curving walkway runs around the outside of the tank from top to bottom and provides viewpoints of the interior of the tank from different levels. Also resident at the aquarium are colonies of penguins, playful harbor seals, anacondas, rays, sea turtles, and mesmerizing seadragons. The facility also includes a superb IMAX theatre.

Edge of the Sea Tidepool
A fiberglass shore recreates a world where the land meets the sea. It is home to animals such as horseshoe crabs and sea urchins.

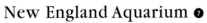

★ Penguin Pool
One of the main attractions of the aquarium, the penguin pool runs around the base of the giant tank. It contains African, rockhopper, and blue penguins.

★ Whale Watch
A naturalist aboard an Aquarium boat explains marine ecology on educational trips to Stellwagen Bank, 75 minutes offshore, to see whales and sea birds.

Main entrance

Ticket booth

Harbor Seals
An outdoor tank covered by a steel canopy is home to a lively colony of harbor seals.

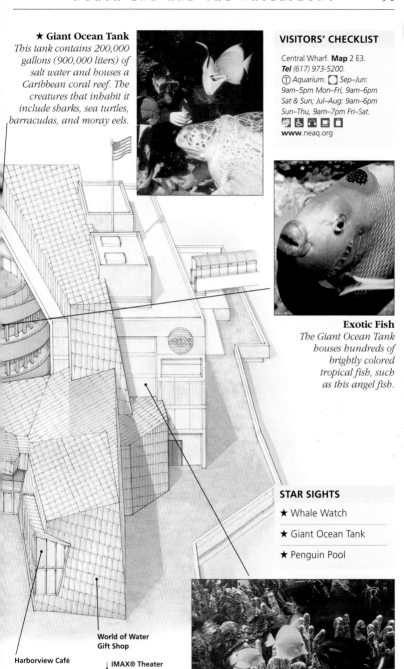

★ **Giant Ocean Tank**
This tank contains 200,000 gallons (900,000 liters) of salt water and houses a Caribbean coral reef. The creatures that inhabit it include sharks, sea turtles, barracudas, and moray eels.

VISITORS' CHECKLIST

Central Wharf. **Map** 2 E3.
Tel (617) 973-5200.
Ⓣ Aquarium. ☐ Sep–Jun: 9am–5pm Mon–Fri, 9am–6pm Sat & Sun; Jul–Aug: 9am–6pm Sun–Thu, 9am–7pm Fri–Sat.
www.neaq.org

Exotic Fish
The Giant Ocean Tank houses hundreds of brightly colored tropical fish, such as this angel fish.

STAR SIGHTS

★ Whale Watch
★ Giant Ocean Tank
★ Penguin Pool

Harborview Café

World of Water Gift Shop

↓ **IMAX® Theater**

Tropical Gallery
This exhibit provides an account of the many types of environment manifested in reefs, starting with a darkened exhibit of deep-water reef fishes and ending with a brightly lit, Pacific coral reef.

BACK BAY AND SOUTH END

Until the 19th century Boston was situated on a narrow peninsula surrounded by tidal marshes. Projects to fill Back Bay began in the 1850s and were made possible by new inventions such as the steam shovel. The Back Bay was filled by 1880, and developers

Sargent mural, Boston Public Library

soon moved in. Planned along French lines, with elegant boulevards, Back Bay is now one of Boston's most exclusive neighborhoods. The more bohemian South End, laid out on an English model of town houses clustered around squares, is home to many artists and Boston's gay community.

SIGHTS AT A GLANCE

Historic Streets and Squares
Boylston Street **8**
Commonwealth Avenue **4**
Copley Square **7**
The Esplanade **1**
Newbury Street **5**

First Baptist Church **3**
Gibson House Museum **2**
Berklee Performance Center **11**
John Hancock Tower **10**
Trinity Church pp98–9 **6**

Historic Buildings, Churches, and Museums
Boston Center for the Arts **12**
Boston Public Library **9**

KEY

Street-by-Street map *see pp94–5*

Ⓣ "T" station

Train station

Bus station

Tourist information

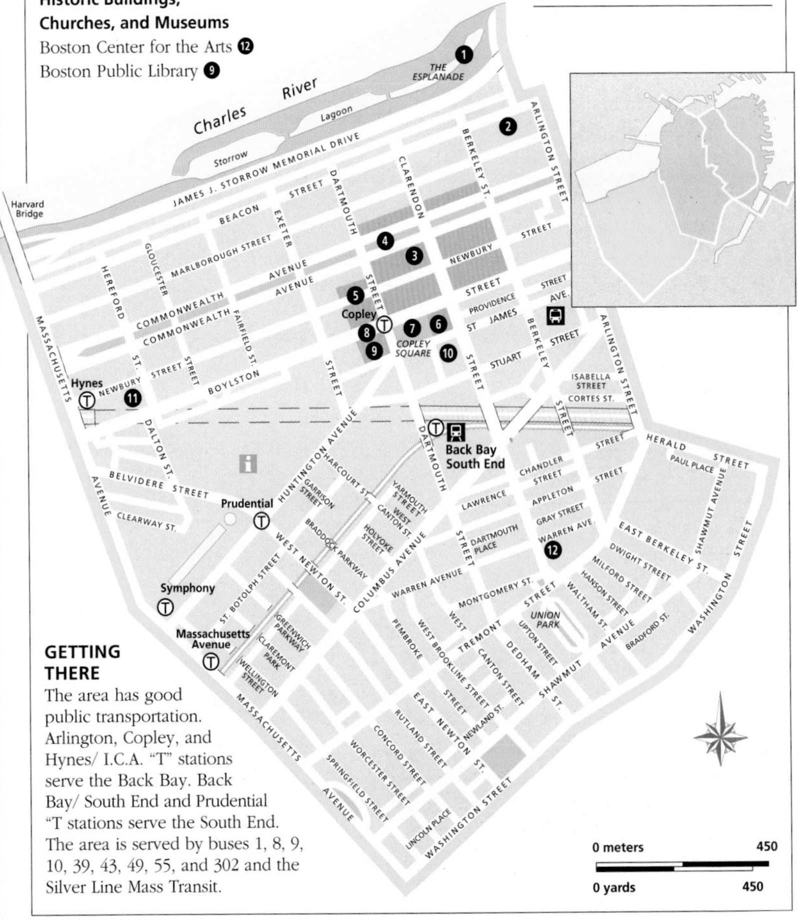

GETTING THERE

The area has good public transportation. Arlington, Copley, and Hynes/ I.C.A. "T" stations serve the Back Bay. Back Bay/ South End and Prudential "T stations serve the South End. The area is served by buses 1, 8, 9, 10, 39, 43, 49, 55, and 302 and the Silver Line Mass Transit.

0 meters   450
0 yards   450

◁ **View of Back Bay's characteristic row houses, from the top of the Prudential Skywalk**

Street-by-Street: Back Bay

This fashionable district unfolds westward from the Public Garden *(see pp64–5)* in a grid that departs radically from the twisting streets found elsewhere in Boston. Commonwealth Avenue, with its grand 19th-century mansions and parkland, and Newbury and Boylston Streets are its main arteries. Newbury Street is a magnet for all of Boston wanting to indulge in some upscale shopping, whereas the more somber Boylston Street bustles with office workers. Copley Square anchors the entire area and is the site of Henry Hobson Richardson's magnificent Trinity Church *(see pp98–9)* and the 60-story John Hancock Tower *(see p101)*, which is the tallest building in New England.

Weekly summer and fall farmers' market, Copley Square

Copley Square
This square was a marsh until 1870. It took on its present form only in the late 20th century as buildings around its edges were completed. A farmers' market, concerts, and folk-dancing feature regularly ❼

COMMONWEALTH AVEN

NEWBU

Fenway Park ←

Boylston Street
The site of the Prudential Center and the Hynes Convention Center, Boylston Street is also the location of the fabulous New Old South Church (see p100) ❽

DARTMOUTH STREET

BOYLSTON STREET

★ Boston Public Library
One of the first free public libraries in the world, this building was designed by Charles McKim. Inside are murals by John Singer Sargent ❾

South End ↓

For hotels and restaurants in this region see pp306–11 and pp332–9

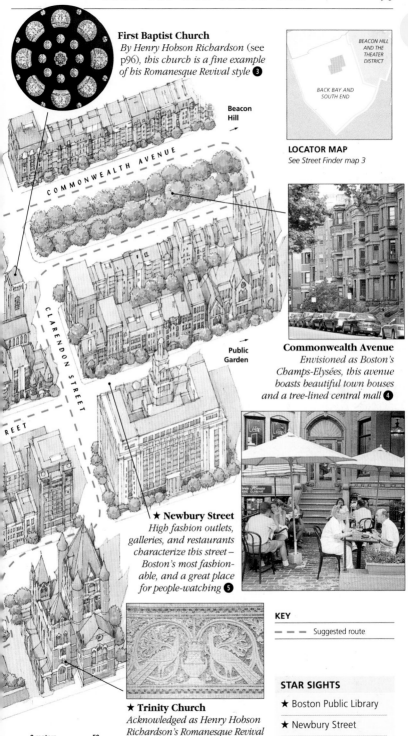

First Baptist Church
By Henry Hobson Richardson (see p96), this church is a fine example of his Romanesque Revival style 3

Beacon Hill

LOCATOR MAP
See Street Finder map 3

BEACON HILL AND THE THEATER DISTRICT

BACK BAY AND SOUTH END

COMMONWEALTH AVENUE

CLARENDON STREET

REET

Public Garden

Commonwealth Avenue
Envisioned as Boston's Champs-Elysées, this avenue boasts beautiful town houses and a tree-lined central mall 4

★ **Newbury Street**
High fashion outlets, galleries, and restaurants characterize this street – Boston's most fashionable, and a great place for people-watching 5

KEY

– – – Suggested route

★ **Trinity Church**
Acknowledged as Henry Hobson Richardson's Romanesque Revival masterpiece, this is one of the most important churches in the US 6

0 meters 50
0 yards 50

STAR SIGHTS

★ Boston Public Library

★ Newbury Street

★ Trinity Church

The Esplanade ❶

Map 1 A4. ⓣ *Charles/MGH.*
◯ *24 hrs daily.* ♿

Running along the Boston
side of the Charles River,
between Longfellow Bridge
and Dartmouth Street, are
the parkland, lagoons, and
islands known collectively as
the Esplanade. The park is
used extensively for in-line
skating, cycling, and strolling.
It is also the access point
for boating on the river,
(including gondola rides) and
the site of the city's leading
outdoor concert space.

In 1929, Arthur Fiedler, then
the young conductor of the
Boston Pops Orchestra, chose
the Esplanade for a summer
concert series that became a
tradition. The Hatch Memorial
Shell was constructed in 1939,
and its stage is widely used
by musical ensembles and
other musical groups throughout the
summer. Fourth of July concerts by the Boston Pops,
which are followed by fireworks, can attract upward
of 500,000 spectators.

**Fountains at the Esplanade,
next to the Charles River**

Gibson House
Museum ❷

137 Beacon St. **Map** 1 A4.
Tel *(617) 267-6338.* ⓣ *Arlington.*
◯ *Tours at 1pm, 2pm & 3pm
Wed–Sun.* 📷 ⌀ 🎫
www.thegibsonhouse.org

Among the first houses
built in the Back Bay, the
Gibson House preserves its
original Victorian decor and
furnishings throughout all six
stories. The 1860 brownstone
and red-brick structure was

The original Victorian-style library of the Gibson House Museum

designed in the popular
Italian Renaissance Revival
style for the widow Catherine
Hammond Gibson, who was
one of the few women to own
property in this part of the
city. Her grandson Charles
Hammond Gibson, Jr., a noted
eccentric, poet, travel writer,
horticulturalist, and bon vivant,
arranged for the house to become a museum after his death
in 1954. As a prelude to this,
Gibson began to rope off the
furniture in the 1930s, thus
inviting his guests to sit on the
stairs to drink martinis made
with his own bathtub gin.

One of the most modern
houses of its day, the Gibson
House boasted such technical
advancements as gas lighting,
indoor plumbing in the basement, and coal-fired central
heating. Visitors can see a full
dinner setting in the dining
room or admire the whimsical
Turkish pet pavilion. It is
Gibson's preservation of the
1860s decor (with some modifications in 1888) that makes
the museum a true time capsule of Victorian life in Boston.

**Detail of Bartholdi's frieze atop the distinctive
square tower of the First Baptist Church**

First Baptist
Church ❸

110 Commonwealth Ave.
Map 3 C2. **Tel** *(617) 267-3148.*
ⓣ *Arlington.* ◯ *for Sunday
worship.* ⬆ *11am Sun.* ⌀ ♿

The Romanesque-style First
Baptist Church on the corner
of Commonwealth Avenue and
Clarendon Street was Henry
Hobson Richardson's first
major architectural commission and became an instant
landmark when it was
finished in 1872. Viewed from
Commonwealth Avenue, it is
one of the most distinctive
buildings of the city skyline.

Richardson considered the
nearly freestanding bell tower,
which he modeled roughly
on Italian campaniles, to be
the church's most innovative
structure. The square tower
is topped with a decorative
frieze and arches protected
by an overhanging roof. The
frieze was modeled in Paris
by Bartholdi, the sculptor who
created the Statue of Liberty,
and was carved in
place by Italian artisans after the stones
were set. The faces
in the frieze, which
depict the sacraments,
are likenesses of prominent Bostonians of
that time, among them
Henry Wadsworth
Longfellow and Ralph
Waldo Emerson. The
trumpeting angels at

the corners of the tower gave the building its nickname, "Church of the Holy Bean Blowers."

Four years after the church was completed, the Unitarian congregation dissolved because it was unable to bear the expense of the building. The church stood vacant until 1881, when the First Baptist congregation from the South End took it over.

Commonwealth Avenue ❹

Map 3 B2. Ⓣ *Arlington, Copley, Hynes Convention Center.*

Back Bay was Boston's first fully planned neighborhood, and architect Arthur Gilman made Commonwealth Avenue, modeled on the elegant boulevards of Paris, the centerpiece of the design. At 200 ft (61 m) wide, with a 10-ft (3-m) setback from the sidewalks to encourage small gardens in front of the buildings, Commonwealth became an arena for America's leading domestic architects in the second half of the 19th century. A walk from the Public Garden to Massachusetts Avenue is like flicking through a catalog of architectural styles. Few of the grand buildings on either side of the avenue are open to the public, but

strollers on the central mall of the avenue encounter a number of historic figures in the form of bronze statues. Some have only tangential relationships to the city, like Alexander Hamilton, the first secretary of the US Treasury. The end of the mall features an heroic bronze of Leif Eriksson, erected as a historically unsupported flight of fancy that the Norse explorer landed at Boston. The patrician statue of abolitionist William Garrison is said to capture exactly the man's air of moral superiority. The best-loved memorial depicts sailor and historian Samuel Eliot Morison dangling his feet from a rock.

William Garrison statue on Commonwealth Avenue

Newbury Street ❺

Map 3 C2. Ⓣ *Arlington, Copley, Hynes Convention Center.*

Newbury Street is a Boston synonym for "stylish." The Taj Boston, formerly the Ritz-Carlton Hotel, at Arlington Street sets an elegant tone for the street that continues with a mix of prestigious and often

well-hidden art galleries, stylish boutiques, and some of the city's most *au courant* restaurants.

Churches provide vestiges of a more decorous era. The Church of the Covenant at No. 67 Newbury contains the world's largest collection of Louis Comfort Tiffany stained-glass windows and an elaborate Tiffany lantern. A chorus and orchestra perform a Bach cantata each Sunday at Emmanuel Church on the corner of Newbury and Berkeley Streets.

Most of Newbury Street was constructed as townhouse residences, but the desirability of these spaces for retail operations has pushed residents to the upper floors, while ground and subsurface levels are devoted to chic boutiques and eateries. Modern-day aspiring celebrities may be spotted at the sidewalk tables of Newbury's "hottest" restaurants, such as Sonsie *(see p333).*

🔒 **Church of the Covenant**
67 Newbury St. **Tel** *(617) 266-7480.*
🕐 *10:30am Sun.*
📷 🚫 ♿ 🎥
www.churchofthecovenant.org

Stylish Newbury Street, with its elegant shops, galleries, and restaurants, the epitome of Boston style

Trinity Church ❻

Routinely voted one of America's 10 finest buildings, this masterpiece by Henry Hobson Richardson dates from 1877. Trinity Church was founded in 1733 near Downtown Crossing, but the congregation moved the church to this site in 1871. The church is a granite and sandstone Romanesque structure standing on wooden piles driven through mud into bedrock, surmounted with granite pyramids. John LaFarge designed the interior, while some of the windows are designed by Edward Burne-Jones and executed by William Morris.

The Bell Tower was inspired by the Renaissance cathedral at Salamanca, central Spain.

Bas-relief in Chancel
On the wall of the chancel, behind the altar, are a series of gold bas-reliefs. This one shows St. Paul before King Agrippa.

★ **North Transept Windows**
Designed by Edward Burne-Jones and executed by William Morris, the three stained-glass windows above the choir relate the story of Christmas.

Parish House

The Pulpit is covered with carved scenes from the life of Christ, as well as portraits of great preachers through the ages.

Chancel
Designed by Charles Maginnis, the present-day chancel was not dedicated until 1938. The seven windows by Clayton & Bell of London show the life of Christ.

David's Charge to Solomon
Located in the baptistry, to the right of the chancel, this beautiful window is also the result of a partnership between Edward Burne-Jones and William Morris. The story shown is one of the few in the church from the Old Testament.

VISITORS' CHECKLIST

Copley Sq. **Map** 3 C2. **Tel** (617) 536-0944. ⓣ Copley. ◯ 10am–3:30pm Mon–Fri, 9am–4pm Sat, 1–5pm Sun. ◷ 🕁 7:45am, 9am, 11:15am, 6pm Sun. 📷 🕭 **Concerts** Sep–mid-June: 12:15pm Fri.

John LaFarge's lancet windows show Christ in the act of blessing. They were designed at the request of Phillips Brooks – he wanted LaFarge to create an inspirational design for the west nave, which he could look at while preaching.

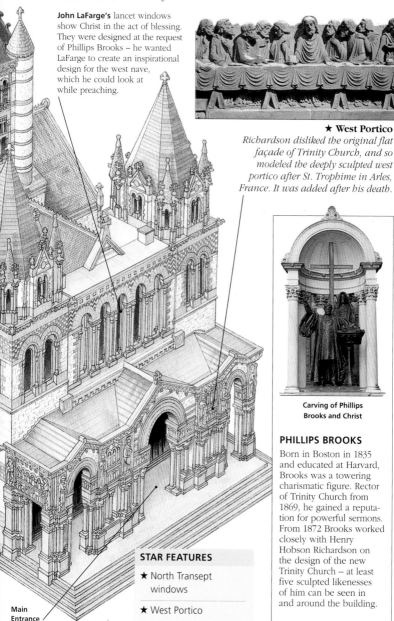

★ West Portico
Richardson disliked the original flat façade of Trinity Church, and so modeled the deeply sculpted west portico after St. Trophime in Arles, France. It was added after his death.

Carving of Phillips Brooks and Christ

PHILLIPS BROOKS

Born in Boston in 1835 and educated at Harvard, Brooks was a towering charismatic figure. Rector of Trinity Church from 1869, he gained a reputation for powerful sermons. From 1872 Brooks worked closely with Henry Hobson Richardson on the design of the new Trinity Church – at least five sculpted likenesses of him can be seen in and around the building.

STAR FEATURES

★ North Transept windows

★ West Portico

Main Entrance

The New Old South Church on the corner of Copley Square

Copley Square ⑦

Map 3 C2. ⓣ Copley.

Named after John Singleton Copley, the great Boston painter born nearby in 1737, Copley Square is a hive of civic activity surrounded by some of Boston's most striking architecture. Summer activities include weekly farmers' markets, concerts, and even folk-dancing.

The inviting green plaza took years to develop; when Copley was born it was just a marshy riverbank, which remained unfilled until 1870. Construction of the John Hancock Tower in 1975 anchored the southeastern side of Copley Square, and the Copley Place development completed the square on the southwestern corner in 1984. Today's Copley Square, a wide open space of trees, grass, and fountains, took shape in the heart of the city in the 1990s, after various plans to utilize this hitherto wasted space were tendered.

A large plaque honoring the Boston Marathon, which ends at the Boston Public Library, was set in the sidewalk in 1996 to coincide with the 100th race. As well as pushcart vendors, the plaza has a booth for discounted theater, music, and dance tickets.

Boylston Street ⑧

Map 3 C2. ⓣ Boylston, Arlington, Copley, Hynes Convention Center.

The corners of Boylston and Berkeley streets represent Boston architecture at its most diverse. The stately French Academic-style structure on the west side was erected for the Museum of Natural History, a forerunner of the Museum of Science (see p67). It has gone on to house upscale shops and restaurants. The east side spouts a Robert A.M. Stern tower and a Philip Johnson office building that resembles a table radio. Boston jeweler Shreve, Crump & Low occupied the Art Deco building at the corner of Arlington Street until relocating to 440 Boylston in 2005.

Some notable office buildings stand on Boylston Street. The lobby of the New England building at No. 501 features large historical murals and dioramas depicting the process of filling Back Bay. The central tower of the Prudential Center dominates the skyline on upper Boylston Street. Adjoining the Prudential is the Hynes Convention Center. It was significantly enlarged in 1988 to accommodate the city's burgeoning business in hosting conventions.

The Italian Gothic-style **New Old South Church**, which is located at the corner of Dartmouth, was built in 1874–5 by the congregation that had met previously at the Old South Meeting House (see p77).

🄝 **New Old South Church**
645 Boylston St. **Tel** (617) 536-1970. ⬭ 9am–7pm Mon–Fri, 10am–4pm Sat, 9am–4pm Sun. 🄵 6pm Thu, 9am, 11am Sun. 🄿 🄐 🄶 🄲 **www**.oldsouth.org

Boston Public Library ⑨

Copley Square. **Map** 3 C2. **Tel** (617) 536-5400. ⓣ Copley. **General Library** ⬭ 9am–9pm Mon–Thu, 9am–5pm Fri–Sat, 1–5pm Sun. 🄐 public hols; Jun–Sep: Sun. 🄵 2:30pm Mon, 6pm Tue & Thu, 11am Fri–Sat (& 2pm Sun Oct–May). 🄐 🄶 **www**.bpl.org

Founded in 1848, the Boston Public Library was America's first metropolitan library for the public. It quickly outgrew its original building, hence the construction of the Italian *palazzo*-style Copley Square building in 1887–95. Designed by Charles McKim, the building is a marvel of fine wood and marble detail. Bates Hall, on the second floor, is particularly noted for its soaring barrel-vaulted ceiling. Sculptor Daniel Chester French fashioned the library's huge bronze doors, Edward Abbey's murals of the Quest for the Holy Grail line the book request room, and John Singer Sargent's murals of Judaism and Christianity cover a third-floor gallery.

The library's collection is housed in the 1971 Boylston Street addition, a modernist structure by architect Philip Johnson.

The vast Bates Hall in the Boston Public Library, noted for its high barrel-vaulted ceiling

For hotels and restaurants in this region see pp306–11 and pp332–9

John Hancock Tower ❿

200 Clarendon St. **Map** 3 C2.
Ⓣ *Copley.*

The tallest building in
New England, the 740-ft
(226-m) rhomboid that is the
John Hancock Tower cuts
into Copley Square, with its
mirrored façade reflecting the
surroundings, including from
one angle the original
Hancock building built in
1947. The innovative design
has created a 60-story office
building with 10,344 windows
that shares the square with its
19th-century neighbors, the
Romanesque Trinity Church
and the Italian Renaissance
Revival Copley Plaza Hotel,
without dwarfing them. It was
designed by Henry Cobb of
the architect firm of I. M. Pei
& Partners and its construction
was completed in 1975.
Unfortunately, the observatory
on the 60th floor has been
closed following the events
of September 11.

View over Back Bay and the Charles River from the John Hancock Tower

Berklee Performance Center ⓫

136 Massachusetts Ave. **Map** 3 A3.
Tel (617) 266-7455. Ⓣ Hynes/
Convention Center. ◯ call or
consult website for concert details.
www.berkleebpc.com

The largest independent
music college in the world,
Berklee College of Music has
produced a number of jazz,
rock, and pop stars, including producer and arranger
Quincy Jones, Dixie Chicks
singer Natalie Maines, and
jazz-pop pianist/vocalist
Diana Krall.
    Berklee students as well
as faculty frequently use
the Berklee Performance
Center as a showcase, and
often as a venue for making
live recordings. The warm
acoustics and intimate rela-
tionship between the per-
formers and the audience
produce what is known
among audiophiles as "the
Berklee sound."

Boston Center for the Arts ⓬

539 Tremont St. **Map** 4 D3.
Tel (617) 426-5000. Ⓣ Back Bay/
South End. **Cyclorama** ◯ 9am–
5pm Mon–Fri. **Mills Gallery**
◯ noon–5pm Wed & Sun; noon–
9pm Thu–Sat. ◯ public hols. 📷 for
performances. 🚫 ♿
www.bcaonline.org

The centerpiece of a resur-
gent South End, the B.C.A.
complex includes four stages,
an art gallery, and artists'
studios as well as the Boston
Ballet Building, home to the
company's educational programs, rehearsal space, and
administrative offices. The
Tremont Estates Building at
the corner of Tremont Street,
an organ factory in the years
after the Civil War, now houses
artists' studios, rehearsal space,
and an art gallery. The largest
of the B.C.A. buildings is the
circular, domed Cyclorama,
which opened in 1884 to
exhibit the 50-ft (15-m) by
400-ft (121-m) painting *The
Battle of Gettysburg* by the
French artist Paul Philipp-
oteaux. The painting was
removed in 1889 and is now
displayed at Gettysburg
National Historic Park. It
now serves as performance
and exhibition space.
    The Stanford Calderwood
Pavilion, with a 360-seat and
a 200-seat theater, opened in
2004 as the first
new theater in
Boston in 75 years.
    The Mills Gallery
houses exhibitions
focusing on emer-
ging contemporary
artists, with a
strong emphasis
on multimedia
installations and
shows with
confrontational,
and often pro-
vocative, themes.

Richardsonian Romanesque is a popular
architectural style in Back Bay

FARTHER AFIELD

Most of Boston's historic sights are concentrated in the central colonial and Victorian city. However, the late 19th and 20th centuries saw Boston expand into the surrounding area. What were the marshlands of the Fenway now house two of Boston's most important art museums, the Museum of Fine Arts and the Isabella Stewart Gardner Museum *(see p105)*. Southeast of the city center, Columbia Point was developed in the mid-20th century and is home to the John F. Kennedy Library and Museum *(see p104)*. West of central

Statue of William Prescott, Bunker Hill Monument

Boston, across the Charles River, lies Cambridge, a city in its own right and sometimes referred to as the "Socialist Democratic Republic of Cambridge," a reference to the politics of its two major colleges, Harvard and the Massachusetts Institute of Technology. Harvard Square *(see p110)* is a lively area of bookstores, cafés, and street entertainers. Charlestown, east of Cambridge, is the site of the Bunker Hill Monument *(see p118)* and the Charlestown Navy Yard, where the US's most famous warship, the USS *Constitution*, is moored.

SIGHTS AT A GLANCE

Towns
Cambridge ❼
Charlestown ❽
Lexington ⓫
Lincoln ⓬
Quincy ⓭

Gardens and Zoos
Arnold Arboretum ❸
Franklin Park Zoo ❷
Broadmoor Sanctuary ❿

Museums and Historic Sites
Isabella Stewart Gardner Museum ❺
John F. Kennedy Library and Museum ❶
John F. Kennedy National Historic Site ❹
Museum of Fine Arts pp106–9 ❻
Wellesley College ❾

KEY

▨	Main sightseeing area
☐	Urban area
✈	Airport
🚇	Train station
══	Highway
══	Major road
═	Minor road
—	Railroad

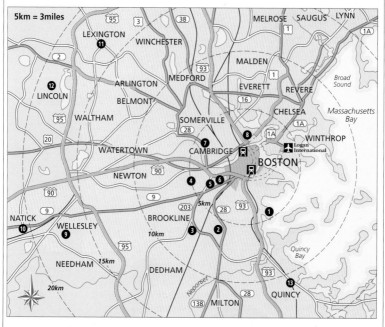

John F. Kennedy Library and Museum ❶

Columbia Point, Dorchester.
Tel *(617) 514-1600.* Ⓣ *JFK/U Mass.*
🚪 *9am–5pm daily.* ⬤ *Jan 1,*
Thanksgiving, Dec 25. 🎟 ♿ 📷 📶
www.jfklibrary.org

The soaring white concrete and glass building housing the John F. Kennedy Library stands sentinel on Columbia Point near the mouth of the Boston Harbor. This striking white and black modern building by the architect I. M. Pei is equally dramatic from the interior, with a 50-ft (15-m) wall of glass looking out over the water. Exhibitions extensively chronicle the 1,000 days of the Kennedy presidency with an immediacy uncommon in many other historical museums. Kennedy was among the first politicians to grasp the power of media. The museum takes full advantage of film and video footage to use the president's own words and image to tell his story: his campaign for the Democratic Party nomination, landmark television debates with Republican opponent Richard M. Nixon (who later became infamous for the Watergate Scandal), and his many addresses to the nation.

Several rooms re-create key chambers of the White House during the Kennedy administration, including the Oval Office; gripping film clips capture the anxiety of nuclear brinksmanship during the Cuban missile crisis as well as the inspirational spirit of the space program and the founding of the Peace Corps. Recently expanded exhibits on Robert F. Kennedy's role as Attorney General touch on both his deft handling of race relations and his key advisory role to his brother. The combination of artifacts, displays, and television footage evoke both the euphoria of "Camelot" and the numb horror of the assassination.

Lowland gorilla with her baby in the simulated natural environment of Franklin Park Zoo

Franklin Park Zoo ❷

1 Franklin Park Rd. **Tel** *(617) 541-5466.* Ⓣ *Forest Hills.* 🚌 *16 from Forest Hills subway.* 🚪 *Apr–Sep: 10am–5pm Mon–Fri, 10am–6pm Sat & Sun; Oct–Mar: 10am–4pm daily.* ⬤ *Jan 1, Thanksgiving, Dec 25.* 🎟 ♿ www.zoonewengland.com

The zoo, originally planned as a small menagerie, has expanded dramatically over the past century and long ago discarded caged enclosures in favor of simulated natural environments. Lowland gorillas roam a forest edge with caves for privacy, lions lounge around a rocky kingdom, while zebras, ostriches, and giraffes are free to graze on open grassland. The seasonal Butterfly Landing is a dense garden within a large enclosure. As many as 1,000 butterflies fly from flower to flower. New Age and light classical music augment the sense of fantasy. In the small petting zoo youngsters can meet farm animals.

Arnold Arboretum ❸

125 Arborway, Jamaica Plain.
Tel *(617) 524-1718.*
Ⓣ *Forest Hills.* 🚌 *39.*
🚪 *sunrise–sunset daily.*
Visitors Center 🚪 *9am–4pm Mon–Fri, 10am–4pm Sat, noon–4pm Sun.* ⬤ *public hols.* ♿
www.arboretum.harvard.edu

Founded by Harvard University in 1872 as a living catalog of all the indigenous and exotic trees and shrubs adaptable to New England's climate, the

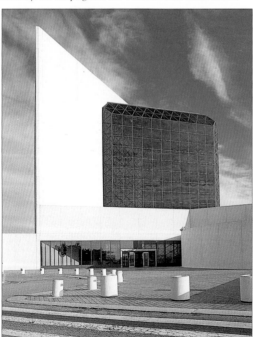

Dramatic, modern structure of the John F. Kennedy Library and Museum

For hotels and restaurants in this region see pp306–11 and pp332–9

Arboretum is planted with more than 15,000 labeled specimens. It is the oldest arboretum in the US and a key resource for botanical and horticultural research. The Arboretum also serves as a park where people jog, stroll, read, and paint.

The park's busiest time is on Lilac Sunday in early May when tens of thousands come to revel in the sight and fragrance of the lilac collection, one of the largest in the world. The range of the Arboretum's collections guarantees flowers from late March into November, beginning with cornelian cherry and forsythia. Blooms shift in late May to azalea, magnolia, and wisteria, then to mountain laurel and roses in June. Sweet autumn clematis bursts forth in September, and native witch hazel blooms in October and November. The Arboretum also has fine fall foliage in September and October.

A large scale model of the Arboretum can be seen in the Visitors' Information Center just inside the main gate.

John F. Kennedy National Historic Site ❹

83 Beals St, Brookline.
Tel (617) 566-7937.
Ⓣ Coolidge Corner. ⬜ late May–
Sep: 10:30am–4:30pm Wed–Sun.
🖼 ⌀ ♿ 🎞 🎧
www.nps.gov/jofi

The first home of the late president's parents, this Brookline house saw the birth of four of nine Kennedy children, including J.F.K. on May 29, 1917. Although the Kennedys moved to a larger house in 1921, the Beals Street residence held special memories for the family, who repurchased the house in 1966 and furnished it with their belongings circa 1917 as a memorial to John F. Kennedy. The guided tour includes a taped interview with J.F.K.'s mother Rose. A walking tour takes in other neighborhood sites relevant to the family's early years.

Central courtyard of the *palazzo*-style Isabella Stewart Gardner Museum

Isabella Stewart Gardner Museum ❺

280 The Fenway. **Tel** (617) 566-1401.
Ⓣ MFA. ⬜ 11am–5pm Tue–Sun.
⬤ Jan 1, Thanksgiving, Dec 25. 🖼
⌀ 🎵 **Concerts** (call for schedule).
www.gardnermuseum.org

The only thing more surprising than a Venetian *palazzo* on The Fenway is the collection of more than 2,500 works of art inside. Advised by scholar Bernard Berenson,

the strong-willed Isabella Stewart Gardner turned her wealth to collecting art in the late 19th century, acquiring a notable collection of Old Masters and Italian Renaissance pieces. Titian's *Rape of Europa*, for example, is considered his best painting in a US museum. The eccentric "Mrs. Jack" had an eye for her contemporaries as well. She purchased the first Matisse to enter an American collection and was an ardent patron of James McNeill Whistler and John Singer Sargent. The paintings, sculptures, and tapestries are displayed on three levels around a stunning skylit courtyard. Mrs. Gardner's will, which was instrumental in the setting up of the museum, stipulates the collection should remain assembled in the manner that she originally intended. Unfortunately, her intentions could not be upheld; in 1990 thieves made off with 13 of these priceless works, including a rare Rembrandt seascape, *Storm on the Sea of Galilee*, then conservatively valued in the region of $200 million.

THE EMERALD NECKLACE

Best known as designer of New York's Central Park, Frederick Law Olmsted based himself in Boston, where he created parks to solve environmental problems and provide a green refuge for inhabitants of the 19th-century industrial city. The Emerald Necklace includes the green spaces of Boston Common and the Public Garden (*see pp64–5*) and Commonwealth Avenue (*see p97*). To create a ring of parks, Olmsted added the Back Bay Fens

Jamaica Pond, part of Boston's fine parklands

(site of beautiful rose gardens and gateway to the Museum of Fine Arts and the Isabella Stewart Gardner Museum), the rustic Riverway, Jamaica Pond (sailing and picnicking), Arnold Arboretum, and Franklin Park (a golf course, zoo, and cross-country ski trails). The 5-mile (8-km) swath of parkland makes an excellent bicycle tour or ambitious walk.

The Museum of Fine Arts ❻

This is the largest art museum in New England and one of the five largest in the United States. Its collection includes around 450,000 items, ranging from Egyptian artifacts to paintings by John Singer Sargent. The original 1909 Classical-style building was augmented in 1981 by the addition of the West Wing, designed by I.M. Pei. The north and east sides have been expanded to create an American Wing, which is scheduled to open in late 2010.

★ Japanese Temple Room
This room was created in 1909 to provide a space in which to contemplate Buddhist art. The M.F.A. has one of the finest Japanese collections outside Japan.

American Silver
The revolutionary Paul Revere (see p44) was also a noted silversmith and produced many beautiful objects, such as this ornate teapot.

First floor

Fenway entrance

★ Egyptian Mummies
Among the museum's Egyptian and Nubian art is this tomb group of Nes-mut-aat-neru (767–656 BC) of Thebes.

Huntington entrance

★ Copley Portraits
John Singleton Copley (1738–1815) painted the celebrities of his day, hence this portrait of a dandyish John Hancock (see p43).

★ **Impressionist Paintings**
Boston collectors were among the first to appreciate French Impressionism. Dance at Bougival *(1883) by Renoir is typical of the M.F.A. collection.*

VISITORS' CHECKLIST

Avenue of the Arts,
465 Huntington Ave.
Tel (617) 267-9300. Ⓣ *MFA.*
☐ *10am–4:45pm Mon–Tue, 10am–9:45pm Wed–Fri, 10am–4:45 Sat–Sun.* ● *most public hols.* ♿ 🔊 📷 ☐
Lectures, concerts, and films.
🍴 🛍 🛈 *www.mfa.org*

KEY

☐ Court level

☐ First floor

☐ Second floor

Sargent Murals
John Singer Sargent spent the last years of his life creating artwork for the M.F.A. Originally commissioned to produce three paintings, Sargent instead constructed these elaborate murals, which were unveiled in 1921 and can still be seen today. He went on to create the works of art in the adjacent colonnade until his death in 1925.

Second floor

Court level

STAR EXHIBITS

★ Copley Portraits

★ Impressionist Paintings

★ Egyptian Mummies

★ Japanese Temple Room

GALLERY GUIDE
The museum is undergoing complete renovation with the addition of a new American Wing designed by Norman Foster. Until its scheduled completion in late 2010 galleries are subject to change – call ahead for the latest information.

Head of Aphrodite
This rare example of Ancient Greek sculpture dates from about 330–300 BC.

Exploring the Museum of Fine Arts

In addition to the major collections noted below, the Museum of Fine Arts has important holdings in the arts of Africa, Oceania, and the ancient Americas. The museum also houses collections of works on paper, contemporary art, and musical instruments. Several galleries are devoted to temporary thematic exhibitions. Other features of the museum include a seminar room, lecture hall, and well-stocked bookstore. Until major renovation work is completed, exhibits are subject to change. Call ahead for the latest information.

11th-century silver Korean ewer

ing decorative arts in a historical context, will be reinstalled in the new American wing, currently under construction. Until the new wing is complete, many objects from these rooms, along with the museum's contemporary crafts, will be housed in temporary galleries.

EUROPEAN PAINTINGS, DECORATIVE ARTS, AND SCULPTURE

This collection of European paintings and sculpture ranges from the 7th to the late 20th century. It showcases numerous masterpieces by English, Dutch, French, Italian, and Spanish artists, including various portraits by the 17th-century Dutch painter Rembrandt. The collection of works from 1550 to 1700 is impressive both for the quality of art and for its size; it includes Francisco de Zurbarán, El Greco, Paolo Veronese, Titian, and Peter Paul Rubens.

Boston's 19th-century collectors enriched the M.F.A. with wonderful French art: the museum features several paintings by Pierre François Millet (the M.F.A. has, in fact, the largest collection of his work in the world), as well as by other well-known 19th-century French artists, such as Edouard Manet, Pierre-Auguste Renoir, and Edgar Degas. Among this collection are the hugely popular *Water-lilies* (1905) by Claude Monet and *Dance at Bougival* (1883) by Renoir. The M.F.A.'s Monet holdings are among the world's largest, and there is also a good collection of paintings by the Dutch artist

Boston Harbor by the Luminist painter Fitz Hugh Lane (1804–65)

AMERICAN PAINTINGS, DECORATIVE ARTS, AND SCULPTURE

The M.F.A. displays a wealth of American art that includes more than 1,600 paintings. The earliest works on show are anonymous portraits painted in the late 17th century. The Colonial period is well represented, with more than 60 portraits by John Singleton Copley, perhaps America's most talented 18th-century painter, as well as works by Charles Willson Peale. Other works on display are 19th-century landscapes, including harbor scenes by Fitz Hugh Lane, an early Luminist painter, lush society portraits by John Singer Sargent, and those of other late 19th-century artists who constituted the "Boston School." There are also notable seascapes by Winslow Homer on show, who often painted on the Massachusetts coast, as well as the muscular

figure portraiture of Thomas Eakins. The M.F.A. also houses a sampling of works by 20th-century masters, including Stuart Davis, Jackson Pollock, Georgia O'Keeffe, and Arthur Dove.

The museum's holdings of American silver are superb. As well as works by John Coney, there are two cases containing tea services and other pieces by Paul Revere *(see p88)*. The M.F.A. also traces the development of the Boston style of 18th-century furniture through a definitive collection of desks, high chests, and tall clocks. Its famed period rooms, display-

Where Do We Come From? What Are We? Where Are We Going? by Paul Gauguin (1848–1903)

Part of the Processional Way of Ancient Babylonia (6th century BC)

Vincent van Gogh. Early 20th-century European art is also exhibited.

The M.F.A. is well known for its extensive collection of European decorative arts. Tableware, ceramics, and glass clustered by period from the early 17th to early 20th century are some examples of the works exhibited.

The construction of the new wing at the museum has temporarily reduced available gallery space. Some prized decorative arts collections have been put into storage as a result. These include the opulent displays of 18th-century French silver normally housed in the Louis XVI-style gallery, and the striking holdings of Chinese export porcelain.

ANCIENT EGYPTIAN, NUBIAN, AND NEAR EASTERN ART

The M.F.A.'s collection of Egyptian and Nubian materials is unparalleled outside of Africa, and it derives primarily from M.F.A.-Harvard University excavations along the Nile, which began in 1905. One of the highlights is a 1998 installation showing Egyptian Funerary Arts, which uses the M.F.A.'s superb collection of mummies from nearly three millennia to illustrate the technical and art-historical aspects of Egyptian burial practices. Also on display are some exceptional Babylonian, Assyrian, and Sumerian reliefs. Works from ancient Nubia, the cultural region around the Nile stretching roughly between the modern African cities of Aswan and Khartoum, encompass gold and silver artifacts, ceramics, and jewels.

Other highlights from the Egyptian and Nubian collections include two monumental sculptures of Nubian kings from the Great Temple of Amen at Napata (620–586 BC and 600–580 BC). A few of the galleries are set up to recreate Nubian burial chambers, which allows cuneiform wall carvings to be displayed in something akin to an original setting; a superb example is the offering chapel of Sekhem-ankh-Ptah from Sakkara (2450–2350 BC).

Tang Dynasty Chinese Horse (8th century)

CLASSICAL ART

The M.F.A. boasts one of America's top collections of Greek ceramics. In particular, the red- and black-figured vases dating from the 6th and 5th centuries BC are exceptional. The Classical galleries of the museum are intended to thematically highlight the influence of Greek arts on both Etruscan and Roman art. The Etruscan collection has several carved sarcophagi, gold jewelry, bronze mirrors, and colorful terracottas, while the Roman collection features grave markers, portrait busts, and a series of wall panel paintings unearthed in Pompeii on an M.F.A. expedition in 1900–01.

ASIAN ART

The Asian collection is one of the most extensive that can be found under one roof. A range of works from India, the Near East, and Central Asia is exhibited. Among the highlights are Indian sculpture and changing exhibitions of Islamic miniature paintings and Indian narrative paintings. Elsewhere, works from Korea feature some Buddhist paintings and sculptures, jewelry, and ornaments.

The museum also boasts calligraphy, ceramics, and stone sculptures from China and the largest collection of Japanese prints outside Japan. Extensive holdings and limited display space mean that exhibitions change often, but the M.F.A.'s collections of Japanese and Chinese scroll and screen paintings are, nevertheless, unmatched in the West. The strength of the M.F.A.'s Japanese art collection is largely due to the efforts of enthusiasts such as Ernest Fenollosa and William Bigelow Sturgis. In the 19th century, they encouraged the Japanese to maintain their traditions, and salvaged Buddhist temple art when the Japanese imperial government had withdrawn subsidies from these institutions. This collection is considered to contain some of the finest examples of Asian temple art in the world.

Roman fresco, excavated from a Pompeian villa (1st century AD)

Cambridge ❼

Part of the greater Boston metropolitan area, Cambridge is, nonetheless, a town in its own right and has the mood and feel of such. Principally a college town, it is dominated by Harvard University and other college campuses. It also boasts a number of important historic sights, such as Christ Church and Cambridge Common, which have associations to the American Revolution. Harvard Square is the area's main entertainment and shopping district.

Site of the Washington Elm, on Cambridge Common

🏛 Longfellow National Historic Site

105 Brattle St. *Tel* (617) 876-4491. ◻ Jun–Oct: 10am–4:30pm Wed–Sun. 🗐 🗐 🗐 🗐 🗐 www.nps.gov/long

This house on Brattle Street, like many around it, was built by Colonial-era merchants loyal to the British Crown during the Revolution. It was seized by American revolutionaries and served as George Washington's head-quarters during the Siege of Boston.

The poet Henry Wadsworth Longfellow boarded here in 1837, was given the house as a wedding present in 1843, and lived here until his death in 1888. He wrote his most famous poems here, including *Tales of a Wayside Inn* and *The Song of Hiawatha*. Longfellow's status as literary dean of Boston meant that Nathaniel Hawthorne and Charles Sumner, among others, were regular visitors.

Street musician, Harvard Square

🏛 Harvard Square

📱 (617) 491-3434. 🗐 www.harvardsquare.com

Even Bostonians think of Harvard Square as a stand-in for Cambridge – the square was the original site of Cambridge from around 1630. Dominating the square is the Harvard Cooperative Society ("the Coop"), a Harvard institution that sells inexpensive clothes, posters, and books. Harvard's large student population is very much in evidence here, adding color to the character of the square. Many trendy boutiques, inexpensive restaurants, and numerous cafés cater to their needs. Street performers abound, especially on the weekends, and the square has long been a place where pop trends begin. Club Passim, for example, has incubated many successful singer-songwriters since Joan Baez first debuted here in 1959.

🏛 Cambridge Common

Set aside as common pasture and military drill ground in 1631, Cambridge Common has served as a center for religious, social, and political activity ever since. George Washington took command of the Continental Army here on July 3, 1775, beneath the Washington Elm, now marked by a stone. The common served as the army's encampment from 1775 to 1776. In 1997 the first monument in the US to commemorate the victims of the Irish Famine was unveiled on the common.

⛪ Christ Church

Garden St. *Tel* (617) 876-0200. ◻ 8am–6pm Mon–Fri & Sun, 8am–3pm Sat. 🕆 7:45am, 10:15am, 5:30pm Sun, 12:10pm Wed. 🗐 🗐 www.cccambridge.org

With its square bell tower and plain, gray shingled edifice, Christ Church is a restrained example of an Anglican church. Designed in 1761 by Peter Harrison, the architect of Boston's King's Chapel (*see p76*), Christ Church came in for rough treatment as a barracks for Continental Army troops in 1775 – British loyalists had almost all fled Cambridge by this time. The army even melted down the organ pipes to cast musket balls. The church was restored for services on New Year's Eve, 1775, when George Washington and his wife, Martha, were among the worshipers. Anti-Anglican sentiment remained strong in Cambridge, and Christ Church did not have its own rector again until the 19th century.

Simple interior of Christ Church, designed prior to the Revolution in 1761

For hotels and restaurants in this region see pp306–11 and pp332–9

🏛 Radcliffe Institute for Advanced Study

Brattle St. **Tel** (617) 495-8601. 🛗
www.radcliffe.edu

Radcliffe College was founded in 1879 as the Collegiate Institution for Women, when 27 women began to study by private arrangement with Harvard professors. By 1943, members of Harvard's faculty no longer taught separate undergraduate courses to the women of Radcliffe, and in 1999 Radcliffe ceased its official existence as an independent college. It is now an institute for advanced study promoting scholarship of women's culture. The first Radcliffe building was the 1806 Federal-style mansion, Fay House, on the northern corner of what became Radcliffe Yard. Schlesinger Library, on the west side of the yard, is considered a significant example of

Stained glass, Radcliffe Institute

Colonial Revival architecture. The library's most famous holdings are an extensive collection of cookbooks and reference works on gastronomy.

🏛 M.I.T.

77 Massachusetts Ave. **Tel** (617) 253-4795. **MIT Museum** ⏰ 10am–5pm daily. 🚇 **Hart Nautical Gallery** ⏰ 10am–5pm daily. **List Visual Arts Center** ⏰ noon–6pm Tue–Sun (to 8pm Thu). 🚻 🛗 🏪 www.mit.edu

Chartered in 1861 to teach "exactly and thoroughly the fundamental principles of positive science with application to the industrial arts," the Massachusetts Institute of Technology has evolved into one of the world's leading universities in engineering and the sciences. Several architectural masterpieces dot M.I.T.'s 135-acre (55-ha) campus along the Charles River, including Eero Saarinen's

VISITORS' CHECKLIST

🚉 Harvard. 🚌 1, 69.
🛈 **Harvard Square Information Booth** (617) 497-1630.
Cambridge Office of Tourism (617) 441-2884 or (800) 862-5678. 📅 Sun. 🎉 late June.
www.harvard.edu or
www.cambridge-usa.org

Kresge Auditorium and Kresge Chapel, built in 1955. The Wiesner Building is a major collaboration between architect I. M. Pei and several artists, including Kenneth Noland, whose relief mural dominates the atrium. The building houses the **List Visual Arts Center**, noted for its avant-garde art.

The **Hart Nautical Gallery** in the Rogers Building focuses on marine engineering, with exhibits ranging from models of ships to exhibits of the latest advances in underwater research. The **M.I.T. Museum** blends art and science with exhibits such as Harold Edgerton's groundbreaking stroboscopic flash photographs, and the latest holographic art.

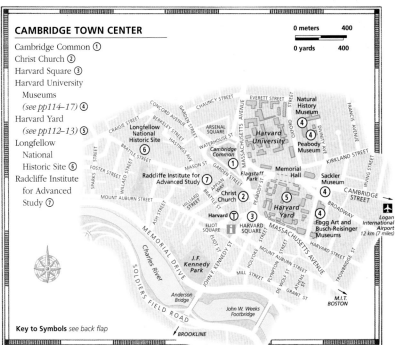

CAMBRIDGE TOWN CENTER

Cambridge Common ①
Christ Church ②
Harvard Square ③
Harvard University Museums
(see pp114–17) ④
Harvard Yard
(see pp112–13) ⑤
Longfellow National Historic Site ⑥
Radcliffe Institute for Advanced Study ⑦

0 meters 400
0 yards 400

Key to Symbols see back flap

Harvard Yard

In 1636 Boston's well-educated Puritan leaders founded a college in Newtowne. Two years later cleric John Harvard died and bequeathed half his estate and all his books to the fledgling college. The colony's leaders bestowed his name on the school and rechristened the surrounding community Cambridge after the English city where they had been educated. The oldest university in the US, Harvard is now one of the world's most prestigious centers of learning. The university has expanded to encompass more than 400 buildings, but Harvard Yard is still at its heart.

Holden Chapel
Built in 1742, the chapel was the scene of revolutionary speeches and was later used as a demonstration hall for human dissections.

Hollis Hall was used as barracks by George Washington's troops during the American Revolution.

Massachusetts Hall, built in 1720, is Harvard's oldest building.

★ **Old Harvard Yard**
This leafy yard dates from the founding of the college in 1636. Freshman dormitories dot the yard, and throughout the year it is a focal point for students.

Harvard University Information Center

★ **John Harvard Statue**
This statue celebrates Harvard's most famous benefactor. Almost a place of pilgrimage, graduates and visitors invariably pose for photographs here.

University Hall,
designed by Charles Bulfinch, was built in 1816.

★ **Widener Library**
This library memorializes Harry Elkins Widener, who died on the Titanic in 1912. With more than 3 million volumes, it is the third largest library in the US.

★ **Memorial Church**
This church was built in 1931 and copies earlier styles. For example, the steeple is modeled on that of the Old North Church (see p87) in Boston's North End.

VISITORS' CHECKLIST

Massachusetts Ave. Ⓣ *Harvard*.
◻ *24 hrs*. ◯ *2nd Thu in Jun (Commencement)*. ♿ 📷 🅿
Lectures, concerts and films.
Harvard Information Center
Tel (617) 495-1573. **Harvard Box Office** *Tel* (617) 496-2222.
Harvard Film Archive *Tel* (617) 495 4700. *Films shown nightly.*
www.harvard.edu

Memorial Hall, a Ruskin Gothic building, memorializes Harvard's Union casualties from the Civil War.

⸻ Sackler and Peabody Museums, and Harvard Museum of Natural History *(see pp116–17)*

Sever Hall
One of the most distinctive of Harvard's Halls, this Romanesque style-building was designed by Henry Hobson Richardson.

Fogg Art and Busch-Reisinger Museums *(see pp114–15)*

Tercentenary Theater

STAR SIGHTS

★ John Harvard Statue

★ Memorial Church

★ Old Harvard Yard

★ Widener Library

0 meters   50

0 yards   50

Carpenter Center for Visual Arts
Opened in 1963, the Carpenter Center is the only building in the US designed by the avant-garde Swiss architect Le Corbusier.

The Harvard University Museums

Harvard's museums were originally conceived to revolutionize the process of education; students were to be taught by allowing them access to artifacts from around the world. Today, this tradition continues, with the museums housing some of the world's finest university collections: art from Europe and America in the Fogg Art and Busch-Reisinger Museums; archaeological finds in the Peabody Museum; Asian, Islamic and Indian art in the Sackler Museum, and a vast collection of artifacts in the Harvard Museum of Natural History.

Main entrance to the Fogg Art and Busch-Reisinger Museums

Fogg Art and Busch-Reisinger Museums

32 Quincy St. *Tel* (617) 495-9400.
🔵 *for renovation until 2013.* 🖼 ♿
🌐 www.artmuseums.harvard.edu
Both these museums are closed for renovation until 2013. Select items are currently on display at the Sackler Museum *(see p117).* The Fogg was created in 1891, when Harvard began to build its own art collection to teach art history more effectively. Both the Fogg and the Busch-Reisinger, which was grafted onto the Fogg in 1991, have select collections of art from Europe and America.

The red-brick Georgian building housing the Fogg was completed in 1927. The collections, which focus on Western art from the late Middle Ages to the present, are organized around a central courtyard modeled on a 16th-century church in Montepulciano, Italy. The ground-floor corridors surrounding the courtyard feature 12th-century capitals from Moutiers St-Jean in Burgundy, France.

Two small galleries near the entrance, and the two-story Warburg Hall, display the Fogg's collections that prefigure the Italian Renaissance. The massive altar-pieces and suspended crucifix in the Warburg are particularly impressive.

The ground floor galleries on the left side of the entrance are devoted to 17th-century Dutch, Flemish, French, and Italian paintings, including four studies for Francesco Trevisiani's *Massacre of the Innocents*, a masterpiece destroyed in Dresden in World War II. Another room details Gian Lorenzo Bernini's use of clay models for his large-scale marbles and bronzes.

The museum's second level features the emergence of landscape as a subject in French 19th-century painting.

Galleries along the front of the building change exhibitions frequently, often focusing on drawings and graphic arts. The highlight of the second level is the Maurice Wertheim collection of Impressionist and Post-Impressionist art, most of it collected in the late 1930s. With a number of important paintings by

Renoir, Manet, and Degas, the Wertheim gallery is the Fogg's most popular.

Surprises lurk in an adjacent gallery of art made in France 1885-1960, often by expatriate artists. Edvard Munch's 1891 painting of *Rue de Rivoli*, for example, is both bright and impressionistic, in contrast with his collection of bleak Expressionist paintings.

The museum also houses rotating displays from its collection of 19th- and 20th-century African art.

Werner Otto Hall, which contains the Busch-Reisinger Museum, is entered through the second level of the Fogg. The museum's collections focus on Germanic art and

Bernini Model (1674-75)
Gian Lorenzo Bernini crafted this clay model of a kneeling angel to guide the artisans casting his larger bronze.

First floor

Main entrance

GUIDE TO THE FOGG ART AND BUSCH-REISINGER MUSEUMS

Western art from the Middle Ages to the present is on the first floor of the Fogg Art Museum. French and American art from the 19th and 20th centuries and 20th-century American art are on the second floor. The Busch-Reisinger focuses on Germanic art.

Light-Space Modulator (1923–30) by the Hungarian Moholy-Nagy

CAMBRIDGE | 115

design from after 1880, with an emphasis on Expressionism. Harvard was a safe haven for many Bauhaus artists, architects, and designers who fled Nazi Germany, and both Walter Gropius and Lyonel Feininger chose the Busch-Reisinger as the depository of their personal papers and drawings.

Periodic exhibitions explore aspects of the work and philosophy of the Bauhaus movement. Although small, the museum owns major paintings and sculptures by 20th-century masters such as Max Beckmann, Lyonel Feininger, Wassily Kandinsky, Paul Klee, Oskar Kokoschka, Emil Nolde, and Franz Marc.

Calderwood Courtyard of the Fogg Art Museum

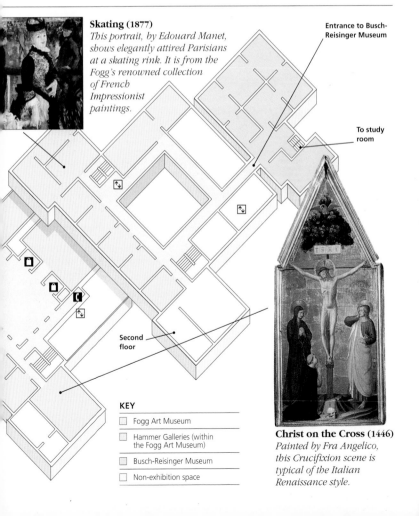

Skating (1877)
This portrait, by Edouard Manet, shows elegantly attired Parisians at a skating rink. It is from the Fogg's renowned collection of French Impressionist paintings.

Entrance to Busch-Reisinger Museum

To study room

Second floor

Christ on the Cross (1446)
Painted by Fra Angelico, this Crucifixion scene is typical of the Italian Renaissance style.

KEY

☐ Fogg Art Museum
☐ Hammer Galleries (within the Fogg Art Museum)
☐ Busch-Reisinger Museum
☐ Non-exhibition space

Peabody Museum of Archaeology and Ethnology

11 Divinity Ave. **Tel** (617) 496-1027.
⬜ 9am–5pm daily.
⬤ Jan 1, Thanksgiving, Dec 24, 25.
🖐 ♿ 📷
www.peabody.harvard.edu

The Peabody Museum of Archaeology and Ethnology was founded in 1866 as the first museum in the Americas devoted solely to anthropology. The many collections, which include several million artifacts and more than 500,000 photographic images, come from all around the world. Initially, in the 19th century, the museum's pioneering archaeological and ethnological research began relatively close to home with excavations of Mayan sites in Central America. The Peabody also conducted some of the first and most important research on the precontact Anasazi people of the American Southwest and on the cultural history of the later Pueblo tribes of the same region. Joint expeditions sponsored by the Peabody Museum and the Museum of Fine Arts (see pp106–9) also uncovered some of the richest finds of dynastic and predynastic Egypt. Research continued in all these areas well into the 20th century and later

Native American totem pole, Peabody Museum

broadened to embrace the cultures of the islands of the South Pacific.

The Hall of the North American Indian on the ground level was completely overhauled in the 1990s. Most of the artifacts are displayed in a way that puts them in the context of the time when they were gathered, when European and Native cultures first came into contact. For example, the Native American tribes of the Northern Plains are interpreted largely through an exhibition detailing the Lewis and Clark expedition of 1804–06; these two explorers undertook to find a route, by water, from East to West Coast, and on their way collected innumerable artifacts. Other outstanding exhibits include totem carvings by Pacific Northwest tribes and a wide range of historic and contemporary Navajo weavings. The third floor is devoted to Central American anthropology, with casts of some of the ruins uncovered at Copán in Honduras and Chichen Itza in Mexico. The fourth floor concentrates on Polynesia, Micronesia, and other islands of the Pacific, with striking collections of ceremonial objects, such as masks. Small vessels used for fishing and near-island trading hang overhead.

Triceratops skull in the Harvard Museum of Natural History

Harvard Museum of Natural History

26 Oxford St. **Tel** (617) 495-3045.
⬜ 9am–5pm daily.
⬤ Jan 1, Thanksgiving, Dec 24, 25.
📷 ♿ 📷
www.hmnh.harvard.edu

The Harvard Museum of Natural History is actually three museums rolled into one, all displayed on a single floor of a turn-of-the-century classroom building. It includes the collections of the Mineralogical and Geological Museum, the Museum of Comparative Zoology, and the Botanical Museum. The straightforward presentation of labeled objects exudes an infectious, old-fashioned charm, yet their initial appearance belies the fact that these are some of the most complete collections of their kind.

The mineralogical galleries include some of Harvard University's oldest specimen collections, the oldest of which dates from 1783. Virtually every New England mineral, rock, and gem type is represented here, including rough and cut gemstones and one of the world's premier meteorite collections.

The zoological galleries owe their inception to the great 19th-century biologist Louis Agassiz and include his personal arachnid collection. The collection of taxidermied bird, mammal, and reptile specimens is comprehensive, and there is also a collection of dinosaur skeletons. Children are most fascinated by the giant kronosaurus (a type of prehistoric sea serpent) and the skeleton of the first triceratops ever described in

Frog mask fom Easter Island in the South Pacific, Peabody Museum

scientific literature. There are also fossil exhibits of the earliest invertebrates and reptiles, as well as skeletons of still-living species, including a collection of whale skeletons.

The collections in the botanical galleries include the Ware Collection of Blaschka Glass Models of Plants, popularly known as the "glass flowers." Between 1887 and 1936, father and son artisans Leopold and Rudolph Blaschka created these 3,000 exacting models of 850 plant species. Each species is illustrated with a scientifically accurate lifesize model and magnified parts. While the handblown models were created as teaching aids, they are a unique accomplishment in the glassblowers' art and are as prized for their aesthetic qualities as their scientific utility.

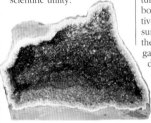

Amethyst specimen in the Harvard Museum of Natural History

Sackler Museum

485 Broadway, Cambridge.
Tel (617) 495-9400.
◷ 10am–5pm Mon–Sat, 1–5pm Sun. ◑ public holidays. 🖼 ♿ 📷
www.artmuseums.harvard.edu

Named after a famous philanthropist, physician, and art collector, the Arthur M. Sackler Museum was built to display Harvard's collection of ancient, Asian, Islamic, and late Indian art. During renovations to the Fogg Art and Busch-Reisinger museums, lasting through 2013, the Sackler will display select items from the collections of all three museums. Be sure to pick up a gallery map and flyers on the configuration of current exhibitions.

Opened in 1985, the Sackler is housed

in a modern building designed by James F. Stirling and his firm of architects based in London, England. The building is itself a bold artistic statement that complements the more traditional Fogg Art Museum that sits directly across from it. Aware that Harvard University had long embarked on a tradition of erecting many unique buildings in the area just north and east of Harvard Yard, Stirling was prompted to introduce the innovatively designed building to the world as "the newest animal in Harvard's architectural zoo." The exterior borrows details and decorative devices from several surrounding buildings, while the starkly modern interior galleries provide optimal display space. The 30-ft (10-m) entrance lobby features a 1997 wall-painting by the late Conceptual artist Sol Lewitt (1928–2007), whose trademark was colorful geometric shapes, which appear to float in space. The original design of the building called for an enclosed walkway over a major street to connect the Sackler to the

Southeast Asian Buddha head, Sackler Museum

Fogg, thereby creating a formal gateway to Harvard, but the plan was thwarted by Cambridge neighborhood activists.

The Sackler is best toured by ascending the long staircase to the galleries on the fourth floor and then working back down to the lobby. Holdings include ancient Greek art with a coin collection from the empire of Alexander the Great, and unusually extensive collections of red and black pottery with decorative friezes. The collections of Chinese art, including many objects which were the gifts of Harvard-affiliated diplomats, are thought to be among the finest of Chinese art in the West. They include Chinese sculpture, Buddhist stone sculpture, and archaic Chinese bronzes, jades, and ceramics. The Southeast Asian collections are particularly interesting for their Buddhist sculptures and figures from Hindu mythology. Also included in the collection are Korean ceramics, Japanese ukiyo-e prints, and former ambassador to India John Kenneth Galbraith's (1908–2006) Indian paintings.

Buddhist sculptures, part of the Sackler's Asian and Indian collections

Charlestown 8

Situated on the north bank of the Charles River,
directly opposite the North End, Charlestown exudes
history. The site of the infamous Battle of Bunker Hill,
when American troops suffered huge losses in their
fight for independence, today the district forms a major
part of Boston's Freedom Trail *(see pp54–57).* As well
as sights from the American Revolution, visitors can
see USS *Constitution*, pride of the post-revolutionary
American Navy, which took part in the 1812 war with
Britain. Also of interest is the Charlestown Navy Yard.

**Granite obelisk of the Bunker Hill
Monument, erected in 1843**

🏛 Bunker Hill Monument

Monument Square. *Tel (617)
242-5641.* ◯ 9am–5pm daily (until
6pm Jul & Aug). ◉ Jan 1, Thanksgiving, Dec 25.
www.nps.gov/bost

In the Revolution's first pitched
battle between British and
colonial troops, which took
place on June 17, 1775, the
British won a Pyrrhic victory
on the battlefield but failed to
create an escape route from
the Boston peninsula to the
mainland. Following the
battle, American irregulars
were joined by other militia
to keep British forces penned
up until the Continental
Army, under the command of
General George Washington,
forced their evacuation by sea
the following March 17, still
celebrated in the Boston area
as Evacuation Day.

Charlestown citizens began
raising funds for the Bunker
Hill Monument in 1823, laid
the cornerstone in 1825 and
dedicated the 221-ft (67-m)
granite obelisk in 1843.
There is no elevator, but

294 steps lead to the top
and great views.

Renovations, completed in
2007, improved ground-level
accessibility for the disabled
and enlarged the on-site
museum which focuses on
the strategies and significance
of the battle. Precision, high-
efficiency lighting was also
installed to fully illuminate
the monument at night and
reveal the pyramid that caps
the obelisk – a design echoed
at the tops of the pylons of
the nearby Leonard P. Zakim
Bunker Hill Bridge.

🏛 City Square

When John Winthrop arrived
with three shiploads of
Puritan refugees
in 1630, they
settled first in the
marshes at the
base of Town Hill,
now City Square.
A small public
park now marks the
site of Winthrop's
Town House, the
very first seat of Boston
government. Today, one
of Boston's most famous
restaurants, Olives *(see p338),*
faces onto the square.

🏛 John Harvard Mall

Ten families founded
Charlestown in 1629, a year
before the rest of Boston
was settled. They built their
homes and a palisaded fort
on Town Hill, a spot now
marked by John Harvard
Mall. Several bronze plaques
within the small enclosed
park commemorate events
in the early history of the
Massachusetts Bay Colony
(see p42), one plaque pro-
claiming "this low mound
of earth the memorial of
a mighty nation." A small
monument pays homage
to John Harvard, the young
cleric who ministered to the
Charlestown settlers and
who left his name, half his
estate, and all his books to
the fledgling college at
Newtowne when he died
in 1638 *(see pp112–13).*

🏛 Warren Tavern

2 Pleasant St. *Tel (617) 241-8142.*
◯ lunch, dinner daily, brunch
Sat–Sun. **www**.warrentavern.com

Dating from 1780, Warren
Tavern was one of the first
buildings erected after the
British burned Charles-
town. It was named
after Joseph Warren,
president of the Pro-
vincial Congress in
1774 and a general
in the Massachusetts
Army. He enlisted
as a private with the
Continental Army for
the Battle of Bunker
Hill, where he was killed.
The tavern, once derelict,
has been restored to its 18th-
century style. By contrast, the
food is modern fare.

**Municipal art in
City Square**

Old-fashioned clapboard houses on Warren Street

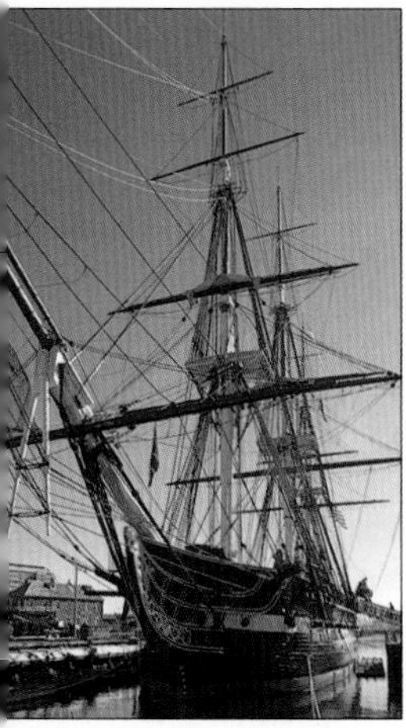

USS *Constitution*, built in 1797, moored in Charlestown Navy Yard

🏛 Charlestown Navy Yard

Visitor Center, Building 5. **Tel** *(617) 242-5601.* 🕘 *9am–5pm daily (till 6pm Jul & Aug).* ⛔ *Jan 1, Thanksgiving, Dec 25.* ♿ 📖 **www**.nps.gov/bost

Boston's deep harbor and long tides made Charlestown a logical site for one of the US Navy's first shipyards, established in 1800. For 174 years, as the Navy moved from wooden sailing ships to steel giants, Charlestown Navy Yard played a key role in supporting the US Atlantic fleet. On decommissioning, the facility was transferred to the National Park Service to interpret the art and history of naval shipbuilding. The yard was designed by Alexander Parris, architect of Quincy Market *(see p80)*, and was one of the first examples of industrial architecture in Boston.

Drydock No. 1, built in 1802, was the one of the first docks that could be drained of water – its first occupant was USS *Constitution*. Visitors can also board the World War II destroyer USS *Cassin Young*.

🏛 USS *Constitution*

Charlestown Navy Yard. **Tel** *(617) 242-5671.* 🕘 *Apr–Oct: 10am–3:50pm Tue–Sun; Nov–Mar: 10am–3:50pm Thu–Sun.* ♿ 📖 **Museum:** 🕘 *Apr–Oct: 9am–6pm daily; Nov–Mar: 10am–5pm daily.* ⛔ *Jan 1, Thanksgiving, Dec 25.* 🚫📷 ♿ **www**.ussconstitutionmuseum.org

The oldest commissioned warship afloat, the USS *Constitution* was built in the North End and christened in 1797. She saw immediate action in the Mediterranean protecting American shipping from the Barbary pirates. In the War of 1812, she won fame and her nickname of "Old Ironsides" when cannonballs bounced off her in a battle with the British ship *Guerriere*. She won 42 battles, lost none, captured 20 vessels, and was never boarded by an enemy. She was nearly scuttled several times, and at one time was reduced to serving as a floating barracks. In 1830, Oliver Wendell Holmes penned the poem *Old Ironsides* that rallied public support to save the ship, while on another occasion, in the 1920s, schoolchildren sent in their pennies and nickels to salvage her. She underwent her most thorough overhaul in time for her 1997 bicentennial, able to carry her own canvas into the wind for the first time in a century. On July 4 each year, she is taken out into the harbor for an annual turnaround that reverses her position at the Navy Yard pier to insure equal weathering on both sides. A small museum documents her history.

VISITORS' CHECKLIST

[T] *Community College.*
🚌 *93.* ⛴ *from Long Wharf.*
🛒 *Wed.* 🎉 *June 24.*

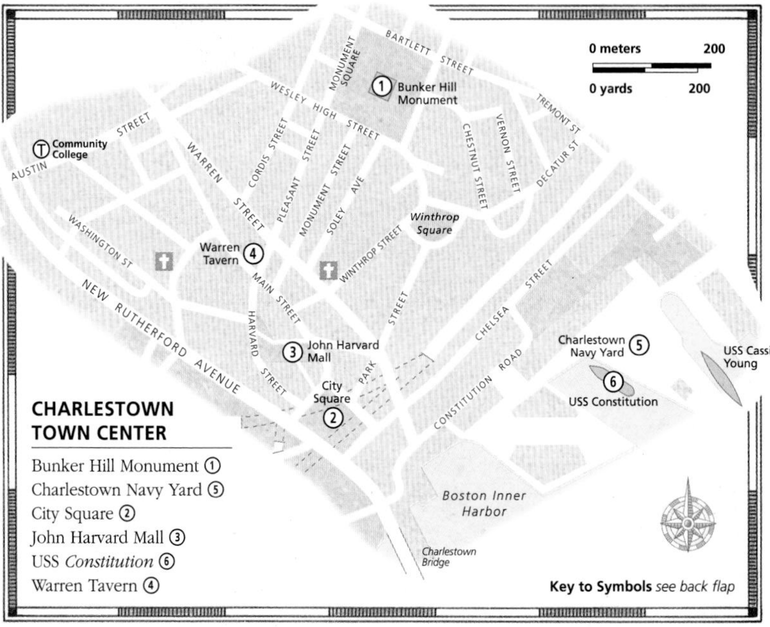
0 meters 200
0 yards 200
Bunker Hill Monument
BARTLETT STREET
MONUMENT SQUARE
WESLEY HIGH STREET
TREMONT ST
Community College
AUSTIN STREET
WARREN STREET
CORDIS STREET
PLEASANT STREET
MONUMENT STREET
SOLEY AVE
CHESTNUT STREET
VERNON STREET
DECATUR ST
WASHINGTON ST
Winthrop Square
WINTHROP STREET
Warren Tavern
MAIN STREET
NEW RUTHERFORD AVENUE
HARVARD STREET
John Harvard Mall
PARK
City Square
CHELSEA STREET
CONSTITUTION ROAD
Charlestown Navy Yard
USS Constitution
USS Cassin Young
Boston Inner Harbor
Charlestown Bridge
CHARLESTOWN TOWN CENTER
Bunker Hill Monument 1
Charlestown Navy Yard 5
City Square 2
John Harvard Mall 3
USS Constitution 6
Warren Tavern 4
Key to Symbols see back flap

Wellesley College 🔟

106 Central St, Wellesley. *Tel (781) 283-1000.* **Museum** *(781) 283-2051.* ◯ *year-round: call for hours.*

Founded in 1875, this top college for women has former First Lady Hillary Rodham Clinton (b.1947), now US Secretary of State, among its graduates. The grounds of the hilly Gothic campus overlooking Lake Waban are a virtual arboretum, with trees tagged for easy identification.

The main attraction is the **Davis Museum and Cultural Center**, with its collection of 5,000 paintings, prints, photos, drawings, and sculptures spanning the ages from classical to contemporary. The dramatic building was the first US project for noted Spanish architect Jose Rafael Moneo (b.1937).

Broadmoor Wildlife Sanctuary 🔟

280 Eliot St, S Natick. 🚻 *(508) 655-2296.* **www**.massaudubon.org **Nature Center** ◯ *9am–5pm Tue–Fri, 10am–5pm Sat, Sun & public hols.* 🌲 **Trails** ◯ *dawn–dusk Tue–Sun.* 📷 ♿

Nine miles (14.5 km) of walking trails go through field, woodland, and wetland habitats at this sanctuary. A boardwalk skirts the bank of Indian Brook before crossing a marsh. The 110-ft (33.5-m) bridge spanning the brook is an ideal lookout from which to photograph beavers, otters, and wood ducks. In winter the sanctuary is popular with snowshoe enthusiasts and cross-country skiers.

US Secretary of State Hillary Rodham Clinton, a Wellesley College grad

Lexington 🔟

🚻 *31,500.* 🏛 *1875 Massachusetts Ave (781) 862-2480.* **www**.lexingtonchamber.org

Lexington and neighboring Concord are forever linked in history as the settings for two bloody skirmishes that acted as catalysts for the Revolutionary War *(see p144)*. It was here on April 19, 1775, that armed colonists, called Minute Men, clashed with British troops on their way to Concord in search of rebel weaponry. The *Minute Man* statue stands on the town common, now known as **Lexington Battle Green**. The battle is reenacted each year in mid-April. The local Historical Society maintains three buildings linked to the battle that now display artifacts from that era. **Buckman Tavern** served as both the

meeting place for the Minute Men before the confrontation and as a makeshift hospital for their wounded. Paul Revere alerted the colonists of the advancing British troops and is said to have stopped here following his historic ride *(see box below)*. Revere also stopped at the **Hancock-Clarke House** to warn Samuel Adams (1722–1803) and John Hancock (1737–93), two of the eventual signatories to the Declaration of Independence. **Munroe Tavern** served as headquarters for British forces.

🏛 **Historical Society Houses** **Hancock-Clarke House** 36 Hancock St. **Buckman Tavern** 1 Bedford St. **Munroe Tavern** 1332 Massachusetts Ave. *Tel (781) 862-1703.* 📷

Lincoln 🔟

🚻 *7,700.*

Located just 13 miles (21 km) from Boston at the midway point between Concord and Lexington, Lincoln was once called "Niptown" because it was comprised of parcels of land that were "nipped" from neighboring towns. Today this wealthy rural community is noted for its interesting array of sightseeing attractions.

Buckman Tavern at Lexington, meeting place of the minute men

PAUL REVERE'S RIDE

Under the cover of night on April 18, 1775, Boston silversmith Paul Revere (1734–1818) took on a daring mission. Rowing silently past British ships in the harbor, he reached Charlestown, borrowed a horse, and rode to Lexington to spread the alarm: the British were approaching to arrest patriots John Hancock and Samuel Adams in Lexington and seize rebel arms in Concord. Detained by British troops on the way to Concord, he was released just in time to see the first shots fired on Lexington Green. Nearly 100 years later, his heroics were immortalized in the 1860 poem "Paul Revere's Ride" by New Englander Henry Wadsworth Longfellow.

Outdoor sculptures at DeCordova Sculpture Park

The **DeCordova Sculpture Park**, the largest park of its kind in New England, displays some 70 contemporary large-scale American sculptures as part of its changing outdoor exhibition. The estate was bequeathed to the town by wealthy entrepreneur and patron of the arts Julian DeCordova (1850–1945). The museum is famous for its collection of contemporary New England artworks.

Walter Gropius (1883–1969), the director of the original Bauhaus school of design in Germany – and one of the 20th century's most influential architects – fled Adolf Hitler's regime and became a professor at Harvard. In 1937 he designed this modest but unique home by combining traditional New England elements, such as clapboard and fieldstone, with modern flourishes of chrome banisters and acoustical plaster. **Gropius House** stands as a prime example of Bauhaus design.

Art and architecture are also celebrated at the **Codman House**, built in 1740 and expanded in the 1790s by merchant John Codman. Home to five generations of the Codman family, the structure was expanded again in 1860, adding 18th-century architectural details to the interior and exterior. The three-story house is set on a 16-acre (6.5-ha) estate and contains wonderful neoclassical furnishings.

At **Drumlin Farm**, which is a Massachusetts Audubon Society property, visitors have an opportunity to see a working New England farm in action as well as to enjoy bird-watching and nature walks.

The farm has hands-on learning activities for children.

🏛 DeCordova Museum and Sculpture Park
51 Sandy Pond Rd. **Tel** (781) 259-8355. **Museum** ◻ 10am–5pm Tue–Sun. 📷 🚻 ♿ 🍴 **Sculpture park** ◻ dawn to dusk daily. 📷 www.decordova.org

🏚 Gropius House
68 Baker Bridge Rd. **Tel** (781) 259-8098. ◻ Jun–mid-Oct: 11am–4pm Wed–Sun; mid-Oct–May: 11am–4pm Sat & Sun. 📷 🚻 hourly. ♿ first floor only. 🚻 🚫

🏚 Codman House
Codman Rd. **Tel** (781) 259-8098. ◻ Jun–mid-Oct: 11am–4pm 2nd & 4th Sat of month. 📷 🚻 hourly.

🦌 Drumlin Farm Education Center and Wildlife Sanctuary
208 South Great Rd. **Tel** (781) 259-2200. **Nature Center** ◻ Mar–Oct: 9am–5pm Tue–Sun; Nov–Feb: 9am–4pm Tue–Sun (trails open same hours). 📷 ♿ 🚻

Quincy ⓲

🏃 84,985. 🛈 (617) 847-1454.

Now a suburb south of Boston, Quincy was once home to four generations of the Adams family, among them the second and sixth presidents of the US. The 12.5-acre (5-ha) **Adams National Historical Park** has 12 buildings, including the John Adams Birthplace, where the second president was born in 1735. His son, John Quincy Adams (1767–1848), was born just steps away at what is now called The John Quincy Adams Birthplace. Other structures include the Old House, home to four generations of the family, and a church, where both presidents and their wives are buried. A trolley provides transportation between sites.

🏚 Adams National Historical Park
1250 Hancock St. **Tel** (617) 770-1175. ◻ mid-Apr–mid-Nov: 9am–5pm daily; Visitor Center open limited hours rest of year. 📷 🚻 ♿ partial. www.nps.gov/adam

Environs

New Bedford, 49 miles (79 km) south, was once a major whaling port. This working-class town lends its name to the **New Bedford Whaling National Historical Park**. The 13-block site was established to commemorate whaling history and heritage. Walking maps and guided tours are available at the visitor center. Among the town's attractions is the excellent **New Bedford Whaling Museum**, which has one of the finest and most comprehensive collections of whaling artifacts in the world, as well as model ships and figureheads. In Fall River, naval veterans at **Battleship Cove** offer year-round tours of a fleet of World War II and Cold War-era warships. In summer, a 1920 vintage wooden carousel operates.

🏚 New Bedford Whaling National Historical Park
33 William St. **Tel** (508) 996-4095. ◻ 9am–5pm daily. ♿ 🚻 www.nps.gov/nebe

🏛 New Bedford Whaling Museum
18 Johnny Cake Hill. **Tel** (508) 997-0046. ◻ 9am–4pm Mon–Sat, noon–4pm Sun. 📷 🚻 ♿ 🚻 www.whalingmuseum.org

🏚 Battleship Cove
5 Water St., Fall River. **Tel** (508) 678-1100. ◻ 9am–4:30pm daily (later in summer). 📷 www.battleshipcove.org

Model ships on display at the New Bedford Whaling Museum

BOSTON STREET FINDER

The key map below shows the area of Boston covered by the *Street Finder* maps, which can be found on the following pages. Map references, given throughout this guide, for sights, restaurants, hotels, shops, and entertainment venues refer to the grid on the maps. The first figure in the map reference indicates which *Street Finder* map to turn to (1 to 4), and the letter and number that follow refer to the grid reference on that map.

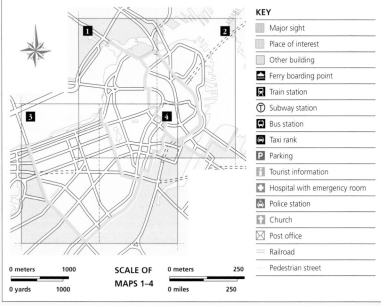

KEY

▓	Major sight
▓	Place of interest
▓	Other building
⚓	Ferry boarding point
🚆	Train station
Ⓣ	Subway station
🚌	Bus station
🚕	Taxi rank
P	Parking
ℹ	Tourist information
✚	Hospital with emergency room
🚔	Police station
✝	Church
⊠	Post office
═	Railroad
	Pedestrian street

0 meters	1000		0 meters	250
0 yards	1000		0 miles	250

SCALE OF MAPS 1–4

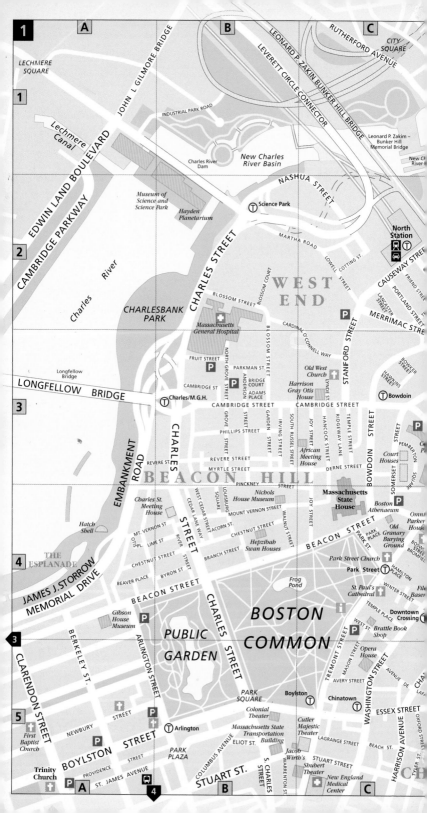

1

A   B   C

LECHMERE SQUARE

JOHN L. GILMORE BRIDGE

RUTHERFORD AVENUE

CITY SQUARE

1

INDUSTRIAL PARK ROAD

LEONARD P. ZAKIN BUNKER HILL BRIDGE

LEVERETT CIRCLE CONNECTOR

Lechmere Canal

EDWIN LAND BOULEVARD

CAMBRIDGE PARKWAY

Charles River Dam

New Charles River Basin

Leonard P. Zakim – Bunker Hill Memorial Bridge

New Ch River

NASHUA STREET

Museum of Science and Science Park

Hayden Planetarium

Ⓣ Science Park

MARTHA ROAD

LOWELL COTTING ST.

North Station
Ⓣ

CAUSEWAY STREE

FRIEND STREET

2

Charles River

CHARLES STREET

WEST END

CHARLESBANK PARK

BLOSSOM COURT

BLOSSOM STREET

CARDINAL O'CONNELL WAY

PORTLAND STREET

LANCASTER STREET

MERRIMAC STRE

Ⓟ

STANIFORD STREET

BOWKER STREET

Longfellow Bridge

Massachusetts General Hospital

FRUIT STREET Ⓟ

NORTH GROVE STREET

PARKMAN STREET

ANDERSON

BRIDGE COURT

ADAMS PLACE

Old West Church

Harrison Gray Otis House

LYNDE ST.

HAWKINS STREET

Ⓣ Bowdoin

3

LONGFELLOW BRIDGE

CAMBRIDGE ST.

CAMBRIDGE STREET

CAMBRIDGE STREET

EMBANKMENT ROAD

CHARLES

REVERE ST.

GROVE STREET

PHILLIPS STREET

GARDEN STREET

SOUTH RUSSEL STREET

IRVING STREET

JOY STREET

HANCOCK STREET

RIDGEWAY LANE

TEMPLE STREET

BOWDOIN STREET

SOMERSET STREET

PEMBERTON

Ⓟ

Court Houses

Co Pl

REVERE STREET

MYRTLE STREET

African Meeting House

DERNE STREET

STREET

Ⓣ Charles/M.G.H.

BEACON HILL

PINCKNEY STREET

Charles St. Meeting House

WEST CEDAR STREET

LOUISBURG SQUARE

CEDAR LANE WAY

MOUNT VERNON STREET

WALNUT STREET

Nichols House Museum

JOY STREET

Massachusetts State House

Boston Athenaeum

Ⓟ

Omni Parker House

Hatch Shell

MT. VERNON ST.

OTIS PL.

LIME ST.

ACORN ST.

RIVER STREET

CHESTNUT STREET

Hepzibah Swan Houses

BEACON STREET

PARK PLACE

Old Granary Burying Ground

BOWDOIN STREET

BROMFIEL

4

THE ESPLANADE

CHESTNUT STREET

BRANCH STREET

BYRON ST.

BEAVER PLACE

BEACON STREET

Frog Pond

Park Street Church

Park Street Ⓣ

HAMILTON PLACE

WINTER STREET

File Base

JAMES J. STORROW MEMORIAL DRIVE

BERKELEY ST.

ARLINGTON STREET

Gibson House Museum Ⓟ

PUBLIC GARDEN

CHARLES STREET

BOSTON COMMON

St. Paul's Cathedral

ⓘ

TEMPLE PLACE

WEST ST.

TREMONT STREET

MASON STREET

Ⓟ

Downtown Crossing Ⓣ

Brattle Book Shop

Opera House

WASHINGTON STREET

AVENUE DE

CHA

3◄

CLARENDON STREET

AVERY STREET

LAFA

5

First Baptist Church

NEWBURY STREET

Ⓟ

BOYLSTON STREET

PROVIDENCE

Trinity Church

Ⓟ
A

ST. JAMES AVENUE

Ⓣ Arlington

BOYLSTON STREET

STREET

Ⓟ

PARK PLAZA

COLUMBUS AVENUE

ELIOT ST.

PARK SQUARE

Massachusetts State Transportation Building

S. CHARLES STREET

WARRENTON ST.

Colonial Theater

Cutler Majestic Theater

Jacob Wirth's

Boylston Ⓣ

Chinatown Ⓣ

LAGRANGE STREET

STUART STREET

Shubert Theater

New England Medical Center

ESSEX STREET

BEACH ST.

HARRISON AVENUE

OXFORD STREET

CH

4

STUART ST.

A   B   C

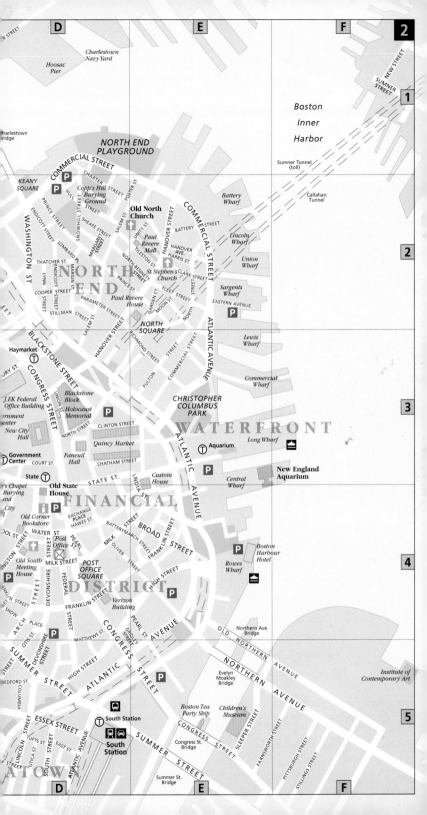

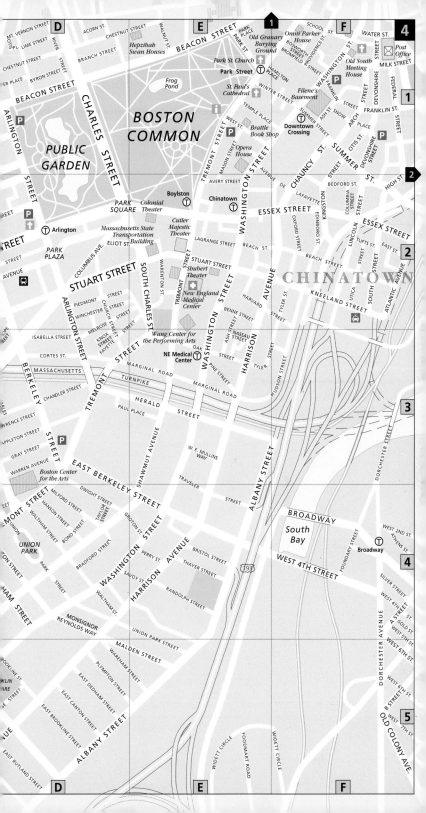

NEW ENGLAND
REGION BY REGION

New England at a Glance

Tucked away in the northeasternmost corner of the United States, New England is rich in history and natural beauty. Many of the country's earliest settlements were established within these six states, with the seeds of the Revolutionary War taking root most firmly in Massachusetts. Interspersed along large tracts of rural countryside, heavy forests, and sweeping coastlines, Ivy League universities and college towns bring an influx of modernity to this historically significant region.

Vermont's fall foliage *usually peaks in mid-October.*

The Towne House *in Old Sturbridge Village was built in 1796. Located in Sturbridge, Massachusetts, the village is one of the New England's most popular living-history museums (see p160).*

Mark Twain House *in Hartford, Connecticut, is where the famous US author penned many of his most beloved works. The house was commissioned in 1873 for the then hefty sum of $45,000 (see pp200–201).*

| 0 kilometers | 100 |
| 0 miles | 50 |

Sugarloaf/USA *is one of Maine's premier ski centers. The mountain has the second-largest vertical drop of all New England ski slopes (see p378–9).*

Lobster boats *dot the waters near Isle au Haut at Ferry Landing.*

The Chase House *is featured in the Strawbery Banke restoration project in Portsmouth, New Hampshire (see pp254–5).*

The Breakers *is one of Newport, Rhode Island's most opulent mansions. Designed after 16th-century palaces in Italy, the 70-room masterpiece was used as the summer "cottage" for the wealthy Vanderbilt family (see pp186–7).*

MASSACHUSETTS

O *f all the New England states, Massachusetts may have the most diverse mix of natural and man-made attractions. Miles of wide sandy beaches beckon along the eastern seaboard; green mountains and rich culture characterize the Berkshire Hills in the west. America's early architecture has been well protected, from the lanes of Boston to villages dotting coast and countryside.*

Many of America's pivotal events have been played out against the backdrop of Massachusetts. In 1620 a group of 102 British Pilgrims sailing to the Virginia Colony were blown off course and forced to land farther north. Their colony at Plymouth *(see pp150–51)* was the first permanent English settlement in North America. More than 100 years later the seeds of the American Revolution took strongest root in Boston, blossoming into the nation of the United States and forever altering the course of world history.

Massachusetts has always been New England 's industrial and intellectual hub. The machinery of the American Industrial Revolution chugged to life in the early 19th century in Lowell *(see p142)* and other mill towns. Later the high-tech labs in Cambridge *(see pp110–11)* would help lead the nation into the computer age. In 1944 scientists at Harvard University *(see pp112–17)*, the oldest and most prestigious college in the nation, developed the world's first digital computer. Today the venerable university attracts visitors from around the world wanting to tour its beautiful campus and explore the multitude of treasures in its magnificent museums.

Travelers can also tread the same ground as some of the country's most influential leaders. Quincy *(see p121)* honors the father and son team of John Adams (1735–1826) and John Quincy Adams (1767–1848), the nation's second and sixth presidents. Fashionable Hyannisport on Cape Cod *(see pp154–9)* is home to the Kennedy clan *(see p159)* compound. Of course, the Cape is best known for its expanse of sand dunes and beaches along the Cape Cod National Seashore *(see pp154–5)*.

Part of the stunning sculpture collection at Chesterwood in Stockbridge

◁ Sunset on Duxbury Beach *(see p149)*

Exploring Massachusetts

Massachusetts is a wonderful destination for travelers in that such a diverse array of attractions is squeezed into a relatively small area. Art, music, theater, and dance can be found in abundance in many of the state's larger urban areas and busy college towns. Scenic seascapes, historic villages, and whale-watching junkets await along the coast and Cape Cod *(see pp154–9)*. Understandably, the coastal beaches are popular spots in summer. Venturing inland, visitors will come upon centuries-old towns, verdant forests and meadows, and count-less opportunities for antiquing. As is the case with all the New England states, fall is one of the most beautiful times of year to visit.

Blooming wildflowers beside the Deerfield River

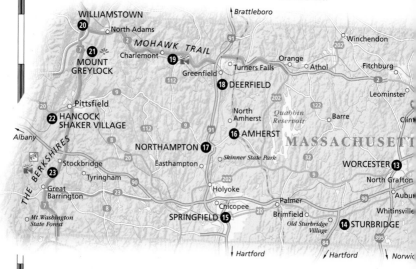

WILLIAMSTOWN **20**
North Adams
MOHAWK TRAIL
21 Charlemont **19**
MOUNT GREYLOCK
Greenfield
18 DEERFIELD
Pittsfield
North Amherst
Quabbin Reservoir
Barre
22 HANCOCK SHAKER VILLAGE
Albany
16 AMHERST
MASSACHUSETTS
NORTHAMPTON **17**
Easthampton
Skinner State Park
WORCESTER **13**
THE BERKSHIRES
23 Stockbridge
Tyringham
North Grafton
Great Barrington
Holyoke
Aubu
Mt Washington State Forest
Chicopee
Palmer
Whitinsville
SPRINGFIELD **15**
Brimfield
Old Sturbridge Village
14 STURBRIDGE
Hartford
Hartford
Norwic
Brattleboro
Winchendon
Orange
Athol
Fitchburg
Turners Falls
Leominster
Clint

GETTING AROUND

Interstate 93 and Interstate 95 are the two largest and most popular north-south routes leading into Boston. Interstate 495 loops outside Boston, thereby bypassing much of the heavy traffic. Highway 2 and Interstate 90 are the two biggest east-west routes. Boston's Logan International Airport is New England's largest airport. Amtrak has rail links between Boston and New York City and Boston and Portland, Maine with stops in between. Bus lines such as American Eagle, Concord Trailways, Greyhound, and Peter Pan service most of Massachusetts. Passenger and car ferries sail year-round from Cape Cod (leaving from Woods Hole) to Martha's Vineyard and from Hyannis to Nantucket. Advance reservations are essential for cars.

Brant Point, at the entrance to Nantucket Harbor

SIGHTS AT A GLANCE

SEE ALSO

- **Where to Stay** pp312–14
- **Where to Eat** pp340–43

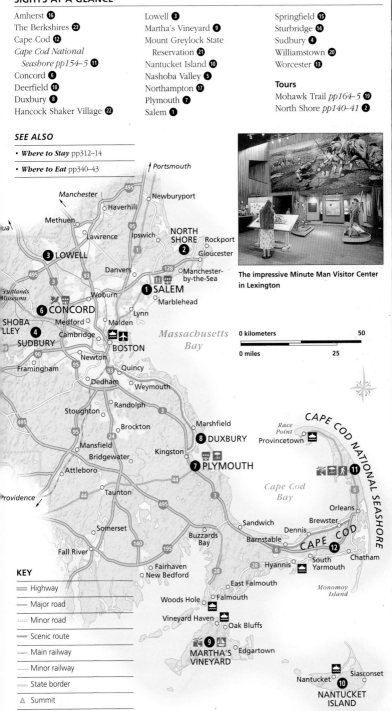

The impressive Minute Man Visitor Center in Lexington

Salem ❶

Although it is best known for the infamous witch trials of 1692, which resulted in the execution of 20 innocent people, this coastal town has other, less sensational claims to fame. Founded in 1626 by Roger Conant (1592–1679), Salem grew to become one of New England's busiest 18th- and 19th-century ports, its harbor filled with clipper ships carrying treasures from around the globe. Present-day Salem is a bustling, good-natured town that has the ability to celebrate its rich artistic and architectural heritage, all the while playing up its popular image as the witchcraft capital of America.

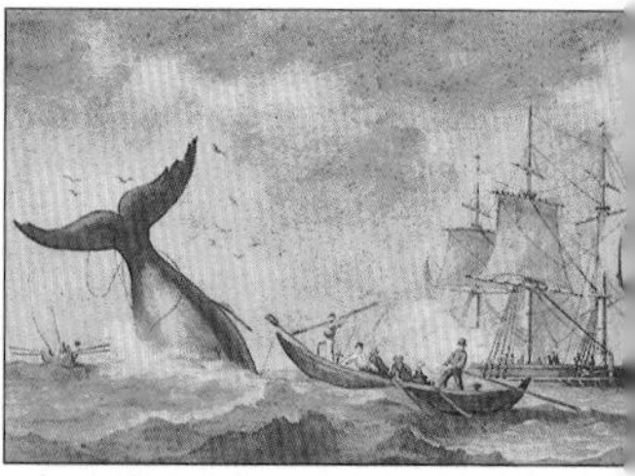
An 1842 whaling scene from the Peabody Essex Museum

Exploring Salem

Salem's main attractions are situated in clusters in the harbor and downtown areas. The historic waterfront can be explored on foot, as can the busy area along Essex and Liberty streets *(see pp138–9)*.

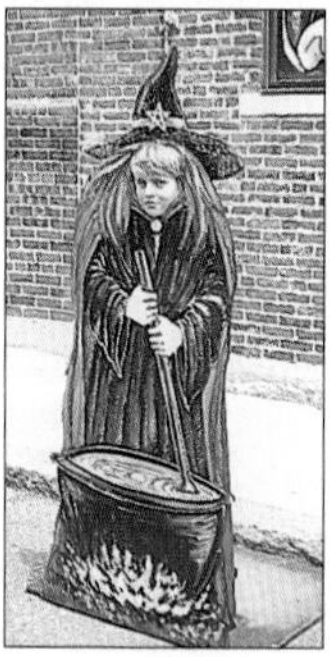
Photo opportunities for Salem visitors

🏛 Peabody Essex Museum

East India Sq.
Tel *(978) 745-9500, (866) 745-1876.*
🕒 *10am-5pm Tue–Sun.*
♿ **www**.pem.org

The dramatic Moshe Safdie building, which opened in 2003, gave the Peabody Essex soaring galleries to display its collection of more than 2.4 million objects, including some of the worlds largest holdings of Asian art and artifacts. Among the exhibits are treasures brought back from the Orient, the Pacific, and Africa by Salem's sea captains. Highlights include jewelry, porcelain figures, ritual costumes, scrimshaw, figureheads, and navigational instruments. Historic East Indian Marine Hall houses portraits and maritime memorabilia.

🏛 Salem Witch Museum

19 1/2 Washington Sq N. ***Tel*** *(978) 744-1692 or (800) 544-1692.* 🕒 *Jul–Aug: 10am–7pm daily; Sep–Jun: 10am–5pm daily.* ● *Jan 1, Thanksgiving, Dec 24 & 25.* ♿
www.salemwitchmuseum.com

Salem's most visited sight commemorates the town's darkest hour. In 1692, 150 people were jailed and 20 executed after being charged with practicing witchcraft. According to some, Nathaniel Hawthorne – who was profoundly disturbed by reports of the events – added

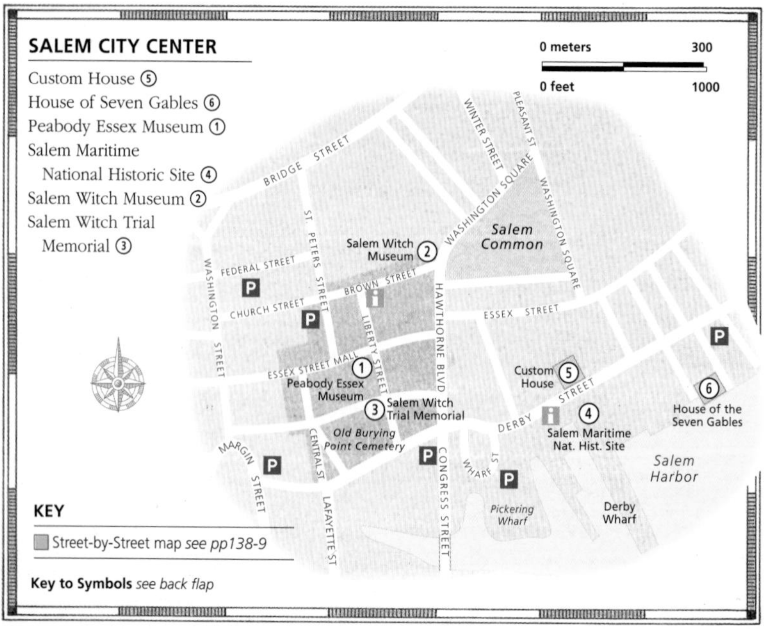
SALEM CITY CENTER
Custom House 5
House of Seven Gables 6
Peabody Essex Museum 1
Salem Maritime National Historic Site 4
Salem Witch Museum 2
Salem Witch Trial Memorial 3
0 meters 300
0 feet 1000
BRIDGE STREET
WINTER STREET
PLEASANT ST
WASHINGTON SQUARE
Salem Common
ST. PETERS STREET
Salem Witch Museum 2
FEDERAL STREET
BROWN STREET
WASHINGTON STREET
CHURCH STREET
LIBERTY STREET
HAWTHORNE BLVD
ESSEX STREET
ESSEX STREET MALL
Peabody Essex Museum 1
Salem Witch Trial Memorial 3
Custom House 5
DERBY STREET
Salem Maritime Nat. Hist. Site 4
House of the Seven Gables 6
Old Burying Point Cemetery
CENTRAL ST
MARGIN STREET
CONGRESS STREET
WHARF ST
Salem Harbor
Pickering Wharf
Derby Wharf
LAFAYETTE ST
KEY
Street-by-Street map see pp138-9
Key to Symbols see back flap

Salem Witch Museum, commemorating the infamous 1692 witch trials

VISITORS' CHECKLIST

38,000. From Boston's Long Wharf. 14 miles (22 km) S in Boston. 2 New Liberty St (978) 740-1650. Maritime Festival (Jul), Haunted Halloween (Oct). www.salem.org

a "w" to his last name to distance himself from descendants of Judge Hathorne, the man who presided over the witch trials. A 30-minute multimedia reenactment of the witch-hunt and subsequent trials gives visitors a chilling look at the frenzy that once gripped Salem. The town capitalizes on its association with witches each year in October with one of the nation's largest and most colorful celebrations of Halloween.

Salem Witch Trial Memorial

Charter St. dawn to dusk.
Located next to the old cemetery, this memorial provides a place for quiet contemplation and public acknowledgment of this tragic event in local history. The memorial was dedicated by Nobel laureate Elie Wiesel in 1992 on the 300th anniversary of the witch trials.

Salem Maritime National Historic Site

Orientation Center 193 Derby St. **Tel** (978) 740-1660. May–Oct: 9am–5pm daily; call for winter hours. Jan 1, Thanksgiving, & Dec 25. www.nps.gov/sama
Salem's heyday as a maritime center has been preserved here. At its peak, the town's harbor was serviced by some 50 wharves. Today this waterfront complex maintains three wharves, including the 2,100-ft (640-m) Derby Wharf. The *Friendship*, a reconstruction of an East Indiaman sailing ship built in 1797, is moored here when it is not on tour during the summer.

Custom House

See Salem Maritime National Historic Site for details.
The federal-style Custom House (1819) was established to collect taxes on imports and now forms part of the Salem Maritime National Historic Site. In the 1840s author Nathaniel Hawthorne (1804–64) worked as a surveyor here. The redbrick structure, described in his novel *The Scarlet Letter* (1850), contains his office and desk.

House of Seven Gables Historic Site

115 Derby St.
Tel (978) 744-0991. mid-Jan–Jun, Nov–Dec 10am–5pm daily; Jul–Oct: 10am–7pm daily. first 2 weeks Jan, Thanksgiving, Dec 25. obligatory. partial. www.7gables.org
Fans of author Nathaniel Hawthorne should make a pilgrimage to this 1668 house. The Salem-born writer was so taken with the Colonial-style home that he used it as the setting in his novel *House of Seven Gables* (1851). As well as its famous seven steeply pitched gables, the house also has a secret staircase. The site contains some other early homes, including Hawthorne's birthplace, a gambrel-roofed 18th-century residence moved from Union Street in 1958.

Environs

Just 4 miles (6 km) from town lies the area's most picturesque spot: Marblehead. When President George Washington (1732–99) visited, he said it had "the look of antiquity." This still holds true. Settled in 1629 and perched on a rocky peninsula, this village displays its heritage as a fisherman's enclave and a thriving port. Crisscrossed by hilly, twisting lanes, the historic district is graced with a wonderful mix of merchants' homes, shipbuilders' mansions, and fishermen's cottages. With more than 200 houses built before the Revolutionary War and nearly 800 built during the 1800s, the district is a catalog of American architecture. Included among the historic buildings is the spired **Abbot Hall**, the seat of local government built in 1876,

Clock Tower at Abbot Hall in Marblehead

where *The Spirit of '76* painting (1875) by Archibald Willard (1836–1918) hangs. Built in 1768 for a wealthy businessman, **The 1768 Jeremiah Lee Mansion** has a sweeping entrance hall, mahogany woodwork, and superb wallpaper. A drive along the shoreline reveals the lighthouse at Point O'Neck (1835).

Abbot Hall

Washington Sq. **Tel** (781) 631-0000. call for hours.

The 1768 Jeremiah Lee Mansion

161 Washington St. **Tel** (781) 631-1768. Jun–Oct: 10am–4pm Thu–Sat.

Street-by-Street: Historic Salem

Like many New England towns, Salem has enjoyed
a rebirth in recent years. Downtown renewal
programs have revitalized the city core, particularly
around Essex Street. Specialty shops, cobblestone
walkways, restaurants, and a pedestrian mall offer
visitors an array of diversions, including stores specializing in the occult. Travelers are best served by
stopping by the Regional Visitor Center operated by
the National Park Service, where they can watch a
27-minute film on the region's history and pick
up maps to guide their tour.

Peabody Essex Museum
*houses the 1765 portrait of
Sarah Erving by John S. Copley.*

Old Town Hall
*The red-brick building
is now a popular
venue for concerts.*

**Old Burying
Point Cemetery**

Salem Witch Village traces
the history of witches by looking
at their traditions, legends, and –
ultimately – their persecution.

DERBY SQUARE

ESSEX STREET

FRONT STREET

LAFAYETTE ST.

CENTRAL STREET

CHARTER STREET

NEW LIBERTY STREET

DERBY STREET

| 0 yards | 50 |
| 0 meters | 50 |

KEY

☐ Pedestrian mall

– – • Suggested route

STAR SIGHTS

★ Essex Street
Pedestrian Mall

★ Gardner-Pingree
House

SALEM WITCH TRIALS

In 1692 Salem was swept by a wave of
hysteria in which 200 citizens were
accused of practicing witchcraft. In all
150 people were jailed and 19 were
hung as witches, while another man
was crushed to death with stones. No
one was safe: two dogs were executed
on the gallows for being witches. Not
surprisingly, when the governor's wife
became a suspect, the trials came to an
abrupt and officially sanctioned end.

**Early accused:
Rebecca Nurse**

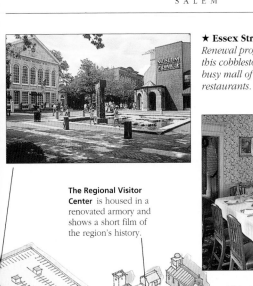

★ Essex Street Pedestrian Mall
Renewal programs have turned this cobblestone walkway into a busy mall of shops, cafés, and restaurants.

The Regional Visitor Center is housed in a renovated armory and shows a short film of the region's history.

★ Gardner-Pingree House
This 1804 house is elegantly decorated and furnished with period pieces.

Salem Witch Museum

Crowninshield Bentley House
Built in 1727, this house typifies the architectural style of mid-18th century dwellings.

Statue of Nathaniel Hawthorne honors the Salem-born author of *The Scarlet Letter* (1850).

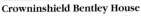

Tour of the North Shore ❷

Fisherman's
Memorial statue

The scenic tip of the North Shore is a favorite escape for harried Bostonians and vacationers who come for the quaint towns, sandy beaches, and whale-watching excursions that are found here in abundance. Ipswich, founded in 1633, still has more than 40 houses built before 1725. It is also known for its sandy beaches, marshes, dunes and seafood, especially clams. The rocky shores of Cape Ann hold diverse pleasures, including artists' colonies, mansions, and opportunities for swimming and boating.

Fishermen casting into the surf on a North Shore beach

Ipswich ⑧
A wealth of 17th century architecture makes this a fine town to explore.

Antiquing
Antique stores can be found throughout the North Shore region, particularly in Essex along Main Street.

Manchester-by-the-Sea ①
A scenic harbor, luxurious mansions, and a wide beach are town highlights.

Chebacco Lake

Essex River

Ipswich River

Castle Neck River

Essex

Magnolia ②
This Gloucester village is known for magnificent summer homes and the Medieval-style Hammond Castle Museum.

KEY

▬ Tour route
═ Other road
☀ Viewpoint

0 kilometers 3
0 miles 3

Gloucester ③
Famous for its *Fisherman's Memorial* statue, this is a lively town with a busy harbor.

THE WORLD'S FIRST FRIED CLAM

The town of Essex has a proud culinary distinction: it was here that the clams were first fried. In 1916 Lawrence "Chubby" Woodman and his wife were selling raw clams by the road. Following a friend's suggestion, they tried deep-frying a clam. The popularity of the new-dish snack helped Woodman open his own restaurant – still one of the region's most popular today.

Fried clams to go from Woodman's restaurant in Essex

TIPS FOR DRIVERS

Tour length: *31 miles (50 km) with detour to Wingaersheek Beach.*
Starting point: *Rte 127 in Manchester-by-the-Sea.*
Stopping-off points: *Seafood abounds in places such as Gloucester, Rockport, Essex, and Newburyport. Lodgings are plentiful, but reservations are advised during the peak period of June to October.*

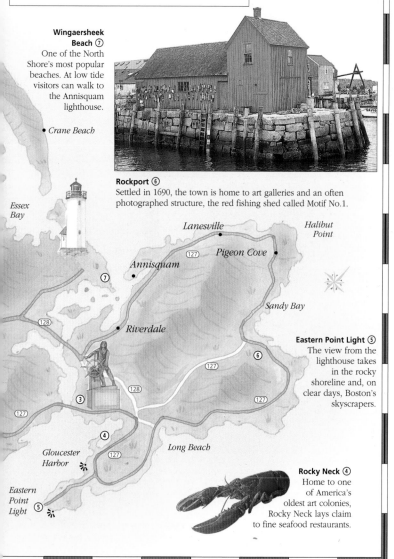

Wingaersheek Beach [7]
One of the North Shore's most popular beaches. At low tide visitors can walk to the Annisquam lighthouse.

Rockport [6]
Settled in 1690, the town is home to art galleries and an often photographed structure, the red fishing shed called Motif No.1.

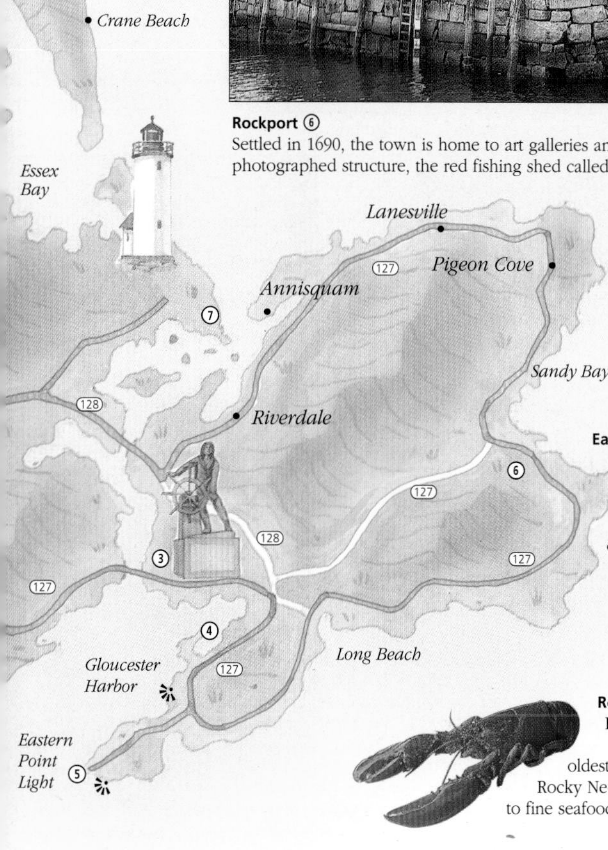
Crane Beach
Essex Bay
Lanesville
Halibut Point
Pigeon Cove
127
Annisquam
7
Sandy Bay
128
Riverdale
6
127
128
3
127
127
4
Long Beach
Gloucester Harbor
127
Eastern Point Light
5

Eastern Point Light [5]
The view from the lighthouse takes in the rocky shoreline and, on clear days, Boston's skyscrapers.

Rocky Neck [4]
Home to one of America's oldest art colonies, Rocky Neck lays claim to fine seafood restaurants.

Power looms on display in the Boott Cotton Mills Museum

Lowell ❸

🏃 103,000. ✈ 30 miles (48 km) S in Boston. 🚉 🚌 9 Central St, Suite 201, Lowell (978) 459-6150 or (800) 443-3332.
www.merrimackvalley.org

Lowell has the distinction of being the country's first industrial city, paving the way for the American Industrial Revolution. In the early 19th century, Boston merchant Francis Cabot Lowell (1775–1817) opened a cloth mill in nearby Waltham and equipped it with his new power loom. The increase in production was so great that the mill quickly outgrew its quarters and was moved to the town of East Chelmsford (later renamed for Lowell). Set on 400 acres (162 ha) and using power provided by a steep drop in the Merrimack River, the business expanded to include 10 giant mill complexes, which employed more than 10,000 workers.

While the town prospered, it was at the expense of its workers, many of whom were unskilled immigrants exploited by the greedy mill owners. Eventually laborers organized and there were many strikes. The most successful was the 1912 Bread and Roses Strike, which began in neighboring Lawrence and spread to Lowell. While that confrontation helped improve conditions for workers, the relief was temporary. In the 1920s companies began to move

south in search of cheaper labor. The death knell came in 1929. The country was rocked by the Great Depression and the mills closed, leaving Lowell a ghost town.

In 1978 the **Lowell National Historical Park** was established to rehabilitate more than 100 downtown buildings and preserve the town's unique history. The Market Mills Visitor Center on Market Street offers a free introductory video show, walking tour maps, guided walks with rangers, and tickets for summer canal boat tours of the waterways. From March to November, antique trolleys take visitors to the **Boott Cotton Mills Museum**, the centerpiece of the park, where 88 vintage power looms produce a deafening clatter. Interactive exhibits trace the Industrial Revolution and the growth of the labor movement. Also in Lowell, the **American Textile History Museum** traces the evolution of textiles, from Colonial-era weavers to today's high-tech fabrics made from recycled materials.

Lowell has non-industrial attractions as well. The **New England Quilt Museum** displays both antique and contemporary examples of the quilt-maker's art, and sponsors talks and symposia on quilt scholarship and trends in current fiber arts. Painter James McNeill Whistler (1834–1903), most famous for his portrait of his mother, was born in Lowell while his father was in

charge of the railroad works for the city's mills. Whistler's birthplace is now a museum that displays prints of some of his work, but focuses more on 19th- and 20th-century American art.

🚩 **Lowell National Historical Park**
246 Market St. **Tel** (978) 970-5000. ⬤ Mar–Oct: 9am–5pm daily, Nov–Feb: 9am–4:30pm Mon–Sat, 10am–5pm Sun. 🎫 for canal tours only. 🅿 ♿ **www**.nps.gov/lowe

🏛 **Boott Cotton Mills Museum**
115 John St. **Tel** (978) 970-5000. ⬤ late May–Oct: 9:30am–4:30pm daily (call for opening hours off-season). 🎫 ♿

🏛 **American Textile History Museum**
491 Dutton St. **Tel** (978) 441-0400. ⬤ 10am–5pm Wed–Sun. ⬤ public hols. 🎫 🅿 ♿ **www**.athm.org

🏛 **New England Quilt Museum**
18 Shattuck St. **Tel** (978) 452-4207. ⬤ 10am–4pm Tue–Sat, also open noon–4pm Sun May–Dec. ⬤ public hols. 🎫 ♿ **www**.nequiltmuseum.org

Bedroom display at the New England Quilt Museum in Lowell

LOWELL'S JACK KEROUAC

Lowell native Jack Kerouac was the leading chronicler of the "beat generation," a term that he coined to describe members of the disaffected Bohemian movement of the 1950s. Although he lived elsewhere for most of his adult life, his remains are buried in the town's Edson Cemetery. Excerpts from Kerouac's most famous novel, *On the Road* (1957), and other of his writings are inscribed on granite pillars in the Kerouac Commemorative Park on Bridge Street.

Jack Kerouac (1922–69)

Part of the Fruitlands Museums' Shaker collection

🏛 Whistler House Museum of Art

243 Worthen St. **Tel** (978) 452-7641. ⬜ 11am–4pm Wed–Sat. 🖼

Sudbury ➍

🏙 16,500. ✈ 24 miles (39 km) E in Boston.

The picturesque town of Sudbury is home to a number of historic sites, including the 1797 First Parish Church and the 1723 Loring Parsonage. Longfellow's Wayside Inn, one of the nation's oldest inns, was built in 1716 and was immortalized in Henry Wadsworth Longfellow's poetry collection entitled *Tales of a Wayside Inn* (1863). In the 1920s the building was purchased by industrialist Henry Ford (1863–1947), who restored it, filled it with antiques, and surrounded it with other relocated structures, such as a rustic gristmill, a schoolhouse, and a general store.

Today, the inn serves both as a mini-museum of Colonial America as well as offering cozy overnight rooms and hearty American fare in its pub-like restaurant.

Nashoba Valley ➎

ℹ 100 Sherman Ave, Devens (978) 772-6976.

Fed by the Nashoba River, Nashoba Valley is an appealing world of meadows and orchards and colonial towns built around village greens. The region is particularly popular in May when the apple trees are in bloom, and again in fall when the apples are ripe for picking and the surrounding hills are ablaze in autumn colors.

The **Fruitlands Museums**, the valley's major attraction, comprises four museums, two outdoor sites, and a restaurant on beautiful hilltop grounds that include nature trails and picnic areas with valley views. Founder Clara Endicott Sears (1863–1960), a philosopher, writer, collector, and early preservationist, built her home here in 1910 and began gathering properties of historical significance. Her first acquisition was Fruitlands, the "New Eden" commune based partly on vegetarianism and self-sufficiency initiated by Bronson Alcott (1799–1888) and fellow Transcendentalists.

**Fruitlands Museums'
rocking horse**

Alcott was the father of author Louisa May Alcott (1832–88) and was the model for the character of Mr. March in her book *Little Women* (1868). The restored farmhouse now serves as a museum and includes memorabilia of Alcott, Ralph Waldo Emerson (1803–82), and other Transcendentalist leaders.

Five years later, Sears acquired a building in nearby Shaker Village. The 1790 structure, the first office building in the village, now houses a collection of traditional Shaker furniture, clothing, and artifacts. The American Indian Museum opened its doors in 1928 to display Sears' personal collection of Native American artifacts.

Another of the region's attractions is the **Nashoba Valley Winery**, a beautiful 55-acre (22-ha) orchard that produces wines from fruits such as apples, pears, peaches, plums, blueberries, strawberries, and elderberries. More than 100 varieties of apples are grown here. On weekends the winery offers tours.

🏕 Fruitlands Museums

102 Prospect Hill Rd, Harvard. **Tel** (978) 456-3924. ⬜ May–Oct: 11am–4pm Mon–Fri, 11am–5pm Sat–Sun. 🖼 🔥 partial. www.fruitlands.org

🍷 Nashoba Valley Winery

100 Wattaquadock Hill Rd, Bolton. **Tel** (978) 779-5521. ⬜ year-round: 10am–5pm daily. **Winery tours**: year-round: 11am–4pm Sat–Sun. 🖼

Henry Wadsworth Longfellow's Wayside Inn, one of the nation's oldest

Concord ❻

The peaceful, prosperous suburban look of modern-day Concord masks an eventful past. This small town was at the heart of two important chapters in US history. The first was marked by a single dramatic event, the Battle of Concord on April 19, 1775, which signaled the beginning of the Revolutionary War. The second spanned several generations, as 19th-century Concord blossomed into the literary heart and soul of the US, with many of the nation's great writers establishing homes here. The influence of both important periods is in full evidence today.

North Bridge in Minute Man National Historical Park

Exploring Concord

At Concord's center lies **Monument Square**. It was also at the center of the battle fought between British troops and Colonists more than 200 years ago. Having seized the gun cache and other supplies of rebel forces, the British soldiers began burning them. Nearby Colonist forces spotted the smoke and, believing the town was being torched, rushed to its defense, precipitating the Revolutionary War.

🏕 Minute Man National Historical Park

North Bridge Visitor Center, 174 Liberty St. **Tel** (978) 318-7810. ⬤ Apr–Oct: 9am–5pm daily; Nov: 9am–4pm daily; Dec–Mar: 11am–3pm daily. ⬤ Jan 1, Thanksgiving, Dec 25.

Minute Man Visitor Center, Rte. 2A Lexington. **Tel** (781) 674-1920. ⬤ Apr–Oct: 9am–5pm daily; Nov: 9am–4pm daily. ⬤ Winter. ♿ www.nps.gov/mima

On April 19, 1775, a group of militia, ordinary citizens, and Colonist farmers known as Minute Men confronted British troops who were patrolling the **North Bridge**. The Minute Men fought valiantly, driving three British companies of troops from the bridge and chasing them back to Boston.

This 990-acre (400-ha) park preserves the site and tells the story of the American victory. The Minute Man Visitor Center also features a massive battle

mural and a 22-minute multimedia show called "Road to Revolution." The Battle Road Trail traces the five-mile (8-km) path followed by the British as they advanced from Lexington to Concord – the same route they took in their retreat back to Boston.

The park's North Bridge Unit is the place where the first major engagement was fought. This so-called "shot heard 'round the world" set off the war. Across the bridge is the famous **Minute Man statue** by Concord native Daniel Chester French (1850–31). A short trail leads from the bridge to the **North Bridge Visitor Center**. A reenactment of the battle takes place every year in April in Concord and Lexington.

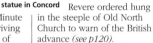

Minute Man statue in Concord

🏛 Concord Museum

Jct of Lexington Rd & Cambridge Tpk. **Tel** (978) 369-9609. ⬤ Jan–Mar: 11am–4pm Mon–Sat, 1pm–4pm Sun; Apr–Dec: 9am–5pm Mon–Sat, noon–5pm Sun (Jun–Aug: 9am–5pm Sun). 🎦 ♿ www.concordmuseum.org

The museum's eclectic holdings include decorative arts from the 17th, 18th, and 19th centuries and the lantern that Paul Revere ordered hung in the steeple of Old North Church to warn of the British advance (see p120).

🏕 The Old Manse

269 Monument St. **Tel** (978) 369-3909. ⬤ mid-April–Oct: 10am–5pm Mon–Sat, noon–5pm Sun. 🎦 www.thetrustees.org

The parsonage by the North

Along the Battle Road, by John Rush, located in the Minute Man Visitor Center

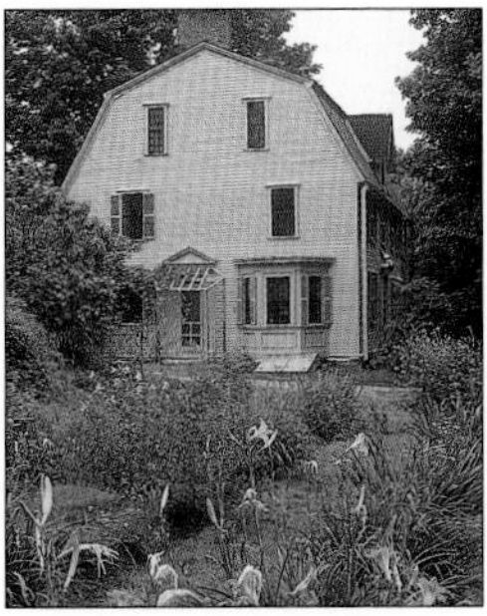

Concord's Old Manse: home to 19th-century literary giants

Bridge was built in 1770 by the grandfather of writer Ralph Waldo Emerson (1803–82), who lived here briefly. Author Nathaniel Hawthorne (1804–64) and his wife rented the house during the first three years of their marriage (loving inscriptions are scratched into the windows). The house got its name from Hawthorne's *Mosses from an Old Manse* (1846), the collection of short stories he wrote here.

🏛 Emerson House

28 Cambridge Tpk. ***Tel*** *(978) 369-2236.* 🕐 *mid-Apr–late Oct: 10am–4:30pm Thu–Sat, 1–4:30pm Sun & public hols.* $

Ralph Waldo Emerson lived in this house from 1835 until his death in 1882, writing essays, organizing lecture tours, and entertaining friends and admirers. Much of Emerson's furniture, writings, books, and family memorabilia is on display.

🍁 Walden Pond State Reservation

915 Walden St. ***Tel*** *(978) 369-3254.* 🕐 *call for hours.* $ 🅿 ♿ **www**.mass.gov/dcr/

Essayist Henry David Thoreau (1817–62) lived in relative isolation at Walden Pond from July 1845 to September 1847. During his stay, he compiled the material for his seminal work *Walden; or, Life in the Woods* (1854). In the book, he called for a return to simplicity in everyday life and respect for nature. Because of Thoreau's deep influence on future generations of environmentalists, Walden Pond is widely considered to be the birthplace of the conservationist movement.

The pond itself is surrounded by 333 acres (135 ha) of mostly undeveloped woodlands. The area is popular for walking, fishing, and swimming, and today is far from the solitary spot that Thoreau described, even though the reservation limits the number of visitors to no more than 1,000 people at one time.

VISITORS' CHECKLIST

👥 17,750. ✈ *21 miles (34 km) W in Boston.* ℹ *58 Main St (978) 369-3120.* 🎉 *Battle of Concord Reenactment (Apr).* **www**. concordchamberofcommerce.org

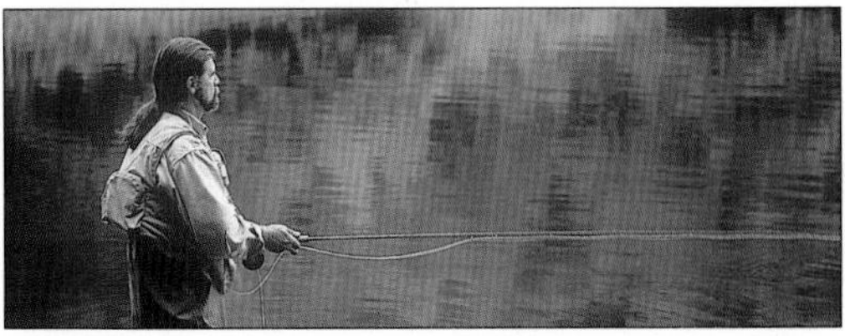

Fisherman on the tranquil waters of Walden Pond

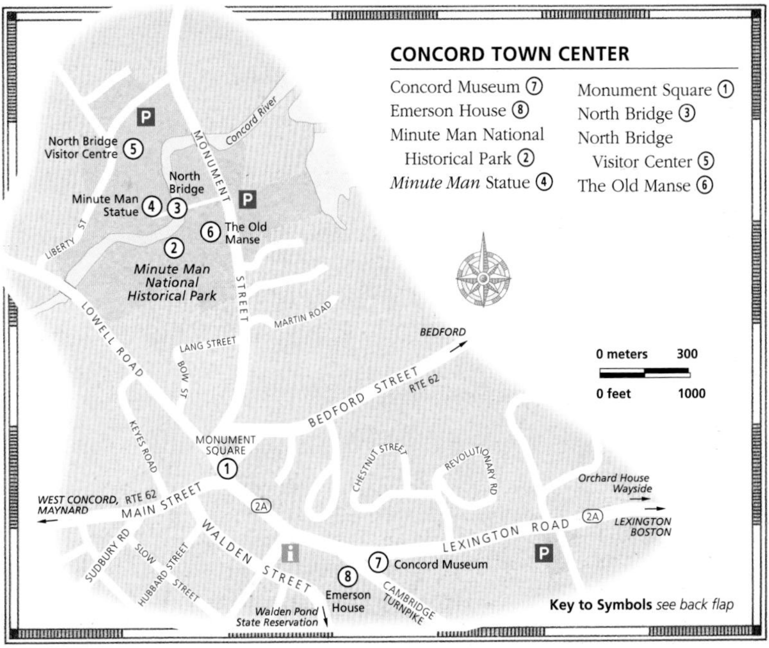
CONCORD TOWN CENTER
Concord Museum 7
Emerson House 8
Minute Man National Historical Park 2
Minute Man Statue 4
Monument Square 1
North Bridge 3
North Bridge Visitor Center 5
The Old Manse 6
North Bridge Visitor Centre 5
North Bridge
Minute Man Statue 4 3
6 The Old Manse
2 Minute Man National Historical Park
Concord River
MONUMENT STREET
LIBERTY ST
LOWELL ROAD
MARTIN ROAD
LANG STREET
BOW ST
KEYES ROAD
BEDFORD
BEDFORD STREET RTE 62
MONUMENT SQUARE 1
CHESTNUT STREET
REVOLUTIONARY RD
WEST CONCORD, MAYNARD RTE 62
MAIN STREET
2A
WALDEN STREET
SUDBURY RD
SLOW
HUBBARD STREET
STREET
LEXINGTON ROAD
2A
Orchard House Wayside
LEXINGTON BOSTON
7 Concord Museum
8 Emerson House
CAMBRIDGE TURNPIKE
Walden Pond State Reservation
0 meters 300
0 feet 1000
Key to Symbols *see back flap*

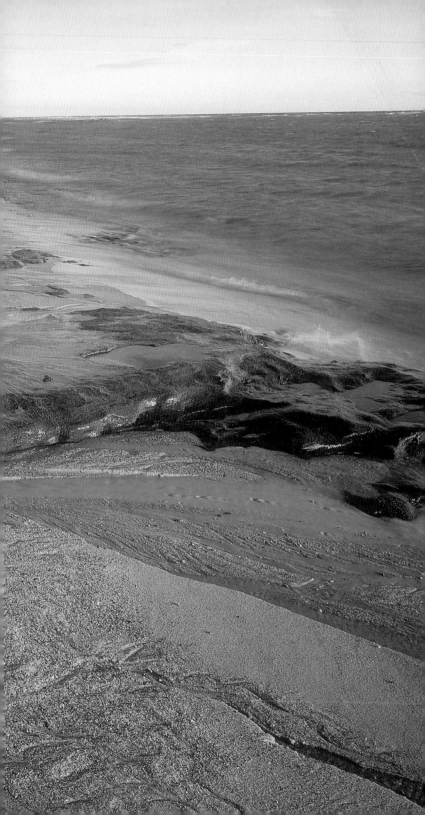

Mayflower II, replica of the original Pilgrim sailing ship

Plymouth ❼

🏠 52,000. ✈ 40 miles (64 km) NW in Boston. ⛴ to Provincetown (seasonal). 🚏 130 Water St (508) 747-7533 or (800) USA-1620. **www**.visit-plymouth.com

In 1620, 102 pilgrims aboard the ship *Mayflower* sailed into Plymouth harbor and established what is considered to be the first permanent English settlement in the New World. Today the town bustles with tourists exploring the sites of America's earliest days, including **Plimoth Plantation** *(see pp150–51),* which is 2.5 miles (4 km) from town. The plantation is a living-history museum of the English colonists and Native Americans of the area. Plymouth itself is a popular sea-side resort, complete with a 3.5-mile-(6-km-) long beach, harbor cruises, and fishing excursions. In the fall, the surrounding bogs turn ruby red as the annual cranberry harvest gets underway. Plymouth is popular for its "Progress," which takes place most Fridays in August at 6pm and on Thanksgiving Day at 10am. Visitors come to witness the solemn re-enactment of the Pilgrims' slow procession to Burial Hill, where a short service is held.

Most of the historic sights can be accessed on foot by the Pilgrim Path that stretches along the waterfront and downtown areas. A seasonal sightseeing trolley connects sights and features a 40-minute history of the town. Ensconced in a monument in the harbor is the country's most famous boulder, Plymouth Rock, marking the spot where the Pilgrims are said to have first stepped ashore. The *Mayflower II,* a replica of the 17th-century sailing ship that carried the Pilgrims over from England, is moored by Plymouth Rock. At just 106 ft (32 m) in length, the vessel seems far too small to have made a transatlantic voyage, especially considering the horrific weather it encountered. Walking along the cramped deck, visitors will marvel at the Pilgrims' courage. Even after surviving the brutal crossing, many Pilgrims succumbed to illness and malnutrition during their first winter in Plymouth. Their remains are buried across the street on Coles Hill, which is fronted by a statue of Massasoit, the Wampanoag Indian chief who allied himself with the newcomers and aided the survivors by teaching them the growing and use of native corn. It was with Massasoit and his people that the Pilgrims celebrated their famous first Thanksgiving. Coles Hill offers a panoramic view of the harbor.

Burial Hill at the head of the Town Square was the site of an early fort and the final resting place of many members of the original colony, including Governor William Bradford (1590–1656). Most Fridays in August, citizens dressed in Pilgrim garb walk from Plymouth Rock to the hill to reenact the church service attended by the 51 survivors of the first winter. Perched on a hilltop overlooking town, the 81-ft (25-m) National Monument to the Forefathers is dedicated to the Pilgrims who made the dangerous voyage to the New World. The Pilgrim Mother Fountain was erected in honor of the women who made the original voyage. Twenty-five women set sail from England, but only four of them survived.

Opened in 1824, the **Pilgrim Hall Museum** is one of America's oldest public museums, housing the largest existing collection of Pilgrim-era artifacts, such as the only known portrait of a *Mayflower* passenger, as well as such personal items as bibles, cradles, and the sword of one of the most colorful Pilgrims,

Statue of Massasoit

Fully functioning water wheel at Jenney Grist Mill

◁ **Cape Cod National Seashore, Head of the Meadow Beach**

Pilgrim Hall exhibits furniture, armor, and art

Myles Standish (c.1584–1656), a former soldier of fortune who went on to found nearby Duxbury. Exhibitions explore Pilgrim history as well as Native American culture and history, and the interactions between the two groups. To appreciate how quickly the Pilgrims progressed from near castaways to hardy settlers, take in the **Jenney Grist Mill**, a 1970 reconstruction of the 1636 original destroyed by fire in 1847. The restored mill grinds cornmeal with power from a 14-ft (4-m) water wheel.

Plymouth has several historic homes of special interest. Among them is **Spooner House**, constructed in 1749 and continuously occupied by one family until 1954, when James Spooner left his home to the Plymouth Antiquarian Society. Its accumulation of artifacts provides a history of Plymouth life. An American crafts shop can be found in the town's oldest home, c.1640 **Richard Sparrow House**.

The original site of the **Mayflower Society House** was built in 1754 and extensively renovated in 1898. What was the old kitchen is now the office for the General Society of Mayflower Descendants. Its research library has one of the finest genealogical collections in the United States.

Travelers will find many cranberry bogs on the roads

outside Plymouth. Nearby, in South Carver, is the **Edaville Railroad**, a family fun park built around old-fashioned train rides, antique cars and locomotive displays, and a modest amusement park. Edaville presents a variety of family-oriented special events and festivals during the summer and fall, including the National Cranberry Festival. The crop was first grown commercially on Cape Cod in the mid-19th century.

🏛 **Mayflower II**
State Pier. **Tel** (508) 746-1622.
⬚ late Mar–Nov: 9am–5pm daily. 🖼

🏛 **Pilgrim Hall Museum**
75 Court St. **Tel** (508) 746-1620.
⬚ year round: 9:30am–4:30pm daily. ◐ Jan. 🖼

🏚 **Jenney Grist Mill**
6 Spring Lane. **Tel** (508) 747-4544.
⬚ Apr–Nov: 9:30am–5pm Mon, Wed–Sat; noon–5pm Sun.

🏚 **Spooner House**
27 North St. **Tel** (508) 746-0012.
◉ for restoration.

🏚 **Richard Sparrow House**
42 Summer St. **Tel** (508) 747-1240.
⬚ Apr–late Dec: 10am–5pm Mon–Tue, Thu–Sun; late Dec–Apr: 10am–5pm Thu–Sat.
🖼 🚹 call first. 🚻

🏚 **Mayflower Society House**
4 Winslow St. **Tel** (508) 746-3188.
⬚ call for hours. 🖼

🏛 **Edaville Railroad**
7 Eda Ave, South Carver.
Tel (508) 866-8190. ⬚ mid-Jun–Oct: call for hours. 🚹 🚻 🖼

Duxbury ❽

🚶 15,350. ✈ 34 miles (54 km) N in Boston. 🛈 130 Water St, Plymouth (508) 747-7533.

Duxbury was settled in 1628 by a group of Pilgrims who found that the Plymouth colony was getting too crowded. Two who made the move, John Alden (c.1598–1687) and Myles Standish (c.1584–1656), were on the *Mayflower* crossing. Today the town is best known for its nine-mile- (14-km-) long beach.

The last home of Alden and his wife was the 1653 **Alden House**. The structure has several features of note, including gunstock beams and a ceiling plastered with crushed clam and oyster shells.

King Caesar House, the home of another prominent resident, is one of the town's grandest structures. Ezra Weston II, an 18th-century shipping magnate, had a fortune large enough to earn him the nickname "King Caesar." It also allowed him the luxury of building this stately Federal mansion in 1808. Today the house is furnished with period pieces, French wallpaper, and a small museum celebrating the region's maritime history.

The **Art Complex Museum** has everything from Asian and European art to Shaker furniture and contemporary New

Shaker piece at Art Complex Museum

England art. A traditional Japanese tea ceremony is held on the last Sunday of the month, June through August.

🏚 **Alden House**
105 Alden St. **Tel** (781) 934-9092.
⬚ mid-May–mid-Oct: noon–4pm Mon–Sat. 🖼 🚹

🏚 **King Caesar House**
120 King Caesar Rd. **Tel** (781) 934-6106. ⬚ Jul–Aug: 1–4pm Wed–Sun; Sep: 1–4pm Sat–Sun. 🖼 🚻

🏛 **Art Complex Museum**
189 Alden St. **Tel** (781) 934-6634.
⬚ Mar–mid-Jan: 1–4pm Wed–Sun.

Plimoth Plantation

Plimoth Plantation is a painstakingly accurate re-creation of the Pilgrims' 1627 village, right down to the 17th-century breeds of livestock. Costumed interpreters portray actual original colonists going about their daily tasks of salting fish, gardening, and musket drills. In the parallel Wampanoag Village, descendants of the people who have lived here for 12,000 years speak in modern language about the experiences of the Wampanoag and explore the story of one 17th-century man, Hobbamock, and his family.

Colony Governor William Bradford

Plimoth Plantation
Costumed interpreters mingle with visitors on the village's busy central street.

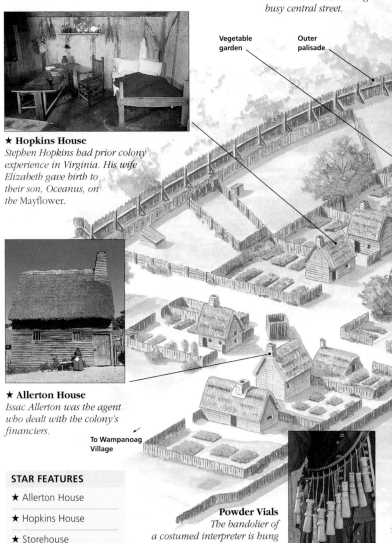

Vegetable garden

Outer palisade

★ Hopkins House
Stephen Hopkins had prior colony experience in Virginia. His wife Elizabeth gave birth to their son, Oceanus, on the Mayflower.

★ Allerton House
Issac Allerton was the agent who dealt with the colony's financiers.

To Wampanoag Village

STAR FEATURES

★ Allerton House

★ Hopkins House

★ Storehouse

Powder Vials
The bandolier of a costumed interpreter is hung with handcarved gunpowder vials.

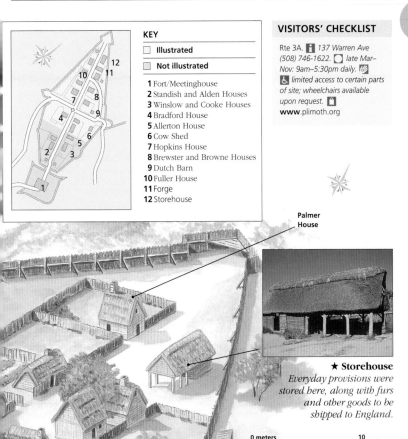

KEY

☐ Illustrated

☐ Not illustrated

1 Fort/Meetinghouse
2 Standish and Alden Houses
3 Winslow and Cooke Houses
4 Bradford House
5 Allerton House
6 Cow Shed
7 Hopkins House
8 Brewster and Browne Houses
9 Dutch Barn
10 Fuller House
11 Forge
12 Storehouse

VISITORS' CHECKLIST

Rte 3A. 🚩 137 Warren Ave (508) 746-1622. ⬜ late Mar–Nov: 9am–5:30pm daily. ♿ limited access to certain parts of site; wheelchairs available upon request. ⬜
www.plimoth.org

Palmer House

★ **Storehouse**
Everyday provisions were stored here, along with furs and other goods to be shipped to England.

0 meters	10
0 yards	10

Local Reeds
Used for thatching, reeds were long-lasting, easily repaired, and virtually waterproof.

Dutch Barn

The Cow Shed
Cows and other livestock were housed in what was often called the "beasthouse." It opens into an enclosed paddock.

Martha's Vineyard scene: fishing boat outside fishing shack

Martha's Vineyard ❾

🏃 13,900. ✈ West Tisbury.
🚢 Woods Hole; Hyannis; Falmouth;
New Bedford. ❢ Beach Rd, Vineyard
Haven (508) 693-0085 or (800) 505-
4815. **www**.mvy.com

The Vineyard, as the locals call it, is the largest of all New England's vacation islands at 108 sq miles (280 sq km). Just a 45-minute boat ride from shore, it is blessed with a mesmerizing mix of scenic beauty and the under-stated charm of a beach resort. Bicycle trails abound here and opportunities for hiking, surf fishing, and some of the best sailing in the region add to the Vineyard's lure. Each town has its own distinctive mood and architectural style, making for interesting exploring.

Vineyard Haven

Most visitors arrive on Martha's Vineyard aboard ferries that sail into this waterfront town, which was largely destroyed by fire in the 1800s. Vineyard Haven is sheltered between two points of land known as East and West Chop, each with its own landmark lighthouse.

Edgartown

As the center of the island's whaling industry in the early 1800s, Edgartown was once home to wealthy sea captains and merchants. The streets are lined with their homes.

The main building of the **Martha's Vineyard**

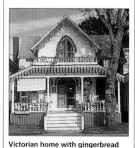

Victorian home with gingerbread ornamentation in Oak Bluffs

Museum complex is the c.1730 Thomas Cooke House. The beautiful 12-room structure is filled with antique furniture, ship models, scrimshaw, and gear used by whalers.

At the eastern end of the waterfront, visitors can catch the ferry to Chappaquiddick Island, a rural outpost that is popular for its beaches and opportunities for bird-watching, surf fishing, canoeing, and hiking. This quiet enclave was made famous by a fatal accident in 1969, when a car driven by Senator Edward Kennedy (b.1932) went off the bridge, killing a young woman passenger.

🏛 **Martha's Vineyard Museum**
59 School St. **Tel** (508) 627-4441.
◯ mid-Jun–mid-Oct: 10am–5pm
Mon–Sat; mid-Oct–mid-Jun: 10am–
4pm Mon–Sat (Jan–mid-Mar: open
Sat only). ◯ public hols. 🅿 ♿ 🗅
www.mvmuseum.org

Oak Bluffs

Tourism began on Martha's Vineyard in 1835 when local Methodists began using the undeveloped area to pitch their tents during their summer revival meetings. The setting proved popular as people came in search of sunshine and salvation. Gradually the tent village gave way to a town of colorful gingerbread cottages, boardinghouses, and stores, and was named Cottage City. In 1907 it was renamed Oak Bluffs. The town is home to the **Flying Horses Carousel**, the oldest continuously operating carousel in the country. Today's children delight in riding on it as much as those of the 1870s.

🎠 **Flying Horses Carousel**
Oak Bluffs Ave. **Tel** (508) 693-9481.
◯ Apr–mid-Oct: call for hours.
♿ 🗅

Western Shoreline

Unlike the Vineyard's busier eastern section, the western shoreline is tranquil and rural. The area, which includes the towns of North and West Tisbury, Menemsha, and Aquinnah (formerly Gay Head but renamed in 1998), is graced by a number of

---

WHALE-WATCHING

Whale off the coast of Martha's Vineyard

From April to mid-October the waters off Nantucket Island and Cape Cod come to life with the antics of finback, right, minke, and humpback whales. These gentle behemoths bang their massive tails, blow clouds of bubbles, and sometimes fling their entire bodies into the air only to come crashing down in mammoth back or belly flops. Whales are most numerous during July and August, and cruises are offered from many ports, including Provincetown and Barnstable on the Cape, Vineyard Haven on Martha's Vineyard, and the Straight Wharf in the town of Nantucket.

For hotels and restaurants in this region see pp312–14 and pp340–43

Colored cliffs of Aquinnah on western shore of Martha's Vineyard

private homes and pristine beaches, many of which are strictly private.

Tiny West Tisbury remains a rural village of picket fences, a white-spired church, and a general store. In Menemsha, a working fishing fleet fills the harbor, and the weathered fishermen's shacks, fish nets, and lobster traps look much as they did a century ago. Windswept Aquinnah at the western edge of the island is famous for its steep multi-hued clay cliffs – a favorite subject of photographers.

Nantucket Island ⑩

🏠 9,000 (year-round). ✈ West Tisbury. ⛴ Hyannis, Harwichport & Oak Bluffs. ⓘ Zero Main St (508) 228-1700. www. nantucketchamber.org

Lying off the southern tip of Cape Cod (see pp156–9), Nantucket Island is a 14-mile- (22-km-) long enclave of tranquility. With only one town to speak of, the island remains an untamed world of kettle ponds, cranberry bogs, and lush stands of wild grapes and blueberries, punctuated by the occasional lighthouse.

In the early 19th century the town of Nantucket was the envy of the whaling industry, with a fleet of about 100

vessels. The town's architecture reflects those glory days, with the magnificent mansions of sea captains and merchants – made rich from their whaling profits – lining Main Street. Today the town has the nation's largest concentration of pre-1850s houses.

The **Nantucket Historical Association** (NHA) operates 11 historical buildings in town. One of the most important sites is the Whaling Museum on Broad Street. The expanded museum features a restored 1847 spermaceti candle factory and a rare complete 46-ft (14-meter) skeleton of a sperm whale recovered from Nantucket beach. Historic exhibits include ship models, tools, ship's logs, portraits, and scrimshaw that highlight the era when Nantucket was the world's leading whaling port. The Hawden House, built in 1845, focuses on the lifestyle of the well-off whaling merchants. The Quaker Meeting House is a reminder that from the first meeting in 1701, Quakerism grew to be the religion of Nantucket's elite – a small group still meets here. Additional sites open for tours are the 1686 Jethro Coffin House, the oldest house on the island, and the 18th-century Old Mill, a wind-powered grain mill still in operating condition.

Brant Point Light on Nantucket Island

🏛 **Nantucket Historical Association (NHA)**
15 Broad St. **Tel** (508) 228-5646. **Historic buildings** ⬚ call for hours. 🖼 📷 ♿ Whaling Museum only. 🅿 www.nha.org

Environs

Just 8 miles (13 km) from the town of Nantucket lies the tiny village of **Siasconset**. The village, which is called "Sconset" by locals, is located on the eastern shore of the island and easily lives up to the description offered by one 18th-century visitor: "Perfectly unconnected with the real world and far removed from its perturbations." Set between cranberry bogs and rose-covered bluffs overlooking the Atlantic Ocean, the village's narrow lanes are lined with miniature cottages that are among the oldest of the island. Many of these fishermen's shanties are constructed of wood rescued from shipwrecks, accounting for Sconset's old nickname, "Patchwork Village."

Once Sconset was a summer colony for actors, attracting such luminaries of the American stage as Lillian Russell (1861–1922) and Joseph Jefferson (1829–1905), who made the 35-minute ride from the town of Nantucket via an island railroad. Today there are only a few inns remaining. The majority of Sconset's summer visitors own or rent homes, a fact that serves to keep the beaches uncrowded and the village peaceful.

Cape Cod National Seashore ⑪

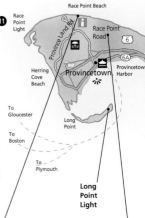

National Park sign

Stretching more than 40 miles (64 km) from Chatham in the south to Provincetown in the north, Cape Cod National Seashore is one of the Eastern Seaboard's true gems. With the backing of President John Kennedy (1917–63) the seashore was established in 1961 to protect the fragile sand dunes and beaches, salt marshes, glacial cliffs, and woodlands. While the delicate landscape has been under federal protection since then, certain features have been added, including bike trails, hiking paths, and specially designated dune trails for off-road vehicles. Historical structures are interspersed among the seashore's softly beautiful natural features.

★ Old Harbor Life-Saving Station

This 1897 station houses a museum containing turn-of-the-century rescue equipment and shipwreck paraphernalia. During the summer months, traditional rescue methods are sometimes demonstrated.

★ Province Lands Area

The barren, windswept landscape of the Province Lands Area has long been an inspiration for writers and artists. Here beech forests give way to horseshoe-shaped dunes and white sand beaches.

Overview
Visitors get an overview of the area in the park's visitor centers.

KEY

▬	Major road
▬	Minor road
‑ ‑	Walking trail
—	Park boundary
ℹ	Tourist information
P	Parking
⛴	Ferry (seasonal)
⛱	Picnic area
☼	Viewpoint

0 kilometers 2

0 miles 2

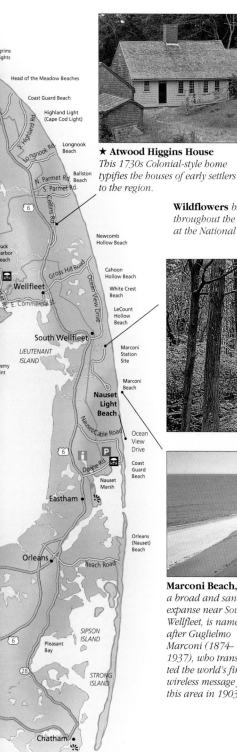

VISITORS' CHECKLIST

Rte 6, Cape Cod. **ℹ** *Salt Pond
Visitor Center, Rte 6, Eastham
(508) 255-3421.* ☐ *9am–
4:30pm daily, with extended
summer hours.* 🏖 *beach (late
Jun–Sep).* **www**.nps.gov/caco

★ Atwood Higgins House
*This 1730s Colonial-style home
typifies the houses of early settlers
to the region.*

Wildflowers *bloom
throughout the seasons
at the National Seashore.*

**★ Atlantic White
Cedar Swamp Trail**
*A nature trail,
part of which is a
boardwalk over
swamp, leads
through forested
swampland and
stands of scrub oak
and pitch pine to
Marconi Station.*

Marconi Beach,
*a broad and sandy
expanse near South
Wellfleet, is named
after Guglielmo
Marconi (1874–
1937), who transmit-
ted the world's first
wireless message from
this area in 1903.*

STAR FEATURES

★ Atlantic White Cedar
Swamp Trail

★ Atwood
Higgins House

★ Old Harbor
Life-Saving Station

★ Province Lands Area

Cape Cod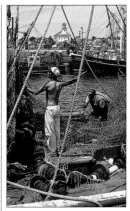

More than 13 million people arrive each summer to
enjoy the boundless beaches, natural beauty, and
quaint colonial villages of Cape Cod. Extending some
70 miles (113 km) into the sea, the Cape is shaped like
an upraised arm, bent at the elbow with the Atlantic
Ocean and the Cape Cod National Seashore (see
pp154–5) and ending with the fist at Provincetown.
Crowds are heaviest along Route 28, where beaches
edge the warmer waters of Nantucket Sound and
Buzzard's Bay. Towns along Route 6A, the old Kings
Highway, retain their colonial charm, with many of
the old homes now serving as antique shops and inns.

Exploring the Lower Cape

First-time visitors to
Cape Cod are almost
always confused when
they are given direc-
tions by locals. This is
because residents have
divided the Cape into
three districts with
names that do not make
much sense. The Mid-
and Upper Cape is actu-
ally the southernmost
portion closest to the
mainland, while the
Lower Cape is the
northernmost section.

Pilgrim
Monument

The Lower Cape takes
in the long elbow of the
peninsula that curls north-
ward and forms Cape Cod
Bay. The towns of Chatham,
Brewster, Orleans, Eastham,
Wellfleet, Truro, and
Provincetown are all located
in this section of Cape Cod.

Provincetown

This picturesque town at the
northern tip of the Cape has
a colorful history. The
Pilgrims first landed here
in 1620 and stayed for five
weeks before pushing on
to the mainland. During
that time they drew up the
Mayflower Compact, a forerunner of the American
Constitution. "P-Town," as
it is called, later grew into a
major 18th-century fishing
center. By the beginning of
the 20th century, P-Town had
become a bustling artists'
colony. Today this popular
and eccentric town is one of
New England's most vibrant
destinations and a popular
gay resort. However, in the
summer months the town's

population can swell
from 3,500 to more
than 30,000.

The place where the
Pilgrims first landed is
marked by a bronze
plaque on Commercial
Street and commemo-
rated by the tallest
granite structure in the
US, the 252-ft (77-m)
Pilgrim Monument.
On a clear day, the
view from the top
extends all the way to
Boston. Eclectic displays
in the adjacent muse-
um include exhibits of
Pilgrim history as well
as marine and Arctic artifacts.

The **Whydah Pirate
Museum** is named for a ship
that sank in a storm off Cape
Cod after being captured by
pirates. It exhibits artifacts
such as gold dubloons,
weapons, clothing, and West
African gold jewelry. The
region's rich cultural history
is celebrated in the galleries
of the **Provincetown Art
Association and Museum**,
where works by local artists

Fishermen on their boat in
Provincetown harbor

are displayed. One of the
town's busiest locales is
MacMillan Wharf, the center of
nautical activity, including the
jumping-off point for whale-
watching cruises (see p152).

🏛 **Pilgrim Monument and
Provincetown Museum**
High Pole Hill Rd. **Tel** (508) 487-
1310. ◯ Apr–Nov: 9am–5pm daily
(Jun–mid-Sep: to 7pm). 🖼 ♿

🏛 **Whydah Pirate Museum**
16 MacMillan Wharf. **Tel** (508)
487-8899. ◯ May–Oct: 10am–5pm
daily (Jun–Aug: extended hours). 🖼
♿ ⬛

🏛 **Provincetown Art
Association and Museum**
460 Commercial St. **Tel** (508) 487-
1750. ◯ call for hours. 🖼 ♿

Environs

Just 17 miles (27 km) south of
Provincetown lies Wellfleet,
an early whaling center that
possesses one of the Cape's
largest concentrations of art
galleries. Farther down the

Busy streets of Cape Cod's Provincetown in the summertime

Cape is Eastham, home to the **Old Schoolhouse Museum**, a one-room school built in 1869. Neighboring Orleans is a commercial center with access to the very beautiful Nauset Beach and its much-photographed lighthouse.

🏛 Old Schoolhouse Museum
Nauset Rd, Eastham. *Tel* (508) 255-0788. ⬚ call for opening hours.

Chatham
Chatham rests on the very point of the Cape's "elbow," the place where Nantucket Sound meets the Atlantic Ocean. An attractive, upscale community, it offers fine inns, a Main Street filled with attractive shops, and a popular summer playhouse. Housed in an 1887 Victorian train station, the **Railroad Museum** contains models, photos, memorabilia, and vintage trains that can be boarded. Fishing boats unload their catch at the pier every afternoon, and the surrounding waters offer good opportunities for amateur anglers to fish for bluefish and bass.

Chatham is also the best place to plan a trip to the **Monomoy National Wildlife Refuge**. Encompassing two islands, this huge reserve attracts migrating birds and is a nesting habitat for such endangered birds as the piping plover and the roseate tern. Deer are spotted here, as are the numerous gray and harbor seals that bask on the rocks.

🏛 Railroad Museum
Depot Rd. *Tel* (508) 945-5199. ⬚ mid-Jun–mid-Sep: 10am–4pm Tue–Sat. ♿

✖ Monomoy National Wildlife Refuge
Wikis Way, Morris Island. *Tel* (508) 945-0594. **Visitor Center** ⬚ 8am–4pm Mon–Sat (Nov–May: Mon–Fri only). Call for info on boat services. **http://**monomoy.fws.gov

Brewster
Named for Elder William Brewster (1567–1644), who was a passenger on the *Mayflower*, Brewster is another town graced with handsome 19th-century houses of wealthy sea captains. It is also home to a particularly lovely church, the 1834 First Parish Brewster Unitarian Universalist Church. Some pews are marked with names of prominent captains.

Children will love the interactive exhibits on display at the **Cape Cod Museum of Natural History**. An observation area looking out on the salt-marsh habitat of birds gives visitors close-up views of the natural world. The 82-acre (33-ha) grounds are laced with three walking trails with boardwalks that cross salt marshes. The museum also offers interesting guided "eco-treks" and cruises to nearby Nauset Marsh and Monomoy Islands.

Naturalists can continue with a more hands-on kind of exploration at any of Brewster's eight beaches along Cape Cod Bay. These strands taper gradually toward the ocean, and about a mile (1.6 km) of tidal flats is revealed at low tide. The dramatic flats attract a wide variety of visitors, from photographers to children who like to search for sea life, to clam diggers.

🏛 Cape Cod Museum of Natural History
869 Rte 6A. *Tel* (508) 896-3867. ⬚ Jun–Sep: 9:30am–4pm daily. Call for winter opening hours. 📷 🎫 ♿ **www**.ccmnh.org

Red and white Nauset Light on the Lower Cape

PROVINCETOWN ARTIST COLONY

Artists, writers, and poets have long been inspired by the sublime natural beauty of Provincetown. The town's first art school opened in 1901 and Hans Hofmann (1880–1966), Jackson Pollock (1912–56), Mark Rothko (1903–70), and Edward Hopper (1882–1967) are among the many prominent artists who have spent time here. Today the town is famous for its art galleries, both large and small. The roster of resident writers includes John Dos Passos (1896–1970), Tennessee Williams (1911–83), Sinclair Lewis (1885–1951), and Eugene O'Neill (1888–1953), whose earliest plays were staged at the Provincetown Playhouse.

Visitor to one of Provincetown's many art galleries

Exploring the Mid- and Upper Cape

Stretching from Bourne and Sandwich in the west to Yarmouth and Harwich in the east, Cape Cod's Mid- and Upper sections offer travelers a broad range of vacation experiences. Be it sunbathing on the tranquil beaches of Nantucket Sound by day or partaking in the fashionable nightlife of Hyannis once the sun has set over Cape Cod Bay, this section of the Cape has a little something for every taste.

Hyannis boatbuilder and his remodeled Russian torpedo boat

Dennis
This gracious village has developed into a vibrant artistic center and is home to the 1927 **Cape Playhouse**, America's oldest professional summer theater, as well as some of the Cape's finest public golf courses. The list of stage luminaries who started their career here is impressive. Playhouse grads include eventual Academy Award-winners Humphrey Bogart, Bette Davis, and Henry Fonda. The Playhouse complex also includes the **Cape Cod Museum of Art**, displaying the works of Cape Cod artists. A short drive to the east, the Scargo Hill Tower is open to the public and offers brilliant views of the surrounding landscape.

Cape Playhouse
820 Rte 6A. *Tel* (508) 385-3911.
☐ call for show times.

Cape Cod Museum of Art
Cape Playhouse grounds. *Tel* (508) 385-4477. ☐ late May–mid-Oct: 10am–5pm Mon–Sat, noon–5pm Sun; call for winter hours. ● public hols; mid-Oct–late May: Mon. ☑ ☒ ☒ www.ccmoa.org

Hyannis
The Cape's largest village is also a busy shopping center and the transportation hub for regional train, bus, and air service. The harbor is full of yachts and sightseeing boats. Surprisingly, one of Hyannis' most popular forms of transportation does not float. The **Cape Cod Central Railroad** takes travelers for a scenic two-hour round-trip to the Cape Cod canal. Hyannis was one of the Cape's earliest summer resorts, attracting vacationers as far back as the mid-1800s. In 1874 President Ulysses S. Grant (1822–85) vacationed here, followed by President Grover Cleveland (1837–1908) years later. The most famous estate is the Kennedy compound, summer playground of one of America's most famous political dynasties. The heavily screened compound is best seen from the water aboard a sightseeing cruise.

After John Kennedy's assassination in 1963, a simple monument was erected in his honor: a pool and fountain and a circular wall bearing Kennedy's profile. The **John F. Kennedy Hyannis Museum** on the ground floor of the Old Town Hall covers the years he spent vacationing here, beginning in the 1930s, and includes photos, oral histories, and family videos.

Cape Cod Central Railroad
Tel (508) 771-3800 or (888) 797-7245. ☐ late May–late Oct: Tue–Sun; call for trip times and departure points. ☑ ☒ ☒ www.capetrain.com

John F. Kennedy Hyannis Museum
397 Main St. *Tel* (508) 790-3077. ☐ call for hours. ☑ ☒

Barnstable
This attractive harbor town is the hub of Barnstable County, a widespread region extending to both sides of the Cape. The **Coast Guard Museum**, located in an 1856 customs house, has a rich display of artifacts from the Lighthouse, Livesaving,

Popular sightseeing mode of transportation: Cape Cod Central Railroad

THE KENNEDY CLAN

The center of the Kennedy compound in Hyannis Port is the "cottage" that multi-millionaire Joseph Kennedy (1888–1969) and his wife Rose (1890–1995) bought in 1926. The much-expanded structure was a vacation retreat for the Kennedys and their nine children. John Fitzgerald Kennedy (1917–63), the country's 35th president, and his brothers and sisters continued to summer here long after they had started families of their own. In 1999, JFK's son, John Jr, was flying to the compound for a family wedding when his plane crashed off Martha's Vineyard.

John and Jacqueline Kennedy at their cottage in Hyannis Port

and Revenue Cutter services. A film shows lifesaving techniques. The harbor is home to whale-watching cruises, and conservation properties offer fine hiking.

🏛 Coast Guard Museum
Rte 6A, 3353 Main St. *Tel (508) 362-8521.* ☐ *mid-Jun–Oct: 10am–3pm Tue–Sat.*

Falmouth

Falmouth, settled by Quakers in 1661, grew into a resort town in the late 19th century. The picturesque village green and historic Main Street reflect a Victorian heritage.

Falmouth's coastline is ideal for boating, windsurfing, and sea kayaking. As well, the town is graced with 12 miles (19 km) of beaches. Old Silver is the most popular beach, but Grand Avenue has the most dramatic views of Vineyard Sound. Nature lovers will find walking and hiking trails, salt marshes, tidal pools, and opportunities for beach-combing and bird-watching. The 3.3-mile (5 km) Shining Sea Bike Path offers vistas of beach, harbor, and woodland on the way to Woods Hole.

Woods Hole

This is home to the world's largest independent marine science research center, the Woods Hole Oceanographic Institution (WHOI).

Visitors to the **WHOI Exhibit Center** can explore two floors of displays and videos explaining coastal ecology and highlighting some of the organization's findings. Exhibits include a replica of the interior of the *Alvin*, one of the pioneer vessels developed for deep-sea exploration.

🏛 WHOI Exhibit Center
15 School St. *Tel (508) 289-2663.* ☐ *Apr–Oct: call for hours.* 🔲 *donation.* 🗹 *Jul–Aug by appt.* ♿

Sandwich

The oldest town on the Cape is straight off a postcard: the First Church of Christ over-looks a picturesque pond fed by the brook that powers the water-wheel of a colonial-era gristmill. The church has what is said to be the oldest church bell in the US, dating to 1675. The **Dexter Grist Mill**, built in 1654, has been restored and is grinding again, producing cornmeal that is available at the gift shop.

Another industry is celebrated at the **Sandwich Glass Museum**. Between 1825 and 1888, local entrepreneurs invented a way to press glass that was prized for its colors. Nearly 5,000 pieces of Sandwich glass are handsomely displayed here.

The most unique attraction in Sandwich is **Heritage Museums and Gardens**, a 75-acre (30-ha) garden and museum built around the collection of pharmaceutical magnate and inveterate collector Josiah

Antique bottle in Glass Museum

Kirby Lilly, Jr (1893–1966). The artifacts fill three buildings. The American History Museum, a replica of a revolutionary war fort, includes military miniatures and antique firearms. A collection of 37 antique cars is displayed in a reproduction of a Shaker barn. The Art Museum contains everything from folk art and a collection of Currier and Ives prints to changing exhibits and a working 1912 carousel – a favorite with visitors. Outside, the grounds are planted with more than 1,000 varieties of trees, shrubs, and flowers, including superb rhododendrons.

🏛 Dexter Grist Mill
Maine & Water Sts. *Tel (508) 888-4910.* ☐ *call for hours.* 🔲

🏛 Sandwich Glass Museum
129 Main St. *Tel (508) 888-0251.* ☐ *Feb–Mar: 9:30am–4pm Wed–Sun; Apr–Dec: 9:30am–5pm daily.* 🔲 🗹 ♿

🏛 Heritage Museums and Gardens
67 Grove St. *Tel (508) 888-3300.* ☐ *Apr–Oct: 9am–5pm daily; Nov–Mar: call for hours.* 🔲 ♿ www.heritagemuseumsandgardens.org

Film star Gary Cooper's 1930 Duesenberg, Heritage Museums and Gardens

Old Sturbridge Village

At the heart of this open-air museum are about 40 vintage buildings that have been restored and relocated from all over New England. Laid out like an early 19th-century village, Old Sturbridge is peopled by costumed interpreters who go about their daily activities. A blacksmith works the forge, farmers tend crops, and millers work the gristmill. Inside buildings visitors will find re-created period settings, early American antiques, and demonstrations of such crafts as spinning and weaving. A gallery, education center, and workshops illuminate 19th-century life.

VISITORS' CHECKLIST

Rte 20, Sturbridge. *Tel (508) 347-3362 or (800) 733-1830.* ☐ *mid-Apr–mid-Oct: 9:30am–5pm daily; mid-Oct–mid-Apr: 9:30am–4pm Tue–Sun.* ● *Dec 25.* 🎟 🎫 *call for times.* ♿ *some bldgs.* 🍴 📷 🚻 **www.osv.org**

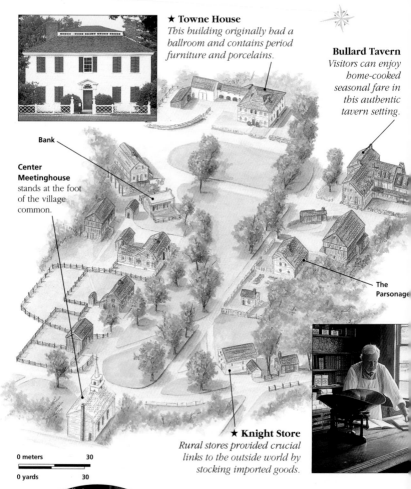

★ **Towne House**
This building originally had a ballroom and contains period furniture and porcelains.

Bullard Tavern
Visitors can enjoy home-cooked seasonal fare in this authentic tavern setting.

Bank

Center Meetinghouse stands at the foot of the village common.

The Parsonage

★ **Knight Store**
Rural stores provided crucial links to the outside world by stocking imported goods.

0 meters   30
0 yards   30

Home-baked goods
Visitors can watch as costumed interpreters go about such daily activities as preparing food.

STAR SIGHTS

★ Knight Store

★ Towne House

Worcester ⓭

🏛 170,000. ✈ Worcester Airport.
🚌 🚆 ℹ Elm St (508) 753-2920.

Worcester has always been on the cutting edge. During the American Industrial Revolution, local designers developed the nation's first mechanized carpet weavers and envelope folders. This spirit of invention reached its pinnacle in 1926, when Worcester native Dr. Robert Goddard (1882–1945) launched the world's first liquid-fuel rocket.

Not all of Worcester's forward thinking has been reserved for the development of new machines, however. Over time this city, which is built on seven hills, became home to 10 colleges and universities plus a center for biological research that in the 1950s developed the first birth-control pill.

Worcester's most unusual attraction is the **Higgins Armory Museum**, a showcase for more than 70 suits of armor and a multitude of ancient weapons. The artifacts date back to medieval and Renaissance Europe, ancient Greece and Rome, and feudal Japan, and are displayed in a hall adorned with stained glass and tapestries. Young museum-goers are allowed to actually don ancient garb from the try-on costume collection.

Housed in a handsome late 19th-century stone building, the **Worcester Art Museum** has distinguished itself as an important repository. Its impressive collection contains some 35,000 objects spanning 5,000 years, including a 12th-century chapter house that was rebuilt stone by stone on the premises. The museum's holdings of East and West Asian art and Japanese woodblock prints are balanced wonderfully by a good number of works by such Western masters as Claude Monet (1840–1926), Thomas

Gainsborough (1728–88), and Pablo Picasso (1881–1973).

Just 2 miles (3 km) from downtown, the **Ecotarium** promotes a better understanding of the region's environment and its wildlife. Interactive exhibits invite hands-on learning experiences. The surrounding grounds contain a wildlife center for injured and endangered animals, and New England's only tree canopy walkway (summer only). The 60-acre (24-ha) grounds also hold a planetarium.

Higgins Armory Museum display

🏛 **Higgins Armory Museum**
100 Barber Ave. *Tel* (508) 853-6015. ◯ year-round: 10am–4pm Tue–Sat, noon–4pm Sun. 🌐 ♿
www.higgins.org

🏛 **Worcester Art Museum**
55 Salisbury St. *Tel* (508) 799-4406.
◯ year-round: 11am–5pm Wed–Fri & Sun, 10am–5pm Sat. ♿ ♿
www.worcesterart.org

🐾 **Ecotarium**
222 Harrington Way. *Tel* (508) 929-2700. ◯ year-round: 10am–5pm Tue–Sat, noon–5pm Sun. 🌐 ♿
www.ecotarium.org

Environs
North Grafton, 10 miles (16 km) southeast, has a long history of clock-making. In the early 19th century brothers Benjamin, Simon, Ephraim, and Aaron Willard were regarded as some of New England's best craftsmen, designing new styles for timepieces. The timepieces were given such names as Eddystone Lighthouse, Skeleton, and Act of Parlia-

ment. Today more than 70 Willard timepieces and elegant tall clocks are on display in the family's original 18th-century homestead.

🏛 **Willard House and Clock Museum**
11 Willard St, North Grafton. *Tel* (508) 839-3500. ◯ Apr–Dec: 10am–4pm Tue–Sat, 1–4pm Sun; Jan–Mar: Fri–Sun only. 🌐 📷 obligatory. ♿ partial.

Sturbridge ⓮

Sturbridge's roots are literally in the land. Soon after its founding in 1729, residents planted apple orchards, some of which are still in operation. The town's main attraction is its living-history museum: Old Sturbridge Village (*see p160*).

The 1748 Parsonage in Old Sturbridge Village

Environs
Located 9 miles (14 km) west, the village of Brimfield blossoms three times each year as America's flea market capital. The Brimfield Antique Show attracts hundreds of dealers, filling every field, sidewalk, and front porch in town. Treasure hunters descend to the village by the thousands to shop for wares ranging from valuable antiques to the truly kitsch.

Scraping recent layers of paint off an antique carousel horse at the Brimfield flea market

Springfield ⑮

🏛 153,000. ✈ 15 miles (24 km) SW in Windsor Locks, CT. 🚌 🚆 🛈 1441 Main St (413) 787-1548 or (800) 723-1548. www.valleyvisitor.com

Now a center for banking and insurance, Springfield owes much of its early success to guns. The **Springfield Armory** – the first armory in the US – was commissioned by George Washington (1732–99) to manufacture arms for the Colonial forces fighting in the Revolutionary War. Today the historic armory is part of the National Park Service and maintains one of the most extensive and unique firearms collections in the world.

In 1891 Dr. James Naismith (1861–1939), an instructor at the International YMCA Training Center, now Springfield College, invented the game of basketball. **Basketball Hall of Fame** traces the development of the game from its humble beginnings, in which peach baskets

Emblem of the Basketball Hall of Fame in Springfield

were used as nets, to its evolution as one of the world's most popular team sports.

Along with its collection of basketball memorabilia, the state-of-the-art museum features interactive displays. Children and adults can play against former stars in virtual reality games or test their own shooting skills.

Court Square on Main Street is the revitalized center of the city, lined with 19th-century churches, civic and commercial buildings, and a 300-ft (91-m) high tower

housing carillon bells. Nearby is **The Quadrangle**, a collection of four museums of art, science, and history. The George Walter Vincent Smith Art Museum displays a noted collection of Oriental decorative arts and Japanese armor, and has a children's activity center. Galleries at the Museum of Fine Arts contain European and American paintings, sculpture, and decorative arts. Children love the Springfield Science Museum, with its hands-on exhibits, Phelon African Hall, planetarium, and Dinosaur Hall, with its life-sized model of *Tyrannosaurus rex*. The Connecticut Valley Historical Museum tells Springfield's story through changing exhibits. The Dr. Seuss National Memorial, commemorating Springfield-native Theodor Geisel (1904–91), better known as popular children's author Dr. Seuss, was opened in June 2002.

🏛 **Springfield Armory National Historic Site**
One Armory Sq. **Tel** (413) 734-8551. ◷ 9am–5pm daily. ● Jan 1, Thanksgiving, Dec 25. 📷 ♿

🏛 **Basketball Hall of Fame**
1000 W Columbus Ave. **Tel** (413) 781-6500. ◷ 10am–4pm Tue–Fri & Sun, 10am–5pm Sat. ● Thanksgiving, Dec 25. 📷 📷 ♿ www.hoophall.com

🏛 **The Quadrangle**
State & Chestnut Sts. **Tel** (413) 263-6800. **Four museums** ◷ year-round: call for hours. 📷 ♿ partial. www.springfieldmuseums.org

Environs
Some 11 miles (18 km) north, the hamlet of South Hadley is home to **Mount Holyoke College** (1837), the nation's oldest women's college. Poet Emily Dickinson (1830–86) was one of Mount Holyoke's most famous graduates. The 800-acre (320-ha) campus encompasses two lakes and a series of nature trails. College sites worth a visit include the **Art Museum** and the **Talcott Greenhouse**, which is located in a Victorian-style greenhouse.

Farther north in Hadley, the summit of 954-ft (291-m) Mount Holyoke in **Skinner**

Dinosaur model dwarfing visitor in Springfield's Science Museum

State Park offers a panorama of the oxbow bend in the Connecticut River. The park is well known for massive laurel displays in June and flaming foliage in autumn.

🏛 **Mount Holyoke College Art Museum**
Mount Holyoke College. **Tel** (413) 538-2245. ◷ 11am–5pm Tue–Fri, 1–5pm Sat–Sun. ♿

🌿 **Talcott Greenhouse**
Mount Holyoke College. **Tel** (413) 538-2116. ◷ year-round: 9am–4pm Mon–Fri, 1–4pm Sat–Sun. ♿

🏕 **Skinner State Park**
Rte 47. **Tel** (413) 586-0350. ◷ May–Oct: dawn–dusk. 📷 on weekends.

Amherst ⑯

🏛 23,000. ✈ 41 miles (66 km) S in Windsor Locks, CT. 🚌 🚆 🛈 28 Amity St (413) 253-0700.

This idyllic college town is home to three different institutes of higher learning. The most popular with visitors is Amherst College, with its central green and traditional ivy-covered buildings. Founded in 1821 for underprivileged youths hoping to enter the ministry, the school has grown into one of the most selective small colleges in the US. The college's excellent **Mead Art Museum** includes the Rotherwas Room, an ornately paneled English hall c.1600. Minerals, fossils, and bones star in the new **Amherst College Museum of Natural History**, which was opened in spring 2006.

Poet Emily Dickinson was one of Amherst's most famous citizens. In her early 20s, Dickinson withdrew from society and spent the rest of her life in the family home, where she died in 1886. The second-floor bedroom of the **Emily Dickinson Homestead** has been restored to the way it was during the years 1855–86, when the reclusive poet wrote her most important verse. Her work remained unpublished until after her death. Over time critics proclaimed it to be the work of a poetic genius. The **Jones Library** has displays on Dickinson's life and works, as well as collections on poet Robert Frost, who taught at Amherst College in the 1940s.

Mead Art Museum
Amherst College. *Tel* (413) 542-2335.
Sep–May: 9am–noon Tue, Thu & Sun, 9am–5pm Fri & Sat. Call for summer hours. mid-Dec–late Jan.

Amherst College Museum of Natural History
Amherst College. *Tel* (413) 542-2165.
year-round: 11am–4pm Tue–Sun.

Emily Dickinson Homestead
280 Main St. *Tel* (413) 542-8161.
Mar–mid-Dec: call for hours.
obligatory.

Jones Library
43 Amity St. *Tel* (413) 256-4090.
9am–5:30pm Mon–Wed, Fri & Sat, 9am–8:30pm Tue & Thu, 1–5pm Sun. Jun–Aug: Sun. **Special collections** year-round: 2–5pm Mon & Sat, 10am–5pm Tue–Fri.

Northampton ⑰

30,000. 36 miles (58 km) S in Windsor Locks, CT.
99 Pleasant St (413) 584-1900.

A lively center for the arts and known for its fine dining, Northampton has a well preserved Victorian-style Main Street lined with craft galleries and shops. The town is also home to the 1871 **Smith College**, the largest privately endowed women's college in the nation. The handsome campus has a notable **Museum of Art** and the **Lyman Plant House and Conservatory**, known for its flower shows and the

Beautiful bloom at Smith College's Lyman Plant House

arboretum and gardens. South of Northampton in Holyoke, visitors can explore the trails in the 1800-acre (728-ha) **Mount Tom State Reservation**. Nearby is the Norwottuck Rail Trail, a popular walking and biking path that runs along an old railroad bed connecting Northampton to neighboring Amherst.

Smith College Museum of Art
Elm St, Northampton. *Tel* (413) 585-2760. 10am–4pm Tue–Sat, noon–4pm Sun.

Lyman Plant House and Conservatory
College Lane, Northampton. *Tel* (413) 585-2740. year-round: 8:30am–4pm daily. Thanksgiving, Dec 25–Jan 1.

Mount Tom State Reservation
125 Reservation Rd, Holyoke. *Tel* (413) 534-1186. year-round: 8am–dusk daily. **Visitors' center** Memorial Day–mid-Oct: Wed–Sun. Call for hours. partial.

Deerfield ⑱

5,300. 52 miles (84 km) S in Windsor Locks, CT. 18 Miner St, Greenfield (413) 773-9393.

A one-time frontier outpost that was almost annihilated by Indian raids in the late 17th century, Deerfield survived and its farmers prospered, building gracious clapboard homes along the mile-long (1.6-km) center avenue known simply as "The Street."

Sixty of these remain within **Historic Deerfield** and are carefully preserved. Some of the buildings now serve as museums, exhibiting a broad range of period furniture and decorative arts, including silverware, ceramics, and textiles. The Flynt Center of Early New England Life schedules changing exhibitions on early life in western Massachusetts. Visitors seeking a photo opportunity can drive to the summit of **Mount Sugarloaf State Reservation** in South Deerfield for views of the Connecticut River Valley.

Historic Deerfield
The Street, Old Deerfield. *Tel* (413) 775-7214. Dec–Mar: 9:30am–4:30pm Sat & Sun, limited access; Apr–Nov: 9:30am–4:30pm daily. Thanksgiving, Dec 24, Dec 25. **www**.historic-deerfield.org

Mount Sugarloaf State Reservation
US 116, South Deerfield. *Tel* (413) 545-5993. May–Dec: 8am–dusk daily.

White clapboard house and picket fence in historic Deerfield

Tour of the Mohawk Trail ⑲

Originally an Indian trade route, this trail was a popular artery for early pioneers. In 1914 the trail, which stretches for 63 miles (100 km) from Orange to North Adams along Route 2, became a paved road. The choicest section of the route, from Greenfield to North Adams, was the first officially designated scenic drive in New England. This twisting road offers magnificent mountain views, particularly in the sharp hairpin curves leading into North Adams, and is one of the most popular fall foliage routes.

Charlemont ②
The town is dominated by the massive statue *Hail to the Sunrise*.

Hairpin Turn ③
This sharp bend in the road offers soaring views of Mount Greylock.

Mount Greylock
Hoosic River

KEY
▭ Tour route
≈ Other road
☀ Viewpoint

North Adams ④
North Adams is near America's only naturally formed marble bridge.

Williamstown ⑳

🏛 8,000. ✈ 47 miles (75 km) W in Albany, NY. 🚌 ℹ Jct Rtes 2 & 7 (413) 458-9077 or (800) 214-3799.

Art lovers make pilgrimages to **The Sterling and Francine Clark Art Institute** to see its private art collection, strong on Old Masters and French Impressionists, including more than 30 Renoirs. Intimate galleries opened in a striking hilltop building in 2008, and the entire campus is undergoing expansion and renovation through 2013. The **Williams College Museum of Art** is also notable for a collection that ranges from ancient Assyrian stone reliefs to Andy Warhol's (1927–87) final self-portrait.

The summertime Williamstown Theater Festival, founded in 1954, is known for its high-quality productions, which often

A 19th-century Steinway at The Sterling and Francine Clark Art Institute

feature big-name Broadway and Hollywood stars.

🏛 **The Sterling and Francine Clark Art Institute**
225 South St. **Tel** (413) 458-2303. ◯ 10am–5pm Tue–Sun (Jul–Aug: daily). 🎫 (Jun–Oct only). 🎥 ⚫ www.clarkart.edu

🏛 **Williams College Museum of Art**
Main St. **Tel** (413) 597-2429. ◯ year-round: 10am–5pm Tue–Sat, 1–5pm Sun. ⚫ www.wcma.org

Environs
More art can be found 7 miles (11 km) east in North Adams

Degas statue at Clark Institute

at the **Massachusetts Museum of Contemporary Art** (MASS MoCA). Seven interconnected buildings, part of a 19th-century factory, with enormous indoor spaces, elevated walkways, and outdoor courtyards display cutting-edge art. The complex is able to house sculptures and paintings that are too large for most conventional museums.

🏛 **Massachusetts Museum of Contemporary Art**
1040 MASS MoCA Way. **Tel** (413) 662-2111. ◯ Jul–Sep: 10am–6pm daily; Oct–Jun: 11am–5pm Wed–Mon. 🎫 ⚫ 🎥 www.massmoca.org

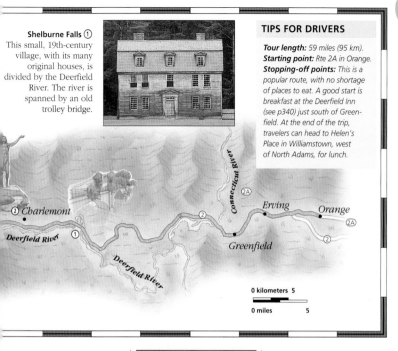

Shelburne Falls ①
This small, 19th-century village, with its many original houses, is divided by the Deerfield River. The river is spanned by an old trolley bridge.

TIPS FOR DRIVERS

Tour length: 59 miles (95 km).
Starting point: Rte 2A in Orange.
Stopping-off points: This is a popular route, with no shortage of places to eat. A good start is breakfast at the Deerfield Inn (see p340) just south of Greenfield. At the end of the trip, travelers can head to Helen's Place in Williamstown, west of North Adams, for lunch.

0 kilometers 5

0 miles 5

Mount Greylock State Reservation ㉑

Off Rte 7, Lanesborough. (Auto road open late-May–late Oct). ℹ *(413) 499-4262.* **www**.mass.gov/dcr/parks

The Appalachian Trail *(see pp22–3)*, the popular 2,000-mile (3,200-km) hiking path running from Georgia to Maine, crosses Mount Greylock's summit. At 3,491 ft (1,064 m), Greylock is the highest peak in Massachusetts and offers panoramic views of five states. The auto road to the summit is open from late May through October. Hiking trails in the 12,500-acre (5059-ha) park remain open and are particularly popular during fall foliage season. At the summit visitors can climb Veterans' Memorial Tower for an even more panoramic view.

Summit Veteran's Memorial Tower atop Mount Greylock

Hancock Shaker Village ㉒

Rte 20, outside Pittsfield. **Tel** *(413) 443-0188.* ☐ *Apr–mid-May: 10am–4pm daily; mid-May–mid-Oct: 10am–5pm daily; mid-Oct–Mar: guided tours only (call for hours).* ● *Jan 1, Thanksgiving, Dec 25.* ☑☑☑☒☒ **www**.hancockshakervillage.org

Founded in 1783, this was the third in a series of 19 Shaker settlements established in the Northeast and Midwest as utopian communities. The Shakers, so-called because

Authentic Shaker door latch at Hancock Shaker Village

they often trembled and shook during moments of worship and prayer, believed in celibacy and equality of the sexes, with men and women living separately but sharing authority and responsibilities. At its peak in the 1830s, there were 300 residents living in the village. Now the community has no resident Shakers.

Twenty of the 100 original buildings have been restored, including the tri-level round stone barn, cleverly designed so that as many as 52 head of cattle could be fed by a single farmhand from a central core. The Brick Dwelling can house up to 100 people, and has a meeting room used for weekday worship and a communal dining room, where traditional Shaker fare is served on select evenings.

Presentations on the Shaker way of life include demonstrations of chair-, broom-, and oval box-making. In the Discovery Room visitors may try on reproduction Shaker clothing and also try their hand at crafts such as weaving. An orientation exhibit and videos in several buildings provide historical background.

Picturesque Bash Bish Falls in
Mount Washington State Forest

The Berkshires 23

🛬 37 miles (60 km) NE in Albany, NY.
🚌 Pittsfield. 🏠 3 Hoosac St, Adams
(413) 743-4500; (800) 237-5747.
www.berkshires.org

Visitors have long been
attracted to the peaceful
wooded hills, green valleys,
rippling rivers, and waterfalls
of this western corner of
Massachusetts. Among the
first tourists were writers
such as Henry Wadsworth
Longfellow (1807–82),
Herman Melville (1819–91),
and Nathaniel Hawthorne
(1804–64). When the three
wrote about the natural
beauty of the area, the location caught the attention of
many of the region's wealthy
people, who began to spend
their summers here. Now
the region is a year-round
playground, popular for
its culture as well as for the

ample opportunities it provides for outdoor recreation.
    The area is speckled with
small towns and country
villages. Great Barrington
to the south and Pittsfield to
the north are the com-
mercial centers of the
region, while Lenox
and Stockbridge are
cultural meccas. The
old cotton and woolen
mills in Housatonic are
finding new life as art
galleries, and Main
Street of Sheffield is
lined with interesting
little antique shops.
    Among the most pop-
ular walking and hiking
trails in the Berkshires are
Bartholemew's Cobble in
Sheffield and Bash Bish Falls
in the **Mount Washington
State Forest**. A trail leads to
the summit of Monument
Mountain and affords beautiful views. Reputedly, it was
on a hike up the mountain
that Herman Melville first
met Nathaniel Hawthorne,
forming a friendship that
resulted in Melville's dedicat-
ing his novel *Moby-Dick* to
his fellow author.

🥾 Mount Washington
State Forest
Rte 41 S. **Tel** (413) 528-0330. ◐
Memorial Day–Columbus Day. 🌐

Pittsfield
Although primarily a commercial hub, Pittsfield has a growing cultural scene, including
the award-winning **Barrington
Stage Company**. The town's
literary shrine is **Arrowhead**,
an 18th-century home in the
shadow of Mount Greylock,

where Herman Melville
lived from 1850 to 1863
and where he wrote his
masterpiece *Moby-Dick*.
    The **Berkshire Museum**,
renovated in 2008, has a large

Life-sized model of Stegosaurus at
Berkshire Museum in Pittsfield

collection of items covering
the disciplines of history,
natural science, and fine art.
The museum's aquarium has
20 tanks for local and exotic
sea creatures. The galleries
are notable for their works by
such 19th-century American
masters as George Inness
(1825–94) and Frederic
Church (1826–1900).

🎭 Barrington Stage
Company
30 Union St. **Tel** (413) 236-8888.
www.barringtonstageco.org

🎪 Arrowhead
780 Holmes Rd. **Tel** (413) 442-
1793. ◐ late May–mid-Oct:
9:30am–4pm daily; rest of year by
appt. 🌐 🎫 ♿ first floor only. 🚫
📷 www.mobydick.org

🏛 Berkshire Museum
39 South St. **Tel** (413) 443-7171.
◐ 10am–5pm Mon–Sat,
noon–5pm Sun. 🌐 ♿ 🚫 📷
www.berkshiremuseum.org

Lenox
In the late 19th century the
gracious village of Lenox
became known as the
"inland Newport" for the
lavish summer "cottages"
built by prominent families
such as the Carnegies and
the Vanderbilts. Before the
1929 Great Depression,
there were more than 70
grand estates gracing the
area. While some of the
millionaires have since
moved away, many of
their lavish homes remain
in service as schools, cultural institutions, resorts,
and posh inns. One of the

Gathering hay by oxcart at Hancock Shaker Village

Typical townhouse in the village of Lenox

more prominent mansions is **The Mount**, built in 1902 by Pulitzer Prize-winning author Edith Wharton (1862–1937).

Lenox gained new status as a center of culture in 1937 when the 500-acre (202-ha) Tanglewood estate became the summer home of the Boston Symphony Orchestra. Music lovers flock for concerts in the 1,200-seat Seiji Ozawa Hall or the open

Figures of *Andromeda* and *Memory* at Chesterwood

Music Shed, where many enjoy picnicking and listening to the music on the surrounding lawn. Jazz and popular concerts are interspersed with the classical program. Tanglewood's name is credited to Nathaniel Hawthorne, who lived in a house on the estate at one time and wrote some of his short stories here.

The Mount
2 Plunkett St. *Tel (413) 551-5111.*
call ahead for details.
www.edithwharton.org

Stockbridge
Stockbridge was founded in 1734 by missionaries seeking to educate and convert the local Mohegan Indians. The

simple **Mission House** (c.1739) was built by Reverend John Sergeant for his bride. Today the house contains period pieces and Indian artifacts.

The town's quaint main street, dominated by the 1897 Red Lion Inn, has been immortalized in the popular paintings of Norman Rockwell (1894–1978), one of America's most beloved illustrators. The painter lived in Stockbridge for 25 years, and the country's largest collection of Rockwell originals can be seen at the **Norman Rockwell Museum**.

Stockbridge has been home to its share of prominent residents, including sculptor Daniel Chester French (1850–1931), who summered at his **Chesterwood** estate. It was here that French created the working models for his famous *Seated Lincoln* (1922) for the Lincoln Memorial in Washington, DC. The models remain in the studio along with other plaster casts. During the summer months the grounds are used to exhibit sculpture.

Naumkeag Museum and Gardens is a graceful 1885 mansion built for Joseph H. Choate, US ambassador to Britain and one of the era's leading attorneys. The 26-room house is appointed with its original furnishings and an art collection that spans three centuries. Of note is the exhibit of Chinese porcelains. The grounds are a work of art also with their formal gardens.

Mission House
19 Main St. *Tel (413) 298-3239.*
Memorial Day–Columbus Day: 10am–5pm daily.

Norman Rockwell Museum
Rte 183. *Tel (413) 298-4100.* *May–Oct: 10am–5pm daily; Nov–Apr: 10am–4pm Mon–Fri, 10am–5pm Sat–Sun.* Jan 1, Thanksgiving, Dec 25.
www.nrm.org

Chesterwood
4 Williamsville Rd. *Tel (413) 298-3579.* *May–Oct: 10am–5pm daily.* partial. www.chesterwood.org

Naumkeag Museum and Gardens
Prospect Hill. *Tel (413) 298-3239.* *Memorial Day–Columbus Day:* 10am–5pm daily.

THE ARTS IN THE BERKSHIRES

The Berkshires region has one of America's richest summer menus of performing arts. As well as Boston Symphony Orchestra concerts at Tanglewood, Aston Magna presents baroque concerts at several locations. The Berkshire Choral Festival is held in Sheffield, and the Barrington Stage Company performs in Pittsfield. The Jacob's Pillow Dance Festival in Becket, the oldest such event in the nation, presents leading international companies. The Berkshire Theater Festival and the Williamstown Theater Festival are among the oldest and most respected summer theaters in the nation. Shakespeare & Company presents acclaimed productions of the Bard's works, as well as thought-provoking new plays.

Relaxed setting for the Tanglewood summer concert series

RHODE ISLAND

With an area of just over 1,200 sq miles (3,100 sq km), Rhode Island is the smallest of the 50 states. However, its historic towns, unspoiled wilderness areas, and a pristine shoreline dotted with inlets and tranquil harbors make the place a lively and easily explored holiday destination.

For such a small state, "Little Rhody" was founded on big ideals. Driven from the Massachusetts Bay colony in 1636 for his outspoken beliefs on religious freedom, clergyman Roger Williams (1604–83) established a settlement on the banks of Narragansett Bay. He called the town Providence and founded it upon the tenets of freedom of speech and religious tolerance – principles that would be formally introduced in the First Amendment to the US Constitution in 1781. This forward-thinking spirit made Rhode Island the site of America's first synagogue and Baptist church and some of the nation's earliest libraries, public schools, and colleges. In May 1776 Rhode Island followed the lead of New Hampshire and formally declared its independence from British rule.

Although its 400-mile (645-km) shoreline is considered small in comparison to those of neighboring states, Rhode Island has earned its nickname, the Ocean State. In the 17th century, its port towns were primary players in the burgeoning maritime trade with the West Indies. Today some 120 public beaches provide opportunities for swimming, scuba diving, boating, windsurfing, and fishing. Pleasure craft can be seen skimming the waters of Narragansett Bay. Home to the America's Cup yacht races between 1930–85, Newport is well known as one of the world's great yachting centers. But not all of Rhode Island's allure is found on the waterfront. More than 50 percent of the state is covered in woodland. The 28 state parks are ideal for outdoor activities; three allow camping.

Fishing at dusk on beautiful Narragansett Bay

◁ The elegant Linden Place mansion in Bristol *(see p173)*

Exploring Rhode Island

Not an island at all, the state of Rhode Island does, however, contain dozens of islets and peninsulas along the Atlantic coastline. They dot Narragansett Bay, which takes a huge bite out of the eastern portion of the state. Craggy cliffs, grass-covered bluffs, and golden sand beaches mark the shoreline of the Ocean State, which offers an abundance of opportunities for fishing, swimming, boating, surfing, and other aquatic activities. Inland numerous lakes, reservoirs, and swamps (in South County) maintain the maritime atmosphere. Most activity in Rhode Island centers around its two major cities, Providence *(see pp174–7)* and Newport *(see pp182–7)*, but the smaller roads across the western part of the state are perfect for tranquil country drives.

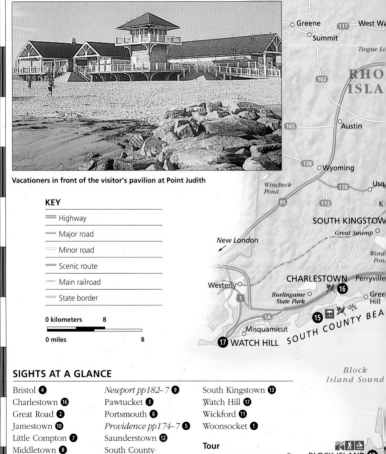

Vacationers in front of the visitor's pavilion at Point Judith

KEY

▬	Highway
—	Major road
⋯	Minor road
—	Scenic route
⊢	Main railroad
—	State border

0 kilometers   8

0 miles   8

SIGHTS AT A GLANCE

Bristol ❹	*Newport pp182–7* ❾	South Kingstown ⓭
Charlestown ⓰	Pawtucket ❸	Watch Hill ⓱
Great Road ❷	Portsmouth ❻	Wickford ⓫
Jamestown ❿	*Providence pp174–7* ❺	Woonsocket ❶
Little Compton ❼	Saunderstown ⓬	
Middletown ❽	South County	**Tour**
Narragansett ⓮	Beaches ⓯	Block Island *pp192–3* ⓲

WOONSOCKET
Diamond Hill
114
295
Lime Rock
Boston
THE GREAT
2 ROAD
aleysville
95
3 PAWTUCKET
146
North
Providence
VIDENCE **5**
East
Providence
195
ton
Roger Williams
Park and Zoo
114
Barrington
95
Warren
Warwick
117
East
Greenwick
Colt
State Park
Fall River
4 BRISTOL
North Tiverton
24
Stafford
Pond
Mount View
1
Tiverton
177
Prudence
Island
b's
Shores
stle
Acres
6 PORTSMOUTH
11 WICKFORD
114
179
Rhode
Island
Adamsville
1A
77
SAUNDERSTOWN
8 MIDDLETOWN
12
138
JAMESTOWN **10**
9 NEWPORT
7
LITTLE
COMPTON
useum of
rimitive Art
nd Culture
Fort Adams
State Park
The Breakers
Sakonnet
kefield
Rhode
Island Sound
14 NARRAGANSETT
1A

oint Judith

Central Providence, notable for its blend of the historic and modern

GETTING AROUND

Highway 146 follows the Blackstone River Valley south to Providence where it connects with Interstate 95, forming the major north-south artery in the state. For scenery, travelers should stay on Route 1 as it hugs Narragansett Bay and Block Island Sound. An alternative route is 114, which island-hops down the eastern region of the state through Bristol *(see pp172–3)* to Newport.

Amtrak operates rail lines running from Boston through Providence and down as far as Westerly.

Rhode Island Public Transit Authority (RIPTA) provides bus services throughout most of the state, with hourly service between Providence and Newport and a summer service to several South County beaches *(see pp190–91).*

Year-round ferry services operated by RIPTA are offered from Providence to Newport. Ferries to Block Island also run year-round and depart from Point Judith *(see pp190–91).*

SEE ALSO

• *Where to Stay* pp314–16

• *Where to Eat* pp343–5

Yachts by the score in the harbour at Newport

Classroom display at the Museum of Work and Culture, Woonsocket

Woonsocket ❶

🏃 44,000. ℹ️ 175 Main St, Pawtucket (401) 724-2200 or (800) 454-2882. **www.**tourblackstone.com

A major manufacturing center located on the busy Blackstone River, Woonsocket was transformed from a relatively small village to a booming mill town by the development of the local textile industry in the 19th and early 20th centuries. Although the textile industry declined after World War II, the city remains one of the major manufacturing hubs.

The **Museum of Work and Culture** focuses on the impact of the Industrial Revolution on the region. The day-to-day lives of the factory owners, managers, and immigrant workers are examined and explained with the help of a re-created 1934 union hall, hands-on displays, models, and multimedia exhibits.

🏛 **Museum of Work and Culture**
42 S Main St. **Tel** (401) 769-9675.
🕘 9:30am–4pm Tue–Fri, 10am–5pm Sat, 1–4pm Sun. 🎟 ♿

The Great Road ❷

ℹ️ (401) 724-2200.
www.tourblackstone.com

An often overlooked gem, the stretch of Great Road (Route 123) between Saylesville and Lime Rock follows the course of the Moshassuck River for

Eleazer Arnold House near Lincoln on the Great Road

0.6 mile (1 km) and yields eight historically significant buildings. Four of these buildings are open by appointment and include the 1680 **Eleazer Arnold House** and the 1704 **Friends Meetinghouse**, New England's oldest Quaker

meeting house in continuous use. Constructed in 1807 as a toll station and later serving as a hotel, **North Gate**, just off the Great Road, now contains a small museum room decked out with early 18th-century furniture. Farther along the road, **Hannaway Blacksmith Shop** is a one-story, 19th-century structure restored for blacksmith demonstrations and special events.

🏚 **Eleazer Arnold House**
487 Great Rd. **Tel** (401) 295-1030.
🕘 Jun–mid-Oct. 🎟 obligatory; call for appt.

🏚 **Friends Meetinghouse**
374 Great Rd. **Tel** (401) 725-2847.
🎟 obligatory; call for appt.

🏚 **North Gate**
Rte 246. **Tel** (401) 725-2847.
🎟 obligatory; call for appt.

🏚 **Hannaway Blacksmith Shop**
671 Great Rd. **Tel** (401) 333-1100.
🎟 obligatory; call for appt.

Pawtucket ❸

🏃 73,000. ℹ️ 175 Main St (401) 724-2200.

This bustling industrial city, built on hills sliced by the Blackstone, Moshassuck, and Ten Mile rivers is generally acknowledged to be the birthplace of America's Industrial Revolution. It was here in 1793 that mechanical engineer Samuel Slater (1768–1835) built the country's first water-powered cotton-spinning mill.

A major historic landmark, the **Slater Mill Living History Museum** includes the restored Slater Mill and the 1810 Wilkinson Mill, complete with an authentic 19th-century machine shop and the only 8-ton (7-tonne) waterwheel in

Pawtucket's Slater Mill Living History Museum, home of the first water-powered cotton-spinning mill in the US

For hotels and restaurants in this region see pp314–16 and pp343–5

McCoy Stadium, playing field of the Pawtucket Red Sox baseball team

the US. Also on the site, the 1758 Sylvanus Brown House is furnished with the machinery and personal effects of Sylvanus Brown, a millwright and pattern-maker.

At the 200-acre (81-ha) **Slater Memorial Park** on the Ten Mile River, there are hiking trails, paddleboats, tennis courts, picnic areas, sunken gardens, and a seasonal 1895 Looff carousel. The park is also home to the city's oldest dwelling, the 1685 **Daggett House**, which contains exhibits of 17th-century furnishings and antiques.

The **Pawtucket Red Sox** baseball team plays games at McCoy Stadium. This minor league team has players who, once they have honed their skills, may move on to play for the Boston Red Sox.

Pawtucket Red Sox logo

🏛 Slater Mill Living History Museum
Roosevelt & Slater Aves. **Tel** (401) 725-8638. ☐ Mar–Apr: 11am–3pm Sat & Sun; May–Oct: 10am–4pm Tue–Sun; Nov–Feb: by appt. 📷 🎫 ♿

♣ Slater Memorial Park
Newport Ave. **Tel** (401) 728-0500 ext 252. ☐ year-round: 8:30am–dusk daily. ♿

🏛 Daggett House
Slater Park off Rte 1A. **Tel** (401) 724-5748. 📷 obligatory; call for appt. 📷

Pawtucket Red Sox
McCoy Stadium, Columbus Ave. **Tel** (401) 724-7300. ☐ Apr–early Sep; call for schedule. 📷 ♿
www.pawsox.com

Bristol ❹

🚹 21,650. 🛈 16 Cutler St, Warren (401) 245-0750.
www.eastbaychamberri.org

Bristol blossomed in the late 18th century when its status as a major commercial, fishing, whaling, and shipbuilding center made it the nation's fourth-busiest port. The many elegant Federal and Victorian mansions lining Hope, High, and Thames streets attest to those prosperous days. One such fine home is the 1810 **Linden Place**, where scenes from *The Great Gatsby* (1974) were filmed. The Federal-style mansion was built by General George DeWolf (1772–1844) with money he had made from his sugar plantations in Cuba and the slave trade. Regular concerts and tours are offered.

The trappings of wealth are also in evidence at **Blithewold Mansion and Gardens**. Built in 1894 for Pennsylvania coal baron Augustus Van Wickle (1856–98), the mansion was rebuilt in 1907. It has many gardens and trees from the Far East. The grounds offer spectacular views of Narragansett Bay (*see p169*).

Boating has always been popular with the rich and famous, and Bristol's history as the producer of America's greatest yachts is traced at the **Herreshoff Marine Museum/America's Cup Hall of Fame**.

The museum is located on Narragansett Bay, at the site of the legendary Herreshoff Manufacturing Company, which built yachts for eight America's Cup races. Photos, models, and restored ships celebrate the golden age of yachting. The museum also operates a sailing school for adults and children, and hosts classic yacht regattas.

Colt State Park, a 460-acre (186-ha) shoreline park features a 3-mile (5-km) shoreline drive along Narragansett Bay, a bicycle trail, many picnic areas, and playing fields. Also on the park grounds is the **Coggeshall Farm Museum**, a restored 1790s coastal farm with a barn, blacksmith shop, and heirloom breeds of domesticated animals. Cyclists and inline skaters can tour the picturesque East Bay Bike Path, leading some 14.5 miles (23 km) from Bristol to Providence along the coast-hugging route of an old railroad line.

The peaceful rural idyll of Coggeshall Farm Museum

🏛 Linden Place
500 Hope St. **Tel** (401) 253-0390. ☐ May–Columbus Day: 10am–4pm Thu–Sat (Sun: call first). 📷 🎫 ♿

🏛 Blithewold Mansion
101 Ferry Rd. **Tel** (401) 253-2707. **Mansion** ☐ mid-Apr–mid-Oct: 10am–4pm Wed–Sun; call for winter hours. ● public hols. **Grounds** ☐ 10am–5pm daily. 🎫 ♿

🏛 Herreshoff Marine Museum/America's Cup Hall of Fame
1 Burnside St. **Tel** (401) 253-5000. ☐ May–Oct: 10am–5pm daily. 📷 🎫 ♿

♣ Colt State Park
Rte 114. **Tel** (401) 253-7482. ☐ daily. ♿

🏛 Coggeshall Farm Museum
Poppasquash Rd off Rte 114. **Tel** (401) 253-9062. ☐ 10am–4pm Tue–Sun. 📷 🎫 **www**. coggeshallfarm.org

Providence ❺

First Unitarian Church bell

Sandwiched between Boston and New York on busy I-95, Providence is often overlooked by hurried travelers. This is a pity, since the city is blessed with a rich history well worth exploring. Perched on seven hills, Providence started life as a farming community before taking advantage of its location on the Seekonk River to develop into a flourishing seaport in the 17th century. The city then evolved into a hub of industry in the 19th century, with immigrants from Europe pouring in to work in the burgeoning textile mills.

Interior courtyard at Rhode Island School of Design's Museum of Art

🏛 **RISD Museum of Art**
224 Benefit St. *Tel* (401) 454-6500.
☐ *year-round: 10am–5pm Tue–Sun, 10am–9pm 3rd Thu of month.* ●
public hols. 🔲 🔲 www.risd.edu

🏛 **Providence Athenaeum**
251 Benefit St. *Tel* (401) 421-6970.
☐ *year-round: 9am–7pm Mon–Thu, 9am–5pm Fri–Sat, 1–5pm Sun.*
● *summer: Sat pm, Sun.*
www.providenceathenaeum.org

🏛 **First Unitarian Church**
310 Benefit St. *Tel* (401) 421-7970.
☐ *daily.* 🔲 🔲 10:30am Sun.

Stately buildings along Benefit Street's Mile of History

Exploring Providence

Providence is bisected by the Providence River, with the Downtown district (*see pp176–7*) on the west bank and College Hill to the east. Walking through College Hill, visitors will pass a large number of 18th-century buildings, including the redbrick colonial Market House, built along the waterway in the 1770s and now part of Rhode Island School of Design (RISD).

🏛 Benefit Street's Mile of History

Benefit St. *Tel* (401) 274-1636.
Along Benefit Street's Mile of History there are more than 100 houses ranging in style from Colonial and Federal to Greek Revival and Victorian. This lovely, tree-lined street passes RISD's **Museum of Art**, which houses a small but comprehensive collection of artworks from Ancient Egyptian to contemporary American. Also on Benefit Street is the 1838 Greek

Revival **Providence Athenaeum**. This is where author Edgar Allen Poe (1809–49) courted Sarah Whitman, the woman who was the inspiration for his poem *Annabel Lee* (1849). The library, one of the oldest in America, has a collection dating back to 1753. Other architectural gems include the **First Unitarian Church**, which possesses a 2,500-lb (1,350-kg) bell, the largest ever cast by silversmith and Revolutionary War hero Paul Revere (*see p120*).

| 0 meters | 250 |
| 0 yards | 250 |

Key to Symbols *see back flap*

Culinary Archives and Museum

Roger Williams Park and Zoo, Johnson and Wales University

Airport
12 miles (19 km) ✈

🏛 First Baptist Church in America

75 N Main St. **Tel** *(401) 454-3418.* 🕐 *call for hours.* 🎫 ♿ ✝ *11am Sun.*
Founded in 1638 by Roger Williams and built in 1774–5, the First Baptist Church in America is noted for its Ionic columns, intricately carved wood interior, and large Waterford crystal chandelier.

🏛 Governor Stephen Hopkins House

15 Hopkins St. **Tel** *(401) 421-0694.* 🕐 *May–Oct: Fri–Sat.* 👥 🎫 *obligatory.*
The 1707 **Governor Stephen Hopkins House** belonged to one of Rhode Island's two signatories to the Declaration of Independence, and contains fine 18th-century furnishings.

Statue on Brown University campus

🏛 Brown University

45 Prospect St. **Tel** *(401) 863-1000.* 🕐 *call for hours.* 🎫 ♿ 🛍 📖
Founded in 1764, Brown is the seventh-oldest college in the US and one of the prestigious Ivy League schools *(see pp28–9)*. The campus, a rich blend of Gothic and Beaux Arts styles, is a National Historic Landmark. The John Hay Library has an eclectic collection that includes artifacts and memorabilia relating to President Abraham Lincoln (1809–65), 5,000 toy soldiers and miniatures, and vintage sheet music. Other buildings of note include University Hall, where French and colonial troops were quartered during the American Revolution; Manning Hall, which houses the University Chapel; the John Carter Brown Library, with its fascinating collection of Americana; and the List Art Center, a striking building designed by Philip Johnson (b.1906) and featuring classical and contemporary art.

🏛 John Brown House

52 Power St. **Tel** *(401) 273-7507.* 🕐 *Jan–Mar: 10:30am–3pm Fri–Sat; Apr–Dec: 1:30–3pm Tue–Fri, 10:30am–3pm Sat.* ● *public hols.* 👥 🎫 🛍
This Georgian mansion was built in 1786 for John Brown (1736–1803) and designed by his brother Joseph (1733–85). A successful merchant and shipowner, John played a lead role in the burning of the British customs ship *Gaspee* in a pre-Revolutionary War raid in 1772. The John Brown House was the most lavish of its era, introducing Providence to many new architectural elements, including the projecting entrance, Doric portico, and the Palladian window above it. There are Neoclassical pediments over paired doorways, a grand staircase with twisted balusters, ornate plaster ornamented ceilings, and intricate detailing inside arches over windows and mantels.

Sparing no expense, Brown ordered wallpapers from France and furniture from famed cabinetmakers Townsend and Goddard. The 12-room house has been impeccably restored and is a repository for some of the finest furniture and antiques of that period.

VISITORS' CHECKLIST

👪 *174,000.* ✈ *TF Green State Airport, Warwick, 12 miles (19 km) S.* 🚆 *Providence Station, 100 Gaspee St.* 🚌 *1 Bonanza Way.* ⛴ *Point St (to Newport).* ℹ *1 Sabin St (401) 751-1177 or (800) 233-1636.* 🎉 *Festival of Historic Houses (Jun–Dec); International Film Festival (Aug).*
www.pwcvb.com

The 1786 John Brown House, an excellent example of Georgian architecture

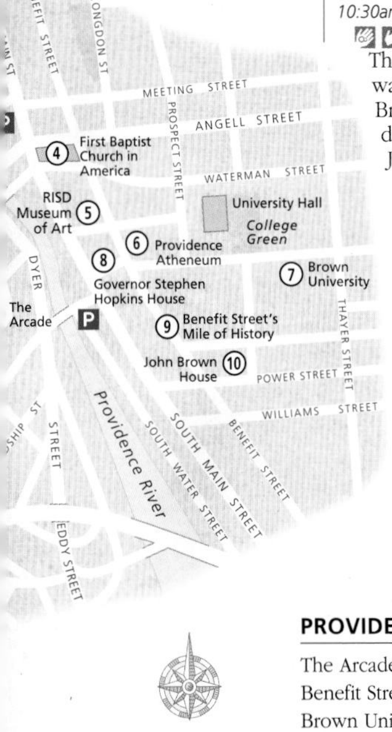
Roger Williams
National Memorial
BENEFIT STREET
CONGDON ST
MEETING STREET
ANGELL STREET
PROSPECT STREET
4 First Baptist Church in America
WATERMAN STREET
RISD Museum of Art 5
University Hall
College Green
6 Providence Atheneum
8 Governor Stephen Hopkins House
7 Brown University
DYER
The Arcade
P
9 Benefit Street's Mile of History
THAYER STREET
John Brown House 10
POWER STREET
WILLIAMS STREET
Providence River
SOUTH WATER STREET
SOUTH MAIN STREET
BENEFIT STREET
EDDY STREET

PROVIDENCE CITY CENTER

The Arcade ③
Benefit Street's Mile of History ⑨
Brown University ⑦
First Baptist Church in America ④
Governor Stephen Hopkins House ⑧
John Brown House ⑩
Providence Athenaeum ⑥
Rhode Island State House ①
RISD Museum of Art ⑤
Waterplace Park ②

Downtown Providence

Downtown Providence, to the west of the Providence River, has undergone several renewal phases. In all, $1 billion has been pumped into the rejuvenation project since 1983. Keeping a balance with the old and the new, Providence municipal officials have managed to clean out previously blighted areas by restoring historic buildings, installing more green spaces, and building pedestrian malls and markets. The reclaimed waterfront and developing arts and entertainment district have helped inject new vitality into the city's core. Visitors are best served by exploring on foot so they are free to poke into the numerous shops, cafés, and restaurants.

Exploring Downtown Providence
Providence's rebirth is more than just physical; it is also cultural. The Trinity Repertory Company on Washington Street is home to one of the best theater groups in the country and has performances year-round. Just a block away, the Providence Performing Arts Center, a 1928 movie palace, features Broadway shows, concerts, entertainment for children, and big-screen films, with free lunchtime organ recitals in the spring and fall.

The Trinity Repertory Company, housed in a 1917 historic theater

⚜ Waterplace Park and Riverwalk
Memorial Blvd. **Tel** *(401) 751-1177.*
◯ *dawn–dusk daily.*
One of the newest and brightest additions to the downtown area is this 4-acre (1.6-ha) walkway at the junction of the Moshassuck, Providence, and Woonasquatucket rivers. Visitors can stroll the park's cobblestone paths, float under footbridges

in rented kayaks, canoes, or gondolas, or enjoy the free concerts and the Waterfire extravaganza during the summer months.

🏛 The Arcade
65 Weybosset St. **Tel** *(401) 598-1199.* ◉ *for renovation.* ♿ 🚻 🎦
Known as the "Temple of Trade," this 1828 Greek Revival building has the distinction of being the first indoor shopping mall in the US. The massive, three-story stone complex covers an entire block in Providence's old financial district and has been acclaimed as "one of the three finest commercial buildings in 19th-century America" by New York's Metropolitan Museum of Art. Similar columns on the Westminster entrance match the six 22-ft- (6.7-m-) high Ionic granite columns on Weybosset. Inside a skylight extends the entire length of the building, providing light even on rainy days. Restored in 1980, the marketplace is currently undergoing another restoration so is not open to visitors.

⛩ Federal Hill
Visitors will know they are in Little Italy once they pass through Federal Hill's impressive arched gateway, decorated with a traditional bronze pine nut. A stripe down the center of the street – in the colors of the Italian flag – confirms that this lively neighborhood in the Federal Hill district is truly Italian in spirit. Bordered by Federal

and Broadway streets and Atwells Avenue, the area is marked by Italian groceries, restaurants, bakeries, import shops, and a pleasant old-world plaza.

The Waterfire show, held every summer at Waterplace Park

⛪ Rhode Island State House
82 Smith St. **Tel** *(401) 222-3983.*
◯ *for tours 9am, 10am & 11am Mon–Fri.* ◉ *public hols.* 🎦 *self-guided, others by appt.* ♿ 🏠 🖥
Dominating the city landscape, this imposing building was constructed in 1904 by the prominent New York firm McKim, Mead, & White. The white Georgian marble dome is one of the largest self-supported domes in the world. A bronze statue called *Independent Man*, a longtime symbol of Rhode Island's free spirit, tops the magnificent dome. Among the displays in the statehouse are a full-length portrait of President George Washington (1732–99) by Gilbert Stuart (1755–1828), a portrait of Providence resident and Civil War General Ambrose Burnside (1824–81)

Rhode Island State House, with its white marble dome

ROGER WILLIAMS (1603–1683)

More than an exponent of religious freedom, Roger Williams was also a friend and champion of the area's indigenous inhabitants. He defied the strict restraints of the Massachusetts Bay Colony, believing that all people should be free to worship as they liked without state interference. Banished from Massachusetts for his outspoken views, he established his own colony of Rhode Island and Providence Plantations, obtaining the land from the Narragansett Indians so that "no man should be molested for his conscience sake." It became the country's first experiment in religious liberty.

by Emanuel Leutze (1816–68), and the original state charter of 1663.

🦌 Roger Williams Park and Zoo

1000 Elmwood Ave. *Tel (401) 785-3510.* 🚉 Kennedy Plaza. **Park** ⬜ dawn to dusk daily. **Zoo** ⬜ 9am–4pm daily. ⬛ Dec 25. 🅿️ zoo. 🎫 ♿ 🏠 🍴 www. rogerwilliamsparkzoo.org

In 1871 Betsey Williams, a direct descendant of Roger Williams, donated 102 acres (41 ha) of prime real estate to the city for use as parkland. Since that time, another 320 acres (130 ha) of property have been added to the site. Once farmland, the park now holds gardens and greenhouses, ponds, a lake with paddleboats and rowboats for rent, jogging and

Historic cookbooks from the Culinary Archives and Museum

cycling paths, and a tennis center. Children especially love the carousel and train, the planetarium, and the Museum of Natural History.

Without a doubt, the highlight of the park is the zoo, which has more than 900 animals and 130 species. Dating back to 1872, the zoo is one of the oldest in the

nation, and is in the midst of an ambitious renovation program. Its Marco Polo Trail, with camels, snow leopards, and Asian black bears, was enhanced with the addition of endangered red pandas, while a raised viewing deck makes it easier to observe the elephants and giraffes in the Plains of Africa exhibit.

🏛 Culinary Arts Museum at Johnson & Wales University

315 Harborside Blvd. *Tel (401) 598-2805.* ⬜ 10am–5pm Tue–Sun. ⬛ Dec 25–Jan 1, public hols. 🅿️ 🎫 www.culinary.org

This one-of-a-kind museum contains half a million items relating to the culinary arts – hardly surprising since Johnson & Wales University is devoted to training chefs. The museum was created in 1979, when Chicago chef Louis Szathmary donated his vast collection of culinary oddities, including a cannibal eating bowl from Fiji and rings worn by bakers that had been excavated at Pompeii. Exhibits include diners that used to be towed from place to place and stoves and ranges.

Roger Williams Park and Zoo, a highlight of downtown Providence

Boats moored at the Sakonnet Wharf near Little Compton

Portsmouth ❻

🏛 *16,850.* ℹ *23 America's Cup Ave, Newport (401) 845-9123 or (800) 976-5122.* **www**.gonewport.com

Portsmouth figures greatly in Rhode Island history. It was the second settlement in the old colony, founded in 1638 just two years after Providence. The town was also the site of the 1778 Battle of Rhode Island, the only major land battle fought in the state during the American Revolution. Bad weather and fierce British resistance forced the US troops to retreat. With the British in hot pursuit, only the courage of the American rear guard enabled most of

Delightful denizens of the Green Animals Topiary Garden

the soldiers to escape to the sanctuary of Butts Hill Fort. Today some of the fort's redoubts are still visible from Sprague Street, where plaques recount the battle.
    The **Green Animals Topiary Garden** is a more whimsical attraction. Located on a Victorian estate, this lighthearted garden is inhabited by a wild array of topiary creations. In all, some 80 animal shapes – including elephants, camels, giraffes, bears, birds, even a dinosaur – have been trimmed and sculpted from a selection of yew, English boxwood, and California privet. Elsewhere on the grounds, formal flower gardens, a rose arbor, and a museum with an extensive collection of Victorian-era toys delight even the very youngest visitors.

    🌑 **Green Animals Topiary Garden**
    Cory's Lane. **Tel** *(401) 847-1000.* ☐ *May–Oct: 10am–5pm daily.* 🏛

Little Compton ❼

🏛 *3,350.* ℹ *23 America's Cup Ave, Newport (401) 845-9123 or (800) 976-5122.*

Residents of Little Compton relish their isolated nook at the end of a peninsula that borders Massachusetts with good reason: Little Compton is one of the most charming villages in the entire state, protected from the outside world by the surrounding farmlands and woods.
    The white-steepled United Congregational Church stands over Little Compton Commons. Beside the church lies the old Commons Burial Ground,

with the gravesite of Elizabeth Padobie (c.1623–1717). The daughter of *Mayflower* Pilgrims Priscilla and John Alden, Padobie was the first white woman born in New England. The 1680 **Wilbor House** was home to eight generations of the Wilbor family. The house is furnished with period pieces and antique household items. Elsewhere on the grounds visitors can explore a one-room schoolhouse and artist's studio. An 1860 barn displays old farm tools, sleighs, a one-horse shay, oxcart, and buggies.
    Nearby **Sakonnet Vineyards** is the largest winery in New England. There are free daily wine tastings and guided tours. Beyond the vineyard on Route 77 is Sakonnet Wharf, where the curious can watch fishermen arrive with their catches.

Sakonnet Vineyards in Little Compton

◁ **Old Harbor, Block Island**

🏛 **Wilbor House**
548 W Main Rd. *Tel (401) 635-4035.*
🗓 *call for hours.* ♿

🍷 **Sakonnet Vineyards**
162 W Main Rd. *Tel (401) 635-
8486.* 🗓 *Jun–Sep: 10am–6pm daily,
Oct–Jan & Apr–May: 11am–5pm
daily; Feb–Mar: Thu–Sun only.* 🗓
call for schedule. ♿ **www**.
sakonnetwine.com

Environs
Four miles (6 km) northeast is
Adamsville. **Gray's Store** dates
back to 1788 and is the oldest
general store in the country.
It contains the first post office
(1804) in the area and still
has its original soda fountain,
candy and tobacco cases,
and ice chest.

Gray's Store, built in 1788, on
Main Street in Adamsville

🏛 **Gray's Store**
4 Main St. *Tel (401) 635-4566.*
🗓 *9am–5pm Mon–Sat, noon–4pm
Sun (Nov–Apr: 9am–5pm Thu–Sat,
noon–4pm Sun).*

Middletown **8**

🏃 19,950. 🛈 *23 America's Cup
Ave, Newport (401) 845-9123 or
(800) 976-5122.*

Nestled between Newport
(see pp182–7) and Portsmouth
on Aquidneck Island,

Middletown's popular Third Beach

Middletown is known
primarily for its two popular
beaches. **Third Beach** is
located on the Sakonnet River
and is outfitted with a boat
ramp. A steady wind and
relatively calm water make
the beach a favorite among
windsurfers and families
with young children.
 Third Beach runs into the
largest and most
beautiful beach
on the island,
Sachuest, or
Second Beach,
is widely con-
sidered one of
the best places to
surf in southern New
England. This spacious
strand is rippled with
sand dunes and
equipped with campgrounds.
Purgatory Chasm, a narrow
cleft in the rock ledges on the
east side of Easton Point,
provides a scenic outlook
over both the beach and 50-ft-
(15-m-) high Hanging Rock.
 Second Beach has yet
another advantage; it is adjacent to the **Norman Bird**

Inhabitant of
Newport
Butterfly Farm

Sanctuary, a 450-acre
(182-ha) wildlife area with
7 miles (11 km) of walking
trails that are ideal for birding.
Some 250 species have been
sighted at this sanctuary,
including herons, egrets,
woodcocks, thrashers, ducks,
and swans. The refuge is
home to numerous four-
legged animals, such as
rabbits and red
foxes. A small
natural history
museum is also
located on the
site, and during
the winter
months the
sanctuary trails are
used by cross-
country skiers.
 Amateur entomolo-
gists will enjoy paying a visit
to the **Newport Butterfly
Farm** in nearby Tiverton.
Colorful species from all
around the world can be
found in a screened-in greenhouse. Visitors are free to walk
among the flowers and observe
the beautiful insects as they
feed on nectar and lay eggs.

🏖 **Third Beach**
Third Beach Rd. *Tel (401) 849-2822.*
🗓 *Memorial Day–Labor Day: life-
guards on duty 9am–5pm daily.* ♿

🏖 **Second Beach**
Third Beach Rd. *Tel (401) 849-2822.*
🗓 *Memorial Day–Labor Day: life-
guards on duty 8am–6pm daily.* ♿

🦋 **Norman Bird
Sanctuary**
583 Third Beach Rd. *Tel (401) 846-
2577.* 🗓 *year-round: 9am–5pm daily.*
⬤ *Thanksgiving & Dec 25.* ♿ 🅿

🦋 **Newport Butterfly Farm**
409 Bulgarmarsh Rd, Tiverton. *Tel
(401) 849-9519.* 🗓 *Jun–Aug: call for
opening hours.* ♿

Waterfowl in Middletown's Norman Bird Sanctuary

For hotels and restaurants in this region see pp314–16 and pp343–5

Newport ❾

A center of trade, culture, wealth, and military activity for more than 300 years, Newport is a true sightseeing mecca. Historical firsts abound in this small city. America's first naval college and synagogue are here, as are the oldest library in the country and one of the oldest continuously operating taverns. Any visit to the city should include a tour of the mansions from the Gilded Age of the late 19th century, when the rich and famous flocked here each summer to beat New York's heat. These summer "cottage" retreats of the country's wealthiest families, the Vanderbilts and Astors among them, are some of America's grandest private homes.

Public grass courts at the International Tennis Hall of Fame

Advertisement for carved whalebone, or whale ivory

Exploring Newport

Like Italy, Newport has a distinctly boot-shaped outline. The city's famous mansions are located on the southeastern side, or the heel of the boot. Newport's harborfront is to the west, where the laces would be. The city's most interesting streets, America's Cup Avenue and Thames Street, are here. Pedestrians will find restaurants, shops, and colonial buildings, including the 1726 **Trinity Church**.

🏛 Brick Market Museum and Shop

127 Thames St. **Tel** (401) 841-8770. ◐ 10am–5pm daily. 🎫 Ⓟ
The Brick Market, a commercial hub during the 18th century, is now a museum that provides an excellent introduction to the city's history and architecture. Self-guided tours include an audiovisual exploration of the downtown in a 19th-century omnibus.

✡ Touro Synagogue

85 Touro St. **Tel** (401) 847-4794. ◐ call for times. ✡ Shabbat and all Jewish hols. Ⓟ Ⓟ
America's oldest synagogue, Touro was erected in 1763 by Sephardic Jews who had fled Spain and Portugal in search of religious tolerance. Designed by architect Peter Harrison (1716–75), it is

considered one of the country's finest examples of 18th-century architecture. Services still follow the Sephardic rituals of its founders.

Redwood Library and Athenaeum's stately interior

⚷ Redwood Library and Athenaeum

50 Bellevue Ave. **Tel** (401) 847-0292. ◐ 9:30am–5:30pm Mon & Fri–Sat, 9:30am–8pm Tue–Thu, 1pm–5pm Sun. ◉ public hols. 🎫 ⚷
www.redwoodlibrary.org
Completed in 1750, the Redwood is the oldest continuously operating library in America and is one of the country's earliest examples of temple-form buildings. It underwent renovation in 2005. The library's museum collections contain colonial portraits, sculpture, and furniture.

🏛 International Tennis Hall of Fame

194 Bellevue Ave. **Tel** (401) 849-3990. ◐ 9:30am–5pm daily. ◉ Thanksgiving & Dec 25. 🎾 courts available to public. 🎫 ⚷ Ⓟ
www.tennisfame.com
The hall is housed in the Newport Casino, once a private club for Newport's elite. Founded in 1880, the club installed grass tennis courts to introduce its members to the latest sports rage. The first US National Lawn Tennis Championship, later known as the US Open, was held here in 1881. Today the hall displays everything from antique rackets to the "comeback" outfit worn by Monica Seles (b.1972). The grass courts are the only ones in the US open to the public.

🥾 Cliff Walk

Begins at Memorial Blvd. **Tel** (401) 845-9123. ◐ year-round: dawn–dusk daily. 🎫
This 3.5-mile (5.5-km) walk along Newport's rugged cliffs offers some of the best views of the Gilded-Age mansions. Local fishermen preserved public access to the trail by going to court when wealthy mansion-owners tried to have it closed. The walk was designated a National Recreation Trail in 1975. The Forty Steps, each step named for someone lost at sea, lead to the ocean.

The breathtaking Cliff Walk, popular with residents as well as visitors

International Yacht Restoration School

449 Thames St. **Tel** (401) 848-5777. 9am–5pm Mon–Sat (longer summer hours). www.iyrs.org

Founded in 1993, this small school provides a fascinating look at yacht restoration. Visitors can observe students from the mezzanine, and tour the waterfront campus to see the *Coronet*, built in 1885. The world's oldest grand yacht is currently undergoing restoration by the school.

Students at work at International Yacht Restoration School

Fort Adams State Park

Harrison Ave. **Tel** (401) 847-2400. sunrise to sunset daily. **Museum of Yachting Tel** (401) 847-1018. Jun–Oct: 10am–6pm Wed–Mon.

Fort Adams is one of the largest military forts in the country. Completed in 1857 at a cost of $3 million, it was

Fort Adams, centerpiece of Fort Adams State Park

designed to house 2,400 troops. The property surrounding the fort is equipped with facilities for swimming, soccer, rugby, and picnicking. Each year Newport's world-famous music festivals *(see p33)* are held here.

The park also is home to the Museum of Yachting, which chronicles Newport's famed yachting history. One of the museum's highlights is its collection of classic luxury boats in its outdoor basin.

Newport Mansions

Preservation Society of Newport County, 424 Bellevue Ave. **Tel** (401) 847-1000. Apr–Dec: 10am–5pm daily; winter: call for hours. Dec 24 & 25. obligatory. partial.

Built between 1748 and 1902, 12 of these summer "cottages," most of them along Bellevue Avenue, are open for guided tours. Modeled on European palaces and decorated with

the finest artworks, the mansions were used for only 10 weeks of the year. The Breakers *(see pp186–7)* is one of the finest examples.

Naval War College Museum

686 Cushing Rd. **Tel** (401) 841-4052. 10am–4:30pm Mon–Fri (Jun–Sep: also noon–4:30pm Sat–Sun).

This site preserves the history, art, and science of naval warfare and the heritage of Narragansett Bay. Founded in 1885, the college is the oldest naval institute of higher learning in the world, where education and research is carried out for the U.S. Navy. The museum houses ship models and maritime art. Due to increased security, visitors must call in advance.

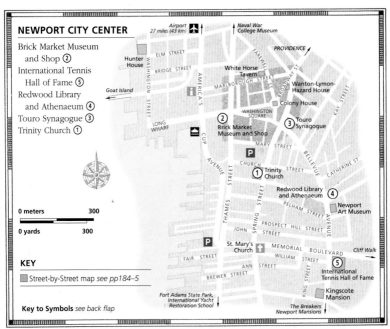

NEWPORT CITY CENTER

Brick Market Museum and Shop ②
International Tennis Hall of Fame ⑤
Redwood Library and Athenaeum ④
Touro Synagogue ③
Trinity Church ①

KEY

Street-by-Street map *see pp184–5*

Key to Symbols *see back flap*

0 meters 300
0 yards 300

Airport 27 miles (43 km)
Naval War College Museum
PROVIDENCE
Hunter House
ELM STREET
WASHINGTON STREET
BRIDGE STREET
Goat Island
White Horse Tavern
AMERICA'S
MARLBOROUGH STREET
FAREWELL STREET
BROADWAY ST
Wanton-Lymon-Hazard House
KAY STREET
Colony House
LONG WHARF
WASHINGTON SQUARE
② Brick Market Museum and Shop
③ Touro Synagogue
CUP
MARY STREET
BELLEVUE
CATHERINE ST
AVENUE
CHURCH STREET
P
① Trinity Church
Redwood Library and Athenaeum ④
Newport Art Museum
THAMES STREET
SPRING STREET
PELHAM STREET
PROSPECT HILL STREET
BELLEVUE AVENUE
JOHN STREET
P
St. Mary's Church
MEMORIAL BOULEVARD
Cliff Walk
FAIR STREET
WILLIAM STREET
KING STREET
ANN STREET
International Tennis Hall of Fame ⑤
BREWER STREET
Kingscote Mansion
Fort Adams State Park, International Yacht Restoration School
The Breakers Newport Mansions

Around Washington Square

Historic marker

Newport's first settlers were religious moderates fleeing persecution at the hands of Puritans in the Massachusetts Bay colony. With its accessible harbor, the town quickly developed into a thriving seaport. However, its location also made it vulnerable. When Rhode Island declared independence from colonial rule in 1776, British forces occupied the city. Before they were driven out in 1780, the occupying army destroyed much of the town. Thanks to preservation efforts, a number of colonial buildings survive. Several of them can be seen on this tour around historic Washington Square, the center of Newport's political and economic life during colonial times.

Architectural detail *is typical of the Washington Square district.*

White Horse Tavern
Granted its liquor license in 1673, the White Horse claims to be the nation's oldest continuously operating tavern. At one time, state legislators gathered here before sitting at Colony House.

St. Paul's Methodist Church was built in 1805. A simple structure, it reflects the continuation of the Colonial style in the decades after independence.

Bank Newport

Rivera House, currently a bank, was once the home of Abraham Rivera, a prominent member of Newport's Jewish and business communities. Rivera laid the cornerstone of Touro Synagogue.

Statue of Oliver Hazard Perry
Oliver Hazard Perry (1785–1819) defeated British forces in a pivotal naval battle in the War of 1812, securing control of Lake Erie for the US. Perry's former home at No. 29 Touro Street faces the statue.

FAREWELL

MARLBOROUGH ST

DUKE STREET

WASHINGTON SQUARE

THAMES STREET

TOURO STREET

STAR SIGHTS

★ Brick Market Museum and Shop

★ Touro Synagogue

★ **Brick Market Museum and Shop**
The Brick Market, once the center of commerce, has been renovated to house this museum (see p182) that brings to life Newport's economic, social, and sporting past.

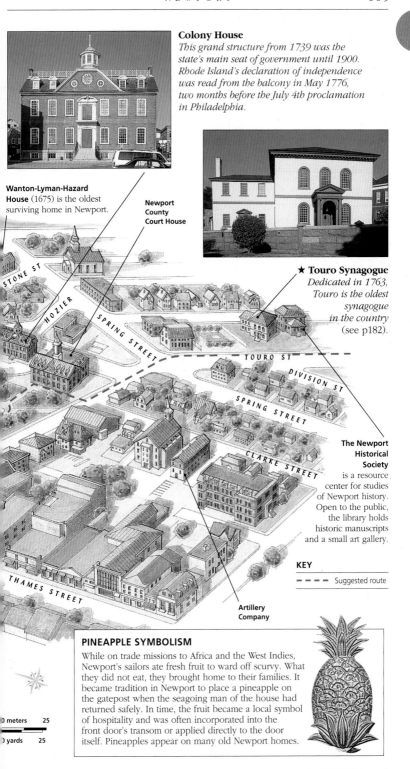

Colony House
This grand structure from 1739 was the state's main seat of government until 1900. Rhode Island's declaration of independence was read from the balcony in May 1776, two months before the July 4th proclamation in Philadelphia.

Wanton-Lyman-Hazard House (1675) is the oldest surviving home in Newport.

Newport County Court House

★ **Touro Synagogue**
Dedicated in 1763, Touro is the oldest synagogue in the country (see p182).

The Newport Historical Society is a resource center for studies of Newport history. Open to the public, the library holds historic manuscripts and a small art gallery.

STONE ST
HOZIER
SPRING STREET
TOURO ST
DIVISION ST
SPRING STREET
CLARKE STREET
THAMES STREET

Artillery Company

KEY

- - - Suggested route

0 meters 25
0 yards 25

PINEAPPLE SYMBOLISM

While on trade missions to Africa and the West Indies, Newport's sailors ate fresh fruit to ward off scurvy. What they did not eat, they brought home to their families. It became tradition in Newport to place a pineapple on the gatepost when the seagoing man of the house had returned safely. In time, the fruit became a local symbol of hospitality and was often incorporated into the front door's transom or applied directly to the door itself. Pineapples appear on many old Newport homes.

The Breakers

The architecture and ostentation of the Gilded Age of the late 1800s reached its pinnacle with the Breakers, the summer home of railroad magnate Cornelius Vanderbilt II (1843–99). Completed in 1895, the four-story, 70-room limestone structure surpassed all other Newport mansions in extravagance. US architect Richard Morris Hunt (1827–95) modeled the building after the 16th-century palaces in Turin and Genoa. Its interior is adorned with marble, alabaster, stained glass, gilt, and crystal.

The Structure
Built in the Italian Renaissance style, the Breakers is alleged to have cost more than $10 million – a huge sum of money in 1895.

The Great Hall The Great Hall rises 50 ft (15 m), or two full stories, providing a majestic welcome to the mansion.

Visitors' entrance, west side

★ Mrs. Vanderbilt's Bedroom
This sumptuous room is decorated in Louis XVI style. Its flowered wall covering and upholstery are reproductions of the original silk and cotton fabrics.

The Music Room This grand room was the scene of many dances and recitals. The bronze and crystal chandeliers, furniture, and gilt decorative touches were modeled on Italian designs.

STAR FEATURES

★ Mrs. Vanderbilt's Bedroom

★ The Dining Room

★ The Morning Room

A MAGNATE'S LIFE

Cornelius Vanderbilt II inherited the mantle as head of the Vanderbilt empire in 1885. He directed the family businesses, mainly railroads, with his brother William for 11 years before suffering a paralyzing stroke. He convalesced at the Breakers, but died in 1899 at the age of 56. At the time of his death, the local gossip held that he had more money than the US Mint.

Cornelius Vanderbilt II

Covered walkway

For hotels and restaurants in this region see pp314–16 and pp343–5

★ The Dining Room
The most richly adorned room in the mansion, the two-story, 2,400-sq-ft (220-sq-m) dining room has two huge crystal chandeliers and a stunning arched ceiling.

VISITORS' CHECKLIST

Ochre Point Ave.
Tel (401) 847-1000. 🚌 67.
⬜ Jan–Mar: 10am–4pm daily;
Apr–Dec: 9am–5pm daily.
⬤ Thanksgiving, Dec 25.
📷 🖼 ♿
www.NewportMansions.org

Upper Loggia
The upper loggia offers a view of the sunrise over the Atlantic Ocean. Its ceiling is painted to look like canopies against a clouded sky.

Sculpted Archways
Ornately carved archways are inspired by Italian Renaissance-style palazzos.

The Billiard Room features several costly wall marbles; the arches and mantel are decorated with yellow alabaster. The mahogany billiard table was built by Baumgarten of New York. Steel beams were needed to support the huge chandeliers.

★ The Morning Room
The ceiling of this east-facing room is adorned with paintings of the Four Seasons, the mahogany doors with the Four Elements. All cornices, pilasters, and panels were made in France and shipped to Newport.

Sunbathing on the rocks at Beavertail Lighthouse and State Park

Jamestown ❿

🏠 5,000. 🚏 23 America's Cup Ave, Newport (401) 845-9123 or (800) 976-5122.

Named for England's King James II (1633–1701), Jamestown is located on Conanicut Island and linked to Newport (see pp182–7) and the mainland by a pair of bridges. During the Revolutionary War, British troops torched much of the town, sparing very few of the houses from that era.

The town is best known for the **Beavertail Lighthouse and State Park**, perched at the southernmost tip of the island. The first lighthouse here was built in 1749 and was subsequently replaced by the present structure in 1856. As with many New England lighthouses, the coastal vistas from Beavertail are beautiful. The winds, currents, and surf can be heavy at times, but on calm days hiking, climbing, and sunbathing on the rocks are favorite pastimes.

Situated on the site of an early fort and artillery battery, **Fort Wetherill State Park** offers great scenic outlooks, picnic tables, and a boat ramp. The park is a popular place for saltwater fishing, boating, and scuba diving. Legend has it that notorious privateer Captain Kidd (1645–1701) stashed some of his plundered loot in the park's Pirate Cave.

🍁 **Beavertail Lighthouse and State Park**
Beavertail Pt. **Tel** (401) 423-9941.
Park ⏰ dawn to dusk daily.
Lighthouse ⏰ call for hours. 🎫 ♿

🍁 **Fort Wetherill State Park**
Fort Wetherill Rd. **Tel** (401) 423-1771. ⏰ dawn to dusk daily. 🎫 ♿

Wickford ⓫

🏠 25,000. 🚏 4808 Tower Hill Rd, Wakefield (401) 789-4422 or (800) 548-4662. **www**.southcountyri.com

Considered a part of North Kingstown, the quaint village of Wickford lies in the northernmost point of Washington County, also known as South County. Wickford's many 18th- and 19th-century houses are a magnet for artists and craftsmen. John Updike (see pp30–31), author of Rabbit Run (1960), had family roots here. The 1745 Updike House on Pleasant Street is just one of some 60 buildings constructed before 1804.

Daytrippers hailing from Providence and Connecticut are apt to jam Wickford's picturesque harbor and shopping streets. At the corner of Brown and Phillips Streets, the Kayak Centre of Rhode Island offers extensive paddling tours on Narragansett Bay.

Old Narragansett Church (more commonly called Old St. Paul's) is one of the oldest Episcopal churches in the US, dating back to 1707, with box pews, an organ from 1660, and an upstairs gallery to which plantation slaves were

Wickford's tranquil harbor

relegated. Artist Gilbert Stuart (1755–1828) was baptized here in a silver baptismal font given to the church as a gift by England's Queen Anne (1665–1714).

Environs
One mile north of town is **Smith's Castle**, one of America's oldest plantation houses. In 1678 settler Richard Smith built a dwelling on the site. Hardly a castle, the structure served as a

Smith's Castle, just outside of Wickford

garrison for the soldiers who had participated in the 1675 Great Swamp Fight against the Narragansett Indians. The battle resulted in a mass slaughter of Indians, which set off a chain of tragic events culminating in the retaliatory destruction of the garrison and the death of 40 soldiers. Later the structure was rebuilt and acquired by the Updike family in 1692. Subsequent additions and renovations transformed the structure into one of the most handsome plantation houses on the Rhode Island shore. The house contains fine paneling, 17th- and 18th-century furnishings, china, and a chair once owned by Roger Williams (see pp169, 177).

🏚 **Smith's Castle**
55 Richard Smith Dr. **Tel** (401) 294-3521. ⬜ call for hours. 🈴 🎫

Saunderstown ⑫

🏠 27,000. 🛈 8045 Post Rd, North Kingstown (401) 295-5566.

Located between Wickford and Narragansett, this town has two main attractions. The gambrel-roofed **Gilbert Stuart Birthplace** was built in 1751 along

the Mattatuxet River. Stuart (1755–1828), whose portraits of US presidents were to bring him lasting fame, was born here. His best-known portrait, that of George Washington, graces the US one-dollar bill.

On the first floor of the house, Stuart's father built a large kitchen and snuff mill, the first in America, powered by a wooden waterwheel. The upstairs living quarters are furnished with authentic period pieces.

Also in town is the 18th-century **Silas Casey Farm**. Still in operation, the farm has been occupied by the same family for 200 years. The 360-acre (146-ha) property is ringed by almost 30 miles (48 km) of stone walls. The house contains original furniture, paintings, and prints, and visitors can tour the family cemetery.

Plaque at Stuart Birthplace

🏚 **Gilbert Stuart Birthplace**
815 Gilbert Stuart Rd. **Tel** (401) 294-3001. ⬜ May–mid-Oct: 11am–4pm Thu–Sat & Mon, noon–4pm Sun. ● mid-Oct–Apr. 🈴 🎫

🏚 **Silas Casey Farm**
2325 Boston Neck Rd. **Tel** (401) 295-1030. ⬜ Jun–mid-Oct: 9am–2pm Sat. ● mid-Oct–May. 🈴 🎫 ♿

South Kingstown ⑬

🏠 26,700. 🛈 230 Old Tower Hill Rd, Wakefield. **Tel** (401) 783-2801.

South Kingstown is a 55-sq-mile (142-sq-km) town that encompasses 15 villages,

including Kingstown, Green Hill, Wakefield, and Snug Harbor. The town is home to the **Museum of Primitive Art and Culture**. Located in an 1856 post office, the museum displays weapons, tools, and implements of aboriginal cultures around the world, including a range of artifacts from prehistoric New England.

After visiting the museum, travelers can enjoy some of the region's outdoor charms. Sightseers, particularly those with cameras, will want to make the trek to the top of the observation post at Hannah Robinson Rock and Tower, where they are greeted with expansive views of the Atlantic Ocean and the Rhode Island seashore.

The South County Bike Path is a 5.6-mile (9-km) paved trail, starting at the Kingstown train station, which takes cyclists through Great Swamp, the scene of the 1675 slaughter of 2,000 Narragansett Indians at the hands of soldiers and settlers – one of the bloodiest battles ever fought in New England. The swamp is now a pristine 3,300-acre (1,335-ha) wildlife refuge called the **Great Swamp Management Area** and is home to creatures such as coyotes, mink, wild turkeys, and ring-necked pheasants. Nature trails lead visitors through dense woodland, past a dike to a boardwalk into a marsh. Birders should pack binoculars and visit the refuge during the spring songbird migration. Avoid hunting season.

🏛 **Museum of Primitive Art and Culture**
1058 Kingstown Rd. **Tel** (401) 783-5711. ⬜ 10am–2pm Wed. 🈴

🦌 **Great Swamp Management Area**
Liberty Lane off Great Neck Rd. **Tel** (401) 789-3094. ⬜ dawn to dusk daily.

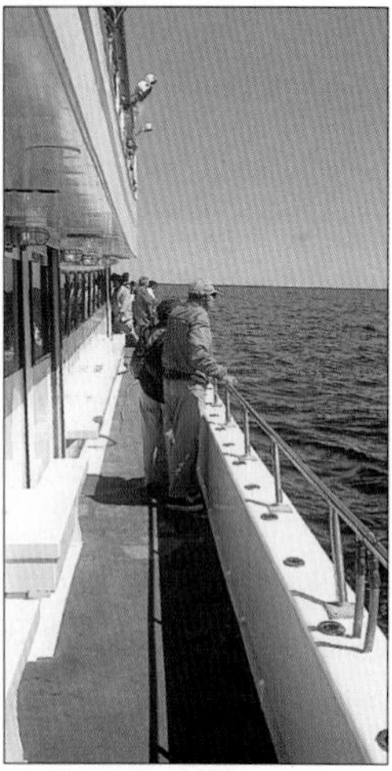

Whale-watching off Point Judith, a popular summer activity

Narragansett ⓮

👥 *18,000.* ✈ *TF Green Airport.* ℹ *36 Ocean Rd (401) 783-7121.*

In the late 19th century this town's waterfront area gained national fame as a fashionable resort, complete with a large casino. In 1900 a devastating fire razed the 1884 casino and many of the lavish hotels. All that remains of the ornate 1884 casino are **The Towers**, two stone towers linked by a Romanesque Revival-style arch.

Today rolling dice have given way to rolling waves, as the town beach offers some of the best surfing on the East Coast. Nearby the **South County Museum** depicts early Rhode Island life with displays of children's toys, farm tools, weapons, a cobbler's shop, a general store, and a working print shop.

The Towers
35 Ocean Rd. ***Tel*** *(401) 782-2597.*
🕘 *call for tours & events schedule or visit the website.*
www.thetowersri.com

South County Museum
Strathmore St off Rte 1.
Tel *(401) 783-5400.* 🕘 *May, Jun, Sep: 10am–4pm Fri–Sat, noon–4pm Sun; Jul–Aug: 10am–4pm Wed–Sat, noon–4pm Sun.* ♿

Environs
Located at the south end of the Narragansett peninsula, **Point Judith** and **Galilee** are departure points for numerous whale-watching cruises, sightseeing boat tours, ferries to Block Island *(see pp192–3)*, and charters for deep-sea fishing. Toward the end of World War II, a German U-boat was sunk just 2 miles (3 km) off the Point Judith Lighthouse. Today the lighthouse affords beautiful views of the ocean. Galilee is famous for its Blessing of the Fleet festival in late July. The Galilee Salt Marsh is popular for birding.

Charlestown ⓰

👥 *6,000.* ✈ 🚌 ℹ *4945 Old Post Rd (401) 364-3878.*

This small town stretches along 4 miles (6.4 km) of lovely beaches, encompassing the largest saltwater marsh in the state and several parks. It is also a convenient base for nature lovers. The 2,000-acre (810-ha) **Burlingame State Park** on Watchaug Pond is equipped with campgrounds, nature trails, swimming and picnic areas, trails for road and mountain bikes, as well as fishing and boating. Birders will enjoy the Audubon Society's **Kimball Wildlife Sanctuary**, located on the south

South County Beaches ⓯

Driving along Highway 1 between Narragansett and Watch Hill, travelers will pass some 100 miles (161 km) of pristine white sand beaches. These thin strands of sand are all that separate Block Island Sound from a series of tidal salt ponds, some of which have been designated national wildlife refuges. The ponds are big lures for bird-watchers hoping to study the egrets, sandpipers, and herons that swim and wade in the salty marshes. Many of the beaches are free to the public, except for parking fees.

KEY
- Major road
- Other road
- Ferry
- Airport
- Viewpoint

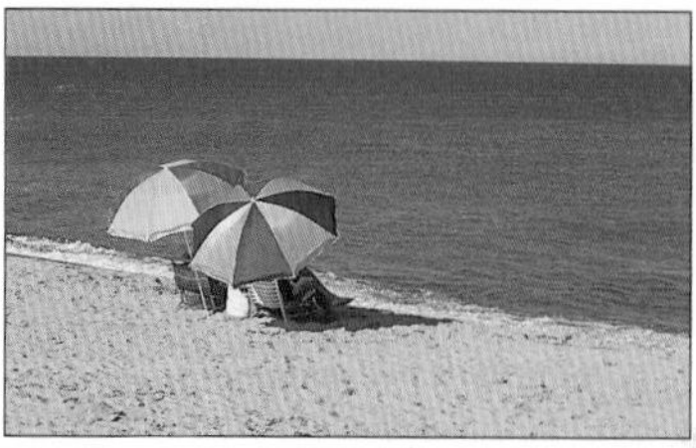

Misquamicut State Beach ⑤
The state's largest beach has gentle surf and a nearby old-time amusement park with rides and diversions for children.

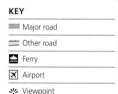

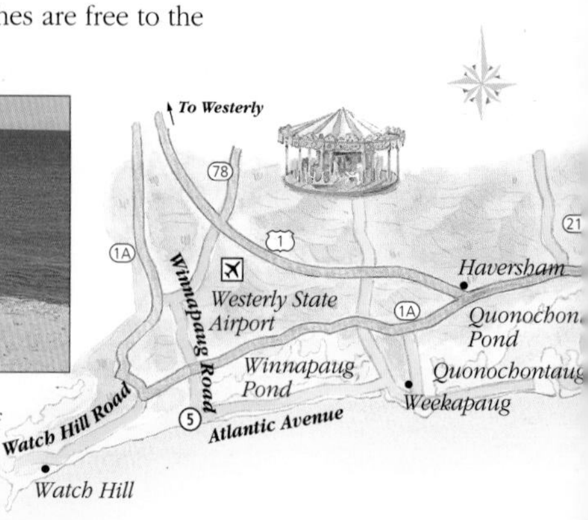
To Westerly
78
1
1A
21
Winnapaug Road
Westerly State Airport
Haversham
Quonochontaug Pond
Winnapaug Pond
Quonochontau
Weekapaug
5
Atlantic Avenue
Watch Hill Road
Watch Hill

side of the park. The sanctuary is a habitat for many kinds of waterfowl and migrating birds, and has a network of easy footpaths.

More outdoor enjoyment can be found at the 172-acre (70-ha) **Ninigret Park**. Tracks lead cyclists and bladers through the grounds, which are graced with a spring-fed swimming pond, tennis courts, and baseball fields. During the winter months, the trails are used by cross-country skiers. Every clear Friday night, the park leaves the gates open to allow visitors to participate

in stargazing activities at the **Frosty Drew Observatory**, which is open year-round. (The facility is unheated, so dress accordingly.)

🔭 Burlingame State Park
Rte 1A. **Tel** (401) 322-8910.
⬜ Apr–early Sep: dawn–dusk daily.
🅿 for camping facilities.

🔭 Kimball Wildlife Sanctuary
Prosser Trail. **Tel** (401) 949-5454.
⬜ dawn–dusk daily.

🔭 Ninigret Park
Rte 1A. **Tel** (401) 364-1222.
⬜ 🅿 ♿

🔭 Frosty Drew Observatory
61 Park Lane, Ninigret Park.
Tel (401) 364-9508. ⬜ year-round:
Fri (weather allowing).
www.frostydrew.org ♿

Watch Hill ❼

ℹ 1 Chamber Way, Westerly
(401) 596-7761.

A village within the town of Westerly, Watch Hill has been an upscale beach haven for the rich and famous since the 19th century. Strolls along Bay Street yield beautiful views of the gingerbread-trimmed Victorian houses on rocky hills above the beach. Visitors to Watch Hill can enjoy the relaxed atmosphere, with a little window shopping or sunbathing at the beach. The 1867 **Flying Horse Carousel** on the beach is a favorite of children. The vantage point of the Watch Hill Lighthouse offers views of neighboring Connecticut's Fishers Island.

🎠 Flying Horse Carousel
Bay St. **Tel** (401) 348-6007. ⬜ mid-Jun–Labor Day: 11am–9pm daily (from 10am Sat–Sun); late May–mid-Jun & Labor Day–mid-Oct: weekends only. 🎫 📷 🍴

Nature trails through the Kimball Wildlife Sanctuary

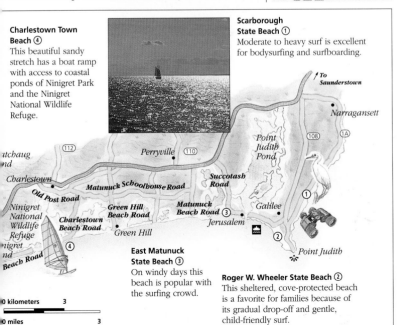

Charlestown Town Beach ④
This beautiful sandy stretch has a boat ramp with access to coastal ponds of Ninigret Park and the Ninigret National Wildlife Refuge.

Scarborough State Beach ①
Moderate to heavy surf is excellent for bodysurfing and surfboarding.

East Matunuck State Beach ③
On windy days this beach is popular with the surfing crowd.

Roger W. Wheeler State Beach ②
This sheltered, cove-protected beach is a favorite for families because of its gradual drop-off and gentle, child-friendly surf.

Tour of Block Island ⑱

Southeast Light

Lying 13 miles (21 km) off the coast, the haven of Block Island has long been a favorite getaway spot for New Englanders. With 25 percent of its wild landscape under protection, Block Island is a wonderful destination for outdoor enthusiasts who enjoy such activities as swimming, fishing, sailing, bird-watching, kayaking, canoeing, and horseback riding. Some 30 miles of natural trails entice hikers and cyclists alike to experience the island's natural beauty firsthand.

Colorful lobster buoys ashore on Block Island

Great Salt Pond ④
Completely protected from the ocean, Great Salt Pond has three marinas and is an excellent spot for kayaking and fishing. New Harbor is Block Island's prime marina and boating center.

Rodman's Hollow ③
Nature trails lead hikers through the glacial depression of Rodman's Hollow Natural Area. The wildlife refuge is home to hawks and white-tailed deer. One path takes visitors to the beach at Black Rock Point at the southern extremity of the island.

KEY

▨ Tour route
⁼ Other road
☼ Viewpoint
🚢 Ferry
✕ Airport

0 meters 500
0 yards 500

Dead Man's Cove
Cormorant Point
Grace Cove Road
Champlin Road
Beacon Hill
West Side Road
Beacon Hill Road
Center Road
Cooneymus Road
Cooneymus Swamp
Dickens Road
Black Rock Road
Lakeside Drive
Black Rock Point
Gr Sa Po

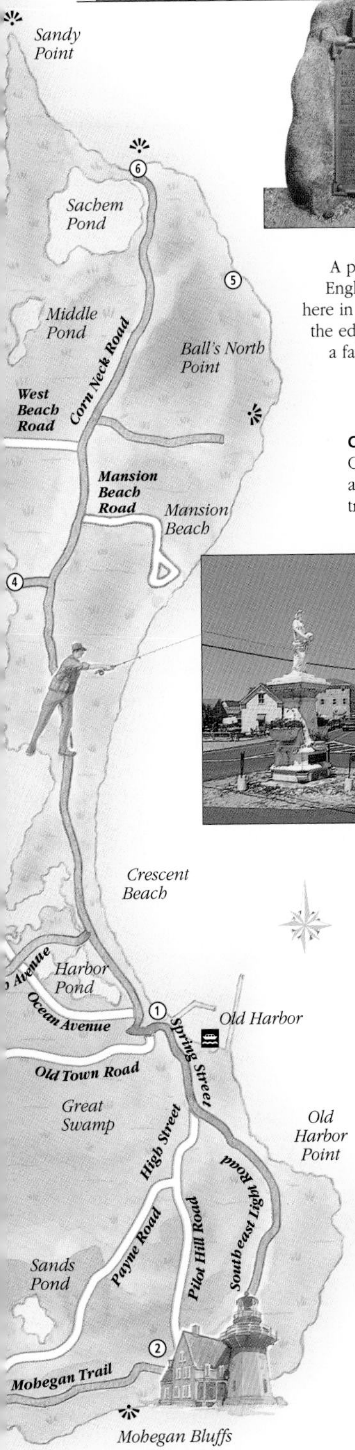

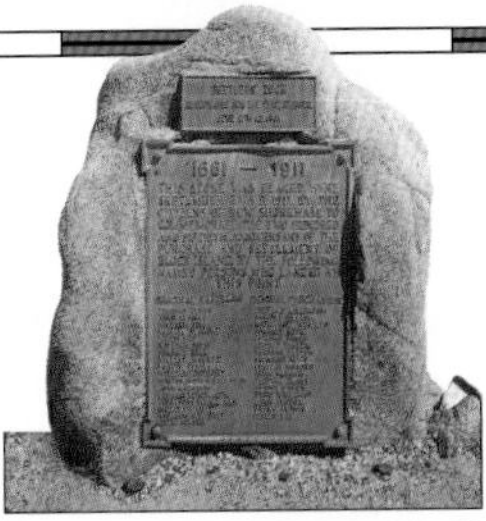

Settlers Rock 6
A plaque honors the 16 Englishmen who landed here in 1661. The rock is at the edge of Sachem Pond, a favorite for swimming and kayaking.

TIPS FOR DRIVERS

Tour length: *18 miles (29 km).*
Getting there: *Regularly scheduled flights from Westerly, RI, and chartered flights from other mainland airports. Year-round ferry service from Point Judith, RI. Ferries carry cars by advance reservations only, (401) 783-7996.*
Stopping-off point: *Old Harbor, the island's only village, has inns and several quaint restaurants overlooking the ocean (see pp314 and 343).*

Clayhead 5
Offers wonderful views of the Atlantic Ocean and is the starting point for a popular nature trail that goes all the way to Settlers Rock.

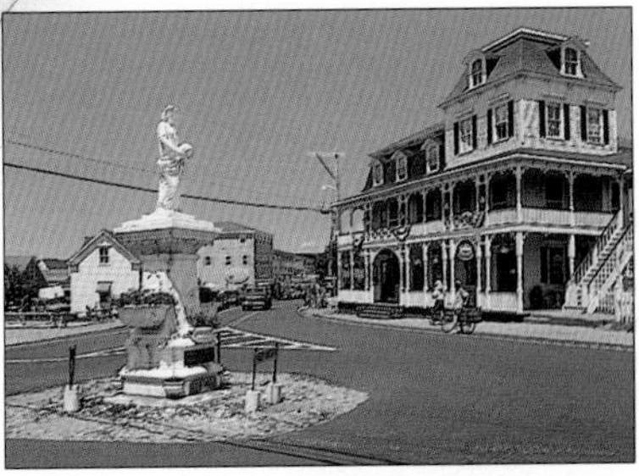

Old Harbor 1
This village is the main hub of activity on the island. Victorian houses, hotels, and shops line the streets, and anglers can charter boats to fish for striped bass, bluefish, flounder, and cod.

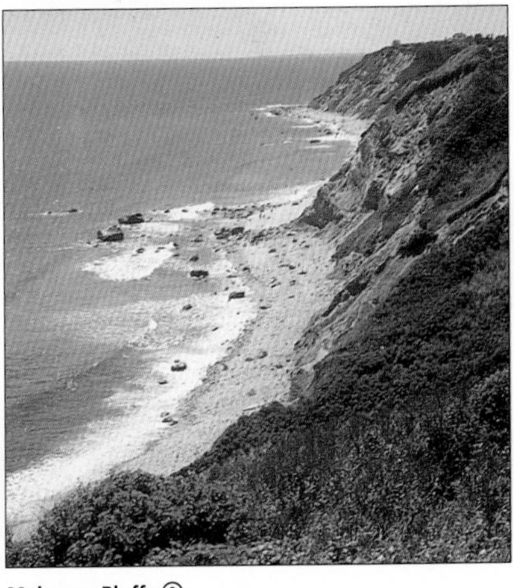

Mohegan Bluffs 2
The name of the bluffs goes back to 1590, when local Manisses Indians tossed 50 Mohegan invaders off these dramatic 200-ft- (61-m-) high red clay cliffs into the waters below. Built in 1875, the Southeast Light was once the most powerful in New England.

CONNECTICUT

*C*onnecticut is quintessential New England. Its quiet charm is evident everywhere, in scenic villages replete with white steepled churches, immaculate village greens, covered bridges, and old-fashioned clapboard houses ringed by stone walls. Even the state's most bustling cosmopolitan centers contain enclaves of picturesque serenity that invite visitors to poke about at their leisure.

The third-smallest state in the US, Connecticut is brimming with history. One of the country's original 13 colonies, Connecticut has always been a trendsetter, beginning with its adoption in 1639 of the Fundamental Orders of Connecticut – the New World's first constitution. It was on Connecticut soil that the nation's first public library, law school, and amusement park were built. Scholars and soldiers can thank the fertile minds of state residents for giving them the first dictionary and pistol, gourmands for the hamburger and corkscrew, and children for the three-ring circus, lollipop, and Frisbee.

Water has played an important role in shaping the state. The Housatonic, Naugatuck, Connecticut, and Thames rivers have been feeding the interior woodlands for thousands of years and acted as the main transportation arteries for early inhabitants. Fueled by waterpower, mill towns sprang up along the rivers, eventually giving way to larger commercial centers. Today these waterways are the arenas of canoeists looking for their next adventure. Houseboats and tour boats offer road-weary passengers unique views of the picturesque towns that hug the banks.

Autumn's annual explosion of color makes it the favorite time of year for visitors to meander along Connecticut's byways, hike the Berkshires, wander the Appalachian Trail *(see pp22–3)*, and indulge in the seasonal bounty of country inns. In addition, the state calendar bulges with eclectic events. Old-fashioned county fairs are held concurrently with cutting-edge performing arts showcases and regattas. When people have had their fill of ballooning and antiquing, they can sample the wares in one of the state's late-summer oyster festivals.

Mystic Seaport's calm harbor

◁ **First Church of Christ Congregational, Farmington, built in 1652** *(see p202)*

Exploring Connecticut

Compact enough to cross in a few hours, Connecticut has treasures that entice travelers to stay for days. The magnificent shoreline, stretching 105 miles (170 km) from Greenwich near the New York State line northeast to Rhode Island, is scalloped by coves, inlets, and harbors, and dotted with state parks, beaches, and marinas. The coast is punctuated by historically significant houses, culminating in Mystic Seaport *(pp214–15)*, a recreated 18th- and 19th-century seafaring village. The area also attracted America's Impressionist artists. Their works are shown in the state's many museums *(pp202–3)*. Inland hills and valleys are dotted with tiny postcard-perfect villages.

Hartford's Bushnell Park

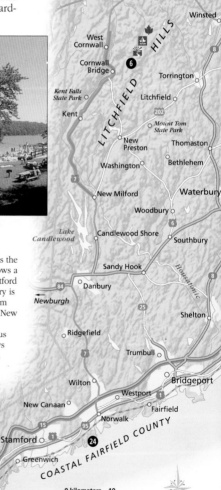

Beach at Mount Tom State Park

GETTING AROUND

Hugging the coast, Interstate 95 serves as the primary east-west link. Interstate 84 follows a similar route from Danbury through Hartford and beyond. The major north-south artery is Interstate 91. Metro North runs trains from New York City to New Haven. Amtrak's New York-Boston line makes stops along Connecticut's shoreline. Several major bus companies, including Peter Pan Trailways and Greyhound, offer interstate services. Seasonal ferries operate New London–Block Island, Rhode Island, and year-round services run New London–Orient Point, New York, as well as Bridgeport–Port Jefferson.

SEE ALSO

0 kilometers   10

0 miles   10

SIGHTS AT A GLANCE

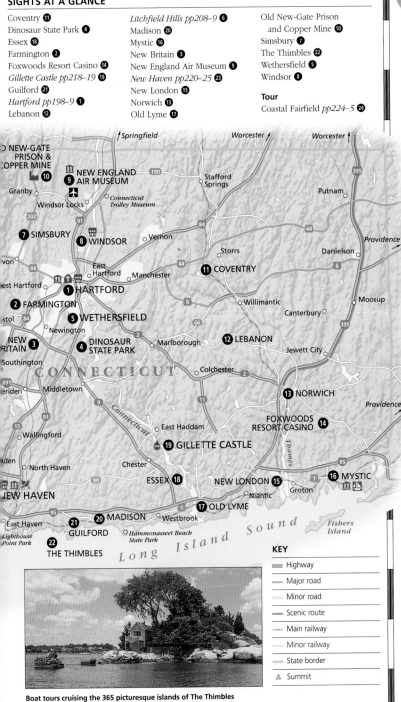

Boat tours cruising the 365 picturesque islands of The Thimbles

KEY

━━ Highway

━━ Major road

╍╍ Minor road

━━ Scenic route

┅┅ Main railway

─── Minor railway

▭▭ State border

△ Summit

Hartford ❶

Elizabeth Park sign

Serving first as an ancient Saukiog Indian settlement and later as a Dutch trading post, Connecticut's capital was founded in 1636 by the Reverend Thomas Hooker (1586–1647) and a group of 100 Englishmen from the Massachusetts Bay Colony. By the late 19th century, Hartford was basking in its Golden Age, thanks to both an economic boom in the insurance industry and a cultural flowering typified by resident authors Mark Twain *(see pp200–201)* and Harriet Beecher Stowe *(see pp30–31)*. In recent decades, an ambitious revitalization program has helped breathe new life into the downtown core.

The imposing façade of the Wadsworth Atheneum

Exploring Hartford

Approaching the city by car, travelers are greeted by sunlight gleaming off the gold-leaf dome of the hilltop **State Capitol**. Many of Hartford's most popular attractions are easily accessed on foot from the Capitol building, which has an information office for tourists.

🏛 Old State House

800 Main St. **Tel** (860) 522-6766.
🕐 year-round: 9am–5pm Mon–Fri.
⬤ public hols. 🎫 ♿ 🏪 📷
www.ctosh.org
The 1796 State House, designed by Charles Bulfinch (1763–1844), is the country's oldest Capitol building. Its graceful center hall, grand staircase, and ornate cupola make the Old State House one of the nation's finest examples of Federal architecture. An interactive audio tour highlights points of interest such as the Great Senate Room and the courtroom where the slave ship *Amistad* trial of 1839 was held. Outdoors there is a seasonal farmers' market.

🔒 Center Church and Ancient Burying Ground

675 Main St. **Church Tel** (860) 249-5631. 🕐 by appt. 🎫 by appt.
Burying Ground Tel (860) 228-1517. 🕐 10am–4pm daily.
Five stained-glass windows designed by US artist Louis Comfort Tiffany (1848–1933) grace the 1807 Center Church (First Church of Christ in Hartford). The church's Ancient Burying Ground contains some 415 headstones dating back to 1648, including that of Hartford's founding father Thomas Hooker. Across Main Street is the 527-ft- (160-m-) high Travelers Tower office building, the tallest man-made observation post in the state.

🏛 Wadsworth Atheneum

600 Main St. **Tel** (860) 278-2670. 🕐 11am–5pm Wed–Sun (from 10am Sat & Sun; to 8pm first Thu of month). ⬤ pub hols. 🎫 (reduced fee 5–8pm first Thu of month). 🎫 ♿ 🏪 📷
www.wadsworthatheneum.org

Alexander Calder's *Stegosaurus*

Established in 1842, this museum has the distinction of being the oldest continuously operating public art museum in the country. Its extensive collection has 45,000 pieces and spans five centuries. It is particularly strong in Renaissance, Baroque, and Impressionist works, as well as in European decorative arts. The museum is noted for its extensive collection of American paintings, including works by Thomas Cole (1801–48) and Frederic Church (1826–1900). Outside in the Burr Mall is the monumental red steel sculpture called *Stegosaurus* (1973) by Connecticut resident Alexander Calder (1898–1976).

🍂 Bushnell Park

Trinity and Elm Sts. **Tel** (860) 232-6710. 🕐 year-round. 🎫 May–Sep.
♿ **Carousel** 🕐 late Apr–mid-Oct: 11am–5pm Tue–Sun. 🎫
Shaded by 100 tree varieties, the 40-acre (16-ha) park is the lush creation of noted landscape architect and Hartford native Frederick Law Olmsted (1822–1903). Children adore the park's 1914 Bushnell Carousel, with its 48 hand-carved horses, ornate "lovers' chariots," and refurbished Wurlitzer band organ. The 115-ft- (35-m-) tall Soldiers and Sailors Memorial Arch honors those who saw duty in the American Civil War (1861–65).

East Senate Chambers of Hartford's Old State House

🏛 State Capitol

210 Capitol Ave. ***Tel*** *(860) 240-0222.* 🕐 *9am–5pm Mon–Fri, tours every hour 9:15am–1:15pm Mon–Fri (& 10:15am–2:15pm Sat Apr–Oct).* ♿ 🖵

The State Capitol was designed by Richard Upjohn (1828–1903) in the high Victorian-Gothic style. It is constructed primarily of marble and granite and has a golden dome. Highlights of the grand interior are the oak woodwork and the ornate oak charter chair.

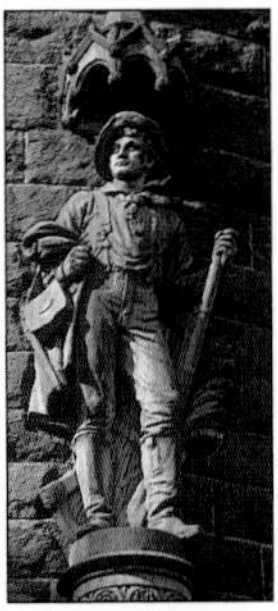

Soldiers and Sailors Memorial

🏛 Bushnell Center for the Performing Arts

166 Capitol Ave. **Box office *Tel*** *(860) 987-5900.* 🚶 *call (860) 987-6033 for tour schedule.*
www.bushnell.org

This leading performing arts venue features Broadway-style extravaganzas as well as more modest productions. Highlights of the free tours include the historic theater, a state-of-the-art modern stage, and a 14-ft (4.27 m) chandelier by Seattle glass artist Dale Chihuly.

🏛 Harriet Beecher Stowe Center

77 Forest St. ***Tel*** *(860) 522-9258.* 🕐 *year-round: 9:30am–4:30pm Wed–Sat (& Tue Jun–Oct), 12pm–4:30pm Sun.* ● *public hols.* 💲 🚶 *obligatory.* ♿ *first floor.* 🛍 📷 **www**. harrietbeecherstowe.org

Located next to the Mark Twain House *(see pp200–201)*, this home is adorned with gingerbread ornamentation typical of late 19th-century Victorian design. Harriet Beecher Stowe's fame as the author of the anti-slavery novel *Uncle Tom's Cabin* (1852) overshadowed her skill as an interior decorator, demonstrated by the elegance of her 1871 home. The Stowes lived here until Harriet's death in 1896.

VISITORS' CHECKLIST

👥 *139,000.* ✈ *Bradley International Airport.* 🚌 🚆 *1 Union Place.* ℹ *31 Pratt St (860) 728-6789 or (800) 446-7811.* 🎪 *Mark Twain Days (summer).* **www**.enjoyhartford.com

🌳 Elizabeth Park Rose Gardens

Prospect Ave. ***Tel*** *(860) 231-9443.* **Gardens** 🕐 *dawn to dusk daily.*

Each year in this 90-acre (28-ha) park more than 900 varieties of roses bloom on around 15,000 bushes. The park has delightful herb, perennial, and rock gardens.

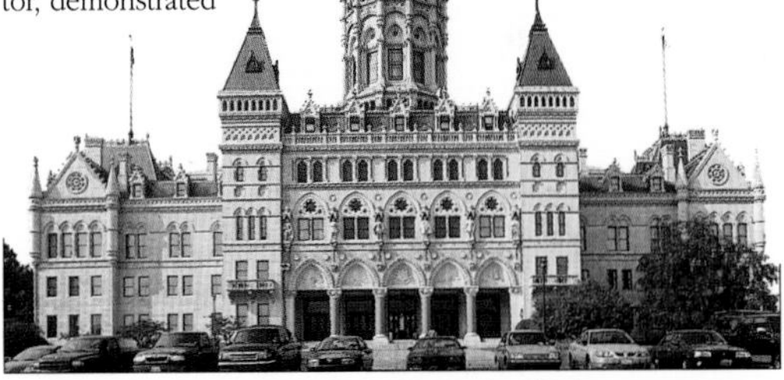

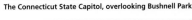

The Connecticut State Capitol, overlooking Bushnell Park

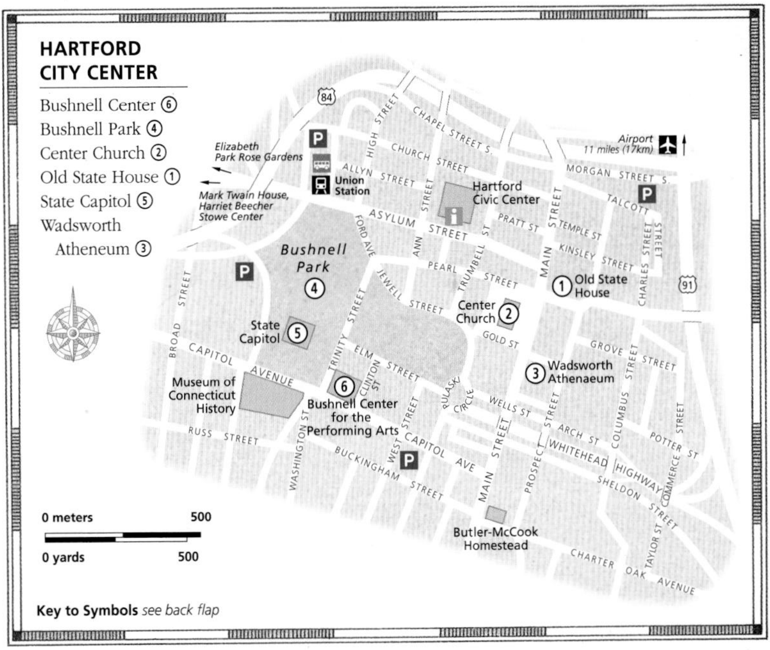

Mark Twain House and Museum

Brickwork

Mark Twain (1835–1910) – a former Mississippi riverboat pilot, humorist, and author – lived here from 1874 to 1891 and penned six novels. Based on a floor plan sketched out by Twain's wife, Olivia, the 19-room home is a masterpiece of the Picturesque-Gothic style. The home's expansive upper balconies, peaked gables, towering turrets, and painted brick combine the sense of high style and playfulness personified by its owners. The adjoining museum has extensive exhibits on Twain and his times, including a film by award-winning New England documentary filmmaker Ken Burns.

North face of Mark Twain House, showing peaked gable and turret

★ Billiard Room
Twain worked on some of his best-known works, including The Adventures of Tom Sawyer *(1876), in the tranquility of the Billiard Room.*

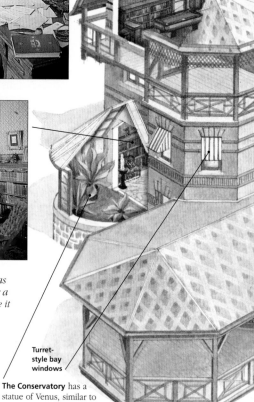

★ Library
The ornate fireplace mantel was carved in Scotland in 1869 for a castle that burned down before it was installed.

STAR FEATURES

- ★ Billiard Room
- ★ Library
- ★ Master Bedroom

Turret-style bay windows

The Conservatory has a statue of Venus, similar to works by Karl Gerhardt (1853–1940). Twain helped finance Gerhardt's studies in Europe.

For hotels and restaurants in this region see pp316–19 and pp346–8

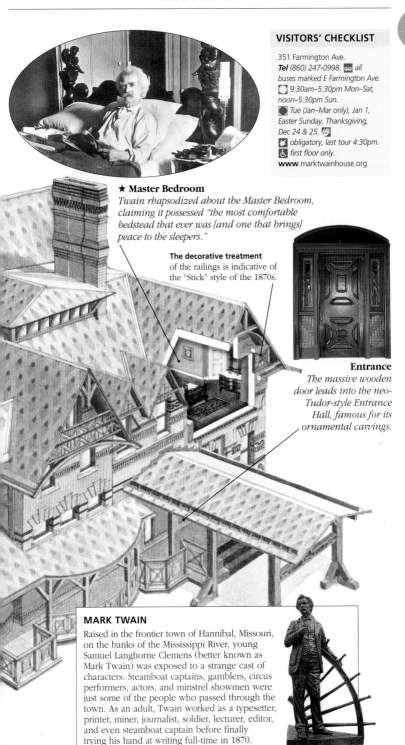

VISITORS' CHECKLIST

351 Farmington Ave.
Tel (860) 247-0998. 🚌 all
buses marked E Farmington Ave.
🕐 9:30am–5:30pm Mon–Sat,
noon–5:30pm Sun.
📅 Tue (Jan–Mar only), Jan 1,
Easter Sunday, Thanksgiving,
Dec 24 & 25. 🎫
🎟 obligatory, last tour 4:30pm.
♿ first floor only.
www.marktwainhouse.org

★ Master Bedroom
Twain rhapsodized about the Master Bedroom, claiming it possessed "the most comfortable bedstead that ever was [and one that brings] peace to the sleepers."

The decorative treatment
of the railings is indicative of the "Stick" style of the 1870s.

Entrance
The massive wooden door leads into the neo-Tudor-style Entrance Hall, famous for its ornamental carvings.

MARK TWAIN
Raised in the frontier town of Hannibal, Missouri, on the banks of the Mississippi River, young Samuel Langhorne Clemens (better known as Mark Twain) was exposed to a strange cast of characters. Steamboat captains, gamblers, circus performers, actors, and minstrel showmen were just some of the people who passed through the town. As an adult, Twain worked as a typesetter, printer, miner, journalist, soldier, lecturer, editor, and even steamboat captain before finally trying his hand at writing full-time in 1870.

Graceful exterior of the Hill-Stead Museum in Farmington

Farmington ❷

👥 21,050. ℹ 31 Pratt St, Hartford (860) 728-6789 or (800) 446-7811.

Perched on the banks of the surging Farmington River, this quiet enclave has long been the starting point for canoeists, fishermen, and bird-watchers. The skies above the Farmington River Valley are also a busy place, popular with hang gliders and hot-air balloonists taking in the spectacular vistas from on high. Several companies offer champagne flights over the scenic valley, while others offer candlelit tours of the town's historic homes.

The interior of the **Hill-Stead Museum** has remained unchanged since the 1946 death of its original owner Theodate Pope Riddle (1867–1946). Pope, one of the country's first female architects, designed the Colonial–Revival mansion, which was completed in 1901. Her will stipulated that upon her death nothing in the house could be changed, altered, or moved. The result is a fascinating home frozen in the Edwardian period. On display is the Pope family's fine collection of French and American Impressionist paintings, including works by Edgar Degas (1834–1917), Édouard Manet (1832–83), Mary Cassatt (1845–1926), and James Whistler (1834–1903). The museum also contains splendid examples of American and European furniture and decorative arts. Particularly noteworthy on the grounds of the 150-acre (61-ha) estate is the sunken garden. The **Stanley-Whitman House** is a well-preserved example of the framed overhang style of early 18th-century architecture of New England. The house, furnished with Colonial pieces, is often used as a venue for craft demonstrations and exhibits. Elsewhere in Farmington, admirers of old cemeteries will find many markers of interest in the Ancient Burying Ground, with gravestones dating back to 1661. In the Riverside Cemetery, one tombstone marks the grave of Foone, an African slave who drowned in the town's canal after being freed in the *Amistad* trial *(see p198)*.

🏛 Hill-Stead Museum
35 Mountain Rd. ***Tel*** *(860) 677-4787.* ○ *May–Oct: 10am–5pm Tue–Sun; Nov–Apr: 11am–4pm Tue–Sun.* ● *public hols.* 🎫 👥 *obligatory.* ♿ *partial.*
www.hillstead.org

🏛 Stanley-Whitman House
37 High St. ***Tel*** *(860) 677-9222.*
○ *May–Oct: noon–4pm Wed–Sun; Nov–Apr: noon–4pm Sat–Sun.* 🎫 👥 ♿ *partial.*

Environs

Twenty miles (32 km) south of Farmington lies the blue-collar town of Waterbury. The town is proud of its ethnic roots, as evidenced by its

Arts of the West **by Thomas Hart Benton at the New Britain Museum of American Art**

IMPRESSIONIST ART TRAIL

Between 1885 and 1930 Connecticut was a magnet for many American artists. Childe Hassam (1859–1935), J. Alden Weir (1852–1919), Willard Metcalf (1858–1925), and others depicted marshes, seascapes, harbors, and farms in a style called American Impressionism. Their works are in nine museums on a self-guided trail that winds from Greenwich to New London.

SIGHTS AT A GLANCE

Bruce Museum, Greenwich ①
Bush-Holley Historic Site, Cos Cob ②
Florence Griswold Museum, Old Lyme ⑧
Hill-Stead Museum, Farmington ⑥
Lyman Allyn Art Museum, New London ⑨
New Britain Museum of American Art, New Britain ⑤
Wadsworth Atheneum, Hartford ⑦
Weir Farm, Ridgefield and Wilton ③
Yale University Art Gallery, New Haven ④

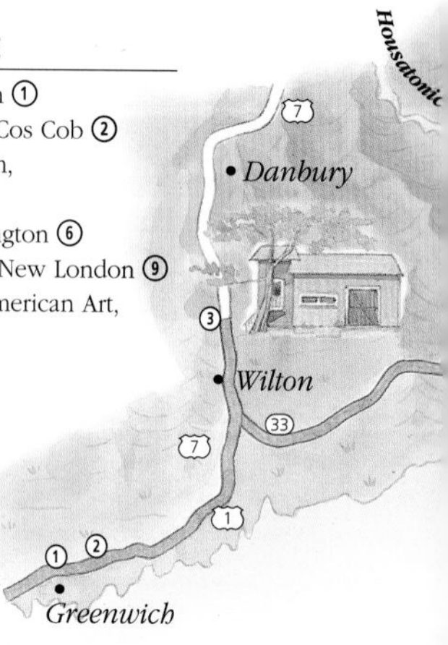

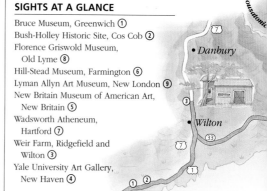

240-ft- (73-m-) tall Clock Tower, modeled on the city hall in Siena, Italy. A hands-on exhibit at the **Mattatuck Museum** relates the state's industrial history, including Waterbury's role as the "Brass City" during the 19th and early 20th century.

🏛 **Mattatuck Museum**
144 W Main St, Waterbury. **Tel** (203) 753-0381. 🕐 year-round: 10am–5pm Tue–Sat, noon–5pm Sun. ⊘ public hols. 📷📹🚻♿ **www**.mattatuckmuseum.org

New Britain ❸

🏙 70,000. 🚏 31 Pratt St, Hartford (860) 728-6789 or (800) 446-7811.

New Britain is midway between Boston and New York. Travelers to either city should stop to visit the **New Britain Museum of American Art**, which opened in 2006. The distinguished collection spans art from the Colonial era to the present. Almost every major US artist is represented, including Georgia O'Keeffe (1887–1986), Andrew Wyeth (b.1917),

Alexander Calder (1898–1976), and Isamu Noguchi (1904–88). The American Impressionist collection is also important. One gallery is dedicated to the seminal "Arts of Life in America" mural series by Thomas Hart Benton.

🏛 **New Britain Museum of American Art**
56 Lexington St, New Britain. **Tel** (860) 229-0257. 🕐 11am–5pm Tue–Wed & Fri; 11am–8pm Thu; 10am–5pm Sat; noon–5pm Sun. 📷 **www**.nbmaa.org

Dinosaur State Park ❹

400 West St, Rocky Hill. **Tel** (860) 529-8423. **Park** 🕐 9am–4:30pm daily. **Exhibit center** 🕐 9am–4:30pm Tue–Sun. ⊘ public hols. 📷 **www**.dinosaurstatepark.org

During the lower Jurassic period some 200 million years ago, the dinosaurs that roamed this region literally left their mark on the land. Today some 500 prehistoric tracks are preserved beneath this park's huge geodesic

One of 500 ancient tracks at **Dinosaur State Park**

dome. Also on display is a life-size model of an 8-ft (2-m) *Dilophosaurus*, the creature that most likely left the prints. Two large dioramas tell the story of the Connecticut Valley during the Triassic and Jurassic periods. Highlights of this exhibit are a model *Coelophysis* and a cast of a skeleton unearthed in New Mexico. A thrill for children and amateur paleon-tologists is the chance to make plaster casts of the tracks from May through October. (Call ahead to find out what to bring.) The park also has 2.5 miles (4 km) of hiking trails through a variety of habitats.

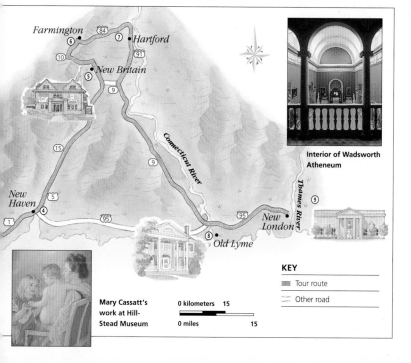

Interior of Wadsworth Atheneum

Mary Cassatt's work at Hill-Stead Museum

KEY
▦ Tour route
═ Other road

0 kilometers 15
0 miles 15

Street-by-Street: Wethersfield 5

Now an affluent Hartford suburb, Wethersfield began as the state's first settlement in 1634. In 1640 its citizens held an illegal public election – America's first act of defiance against British rule. The town also hosted the 1781 Revolutionary War conference between George Washington (1732–99) and his French allies, during which they finalized strategies for the decisive American victory in Yorktown. Preserved within a 12-block area, Old Wethersfield stands as a primer of American architecture, with numerous houses from the 18th to 20th centuries. The centerpiece is the Webb-Deane-Stevens Museum, a trio of dwellings depicting the differing lifestyles of three 18th-century Americans: a wealthy merchant, a diplomat, and a leather tanner.

A Connecticut River-style entrance built in 1767

133 Main Street
This 1787 house was the home of Reverend Joseph Emerson, who ran the Female Seminary at the Old Academy at 150 Main.

Church and Main
The house atop the street sign marks the area of one of Connecticut's first suburban subdivisions.

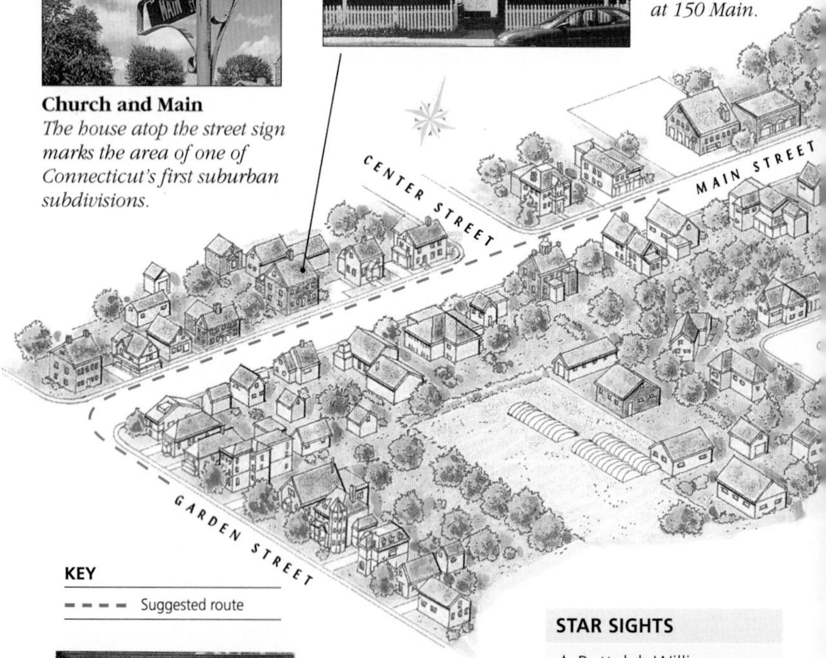

KEY

- - - - Suggested route

Memorial Plaque
This simple plaque pays tribute to the Massachusetts adventurers who settled here in 1634.

STAR SIGHTS

- ★ Buttolph Williams House
- ★ First Church of Christ
- ★ Webb-Deane-Stevens Museum

◁ **Cruising through The Thimbles, a collection of 365 islands and islets**

WETHERSFIELD

★ First Church of Christ

One of only three Colonial meeting houses left in the state, the 1761 church included presidents George Washington (1732–99) and John Adams (1735–1826) among its worshipers.

VISITORS' CHECKLIST

26,000. Bradley International Airport, 17 miles (27 km) N in Windsor Locks. from Hartford. Connecticut Heritage River Valley, (860) 244-8181 or (800) 793-4480. www.visitctriver.com and www.historicwethersfield.org

Ancient Burying Ground

Legend has it that the graves of nine victims of the 1637 Pequot Massacres are buried here.

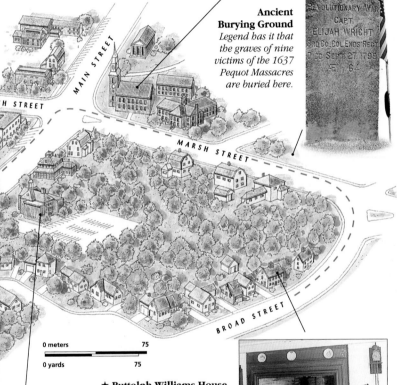

Wethersfield Museum & Visitors' Center

★ Buttolph Williams House

Built c.1720, this house exemplifies the era's austere architecture. The parlor is shown at right.

Webb-Deane-Stevens Museum

The Joseph Webb House, built in 1751, is part of the Webb-Deane-Stevens Museum. Shown at right is wallpaper from one of the upstairs bed chambers.

For hotels and restaurants in this region see pp316–19 and pp346–8

Litchfield Hills ❻

Nestled in the folds and foothills of the Berkshire Hills and Taconic Mountains in the northwesternmost section of Connecticut, the Litchfield Hills region covers some 1,000 sq miles (2,590 sq km), or one-quarter of the state. Many people consider this to be the most scenic part of Connecticut. Anchored by the Housatonic River, the bucolic landscape of woods, valleys, lakes, and wildlife offers unparalleled opportunities for canoeing, kayaking, white-water rafting, tubing, fly-fishing, and hiking. In autumn, traffic along the winding roads can slow as the brilliant

American Clock and Watch Museum

fall foliage entrances sightseers. A steady influx of the wealthy into the area has resulted in the gentrification of Litchfield's 26 towns and villages, with boutiques and bistros popping up beside traditional craft shops and historic homes and gardens.

Fishing at Mount Tom State Park outside Litchfield

Bristol

🏙 62,000. 🏛 *Litchfield (860) 567-4506.*

Bristol's past as a premier clock manufacturing center is celebrated at the American Clock and Watch Museum on Maple Street. Housed in an 1801 mansion, this vast collection includes 5,000 clocks and watches.

Bristol is also home to the Lake Compounce Theme Park, the nation's oldest amusement park. Complete with the fastest and longest wooden roller coaster on the East Coast, a white-water raft ride and a new 185-ft- (56-m-) drop tower, the park on Lake Avenue has been entertaining families since 1846. More family fun can be found on Riverside Avenue in the form of the Carousel Museum of New England. Its collection of antique carousel pieces is one of the finest in the world.

Woodbury

🏙 9,400. 🏛 *Litchfield (860) 567-4506.*

With many shops and dealers, this is a popular haunt for antique lovers. Antique furnishings from the late 18th century can also be found at the Glebe House on Hollow Road. This minister's farmhouse is surrounded by the Gertrude Jekyll Garden, the noted English landscaper's only garden on US soil. The

town is also blessed with five churches from various eras that have been wonderfully preserved.

New Preston

🏛 *Litchfield (860) 567-4506.*

New Preston offers access to 95-acre (38-ha) Lake Waramaug State Park. The lake is especially beautiful in the autumn, when the glorious colors are reflected on its mirrorlike surface. Visitors can rent canoes for peaceful paddles around the shoreline, and some 80 campsites cater to enthusiasts who want to linger and enjoy the great outdoors. The Hopkins Vineyard, perched

above the lake, offers wine tastings along with tours of its facilities.

Litchfield

🏙 8,850. 🏛 *Northwest Connecticut (860) 567-4506.* **www**.litchfieldhills.com

Picturesque Litchfield has many noteworthy historic buildings, such as South Street's 1784 Tapping Reeve House and Law School, the country's first law school.

Just on the outskirts of town on Route 202, Mount Tom State Park has trails leading to the 1,325-ft (404-m) summit. The lake is ideal for scuba diving, swimming, boating, and fishing.

Elegant Bellamy-Ferriday House and Garden in Bethlehem

For hotels and restaurants in this region see pp316–19 and pp346–8

Bethlehem

🏃 3,700. 🏛 Litchfield.

One of the town's highlights is the Bellamy-Ferriday House and Garden, the 18th-century home of Reverend Joseph Bellamy (1719–90), founder of the first theological seminary in America. Located on Main Street, this 13-room house displays Ferriday family delftware, furniture, antiques, and Oriental art.

West Cornwall

🏛 Litchfield.

Tiny West Cornwall is best known for its covered bridge. The 1841 bridge, which spans the Housatonic River, is only one of two such spans in the state open to car traffic.

Norfolk

🏃 2,000. 🏛 Litchfield.

Founded in 1758, this small village is located in the northwest corner of the state. Its village green is known for two key reasons: a monument that was designed by architect Stanford White (1853–1906) and US sculptor Augustus Saint-Gaudens (see pp262–3); and the Music Shed. The latter is an auditorium on the Ellen Batell Stoeckel Estate that hosts the highly acclaimed annual Norfolk Chamber Music Festival.

Re-created Algonkian village at the Institute for American Indian Studies

Washington

🏃 3,950. 🏛 Litchfield.

At the Institute for American Indian Studies, situated on Curtis Road, those with a bent for history can examine a pre-contact Algonkian village, artifacts from 10,000 years ago, and exhibits of northwest Connecticut's Woodland Indians. The grounds contain a re-created archaeological dig.

Kent

🏃 2,900. 🏛 Litchfield.

Art lovers should go out of their way to visit this small community. It is well known for having the highest concentration of galleries in the region, including the interesting Heron American Craft Gallery and the Kent Art Association Gallery.

North of town travelers indulge in outdoor fun at Kent Falls State Park. A short hike into the 295-acre (119-ha) park will reward visitors with stunning views of what many people consider the most impressive waterfall in Connecticut. Picnic facilities overlook the idyllic scene.

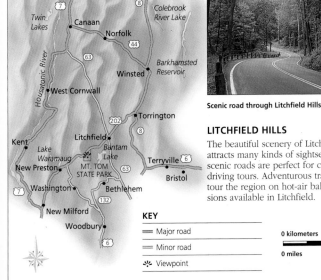

Scenic road through Litchfield Hills

LITCHFIELD HILLS

The beautiful scenery of Litchfield County attracts many kinds of sightseers. Its scenic roads are perfect for cycling and driving tours. Adventurous travelers can tour the region on hot-air balloon excursions available in Litchfield.

KEY

━━ Major road

━━ Minor road

🌿 Viewpoint

0 kilometers   15

0 miles   15

Picturesque bridge over the Connecticut River outside the town of Windsor

Simsbury ❼

🏛 22,000.

Originally a quiet colonial farming community, Simsbury grew into something of a boomtown in the early 18th century with the discovery of copper in the region. The wheels of US industry started turning here with the opening of the nation's first steel mill in 1728.

Three centuries of local history are squeezed into the **Phelps Tavern Museum**. The museum is located in the home of sea Captain Elisha Phelps. Period rooms and galleries have been used to create an authentic inn from 1786 to 1849, an era when such wayside inns were central to New England's social life. The tavern museum is part of a 2-acre (1-ha) complex that includes a museum store and award-winning period gardens.

🏛 **Phelps Tavern Museum**
800 Hopmeadow St.
Tel (860) 658-2500.
◯ year-round: noon–4pm Tue–Sat.
● public hols. 🅰 🅰

Sea captain's home, Phelps Tavern Museum

Windsor ❽

🏛 27,800. ℹ Hartford (860) 728-6789.

Windsor was settled in the early 1630s by Pilgrims from Plymouth *(see pp148–9)*, making it the oldest permanent English settlement in the state – a claim disputed by the residents of nearby Wethersfield *(see pp206–07)*. A drive along Palisado Avenue passes several historic houses.

The 1758 **John & Sarah Strong House** is an old surviving frame structure named after the newlyweds who built it and lived in it for four years before heading west to settle. It has an excellent collection of furnishings reflecting the history of Windsor. Next door is the **Dr. Hezekiah Chaffee House**, a three-story brick Georgian-Colonial built in the mid-18th century. The home is appointed with period furniture and features changing exhibits. Visitors may also tour the adjoining Palisado Green. Here nervous settlers built a walled stockade during the 1637 war with the Pequot Indians. Further down the road stands the

1780 Georgian home of the state's first senator, Oliver Ellsworth (1745–1807). Today the **Oliver Ellsworth Homestead** contains interior design details from the era, including the original wallpaper.

🏛 **John & Sarah Strong House**
96 Palisado Ave. **Tel** (860) 688-3813. ◯ year-round: 10am–4pm Tue–Sat. ● public hols. 🅰 includes admission to Dr. Hezekiah Chaffee House. 🅰

🏛 **Dr. Hezekiah Chaffee House**
108 Palisado Ave. **Tel** (860) 688-3813. ◯ year-round: 10am–4pm Tue–Sat. ● public hols. 🅰 includes admission to John & Sarah Strong House. 🅰

🏛 **Oliver Ellsworth Homestead**
778 Palisado Ave. **Tel** (860) 688-8717. ◯ mid-May–mid-Oct: noon–4pm Wed, Thu & Sat. 🅰

Environs
Fifteen miles (24 km) north of Windsor, the **Connecticut Trolley Museum** takes visitors on a nostalgic journey. A round-trip through the grounds on an antique trolley highlights permanent displays of classic trolley cars dating from 1894 to 1949. The Connecticut Fire Museum and a new Bus Museum are also part of the complex.

🏛 **Connecticut Trolley Museum**
58 North Rd, East Windsor. **Tel** (860) 627-6540. ◯ Apr–mid-Jun: 10am–4pm Sat, noon–4pm Sun; mid-Jun–Labor Day: 10am–4pm Mon, Wed–Fri, 10am–5pm Sat, noon–4pm Sun; off season: call for hours. 🅰 access to both museums. **www**.ceraonline.org

New England Air Museum ❾

Bradley International Airport, Windsor Locks. *Tel (860) 623-3305.* 〇 *10am–5pm daily.* ● *Jan 1, Thanksgiving, & Dec 25.* 🖼 🎫 ♿ ⬛ **www**.neam.org

Aviation fans can indulge their flights of fancy at the largest aviation museum in the Northeast. The impressive collection of 80 aircraft spans the complete history of aviation beginning with pre-Wright Brothers flying machines right up to present-day jets and rescue helicopters. Located near Bradley International Airport, the museum is housed in and around two cavernous hangars. Highlights include a Bunce-Curtiss Pusher, a vintage 1909 Blériot and a Sikorsky VS-44 Flying Boat, the last of the four-engined flying boats.

To experience the thrill of flying, visitors can strap themselves into a simulator of the Grumman Tracer.

One of the planes on display at the New England Air Museum

Old New-Gate Prison and Copper Mine insignia

Old New-Gate Prison and Copper Mine ❿

🏛 *115 Newgate Rd, East Granby.* *Tel (860) 653-3563.* 〇 *May–Oct: 10am–4pm Fri–Sun.* 🖼 🎫 ♿ ⬛

When financial woes forced the sale of this less than prosperous 18th-century copper mine, its new proprietors found a novel but grim use for the dark hole in the ground. In 1773 the local government transformed the nation's first chartered copper mine into the state's first colonial prison. Over the course of its infamous career, the jail

held everyone from horse thieves to captured British soldiers. New-Gate represented a particularly brutal form of punishment, with prisoners living and sleeping in damp, sunless tunnels. Mercifully, the prison was abandoned in 1827, although tours of its lower chamber still inspire shivers.

Coventry ⓫

🌆 *11,350.* 🚉 *New London (860) 444-2206.*

Coventry is the birthplace of Nathan Hale (1755–76), one of the inspirational heroes of the American Revolution (1775–83). Just minutes before he was to be hanged by the British for being a spy, the 21-year-old Coventry schoolteacher uttered his now famous last words, "I only regret that I have but one life to lose for my country."

The **Nathan Hale Homestead** is an anomaly in that its namesake never actually lived

in the house. The existing structure, located on the site where Hale was born, was built by Hale's brothers and father in 1776, the same year he was executed.

Some of Hale's belongings are on display, including his Bible, army trunk and boyhood "fowling piece." Nearby, Strong-Porter House was built by Hale's great uncle in 1730.

Coventry is also home to the **Caprilands Herb Farm**, a 20-acre (8-ha) operational farm with more than 30 herb gardens. The greenhouse and grounds are open to the public, as is the restored 18th-century barn. At the end of a visit, some of the more than 300 types of herbs grown here can be purchased.

🏛 **Nathan Hale Homestead** 2299 South St. *Tel (860) 742-6917.* 〇 *mid-May–mid-Oct: 11am–4pm Wed–Sun & by appt.* 🖼 🎫 ♿ *partial.*

🏛 **Caprilands Herb Farm** 534 Silver St. *Tel (860) 742-7244.* 〇 *year-round: 10am–5pm daily (weekends only in winter).* ● *public hols.*

The 1730 Strong-Porter House in Coventry

Lebanon ⓬

🏛 6,500. ✈ Hartford. 🚌 🚊 New London. ℹ (860) 444-2206 or (800) 863-6569.

This Eastern Connecticut community is steeped in American Revolution history. It was here on the 160-acre (65-ha) common that French hussars trained before joining their American allies in Yorktown for the climactic battle of the conflict. Lebanon native and artist John Trumbull (1756–1843), whose paintings can be seen in Hartford's Wadsworth Atheneum (see p198) and New Haven's Yale University Art Gallery, put down his paintbrush long enough to design the town's 1807 Congregational Church.

Also overlooking the green is the **Governor Jonathan Trumbull's House**. Father to John and governor of the colony and the state of Connecticut from 1769 to 1784, Trumbull was the only governer of the 13 colonies to remain in office before, during and after the Revolutionary War. Behind the house is the **Doctor William Beaumont Homestead**, birthplace of one of the world's pioneers of gastric medicine.

🏛 **Governor Jonathan Trumbull's House**
169 W Town St. **Tel** (860) 642-7558. ◐ mid-May–mid-Oct: noon–4pm Wed–Sun. 🎟

🏛 **Doctor William Beaumont Homestead**
169 W Town St. **Tel** (860) 642-6579. ◐ mid-May–mid-Oct: noon–4pm Sat. 🎟

Environs
Twelve miles (19 km) to the east, Canterbury is home to the **Prudence Crandall Museum**. Crandall (1803–90) raised the ire of citizens when, in 1832, she admitted a young black student to her private school for girls. Undaunted by threats of boycotts, Crandall kept the school open and attracted students, many of whom were black, from other states. Public outcry was such that the local government pushed through a law forbidding private schools to admit black children from out of state. Crandall was subsequently jailed and brought to trial. It was only after an angry mob attacked the school in 1834 that the heroic Quaker woman reluctantly closed its doors forever. Today the museum commemorates Crandall's struggle and traces local black history.

🏛 **Prudence Crandall Museum**
Canterbury Green. **Tel** (860) 546-7800. ◐ call for hours. ● mid-Dec–Mar. 🎟

Norwich ⓭

🏛 35,000. ℹ 69 Main St (860) 886-4683.

Norwich has the dubious distinction of being the birthplace of Benedict Arnold (1741–1801), forever synonymous with traitor for betraying Colonial forces during the American Revolution. In contrast, the Colonial Cemetery contains graves of soldiers, both American and French, who died fighting for the American cause during the war.

A two-story colonial structure consisting of a pair of annexed saltboxes, the **Christopher Leffingwell House**, is named after a financier of the Colonial side in the American Revolution. During the war, Leffingwell's house and tavern were used for secret meetings. The interior, full of late 17th- and 18th-century furniture, has never been remodeled, making it of special interest.

🏛 **Christopher Leffingwell House**
348 Washington St. **Tel** (860) 889-9440. ◐ mid-Apr–mid-Oct: 1–4pm Sat–Sun. ● public hols. 🎟 📷

Environs
Located 5 miles (8 km) south of Norwich is the **Shantok Village of Uncas**, final resting place of Native American leader Uncas (d.1683). Inspiration for James Fenimore Cooper's novel *Last of the Mohicans* (1826), Uncas provided early colonists with the plot of land for the original Norwich settlement and sided with them during the Pequot War of the 1630s. An obelisk memorializing Uncas was erected here in 1840.

A Leffingwell sculpture

🏛 **Shantok Village of Uncas**
Rte 32 S of Norwich. ◐ dawn to dusk daily. 📷

Foxwoods Resort Casino ⓮

Rte 2. **Tel** (800) PLAYBIG. **Casino** ◐ 24 hrs daily. ♿ 🏨 🍴 🍽 🚭 🛍 🎰

First of the Native American-operated casinos in New England, this gaming facility has hundreds of games tables, more than 5,800 slot machines, and high-stakes bingo and poker. In addition, the 1,500-seat Fox Theater attracts international stars.

Also on casino grounds is the **Mashantucket Pequot Museum**, a state-of-the-art research and exhibition center of Native American history. Multimedia displays and touch-screen computers provide a detailed study of the natural history of the area and

The War Office in Lebanon, once Jonathan Trumbull's store

Life-size Native American figures at the Mashantucket Pequot Museum

its earliest inhabitants. Walking through a replica Pequot Village c.1500, visitors come upon life-size figures depicting local Native American life.

Mashantucket Pequot Museum
110 Pequot Trail. **Tel** (860) 396-6800 or (800) 411-9671. 10am–4pm Wed–Sat. Jan 1, Thanksgiving Eve, Thanksgiving, Dec 24 & 25. www.pequotmuseum.org

New London ⑮

26,000. 32 Huntington St (860) 444-2206 or (800) 863-6569.

British forces led by traitor Benedict Arnold razed New London during the American Revolution. Rebounding from the attack, the town enjoyed new-found prosperity with the whaling industry during the 19th century. The four colonnaded Greek Revival mansions along Whale Oil Row attest to the affluence of that era.

Remarkably, many homes survived Arnold's torching, including the **Joshua Hempsted House**. Built in 1678, the dwelling is insulated with seaweed and represents one of the few 17th-century homes left in the state. Connecticut College houses the **Lyman Allyn Art Museum**, particularly known for its 19th-century American paintings. Also on campus, the 750-acre (303-ha) college Arboretum encompasses a variety of ecosystems, native trees and shrubs, trails, and ponds. At the edge of town is **Monte Cristo Cottage**, boyhood home of Nobel Prize-winning playwright Eugene O'Neill (1888–1953). The two-story cottage, which served as the setting for his Pulitzer Prize-winning play *Long Day's Journey into Night* (1957), is now a research library, with some of O'Neill's belongings on display.

Joshua Hempsted House
Jct of Hempstead, Jay, & Truman Sts. **Tel** (860) 443-7949. mid-May–mid-Oct: noon–4pm Sat & Sun (Jul–Aug: also Fri). obligatory.

Lyman Allyn Art Museum
625 Williams St. **Tel** (860) 443-2545. year-round: 10am–5pm Tue–Sat, 1–5pm Sun. public hols. by appt.

Monte Cristo Cottage
325 Pequot Ave. **Tel** (860) 443-5378 ext 227. late May–early Sep: noon–4pm Thu–Sat, 1–3pm Sun.

Environs

Directly across the river Thames from New London is the town of Groton. The USS *Nautilus*, the world's first nuclear-powered submarine is berthed at the **Submarine**

Force Museum on the Naval Submarine Base. **Fort Griswold Battlefield State Park** is where British troops under Benedict Arnold killed surrendered American soldiers in 1781. A 134-ft (41-m) obelisk memorial and a battle diorama mark the event.

Submarine Force Museum
Crystal Lake Rd. **Tel** (860) 694-3174. mid-May–Oct: 9am–5pm daily (from 1pm Tue); mid-Nov–mid-Apr: 9am–4pm Wed–Mon. first week Nov.

Fort Griswold Battlefield State Park
Monument & Park Aves. **Tel** (860) 449-6877. **Museum** late May–Labor Day: 9am–5pm Wed–Sun. **Park** year-round: 8am–sunset daily.

Sea lion sculpture on the rocks at Mystic Aquarium

Mystic ⑯

2,600. 14 Holmes St (860) 572-9578.

When shipbuilding waned, Mystic turned to tourism. Today Mystic Seaport (see pp214–15) and **Mystic Aquarium**, a world-class venue, make the town bustle. Seals and sea lions cavort in the outdoor Seal Island; indoors is a colony of African black-footed penguins and 3,500 sea creatures. They have the world's largest outdoor beluga tank and the 14,000-seat theater has daily shows.

Mystic Aquarium
55 Coogan Blvd. **Tel** (860) 572-5955. Mar–Nov: 9am–6pm daily; Dec–Feb: 10am–5pm Mon–Fri, 9am–6pm Sat & Sun. Jan 1, Thanksgiving, Dec 25. www.mysticaquarium.org

World's first nuclear-powered sub, USS *Nautilus*, berthed at Groton

Mystic Seaport

Museum logo

What began as a modest collection of nautical odds and ends housed in an old mill in 1929 has grown into the world's largest maritime museum. The 19-acre (7-ha) working replica of a 19th-century port is a complex of more than 40 buildings open to the public, including a bank, chapel, tavern, rope-making shops, and one-room schoolhouse from the 19th century. Despite its fascinating exhibits of ship models and authentic scrimshaw, Mystic Seaport's main attraction remains its preservation shipyard and its fleet of antique ships, including the *Charles W. Morgan*, the last remaining vessel in the nation's fleet of 19th-century whalers.

Seagoing Connection
Almost every building sports a nautical motif.

Whaleboat Exhibit
A fully equipped whaleboat contains all the gear carried in such vessels in the late 19th century. It is housed in a shed on Chubb's Wharf.

Burrows House
The early 19th century home of a shopkeeper and his milliner wife re-creates coastal domestic life.

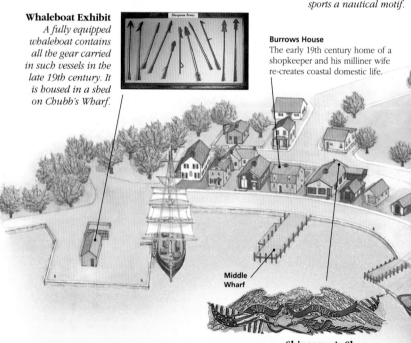

Middle Wharf

Shipcarver's Shop
Independent craftsmen carved figureheads and other decorations, such as this American eagle, for shipbuilders.

★ The *Charles W. Morgan*
The last wooden whaling ship in the world was built in 1841. During restoration of the Charles W. Morgan *visitors can still board the vessel and walk the deck.*

STAR SIGHTS

★ The *Charles W. Morgan*

★ Mystic River Scale Model

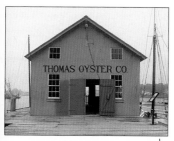

Thomas Oyster House
Initially used as a culling shop to sort oysters by size, the 1874 building was later used to shuck oysters before shipping them on ice.

VISITORS' CHECKLIST

75 Greenmanville Ave (Rte 7). **Tel** (888) 973-2767 or (860) 572-5315. ☐ Apr–Oct: 9am–5pm daily; Nov–Mar: 10am–4pm daily. ● Dec 24 & 25. 🎫 **ff**
www.mysticseaport.org

Village Green Bandstand
Sometimes used as a concert venue, especially for July 4th celebrations.

The *L.A. Dunton*
This 1921 schooner is one of the last existing examples of the once-popular New England round-bow fishing vessels.

The *Sabino*
Built in 1908 in East Boothbay, Maine, the coal-fueled steamship Sabino *takes passengers on cruises along the Connecticut coast.*

The *Joseph Conrad*
Built in Denmark in 1882, this is one of the museum's three largest ships. It serves as a training vessel.

★ Mystic River Scale Model
Inside is a 50-ft- (17-m-) long model giving a bird's-eye view of Mystic in 1870. It has more than 250 detailed buildings.

Lighthouse
This copy of the 1746 Brant Point Lighthouse on Nantucket, houses a multimedia exhibit on lighthouse history (open Apr–Oct).

The Harpist by Alphonse Jongers at the Florence Griswold Museum

Old Lyme ⑰

🏠 6,800. 🛈 *Southeast Connecticut 32 Huntington St, New London (860) 444-2206.*

Once a shipbuilding center, Old Lyme is home to numerous 18th- and 19th-century houses. Originally built for merchants and sea captains, many became residences of the artists who established a colony here in the early 1900s.

The **Florence Griswold Museum** is intimately linked to the arts. The mansion became the home of Captain Robert Griswold and his daughter Florence. An art patron, Florence began letting rooms in the 1890s to New York artists looking for a summer by the sea. She hosted Henry Ward Ranger (1858–1916), Childe Hassam (1859–1935), and Clark Voorhees (1871–1933), spawning the Old Lyme Art Colony.

This stop on the American Impressionist Art Trail *(see pp202–203)* features more than 900 works by artists who at one time lived in the house or nearby. Many of Griswold's guests painted on the wall panels of the dining room as thanks for her generosity.

There is also a modern gallery which houses changing exhibitions. It is a work of art in itself, with a rippling aluminum canopy entrance, curvilinear walls and skylights to provide soft illumination.

🏛 **Florence Griswold Museum**
96 Lyme St, Old Lyme. *Tel (860) 434-5542.* 🕐 *year-round: 10am–5pm Tue–Sat, 1–5pm Sun.* 🅿 ⬛ ♿

Essex ⑱

🏠 2,500. 🛈 *32 Huntington St, New London (860) 444-2206.*

In surveys naming America's top small towns, Essex is often found at the head of the list. Sited on the Connecticut River, the village is surrounded by a series of sheltered coves and has a bustling marina and tree-lined, virtually crime-free streets.

The **Connecticut River Museum**, a restored 1878 warehouse, is perched on a dock overlooking the water. Its collection and exhibits of maritime art and artifacts tell the story of this once-prominent shipbuilding town, where the *Oliver Cromwell* – the first warship built for the American Revolution (1775–83) – was constructed. The museum's conversation piece is a replica of the world's first submersible craft, the *Turtle*, a squat, single-seat vehicle built in 1775. Transportation is also the focus at the **Essex Steam Train & Riverboat Ride**, where guests take an authentic, coal-belching steam engine for a 12-mile (19-km) scenic tour. At the midpoint, passengers can take a 90-minute cruise down the river aboard a riverboat.

🏛 **Connecticut River Museum**
67 Main St. *Tel (860) 767-8269.* 🕐 *year-round: 10am–5pm Tue–Sun (to 4pm in winter).* ● *Jan 1, Labor Day, Thanksgiving, Dec 24 & 25.* 🅿 ⬛ ♿

🚂 **Essex Steam Train & Riverboat Ride**
Exit 3 off Rte 9. *Tel (860) 767-0103 or (800) 377-3987.* 🕐 *May–Dec: call for ride times.* 🅿 ⬛ 🕚 www.essexsteamtrain.com

Environs
Five miles (8 km) north of Essex is Chester, home to **The Norma Terris Theatre**, a theater that presents new musicals. Across the Connecticut River the town of East Haddam offers spectacular views of river traffic from the **Goodspeed Opera House**. This late-Victorian "wedding cake" gem is the setting for new musicals and revivals, which are staged from April to December.

🎭 **The Norma Terris Theatre**
N Main St / Rte 82, Chester. *Tel (860) 873-8668.* 🕐 *call for show times.* 🅿 ♿

🎭 **Goodspeed Opera House**
Rte 82, East Haddam. *Tel (860) 873-8668.* 🕐 *call for show times.* 🅿 ♿

Replica of the first submersible at Connecticut River Museum

Gillette Castle ⑲

See pp218–19.

Madison ⑳

🏠 16,000. 🛈 *169 Orange St, New Haven (203) 777-8550 or (800) 332-7829.*

Madison is a resort town full of antique stores and boutiques, including a specialty store that stocks British kippers, bangers, and pork pies. Several historic homes are open for viewing, including the 1685 **Deacon John Grave House**. The structure has served as tavern, armory, courthouse, and infirmary, but has always belonged to the Graves. One of the oldest artifacts on display is the family's bookkeeping ledger, with entries from 1678 to 1895.

Madison is also home to **Hammonasset Beach State Park**, the largest shoreline park in the state. Poking into Long Island Sound, the peninsula has a 2-mile- (3-km-) long beach that attracts swimmers, sailors, scuba divers, and sunbathers. The park has walking trails, picnic areas, and a 550-site campground.

Deacon John Grave House
581 Boston Post Rd. *Tel (203) 245-4798.* mid-Jun–early Sep: 1–4pm Sat.

Hammonasset Beach State Park
I-95, exit 62. **Park** *Tel (203) 245-2785.* **Campground reservations** *Tel (877) 668-2267.* **Park** 8am–dusk daily.

The boardwalk at Hammonasset Beach State Park in Madison

Guilford ㉑

20,000. 169 Orange St, New Haven (203) 777-8550 or (800) 332-7829. www.visitnewhaven.com

In 1639 Reverend Henry Whitfield (1597–1657) led a group of Puritans from Surrey, England, to a wild parcel of land near the West River. There they established the town of Guilford. A year later, fearing an attack by local Mennuncatuk Indians, the colonists built a three-story stronghold out of local granite. The Tudor Gothic-style fort, the oldest stone dwelling of its type in New England, now serves as the **Henry Whitfield State Historical Museum**. The austere interior has a 33-ft- (10-m-) long great hall and 17th-century furnishings.

Guilford is graced by dozens of historic 18th-century homes. Both the **Hyland House**, a classic early saltbox *(see p26)*, and the 1774 **Thomas Griswold House** are open to view. **Dudley Farm**, a 19th-century working farm

and living history museum, demonstrates agricultural techniques of the era. In mid-July craftsmen gather on Guilford Green for the Guilford Handcraft Exposition *(see p33)*.

Henry Whitfield State Historical Museum
248 Old Whitfield St. *Tel (203) 453-2457.* Apr–mid-Dec: 10am–4:30pm Wed–Sun; mid-Dec–Jan: by appt only.

Hyland House
84 Boston St. *Tel (203) 453-9477.* Jun–Labor Day: 10am–4:30pm Tue–Sat, noon–4:30pm Sun. Columbus Day. obligatory.

Thomas Griswold House
171 Boston St. *Tel (203) 453-3176.* Jul–Aug: 11am–4pm Tue–Sat, noon–4pm Sun; Jun & Sep: Sat & Sun only.

Dudley Farm
2351 Durham Rd. *Tel (203) 457-0770.* Apr–Oct: 10am–1pm Mon–Sat.

The Thimbles ㉒

from Stony Creek Dock (203) 488-8905. (203) 777-8550.

From Stony Creek, travelers can cruise to the Thimble islands aboard one of several tour boats that operate in the area. Many of the 365 islands are little more than large boulders visible only at low tide. Some of the privately owned islands sport small communities. One colorful legend about this clutch of islands centers on circus midget General Tom Thumb (1838–83) courting a woman on Cut-In-Two Island. Another has the privateer Captain Kidd (1645–1701) hiding plundered treasure on Money Island while being pursued by the British fleet. Today cruisers watch seals or take in glorious fall colors.

The Thimbles, home to seals, whales, and colorful legends

Gillette Castle ⑲

Entrance sign

Ostentatious and bizarre, Gillette Castle is the antithesis of New England architectural grace. However, visitors to the 24-room granite mansion always leave with a smile. Actor William Gillette (1853–1937) based the design of his 1919 dream home on medieval castles, complete with battlements and turrets. The castle is rife with such oddities as Gillette's homemade trick locks, furniture set on wheels and tracks, a cavernous 1,500-sq-ft (139-sq-m) living room, and a series of mirrors starting in his bedroom that permitted him to see who was arriving downstairs in case he wished to be "indisposed" or make a grand entrance.

Park and goldfish pond, a pleasing vista

Servants' quarters

The View
The castle has a view of the Connecticut River and its traffic. Gillette lived on a houseboat for five years while the castle was constructed.

The Study
Gillette spent much of his time in the Study. The chair at his desk is on a set of small tracks so it can be easily moved back and forth.

Castle Grounds
Following Gillette's death, the castle and its 117 acres (47 ha) became a state park. His railroad with its two locomotives used to carry guests on a three-mile (5-km) tour through the property. Now visitors walk the trails.

STAR FEATURES

★ Library

★ The Great Hall

Main Entrance
The huge oak door through which visitors must pass is equipped with an elaborate homemade lock.

For hotels and restaurants in this region see pp316–19 and pp346–8

WILLIAM GILLETTE

An eccentric playwright and actor, Gillette caught the acting bug early, leaving college at age 20 to tread the boards. His most famous role, repeated many times in repertory, was Sherlock Holmes. He was reputed to have made $3 million playing the fictional sleuth. Gillette spent $1 million to build his folly. His will stipulated that it should never fall into the hands of "any blithering saphead."

VISITORS' CHECKLIST

67 River Rd off Rte 82, Hadlyme. **Tel** (860) 526-2336.
☐ **Castle** late May–Columbus Day: 10am–4:30pm daily. **Park** 8am–sunset daily. 🚭 📷 castle only. ♿ first floor and terrace.

★ Library
The self-educated Gillette's book collection ranges far and wide.

Mezzanine

Castle Exterior
Constructed on a steel framework, the castle is built of fieldstone bought from local farmers and lifted up the hill on an aerial tram designed by Gillette.

Outdoor terrace

Outdoor terrace

★ The Great Hall
Exposed stone walls are five feet (1.5 m) thick in some places, and heavy oak covers steel beams. Gillette had a generator installed to provide power, but the castle is still dark and baronial.

New Haven ㉓

The land on which Connecticut's third most populous city stands was purchased from the Quinnipiac Indians in 1638 for a few knives, coats, and hatchets. The city's location on the coast where the West, Mill, and Quinnipiac rivers flow into Long Island Sound has helped make it one of the state's major manufacturing centers. Over the centuries, items ranging from clocks and corsets to musical instruments, carriages, and Revolutionary War cannonballs have been made here. In 1716 Yale University *(see pp222–5)* moved from Saybrook to New Haven, establishing the city as a center for education, technology, and research. Today New Haven also offers opportunities for attending theater, opera, dance performances, and concerts.

Amistad Memorial

Exploring Downtown New Haven

The 16-acre (6-ha) New Haven Green is the central section of the original nine symmetrical town squares the Puritans laid out in New Haven, the first planned city in America. The Green has been the focal point of local life ever since, serving as the setting for many of New Haven's activities and festivals. Three churches, all built between 1812 and 1815, sit on the Green on Temple Street. United Church on the Green (often called North Church for its northern location) is in the style of London's St. Martin-in-the-Fields. Graced by a beautiful Tiffany stained-glass window, the First Church of Christ (Center Church) is considered an architectural masterpiece of the American Georgian style. The crypt beneath the church holds the remains of some of the city's original colonists. Among the notables buried here are Benedict Arnold's first wife, Margaret, and James Pierpont (1659–1714), one of the founders of Yale University. Trinity Church on the Green was one of the first Gothic-style churches in America.

Looming on the corner of Court and Church streets is the monumental Greek

Tiffany stained-glass window at First Church of Christ

Revival post office, now the Federal District Court, designed in 1913 by James Gamble Rogers (1867–1947), architect of many of Yale University's Gothic Revival buildings. City Hall faces the Green on Church Street and epitomizes high Victorian style, with its polychrome limestone-and-sandstone facade. In front of City Hall, the 14-ft- (4-m-) tall bronze Amistad Memorial, which honors Senghe Pieh (also known as Joseph Cinque), leader of the *Amistad* revolt *(see p198)*, is on the exact site of the jail where the mutinous slaves were held.

In late April the Green becomes the stage for Powder House Day, a reenactment of one of Benedict Arnold's few celebrated moments. At the start of the American Revolution, Arnold, then a captain in the militia, seized control of a municipal arsenal and led his troops to Boston to help bolster the sagging Colonial forces.

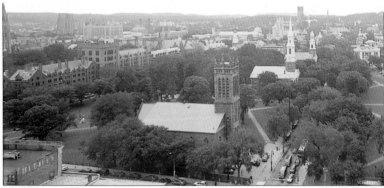

Church spires around New Haven Green

🏛 New Haven Museum and Historical Society

114 Whitney Ave. **Tel** (203) 562-4183. ◯ 10am–5pm Tue–Fri, noon–5pm Sat. ⬤ public hols. 🎫 🏠

This handsome Colonial Revival house traces the city's cultural and industrial growth from 1638 to the present. Exhibits include such items as Eli Whitney's cotton gin, the sign that hung over Benedict Arnold's George Street shop, a fine collection of colonial pewter and china, and permanent galleries on the *Amistad* and the city's maritime history.

🏛 Grove Street Cemetery

227 Grove St, gate at N end of High St. **Tel** (203) 787-1443. ◯ year-round: 8am–3:30pm daily. 🎫 ♿

Established in 1797 and covering 18 acres (7 ha), this was the first cemetery in the US to be divided into family plots. Walking through its 1848 Egyptian Revival gate, visitors will find a veritable who's who of New Haven. Eli Whitney (1765–1825), Noah Webster (1758–1843), Charles Goodyear (1800–1860), and Samuel F.B. Morse (1791–1872) are just some of the distinguished citizens buried in this cemetery.

The colorful 1916 carousel at Lighthouse Point Park

New Haven Parks

Among New Haven's many attractive parks, the 84-acre (34-ha) **Lighthouse Point Park** on Long Island Sound is a standout. The park has nature trails, a picnic grove, a splash pad, swimming facilities, a 1916 Coney Island-style carousel, and an 1847 lighthouse. **East Rock Park** offers

a spectacular view of Long Island Sound, New Haven, and the harbor and is criss-crossed by 10 miles (16 km) of nature trails. The 123-acre (50-ha) **Edgewood Park** has a duck pond, nature trail, in-line skating rink, and playground. Black Rock Fort, from the Revolutionary War period, and Fort Nathan Hale, vintage Civil War era, offer splendid views of New Haven Harbor.

🏞 Lighthouse Point Park

2 Lighthouse Rd. **Tel** (203) 946-8790. **Park** ◯ year-round: dawn–dusk daily. **Beach** ◯ Memorial Day–Labor Day: dawn–dusk daily. 🎫 ♿

🏞 East Rock Park

E Rock Park. **Tel** (203) 946-6086. ◯ year-round: 8am–dusk daily.

🏞 Edgewood Park

Edgewood Ave. **Tel** (203) 946-8028. ◯ year-round: dawn–dusk daily. ♿

🏛 Eli Whitney Museum

915 Whitney Ave, Hamden. **Tel** (203) 777-1833. ◯ noon–5pm Wed–Fri & Sun, 10am–3pm Sat. ⬤ public hols. 🎫 ♿ www.eliwhitney.org

On the northern outskirts of New Haven in the suburb of Hamden is the Eli Whitney Museum. One of the nation's earliest inventors, Whitney (1765–1825) was best known for developing the cotton gin, thereby automating the labor-intensive task of separating cotton from its seeds. Another of his inventions, a musket with interchangeable parts, revolutionized manufacturing. The museum contains examples of Whitney's achievements but the primary emphasis is on hands-on children's learning activities which emphasize creativity and inventiveness.

🦅 Connecticut Audubon Coastal Center

1 Milford Point Rd, Milford. **Tel** (203) 878-7440. **Center** ◯ year-round: 10am–4pm Tue–Sat, noon–4pm Sun. ⬤ gate closed at dusk. 🎫 🎫 ♿ 🏠 www.ctaudubon.org

Just 15 miles (16 km) south-west of New Haven, travelers come upon the Connecticut Audubon Coastal Center, one of the state's best birding sites. This 8.4-acre (3-ha) bird and wildlife sanctuary and nature center is situated on Long Island Sound at the mouth of the Housatonic River. Visitors can take nature walks along the beach or around the salt marsh and climb a 70-ft (21-m) tower overlooking Long Island Sound.

Eli Whitney Museum in Hamden, just north of New Haven

🏛 Shore Line Trolley Museum

17 River St, East Haven. **Tel** (203) 467-6927. ◯ Apr–Dec: call for hours. 🎫 ♿ partial. 🏠 www.bera.org

Five miles (8 km) to the east of New Haven in East Haven is the Shore Line Trolley Museum. The oldest rapid-transit car and first electric freight locomotive are among 100 vintage trolleys from 1878 onward on display. The museum also offers a 3-mile (5-km) trolley ride through salt marshes and woods on the oldest suburban trolley line in the country.

The 1840 lighthouse at Lighthouse Point Park

Yale University

Founded in 1701, this Ivy league school is one of the most prestigious institutions of higher learning in the world. The list of Yale's distinguished alumni includes Noah Webster (1758–1843), who compiled the nation's first dictionary, Samuel Morse (1791–1872), inventor of Morse code, and five US presidents, including George W. Bush (b.1946). While its law and medical schools attract much of the attention, Yale's other graduate programs (ranging from divinity to drama) are no less demanding. In some ways avant-garde, in others staunchly traditional, Yale admitted its first female Ph.D. student before the turn of the 20th century, but didn't become fully co-educational until 1969.

VISITORS' CHECKLIST

Across from New Haven Green.
ℹ️ 149 Elm St (203) 432-2300.
Call individual sites for hours.
🚻 ♿ 🅿️ International Festival
of Arts and Ideas (Jun).
www.yale.edu

Stiles and Morse Colleges at Broadway and Tower is by architect Eero Saarinen (1910–61), who based the design on an Italian mountain village. Philip Johnson's Kline Biology Tower, Yale's skyscraper, was completed in 1965.

🏛 **Yale Center for British Art**
1080 Chapel St. **Tel** (203) 432-2800.
🕐 year-round: 10am–pm Tue–Sat, noon–5pm Sun. 🔴 public hols. 🚻
♿ 🅿️ www.yale.edu/ycba
In 1966 Philanthropist Paul Mellon (1907–99)

Wrexham Tower, Branford College, on the Yale campus

Exploring Yale Campus
Yale's campus comprises much of New Haven's downtown core, with the main section located on the western flank of the New Haven Green. Campus buildings reflect the architectural eclecticism that runs through the university. **Connecticut Hall** is Yale's oldest building and the only one left of a row of Georgian buildings on the **Old Campus**, Yale's original quadrangle. Nathan Hale (see p211) and US President William Howard Taft (1857–1930) had rooms here when they were students.

Yale's oldest building, Connecticut Hall, constructed in 1717

After World War I, James Gamble Rogers (1867–1947) designed the **Memorial Quadrangle**, a beautiful Gothic complex that is now the heart of the campus. Another Rogers design, **Harkness Tower**, completed in 1921, was modeled on St. Botolph's Tower in Boston, England, and has a facade covered with sculptures celebrating Yale's history and traditions. Each day at noon and again at 6pm the beautiful sounds of the bell tower's carillon can be heard throughout New Haven. On the Memorial Gate near the tower, the school's motto is inscribed: "For God, for country, and for Yale."

Post-World War II architects have left their mark on campus, too. The **Yale School of Art and Architecture** is as controversial today as when it was built in the 1960s. From the outside this 36-level building seems to stand only seven stories tall. The collection of buildings that makes up Ezra

donated his collection of British art to the university. This was no small gift, considering it consisted of more than 50,000 paintings, prints, drawings, watercolors, and rare books and documents. Needing the right space to display its artistic windfall, the university hired American architect Louis Kahn (1901–74) to design an elegant new center. Thus was born this important collection covering the major art

Library Court in the Yale Center for British Art

schools and masters from Tudor times to the present. The museum has the largest collection of British art outside the UK. Included among the paintings are works by William Hogarth (1697–1764), Thomas Gainsborough (1727–88), and Joseph Turner (1775–1851). The fourth floor of the museum is arranged chronologically so that visitors are given an overview.

Statue of Elihu Yale (1649–1721)

0 meters 200

0 yards 200

Key to Symbols *see back flap*

YALE UNIVERSITY CAMPUS

Beinecke Library ②
Connecticut Hall ⑦
Harkness Tower ⑤
Memorial Quadrangle ④
Old Campus ⑥
Sterling Memorial Library ③
Yale Center for British Art ⑧
Yale Collection of Musical Instruments ①
Yale School of Art and Architecture ⑩
Yale University Art Gallery ⑨

🏛 Sterling Memorial Library

128 Wall St. ***Tel*** *(203) 432-2798.* ● *to the public.*

This striking library boasts stained-glass windows and Gothic arches and is the largest on the Yale University campus. It contains some 4 million items, including rare Babylonian tablets.

Gothic entrance to the Sterling Memorial Library

🏛 Beinecke Rare Book and Manuscript Libraries

121 Wall St. ***Tel*** *(203) 432-2977.* □ *year-round: 8:30am–8pm Mon–Thu, 8:30am–5pm Fri, 10am–5pm Sat.* ● *Sat in Aug & public hols.*

American architect Gordon Bunshaft (1909–90) built the walls of this library out of translucent marble. This unique design helps filter the sunlight, which could harm the library's illuminated medieval manuscripts and 7,000 books. The library owns a host of rare books and manuscripts, but its prized possession is one of the world's few remaining Gutenberg Bibles.

🏛 Yale University Art Gallery

1111 Chapel St. **Tel** *(203) 432-0600.*
◯ *10am–5pm Tue–Sat (Sep–Jun: until 8pm Thu), 1–6pm Sun.* ● *public hols.*
📷 ♿ 🛍 **www**.artgallery.yale.edu

This major collection of Asian, African, European, American, and pre-Columbian art comprises more than 100,000 objects and reflects the generosity and taste of Yale alumni and benefactors. While the museum was founded in 1832, its main building was completed in 1953 and is considered architect Louis Kahn's first masterpiece. A three-year, $44 million renovation, completed in 2006, replaced the signature window walls, refurbished the geometric ceilings, and reinstated Kahn's open plan to the galleries.

The gallery's vast collection highlights art as far back as ancient Egypt. It is famous for its American paintings, furniture, and decorative arts. Among its prized American pieces is John Trumbull's *The Battle of Bunker Hill* (1786). It also includes works by artists such as Picasso, Van Gogh, Monet, and Pollock.

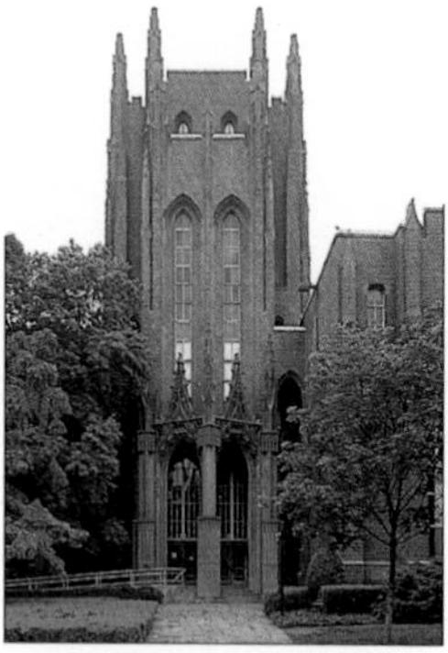

Entrance to the Peabody Museum of Natural History

🏛 Peabody Museum of Natural History

170 Whitney Ave. **Tel** *(203) 432-5050.*
◯ *year-round: 10am–5pm Mon–Sat, noon–5pm Sun.* ● *public hols.* 🎫
📷 ♿ 🛍 **www**.yale.edu.peabody

Visitors entering the museum are dwarfed by the imposing skeleton of a 67-ft- (20-m-) high *Brontosaurus* – an apt introduction to this outstanding museum, famous for its collection of dinosaurs.

Children migrate to the Great Hall of Dinosaurs, where they can mingle with the mastodon and socialize with the *Stegosaurus*. Included among the many fossils and realistic dioramas is a 75-million-year-old turtle.

Tour of Coastal Fairfield County [24]

P.T. Barnum

Travelers following Interstate 95 are bound to strike it rich along the "Gold Coast," so nicknamed because of the luxurious estates, marinas, and mansions concentrated between Greenwich and Southport. This, the southernmost corner of the state, has attractions sure to meet everyone's taste. The shoreline is dusted with numerous beaches offering a variety of summer recreation opportunities. Nature preserves, arboretums, planetariums, and the state's only zoo will appeal to naturalists of all ages. People of a more artistic bent can visit the area's numerous small galleries or visit some of its larger, well-established museums.

New Canaan Historical Society building

Stamford's First Presbyterian Church has the largest mechanical-action organ in the state.

Greenwich [6]
Blessed with a stunning coastline, this town is home to the Bush-Holley Historic Site, the state's first Impressionist art colony.

Stamford [5]
This major urban area has a lively downtown and the First Presbyterian Church, which is shaped like a fish.

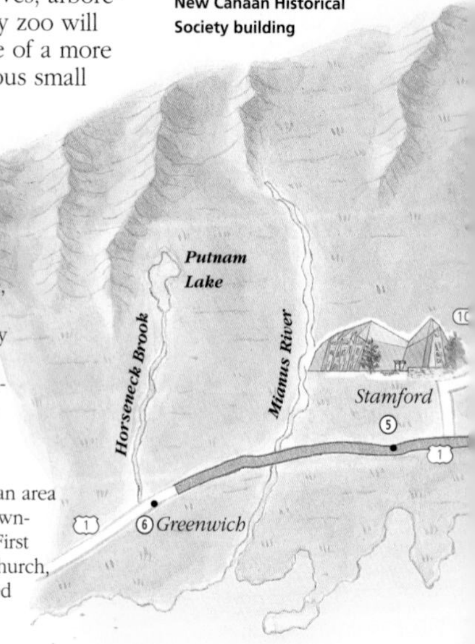
Putnam Lake
Horseneck Brook
Mianus River
Stamford
[5]
[1]
[6] Greenwich

Archelon, at 10 ft (3 m), ranks as the largest turtle that ever roamed the planet.

The Peabody's third floor has a slightly more contemporary feel, with displays ranging near and far – from daily life in Ancient Egypt to modern biodiversity in Connecticut. Elsewhere, visitors can admire exhibits on Native American or Pacific Island cultures, or examine minerals, meteorites, and exhibits on the solar system.

🏛 Yale Collection of Musical Instruments

15 Hillhouse Ave. **Tel** *(203) 432-0822.* ⬜ *Sep–Jun: 1pm–4pm Tue–Fri, 1–4pm Sun.* ⬤ *Jul–Aug.* 📷 📹 *by appt.* ♿ *partial.* **www**.yale.edu/musicalinstruments A must stop for the musically inclined, this stunning

collection of instruments, considered among the top ten of its kind, has 800 objects, including historic woodwind and stringed instruments. The collection was started by New Haven piano manufacturer Morris Steinert (1831–1912). Steinert's love of music (he also founded the New Haven Symphony) saw him travel to Europe to

collect and restore antique instruments, especially claviers and harpsichords, forerunners to his beloved piano. Some of the collection's violins and harpsichords date back centuries. The museum holds a series of concerts from September to April. Many of the concerts are performed using the historic instruments.

Angelic detail on Yale's graceful High Street Bridge

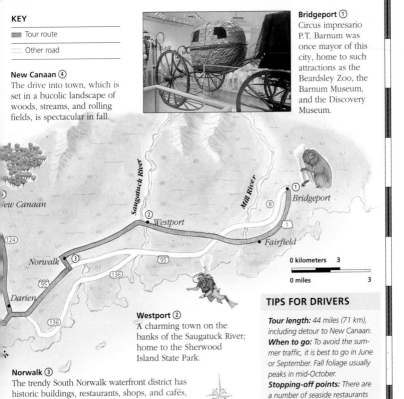

KEY

▬ Tour route

⋯⋯ Other road

New Canaan ④
The drive into town, which is set in a bucolic landscape of woods, streams, and rolling fields, is spectacular in fall.

Bridgeport ①
Circus impresario P.T. Barnum was once mayor of this city, home to such attractions as the Beardsley Zoo, the Barnum Museum, and the Discovery Museum.

ew Canaan

Saugatuck River

Mill River

① Bridgeport

② Westport

Fairfield

124

Norwalk ③

95

136

95

0 kilometers   3

0 miles   3

95

Darien

136

Westport ②
A charming town on the banks of the Saugatuck River; home to the Sherwood Island State Park.

Norwalk ③
The trendy South Norwalk waterfront district has historic buildings, restaurants, shops, and cafés, as well as the Maritime Aquarium at Norwalk.

TIPS FOR DRIVERS

Tour length: *44 miles (71 km), including detour to New Canaan.*
When to go: *To avoid the summer traffic, it is best to go in June or September. Fall foliage usually peaks in mid-October.*
Stopping-off points: *There are a number of seaside restaurants in Greenwich and Norwalk.*

VERMONT

Vermont was given its name by explorer Samuel de Champlain in 1609. The word means "Green Mountain" in French, and must have seemed most suitable when he gazed upon the fertile landscape. Almost 400 years later, Vermont is still very much an enclave of unspoiled wilderness, with thick forests blanketing the rolling hills and the valley lowlands.

In all there are just over a half a million people living in Vermont, one of the most rural states in the Union. The countryside is replete with manicured farms where the state's trademark black and white Holstein cattle graze against a backdrop of natural beauty. The pastoral landscape, dotted with pristine villages and covered bridges, evokes the idealized images found in paintings by longtime resident Norman Rockwell *(see p241)*. An anti-billboard law ensures that the countryside is not blighted by obtrusive advertisements.

Vermonters may be small in number, but they are nationalistic and often have led the country's conscience on social and political issues. The Stars and Stripes are a familiar sight in Vermont; the American flag, "Old Glory" as is it known, decorates many a front porch.

It is hardly surprising that people from around the world are attracted to this green corner of the US. Each season brings new opportunities to enjoy nature. When the countryside is covered in a blanket of snow, picturesque towns are transformed into bustling ski centers. Outdoor enthusiasts have long known that Vermont possesses some of the best boating, hiking, camping, and fishing in the country. Vermont is also a magnet for painters, writers, musicians, and poets who enrich the cultural life of the state. Regional theaters, museums, and art galleries are prominent attractions. But Vermont is at its scenic best in the fall, when thousands of "leaf peepers" come to see the natural phenomenon of leaves changing color *(see pp20–21)*. What makes the season so special here is the variety of colors that the trees manifest, from the palest mustard to flaming scarlet.

Grazing Holstein cows, a favorite breed in Vermont, in a typical state setting

◁ Vermont's trademark rural landscape

Montreal

Exploring Vermont

Unlike New England's coastal states, with attractions most often found along the water's edge, Vermont's highlights are sprinkled liberally throughout the state. The northeastern region boasts mountains, forests, and the fjordlike Lake Willoughby *(see pp230–31)*. Snaking down the western border, Lake Champlain and its islands *(see p236)* provide the backdrop for the collegial spirit of Burlington *(see pp232–5)* and the one-of-a-kind Shelburne Museum *(see pp238–9)*. Pre–Revolutionary War villages grace the south and provide good base camps for hikers looking to trek the Appalachian Trail *(see pp22–3)* or enjoy the splendor of the Green Mountain National Forest *(see p244)*.

Burlington's waterfront, well used by sailors and boaters

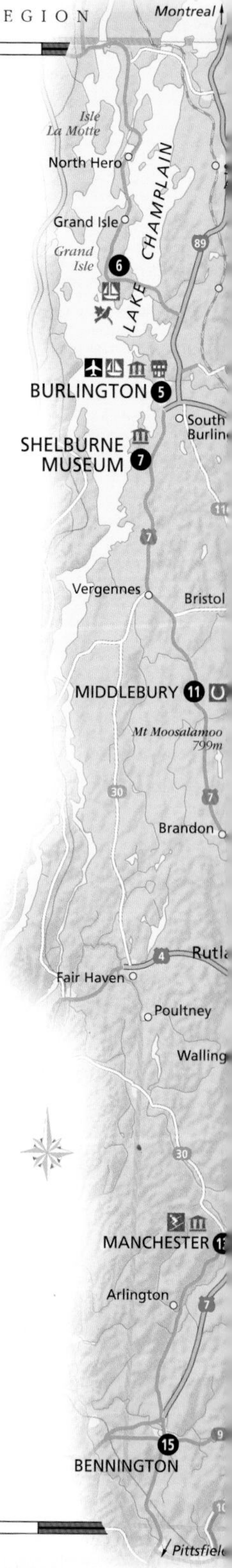

KEY

═══ Highway

─── Major road

∷∷∷∷ Minor road

━━━ Scenic route

━━━ Main railway

──── Minor railway

▭▭▭ International border

═══ State border

△ Summit

0 kilometers 25

0 miles 25

SEE ALSO

• **Where to Stay** pp319–22

• **Where to Eat** pp349–51

SIGHTS AT A GLANCE

Ben & Jerry's Ice
  Cream Factory **8**
Bennington **15**
Brattleboro **17**
Bread and Puppet Museum **3**
Burlington pp232–5 **5**
Grafton **18**
Green Mountain
  National Forest **14**
Killington **12**
Lake Champlain **6**

Lake Willoughby **2**
Mad River Valley **10**
Manchester **13**
Middlebury **11**
Montpelier **9**
St. Johnsbury **1**
Shelburne Museum
  pp238–9 **7**
Stowe **4**
Wilmington **16**
Woodstock **19**

Isle
La Motte

North Hero

Grand Isle

Grand
Isle **6**

LAKE CHAMPLAIN

BURLINGTON 5

South
Burlin

**SHELBURNE
MUSEUM 7**

Vergennes

Bristol

MIDDLEBURY 11

Mt Moosalamoo
799m

Brandon

Rutl

Fair Haven

Poultney

Walling

MANCHESTER 13

Arlington

**15
BENNINGTON**

Pittsfiel

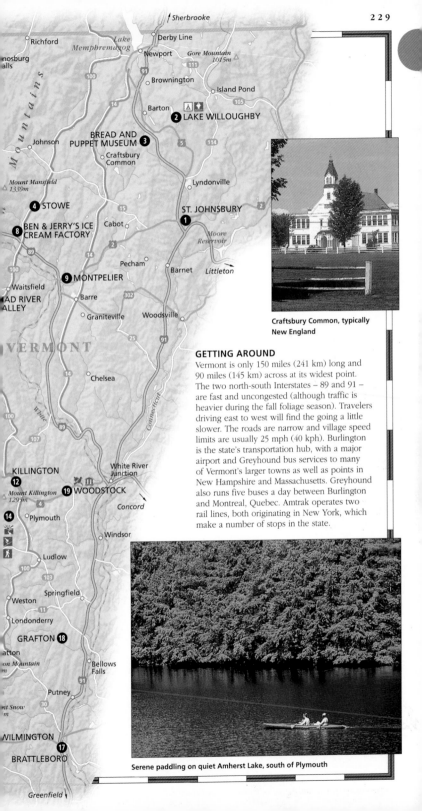

Craftsbury Common, typically New England

GETTING AROUND

Vermont is only 150 miles (241 km) long and 90 miles (145 km) across at its widest point. The two north-south Interstates – 89 and 91 – are fast and uncongested (although traffic is heavier during the fall foliage season). Travelers driving east to west will find the going a little slower. The roads are narrow and village speed limits are usually 25 mph (40 kph). Burlington is the state's transportation hub, with a major airport and Greyhound bus services to many of Vermont's larger towns as well as points in New Hampshire and Massachusetts. Greyhound also runs five buses a day between Burlington and Montreal, Quebec. Amtrak operates two rail lines, both originating in New York, which make a number of stops in the state.

Serene paddling on quiet Amherst Lake, south of Plymouth

St. Johnsbury ❶

🏘 7,800. ✈ 77 miles (125 km)
W in Burlington. 🚉 ℹ️ 51 Depot Sq
(802) 748-3678 or (800) 639-6379.
www.nekchamber.com

This small industrial town,
which is the unofficial capital
of Vermont's northeast region
– also called the "Northeast
Kingdom" – sits on a
promontory at the conver-
gence of the Moose, Sleeper,
and Passumpsic rivers. The
town is named for Saint Jean
de Crèvecour, who was a
friend of Revolutionary War
hero Ethan Allen. It was the
Frenchman who suggested
that "bury" be added to the
name because there were too
many towns called St. John.

It was here in 1830 that
mechanic Thaddeus Fairbanks
(1796–1886) invented the platform scale, an easier and more
accurate method of weighing
than the balances of the time.
The Fairbanks scale, as it came
to be known, put St. Johnsbury
on the map and boosted the
growth of other pioneer industries, notably the manufacturing of maple products.

The Fairbanks family
collected art and antiques,
which now are housed in
the **Fairbanks Museum and
Planetarium** – one of the
area's finest natural history
museums. This Romanesque-
style brick Victorian building,
now on the National Historic
Register, contains over
150,000 artifacts, including
4,500 stuffed birds and
animals, and tools, dolls, and

Tranquil waters of Lake Willoughby

toys. Also on Main Street is the
**St. Johnsbury Athenaeum Art
Gallery**, a Victorian gem with
gleaming woodwork, paneled
walls, and circular staircase.
The gallery highlights the
landscapes of the Hudson
River School of painting.
Popular in the 19th century,
the movement was the first
native school of American art,
and focuses on the beauty of
the natural world. Albert Bier-
stadt (1830–1902), whose
massive canvas *Domes of
Yosemite* (1867) hangs here,
was one of its leaders.

🏛 **Fairbanks Museum and
Planetarium**
1302 Main St. **Tel** (802) 748-2372.
Museum ⬜ 9am–5pm Tue–Sat,
1–5pm Sun (& mid-Apr–mid-Oct:
9am–5pm Mon). **Planetarium** ⬜
call for show times. 📷 ♿ ⬜
www.fairbanksmuseum.org

🏛 **St. Johnsbury Athenaeum
Art Gallery**
1171 Main St. **Tel** (802) 748-8291.
⬜ year-round: 10am–5:30pm
Mon–Fri, 9:30am–5pm Sat.
📷 ♿ ⬜ **www**.stjathenaeum.org

Environs
Nineteen miles (30 km) to
the west is Cabot, where one
of the state's best-known
agricultural products – cheddar
cheese – is made. The **Cabot
Creamery**, a farmers'
cooperative, was started in
1919 and now produces a
mind-boggling 100 million lbs
(45.5 million kg) of cheese a
year. The creamery offers
tours and free tastings.

🧀 **Cabot Creamery**
Main St, Cabot, Rte 215. **Tel** (802)
563-3393 or (800) 837-4261.
⬜ Jun–Oct: 9am–5pm daily;
Nov–Dec & Feb–May: 9am–4pm
Mon–Sat; Jan: 10am–4pm
Mon–Sat. ⬜ Jan 1, Thanksgiving.
📷 ♿ **www**.cabotcheese.com

Lake Willoughby ❷

Rte 5A near Barton. **Tel** (802) 748-
6687.

Travelers heading east
from Barton climb a crest on
the road only to be met with
the breathtaking view of this
beautiful body of water. The
narrow glacial lake, which
plunges 300 ft (90 m) in
certain areas, is flanked by
two soaring cliffs: Mount
Pisgah at 2,750 ft (840 m)
and Mount Hor at 2,650 ft
(810 m). Jutting straight out of
the water, the mountains give
the lake the appearance of a
rugged Norwegian fjord
or a resort in Switzerland,
garnering it the nickname
the "Lucerne of America."

With trails leading around
both promontories, this is a
haven for hikers and swimmers looking for a secluded
spot. There are wonderful
picnic and camping areas
along the beaches at either
end of the 5-mile (8-km) lake.
Several resorts and bed and
breakfast establishments ring
the shores. The lake itself
offers plenty of recreational
opportunities – fishing, boating, scuba diving – and there
are three nearby golf courses.

Environs
Because of its isolated
location 11 miles (18 km)
northwest of Lake Willoughby,
Brownington has retained the
look of an 18th-century
village, with few modern
touches. The **Old Stone House**
museum documents the
history of the region. Twenty-
two miles (35 km) to the
north of the lake lies Derby
Line – really two communities
in one. The northern half,
which is in Quebec, Canada,

Art on walnut wall panels at St.
Johnsbury Athenaeum Art Gallery

is called Rock Island. The border between Canada and the US runs through the middle of the **Haskell Free Library and Opera House**, a stately granite and brick building constructed in 1904.

Part of the audience sits in the US, but the stage is in Canada. The building's wealthy benefactor, Mrs. Martha Stewart Haskell (1831–1906), wanted both communities to enjoy her gift.

Old Stone House
109 Old Stone House Rd. *Tel (802) 754-2022.* ☐ *call for hours.* 🗓 *obligatory.* ♿ 🔲

Haskell Free Library and Opera House
93 Caswell Ave. *Tel (802) 873-3022.*
Library ☐ *year-round: 10am–5pm Tue–Wed & Fri–Sat, 10am–8pm Thu.*
Opera House ☐ *May–Oct: call for hours.* ● *Sun & Mon.* 🔲

Bread and Puppet Museum ❸

Exit 25 Rte 122 near Glover.
Tel (802) 525-3031 or (802) 525-1271. ☐ *Jun–Oct: call for hours and show times.* 🔲

An extraordinary place down a quiet rural road, this museum is a century-old, two-story building, which once served as a barn to shelter dairy cattle. The cattle

A selection of fanciful creatures at the Bread and Puppet Museum

have gone, but every inch of space is taken up by paintings, masks, and other theatrical knickknacks, most notably puppets of all shapes and sizes, dressed in outlandish costumes in every style. The props belong to the internationally famous Bread and Puppet Theater company, founded in 1962. Guided tours of the museum are the best way to glimpse the history behind the artistry. The troupe members live communally on the surrounding farm. Their productions are notable for the masterful use of giant puppets.

Typical Vermont church in Craftsbury Common

Environs
Small and graceful Craftsbury Common, just 14 miles (22 km) southwest, is pure Americana. Gnarled old trees, planted in 1799 to commemorate the death of George Washington (1732–99), the first president of the US, line the main street. The village green is flanked by handsome clapboard homes with black shutters, and is anchored at one corner by a typical New England church with a white wooden steeple. In winter the area is popular with cross-country skiers.

The Austrian-style Trapp Family Lodge

Stowe ❹

🏠 *3,500.* ✈ *40 miles (64 km) W in Burlington.* ℹ *51 Main St (802) 253-7321 or (877) 467-8693.* **www**.gostowe.com

It is hardly surprising that the Von Trapp family, whose daring escape from Austria during World War II was the inspiration behind the 1965 movie *The Sound of Music*, chose Stowe as their new home. The pretty village is ringed by mountains, which reminded them of the Alpine region they had left behind. Their Trapp Family Lodge *(see p322)* is part of the 2,700-acre (1,092-ha) estate. The giant wooden chalet is one of the area's most popular hotels.

The village has been a major ski and outdoor activity center since the 1930s. In winter it draws hordes of skiers looking to enjoy the region's best slopes *(see pp378–9).* Mountain Road begins in the village and is lined with chalets, motels, restaurants, and pubs; it leads to the area's highest peak, 4,393-ft (1,339-m) Mount Mansfield. Many local spas and resorts offer gourmet meals, and massages and other health treatments.

In summer there are still opportunities to enjoy the outdoors. Visitors can hike, rock-climb, fish, and canoe, or walk, cycle, or inline skate along the paved, meandering 5.5 mile (8.5 km) Stowe Recreational Path. It winds from Stowe's village church across the West Branch River, then through woodlands.

Burlington ❺

Burlington is one of Vermont's most popular tourist destinations. It is a lively university town with almost half of its population of just under 40,000 made up of students or people associated with the University of Vermont (UVM) and the city's four colleges. One of the oldest universities in the country, UVM was founded in 1791, the same year that Vermont officially joined the United States. Burlington's strategic location on the eastern shore of Lake Champlain *(see p236)* helped it prosper in pioneer times, and today it is Vermont's center of commerce and industry. The town is also rich in grand old mansions, historic landmarks, interesting shops, and restaurants and has an attractive waterfront. The famed American Revolution patriot Ethan Allen (1738–89), omnipresent throughout the state, has his final resting place here in Greenmount Cemetery.

The restored Flynn Theater, close to City Hall Place

Exploring Burlington

The center of Burlington is compact and easy to explore on foot. Battery Street, near the waterfront, is the oldest, most historic part of the city and a jumping-off point for ferries to New York State and sightseeing trips around Lake Champlain. More than 200 buildings in the downtown core have been renovated in recent years, and visitors will find many architectural landmarks, including the First Unitarian Church *(see pp234–5)*.

Battery Park, at the north end of Battery Street where it meets Pearl Street, was the site of a battle between US soldiers and the British Royal Navy. Burlington saw several skirmishes during the War of 1812, and scuba divers have found military artifacts at the bottom of the lake. Five shipwrecks, three lying close to Burlington, can be explored by divers who register with the Waterfront Diving Center on Battery Street.

These days Battery Park is a much more peaceful place. Lake Champlain is at its widest point here, and visitors who stroll through the park are rewarded with lovely views of Burlington Bay and the backdrop

of the Adirondack Mountains on the other side of the lake. Entertainment is presented in the park on Thursday evenings in summer.

Burlington's cultural life comes to the fore during its annual jazz festival in June. Venues for this popular

concert series include City Hall Place, Waterfront Park, the Church Street Marketplace *(see pp234–5)*, and the Flynn Theater. A former vaudeville theater and movie palace, the Flynn has had its Art Deco interior carefully restored, and now stages a variety of cultural events throughout the year.

Statue in Battery Park

Key to Symbols *see back flap*

KEY

⬜ Street-by-Steet map *see pp234–5*

| 0 meters | | 250 |
| 0 yards | | 250 |

Lake steamer with a full complement of sightseers

A Mozart festival, which started here at the University of Vermont, runs for three weeks in the summer and has spread to other communities. There are concerts held at Basin Harbor, UVM's Recital Hall, City Hall Park, and Shelburne Farms south of the city.

Tall-stack steamers used to ply the waters of Lake Champlain. Today visitors can board the three-decker cruise ship, *Spirit of Ethan Allen III*, which holds 425 passengers. Its 90-minute trip gives a good historical overview as the captain narrates entertaining tales of the Revolutionary War.

🚢 Spirit of Ethan Allen III
Burlington Boat House, College Street. **Tel** (802) 862-8300. ◯ May–Oct: 10am–6:30pm daytime and sunset dinner cruises (reservations necessary). **www**.soea.com

🏛 Robert Hull Fleming Museum
61 Colchester Ave. **Tel** (802) 656-0750. ◯ May–mid-Sep: noon–4pm Tue–Fri; mid-Sep–May: 9am–4pm Tue–Fri; year-round: 1–5pm SatSun. ◯ mid-Dec–mid-Jan, pub hols.

The museum is located on the campus of the **University of Vermont**, up on a hillside overlooking the city. Built in 1931, the elegant Colonial Revival building houses a huge collection of artifacts – more than 19,000 items – ranging from ancient Mesopotamia to modern times. Some of the items on display include European

Statue of Penelope in the Fleming Museum

and American paintings and sculptures, as well as Native Indian crafts and glassware.

🚍 Shelburne Farms
1611 Harbor Rd. **Tel** (802) 985-8686. **Dairy** ◯ mid-May–mid-Oct: 9:30am–3:30pm daily. **Farm Store** ◯ year round: 10am–5pm daily. partial. **www**.shelburnefarms.org Seven miles (11 km) south of town are Shelburne Museum (*see pp238–9*) and Shelburne Farms, a historic 1,400-acre (566-ha) estate. The parklike grounds of the latter include rolling pastures, woodlands, and a working farm. Tours are given of the dairy. There is a children's farmyard.

BURLINGTON TOWN CENTER

Part of the stately University of Vermont campus

Street-by-Street: Historic District

The four-block section known as the Church Street Marketplace is located at the center of the city's historic district. The neighborhood has been converted into a pedestrian mall complete with trendy boutiques, patio restaurants, specialty stores, factory outlets, craft shops, and, naturally, a Ben & Jerry's *(see p236)*. The marketplace, thronged with shoppers and sightseers at the best of times, is at its most vibrant in the summer months, with numerous street performers and musicians adding color and action. The district also has its share of historical attractions, including the 1816 First Unitarian Church.

Richardson Building
This 1895 chateau-style building was a 19th-century department store.

PEARL STREET

CHERRY STREET

CHURCH STREET

The Masonic Temple is Church Street's tallest structure.

★ First Unitarian Church
Standing at the head of Church Street, the First Unitarian Church was built in 1816 and stands as the oldest house of worship in Burlington.

The Burlington Montgomery Ward Building, built in 1929, is on the National Register of Historic Places. Its graceful lines and colorful facade typify pre-Depression architecture.

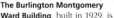

Central-Union Blocks
This was the first major development on upper Church Street. It now houses restaurants and pubs.

STAR SIGHTS

★ City Hall

★ First Unitarian Church

For hotels and restaurants in this region see pp319–22 and pp349–51

Pedestrian Mall

This section of the mall – particularly lively on weekends – is popular among students and tourists for its many shops and terraces. Cafés, pubs, and restaurants are housed in Queen Anne-style buildings from the late 1800s.

Merchants Bank

was built in 1895 by Burlington architect Sydney Greene.

★ City Hall

This 1928 building marks the southern boundary of the marketplace and is made of local brick, marble, and granite.

KEY

▢	Pedestrian mall
– – –	Suggested route

0 meters 25

0 yards 25

WOOSKI AVENUE

K STREET

COLLEGE STREET

MAIN STREET

Abraham Block was once considered the most striking commercial block in the state.

City Hall Park

The park is a popular outdoor concert venue. It features a poured concrete fountain and two granite monuments. One honors those who died in the Civil War; the other, soldiers who died in World War II.

Sailing and boating, popular on beautiful Lake Champlain

Lake Champlain ⑥

Vermont-New York border from
Whitehall to Alburg. ✈ *Burlington.*
🚌 ℹ️ *60 Main St, Burlington (802)
863-3489 or (877) 686-5253.*
www.vermont.org

Said to be the home of
"Champ," a water serpent
that could be a distant cousin
of Scotland's Loch Ness
Monster, Lake Champlain was
named for French explorer
Samuel de Champlain
(1567–1635). He discovered
and explored much of the
surrounding region. Some 120
miles (190 km) long and 12
miles (19 km) wide, the lake
has its western shore in New
York State, while the eastern
sector is in Vermont. Seasonal
hour-long ferry rides run
regularly between Burlington
and Port Kent, New York.

Sometimes called the sixth
Great Lake because of its size,
Champlain has 500 miles (800
km) of shoreline and about 70
islands. At the lake's northern
end, the Alburg Peninsula and
a group of thin islands (North
Hero, Isle La Motte, and Grand
Isle) give glimpses of the
region's colorful past.

At Ste. Anne's Shrine on
Isle La Motte is a statue of
Champlain. Grand Isle is home
to America's oldest log cabin
(1783). The villages of North
and South Hero were named
in honor of brothers Ethan and
Ira Allen. Their volunteers, the
Green Mountain Boys, helped
secure Vermont's status as a
separate state.

Some of Lake Champlain's
treasures are underwater, preserved in a marine park where
scuba divers can explore shipwrecks resting on sandbars
and at the bottom of the lake.

The **Lake Champlain Maritime
Museum** at Basin Harbor
gives an overview of the
region's marine history. On
display are ship models, old
divers' suits, and photographs
of Lake Champlain
steamers, the
most famous
of which
was the SS
Ticonderoga,
built in 1906.
Visitors can
board a full-scale
replica of a 1776
gunboat.

Ben & Jerry's bus, gaily
decorated with dairy cows

🏛 **Lake Champlain
Maritime Museum**
4472 Basin Harbor Rd, Vergennes.
Tel (802) 475-2022. ⏰ *late May–
Oct: 10am–5pm daily.* ♿
www.lcmm.org

Shelburne Museum ⑦

See pp238–9

Gold dome of the Vermont State
House in Montpelier

Ben & Jerry's Ice Cream Factory ⑧

Rte 100, Waterbury. **Tel** (802) 882-
1240 or (866) BJTOURS. ⏰ tours:
Jun: 9am–5pm daily; Jul–mid-Aug:
9am–9pm daily; mid-Aug–Oct: 9am–
7pm daily; Nov–May: 10am–5pm daily.
🅿️ ♿ 🚻 🏠 **www**.benjerry.com

Although Ben Cohen and
Jerry Greenfield hail from
Long Island, New York, they
have done more than any
other "flatlanders" to put
Vermont's dairy industry on
the map. In 1977 these child-
hood friends paid $5 for a cor-
respondence course on making
ice cream and parlayed
their knowledge into a
hugely successful
franchise.
Ben and
Jerry use the
richest cream
and milk from
local farms to
produce their ice
cream and frozen
yogurt. The Ben & Jerry
trademark is the black and
white Holstein cow, embellish-
ing everything in the gift shop.

Tours of the factory start
every 15 minutes and run
for 30 minutes. Visitors learn
all there is to know about
making ice cream. They are
given a bird's-eye view of
the factory floor, and at the
end of the tour a chance to
sample the products and
sometimes test new flavors.

Montpelier ⑨

🏠 8,400. ✈ 40 miles (64 km) NW
in Burlington. 🚌 🚉 ℹ️ (877) 887-
4968. **www**.central-vt.com

Montpelier is the smallest
state capital in the US,
but its diminutive stature is
advantageous: The city is
impeccably clean, friendly,
and easily seen on foot.
Despite its size, Montpelier has
a grand, imposing building to
house its state politicians and
legislators. The **Vermont State
House**, which dates back
to 1859, replaced an earlier
building that was destroyed
by fire. It is now a formidable

Greek Revival structure, complete with a gilt cupola and giant fluted pillars of granite that were hewn from one of the quarries at neighboring Barre.

The **Vermont Historical Society Museum**, run by the local historical society, is housed in a replica of a 19th-century hotel. The museum has also opened an additional center in Barre.

Vermont State House
115 State St. **Tel** (802) 828-2228.
year-round: 8am–4pm Mon–Fri.
Jul–mid-Oct: 10am–3:30pm Mon–Fri, 11am–2:30pm Sat.
public hols.

Vermont Historical Society Museum
109 State St. **Tel** (802) 828-2291.
10am–4pm Tue–Fri; May–Oct: also 10am–4pm Sat.

Environs
Seven miles (11 km) to the south, Barre (pronounced "berry") is the self-proclaimed granite capital of the world. In the 19th century, Italian and Scottish stonemasons came here to work the pale, white and blue-gray rock.

The region still is a hive of granite-related activity, with several large plants producing stone for tombstones (many have ended up in Barre's Hope Cemetery on Merchant Street), statues, and monuments. In nearby Graniteville, the **Rock of Ages Quarry** is the biggest such operation. Visitors can watch – from the safety of an observation deck – as the stone is being

hewn from the huge 475-ft (134-m) pit. On weekdays visitors can also take a self-guided tour to see artisans at work.

Rock of Ages Quarry
773 Main St, Graniteville.
Tel (802) 476-3119. late May–mid-Sep: 9:15am–3:35pm Mon–Sat; mid-Sep–mid-Oct: 9:15am–3:35pm daily. Jul 4.
www.rockofages.com

Mad River Valley ⑩

Central VT along Rte 100.
Rte 100, Waitsfield (802) 496-3409 or (800) 828-4748. Waitsfield, mid-May–Columbus Day: 9:30am–1pm Sat.
www.madrivervalley.com

Located in central Vermont, Mad River Valley is most famous for outdoor activities that include hiking, cycling, hunting, and especially skiing.

One popular stop is the Mad River Glen ski area (see p.378), which attracts die-hard traditionalists who enjoy their sport the old-fashioned way – without fancy high-speed gondolas (though there are four chairlifts) and snow-making equipment. With only a couple of dozen trails, Mad River Glen caters to the country's most skilled skiers – in fact, its motto is "Ski it if you can."

Sugarbush, on the other hand, has more than 100 trails and a vertical drop of 2,650 ft (800 m). It is the polar opposite of Mad River Glen. This trendy resort, which caters to beginners and intermediate skiers as well as those who are

Moss Glenn Falls near Warren in Mad River Valley

more advanced, has the most modern snowmaking facilities and lifts. It was very popular with the 1960s "jet set," but now a more "retro" crowd who own time-share condos frequents the slopes. A state-of-the-art express "people mover" connects what used to be two separate ski areas: Lincoln Peak and Mount Ellen.

Activities in and around Waitsfield, the small, fashionable, and wealthy community that is the center of this tourist region, include hiking, hunting, and – of all things – polo. The local landmark is a round barn, which is one of only a dozen remaining in the state. It is a venue for cultural functions and art exhibits. It sits next to an elegant inn and restaurant that have been converted from an 1806 farmhouse.

Bucolic scenery outside of Waitsfield, a popular summer destination

Shelburne Museum **❼**

More than just an eclectic repository, the Shelburne Museum celebrates three centuries of American ingenuity, creativity, and diversity. Here folk art, antique tools, duck decoys, and circus memorabilia are displayed on the same grounds as scrimshaw, Native American artifacts, and paintings by such US artists as Winslow Homer (1836–1910) and Grandma Moses (1860–1961). Established in 1947 by collector Electra Webb (1888–1960), the museum's 39 exhibition buildings and their contents constitute one of the nation's finest museums.

Big Chief statue

★ **Circus Building**
The horseshoe-shaped building houses a 500-ft- (152-m-) long miniature circus parade. The west entrance foyer features this 3,500-piece miniature circus.

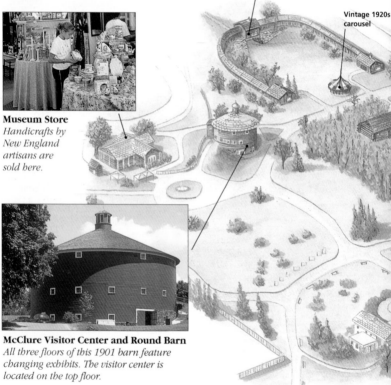

Vintage 1920s carousel

Museum Store
Handicrafts by New England artisans are sold here.

McClure Visitor Center and Round Barn
All three floors of this 1901 barn feature changing exhibits. The visitor center is located on the top floor.

KEY

- ☐ Illustrated
- ☐ Not illustrated

1 Museum Store and Entrance
2 McClure Visitor Center and Round Barn
3 Circus Building and Carousel
4 Railroad Station
5 Beach Gallery
6 Beach Lodge
7 SS *Ticonderoga*
8 Electra Havemeyer Webb Memorial Building
9 Lighthouse
10 Webb Gallery
11 Covered Bridge
12 Meeting House
13 Horseshoe Barn

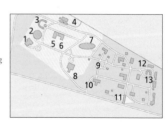

★ Railroad Station
The station was built in 1890 in Shelburne, Vermont, and relocated here. It houses a variety of railroad memorabilia, including telegraphy systems, vintage railroad maps, a restored stationmaster's office, and men's and women's waiting rooms.

VISITORS' CHECKLIST

Rte 7, 7 miles (11 km)
S of Burlington.
Tel (802) 985-3346.
◻ mid-May–late Oct: 10am–5pm daily. ● late Oct–mid-May.
🖼 ♿ 🍴 📷 🎞 *flash photography restricted in some buildings.*
www.shelburnemuseum.org.

Beach Lodge contains a variety of big-game trophies and Native American artifacts.

Locomotive 220, a 1915 10-wheel steam locomotive, hauled freight and passenger trains. Engine 220 could pull 12.5 tons (11 tonnes) of dead weight.

1871 Lake Champlain Lighthouse
Built to warn ships off reefs in the lake, the building now tells of the life led by lighthouse keepers.

★ SS *Ticonderoga*
A National Historic Landmark, the SS Ticonderoga was still in operation when Webb bought it in 1951. Today the former Lake Champlain steamship is open for visitors to explore.

STAR FEATURES

★ Circus Building

★ Railroad Station

★ SS *Ticonderoga*

Middlebury ⓫

🏛 8,500. ✈ 36 miles (58 km)
N in Burlington. 🚌 ℹ 2 Court St
(802) 388-7951 or (800) 733-8376.
www.midvermont.com

Middlebury, founded in 1761, is the archetypal New England town. It has not one, but two village greens, or "commons," tall-spired churches, a prestigious college, and a collection of Colonial-era homes. In all Middlebury lays claim to more than 300 buildings that were constructed during the 18th and early 19th centuries. Chief among them are the Congregational Church, the Battell and Beckwith commercial blocks, and the Middlebury Inn, a classic brick Georgian-style hostelry with shuttered windows that dates back to 1827.

Peaceful campus of Middlebury College

The town sits on Otter Creek, which at one time powered the machinery for a thriving wool and grain industry. But the town gets its name from the days of stage coaches when Middlebury served as the transit point on Vermont's main north-south and east-west routes. Morgan horses, one of the first US native breeds, were often seen on this route. Today visitors can tour the **University of Vermont Morgan Horse Farm**, which is dedicated to the preservation and improvement of this versatile and historic breed. Between 60 and 80 stallions, mares, and foals are cared for by agricultural science students.

History buffs will enjoy the **Henry Sheldon Museum of Vermont History**, an 1829 house that documents the early 19th century through its collection of furniture, textiles and clothing, and portraits.

Folk art and folk ways meet the 21st century at the **Vermont Folklife Center** where multi-media exhibits using computers and iPods help bring rural culture to life.

Morgan Horse Farm

The center's Heritage Shop features quilts, decoys, baskets, and other objects made by contemporary folk artists. The 500-acre (200-ha) campus of **Middlebury College** is a delightful place to explore, with graceful architecture, an art gallery, and green spaces.

The college's Bread Loaf campus in nearby Ripton is nestled in the Green Mountain National Forest *(see p244)* near the scenic Robert Frost Interpretive Trail. Named for the famous American poet who spent summers here from 1938 to 1962, the path is flanked with quotations from Frost's poems set on plaques.

🅤 **University of Vermont Morgan Horse Farm**
Rte 23 NW of Middlebury in Weybridge. **Tel** (802) 388-2011.
◯ May–Oct: 9am–4pm daily. 🏛
🗲 🕭

🏛 **Henry Sheldon Museum of Vermont History**
1 Park St. **Tel** (802) 388-2117. ◯ 10am–5pm Tue–Sat, 1–5pm Sun (call for winter hours). ◐ Feb. 🏛 🕭

🏛 **Vermont Folklife Center**
88 Main St. **Tel** (802) 388-4964.
◯ Jan–late May: 10am–5pm Tue–Sat; late May–Dec: 10am–5pm Mon–Sat, noon–4pm Sun. 🕭

🏫 **Middlebury College**
College St. **Tel** (802) 443-5000.
◯ year-round: Mon–Fri.
🗲 🕭

Killington ⓬

🏛 1,000. ✈ 5 miles (8 km) W in Rutland. ℹ Rte 4, West Killington (802) 422-3333 or (800) 621-6867.

Sporty types who like outdoor adventure and a lively social life head for this year-round resort. Killington has a highly developed tourism infrastructure, with hundreds of condominiums, vacation homes, ski lodges and B&Bs, golf courses, hiking and bike trails, and an adventure center with water slides and a climbing wall. It operates the largest ski center *(see p378)* in the eastern United States, with 200 runs for alpine skiing and snowboarding spread across seven peaks including nearby Pico Mountain. Killington itself is the second-highest peak in Vermont at 4,240 ft (1,295 m). Two of the best cross-country ski centers in the eastern US – Mountain Top Ski and Mountain Meadows Ski

One of the numerous trails at Killington, Vermont

Touring – are also situated in the Killington area.

The ski season here usually lasts eight months, longer than anywhere else in Vermont, and one of the gondolas that ferry skiers to the peaks runs during the summer and fall as well. It is worth taking a ride to the top for the spectacular views. On a clear day, visitors can glimpse parts of five states and distant Canada. Killington also keeps busy throughout the summer with arts and crafts shows, barbecues, and music festivals.

Manchester ⑬

🏠 3,860. ✈ 33 miles (53 km) N in Rutland. 🚌 🛈 Suite 1, 5046 Main St (802) 362-2100 or (800) 362-4144. **www**.manchestervermont.net

Manchester is actually made up of three separate communities: Manchester Depot and Manchester Center, the outlet centers of New England, and Manchester Village. The sum of these parts is a picturesque destination surrounded by mountains, typical of scenic southern Vermont. There are two major ski areas: Stratton, a large complex with more than 90 trails and a hillside ski village with shops and restaurants; and Bromley, a busy, family-oriented ski area.

Manchester has been a popular vacation resort since the 19th century, when wealthy urbanites used to head to the mountains to escape the summer heat. The town's marble sidewalks fringed by old shade trees, the restored Equinox Resort *(see p321)*, and several stately homes evoke that era. Today's tourists take pleasure in following the Equinox Skyline Drive, a toll road, with its panoramic view of the countryside from the crest of Mount Equinox. Many visitors spend their time hunting for brand-name bargains in the designer outlets and factory stores.

One of Manchester's largest and most elegant houses is **Hildene**, a 24-room Georgian Revival manor house built by Robert Lincoln (1843–1926), a lawyer, diplomat, and the son of President Abraham Lincoln (1809–65). Among the mansion's most notable features are its 1,000-pipe Aeolian organ and Lincoln family memorabilia. The grounds are graced with an impeccable formal garden. In winter, 8 miles (14 km) of trails are open to cross-country skiers.

Also housed in a stately Georgian mansion, the **Southern Vermont Arts Center** rotates its permanent collection of 700 paintings and photographs. The hilly 400 acres (160 ha) also contain a striking sculpture garden. Elsewhere the **American Museum of Fly Fishing**, which moved to larger quarters in 2004, claims to house the largest collection of fly-fishing paraphernalia in the world.

Antique kitchenware on display at elegant Hildene

The collection includes hundreds of rods, reels, and flies used by famous people such as singer Bing Crosby, literary giant Ernest Hemingway, and former US president Jimmy Carter.

🏛 **Hildene**
Rte 7A. **Tel** (802) 362-1788.
◯ year-round: 9:30am–4:30pm daily. ● Easter, Thanksgiving, Dec 25–27. 📷 🚻
www.hildene.org

🏛 **Southern Vermont Arts Center**
West Rd. **Tel** (802) 362-1405.
◯ May–Dec: 10am–5pm Tue–Sat, noon–5pm Sun. 📷 🚻 🍴

🏛 **American Museum of Fly Fishing**
4104 Main St. **Tel** (802) 362-3300.
◯ Jan–Apr: 10am–4pm Tue–Sat; May–Dec: 10am–4pm Tue–Sun.
📷 🚻

Environs
Nine miles (14 km) southwest lies little Arlington, with two major claims to fame: angling and art. Nearby Battenkill River is considered by experienced fishermen to be one of the best trout rivers in the state, if not the whole of New England. Local anglers have served as subjects for artist Norman Rockwell (1894–1978) during the years that he lived here. The **Norman Rockwell Exhibition** houses a collection of his work and photographs of some of the townsfolk he used as models.

🏛 **Norman Rockwell Exhibition**
Rte 7A. **Tel** (802) 375-6423.
◯ May–Oct: 10am–4pm daily.
📷 🚻

NORMAN ROCKWELL IN VERMONT

Painter and illustrator Norman Rockwell, famous for idealized depictions of small-town America, lived in Arlington at the height of his career, from 1939 to 1954. His paintings were so detailed they looked almost like photographs, and the magazine covers that he designed for publications such as

Norman Rockwell surveys his work surrounded by friends and his son c.1944

Saturday Evening Post, the *Ladies' Home Journal*, and *Look*, have become collectors' items. Admirers of his work should be sure to visit the Norman Rockwell Museum in Stockbridge, Massachusetts *(see pp166–7)*, and Arlington *(see right)*.

Green Mountain National Forest ⓮

ℹ️ *Forest Supervisor, Green Mountain National Forest, 231 N Main St, Rutland.* **Tel** *(802) 747-6700.* **Hapgood Campground Tel** *(877) 444-6777 for reservations (all other campgrounds on first-come, first-served basis).* ☐ *year-round.* ♿ *to campgrounds.* **www**.recreation.gov

This huge spine of greenery and mountains runs for 350,000 acres (142,850 ha) – almost the entire length of the state – along two-thirds of the Green Mountain range. The mountains, many more than 4,000 ft (1,200 m) high, have some of the best ski centers in the eastern United States, including Sugarbush *(see p237)* and Mount Snow *(see p246)*. A large network of snowmobile and cross-country ski trails are also maintained throughout the winter months.

The National Forest is divided into northern and southern sectors, and encompasses six wilderness areas; sections of the forest have remained entirely undeveloped – no roads, no electricity, and even paths may be poorly marked or non-existent. While hard-core backcountry hikers and campers may enjoy this challenge, the majority of

Woodward Reservoir in the Green Mountain National Forest

travelers will prefer to roam the less primitive areas of the forest. Picnic sites and camp-grounds are found through-out, along with more than 500 miles (805 km) of hiking paths, including the challenging Long and Appalachian trails *(see pp22–3)*.

Many lakes, rivers, and, reservoirs offer excellent boating and fishing opportunities. On land, bike paths (both mountain and road) are numerous and specially designated paths are open to horseback riders. Regardless of their mode of transportation, visitors are encouraged to stay on the paths in order to preserve the delicate ecosystem. Markers indicate designated lookout points and covered bridges. The town of Stratton in the

southern portion of the Green Mountain range offers recreational activities such as golf, horseback riding, sailing, and fly fishing, as well as alpine and cross-country skiing. The Stratton Arts Festival is held in the fall. Nearby Bromley Mountain Ski Center has been a popular family resort since the 1930s.

Bennington ⓯

🚶 16,800. ✈️ 🚌 ℹ️ *100 Veterans Memorial Dr (802) 447-3311 or (800) 229-0252.* 🏛️ *Wed & Fri.* **www**.bennington.com

Although it is tucked away in the southwest corner of the Green Mountain National Forest bordering Massachusetts and New York

Dense woodlands of the Green Mountain National Forest

◁ **Paper Mill Village Bridge, originally built in 1889, near Bennington**

State, Bennington is no backwoods community. The third-largest city in the state, Bennington is an important manufacturing center and home to Bennington College, the faculty of which once included cutting-edge engineer Buckminster Fuller (1895–1983).

Three covered bridges (just off Route 67) herald the approach to town. These 19th-century wooden structures, built with roofs to protect them against the harsh Vermont winter, were nicknamed "kissing bridges" because in the days of horses and buggies they provided a discreet shelter for courting couples to embrace.

Bennington was established in 1749 and a few decades later Ethan Allen arrived on the scene to lead the Green Mountain Boys, a citizen's militia originally created to protect Vermont from the expansionist advances of neighboring New York. Allen would later make his name as a patriot during the Revolutionary War by leading his men into battle and scoring several decisive victories against British forces.

The revolutionary era comes alive during a walking tour of the **Old Bennington Historic District** just west of the downtown core, where a typical New England village green is ringed by pillared Greek Revival structures and Federal-style brick buildings. The 1806 **First Congregational Church**, with its vaulted plaster and wood ceilings, is a striking and much-photographed local landmark. Next to it is the Old Burying Ground, resting place of five Vermont governors

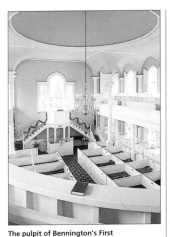

The pulpit of Bennington's First Congregational Church

and the beloved poet Robert Frost (see pp30–31).

Looming over the Historic District is the 306-ft- (93-m-) high **Bennington Battle Monument**, a massive stone obelisk that, when it was built in 1891, was the tallest war monument in the world. It commemorates a 1777 battle in nearby Willoomsac Heights, when the colonial forces defeated the British army and their allies, leading to the surrender of their commander, General John Burgoyne (1722–92). An elevator takes visitors to an observation area that affords panoramic views of Vermont and the neighboring states of New York and Massachusetts.

The turbulent times of the Revolutionary and Civil wars are also recalled at the **Bennington Museum and Grandma Moses Gallery**. The museum houses several dozen paintings by famed folk artist Anna Mary "Grandma" Moses (1860–1961), who lived in the Bennington area. A farmer's wife with no formal training in art, Moses started

The 1891 Bennington Battle Monument

painting landscapes as a hobby when she was in her mid-70s. She was "discovered" by the critics in 1940, when a collection of her art was shown at a private exhibition in the Museum of Modern Art in New York City. At that time the 79-year-old primitive artist was being hailed as an important new talent. By the time she died in 1961 at the age of 101, Grandma Moses had produced some 1,600 works of art, including a series of tiny country scenes painted on mushrooms. The collection in Bennington includes her only known self-portrait.

The Museum's comprehensive collection of Americana also includes uniforms, furniture, and examples of pottery from Bennington's ceramics industry, which reached its peak in the mid-19th century. The display of American glassware includes examples of the decorative Art Nouveau style that was popularized by Louis Comfort Tiffany (1848–1933).

Portrait of Governor Paul Brigham

🏛 **Old Bennington Historic District**
Tel (802) 447-3311 or (800) 229-0252.

🏛 **First Congregational Church**
Monument Ave. *Tel* (802) 447-1223.
🕆 11am Sun (also 9:30am Jul–Aug). 🅿

🏛 **Bennington Battle Monument**
15 Monument Circle. *Tel* (802) 447-0550. 🕐 mid-April–late Oct: 9am–5pm daily. 🅿 🚻

🏛 **Bennington Museum and Grandma Moses Gallery**
75 Main St. *Tel* (802) 447-1571.
🕐 10am–5pm Thu–Tue. 🕐 Jan 1, Thanksgiving, Dec 25. 🅿 🚻 📷
www.benningtonmuseum.com

For hotels and restaurants in this region see pp319–22 and pp349–51

Wilmington 16

🏛 *1,950.* ✈ *8 miles (13 km) NW in West Dover.* 🚉 *21 W Main St (802) 464-8092 or (877) 887-6884.*

Wilmington is the largest village in the Mount Snow Valley, with several dozen restaurants and stores catering to the tourists who come to enjoy outdoor sports at the nearby mountain. Like so many of Vermont's small towns, its Main Street is lined with restored 18th- and 19th-century buildings, many listed on the National Register of Historic Places.

Standing 3,600 ft (1,100m) tall, **Mount Snow** is named after the original owner of the land, farmer Reuben Snow, although most visitors believe the name refers to the abundance of white stuff that during winter is the resort's *raison d'être.*

In the late 1990s, more than $35 million was spent on upgrading the ski center, which now has 102 trails, many of them wooded, spread over 610 acres (247 ha). Mount Snow was one of the first ski resorts in the US to provide facilities for snowboarders, with dedicated learning areas for beginners and facilities for advanced surfers. The center also opened the first mountain-bike school in the country. Outdoor summer attractions include 45 miles (72 km) of challenging bike trails (some are also ski runs), hiking

routes, an inline skate and skateboard park, and a climbing wall. The 18-hole **Mount Snow Golf Club** provides a more sedate diversion.

🏂 **Mount Snow**
Rte 100. **Tel** *(802) 464-3333 or (800) 245-7669.* ☐ *year-round.* 🌐 ⛷
www.mountsnow.com

⛳ **Mount Snow Golf Club**
Rte 100. **Tel** *(802) 464-4254; call for tee times.* ☐ *7am–dusk Mon–Fri, 6am–dusk Sat–Sun & public hols.* 🌐

Brattleboro 17

🏛 *12,500.* ✈ *20 miles (32 km) NE in Keene, NH.* 🚌 🚉 🚉 *180 Main St (802) 254-4565 or (877) 254-4565.* 📅 *May–Oct: Wed & Sat.*
www.brattleborochamber.org

Perched on the banks of the Connecticut River on the New Hampshire border, Brattleboro is the first major town that northbound travelers encounter as they enter the state. Fort Dummer was established here in 1724, making it the state's first European settlement. For that reason, Brattleboro has adopted the slogan "Where Vermont Begins."

A bustling center of commerce and industry, the town is also a hub of tourism. As is the case with so many other Vermont towns, there is a historic district with many Colonial-era buildings of architectural interest. In the 1840s, after the Vermont Valley Railroad was laid to provide a vital link to the outside world, natural springs were discovered in the area and Brattleboro took on a new personality as a spa town where people came for "cures" and health treatments.

The former railroad station is now home to the **Brattleboro Museum and Art Center**, which offers rotating exhibitions by artists of regional and international stature. The Brattleboro Music Center, on Walnut Street, stages a broad range of programs,

Estey organs were manufactured in Brattleboro for more than 100 years

including a chamber music series. An organ museum is being built. It will hold a collection of organs manufactured by the Estey family, whose instruments were exported around the world.

🏛 **Brattleboro Museum and Art Center**
10 Vernon St. **Tel** *(802) 257-0124.* ☐ *Apr–mid-Feb: 11am–5pm Wed–Mon.* 🌐 ⛷
www.brattleboromuseum.org

Grafton 18

🏛 *600.* ✈ *47 miles (76 km) N in Rutland.* 🚉 *(877) 887-2378.*

A thriving industrial center 200 years ago, Grafton suffered a steady decline until by the 1960s it was almost a ghost town. But in 1963 Dean Mathey (1890–1972), a wealthy investment banker, established a foundation with the mandate to restore historic structures and revitalize commercial life. Today the village is an architectural treasure trove of 19th-century buildings.

Grafton mailbox

Two tourist attractions are also thriving commercial enterprises: the **Grafton Village Cheese Company**, with its hearty cheddars, and the Old Tavern at Grafton *(see p320),* a hostelry since 1801. Over the years, the inn has hosted author Rudyard Kipling (1865–1936), and President Theodore Roosevelt (1858–1919).

Verdant farmlands around the town of Wilmington

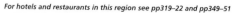

Grafton Village Cheese Company

533 Townshend Rd. *Tel (800) 472-3866.* ◯ *year-round: 10am–5pm daily.*

Environs

Eighteen miles (29 km) to the north lies the hamlet of Plymouth Notch. The tiny community was the birthplace of Calvin Coolidge (1872–1933), the 30th president of the US. The **Calvin Coolidge State Historic Site** encompasses an 1850s general store and post office once run by Coolidge's father, a cheese factory, a schoolhouse, and the Coolidge family home.

In Weston, 21 miles (34 km) west of Plymouth Notch, visitors will find the **Vermont Country Store**. The store is famous for its enormous and eclectic array of merchandise, selected by its owners, the Orton family. Not only are these items highly original – be they badger-hair shaving brushes or handblown glasses that sea captains once used to forecast the weather – they are also always of the highest quality.

Calvin Coolidge State Historic Site

Rte 100A. *Tel (802) 672-3773.* ◯ *late May–mid-Oct: 9:30am–5pm daily.*

One of the many beautiful homes in the village of Woodstock

Vermont Country Store

Rte 100, Weston. *Tel (802) 824-3184.* ◯ *year-round: 9am–5:30pm daily.*

Woodstock ⑲

🏘 *1,000.* ✈ *31 miles (50 km) W in Rutland.* 🚌 🛈 *Mechanic St (802) 457-3555 or (888) 496-6378.* **www**.woodstockvt.com

Even in Vermont, a state where historic, picturesque villages are common, Woodstock stands out. Founded in 1761, the town is an enclave of renovated brick and clapboard Georgian houses. The restoration of the town came about as a result of the generosity of philanthropists such as the Rockefeller family and railroad magnate Frederick Billings (1823–90). An early proponent of reforestation, Billings personally financed the planting of 10,000 trees.

Billings Farm & Museum is still a working entity. The 1890 farmhouse has been restored and there are seasonal events such as plowing competitions in the spring and apple-cider pressing in the fall. The museum also traces Vermont's agricultural past with old photographs and exhibits of harvesting implements, butter churns, and ice cutters.

The **VINS Nature Center** is a reserve where injured birds of prey are cared for until they can be returned to the wild. As well as operating conservation programs and summer day camps for children, the naturalists here give frequent presentations about the owls, falcons, and eagles that have come under their care.

Billings Farm & Museum

River Rd. *Tel (802) 457-2355.* ◯ *May–Oct: 10am–5pm daily; call for winter hours.* **www**.billingsfarm.org

VINS Nature Center

Rte 4, Quechee. *Tel (802) 359-5000.* ◯ *May–Oct: 10am–5pm daily; Nov–Apr: call for hours.* **www**.vinsnaturecenter.org

Environs

Six miles (10 km) east of town is the stunning Quechee Gorge. The best view of the chasm is on Route 4, which crosses the gorge via a steel bridge. A short hiking trail leads from the parking lot on the east side down to the Ottauquechee River below.

THE RISE OF CALVIN COOLIDGE

Calvin Coolidge was born in tiny Plymouth to parents who ran a general store. His humble upbringing endowed him with traits that would carry him to the presidency in the 1920s: honesty, frugality, and industry. Known as "Silent Cal," because he wasted little time on small talk, Coolidge guided the US to a period of economic prosperity before the onset of the Great Depression of 1929.

Boyhood home of Calvin Coolidge

NEW HAMPSHIRE

N ew Hampshirites are known for their fiercely independent nature, born of necessity in the early 1600s when European settlers established outposts in this mountainous and heavily forested region. This natural beauty is still in evidence, in the soaring peaks of the White Mountains, the pristine water of Lake Winnipesaukee, and the small, but scenic coastline.

There can be no better expression of New Hampshire's individualistic spirit than the state motto, "Live Free or Die," which is stamped on every state license plate. Six months before the July 4, 1776 signing of the Declaration of Independence, New Hampshire became the very first state to formally declare its separation from Great Britain. Ever cautious of centralized government, modern New Hampshirites proudly point out that they pay no personal state income tax, nor is sales tax levied on most consumer goods in the state – a boon for tourists looking for bargains.

The landscape that helped forge the determined mindset of early settlers has changed little in the ensuing centuries. It is estimated that more than 90 percent of the state is undeveloped, with dense forest covering more than three-quarters of its land.

The northern part of the state is wild country, its woodlands bisected by the mighty Connecticut River and rippled by the tall peaks of the White Mountains *(see p265)*. Campers, climbers, and canoeists reign here. The hundreds of lakes and ponds that quilt central New Hampshire attract vacationers year-round looking to boat, fish, cross-country ski, and snowmobile. In the southwest, sightseers drive across rolling farmland that is punctuated by scenic villages and covered bridges. Even the industrial heartland of the Merrimack Valley is predominantly rural. A mere 15-minute drive from the downtown cores of the state's major commercial centers of Concord *(see pp258–9)* and Manchester *(see p258)* will transport travelers to the tranquility of dairy farms or quiet country roads.

Early October view of the Presidential Range in the White Mountains

◁ Canterbury Shaker Village *(see pp260–61)*, founded in 1792

Exploring New Hampshire

New Hampshire's compact borders make it ideal for sightseeing. Some attractions can be enjoyed on foot, as with the spectacular boardwalked chasm of Franconia Notch *(see pp272–3)*, or by car, as with a breathtaking fall-foliage tour along the Kancamagus Highway *(see p270)*. The remains of colonial battlements, the Shaker villages at Enfield *(see p262)* and Canterbury *(see pp260–61)*, and the historic homes of poets, politicians, and presidents are sprinkled throughout the state. Called the Granite State for its extensive granite formations and quarries, New Hampshire's rough edges are softened somewhat in its many fine museums. The Currier Gallery of Art *(see p258)* is one such establishment, giving visitors the chance to view work by some of the world's great masters.

Bridge over the Flume Gorge in Franconia Notch State Park

Lengthy Cornish-Windsor Bridge outside Cornish

GETTING AROUND

Interstates 93 and 89 are the largest and most popular north-south routes in the state, with numerous smaller roads branching off to more remote areas. Drivers should be aware of two New Hampshire realities: heavier traffic during peak fall-foliage season, especially on the weekends; and moose crossings. While moose sightings are thrilling, collisions with the huge animals can be extremely dangerous. Travelers should drive with caution at all times. The Amtrak "Northeastern" service stops in Exeter, Durham, and Dover. Travelers may also take Amtrak to White River Junction, Vermont, or to Boston and link up with a bus line from there. Commercial bus lines servicing the area include C&J Trailways, Concord Trailways, and Greyhound bus lines *(see p375)*. The state's largest airport is found in the south in Manchester *(see p258)*, although Maine's Portland International Airport is a good jumping-off point for northeastern New Hampshire.

St. Joh
Me
Re
Littleton
302
Lisbon
**FRANCONIA NOTC
STATE PARK**
10
**LINCOL
WOODSTOC**
25
Warren
Plym
HANOVER 15
Lebanon
**13 ENFIELD SHAKER
MUSEUM**
Bris
**SAINT-GAUDENS
NAT. HISTORIC SITE**
14
89
Cornish
4
12A
**12 NEW
LONDON**
Claremont   Newport   *Sunapee Lake*
**LAKE SUNAPEE
REGION 10**
Charlestown
Henniker
10
Hillsbo
12
9
202
7 KEENE
101
9
Peterborou
**MONADNOCK
STATE PARK 5**
12
6   Jaffrey
119
Winchester   **RHODODENDRON
STATE PARK**
Fitchburg

Pittsburg

Connecticut Lakes

Colebrook

Blue Mountain 998m

Errol

Groveton

ancaster

Berlin

Androscoggin

TTON OODS

21

Mount Washington 1917m

20 PINKHAM NOTCH

RAWFORD OTCH **24**

19 JACKSON

HITE MOUNTAINS

17 **18** NORTH CONWAY

CAMAGUS HWY

22

Conway

NEW AMPSHIRE

quam ake

23 **25**

Meredith

16 LAKE WINNIPESAUKEE

Wolfeboro

Laconia

Farmington

CANTERBURY SHAKER VILLAGE

Rochester

Somersworth

Dover

CONCORD

Suncook

Portland

Newmarket

1 PORTSMOUTH

town

8 MANCHESTER

EXETER **2**

3 HAMPTON

Derry

AMERICA'S STONEHENGE

Hampton Beach

4

Salem

Nashua

Boston

SIGHTS AT A GLANCE

America's Stonehenge **4**
Bretton Woods **21**
Canterbury Shaker Village pp260–61 **11**
Concord **9**
Crawford Notch State Park **24**
Enfield Shaker Museum **13**
Exeter **2**
Franconia Notch State Park pp272–3 **25**
Hampton **3**
Hanover **15**
Jackson **19**
Kancamagus Highway **22**
Keene **7**

Lake Sunapee Region **10**
Lincoln Woodstock **23**
Manchester **8**
Monadnock State Park **5**
New London **12**
North Conway **18**
Pinkham Notch **20**
Portsmouth **1**
Rhododendron State Park **6**
Saint-Gaudens National Historic Site **14**
White Mountains/White Mountain National Forest **17**

Tour
Lake Winnipesaukee *p264* **16**

KEY

═══ Highway
─── Major road
∷∷∷ Minor road
─── Scenic route
-■- Main railway
─── Minor railway
▬▬▬ International border
▬▬▬ State border
△ Summit

Panorama of Saco River Valley from North Conway

SEE ALSO

- *Where to Stay* pp322–5
- *Where to Eat* pp351–3

0 kilometers   30

0 miles   30

Portsmouth ❶

When settlers established a colony here in 1623, they called it Strawbery Banke *(see pp254–5)* in honor of the berries blanketing the banks of the Piscataqua River. In 1653 the name was changed to Portsmouth, a reflection of the town's reputation as a hub of maritime commerce. First a fishing port, the town enjoyed prosperity in the 18th century as a link in the trade route between Great Britain and the West Indies. During the years leading up to the American Revolution, the town was a hotbed of revolutionary fervor and the place where colonial naval hero John Paul Jones (1747–92) built his warship, the *Ranger*.

Favorite with tourists: Portsmouth's Market Street

Exploring Portsmouth
Girded by the Piscataqua River and the North and South Mill ponds, compact Portsmouth is easily explored on foot. The town's past permeates the downtown core, especially along busy Market Street. Historic buildings, some constructed in the 19th-century by wealthy sea captains, have been restored and turned into museums, boutiques, and restaurants. The city also has a number of brew pubs and microbreweries that produce local ales. More than 70 historic sites, including houses and gardens, can be found along the Portsmouth Harbor Trail, a walking tour of the Historic District.

Beautiful exterior of Moffatt-Ladd House in Portsmouth

🏠 Governor John Langdon House
143 Pleasant St. *Tel (603)-436-3205.*
⏱ Jun–mid-Oct: 11am–4pm Fri–Sun.
● Labor Day. 🎨 📷 ♿
The son of a farmer of modest means, John Langdon (1741–1819) became one of Portsmouth's most prominent citizens. Langdon enjoyed great prosperity as a ship captain, merchant, and shipbuilder before becoming the governor of New Hampshire and a US senator. In 1784 he built this imposing Georgian mansion. The house is known for its ornate Rococo embellishments. The grounds feature a grape arbor and a large rose garden.

🏠 Moffatt-Ladd House
154 Market St. *Tel (603) 436-8221.*
⏱ mid-Jun–mid-Oct: 11am–5pm Mon–Sat, 1–5pm Sun. 🎨 📷 ♿
One of Portsmouth's first three-story homes, this elegant 1763 mansion was built for wealthy maritime trader and sea captain John Moffatt. The house's boxy design was a precursor to the Federal style of architecture that would later become popular throughout the country. The house, located on the Portsmouth Harbor Trail, is graced by a grand entrance hall, a series of family portraits, and period furnishings.

🏠 Wentworth-Gardner House
50 Mechanic St. *Tel (603) 436-4406.*
⏱ mid-Jun–mid-Oct: noon–4pm Wed–Sun. ● public hols. 🎨 ♿
Also located on the Portsmouth Harbor Trail, this 1760 house is considered to be one of the best examples of Georgian architecture in the country. The house's beautiful exterior has rows of multi-paned windows, symmetrical chimneys, and a pillared entrance. The interior has 11 fireplaces, hand-painted wallpaper, and graceful carvings that took artisans a year to complete.

JOHN PAUL JONES

Born in Scotland, John Paul Jones (1747–92) went to sea as a cabin boy when he was only 12 years old. He worked his way up to being the first mate on a slave ship, then later the commander of a merchant vessel in Tobago. A hard taskmaster, Jones escaped to America before he was to go on trial for the deaths of several sailors he had punished. Regarded as an outlaw by the British, Jones went on to become an illustrious naval commander for the US. During the American Revolution, Jones led a series of daring raids up and down the British coast for which he was awarded a gold medal by Congress.

USS *Albacore*

Albacore Park, 600 Market St. **Tel** (603) 436-3680. ☐ mid-May–mid-Oct: 9:30am–5pm daily; mid-Oct–mid-Jan & mid-Feb–mid-May: 9:30am–4pm Thu–Mon. ☒
www.ussalbacore.org
This sleek submarine was the fastest underwater vessel of its type when it was launched from the Portsmouth Naval Shipyard in 1953. It gives visitors access to the cramped quarters of submariners and an idea of what life was like for the 55 crew members. Exhibits in the visitor center trace the vessel's history.

🌊 Water Country

Rte 1 S of Portsmouth. **Tel** (603) 427-1111. ☐ Jun–Labor Day: call for hours. ☒ ⛔
Thrilling water rides, a huge wave pool, a pirate ship, and a man-made lagoon await visitors to New England's largest water park. Smaller children can enjoy the slides and fountains in designated areas, while the more adventurous thrill-seekers can career down looping water slides.

VISITORS' CHECKLIST

🏙 26,000. ✈ 10 Ladd St.
🛬 36 Airline Ave. ℹ 500 Market St or Market Sq (603) 436-1118. ☐ mid-May–Oct: 8:30am–1pm. 🎭 Market Square Day (Jun), Prescott Park Arts Festival (Jul–Aug daily).
www.portsmouthchamber.org

🏛 Children's Museum of New Hampshire

6 Washington St, Dover (12 miles/20 km N of Portsmouth). **Tel** (603) 742-2002. ☐ 10am–5pm Tue–Sat (& Mon in summer), noon–5pm Sun. ☒ ♿ www.childrens-museum.org
This facility features a riverside playground as well as interactive exhibits where kids can command a submarine, don lab coats to excavate dinosaur fossils, play musical instruments from around the world, and explore visual and textural patterns. There is also a human-scale kaleidoscope.

Popular destination on summer days: Water Country

PORTSMOUTH CITY CENTER

Gov. John Langdon House ①
Moffatt-Ladd House ②
Wentworth-Gardner House ③

KEY

▮ Street-by-Street map *see pp254–5*

Key to Symbols *see back flap*

Street-by-Street: Strawbery Banke

Aldrich Garden bloom

This outdoor museum near the waterfront is located on the very spot on which Portsmouth was founded. Tracing the history of the town, this 10-acre (4-ha) site contains 40 historic buildings that depict life from 1695 to 1955. Those houses open to the public are furnished in period style and contain interesting collections of decorative arts, ceramics, and assorted artifacts. Many of the buildings are set amid gardens cultivated according to their eras, from early pioneer herb gardens to formal Victorian flower beds.

Pitt Tavern
This Revolutionary War-era inn was frequented by George Washington.

Aldrich House and Garden
The garden of the restored Colonial Revival home of poet Thomas Bailey Aldrich (1836–1907) blooms with flowers celebrated in his verse.

COURT STREET

ATKINSON STREET

COURT STREET

JEFFERSON STREET

WHIDDEN PLACE

WASHINGTON STREET

0 meters   50

0 yards   50

STAR SIGHTS

★ Chase House

★ Jones House

★ Sherburne House

★ **Chase House**
Built c.1762, this elegant home is furnished with sumptuous pieces from several periods.

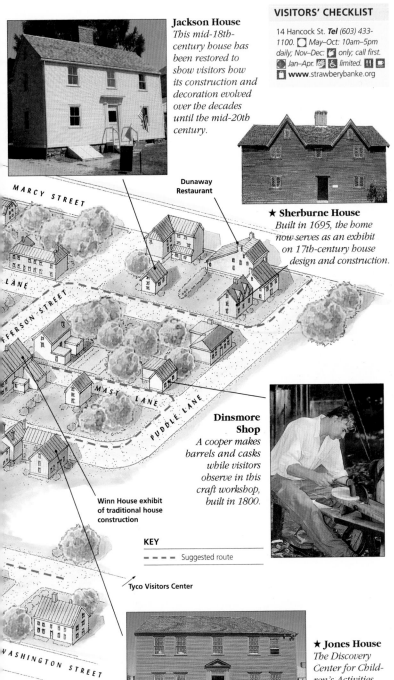

Jackson House

This mid-18th-century house has been restored to show visitors how its construction and decoration evolved over the decades until the mid-20th century.

VISITORS' CHECKLIST

14 Hancock St. **Tel** (603) 433-1100. May–Oct: 10am–5pm daily; Nov–Dec: only; call first. Jan–Apr. limited. www.strawberybanke.org

Dunaway Restaurant

MARCY STREET

LANE

FFERSON STREET

MAST LANE

PUDDLE LANE

Winn House exhibit of traditional house construction

WASHINGTON STREET

★ **Sherburne House**
Built in 1695, the home now serves as an exhibit on 17th-century house design and construction.

Dinsmore Shop

A cooper makes barrels and casks while visitors observe in this craft workshop, built in 1800.

KEY

– – – Suggested route

Tyco Visitors Center

★ **Jones House**
The Discovery Center for Children's Activities entertains and educates youngsters in this circa 1790 structure.

Exeter ②

14,500. ✈ 15 miles (24 km) E in Portsmouth. ℹ 24 Front St (603) 772-2411. www.exeterarea.org

The quiet little town of Exeter southwest of Portsmouth was much less tranquil during the century and a half leading up to the American Revolution (1775–83). The community sprang up around the falls linking the freshwater Exeter River and the salty Squamscott River. It was founded in 1638 by the Reverend John Wheelwright (1592–1679), an outspoken cleric who was thrown out of the Massachusetts colony for his radical views.

During the turbulent years leading up to American Independence, outraged townspeople openly defied the British government. They drove off officials who had been dispatched to cut down trees for the British Navy, burned their leaders in effigy, and finally declared independence from Britain, setting a precedent for the rest of the colonies.

Dominating the center of town, Phillips Exeter Academy stands as one of the country's most prestigious preparatory schools. The complex of more than 100 ivy-clad brick buildings fronted by manicured lawns was founded in 1781.

Other points of interest include the **Gilman Garrison**

Exeter farmers market sign

House, a late 17th-century fortified log building, and the **American Independence Museum**, which displays an original copy of the Declaration of Independence each year on July 22, and also owns two drafts of the US Constitution.

🚇 **Gilman Garrison House**
12 Water St. **Tel** (603) 436-3205. ⬚ call for opening hours. 🎫 📷 obligatory. ♿

🏛 **American Independence Museum**
1 Governors Lane. **Tel** (603) 772-2622. ⬚ late May–Oct: 10am–4pm Wed–Sat. 🎫 📷 obligatory. 🎒 🚫

Hampton ③

15,000. ✈ 12 miles (19 km) N in Portsmouth. ℹ 1 Lafayette Rd (603) 926-8718. www.hamptonchamber.com

One of New Hampshire's oldest towns, Hampton is situated at the geographic center of the many state parks and public beaches that line Highway 1A, the coast road. Public recreation areas stretch from Seabrook Beach, a sandy shore dotted with dunes, to the rugged shoreline of **Odiorne Point State Park** in Rye to the north. The park has biking trails, tidal pools, and a boardwalk spanning a saltwater marsh. The park's Science Center also runs interpretive nature programs that are especially appealing to young visitors.

Exterior of the American Independence Museum in Exeter

Ten miles (6 km) to the south of the factory outlet shopping mecca of North Hampton, travelers will come upon the popular **Hampton Beach**. This miniature version of Atlantic City (without the gambling) comes complete with a venue that hosts big-name entertainers and an old-fashioned boardwalk lined with video arcades, ice-cream shops, and stalls selling T-shirts and tacky souvenirs. Open year-round, Hampton Beach is busiest during hot summer months, when vacationers come to enjoy the miles of clean, golden beaches, including a separate area designated for surfers. Swimmers and jet skiers test the waters, para-sailers soar overhead, and deep-sea fishing and whale-watching charter boats are available from Hampton Harbor. Hampton Beach is not the place for people looking for quiet, but it is geared toward family fun, with game arcades, water slides, magic shows, and a series of free concerts and fireworks.

Away from the casino and busy boardwalk, the blue skies and tranquil surf of Hampton Beach

For hotels and restaurants in this region see pp322–5 and pp351–3

⚓ Odiorne Point State Park
Rte 1A, Rye Beach. *Tel (603) 436-7406.* 🅿 **Science Center** *Tel (603) 436-8043.* 🕐 *10am–5pm daily (Nov–Mar: only Sat–Mon).* ● *Jan 1, Thanksgiving, & Dec 25.* 🅿
Park 🕐 *year-round: 8am–dusk.* 🅿

🚌 Hampton Beach
Tel (603) 926-8717.
www.hamptonbeach.org

America's Stonehenge ❹

Haverhill Rd, N. Salem. *Tel (603) 893-8300.* 🕐 *9am–5pm daily.* ● *Thanksgiving, Dec 25.* 🅿
www.stonehengeusa.com

Although not nearly as imposing as its British namesake, this is an intriguing place nonetheless. Believed to be one of the oldest man-made complexes this side of the Atlantic, the 30-acre (12-ha) grounds of America's Stonehenge are scattered with standing stones, walls, and stone chambers. Archeologists, historians, and astronomers have argued for decades about the origins of the site, with credit going to everyone from ancient Greeks to wayward aliens. Today one of the most popular theories has Native American tribes constructing this megalithic complex as a giant calendar to measure the movements of the sun and the moon. Excavations have turned up a wealth of ancient remains, including stone pottery, tools, and petroglyphs that have been carbon-dated to between 3,000 and 4,000 years old. One of the more gruesome parts of the site is the 5-ton (4.5-tonne) Sacrificial Table, carved with grooves that researchers believe may have been troughs for collecting the blood of victims. Special events are held at the site during the spring and fall equinox and at the winter and summer solstice.

Mount Monadnock, popular with climbers and hikers

Monadnock State Park ❺

Off Rte 124, W of Jaffrey. *Tel (603) 532-8862. Campground reservations: (877) 647-2757.* 🕐 *year-round.* 🅿
🅿 🅿 **www**.nhstateparks.org

Standing some 3,165 ft (965 m) high, Mount Monadnock has two claims to fame. It is said to be one of the world's most climbed mountains (it is not unusual to find several hundred hikers milling around its peak) and it has spawned a geological term. A "monadnock" is an isolated hill or mountain of resistant rock rising above a plain that has been created by glacial activity.

The mountain's popularity has a lot to do with its campsites, scenic picnic areas, and numerous hiking trails. Within the 5,000-acre (2,000-ha) park, there are 40 miles (64 km) of trails, many of which lead to the summit. The climb to the peak of the metamorphic schist pinnacle takes more than three hours, but on clear days intrepid hikers are rewarded with gorgeous views of all six New England states. Markers along the trails have been erected in memory of such men of letters as

Ralph Waldo Emerson (1803–82) and Henry David Thoreau (1817–62), both of whom climbed to the peak. The visitor's center gives an overview of the hiking trails and information about the local flora and fauna. The campsites are open year-round and in the winter months the trails are popular with cross-country skiers.

Rhododendron State Park ❻

Off Rte 119, W of Fitzwilliam. *Tel (603) 532-8862.* 🕐 *year-round: dawn–dusk daily.* 🅿 🅿 *partial.*

New England's largest grove of wild rhododendrons bursts into a celebration of pink and white in June through mid-July. The 2,700-acre (1,095-ha) park has more than 16 acres (6 ha) of giant rhododendron bushes. Walking through the rhododendrons, some of which grow to more than 20 ft (6 m) high, is a feast for the senses in summer, but there are floral highlights in other seasons as well. In the spring the woodland park is carpeted with trilliums. By May the apple trees are heavy with blossoms. During summer, visitors will find flowering mountain laurel and wildflowers such as jack-in-the-pulpit and delicate pink lady slippers. The park is equipped with picnic areas and hiking trails that offer spectacular views of Mount Monadnock and the surrounding peaks.

Ancient ruins of America's Stonehenge

Keene ❼

🏠 25,350. ✈ 58 miles (93 km) E in Manchester. 🚌 🛈 48 Central Sq (603) 352-1303.

Keene is the largest town in southern New Hampshire's Monadnock region. The nation's first glass-blowing factory was founded in nearby Temple in 1780, and soon after Keene became one of the region's hotbeds of arts and crafts. By the 19th century the town was famous for the production of high-quality glass and pottery and for its thriving wool mill. The **Horatio Colony Museum** is the former home of a descendant of the mill-owning family. Its period furnishings give a good idea of upper-class life in the mid-19th century. Today the focus of Keene's thriving cultural life is Keene State College, located on what is reputed to be the widest Main Street in the world. The college has several theaters and art studios where events are staged throughout the year.

🏛 Horatio Colony Museum
199 Main St. **Tel** (603) 352-0460. 🕐 May–mid-Oct: 11am–4pm Wed–Sun. 📷 obligatory.

Environs
Half a dozen covered bridges (*see p263*) lie within a 10-mile (16-km) radius of Keene, giving the region the nickname "Currier and Ives country." Road markers direct drivers to each span. These "kissing bridges," where young couples would steal secret embraces as they rode their buggy through them, have long been favorite subjects of photographers.

West Swanzey or Thompson Covered Bridge near Keene

Manchester ❽

🏠 105,250. ✈ 1 Airport Rd. 🚌 🛈 889 Elm St (603) 666-6600. 📧 (603) 622-7531.

In 1805 a modest mill was built on the east bank of the Merrimack River. Fueled by waterpower, the Amoskeag Mill continued to expand until by the beginning of the 20th century it claimed the title as the largest textile mill in the world. At its peak, the operation employed some 17,000 people and its complex of brick buildings stretched for more than 1 mile (1.5 km). Today the structures that once held workers and heavy machinery are used for restaurants, college classrooms, and even residential housing.

This former industrial center is now known for the **Currier Museum of Art**, New Hampshire's premier art museum. In order to display more of its impressive collection of fine and decorative arts, the museum has undergone an ambitious renovation program that added a massive 33,000 sq ft (3,066 square meters) of space. The entire second floor is dedicated to 18th- and 19th-century American artists, including the Impressionists and members of the Hudson River School. The museum's holdings of modern paintings and sculptures include works by Pablo Picasso (1881–1973) and Henri Matisse (1869–1954). A gallery features regional artists, while a café occupies the sky-lit Winter Garden.

The museum's largest piece is the nearby Zimmerman House, designed in 1950 by pioneering American architect Frank Lloyd Wright (1867–1959) as an exemplar of his Usonian homes. Shuttles take visitors from the museum to the house, and guided tours (by advance reservation April through December) of its interior highlight textiles and furniture designed by Wright.

🏛 Currier Museum of Art
150 Ash St. **Tel** (603) 669-6144. 🕐 11am–5pm Wed–Mon (from 10am Sat). 🏛 **Zimmerman House** 🕐 Apr–Dec (call for tour hours). 📷 🚻 🛗 🏠 🅿 🚫 www.currier.org

Concord ❾

🏠 37,500. ✈ 25 miles (49 km) S in Manchester. 🚌 🛈 40 Commercial St (603) 224-2508.

New Hampshire's capital is a quiet little town, but thanks to its prominent political position, it has been associated with a number of important historical

The granite and marble façade of State House, in Concord

CONCORD COACHES

In 1827 Concord-based wheelwright Lewis Downing and coach builder J. Stephens Abbot built the first Concord Coach, designed to withstand the unforgiving trails of the undeveloped West. The 1-ton (1-tonne) stagecoaches were, in their own way, as revolutionary as the Internet is today because they helped facilitate communications across the vast emerging hinterland. Wells Fargo, the famous transportation company, relied heavily on the coaches during the California Gold Rush (1848–55) to carry mail and passengers on parts of the route between New York City and San Francisco.

figures. Mary Baker Eddy (1821–1910), founder of the Christian Science Church, spent much of her life here. The **Pierce Manse** was the one-time home of Franklin Pierce (1804–69), the 14th president of the US.

The 1819 **State House**, built from New Hampshire granite and Vermont marble, is one of the oldest in America. Inside the building are several hundred paintings of the state's better known residents and political figures.

In its heyday, the Eagle Hotel on Main Street, which is now used as an office building, hosted the likes of presidents Andrew Jackson and Benjamin Harrison, as well as aviator Charles Lindbergh, and former first lady Eleanor Roosevelt.

Concord schoolteacher Christa McAuliffe (1948–86) unfortunately gained her fame through tragedy. On January 28, 1986, McAuliffe boarded the *Challenger* space shuttle as the first civilian to be launched into space by NASA. Seventy-three seconds after the lift-off, with her husband and children watching from the ground, the shuttle exploded into a fireball and crashed, killing McAuliffe and her six fellow astronauts.

McAuliffe's memory lives on at **The McAuliffe-Shepard Discovery Center**, which also honors New Hampshire native and astronaut Alan Shepard, who was the first American to be launched into space. The futuristic center is capped by a giant glass pyramid. In addition to exhibits and planetarium shows, visitors can see a scale model of a space shuttle and a replica of the Mercury-Redstone rocket from Shepard's flight on May 5, 1961. Special astronomy programs are offered on Friday evenings.

🚏 Pierce Manse
14 Horseshoe Pond Lane. *Tel* (603) 225-4555. ⬤ mid-Jun–early Aug: 11am–3pm Tue–Sat. 🔲 🔲

🚏 State House
107 N Main St. *Tel* (603) 271-2154. **Visitor center** ⬤ year-round: 8am–4:30pm Mon–Fri. 🔲 🔲

🏛 The McAuliffe-Shepard Discovery Center
2 Institute Dr. *Tel* (603) 271-7827. ⬤ 10am–5pm Mon–Thu, 10am–9pm Fri, 10am–5pm Sat & Sun. Call for show times. 🔲🔲🔲🔲 week after Labor Day. **www**.starhop.com

Lake Sunapee Region ❿

ℹ 143 Main St, New London (603) 526-6575 or (877) 526-6575.

This scenic region, dominated by 2,743-ft- (835-m-) high Mount Sunapee and the 10-mile- (16-km-) long lake at its feet, is a major drawing card for outdoor enthusiasts, particularly boaters and skiers. Many locals have vacation and weekend homes here, and an increasing number of retirees are also moving to the region, attracted not only by the scenery but also by the activity-oriented lifestyle.

Lake Sunapee (its name is said to be derived from the Penacook Indian words for "wild goose water") has been attracting visitors for well over a century. In the mid-19th century, trains and steamships used to transport tourists to hotels that rimmed the lake. The steamships have long since gone, but vacationers can rent canoes, picnic on the beach, or take a narrated trip on a sightseeing boat. **Mount Sunapee State Park**'s namesake peak attracts hikers and climbers during the summer months and skiers during the winter. The Mount Sunapee resort in the park is the largest ski area between Boston and the White Mountains.

🎿 Mount Sunapee State Park
Rte 103. *Tel* (603) 763-5561. ⬤ mid-Jun–Labor Day. 🔲 🔲 **Mount Sunapee Resort** *Tel* (603) 763-4020.

Sightseeing boat on Lake Sunapee

Canterbury Shaker Village ⓫

When founded in 1792, this village was occupied
for 200 years, making it one of the longest-lasting
communities of the religious group in the country.
Shakers also lived in nearby Enfield *(see p262)*. Their
belief in strict separation from the rest of the world
and in celibacy eventually led to their demise. The
last member of this colony died in 1992, and now
25 of the original buildings are part of the village.
Millponds, nature trails, and traditional gardens
punctuate the 690-acre (280-ha) site. Skilled artisans
re-create Shaker crafts, herbal products, and cooking.

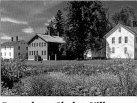

Canterbury Shaker Village
*The village is dominated by the
central Dwelling House (below).*

The belfry
is a distinctive
shape and contains
a bell made by
Revere and Sons.

Shaker Brooms
*The common flat broom was
invented in 1798 by Shaker
Brother Theodore Bates. Shakers
believed that cleanliness
mirrored spiritual purity.*

Shaker Table
*Open for lunch, dinner, and
Sunday brunch, this
restaurant features delicious
Shaker-inspired cuisine.*

**Brethren's
retiring room**

STAR SIGHTS

★ Dining Room

★ Old Library and
Museum

★ Sisters' Retiring Room

★ **Dining Room**
*This area once
held as many as 60
Shakers per sitting.*

KEY

☐ Illustrated building

1 Trustees' Office
2 The Infirmary
3 Meeting House
4 Dwelling House
5 Sisters' Shop
6 Carriage House
7 Creamery
8 Carpenter Shop
9 Fire House/Power House
10 Laundry
11 Horse Barn
12 School House
13 Syrup Shop
14 Shaker Table

VISITORS' CHECKLIST

288 Shaker Rd, Canterbury.
Tel (603) 783-9511; Shaker
Table (603) 783-4238. ☐ mid-
May–Oct: 10am–5pm daily; Nov:
10am–4pm Fri–Sun. 🚭 ✔ ‖
📷 🖼 www.shakers.org

Welcome to
CANTERBURY
Shaker Village

CREAMERY RESTAURANT
SHAKER GIFT SHOP
OPEN DAILY 10AM - 5PM

Dormer rooms were used
for summer sleeping and as
clothes cupboards.

Popular Stop
*Historic buildings, a
restaurant, and a gift
shop make Canterbury a
favorite tourist destination.*

**★ Sisters'
Retiring Room**
*Men and women had
separate sleeping quarters.
Each one is equipped with
traditional Shaker furniture.*

★ Old Library and Archives
*The library contains 1,500
Shaker books and docu-
ments, and is open by
appointment only.*

The Infirmary
*Built in 1811, this building served as the
hospital, pharmacy, dental office, and morgue.*

New London ⑫

🏛 3,700. ✈ 28 miles (45 km) NW in Lebanon. 🚌 ℹ Main St (603) 526-6575 or (877) 526-6575.
www.sunapeevacations.com

New London's perch atop a crest gives it an enviable view of the surrounding forests during the fall foliage season. The bucolic setting also serves as a wonderful backdrop for the town's rich collection of colonial and early 19th-century buildings. Of these, the architectural centerpiece is **Colby-Sawyer College**, an undergraduate liberal arts school founded in 1837. The college organizes numerous cultural programs, including plays, lectures, films, concerts, and art exhibitions. More cultural fun can be had farther down the street at the **New London Barn Playhouse**. Housed in a refurbished 1820s barn, the theater stages popular plays and musicals during the summer months.

🏛 **Colby-Sawyer College**
Main St. **Tel** (603) 526-2010.
☐ year-round: 9am–5pm
Mon–Fri. ♿ ℹ 🍴

🎭 **New London Barn Playhouse**
84 Main St. **Tel** (603) 526-4631 or (603) 526-6710. ☐ mid-Jun–Sep:
call for hours. 🅿

Enfield Shaker Museum ⑬

Rte 4A, Enfield. **Tel** (603) 632-4346.
☐ 10am–5pm Mon–Sat, noon–5pm
Sun (winter: closes 4pm). 🎫 🅿 ♿
🅿 🍴

Facing religious persecution in Britain in the mid-18th century, several groups of Shakers, a sect that broke away from the Quakers, fled to North America under the spiritual guidance of Mother Ann Lee (1736–84). The Shaker village at Enfield was founded in 1793, one of 18 such communities in the US.
Between the founding of Enfield and the 1920s, the Shakers constructed more than 200 buildings, of which 13 remain. And while they

Colby-Sawyer College in New London

farmed more than 3,000 acres (1,200 ha) of land, property was under the ownership of the community, not individuals. Members were celibate and they were strict pacifists, devoting their "hands to work and hearts to God." At one time the Enfield Shakers numbered over 300, but, as in similar communities, their numbers gradually dwindled. In 1923 the last 10 members moved to the Canterbury Shaker Village *(see pp260–61)* north of Concord. The last Canterbury Shaker died as recently as 1992 at the age of 96.
The exhibits at the museum illustrate how the Shakers lived and worked. Visitors will come across fine examples of Shaker ingenuity, including one of their many inventions: sulfur matches. The buildings are filled with the simple but practical wooden furniture for which the Shakers, who were consummate craftspeople, were famous. The 160-year-old

Saint-Gaudens' angel

Great Stone Dwelling, the largest such structure ever built by these industrious people, is a model of stately workmanship.

Saint-Gaudens National Historic Site ⑭

Rte 12A N of Cornish-Windsor Bridge.
Tel (603) 675-2175. **Buildings**
☐ late May–Oct: 9am–4:30pm daily.
Grounds ☐ year-round. 🎫 🅿 🅿
www.nps.gov/saga

This national historic site celebrates the life of Augustus Saint-Gaudens (1848–1907), the preeminent US sculptor of his time. When he began to summer here in 1885, it marked the beginning of the town's evolution into an art colony. Artists, writers, and musicians alike were attracted to the town by the talent of Saint-Gaudens, whose family had emigrated to the US from Ireland when he was just a baby. Something of a world traveler, Saint-Gaudens became an apprentice cameo cutter in New York and later studied at the École des Beaux-Arts in Paris. He also won several commissions in Rome. By the time that he returned to New York, his reputation as a brilliant sculptor had been well established. His work, usually of heroic subject matter, can

Great Stone Dwelling in the Enfield Shaker Museum

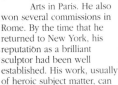

be found throughout the country. New England is home to many Saint-Gaudens masterpieces, including Boston's Shaw Memorial (1897).

Eventually Saint-Gaudens grew tired of the big-city pace, buying an old tavern near the Connecticut River and turning it into a home and

Model for Boston's Shaw Memorial

studio. Many of his greatest works were created here, including the famous statue of Abraham Lincoln (1809–65) in Lincoln Park, Chicago. Today this historic 1805 structure is filled with the sculptor's furniture and samples of his small, detailed sketches for large bronzes. A number of his sculptures are scattered around the 150-acre (61-ha) property, which is laid out with formal gardens and pleasing walking trails flanked by tall pines and hemlocks.

Environs

Just 2 miles (3 km) south of the Saint-Gaudens site, visitors will come upon the Cornish-Windsor Bridge. Spanning the Connecticut River between New

Hampshire and Vermont, the structure is the longest covered bridge in New England at 460 ft (140 m). Three other covered bridges can be found in the vicinity of Cornish.

Hanover 🚩

 9,200. ✈ 6 miles (10 km) SE in Lebanon. 🚌 ℹ 216 Nugget Arcade Building (603) 643-3115. **www**.hanoverchamber.org

Hanover, with a traditional village green ringed by historic brick buildings, is the archetypal New England college town. Situated in the upper valley region of the Connecticut River, it is a pleasant stop for visitors following the Appalachian

Trail, which goes right through the center of town. Hanover is the home of **Dartmouth College**, the northernmost of the country's Ivy League schools. The college was originally known as Moor's Indian Charity School, and was founded in 1769 to educate and convert Abenaki Natives. Today some 4,500 students participate in programs that include one of the oldest medical schools in America, the Thayer School of Civil Engineering (1867), and the Amos Tuck School of Business Administration (1900). The school's famous graduates include statesman Daniel Webster (1782–1852) and former vice president Nelson Rockefeller (1908–79).

The college has a number of noteworthy sights. The **Baker/Berry Memorial Library** is decorated by a series of thought-provoking murals tracing the history of the Americas painted by Mexican artist José Clemente Orozco (1883–1949) in the early 1930s. The **Hood Museum of Art** has a diverse collection that includes Native American and African art, early American and European paintings, and works by such noted modern artists as Pablo Picasso (1881–1973).

🏛 **Dartmouth College**
Tel (603) 646-1110. 📷 ♿

🏛 **Baker/Berry Memorial Library**
Dartmouth College. **Tel** (603) 646-2560. ⏲ year-round: call for hours. ♿

🏛 **Hood Museum of Art**
Dartmouth College. **Tel** (603) 646-2808. ⏲ year-round: 10am–5pm Tue & Thu–Sat, 10am–9pm Wed, noon–5pm Sun. 📷 ♿ 🚫 🏪
www.hoodmuseum.dartmouth.edu

Gallery in Dartmouth's Hood Museum of Art in Hanover

COVERED BRIDGES

American bridge builders began covering their wooden spans in the early 19th-century to protect the truss work and planking from the harsh weather. Originally the bridges were built by locals, meaning that each one had design elements specific to its region. Covered bridges built in farming communities were wide enough and tall enough to accommodate a wagon loaded with hay. Bridges leading into town had the added luxury of pedestrian walkways. The bridges, though, were more than just river crossings. Fishermen cast their lines beneath the spans, children used them as platforms from which to dive into the water below, birds nested among the rafters, and social dances were sometimes held beneath their roofs.

One of New Hampshire's covered bridges outside Cornish

Tour of Lake Winnipesaukee ⓰

Flashy sign at Weirs Beach

This stunning lake has a shoreline that meanders for 240 miles (386 km), making it the biggest stretch of waterfront in New Hampshire. Ringed by mountains, Winnipesaukee is scattered with 274 islands. Around its shores are sheltered bays and harbors, with half a dozen resort towns where visitors can enjoy activities ranging from canoeing to shopping for crafts and antiques.

TIPS FOR DRIVERS

Tour length: *70 miles (113 km).*
Starting point: *Alton, at junction of Hwys 11 & 28.*
Stopping-off points: *Popular Weirs Beach eateries include Donna Jean's Diner and Patio Garden Restaurant. In Center Sandwich, Corner House Inn oozes historic Yankee style. Wolfeboro has many places to eat, including Wolfetrap Grill, Bailey's, and West Lake Asian Cuisine.*

Squam Lake ④
This pristine body of water was where the movie *On Golden Pond* (1981) was filmed. The lake is ideal for boating and fishing.

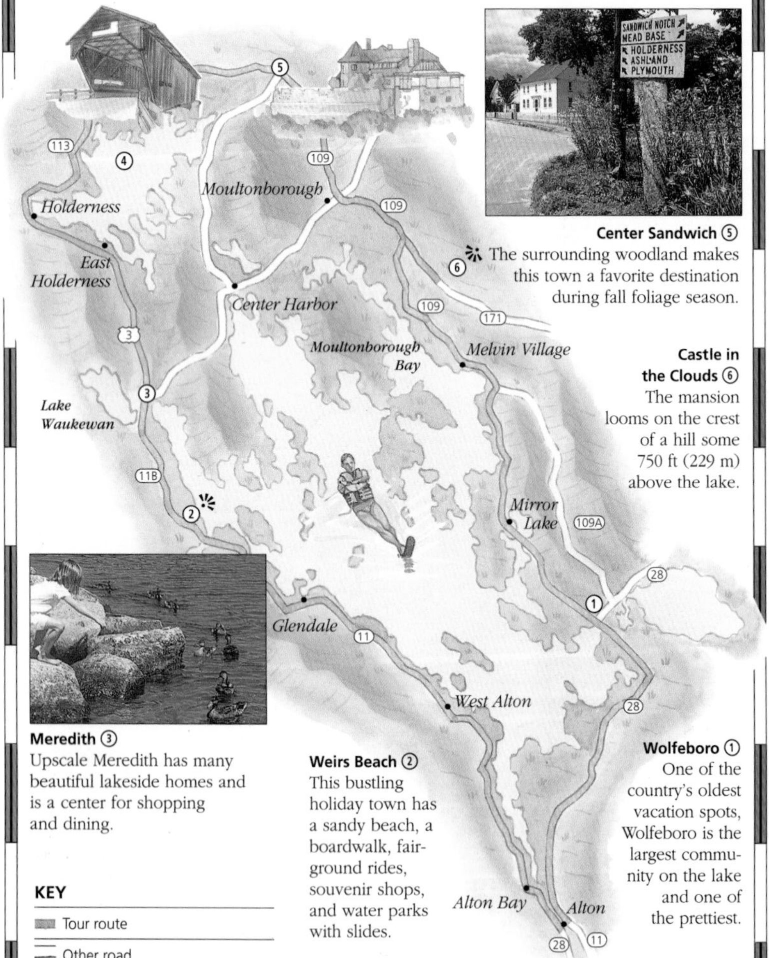

Center Sandwich ⑤
The surrounding woodland makes this town a favorite destination during fall foliage season.

Castle in the Clouds ⑥
The mansion looms on the crest of a hill some 750 ft (229 m) above the lake.

Meredith ③
Upscale Meredith has many beautiful lakeside homes and is a center for shopping and dining.

Weirs Beach ②
This bustling holiday town has a sandy beach, a boardwalk, fairground rides, souvenir shops, and water parks with slides.

Wolfeboro ①
One of the country's oldest vacation spots, Wolfeboro is the largest community on the lake and one of the prettiest.

KEY
Tour route
Other road
Viewpoint

0 kilometers 5
0 miles 5

White Mountains/ White Mountain National Forest ⓱

ℹ 719 North Main St, Laconia (603) 528-8721. ♿ ✉
www.fs.fed.us/r9/white/
Camping reservations Tel (877) 444-6777. **www**.recreation.gov

New Hampshire's heavily forested northland is an outdoor paradise, encompassing a national park, several state parks, more than 1,200 miles (1,900 km) of hiking trails, several dozen lakes, ponds and rivers, and 23 campgrounds. The White Mountain National Forest, a small portion of which lies in neighboring Maine, sprawls over 770,000 acres (311,600 ha).

The most beautiful wilderness area in the state, the National Forest is home to an abundance of wildlife, including a large population of moose. These giant members of the deer family are very shy, but they can be seen from the road at dawn or dusk, lumbering back and forth from their feeding grounds or standing in a swampy pond.

This region offers all manner of outdoor activities – from bird-watching and skiing to rock climbing and kayaking – but even less sporty travelers will revel in the spectacular scenery visible from their car. More than 20 summits soar to over 4,000 ft (1,200 m). Driving through the White Mountains,

Brightly colored engine of the Conway Scenic Railroad

visitors encounter one scenic vista after another: valleys flanked by forests of pine, waterfalls tumbling over rocky outcrops, and trout rivers hissing alongside the meandering roads.

In 1998 a stretch of road, the 100-mile- (161-km-) long White Mountains Trail, was designated as a National Scenic and Cultural Byway. The trail loops across the Mount Washington Valley, through Crawford Notch *(see p271)*, North Conway, and Franconia Notch *(see pp272–3)*.

Ranger station marker

Brilliant fall foliage colors, interspersed with evergreens, transform the rugged countryside into a living palette. The leaves of different trees manifest a rich variety of shades – flaming red maples, golden birch, and maroon northern red oaks. Driving during the fall can be a beautiful but slow-moving experience since thousands of "leaf peepers" are on the

roads. Accommodations can also be difficult to find unless booked well in advance.

North Conway ⓲

🏙 2,500. ✈ 70 miles (112 km) SE in Portland, ME. ℹ 2617 Main St (603) 356-3171 or (800) 367-3364.

The gateway to the sublime beauty of the White Mountains, North Conway is, surprisingly, also a bustling shopping center. This mountain village now has more than 200 factory outlets and specialty shops lining its Main Street. Prices are low in the first place, even for designer names such as Calvin Klein, Ralph Lauren, and Tommy Hilfiger, but because there is no sales tax in New Hampshire, all purchases become even better bargains.

Locals are quick to point out that there are many other attractions in and around North Conway, including canoe trips on the Saco River and a ride into the mountains in an old-fashioned train aboard the **Conway Scenic Railroad**. At the **Story Land** theme park children can ride on an antique German carousel, a pirate ship, or Cinderella's coach.

🚂 Conway Scenic Railroad
Rte 16 in North Conway. **Tel** (603) 356-5251 or (800) 232-5251. ◐ call for schedule. ✉ ☑ ♿ **www**.conwayscenic.com

🚃 Story Land
Rte 16 in Glen. **Tel** (603) 383-4186. ◐ Jul–Aug: 9am–6pm daily; late May–Jun & Labor Day–Columbus Day: 10am–5pm Sat–Sun. ✉ ♿

Breathtaking view from Cathedral Ledge just outside North Conway

Red and white covered bridge leading into Jackson

Jackson ⑲

🏘 750. ✈ 77 miles (125 km) SE in Portland, ME. 🏢 Rte 16B (603) 383-9356 or (800) 866-3334.

This mountain village is tucked away on a back road off Route 16B, but drivers will not miss it because the entrance is marked by its distinctive red and white covered bridge. The picturesque 200-year-old community is, along with the nearby villages of Intervale, Bartlett, and Glen, the main center for accommodation in the Mount Washington area.

Jackson was at one time a favorite getaway spot for big-city Easterners, but the hard times of the Great Depression of the 1930s saw the town slip into disrepair. Developers rediscovered this quiet corner of New Hampshire in the 1980s and began restoring several of the town's best hotels.

Jackson is a popular base camp for winter sports enthusiasts because the region is blessed with more than 110 downhill ski runs and a network of more than 200 miles (320 km) of cross-country trails. The main ski centers are Black Mountain, the Wildcat Ski Area, and the recently enlarged Attitash Bear Peak *(see p379)*. With 273 acres (113 ha) of skiable terrain served by 12 lifts, Attitash is the state's biggest ski center.

Summer sports abound here as well. The region's numerous peaks and valleys make this prime hiking and mountain-biking country, and a restored 18-hole course gives golfers the chance to play a round against one of the most scenic backdrops in New England. After having worked up a sweat, bikers and hikers can cool off under the waterfalls of the Wildcat River in Jackson Village.

Pinkham Notch ⑳

🛈 Rte 16 N of North Conway (603) 466-2721. ⏱ 6:30am–10pm daily.

Named after Joseph Pinkham, who according to local lore explored the area in 1790 with a sled drawn by pigs, this rocky ravine runs between Gorham and Jackson. The lofty Presidential Range girds the western flank of Pinkham Notch, while the 4,415-ft (1,346-m) Wildcat Mountain looms to the east.

Backcountry adventurers love this part of the state because of its great variety of activities. Skiing at the Wildcat Ski Area is among the best in the state, and its high elevation makes for a long season, running from November to April. In the summer, visitors can ride to the summit aboard the aerial gondola. Picnic areas at the top offer great views of Mount Washington and the Presidential Range.

Hiking trails lace Pinkham Notch, including a section of the fabled Appalachian Trail *(see pp22–3)*. These well-maintained paths range from less demanding nature walks suitable for whole families to lung-testing climbs best attacked by serious hikers. Along the way, visitors are led past some of the region's most captivating sights, including waterfalls, rivers, scenic overlooks, and pristine ponds tucked away in thick woodland. Lucky

Sublime beauty of the Presidential Range from Pinkham Notch

For hotels and restaurants in this region see pp322–5 and pp351–3

Striking exterior of the Mount Washington Hotel and Resort

travelers may spot raccoons, beaver, deer, and even the occasional moose.

Bretton Woods ㉑

🏠 550. ✈ 96 miles (155 km) SE in Portland, ME. 🛈 (603) 745-8720 or (800) 346-3687. 🗺 www.visitwhitemountains.com

This tiny enclave situated on a glacial plain at the base of the Presidential Range has an unusual claim to fame: it hosted the United Nations Monetary and Financial Conference in 1944. The meetings established the International Monetary Fund and laid the groundwork for the World Bank, a response to the need for currency stability after the economic upheavals of World War II. The delegates also set the gold standard at $35 an ounce and chose the American dollar as the international standard for monetary exchange.

The setting for this vital meeting was the **Mount Washington Hotel and Resort** (see p322). It is easy to imagine the reaction of delegates when they first caught sight of this grand Spanish Renaissance-style hotel from a sweeping curve in the road. Opened in 1902, the hotel's sparkling white exterior and crimson roof stand out in stark contrast to Mount Washington, looming 6,288 ft (1,917 m) skyward behind the edifice. The hotel has entertained a host of distinguished guests, including British Prime Minister Sir Winston Churchill (1874–1965), inventor Thomas Edison (1847–1931), baseball star Babe Ruth (1895–1948), and three presidents.

Apart from its sublime setting, what makes the hotel so impressive is its sheer size. Designated a National Historic Landmark, the 200-room structure was built by 250 skilled craftsmen from Italy. Today the hotel is surrounded by more than 17,300 acres (7,000 ha) of parkland, and its facilities include a 27-hole golf course laid out by the famous Scottish designer Donald Ross (1872–1948). Nearby Bretton Woods ski area (see p379) offers alpine skiing along with 62 miles (100 km) of cross-country trails.

🏨 **Mount Washington Hotel and Resort**
Rte 302, Bretton Woods. *Tel* (603) 278-1000 or (800) 314-1752. 🚶 🗒 www.mtwashington.com

Environs

The Mount Washington Valley, in which Bretton Woods is located, is dominated by the 6,288-ft (1,917-m) peak of Mount Washington, the highest in the northeastern United States. Other imposing peaks belonging to the Presidential Range – Adams, Jefferson, Madison, Monroe, and Eisenhower – surround Mount Washington, which has the dubious distinction of having the worst weather of any mountain in the world. Unpredictable snowstorms are not unusual, even during the summer months; the highest wind ever recorded on Earth was clocked here in April 1934: 230 mph (370 kph). During the last century, the mountain has claimed the lives of almost 100 people caught unaware by Mount Washington's temper-amental climate.

On clear days, however, when the mountain is in a good mood, nothing compares to the panoramic view from the top.

Sir Winston Churchill, a Mount Washington visitor

Brave souls hike to the summit by one of the many trails, drive their own cars up the winding Mount Washington Auto Road, or puff their way slowly to the top in the deservedly famous **Mount Washington Cog Railroad**. Billed as "America's oldest tourist attraction," the railroad started operating in 1869.

The train, powered by steam locomotives, chugs its way up the cog track to the top of the mountain belching steam. The 3.5-mile (5.6-km) route to the top is one of the steepest tracks in the world, climbing at a heart-stopping 37 percent grade at some points. At the top, passengers can visit the Sherman Adams Summit Building, with the Summit Museum, and Mount Washington Observatory, which records weather conditions and conducts research.

🏨 **Mount Washington Cog Railroad**
Off Rte 302, Marshfield Base Station. *Tel* (603) 278-5404 or (800) 922-8825. 🕐 year-round: call for hours and train schedule. 🚶 🗒 www.thecog.com

Mount Washington Cog Railroad

Perfect spot on Chocorua Lake for the view of Mount Chocorua

Kancamagus Highway ㉒

Rte 112 between Lincoln & Conway.
🛈 *Saco District Ranger Station, 33 Kancamagus Hwy (603) 447-5448.*

Touted by many as the most scenic fall-foliage road in New England, this stretch of highway runs through the White Mountain National Forest *(see p265)* between Lincoln and Conway. The road covers about 34 miles (55 km) of Route 112 and offers exceptional vistas from the Pemi Overlook as it

Sabbaday Falls, a highlight of the Kancamagus Highway

climbs 3,000 ft (914 m) through the Kancamagus Pass. Descending into the Saco Valley, the well-traveled road joins up with the Swift River, following the aptly named waterway into Conway. The highway provides fishermen with easy access to the river, home to brook and rainbow trout.

Campgrounds and picnic areas along the entire length of highway give travelers ample opportunity to relax and eat lunch on the banks of cool mountain streams. Maintained by the US Forest Service, the campgrounds are equipped with toilets and one has shower facilities; most are operated on a first-come, first-served basis. Well-marked trails also allow drivers to stretch their legs in the midst of some of the most beautiful scenery in the state. One of the most popular trails is the short loop that leads travelers to the oft-photographed Sabbaday Falls. Closer to Conway, road signs guide drivers to several scenic areas that afford views of cascades, rapids, and rivers.

The area is home to a wide variety of wildlife, including resident birds such as woodpeckers and chickadees, as well as migratory songbirds who breed here in the summer. Larger inhabitants include deer, moose, and the occasional black bear.

Clark's Trading Post in North Woodstock

Lincoln Woodstock ㉓

🚹 1,300. ✈ 66 miles (106 km) SW in Lebanon. 🛈 Rte 112 & Connector Rd, Lincoln (603) 745-6621 or (800) 227-4191. www.lincolnwoodstock.com

Not including its convenient location near the White Mountains *(see p265)*, the region's main attraction is **Clark's Trading Post**, a strange combination of circus acts, amusement park rides, and museums. Children especially love the trained bears and the over-the-top performers. A session at Clark's "bumper boat" marina, in which participants try to ram each other's boat, is where the younger set can blow off the steam that may have built up on a leaf-peeping drive.

🏛 **Clark's Trading Post**
Rte 3, Lincoln. *Tel* (603) 745-8913.
🕐 *late May–mid-Oct: call for hours & show times.* 📷

◁ Silver Cascades, Crawford Notch State Park, in the autumn

Environs

Tiny Lincoln is located just
3 miles (5 km) northwest of
North Woodstock. The town's
location at the western end of
the Kancamagus Highway and
at the southern entrance to
Franconia Notch State Park *(see
pp272–3)* have turned it into a
base camp for both backwoods
adventurers and stick-to-the-
road sightseers. Nearby **Loon
Mountain** is one of the state's
premier ski resorts. However,
in the summer it offers a
number of activities, from
guided nature walks and tours
of caves to horseback riding,
mountain biking, and a
gondola ride to the summit.

Challenging climbing wall at Loon Mountain outside of Lincoln

🎿 **Loon Mountain**
E of I-93, near Lincoln. **Tel** *(603)
745-8111 or (800) 229-5666.* ♿
♿ 🚻 **www.loonmtn.com**

View from the Willey House in
Crawford Notch State Park

Crawford Notch State Park ㉔

Rte 302 between Twin Mountains
& Bartlett. 🚻 *(603) 374-2272 or
(877) 647-2757.*
Camping Tel *(877) 647-2757 for
reservations.* 🔲 *mid-May–mid-Oct;
(campground until mid-Dec).* ♿

This narrow pass, which
squeezes through the sheer
rock walls of Webster and
Willey mountains, gained
notoriety in 1826. One night
a severe rain sent tons of mud
and stone careening into the
valley below, heading straight
for the home of innkeeper
Samuel Willey and his family.
Alerted by the sounds of the
avalanche, the family fled
outdoors, where all seven
were killed beneath falling
debris. Ironically the lethal
avalanche bypassed the
house, leaving it unscathed.
Several writers, including
New Englander Nathaniel
Hawthorne *(see p30)*, have
immortalized the tragedy in
literature. The house still
stands today and is now in
service as a visitors center.

Once the notch was threat-
ened by overlogging. However, the establishment of the
state park in 1911 has ensured
protection of this rugged wilderness. Today white-water
boaters come here to test
their mettle on the powerful
Saco River, which carves its
way through the valley. Fishermen ply the park's more
tranquil ponds and streams
in search of sport and a tasty
dinner of trout or salmon.

People who prefer to keep
their feet dry can still enjoy
the water on a short hiking
trail leading to the Arethusa
Falls. Towering more than
200 ft (61 m) in the air, this
magnificent cascade is New
Hampshire's tallest waterfall.
Elsewhere drivers will get
wonderful views of the Silver
Cascades and Flume Cascades
waterfalls without leaving the
comfort of their car.

ROBERT FROST AND NEW HAMPSHIRE

The natural beauty of New Hampshire
was an inspiration to one of America's
best-loved poets: Robert Frost (1874–
1963). Born in San Francisco, California,
the four-time winner of the Pulitzer
Prize moved to Massachusetts with his
family when he was 11. After working
as a teacher, a reporter, and a mill hand,
Frost moved to England in 1912. Upon
his return to the US in 1915, Frost settled in the Franconia Notch area *(see
pp272–3)*. The majestic setting inspired
him to pen many of his greatest works,
including his famous poem *Stopping by
Woods on a Snowy Evening* (1923).

Robert Frost farm in Derry, New Hampshire

Franconia Notch State Park ㉕

**Canoeing on
Profile Lake**

This spectacular mountain pass carved between the Kinsman and Franconia ranges is graced with some of the state's most spectacular natural wonders. Foremost among them was the Old Man of the Mountain, a rocky outcropping on the side of a cliff that resembled a man's profile, until the nose and forehead came crashing down in May 2003. Other attractions compensate for the loss including a boardwalk and stairways which lead visitors through the Flume Gorge, a narrow, granite chasm slashed in two by the Flume Brook, while an aerial tramway carries passengers to the summit of Cannon Mountain in eight minutes. Also within the park is Boise Rock, a picnic area by a mountain spring that offers views of the Cannon Cliffs and Echo Lake.

Glacial Boulder
*This glacial boulder is one of
the sights on the Flume Trail.*

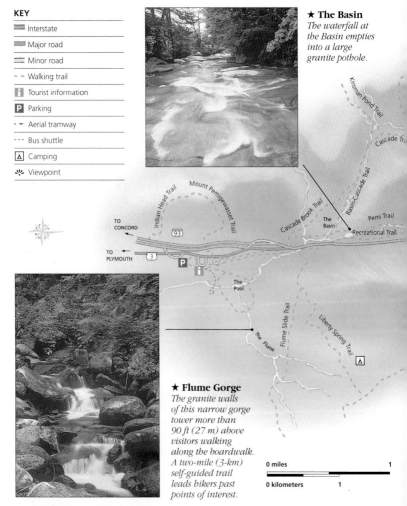

KEY

▨▨	Interstate
▨▨	Major road
▨▨	Minor road
- -	Walking trail
🛈	Tourist information
P	Parking
· -	Aerial tramway
· · ·	Bus shuttle
Ⓐ	Camping
❊	Viewpoint

★ The Basin
*The waterfall at
the Basin empties
into a large
granite pothole.*

TO
CONCORD

TO ◀
PLYMOUTH

★ Flume Gorge
*The granite walls
of this narrow gorge
tower more than
90 ft (27 m) above
visitors walking
along the boardwalk.
A two-mile (3-km)
self-guided trail
leads hikers past
points of interest.*

0 miles   1

0 kilometers   1

Scenic Views
Hikers are rewarded with many beautiful panoramas along the park's trails.

VISITORS' CHECKLIST

I-93, Franconia Notch Parkway. (603) 823-8800. **Park** year-round. **Flume Gorge Visitor Center Tel** (603) 745–8391. May–late Oct: 10am–5pm daily. for Flume Gorge & Visitor Center and campsites. **www. nhparks.state.nh.us Cannon Mountain Tramway Tel** (603) 823 8800. **www**.cannonmt.com

Cannon Mountain

Wild Bunchberries
This fruit can be found throughout the lush Franconia Notch region.

Kinsman Ridge Trail

Recreational Trail

Pemi Trail

Profile Lake

Echo Lake

Artists Bluff

Skookumchuck Trail

Greenleaf Trail

Lafayette Brook

Old Bridge Path

TO FRANCONIA

TO LITTLETON

TO TWIN MOUNTAINS

Echo Lake
The 28-acre (11-ha) lake is great for picnicking, boating, and swimming.

STAR FEATURES

★ The Basin

★ Flume Gorge

★ Profile Lake

★ **Profile Lake**
A favorite among fly-fisherman looking for brook trout, Profile Lake reflects the brilliant colors of fall foliage on the rounded slopes of Cannon Mountain.

MAINE

Maine truly is the great outdoors. More than 5,500 miles (8,850 km) of inlets, bays, and harbors make up its spectacular coastline. Inland deep forests and jutting mountain peaks complement 32,000 miles (51,500 km) of rivers and 6,000 glacial lakes. However, for all its wild mystique, Maine also includes quaint villages, appealing cities, and discount shopping meccas.

Maine has a long and rich history. While some historians maintain that the Vikings probed the rocky coast as early as the 11th century, European settlement began in earnest 500 years later, beginning with the Popham Beach colony of 1607. Although this original colony was short-lived, it spawned a succession of similar settlements at Monhegan (1622), Saco (1623), and Georgeana (1624). The last – renamed York *(see p278)* in 1652 – became the English America's first chartered city in 1642.

While Maine has always been one of the more sparsely populated states in the Union, it has been at the center of numerous territorial disputes, beginning with its abrupt seizure by Massachusetts in 1652 (an unhappy forced marriage, which ended in 1820 when Maine was granted statehood). Between 1675 and 1748 a series of four bloody wars was fought between British colonials and their French counterparts in Quebec. At the outset of the Revolutionary War (1775–83), Portland *(see pp280–83)* was bombarded and burned by the British as an example to other colonies harboring similar anti-Loyalist sentiments.

Traveling through Maine it is easy to see what all the fuss was about. The state's trove of unspoiled wilderness is interspersed with wonderfully preserved relics of its past. Beautiful Colonial homes can be found throughout the state. The importance of seafaring in the region's history is evident in the lighthouses *(see p279)*, maritime museums, and the sea captains' mansions found up and down the coast. And although tourism is now Maine's number one industry, the state has remained remarkably undeveloped, retaining much of the natural splendor that first attracted settlers so many centuries ago.

Hot summer shoreline along Old Orchard Beach

◁ **Nubble Lighthouse at York Beach** *(see p279)*

Exploring Maine

Maine's most popular attractions are found dotted along its coast, beginning in the southeast with the beach playgrounds of Ogunquit *(see pp278–9)*, Old Orchard *(see p279)*, and the resort towns of the Kennebunks *(see p279)*. The scenery gets more dra-matic as travelers move north through Boothbay Harbor *(see p285)*, Pemaquid Point *(see p285)*, and Muscongus Bay. The tiny villages are perfect starting points for sailing and kayaking excursions. Yachts and windjammers ply the waters of the Penobscot Bay region *(see pp286–7)*, while Acadia National Park *(see pp288–9)* stands as Maine's coastal jewel. Farther north, the rising sun first strikes the US at Cobscook Bay. World-class hiking, boating, and mountain-biking opportunities are found inland among the state's many mountains, lakes, and rivers.

KEY

▬▬ Highway

▬ Major road

▭▭▭ Minor road

▬ Scenic route

– – Track

▬▬ Main railway

▬ Minor railway

▬▬ International border

▬ State border

△ Summit

Stone fortifications at Fort William Henry on Pemaquid Point

GETTING AROUND

Interstate 95 is the only major artery in the state. As a result, the smaller scenic routes along the coastline are often congested with summer traffic. Many coastal towns can be reached from Boston by Concord Trailways bus lines. Amtrak runs a service from Boston to Portland with stops en route. Maine State Ferry Service has numerous routes to and from various seashore destinations. Both Portland and Bangor have international airports. The scarcity of public roads in northern Maine means that occasionally logging roads are used, which are operated much like toll roads and are best tackled with four-wheel drive vehicles.

0 kilometers   30

0 miles   30

Québec

Boundary Bald Mountain △
1109m

Jackman   Rockhead ○ ②

MOOSE
LA

Moose   Big Squaw Mountain △
974m

Tumbledown Mountain △
1080m

201   Greenv

27   Flagstaff Lake

Stratton

*Aziscohos
Lake*

RANGELEY
LAKES REGION
⑳   16

⑲ SUGARLOAF
SKI RESORT

Saddleback Mountain △
1252m

*Rangeley
Lake*

27

Skowhegan

17   Farmington ○

Grafton Notch
State Park ○ Old Speck Mountain △
1274m   Wilton

Watervi

Winslo

26   2   Rumford   Livermore Falls

Androscoggin   ⑱ BETHEL   4

Littleton   26   AUGUSTA ⑰   202

Norway ○

Bridgton   202

Lewiston
95

○ Wiscasset

New Gloucester   302   BRUNSWI
⑦ ○ Bath

Laconia   *Sebago
Lake*   FREEPORT ⑥

BOO
HA

Gorham ○   25   ⑤ PORTLAND
✈ ⩎ ⌂

Alfred ○   Saco ○ ④ OLD ORCHARD
BEACH

Sanford ○   ③ THE
KENNEBUNKS

Gulf

Rochester   95

② OGUNQUIT

○ York Village

Boston   ① KITTERY

View of Mount Katahdin, centerpiece of Baxter State Park

SIGHTS AT A GLANCE

Acadia National Park
    pp288–9 **10**
Aroostook County **23**
Augusta **17**
Bangor **16**
Bar Harbor **11**
Baxter State Park **22**
Bethel **18**

Boothbay Harbor **8**
Brunswick **7**
Calais **15**
Campobello Island
    p292 **14**
Freeport **6**
The Kennebunks **3**
Kittery **1**
Machias **13**
Moosehead Lake **21**
Northeast Harbor **12**
Old Orchard Beach **4**
Penobscot Bay **9**
Portland **5**
Rangeley Lakes
    Region **20**
Sugarloaf Ski Resort **19**

Picturesque Stonington village on Deer Isle

Kittery ❶

🚶 9,500. ✈ 49 miles (78 km) NE in Portland. 🚌 I-95 and US Rte 1, (207) 439-1319. **www**.mainetourism.com

The southern coast of Maine begins at the Piscataqua River and Kittery, a town with a split personality. Founded in 1647, Kittery boasts the oldest church in the state, the 1730 **First Congregational Church**. Many fine old mansions line the streets, including the John Bray House, one of the oldest dwellings in Maine. **Fort McClary**, now a state historic site, has fortifications dating to the early 1800s and a hexagonal blockhouse, and the **Kittery Historical and Naval Museum** is filled with ship models and exhibits explaining maritime history. Despite its wealth of historical attractions, Kittery is best known for a more contemporary lure – the more than 100 factory outlet stores promising bargains along Route 1, where shoppers can buy name brands at a discount.

🏛 **First Congregational Church**
23 Pepperrell Rd. **Tel** (207) 439-0650. 🚪 8am & 10am Sun.

🏯 **Fort McClary State Historic Site**
Rte 103 E of Kittery.
Tel (207) 384-5160. 🕐 late May–Sep: 9am–dusk daily. 🚻

🏛 **Kittery Historical and Naval Museum**
Rogers Rd. **Tel** (207) 439-3080.
🕐 Jun–mid-Oct: 10am–4pm Tue–Sat; call for winter hours.
🚻 🚻 partial.

Hexagonal Fort McClary block-house in Kittery

Environs

Four miles (6 km) from Kittery, visitors will come upon York Village. Settled in the 1630s, the village later grew into an important trading center, its wharves and warehouses filled with treasures from the lucrative West Indies trade. A collection of nine historic buildings maintained by the Old York Historical Society, **Old York** traces town history over three centuries. A repository for historical items, Old York has a superb collection of regional decorative arts housed in more than 30 period rooms and galleries. Tours begin at Jefferds' Tavern, a colonial hostelry, and include two historic homes, a 1745 one-room schoolhouse, and the John Hancock Warehouse, named after its owner, an original signatory of the Declaration of Independence. Down the street, the 1719 Old Gaol (jail) stands as one of the country's oldest public buildings. Dark, foreboding dungeons tell of

harsh conditions faced by the felons who served their sentences within the jail's 3-ft- (1-m-) thick walls.

🏯 **Old York**
Lindsay Rd. **Tel** (207) 363-4974.
🕐 Jun–mid-Oct: 10am–5pm Mon–Sat. 🚻 🚻 last tour at 4pm.
🚻 🚻 indoors. **www**.oldyork.org

Ogunquit ❷

🚶 900. ✈ 36 miles (58 km) NE in Portland. 🚌 36 Main St (207) 646-2939. **www**.ogunquit.org

It is easy to see why the Abenaki Indians called this enclave Ogunquit, or "Beautiful Place by the Sea." Maine beaches do not come any better. From mid-May to Columbus Day, trolleys shuttle visitors to this powdery three-mile (5-km) stretch of sand and dunes that curves around a backdrop of rugged cliffs. Atop the cliffs is the 1.25-mile (2-km) Marginal Way, a footpath that offers walkers dramatic vistas of the ocean. Perkins Cove, home of the only pedestrian draw-bridge in the US, is

Lobster trap buoys

a quaint jumble of fishermen's shacks now transformed into shops, art galleries, restaurants, and docks with fishing and cruise boats.

This picturesque outpost attracted an artist's colony as early as 1890, establishing it as a haven for the arts. The handsome **Ogunquit Museum**

Scenic ocean vista at Marginal Way in Ogunquit

of American Art was built in 1952 by the eccentric but wealthy Henry Strater, who served as its director for more than 30 years. Constructed of wood and local stone, the museum has wide windows to allow views of the rocky cove and meadows. A 3-acre (1-ha) sculpture garden and lawns also make the most of the breathtaking setting. The permanent collection includes art by many notable American painters.

🏛 **Ogunquit Museum of American Art**
543 Shore Rd. *Tel* (207) 646-4909.
◯ Jul–Oct: 10:30am–5pm Mon–Sat, 2–5pm Sun. ● Labor Day.
www.ogunquitmuseum.org

The Kennebunks ❸

🛬 30 miles (48 km) NE in Portland. 🛈 17 Western Ave, Kennebunk (207) 967-0857. www.visitthekennebunks.com

First a thriving port and busy shipbuilding center, then a summer retreat for the wealthy, the Kennebunks are made up of two villages, Kennebunkport and Kennebunk.

The profusion of fine Federal and Greek Revival structures in Kennebunkport's historic village is evidence of the fortunes made in shipbuilding and trading from 1810 to the 1870s. With its 100-ft- (30-m-) tall white steeple and belfry, the 1824 South Congregational Church is a favorite subject for photographers. History of a different sort can be found at the **Seashore Trolley Museum**, where some 200 antique streetcars are housed, including one vehicle from New Orleans named "Desire." Visitors can embark on a tour of the countryside aboard one of the restored trolleys.

The scenic drive along Route 9 offers views of surf along rocky Cape Arundel. At Cape Porpoise hungry travelers can sample lobster pulled fresh from

MAINE'S LIGHTHOUSES

For centuries mariners have been guided to safety by Maine's picturesque lighthouses. The coast is dotted with 63 such beacons, some accessible from the mainland and others perched on offshore islands. Portland Head Light was commissioned by the country's first president, George Washington (1732–99), and built in 1791, making it the oldest lighthouse in the state. It, like several other beacons, is open to the public and houses a small museum focusing on local marine and military history.

Nubble Lighthouse near Old York

the Atlantic. Kennebunk is famous for its beaches, most notably Kennebunk Beach, which is actually three connected strands. One of the town's most romantic historic homes is the 1826 Wedding Cake House. According to the local lore, George Bourne was unexpectedly called to sea before his marriage. Although a very hastily arranged wedding took place, there was no time to bake the traditional wedding cake. Instead, the shipbuilder vowed to his bride that upon his return he would remodel their home to look like a wedding cake. Today the Gothic spires, ornate latticework, and gingerbread trim offer proof that Bourne was a man of his word. Housed in four restored 19th-century buildings, **The Brick Store Museum** offers glimpses into the past with displays of decorative arts. It also offers architectural

Kennebunkport signpost

walking tours of the town's historic area (May–October).

🏛 **Seashore Trolley Museum**
195 Log Cabin Rd, Kennebunkport.
Tel (207) 967-2712. ◯ late May–Oct: 10am–5pm daily; early May & late Oct: 10am–5pm Sat–Sun.
www.trolleymuseum.org

🏛 **The Brick Store Museum**
117 Main St, Kennebunk. *Tel* (207) 985-4802. ◯ year-round: 10am–4:30pm Tue–Fri, 10am–1pm Sat. ● pub hols.
www.brickstoremuseum.org

Old Orchard Beach ❹

👥 9,000. 🛬 13 miles (21 km) NE in Portland. 🚉 🛈 11 First St (207) 934-2500 or (800) 365-9386.

One of Maine's oldest seashore resorts, Old Orchard Beach's 7 miles (11 km) of sandy shoreline and low surf make it a favorite spot for swimming. Kids love the pier lined with game booths, food stands, a roller coaster, a 60-ft (18-m) water slide, and a 36-hole miniature golf course with waterfalls. A floating marina caters to water sports.

Fresh lobster from the Cape Porpoise area in southern Maine

Portland ⑤

Children's Museum banner

Poet and Portland native Henry Wadsworth Longfellow (1807–82) described Maine's largest city as "the beautiful town that is seated by the sea." Longfellow was inspired by Portland's fortunate location on the crest of a peninsula with expansive views of Casco Bay and the Calendar Islands on three sides. Once a prosperous port and an early state capital, Portland has been devastated by no less than four major fires, resulting in a preponderance of sturdy stone Victorian buildings that line many of its streets today.

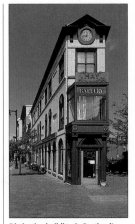

Distinctive building in Portland's downtown arts district

Exploring Portland

A thriving arts community and a downtown with interesting shopping and dining are all part of a stroll along Congress Street and through the restored Old Port Exchange area *(see pp282–3)*. The West End has fine homes and a splendid Western Promenade overlooking the water. The working waterfront and nearby beaches all add to the city's charm and atmosphere.

⚑ Neal Dow Memorial

714 Congress St. *Tel* (207) 773-7773. ☐ 11am–4pm Mon–Fri. Neal Dow (1804–97), one of Portland's prominent citizens, built this Federal-style mansion in 1829. Twice serving as the city's mayor, Dow was an abolitionist and prohibitionist who also championed the causes of women's rights and prison reform. The Dow family's furnishings, paintings, china, and silver are displayed. The home is also the headquarters of The Maine Women's Christian Temperance Union.

⚑ Victoria Mansion

109 Danforth St. *Tel* (207) 772-4841. ☐ May–Oct: 10am–4pm Mon–Sat, 1–5pm Sun; late Nov & Dec: 11am–5pm Tue–Sun. ● Jan–Apr, Jul 4, Nov & Dec 25. ▣ ☑ every half hour. ▣ This sumptuous brownstone villa was completed in 1860 to serve as the summer home of Ruggles hotelier Sylvester Morse (c.1816–93). The interior has extraordinary interior detail, such as painted *trompe l'oeil* walls and ceilings, wood paneling, marble mantels, and a flying staircase.

⛫ Portland Museum of Art

7 Congress Sq. *Tel* (207) 775-6148. ☐ year-round: 10am–5pm Tue, Wed, Thu, Sat, Sun, 10am–9pm Fri; late May–mid-Oct: 10am–5pm Mon. ▣ ☒ www. portlandmuseum.org Portland's premier fine art collection fills three distinctive buildings, spanning Federal, Beaux-Arts, and postmodern design. One

gallery showcases paintings and extensive graphic art by the Portland area's most famous artist, Winslow Homer (1836–1910). Other highlights include works by Andrew Wyeth (1917–2009), Paul Gauguin (1848–1903), and Pablo Picasso (1881–1973). Also on display are glass, ceramics, and furniture.

(map labels:) Frost Gully Gallery; Portland Public Market; Portland Public Library; Wadsworth Longfellow House ⑤; Maine College of Art; Children's Museum & Theatre of Maine ④; Portland Museum of Art ③; Victoria Mansion ②; Neal Dow Memorial ①; CUMBERLAND AVENUE; OAK STREET; FOREST AVENUE; CONGRESS STREET; FREE STREET; CASCO ST; BROWN ST; PREBLE ST; FEDERAL ST; COTTON ST; CENTER ST; HIGH STREET; STATE STREET; SPRING STREET; PARK STREET; DANFORTH STREET; PLEASANT STREET; YORK STREET; ✈ Airport 4 miles (7 km); Bus Station 5 miles (8 km); George Tate House; Fort Will Park; 77

Victoria Mansion, with its lavishly decorated interior

PORTLAND CITY CENTER

Coastal fishing on the outskirts of Portland

Constructed in 1807, this
octagonal landmark is the last
surviving 19th-century signal
tower on the Atlantic. The
102-step climb to the upper
deck is worth the effort.

🏛 Children's Museum & Theatre of Maine

142 Free St. *Tel* (207) 828-1234.
☐ year-round: 10am–5pm Tue–Sat,
noon–5pm Sun; May–Sep: 10am–
5pm Mon. ⬤ public hols. 🅿 🚹
This historic brick building
houses three floors of interactive exhibits, including a
tidepool touch tank, a replica
space shuttle, and an observation beehive. Young actors
occasionally perform
shows in the Chil-
dren's Theatre.

🏚 Wadsworth-Longfellow House

489 Congress St. *Tel* (207) 879-0427.
☐ May–Oct: 10am–5pm daily (from
noon Sun). 🅿 🚹 🚹 first floor. 🚹
Poet Henry Wadsworth
Longfellow grew up in this
1785 house, which contains
family mementos, portraits,
and furnishings.

🏚 George Tate House

1270 Westbrook St. *Tel* (207) 774-
6177. ☐ Jun–mid-Oct: 10am–4pm
Tue–Sat, 1–4pm 1st Sun of month.
⬤ Oct–May, Jul 4, & Labor Day. 🅿
In 1755 George Tate, an agent
of the British Royal Navy, constructed an elegant gambrel-
roofed home with rich wood
paneling, patterned floors, a
dogleg staircase, and eight
fireplaces. Now a National
Historic Landmark, the
house has fine period
furnishings. Tours of the
18th-century garden are
offered on Wednesdays.

🏛 Maine Narrow Gauge Railroad Co. & Museum

58 Fore St. *Tel* (207) 828-0814.
☐ 10am–4pm Mon–Fri (daily during
train season). 🚹 **Train ride** ☐ mid-
May–mid-Oct on the hour; call for
other times. 🅿
Scenic trips along a 3-mile
(5-km) stretch of the waterfront are the highlight of
this museum dedicated to
the railroad that served much
of Maine from the 1870s to
the 1940s. Exhibits include
vintage locomotives.

🏚 Portland Observatory

138 Congress St. *Tel* (207) 774-5561.
☐ late May–mid-Oct: 10am–4:30pm
daily. ⬤ Jul 4. 🅿 🚹 🚹 🚹

🏛 Museum at Portland Head Light at Fort Williams Park

1000 Shore Rd. *Tel* (207) 799-2661.
☐ late May–mid-Oct: 10am–4pm
daily; mid-Apr–May & mid-Oct–Dec:
10am–4pm Sat & Sun. 🅿 🚹
First illuminated in 1791 by
order of President George
Washington (1732–99), the
lighthouse has been the subject of poetry, postage stamps,
and photographs. The keeper's
house is now a museum with
exhibits on the history of the
world's beacons. The large
surrounding park, just 4 miles
(6.5 km) from downtown, has
a beach and picnic areas.

Portland Observatory atop Munjoy Hill

KEY

▢ Street-by-Street map *see pp282-3*

Key to Symbols *see back flap*

Street-by-Street: Old Port

This once-decaying neighborhood near the harbor has been restored and is now the city's liveliest area, filled with shops, art galleries, restaurants, and bars. The Old Port's narrow streets are lined with classic examples of Victorian-era commercial architecture. From the docks, ships take passengers out for deep-sea fishing excursions and harbor tours; ferries to Nova Scotia, Canada, save travelers some 850 miles (1,370 km) of driving. Cruises include mail-boat rides and excursions to the Calendar Islands, where visitors can enjoy everything from cycling to sea kayaking.

Lively District
The Old Port has numerous pubs and outdoor terraces.

Centennial Block
has a facade made of Maine granite.

Charles Q. Clapp Block
This distinctive building was designed by self-taught architect Charles Quincy Clapp in 1866.

First National Bank
is a typical example of Queen Anne commercial style. Its sandstone and brick exterior features a corner tower and tall chimneys.

Dolphins Statue
The statue is situated in the small cobblestone area in the middle of the Old Port district.

Mary L. Deering Block,
built for the prominent Deering family, is a mix of Italian and Colonial Revival styles.

Seaman's Club
Built after the devastating fire of 1866, the building is known for its striking Gothic windows.

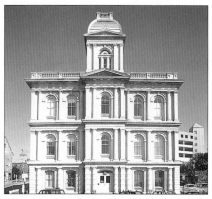

★ United States Custom House
*Built following the Civil War (1861–5), this
regal building contains gilded ceilings,
marble staircases, and chandeliers.*

State of Maine Armory was designed to
resemble a fortress and once was home to
several units of the reserve militia known as
the National Guard.

Antique shops *can be
found throughout the Old
Port district.*

| 0 meters | 50 |
| 0 yards | 50 |

KEY

– – – Suggested route

★ Mariner's Church
*Built in 1828, the building is an eclectic mix
of Greek Revival and Federal styles, and is
now used to house a variety of shops
and businesses.*

Freeport ❻

🏃 7,000. ✈ 17 miles (31 km)
SW in Portland. 🚊 23 Depot St
(207) 865-1212 or (800) 865-1994.
www.freeportusa.com

Although Freeport dates
back to 1789, shoppers
would argue that it did not
arrive on the scene until
1917, when the first L.L.
Bean clothing store opened
its doors. Today this retail
giant is open 24 hours a day,
365 days a year, and, with
more than 3.5 million customers annually, L.L. Bean
is easily Maine's biggest
man-made attraction. Since
the 1980s more than 150
other brand-name outlets
have opened here.

Travelers who make it past
the shops will discover a working harbor in South Freeport,
where seal-watching tours and
sailing cruises depart. The
shoreline includes **Wolfe's
Neck Woods State Park**, 233
acres (94 ha) of tranquility
wrapped along Casco Bay.

Freeport's most unusual
sight is the **Desert of Maine**.
Originally a late-1700s farm,
the area was severely over-
tilled and over-logged. The
topsoil eventually disappeared
altogether, giving way to
glacial sand deposits and creating a 40-acre (16-ha) desert
of sand dunes. Visitors can
walk the nature trails with a
guide who narrates the history
of the area, or ride on an
open cart. The farm museum
is housed in a 1783 barn.

L.L. BEAN AND OUTLET SHOPPING

Leon Leonwood Bean (1872–1967) likely
would be amazed if he could see the result
of his dislike for cold, wet feet. The hunting shoe he developed in 1912 with leather
uppers on rubber overshoe bottoms began
a company that now claims more than a
billion dollars in sales worldwide and
carries anything needed for outdoor
excursions. Bean's showroom has
grown into a mammoth flagship store
that includes a 785-sq-ft (73-sq-m-)
pond stocked with trout.

Bust of L.L. Bean

🌺 **Wolfe's Neck Woods
State Park**
Wolfe's Neck Rd. **Tel** (207) 865-
4465. ⬜ Apr–Oct: 9am–dusk daily.
♿ 🚻 ♿

🏛 **Desert of Maine**
95 Desert Rd. **Tel** (207) 865-6962.
⬜ May–mid-Oct: tours 9am–
4:30pm daily. ♿ ♿
www.desertofmaine.com

Brunswick ❼

🏃 21,000. ✈ 33 miles (53 km)
SW in Portland. 🚆 🚊 2 Main St,
Topsham (207) 725-8797.

Brunswick is best known
as the home of Bowdoin
College and the land entry
for the scenic panoramas of
the town of Harpswell – a
peninsula and three islands
jutting out into Casco Bay.

Founded in 1794, the col-
lege claims a number of
distinguished alumni, including explorers Robert Peary
(1856–1920) and Donald
MacMillan (1874–1970).
The **Peary-MacMillan Arctic**

**Peary-MacMillan Arctic Museum
on Bowdoin College campus**

Museum honors the two,
who in 1909 became the first
to reach the North Pole.
Exhibits trace the history of
polar exploration and display
the journals of both men.

The **Pejepscot Historical
Society** offers displays of
Brunswick history in its three
museums and offers tours of
both Skolfield-Whittier House,
a 17-room Italianate mansion
built in 1858 by a shipyard

Seemingly endless acres of sand in Desert of Maine, Freeport

For hotels and restaurants in this region see pp325–7 and pp353–5

owner, and the Joshua L. Chamberlain House, a Civil War museum.

🏛 Peary-MacMillan Arctic Museum
Hubbard Hall, Bowdoin College. **Tel** *(207) 725-3416.* ⏷ *year-round: 10am–5pm Tue–Sat; 2–5pm Sun.* ● *public hols.* ♿

🏛 Pejepscot Historical Society
159 Park Row. **Tel** *(207) 729-6606.* ⏷ *Jun–Oct: call for opening hours and tour times.* 📷

Environs
Nine miles (14 km) east lies Bath, long a shipbuilding center. Its stately homes were built with the profits from this lucrative industry. In 1608 colonists constructed the *Virginia*, the first British boat produced in the New World. Since then, some 4,000 ships have been constructed here. The **Maine Maritime Museum** operates one of the country's few surviving wooden shipbuilding yards. The modern Maritime History Building annex is a repository of nautical models, paintings, and memorabilia.

Nautical art from the Maine Maritime Museum in Bath

🏛 Maine Maritime Museum
243 Washington St. **Tel** *(207) 443-1316.* ⏷ *9:30am–5pm daily.* ● *Jan 1, Thanksgiving, & Dec 25.* 📷 📷 *call for times.* ♿ *partial.* ▯

Boothbay Harbor ❽
🏛 *2,500.* ✈ *38 miles (61 km) N in Augusta.* 🚩 *192 Townsend Ave (207) 633-2353 or (800) 266-8422.* **www**.boothbayharbor.com

The boating capital of the mid-coast, Boothbay Harbor bustles with the influx of summer tourists. Dozens of boating excursions cast off from the dock. Visitors might choose to take an hour's sail along the coast aboard a majestic

Boothbay Harbor's busy boardwalk area

windjammer, a 41-mile (66-km) cruise up the Kennebec River, or the popular day trip to the artists' retreat on Monhegan Island *(see p287)*. Sightseers can participate in a wide range of activities, including puffin and whale-watching expeditions. The harbor is at its best in late June, when majestic tall ships parade in under full sail for the annual Windjammer Days festival.

Boothbay Harbor whale watch sign

The town itself is chock-a-block with shops and galleries. **Maine State Aquarium**, a haven for parents of restless children on rainy days, is equipped with a large touch tank filled with sea creatures, which can be touched.

🐟 Maine State Aquarium
194 McKown Point Rd, West Boothbay Harbor. **Tel** *(207) 633-9674.* ⏷ *late May–early Sep: 10am–5pm daily.* 📷 📷 ♿

Environs
A scenic 30-mile (48-km) drive up the coast brings travelers to Pemaquid Point, complete with shelves of granite cliffs that jut from the sea. Rising dramatically above a bluff and offering panoramic views of the coastline, the 1827 **Pemaquid Point Light** houses the **Fisherman's Museum** in the old light-keeper's home. The **Pemaquid Art Gallery** is on the grounds and shows the work of local artists. There is a bonus for history buffs at the 8-acre (3-ha) **Colonial Pemaquid State Historic Site**, which

includes a 1695 graveyard and a replica of **Fort William Henry**. English colonists fought French invaders at this spot in several forts that date from the early 17th century onward. A small museum contains a diorama of the original 1620s settlement and displays a collection of tools, pottery shards, and household items that reflect the rustic lives of the early settlers.

🗼 Pemaquid Point Light
Rte 130. **Tel** *(207) 677-2492.* ⏷ *mid-May–mid-Oct: 10am–5pm daily.* 📷 ♿ **Fisherman's Museum** **Tel** *(207) 677-2494.* ⏷ *May–Oct: call for hours.* ♿ **Pemaquid Art Gallery** **Tel** *(207) 677-2494.* ⏷ *May–Oct: call for hours.*

🗼 Colonial Pemaquid State Historic Site/Fort William Henry
Off Rte 130. **Tel** *(207) 677-2423.* ⏷ *late May–early Sep: dawn to dusk.* 📷

Pemaquid Point Light and the Fisherman's Museum

Penobscot Bay **⑨**

Penobscot Bay is picture-book Maine, with high hills seemingly rolling straight into the ocean, wave-pounded cliffs, sheltered harbors bobbing with fishing boats, and lobster traps piled high on the docks. Windjammer sailboats, ferries, and numerous cruise ships carry passengers to offshore islands, setting sail from ports such as Rockland, Camden, and Lincolnville, popular stops on the bay's western shore. The former shipbuilding centers of Searsport and Bucksport lie beyond. The more remote eastern shore leads to serene, perfectly preserved villages such as Castine and Blue Hill.

Sailboats moored in the safe confines of Camden Harbor

Secluded cliff-top view of Penobscot Bay

Exploring Penobscot Bay

To sail across Penobscot Bay covers a mere 35 miles (56 km) from its southernmost outpost of Port Clyde to its northern tip at Stonington. However, typical of Maine's ribboned coast, the same voyage takes almost 100 miles (160 km) by car. Either mode of transportation will offer stunning views of one of Maine's coastal highlights.

Rockland

🛈 *1 Park Drive (207) 596-0376 or (800) 562-2529.*

Long a fishing town and commercial center, Rockland is now evolving into a tourist destination. These days lobster boats share the harbors with excursion boats, state ferries, and the schooners of Maine's windjammer fleet. However, the Lobster Festival, on the first full weekend of August, remains the town's biggest event.

On land the Farnsworth Art Museum and Wyeth Center showcases artists inspired by the Maine landscape,

including Rockwell Kent (1882–1971), Edward Hopper (1882–1967), and N.C. (1882–1945), Andrew (1917–2009), and Jamie (b.1946) Wyeth. The Maine Lighthouse Museum has a superb collection of lenses and other artifacts as well as a lighthouse-themed gift shop. Two miles (3.2 km) south of Rockland on Route 73, the Owls Head Transportation Museum houses aircraft, cars, bicycles, and carriages and occasionally hosts air shows.

Camden

🛈 *Commercial St, Public Landing (207) 236-4404 or (800) 223-5459.* **www.**visitcamden.com

The compact village is ideal for exploring on foot. Shady streets are lined with elegant homes and spired churches, and a host of shops border the waterfront. Among the fine inns on High Street is the Whitehall, with a room dedicated to Pulitzer Prize-winning poet Edna St. Vincent Millay (1892–1950), who went to school in Camden.

From mid-May to mid-October a short road at Camden Hills State Park on Route 1 is open to the top of

796-ft (242-m) Mount Battie. Standing on this point overlooking Penobscot Bay, Millay was inspired to write her first volume of poetry.

Searsport

🛈 *Main & Steamboat (207) 548-6510.*

Searsport was once a major shipbuilding port. Now a handful of restored sea captains' homes on Church Street house the collection of the Penobscot Marine Museum (open late May to late October). An extensive collection of maritime art, ship models, navigational instruments and imported goods and displays of shipbuilding tools help tell the story of those glory days.

Considered to be the antiques capital of Maine, the town is chock-a-block with shops and has large flea markets on weekends in the summer.

Bucksport

🛈 *52 Main St (207) 469-6818.* 🛥

Bucksport looks across the Penobscot River to the 125-acre (51-ha) Fort Knox State Park that surrounds a pentagonal Civil War-era fortress.

Vintage aircraft at Owls Head Transportation Museum

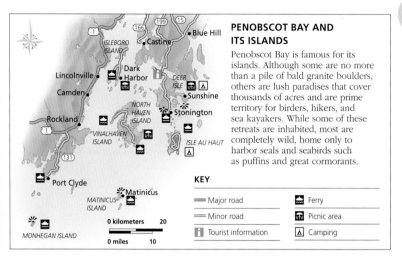

PENOBSCOT BAY AND ITS ISLANDS

Penobscot Bay is famous for its islands. Although some are no more than a pile of bald granite boulders, others are lush paradises that cover thousands of acres and are prime territory for birders, hikers, and sea kayakers. While some of these retreats are inhabited, most are completely wild, home only to harbor seals and seabirds such as puffins and great cormorants.

KEY

═══ Major road

─── Minor road

ℹ️ Tourist information

⛴ Ferry

🏞 Picnic area

△ Camping

0 kilometers 20

0 miles 10

From May through October, visitors can explore barracks, storehouses, and underground passages. The park also features the Penobscot Narrows Bridge Observatory, which provides 360-degree views from 420 ft (128 m) above the river.

Castine

ℹ️ *Emerson Hall, Court St (207) 326-4502.*
Founded in the early 17th century and coveted for its strategic location overlooking the bay, Castine has flown the flags of France, Britain, Holland, and the US.

Relics of Castine's turbulent past can still be seen at Fort George on Wadsworth Cove Road, the highest point in town. Fort George was built by the British in 1779 and witnessed the American Navy's worst defeat during the Revolutionary War, a battle in which more than 40 colonial ships were either captured or destroyed. The fort is always open. Across from Fort George on Battle Avenue is the Maine Maritime Academy.

On Perkins Street, the two-story Wilson Museum has a collection that includes everything from Balinese masks and pre-Inca pottery to minerals and farm tools. It is closed during the fall and winter months.

Blue Hill

ℹ️ *Blue Hill Town Hall (207) 374-3242.*
Surrounded by fields of blueberries and with many of its white clapboard buildings listed on the National Historic Register, Blue Hill is a living postcard. Visitors will get a great view if they climb up Blue Hill Mountain.

Deer Isle

ℹ️ *Rte 15 at Eggemoggin Rd (207) 348-6124.* ⛴
Deer Isle, reached from the mainland via a graceful suspension bridge, is actually a series of small islands linked by causeways. Island highlights include the towns of Deer Isle and Stonington, and the famous Haystack Mountain School of Crafts.

Isle au Haut

ℹ️ *Rte 15 at Eggemoggin Rd (207) 348-6124.* ⛴
A mail boat from Stonington covers the 8 miles (13 km) to Isle au Haut. Almost half the island, some 2,800

White-tailed deer, a common sight throughout the Penobscot Bay area

wooded acres (1,133 ha), belongs to Acadia National Park *(see pp288–9)* and offers 20 miles (32 km) of hiking.

Monhegan Island

ℹ️ *(207) 596-0376 or (800) LOBCLAW.*
This unspoiled enclave has no cars, no commotion, and until recently no electricity. Only a half mile (0.8 km) wide and 1.7 miles (2.7 km) long, this island is smaller than New York City's Central Park, and is a favored retreat for birders and hikers who enjoy rough trails along rocky cliffs and through deep forest. Painter Jamie Wyeth is one of the prominent current residents of a summer artists' colony. Cruise companies operate round-trip excursions from Port Clyde, Boothbay Harbor, and New Harbor.

North Haven Island

ℹ️ *(207) 867-4433.* ⛴
Eight miles (13 km) long and 3 miles (5 km) wide, North Haven is a refined summer colony and home to 350 hardy year-round residents. Much of the island remains open fields and meadows filled with wildflowers.

Vinalhaven

ℹ️ *(207) 863-4826.* ⛴
Tiny Vinalhaven is a perfect place for a swim or a hike. Inland moors and green spaces are balanced by a granite shoreline and a harbor bustling with lobster boats.

For hotels and restaurants in this region see pp325–7 and pp353–5

Acadia National Park ⑩

Located primarily on Mount Desert Island, the 35,000-acre (14,164-ha) Acadia National Park, a wild, unspoiled paradise, is heavily visited in summer. Wave-beaten shores and inland forests await travelers. The park's main attraction is the seasonal Loop Road, a 27-mile (43-km) drive that climbs and dips with the pink granite mountains of the east coast of the island before swinging inland past Jordan Pond, Bubble Pond, and Eagle Lake. Visitors who want a closer, more intimate look at the flora and fauna can do so on foot, bike, or horseback.

Vintage Carriage Roads
Forty-five miles (72 km) of old broken-stone carriage roads can be used for hiking and cycling.

Acadia's Wildlife
The park is home to numerous animals including woodchucks, white-tailed deer, red foxes, and the occasional black bear.

★ Bass Harbor Head
Craggy Bass Harbor Head exemplifies Maine's rock-bound shoreline. The 1858 Bass Harbor Head lighthouse affords magnificent views of the ocean.

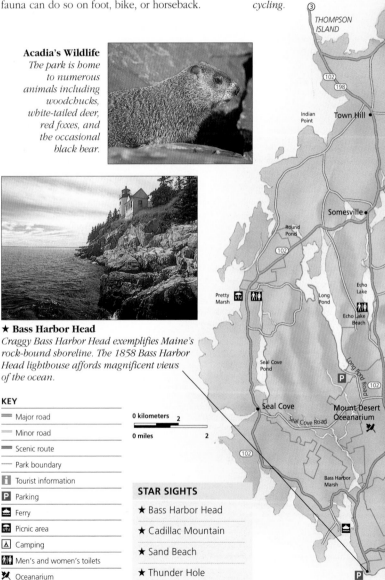

KEY

▬▬	Major road
━━	Minor road
▬▬	Scenic route
— —	Park boundary
🛈	Tourist information
🅿	Parking
⛴	Ferry
⛱	Picnic area
△	Camping
🚻	Men's and women's toilets
🍴	Oceanarium

0 kilometers   2

0 miles   2

STAR SIGHTS

★ Bass Harbor Head

★ Cadillac Mountain

★ Sand Beach

★ Thunder Hole

VISITORS' CHECKLIST

Hulls Cove Visitor Center, off Rte 3 in Hulls Cove. ***Tel*** *(207) 288-3338. mid-Apr–Oct: 8am–4:30pm daily (Jul–Aug: to 6pm). Bangor-Bar Harbor.* **www**.nps.gov/acad

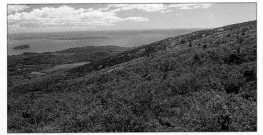

★ Cadillac Mountain

The 1,527-ft- (465-m-) tall Cadillac Mountain is the highest point on the Atlantic Coast. Hiking trails and an auto road lead to spectacular panoramas at the summit.

Salsbury Cove
Hamilton Pond
Hulls Cove
MOUNT DESERT ISLAND
BAR ISLAND
SHEEP PORCUPINE ISLAND
BALD PORCUPINE ISLAND
Bar Harbor
233
3
Aunt Betty Pond
Eagle Lake
The Tarn
Bubble Pond
Cadillac Mountain
Schooner Head
Jordan Pond
Sand Beach
Great Head
Thunder Hole
198
Otter Creek
Otter Point
Seal Harbor
Hunters Beach Cove
Northeast Harbor
Ingraham Point
LITTLE CRANBERRY ISLAND
CRANBERRY ISLES
GREAT CRANBERRY ISLAND
BAKER ISLAND

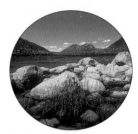

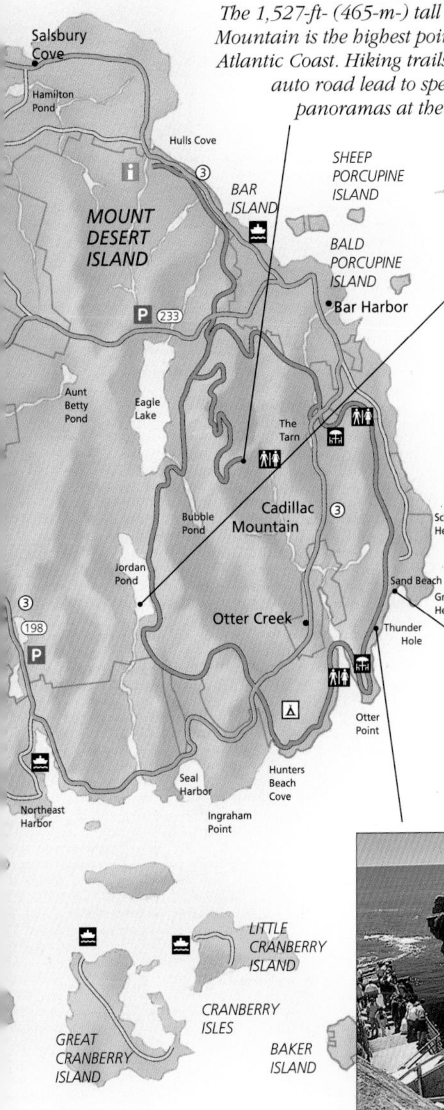

Jordan Pond

Many visitors stop at beautiful Jordan Pond, where a restaurant serves lunch, tea, and dinner from late May to late October.

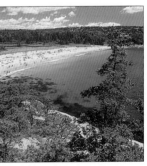

★ Sand Beach

Sand Beach is one of only two lifeguarded beaches in the park, but the ocean water, which rarely exceeds 55° F (15° C), discourages many swimmers.

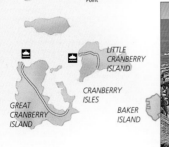

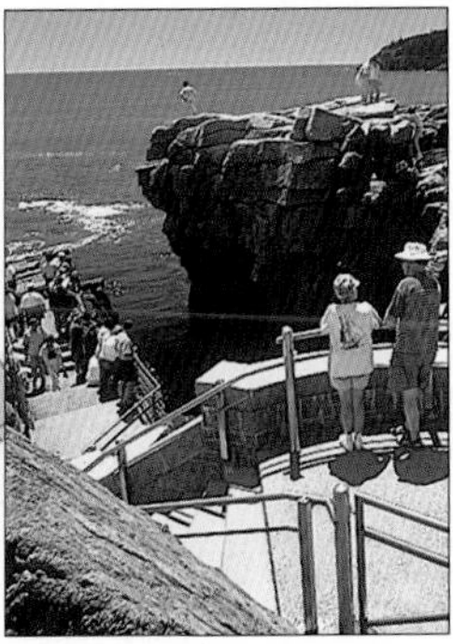

★ Thunder Hole

The ocean's relentless pounding on the island's cliffs has created the natural phenomenon known as the Thunder Hole. When the tide rises during heavy winds, air trapped in this crevice is compressed and expelled with a resounding boom.

Rolling hills near Eagle Lake on the outskirts of Bar Harbor

Bar Harbor ⓫

🏃 5,000 ✈ 11 miles (17 km) NW in Trenton. 🚌 Island Explorer (free). ℹ 1201 Bar Harbor Rd, Trenton, (800) 345-4617 or 1 West St, Bar Harbor (mid-May–mid-Oct only). www.barharbormaine.com

With a commanding location on Frenchman Bay, Bar Harbor is Mount Desert Island's lively tourist center. Artists Thomas Cole (1801–48) and Frederic Church (1862–1900) discovered the area's beauty in the 1840s and their brilliant work attracted the wealthy. In the 19th century, the town was a haven for the Astors and the Vanderbilts, among other rich American families.

Today Bar Harbor is a thriving waterside resort that attracts 5 million visitors a year. From here people can explore Acadia National Park (see pp288–9) or the mid-Maine coastline or grab a ferry to Nova Scotia, Canada.

🏛 Bar Harbor Historical Society Museum

33 Ledgelawn Ave. Tel (207) 288-0000. ⌚ Jun–Oct: 1–4pm Mon–Sat. In 1947 a fire destroyed 17,000 acres (6,880 ha) of

wilderness and a third of Bar Harbor's lavish summer homes, all but ending the village's reign as a high-society enclave. A display of early photographs shows the grand old days and the devastating effects of the fire. Happily for visitors, several of the remaining summer showplaces have been turned into gracious inns.

🎬 Criterion Theater

35 Cottage St. Tel (207) 288-3441. 📷 A perennial favorite, this is an Art Deco gem that is listed on the National Register of Historic Places. The theater offers films, live music, and theater performances.

🏛 Abbe Museum

26 Mount Desert St. Tel (207) 288-3519. ⌚ early Jun–Oct: 10am–6pm daily; call for winter hours. ⬤ Jan. 📷 ♿ This museum celebrates Maine's Native American heritage with exhibits, hands-on programs and workshops taught by Native artists. There is a seasonal branch next to the Wild Gardens of Acadia, which has some 300 species of local plants.

🦞 Bar Harbor Oceanarium & Lobster Hatchery

Rte 3. Tel (207) 288-5005. ⌚ mid-May–Oct: 9am–5pm Mon–Sat. 📷 🎫 ♿ 🅿 Bar Harbor Oceanarium, 8.5 miles (14 km) northwest of town, is where to see harbor seals, explore a salt marsh on Thomas Bay Marsh Walk, or visit the Maine Lobster Museum and separate lobster hatchery, where the hatching and raising process is explained. Children can enjoy the touch tank.

🦌 Acadia Zoo

Rte 3 in Trenton. Tel (207) 667-3244. ⌚ May–late Dec: 9:30am–dusk daily. 📷 ♿ A popular family attraction, the Acadia Zoo is located in Trenton across the bridge from Mount Desert Island, where pastures, streams, and woods shelter some 45 species of animals, including reindeer, wolves, monkeys, and moose. A barn has been converted into a rain-forest habitat for monkeys, birds, reptiles, and other denizens of the Amazon.

Northeast Harbor ⓬

✈ 12 miles (19 km) N in Trenton. ℹ 18 Harbor Dr (207) 276-5040. www.mountdesertchamber.org

Northeast Harbor is the center of Mount Desert Island's social scene. The village has a handful of upscale shops, a few dining places, many handsome but rambling summer mansions and a scenic harbor where boats set sail for nearby Cranberry Islands.

Chartered cruise boat in Bar Harbor

🍁 Asticou Terrace and Thuya Lodge and Gardens

Rte 3 S of Rte 198 jct. *Tel (207) 276-3727.* ☐ *May–Oct: dawn to dusk.* 🖼 *for gardens.* **www**.gardenpreserve.org

The Harbor can best be admired from the stunning Asticou Terraces. A granite path snakes along the hillside, yielding ever-wider vistas as it ascends, with benches and a gazebo placed at strategic viewpoints. At the top of the hill are Thuya Lodge, with collections of paintings and books, and Thuya Gardens, with flowers beds and a reflecting pool that descends to the harbor's edge.

Environs

Somes Sound, a finger-shaped natural fjord that juts 5 miles (8 km) into Mount Desert Island, separates Northeast Harbor from quiet Southwest Harbor, famed for its yacht-builders Hinckley and Morris. The village is also home to the **Wendell Gilley Museum of Bird Carving.** The village artisan was a pioneer in the art of decorative bird carving, and the museum preserves about 100 of more than 10,000 birds he carved. It's a good introduction to local species. Museum workshops range from introductory classes to projects focused on specific birds. A drive or bike ride beyond Southwest Harbor leads to unspoiled villages, including Bass Harbor, where tourists are few and visitors can explore the 1858 Bass Harbor Head Light.

Footbridge in Bad Little Falls Park in Machias

🏛 Wendell Gilley Museum of Bird Carving

Main St. *Tel (207) 244-7555.* ☐ *Jul–Oct: 10am–4pm Tue–Sat; May & Nov–Dec: 10am–4pm Fri–Sun.*

Machias ⓭

🏚 2,900. ✈ 91 miles (146 km) W in Bangor. 🛈 12 East Main St (207) 255-4402.

Situated at the mouth of the river of the same name, Machias retains many of the handsome old homes that sprang up during its days as a prosperous 19th-century lumber center. The town's name comes from the Micmac Indians and means "bad little falls," a reference to the waterfall that cascades in the center of town. There is a good view of the falls from the footbridge in Bad Little Falls Park.

Machias proclaims itself as the wild blueberry capital of Maine. It also lays claim to the region's oldest building, the 1770 **Burnham Tavern**, now a museum with period furnishings, paintings, and historic photographs. It was here that plans were made for the first naval battle of the Revolutionary War in 1775 (*see pp43–45*). Following that heated meeting, local men sailed out into Machias Bay on the small sloop *Unity* and captured the British man-of-war HMS *Margaretta*. Models of the two ships can be seen at the **Gates House**, a restored

Whimsical sculpture in Asticou Gardens

THE LOBSTER INDUSTRY

Harbors filled with lobstering boats and piers piled high with traps are familiar sights in the state that is America's undisputed lobster capital. Maine harvests over 50 million lbs (23 million kg) of this tasty crustacean each year. No visit is complete without a trip to a lobster pound, where patrons pick a live lobster from the tank, wait for it to be steamed, and savor the sweet meat at a picnic table overlooking the ocean.

Lobster fishermen

1807 Federal-style home in nearby Machiasport.

The town is set on the Machias River, a demanding canoeing route. **Roque Bluffs State Park** to the southwest of town offers swimming in a 60-acre (24-ha) freshwater pond and a 1-mile- (1.6-km-) long sweep of beach. The park has a launching ramp for sea kayaks, which are popular in Machias Bay. Birders go to nearby Jonesport for boat trips to Machias Seal Island, home to puffins, Arctic terns, and razorbill auks.

🏛 Burnham Tavern

Main St. *Tel (207) 255-6930.* ☐ *mid-Jun–Sep: 9:30am–4pm Mon–Sat.* 🖼 🎥

🏚 Gates House

Rte 92, Machiasport. *Tel (207) 255-8898.* ☐ *Jul–Aug: 12:30–4:30pm Tue–Fri.* 🖼

🍁 Roque Bluffs State Park

Roque Bluffs Rd, Roque Bluffs. *Tel (207) 255-3475.* ☐ *mid-May–Sep: 9am–dusk.* 🖼 ♿

Campobello Island ⓮

In 1964 2,800 acres (1,133 ha) of Campobello Island were designated as a memorial to President Franklin Delano Roosevelt (1882–1945). The main settlement of Welshpool was where the future president spent most of his summers, until 1921 when he contracted polio. Undaunted, Roosevelt went on to lead the US through the Great Depression and World War II. The highlight of the park – which actually lies in Canada – is Roosevelt Cottage, a 34-room summer home that displays Roosevelt's personal mementos. A passport is required for border crossing.

VISITORS' CHECKLIST

ℹ️ Rte 774. **Tel** (506) 752-2922.
Cottage ⬜ late May–mid-Oct:
9am–5pm daily. **Grounds** ⬜ year-round. 🎦 ♿ **www**.fdr.net

KEY

═══ Major road

─── Minor road

═══ Scenic route

─── Park boundary

– – Walking trail

ℹ️ Tourist information

🅿️ Parking

🎪 Picnic area

🅰️ Camping

🔆 Viewpoint

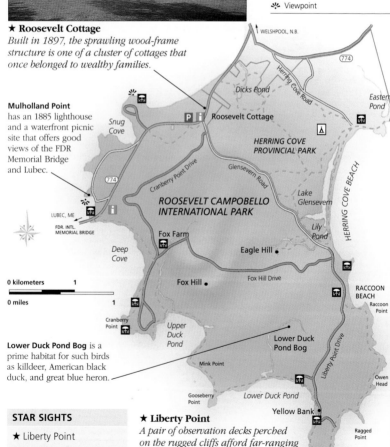

★ **Roosevelt Cottage**
Built in 1897, the sprawling wood-frame structure is one of a cluster of cottages that once belonged to wealthy families.

Mulholland Point
has an 1885 lighthouse and a waterfront picnic site that offers good views of the FDR Memorial Bridge and Lubec.

Lower Duck Pond Bog is a prime habitat for such birds as killdeer, American black duck, and great blue heron.

STAR SIGHTS

★ Liberty Point

★ Roosevelt Cottage

★ **Liberty Point**
A pair of observation decks perched on the rugged cliffs afford far-ranging views of the coastline and the ocean.

Privately owned Hamilton's Folly mansion in Calais

Calais ⑮

🏛 4,000. ✈ 229 miles (424 km) W in Bangor. ℹ 39 Union St (207) 454-2211.

Perched on the west bank of the St. Croix River opposite St. Stephen, New Brunswick, Calais is Maine's busiest border crossing to Canada. The two countries share jurisdiction over nearby St. Croix Island, where in 1604 explorers Samuel de Champlain (1567–1635) and the Sieur de Monts (c.1560–1630) established the first white settlement in North America north of Florida. The island is accessible only by boat, a difficult trip due to strong currents and tides that can run as high as 28 ft (8.5 m).

Calais was devastated by a gigantic fire in 1870. One of the few buildings that survived the conflagration is Hamilton's Folly mansion at No. 78 South Street. The Victorian house was so dubbed by locals because of its ostentatious design – a tribute to excess that bankrupted its owner.

Outdoor activities abound here. The St. Croix River is a challenging waterway for canoeists and a prime spot for salmon fishing. Three miles (5 km) southwest of Calais is the Baring Unit of the **Moosehorn National Wildlife Refuge**, 17,000 acres (6,900 ha) of wilderness that beckons hikers, birdwatchers, and naturalists. Man-made eagle nesting platforms have been erected

along Route 1 north of town. Visitors should watch for the 400-sq-ft (120-sq-m) observation deck on this road for the best views. Also, there are a number of commercial farms that allow visitors to pick their own blueberries.

Ripe blueberries in Calais

🦌 **Moosehorn National Wildlife Refuge**
Charlotte Rd S of Calais. **Tel** (207) 454-7161. **Park** ◌ year-round: sunrise–sunset daily. **Office** ◌ year-round: 8am–4:30pm Mon–Fri. ♿

Bangor ⑯

🏛 33,200. ✈ 287 Godfrey Blvd. ℹ 519 Main St (207) 947-0307.

The world's leading lumber port in the 1850s, Bangor remains the commercial center of northern Maine. The town's Penobscot River harbor was once loaded with ships carrying pine logs from nearby sawmills. This past is saluted with a 31-ft (9.5-m), 3,200-lbs (1,450-kg) statue of the mythical lumberjack Paul Bunyan on Main Street. Industrial might aside, Maine's second-largest city also draws visitors because of its ideal location as a base camp for treks to Acadia National Park (see pp288–9) and the forestlands that stretch to the north.

The city has a number of noteworthy residences from both the past and the

present. The stately homes spared by a 1911 fire still line the West Market Square Historic District and the Broadway area. Maine-born horror author Stephen King lives in a mansion at No. 47 West Broadway, complete with a wrought-iron fence festooned with iron bats and cobwebs. The Greek Revival 1836 Thomas Hill House is headquarters for the **Bangor Museum and Center for History**, and offers historic walking tours.

One of Bangor's most pleasant green spaces is the **Mount Hope Cemetery**. Established in 1834, the cemetery is beautifully landscaped with ponds, bridges, and paved paths that attract strollers and inline skaters. This spirit of movement is also celebrated at the **Cole Land Transportation Museum**. The museum's collection contains more than 200 vehicles dating from the 19th century, ranging from fire engines and horse-drawn logging sleds to antique baby carriages.

🏛 **Bangor Museum and Center for History**
159 Union St. **Tel** (207) 942-5766. ◌ Jun–Sep: 10am–4pm Tue–Fri. 🖼 **www**.bangormuseum.org

🏛 **Mount Hope Cemetery**
State St. ◌ 7:30am–dusk Mon–Fri. 🖼 ♿

🏛 **Cole Land Transportation Museum**
405 Perry Rd. **Tel** (207) 990-3600. ◌ May–early Nov: 9am–5pm daily. 🖼

Bangor's West Market Historic District

Augusta ⑰

🏚 20,0300. ✈ 75 Airport Rd. 🚌
ℹ 21 University Dr (207) 623-4559.

Maine's state capital is a relatively quiet city of 20,000. The 1832 Maine State House, the centerpiece of the government complex on the Kennebec River, was built of granite quarried from neighboring Hallowell. Major expansions have left only the center block from the original design by Boston architect Charles Bulfinch (1763–1844). Exhibits include political portraits and battle flags. Across the street, the Blaine House has been serving as the governor's mansion since 1919. The 28-room Colonial-style home was built in 1832 for a local sea captain.

Costumed interpreter at Old Fort Western in Augusta

The **Maine State Museum** has exhibits spanning "12,000 years of Maine history." One highlight is the "Made in Maine" exhibit, which re-creates a water-powered woodworking mill. The **Old Fort Western** is a restoration of one of New England's oldest surviving wooden forts, dating from 1754. The fort was built on the site where the Plymouth Pilgrims (see pp150–51) had established their trading post the previous century.

🏛 Maine State House
State & Capitol Sts. **Tel** (207) 287-1400. ◯ year-round: 8am–5pm Mon–Fri. 🎦 ♿

Imposing facade of the Maine State House in Augusta

🏛 Blaine House
192 State St. **Tel** (207) 287-2121. ◯ year-round: 2pm–4pm Tue–Thu & by appt. 🎦 call to arrange. ♿

🏛 Maine State Museum
State Capitol Complex, State St. **Tel** (207) 287-2301. ◯ year-round: 9am–5pm Mon–Fri, 10am–4pm Sat. ◉ public hols. 🎦🎦♿
www.maine.gov/museum/

🏛 Old Fort Western
16 Cony St. **Tel** (207) 626-2385. ◯ late–May–mid-Oct: call for hours. 🎦♿
www.oldfortwestern.org

Environs

Heading southwest from Augusta, travelers will get a rare look at the last active Shaker community in the US. Established in the 18th century, the Sabbathday Lake Shaker Community is home to a handful of residents who still adhere to their traditional beliefs of simplicity, celibacy, and communal harmony. Tours of the 18-building village include a stop at the **Shaker Village Museum** to see the beautiful furniture and ingenious inventions that became Shaker trademarks.

Nestled at the feet of Maine's western mountain ranges, Poland Springs is famous for its water. Farther west is Sebago Lake, a favorite among fishermen for its delicious salmon.

Lifeguard's chair on the shore of tranquil Sebago Lake

🏛 Sabbathday Shaker Village Museum
707 Shaker Rd, New Gloucester. **Tel** (207) 926-4597. ◯ late May–mid-Oct: 10am–4:30pm Mon–Sat. 🎦🎦♿ www.shaker.lib.me.us

Bethel ⑱

🏚 2,500. ✈ 70 miles (113 km) S in Portland. ℹ 8 Station Place (207) 824-2282 or (800) 442-5826. www.bethelmaine.com

A picturesque historic district, a major New England ski resort, and proximity to the White Mountains give Bethel year-round appeal. First settled in 1796, the town grew into a farming and lumbering center, and with the coming of the railroad in 1851 quickly became a popular resort. The line-up of classic clapboard mansions on the town green includes the Federal-style **Moses Mason House** (c.1813), which has period pieces and Rufus Porter murals on two floors.

Scenic drives are found in all directions, taking in tiny, unspoiled colonial hamlets such as Waterford to the south and beautiful mountain terrain to the north. **Sunday River Ski Resort** (see p378), 6 miles (10 km) north of town in Newry, has 8 mountains and more than 100 ski trails. Evans Notch, a natural pass through the White Mountain peaks, offers many memorable views, including the Roost, a suspension bridge high above the Wild River and a favorite with photographers. **Grafton Notch State Park** has even more spectacular scenery along its drives, hiking trails and picnic areas. The park's special spots include waterfalls bearing such fanciful names as Screw Auger and Mother Walker, and beautiful panoramic views from Table Rock and the top of Old Speck Mountain.

⌂ Moses Mason House
10–14 Broad St. *Tel* (207) 824-2908.
◯ Jul–Aug: 1–4pm Tue–Sun, or by appointment year-round. 🅿 🖼 ♿
www.bethelhistorical.org

⛷ Sunday River Ski Resort
Off Rte 2 in Newry. *Tel* (207) 824-3000 or (800) 543-2SKI. ◯ 9am–4pm Mon–Fri, 8am–4pm Sat–Sun. 🖼

♣ Grafton Notch State Park
Rte 26 NW of Newry. *Tel* (207) 824-2912. ◯ mid-May–mid-Oct. 🖼

Sugarloaf ⑲

ℹ (207) 237-2000 or (800) 843-5623.

Maine's highest ski mountain, Sugarloaf is the centerpiece of this touristic village packed with hotels, restaurants, and hundreds of condominiums. Downhill skiers have been flocking to the **Sugarloaf/USA** ski center *(see p378)* for years, attracted by the more than 100 trails and a vertical drop of 2,800 ft (870 m). The center also offers cross-country skiing, snowshoeing, and ice skating.

In summer, the emphasis shifts to the resort's 18-hole golf course, boating on the lakes and rivers, and hiking in the surrounding Carrabassett Valley. The resort is also famous for a network of more than 50 miles (80 km) of mountain-biking trails through terrain ranging from flat trails to challenging circuits full of steep climbs and descents.

Screw Auger Falls in Grafton Notch State Park

⛷ Sugarloaf/USA
Carrabassett Valley. *Tel* (207) 237-2000 or (800) 843-5623. ◯ 8:30am–3:50pm daily. 🖼 🅿 ♿ in lodge. 🖼

Rangeley Lakes Region ⑳

ℹ 6 Park Rd (207) 864-5364 or (800) 685-2537.
www.rangeleymaine.com

Set against a backdrop of mountains, this rustic area encompasses a series of pristine lakes that have long been a magnet for any kind of outdoor enthusiast. In summer fishermen ply the waterways for trout and salmon, while canoeists frequently spot a moose or two lumbering along the shoreline. While the area has

Moose crossing sign

become popular with mountain bikers recently, the beauty of the place is no secret. Hikers have been enjoying the vistas from the summit of **Bald Mountain** and tramping the section of the Appalachian Trail running along **Saddleback Mountain** for decades.

Elsewhere, the popular **Rangeley Lake State Park** provides vacationers with facilities for swimming, fishing, birding, boating, and camping, and 1.2 miles (2 km) of lakefront. Toward the southeast, **Mount Blue State Park** is home to Lake Webb, a favorite haunt of fishermen because of its plentiful population of black bass, trout, and salmon. The park is dominated by the towering 3,187-ft (971-m) Mount Blue.

⛰ Bald Mountain
Tel (207) 864-7311.

⛰ Saddleback Mountain
Tel (207) 864-5671. ◯ 9am–4pm Mon–Fri; daily during the ski season.

♣ Rangeley Lake State Park
South Shore Dr, Rangeley. *Tel* (207) 864-3858. ◯ mid-May–Oct: 9am–dusk. 🖼

♣ Mount Blue State Park
West Rd, Weld. *Tel* (207) 585-2347. ◯ daylight hours. **Camping** *Tel* (207) 624-9950. 🖼 🅿 ♿

Challenging snowboarding on Sugarloaf, Maine's second-highest mountain at 4,237 ft (1,290 m)

The dramatic 1,800-ft- (550-m-) high cliffs of Mount Kineo on Moosehead Lake

Moosehead Lake ㉑

🛈 Rte 15, Greenville (207) 695-2702 or (888) 876-2778.
www.mooseheadlake.org

Forty miles (64 km) long and blessed with 320 miles (515 km) of mountain-rimmed shoreline, Moosehead Lake is one of the largest bodies of fresh-water within any state in the Northeast. A popular destination for hunters, fishermen, hikers, and canoeists since the 1880s, the region is attracting a whole new breed of outdoor enthusiasts: mountain bikers, skiers, and snowmobilers.

Greenville, the region's largest town, is the starting point for excursions into the deep boreal forests known as the Great North Woods, including seaplane services that fly visitors to remote fishing camps. **Big Squaw Mountain Resort** in Greenville offers affordable skiing and its chairlift provides panoramic views of the countryside all year.

The **Moosehead Marine Museum** tells of the history of the steamboat in Greenville, beginning in 1836 when the town was a logging center. One of the museum's prized possessions is the *Katahdin*, a restored 1914 steamboat and the last of a fleet of 50 such boats that plied the lake during the peak lumbering years. The *Katahdin* offers lake cruises and excursions to Mount Kineo, the sheer cliff face of which is the most prominent landmark on the lake. Local Native Americans considered the mountain sacred. The tiny settlement

of Rockwood, the closest town to Mount Kineo, provides views of the mountain from rustic lakeside lodgings.

🎿 Big Squaw Mountain Resort
Rte 15 between Greenville & Rockwood. *Tel* (207) 695-1000. **Chairlift** ☐ *ski season: 9am–4pm; Jul–mid-Oct: weekends.* 🏨 🛍

🏛 Moosehead Marine Museum
12 Lily Bay Rd, Greenville. *Tel* (207) 695-2716. **Museum** ☐ *late Jun–mid-Oct: 10am–2pm daily.* 🏨 **Cruises** ☐ *Tue–Thu & Sat–Sun: call for times.* 🛍 **www**.katahdincruises.com

Baxter State Park ㉒

🛈 64 Balsam Dr, Millinocket (207) 723-5140. **Office** ☐ *8am–4pm Mon–Fri; late May–mid-Oct: 8am–4pm daily.* **Park** ☐ *mid-May–mid-Oct & Dec–Mar.* 🏨 **www**.baxterstatepark authority.com

This park was named for Governor Percival Proctor Baxter (1876–1969). Baxter was instrumental in the effort to preserve this magnificent land, purchasing more than 200,000 acres (81,000 ha) and donating it to the state over 30-odd years with the stipulation that it was never to be developed. The park encompasses 46 mountain peaks, 18 of them over 3,000 ft (900 m), including Katahdin, Maine's tallest.

The park's 200 miles (320 km) of hiking

trails are unsurpassed, and range from demanding climbs to easy family walks. Henry David Thoreau *(see p30)* tried the trek in 1846, but never made it to the 5,267-ft (1,605-m) summit of Katahdin. However, thousands of hikers are successful each year, and the trails are crowded with climbers in summer and fall. Some hardy souls can be seen completing the last steps of the famous Appalachian Trail *(see pp22–3)*, which runs from Springer Mountain, Georgia, to its terminus atop Katahdin.

Deer, bear, raccoons, and other wildlife are abundant in this park, and ponds such as Grassy, Sandy Stream, and Russell are favorite watering spots for Maine's official state animal: the moose.

Majestic Mount Katahdin, a popular hiking destination

◁ Monhegan Harbor, with Manana Island in the distance

Autumn colors in Aroostook State Park

Aroostook County ㉓

🏠 11 W. Presque Isle Rd, Caribou (207) 498-8736 or (888) 216-2463.
www.visitaroostook.com

Maine's largest and most northern county, Aroostook covers an area greater than the combined size of Connecticut and Rhode Island. The region is best known for agriculture, with some 1 million acres (405,000 ha) producing nearly 2 billion lbs (907 million kg) of potatoes each year, plus lush crops of clover, oats, barley, and broccoli. In summer endless acres of potato fields are covered with blossoms, a vision in pink and white. Another 4 million acres (1,620,000 ha) of land is forested, mostly owned by paper companies that process the lumber in 50 local pulp and paper mills.

In summer hikers trek the trails in **Aroostook State Park**, fly fishermen plumb the streams for salmon and trout, and canoeists and kayakers paddle the Allagash River. When the heavy winter snows come, snowmobilers arrive in large numbers to explore the entire 1,600 miles (2,500 km) of the Interstate Trail System.

Aroostook County begins in the south in Houlton, a quiet town with a Market Square Historic District of 28 19th-century buildings. A French dialect can be heard in the northern St. John Valley, the legacy of Acadians who settled here in 1785. The **Acadian Village** consists of 16 original and reconstructed buildings from the early days. In New Sweden, a cluster of historic buildings, including a log house and a one-room school, recalls a Swedish colony that settled not far from Caribou in the late 19th century.

🌿 **Aroostook State Park**
87 State Park Rd, S of Presque Isle. **Tel** (207) 768-8341. ◻ year-round: for camping; mid-May–mid-Oct: daylight hours; accessible for cross-country skiing and snow-mobiling in winter.

🏛 **Acadian Village**
Rte 1, Van Buren. **Tel** (207) 868-5042. ◻ mid-Jun–mid-Sep: noon–5pm daily.

Finely crafted tools of the trade for fly fisherman

Environs
Starting at Lake Chamberlain and extending north for more than 90 miles (145 km), the **Allagash Wilderness Waterway** is one of New England's most stunning natural areas. The waterway and its many lakes and streams have been protected since 1966. The Allagash has

also been designated a National Wild and Scenic Rivers System.

The state owns the land flanking the waterway for 500 ft (150 m) on each side, assuring a protected habitat for dozens of animals and more than 120 bird species. Anglers will find numerous brook trout and whitefish.

A trek up or down the Allagash system is the ultimate canoe trip in the state, and one that generally takes between five and ten days. Especially beautiful spots are Allagash Lake, a tranquil side trip where no motors are allowed, and Allagash Falls, a dramatic 40-ft (12-m) drop that necessitates carrying the canoe (called "portaging") for about a third of a mile (0.5 km). The canoeing season runs from late May to early October.

🛶 **Allagash Wilderness Waterway**
🏠 Maine Bureau of Parks and Lands, 106 Hogan Rd, Bangor (207) 941-4014. ◻ year-round.

Frog in the protected habitat of the Allagash Wilderness Waterway

MAINE'S GREAT RAFTING RIVERS

Maine is famous for three whitewater rivers, the Kennebec, the Dead, and the west branch of the Penobscot. The first two rivers meet near the town called The Forks, southwest of Moosehead Lake, where more than a dozen rafting companies offer equipment and guided trips (see p373). The Millinocket area services paddlers bound for the Penobscot, famed among rafters for its challenging drop through a vertical walled canyon below the Ripogenus Dam.

Kennebec River rafters in the challenging whitewater

TRAVELERS' NEEDS

WHERE TO STAY

The incredibly varied accommodations of the New England states are tailored to suit virtually all tastes and budgets. If you are looking to commune with nature and save a few dollars at the same time, you can take your pick of campsites *(see pp372–5)* sprinkled liberally

Ritz-Carlton doorman *(see p308)*

throughout the six states. Rustic country inns and bed and breakfasts (B&Bs) are plentiful, offering travelers quaint facilities and a more personal touch. Hotels and motels are also popular

choices, conveniently located in or around busy tourist destinations and on major roads throughout the region. From the most posh hotel in Boston to a historic Vermont B&B or a rugged backcountry camping experience in Maine, New England has suitable accommodations for everyone. During the summer vacation season, lodgings can sometimes be hard to come by, so it is always best to book in advance. This is also true during the busy fall-foliage season.

Luxurious Foxwoods Resort Casino near Mystic, Connecticut *(see p318)*

HOTELS

New England has no shortage of hotel chains. The majority of the large chains, such as Holiday Inn, Hilton, Hyatt, Marriott, and Ramada, offer standard amenities that include such things as a bar, dining room, and exercise facilities. Although one hotel room is generally indistinguishable from the next, they are all impeccably clean and come equipped with a television, room service, and a private bathroom – comforts not always found in B&Bs.

The luxury hotels, usually found in city centers, can be very lavish. Lush decor, fine dining, and valet services are the earmarks of such establishments. The area's large casinos and resorts are also known for their lavishness.

It is always best to notify the reservation clerk should you be arriving late. Most hotels will hold your reservation only until 6pm, especially during the tourist season.

MOTELS

If you are on a budget, motels offer you the best and most flexible value for your money. Often found on the outskirts of cities and towns, motels also dot the New England roads most frequented by travelers. While you will not find the same amenities as in the big hotels, motels will offer you convenience and comfort at significantly lower prices. The standard motel room is equipped with a private bathroom, color TV, and heat and air

conditioning. The more modern places usually have two double beds, making it easier to accommodate your whole family in a single room.

BED AND BREAKFASTS AND INNS

American B&Bs can differ greatly from their European counterparts. Very often they are not the cozy one- or two-room guest lodgings located in the owner's personal residence like those you would come across in Europe. Increasingly, New England B&Bs are professionally operated businesses in which guests live in separate accommodations from the owner or caretaker. This style of B&B tends to be larger in size and have more rooms than its more traditional counterpart. The loss of intimacy usually comes with the added bonus of private bathrooms and added services. Of course, traditionalists can still find small, cozy B&Bs throughout New England. Regardless of the size, all B&Bs offer distinctive lodgings and a breakfast, which may vary in size and style from one establishment to another.

Like B&Bs, inns come in all shapes and sizes, from the very rustic to the large resort-style lodging. Not only do inns serve breakfast and

Rose Farm Inn *(see p314)*, in a quiet country setting on Rhode Island's Block Island

Mount Washington Hotel and Resort in Bretton Woods, New Hampshire *(see p322)*

dinner, the larger ones can come with such "extras" as swimming pools, gardens, and taverns. Depending on their location, many inns are affiliated with local tennis or golf clubs.

Because some B&Bs and inns are historic homes appointed with beautiful antique furniture, they usually prohibit smoking and often do not allow children. The **New England Inns and Resorts Association**, or one of its state branches, is a good lodging resource.

The nautical Steamboat Inn *(see p318)*, in Mystic Connecticut

PRICES AND RESERVATIONS

Rates and availability can fluctuate from season to season. Prices are generally highest in the peak tourist periods (July–August and mid-September–late October) and in the cities, coastal areas, and other prime vacation destinations. The reverse is true with ski resorts, when winter months are the most expensive. Booking your accommodations well in advance is always the safest way to avoid complications. This is especially true if you are looking forward to staying at a B&B or inn in which rooms are limited.

To save money you should try booking in cities on the weekend and in the country during the week. Many hotels in urban areas such as Boston cater to business travelers and may offer reduced rates from Friday to Sunday. Conversely, many of the rural lodgings, popular with the weekend crowd, slash their prices substantially during the week.

Always inquire about package deals offered by motels and hotels. Discounted meals and free passes to local attractions are sometimes thrown in as added incentive for you to stay with them. Some inns and B&Bs also work in conjunction with each other to promote inn-to-inn tours for cyclists and cross-country skiers, offering special rates

for accommodations along the tour route. To avoid unpleasant surprises, it is always prudent to ask about any restrictions, including those on children, pets, and smoking.

HOW TO MAKE RESERVATIONS

Most hotels have toll-free reservation numbers, and some offer discounts for Internet bookings. Room rates are usually quoted for two people sharing a room, including tax (and breakfast, if it is offered); all B&Bs, of course, provide a morning meal. For longer stays, it is customary to pre-pay one night in advance.

Beautiful room at the Red Lion Inn in Stockbridge, Maine *(see p314)*

HIDDEN EXTRAS

You should be aware that the prices quoted for many accommodations do not include taxes, which can increase the bill significantly – even in the haven of New Hampshire, which has no sales tax, but does have lodging and restaurant taxes. Hotels in large urban areas often charge for their parking facilities, sometimes substantially. In Boston, for example, parking costs could amount to $20–$25 per day. Also be aware of added service fees which can sometimes be as high as 15 percent.

BUSINESS TRAVELERS

As access to high-speed wireless Internet rapidly becomes a common amenity, even in modest motels and many B&Bs, the modern business traveler can stay connected to the office and the world at large. Most properties also have the ability to send and receive faxes, although sometimes at a significant charge. Internet access is often free at small properties but pricey at major chain hotels. Some newly refurbished urban hotels offer multi-line phones, in-room fax machines, and private voice mail.

DISABLED TRAVELERS

Although federal law requires that all businesses provide access and facilities for the disabled, the practical reality is that this is not always the case. The vast majority of large private and chain hotels are modern enough to be equipped with the necessary facilities, including visual notification of the fire alarm, incoming phone calls, and the doorbell. Many also have some suites designated specifically for the disabled. However, many of New England's older buildings and B&Bs have narrow hallways that can obstruct wheelchairs and have no ramps. As always, it is best to check in advance.

WHERE TO STAY IN BOSTON

The centrally located Back Bay has the greatest concentration of hotels, convenient for tourists as well as for business travelers. In the gentrifying South End, an increasing number

Bedroom at the Inn on Covered Bridge Green *(see p319)* in Arlington, Vermont

of restored Victorian townhouses have been converted into B&Bs. Accommodations in the downtown financial district near the waterfront cater to business people during the week, but often offer good value to vacationers on the weekends. Across the Charles River, Cambridge has a large number of hotels, particularly around Harvard Square and among the Kendall Square office towers. In more suburban Brookline along the Green Line Trolley routes west of the Back Bay, several guesthouses as well as more upscale B&Bs offer additional alternatives. One plus for travelers: Boston hotels now house many of the city's top restaurants, including Clio in the Eliot Hotel, Mooo at Fifteen Beacon, Cafe Fleuri at the Langham Hotel, and Aujourd'hui at the Four Seasons Hotel.

Boston hotels are particularly busy in May and June for college graduations, July and August for summer vacations, and September and October for the fall-foliage season. Throughout

the course of a year, many Boston hotels cater to business travelers, including the hotels downtown around the Hynes Convention Center, and in Cambridge's Kendall Square. This means that the rates are often lowest on weekends.

The city does have a good selection of smaller hotels and B&Bs, often offering more personal service and charm than the big convention hotels. If you are looking for a classic B&B – a room or two in the owner's home – you should contact one of the B&B booking agencies, such as the **Bed & Breakfast Agency of Boston, Host Homes of Boston,** or the **Bed and Breakfast Associates Bay Colony, Ltd.** A recent trend is the "boutique" hotel, a small, elegantly appointed accommodation with solicitous service. Be warned: these luxury boutiques are among the most expensive lodging options.

Like most American cities, Boston has its share of chain hotels in all price categories. There are few budget chain properties located within the city itself, although visitors will find lower-priced chains, such as **Fairfield Inn**, in surrounding communities. In fact, this chain is popular throughout

Boston's Seaport Hotel *(see p311)*, busy during the summer

the New England region. While short on charm, these accommodations offer functional budget lodgings. Good-value B&B accommodations near Boston can be found in the North Shore towns of Rockport *(see p141)* and Salem *(see pp136–9)*. Both of these attractive seaside towns have good selections of mid-priced B&Bs, and are easily accessible by the MBTA commuter rail. Contact the **North of Boston Convention and Visitors Bureau** for more detailed information.

The Middlebury Inn *(see p321)*, located in Vermont

The stylish Hotel Pemaquid *(see p327)* in New Harbor, Maine

HOSTELS

Hostels have long been a way for people – especially students – to slash their traveling budget. However, unlike the more extensive European model, New England's hostel network is somewhat underdeveloped. Rhode Island, for example, has no facilities at all. The good news is that some of the region's prime locations (including Boston and Cape Cod) do have hostels. A list of member hostels and their locations is available from **Hostelling International– American Youth Hostels (HI/AYH)**. **HI/AYH Eastern New England Council** provides information on hostels in New Hampshire, Maine, and Massachusetts. Connecticut and Vermont are covered by the **HY/AYH Yankee Council**. A short walk from the Hynes Convention Center, the **Boston International Youth Hostel** offers a variety of rooms, including some very affordable six-bed dormitories and several private doubles.

DIRECTORY

BED AND BREAKFAST AND INN AGENCIES

Bed & Breakfast Agency of Boston
Tel (800) 248-9262 or (617) 720-3540; (0800) 89-5128 from UK.
www.boston-bnbagency.com

Bed and Breakfast Associates Bay Colony, Ltd.
PO Box 57166, Babson Park Branch, Boston, MA 02457-0166.
Tel (888) 486-6018 or (781) 449-5302.
www.bnbboston.com

Host Homes of Boston
PO Box 117, Waban Branch, Boston, MA 02468-0001.
Tel (800) 600-1308 or (617) 244-1308.
www.hosthomesofboston.com

New England Inns and Resorts Association
PO Box 1089, North Hampton, NH 03862-1089.
Tel (603) 964-6689. www.newenglandinnsandresorts.com

HOSTELS AND BUDGET ACCOMMODATIONS

Best Western International
Tel (800) 528-1234.
www.bestwestern.com

Boston International Youth Hostel
12 Hemenway St, Boston, MA 02115.
Tel (617) 536-9455.
www.bostonhostel.org

Days Inn
Tel (800) 329-7466.
www.daysinn.com

Fairfield Inn
Tel (800) 228-2800. www.marriott.com/fairfield-inn/travel.mi

Hostelling International
8401 Colesville Rd, Suite 600, Silver Spring, MD, 20910.
Tel (301) 495-1240. (membership information).
Tel (800) 909-4776. (reservation service).
www.hiusa.org

Hostelling International Eastern New England Council
218 Holland St, Somerville MA 02144.
Tel (617) 718-7990.
www.usahostels.org

Hostelling International Yankee Council
PO Box 87, Windsor, CT 06095.
Tel (860) 683-2847.
http://yankeehostels.org

North of Boston Convention and Visitors Bureau
17 Peabody Sq, Peabody, MA 01960. *Tel (978) 977-7760 or (800) 742-5306.*
www.northofboston.org

Choosing a Hotel

These hotels have been selected for their excellent facilities, good location, and value. They are listed by region in the same order as the chapters in the guide. Within each region, entries are listed alphabetically within each price category, from the least to the most expensive. For map references to central Boston hotels, *see pp122–7.*

PRICE CATEGORIES
For a standard double room and taxes per night, inclusive of breakfast, service charges, and any additional taxes:

$ under $125
$$ $125–$175
$$$ $175–$225
$$$$ $225–$300
$$$$$ over $300

BOSTON

BACK BAY AND SOUTH END 463 Beacon Street Guest House 🅿 $$
463 Beacon St., 02115 **Tel** *(617) 536-1302* **Fax** *(617) 247-8876* **Rooms** *20*   **Map** *3 A2*

Budget lodging especially popular with young European travelers offers studio rooms and small furnished apartments (with some cooking facilities) by the day, week or month. This Back Bay brownstone is a handsome building closer to the Charles River Esplanade than Back Bay attractions, but rates, especially off-season, can be a steal. **www.463beacon.com**

BACK BAY AND SOUTH END Commonwealth Court Guest House $$
284 Commonwealth Ave., 02116 **Tel** *(617) 424-1230, (888) 424-1230* **Fax** *(617) 424-1510* **Rooms** *17* **Map** *3 A2*

The Commonwealth is convenient to upper Back Bay, especially the Hynes Convention Center and Berklee College of Music. The former brownstone residence oozes historic architectural detail inside and out. Rooms may be rented by the week or month and include kitchenettes. Maid service twice weekly. **www.commonwealthcourt.com**

BACK BAY AND SOUTH END Copley Inn $$
19 Garrison St., 02116 **Tel** *(617) 236-0300* **Fax** *(617) 536-0816* **Rooms** *20*   **Map** *3 B3*

A former rooming house in the shadow of Copley Place, this budget lodging features studio rooms, each with a queen bed, kitchenette, and private bath. Clean and bright, the décor is utilitarian but some rooms retain charming old-fashioned touches, such as decorative fireplaces. **www.copleyinn.com**

BACK BAY AND SOUTH END Hotel 140 🖫 👤 📺 🅿 $$
140 Clarendon St., 02116 **Tel** *(617) 585-5600, (800) 714-0140* **Fax** *(617) 585-5699* **Rooms** *54*   **Map** *3 C3*

Literally around the corner from the Back Bay Amtrak/commuter rail station, Hotel 140 is a stylish budget-priced renovation of America's first YWCA building. Rooms are small, but the trendy minimalist design makes efficient use of space. Secure key card access system for both rooms and elevator. **www.hotel140.com**

BACK BAY AND SOUTH END Best Western Roundhouse Suites 🖫 👤 📺 🅿 $$$
891 Massachusetts Ave., 02118 **Tel** *(617) 989-1000; (888) 468-3562* **Rooms** *92*

This unique 1871 round building was transformed into an all-suites hotel in 2001. Sofa beds, microwaves, and refrigerators make Roundhouse Suites an appealing option for families. The hotel is far from major attractions but there is a shuttle service available and parking is free for those who arrive by car. **www.bestwesternboston.com**

BACK BAY AND SOUTH END Chandler Inn 📶 $$$
26 Chandler St., 02116 **Tel** *(617) 482-3450, (800) 842-3450* **Fax** *(617) 542-3428* **Rooms** *55*   **Map** *4 D3*

Located in the South End just two short blocks from Tremont Street's restaurant row, this inn is well-situated for walking to most of Back Bay as well. The immediate neighborhood is primarily low-rise residential, giving the Chandler a homey feel in the heart of the city. **www.chandlerinn.com**

BACK BAY AND SOUTH END Charlesmark Hotel 📶 🖫 $$$
655 Boylston St., 02116 **Tel** *(617) 247-1212* **Fax** *(617) 247-1224* **Rooms** *33*   **Map** *3 C2*

In the mode of a contemporary European boutique hotel, the Charlesmark occupies an 1892 Back Bay townhouse on Copley Square. The smallish rooms have custom-made furniture and light-toned woodwork, imported Italian tiles and European lighting fixtures. Low prices for the location. Breakfast included. **www.thecharlesmarkhotel.com**

BACK BAY AND SOUTH END Newbury Guest House 📶 🅿 $$$
261 Newbury St., 02116 **Tel** *(617) 437-7666, (800) 437-7668* **Fax** *(617) 670-6100* **Rooms** *32*   **Map** *3 B2*

When three Victorian homes were linked to form this inn, owners were careful to preserve such period details as ceiling medallions, parquet floors, and decorative fireplaces. The rooms feature a comfortable mix of older furniture. Newbury Street can be noisy; ask for a room at the back. Breakfast is included. **www.newburyguesthouse.com**

BACK BAY AND SOUTH END Clarendon Square Inn 🅿 $$$$
198 West Brookline St., 02118 **Tel** *(617) 536-2229* **Rooms** *3*   **Map** *3 C4*

This 19th-century townhouse in the heart of the South End offers a peek into historic Boston architecture. Truly boutique, and exquisitely decorated with modern furnishings, this upscale B&B offers full amenities and personal attention to guests' needs. The rooftop hot tub with Boston skyline is not to be missed. **www.clarendonsquare.com**

Key to Symbols *see back cover flap*

BACK BAY AND SOUTH END The Colonnade Hotel $$$$
120 Huntington Ave., 02116 **Tel** *(617) 424-7000, (800) 962-3030* **Fax** *(617) 425-3222* **Rooms** *285*   **Map** *3 B3*

Next door to the Prudential and Copley Place malls, this hotel features spacious and comfortable rooms with rich colors and modern style. Popular with families and upscale bus groups. Bostonians gravitate to the rooftop pool in summer, and Brasserie Jo year-round. **www.colonnadehotel.com**

BACK BAY AND SOUTH END Courtyard Boston Copley Square $$$$
88 Exeter St., 02116 **Tel** *(617) 437-9300, (800) 321-2211* **Fax** *(617) 437-9330* **Rooms** *81*   **Map** *3 B3*

When Marriott transformed this older building in the heart of Copley Square, they chose wisely to take advantage of its variety of room sizes and shapes to avoid the cookie-cutter look of newer Courtyards. Designed for extended stays, each room has a fridge and coffee machine. Location rivals more expensive hotels. **www.marriott.com**

BACK BAY AND SOUTH END Gryphon House $$$$
9 Bay State Rd., 02215 **Tel** *(617) 375-9003, (877) 375-9003* **Fax** *(617) 425-0716* **Rooms** *8*

Built in the Richardsonian Romanesque style, this 1895 townhouse features unusually large guest rooms. All have fireplaces and wet bars, and some have river views. Guests can walk two blocks to Kenmore "T" station or continue on foot to sites in Back Bay or Fenway. **www.innboston.com**

BACK BAY AND SOUTH END Midtown Hotel $$$
220 Huntington Ave., 02115 **Tel** *(617) 262-1000, (800) 343-1177* **Fax** *(617) 262-8739* **Rooms** *159*   **Map** *3 B4*

This classic 1960s-era motor inn is a rarity in Back Bay. Rooms offer simple style and good value in an otherwise expensive area near the Christian Science complex and Symphony Hall. Outdoor swimming pool and low-cost parking are significant bonuses. Pet friendly. **www.midtownhotel.com**

BACK BAY AND SOUTH END Copley Square Hotel $$$$
47 Huntington Ave., 02116 **Tel** *(617) 536-9000, (800) 225-7062* **Fax** *(617) 421-1402* **Rooms** *143*   **Map** *3 C3*

Opened in 1891, this hotel is a favorite with business and leisure travelers, it has smoke-free rooms with efficient workspaces as well as fine linens and big televisions. Ask for an interior room for the utmost tranquility. Basement-level Saint is one of the city's trendiest nightspots. **www.copleysquarehotel.com**

BACK BAY AND SOUTH END Eliot Suites Hotel $$$$
370 Commonwealth Ave., 02215 **Tel** *(617) 267-1607, (800) 443-5468* **Fax** *(617) 536-9114* **Rooms** *95* **Map** *3 A2*

Suites with separate sleeping and sitting rooms are equally convenient for guest musicians playing at nearby Symphony Hall, business people, and families (children under 18 stay free). Guests enjoy complimentary access to Boston Sports Club and the short stroll to Fenway Park. Restaurant Clio is one of the city's best. **www.eliothotel.com**

BACK BAY AND SOUTH END Fairmont Copley Plaza Hotel $$$$$
138 St. James Ave., 02116 **Tel** *(617) 267-5300, (866) 540-4177* **Fax** *(617) 267-7668* **Rooms** *383*   **Map** *3 C2*

A red carpet leads guests into the opulent lobby of this 1912 Boston landmark. Interior rooms can be small, but a $34 million restoration updated the traditional style of dark woods and rich fabrics. Extravagant furnishings and comfortable banquette seating help make the Oak Room the city's favorite steak house. **www.fairmont.com**

BACK BAY AND SOUTH END Hotel Commonwealth $$$$$
500 Commonwealth Ave., 02215 **Tel** *(617) 933-5000, (866) 784-4000* **Fax** *(617) 266-6888* **Rooms** *150*

The opening of this ultra-modern hotel in 2002 signaled the gentrification of student-oriented Kenmore Square. French Second Empire décor is combined with hi-tech amenities. The Foundation Lounge is a popular drinking spot. Lunch and dinner are served outdoors in good weather. **www.hotelcommonwealth.com**

BACK BAY AND SOUTH END Jurys Boston Hotel $$$$
350 Stuart St., 02116 **Tel** *(617) 266-7200, (866) 534-6835* **Fax** *(617) 266-7203* **Rooms** *225*   **Map** *3 D2*

An Irish boutique hotel chain took the elegance of this limestone-faced former Boston Police headquarters, doubled its size to add more rooms, and threw in all the right touches (feather pillows and duvets, heated towel racks, 24-hour room service) to make a modest-priced hotel feel like a luxury stay. **www.jurys-boston-hotels.com**

BACK BAY AND SOUTH END Lenox Hotel $$$$$
61 Exeter St., 02116 **Tel** *(617) 536-5300, (800) 225-7676* **Fax** *(617) 236-0351* **Rooms** *214*   **Map** *3 B2*

This landmark hotel near the Boston Public Library features sumptuous Edwardian detail in the public areas. Several deluxe corner suites with woodburning fireplaces rival any upscale room in town. Mahogany furniture, marble baths and muted fabrics create a soothing, elegant atmosphere. **www.lenoxhotel.com**

BACK BAY AND SOUTH END Taj Boston $$$$$
15 Arlington St., 02116 **Tel** *(617) 536-5700, (877) 482-5267* **Fax** *(617) 536-1335* **Rooms** *273*   **Map** *4 D2*

Overlooking Boston's Public Garden, this 1927 hotel was the first hotel of the Ritz-Carlton chain. The premises became part of the Taj Hotel Group in 2007 but the hotel continues to epitomize the elegance and excellent service of its predecessor. **www.tajhotels.com**

BEACON HILL & THEATER DISTRICT John Jeffries House $$
14 David Mugar Way, 02114 **Tel** *(617) 367-1866* **Fax** *(617) 742-0313* **Rooms** *46*   **Map** *1 B3*

This red brick building opened in 1909 as housing for nurses at the Massachusetts Eye and Ear Infirmary. Hardwood floors, original moldings, and traditional furnishings give the feel of a well-lived-in Beacon Hill townhouse. Popular with families of patients at local hospitals and visitors alike. Continental breakfast included. **www.johnjeffrieshouse.com**

BEACON HILL & THEATER DISTRICT Beacon Hill Hotel & Bistro ⚅ ⑪ $$$$

25 Charles St., 02114 **Tel** *(617) 723-7575* **Fax** *(617) 723-7525* **Rooms** *13*   **Map** *1 B4*

Paris meets Beacon Hill in this smart renovation of a townhouse steps from Boston Common and the Public Garden. Rooms are fairly small but chic with soothing colors, framed photos, plantation shutters and flat-panel TVs. Guests can spread out in the second floor sitting room or on a private roof deck. Breakfast included. **www.beaconhillhotel.com**

BEACON HILL & THEATER DISTRICT Boston Park Plaza Hotel & Towers ⚅ ⑪ 🖬 🅿 $$$$

64 Arlington St., 02116 **Tel** *(617) 426-2000, (888) 625-5144* **Fax** *(617) 426-5545* **Rooms** *941*   **Map** *4 D2*

Opened in 1927, the 15-floor hotel is the city's largest historic lodging. Two ballrooms and an oversized but elegant lobby make the Park Plaza the scene of many local celebrations as well as business meetings and small conventions. Watch the action over afternoon tea in Swan's Cafe. **www.bostonparkplaza.com**

BEACON HILL & THEATER DISTRICT Holiday Inn Boston at Beacon Hill ⚅ ⑪ 🖬 🖬 🅿 $$$$

5 Blossom St., 02114 **Tel** *(617) 742-7630, (800) 465-4329* **Fax** *(617) 742-4192* **Rooms** *305*   **Map** *1 B3*

It's worth walking the few extra steps away from Beacon Hill and Quincy Market for the savings that you make on the price of a room in this cluster of office buildings. Functioning largely as a tour group and conference facility, but it caters for individual travelers too. **www.ichotelsgroup.com**

BEACON HILL & THEATER DISTRICT Bulfinch Hotel ⚅ ⑪ 🖬 🅿 $$$$$

107 Merrimac St., 02114 **Tel** *(617) 624-0202, (877) 267-1776* **Fax** *(617) 624-0211* **Rooms** *80*   **Map** *1 C2*

This flatiron building near TD Garden *(see pp368-9)* and a short stroll to the North End was renovated to ensure that its Beaux-Arts windows flood the sleek, contemporary rooms with light. The lobby is minimal, but the rooms and mini-suites have large, soft beds and modern technology, including flat-screen TVs. **www.bulfinchhotel.com**

BEACON HILL & THEATER DISTRICT Charles Street Inn ⚅ 🅿 $$$$$

94 Charles St., 02114 **Tel** *(617) 314-8900, (877) 772-8900* **Fax** *(617) 371-0009* **Rooms** *9*   **Map** *1 B4*

This time capsule was built in 1860 as a demonstration showpiece for new homes under construction in the Back Bay. Victorian features such as carved marble fireplaces harmonize with European furnishings and modern whirlpool tubs, mini-fridges and CD players. Good base for exploring the antiques shops. Breakfast included. **www.charlesstreetinn.com**

BEACON HILL & THEATER DISTRICT Courtyard Boston Tremont Hotel ⚅ ⑪ 🖬 🅿 $$$$$

275 Tremont St., 02116 **Tel** *(617) 426-1400, (800) 321-2211* **Fax** *(617) 482-6730* **Rooms** *315*   **Map** *4 D3*

The renovation of this 1920s tower hotel in the Theater District was completed in early 2006. The dramatic lobby features marble columns, carved granite details, and glittering crystal chandeliers. Guest rooms are more simply furnished but with modern amenities including walk-in showers. **www.courtyardbostontremont.com**

BEACON HILL & THEATER DISTRICT Four Seasons Hotel Boston ⚅ ⑪ 🖬 🖬 🅿 $$$$$

200 Boylston St., 02116 **Tel** *(617) 338-4400, (800) 819-5053* **Fax** *(617) 423-0154* **Rooms** *274*   **Map** *4 E2*

The low-key luxury at this modern hotel on a corner of the Public Garden at the edge of the Theater District draws rock stars, best-selling authors, corporate bigwigs and visiting dignitaries. Lobby-level Bristol Lounge offers afternoon tea, full menu for children, and a fireplace ambience conducive to making business deals. **www.fourseasons.com**

BEACON HILL & THEATER DISTRICT Hyatt Regency Boston ⚅ ⑪ 🖬 🅿 $$$$$

1 Avenue de Lafayette, 02111 **Tel** *(617) 912-1234, (800) 233-1234* **Fax** *(617) 451-2198* **Rooms** *471*   **Map** *4 D2*

Spacious rooms with modern décor plus an excellent fitness center and pool make this downtown Hyatt a good place to unwind. This 4-star 4-diamond hotel is within walking distance of many attractions, including Boston Common, Chinatown, and the Theater District. **regencyboston.hyatt.com**

BEACON HILL & THEATER DISTRICT Onyx Hotel ⚅ ⑪ 🎿 🖬 🅿 $$$$$

155 Portland St., 02114 **Tel** *(617) 557-9955, (866) 660-6699* **Fax** *(617) 557-0005* **Rooms** *112*   **Map** *1 C2*

This contemporary boutique hotel near North Station features modest-sized rooms decorated in a warm palette of black, taupe, and Chinese-lacquer red. Onyx has comfortable beds with feather and down pillows and a true working desk. Town car service to the financial district each morning. Pet-friendly. **www.onyxhotel.com**

BEACON HILL & THEATER DISTRICT Radisson Boston ⚅ ⑪ 🖬 🅿 $$$$$

200 Stuart St., 02116 **Tel** *(617) 482-1800, (888) 201-1718* **Fax** *(617) 451-2750* **Rooms** *356*   **Map** *4 D2*

Its Theater District location makes this Radisson a popular choice for bus tour groups, while proximity to Chinatown makes it convenient for inexpensive and late-night dining. The hotel also hosts many small conferences at nearby medical and dental schools, and rooms are fitted with oversized work desks. **www.radisson.com/bostonma**

BEACON HILL & THEATER DISTRICT The Ritz-Carlton, Boston Common ⚅ ⑪ 🖬 🅿 $$$$$

10 Avery St., 02111 **Tel** *(617) 574-7100, (800) 241-3333* **Fax** *(617) 574-7200* **Rooms** *193*   **Map** *4 E2*

Boston's new Ritz-Carlton is located in center stage of the Theater District and near the Financial District. Directly connected to The Sports Club/LA spa, fitness center and Olympic pool, this ultra-modern hotel offers both pampering and the latest in technical conveniences. Adjacent to multi-screen cinema. **www.ritzcarlton.com**

BRIGHTON Days Hotel Boston ⚅ ⑪ 🖬 🎿 🖬 🅿 $$

1234 Soldiers Field Rd., 02135 **Tel** *(617) 254-1234; (800) 329-7466* **Fax** *(617) 254-4300* **Rooms** *117*

This hotel along the Charles River provides easy access to the popular river banks and their jogging paths. The rooms are cheerful and spacious. Fitness buffs may want to undertake the one-mile walk to Harvard Square. **www.dayshotelboston.com**

Key to Price Guide *see p306* **Key to Symbols** *see back cover flap*

BROOKLINE Beechtree Inn
P **$$**

83 Longwood Ave., Brookline, 02446 **Tel** *(617) 277-1620, (800) 544-9660* **Rooms** *10*

This rambling Victorian home is located in a leafy neighborhood near Longwood Medical Center and the Green Line. The rooms have an old-fashioned décor with solid furnishings and a television set, but some rooms share bathrooms. Read a book and sip tea under the backyard apple tree. **www.thebeechtreeinn.com**

BROOKLINE Bertram Inn
P **$$$**

92 Sewall Ave., Brookline, 02446 **Tel** *(617) 566-2234, (800) 295-3822* **Fax** *(617) 277-1887* **Rooms** *14*

This beautiful B&B, built in 1907, has an elegant parlor and antiques-filled rooms. Some of the bedrooms feature working wood-burning fireplaces. Located 2 miles (3 km) from the center of Boston, Bertram Inn is a perfect retreat from the hubbub of the city. **www.bertraminn.com**

BROOKLINE Inn at Longwood
P **$$$**

342 Longwood Ave., 02115 **Tel** *(617) 731-4700, (800) 468-2378* **Fax** *(617) 731-4870* **Rooms** *161*

This modern hotel is often booked by families of patients in the hospitals of the Longwood Medical Area. But the standard guest rooms and one- and two-bedroom suites are equally convenient for families on vacation. Fenway Park and the Museum of Fine Arts are within walking distance. On the E branch of the T's Green Line. **www.innatlongwood.com**

CAMBRIDGE Irving House
P **$$**

24 Irving St., Cambridge, 02138 **Tel** *(617) 547-4600, (800) 547-4600* **Fax** *(617) 576-2814* **Rooms** *44*

This rambling Victorian building is a short walk from Harvard University's main campus. The rooms in the older rooming house turned bed and breakfast vary greatly in size and amenities. The Irving's quiet location and proximity to Harvard Yard and Harvard Square make it a favorite with visiting scholars on a budget. **www.irvinghouse.com**

CAMBRIDGE Isaac Harding House
P **$$**

288 Harvard St., Cambridge, 02138 **Tel** *(617) 876-2888, (877) 489-2888* **Fax** *(617) 497-0953* **Rooms** *14*

This bed and breakfast occupies an 1860s Victorian house in a quiet Cambridge residential neighborhood halfway between Central and Harvard squares. Public areas combine comfort with elegance. Guest rooms are spacious and bright, some share baths. Free parking is available. **www.harding-house.com**

CAMBRIDGE A Friendly Inn
P **$$$**

1673 Cambridge St., Cambridge, 02138 **Tel** *(617) 547-7851* **Fax** *(617) 547-0202* **Rooms** *17*

Visiting scholars, prospective students, and parents visiting their Ivy League offspring tend to frequent this aptly named bed and breakfast. It is located in a quiet residential neighborhood just north of Harvard Yard and east of Harvard Divinity School. **www.afinow.com**

CAMBRIDGE Kendall Hotel
P **$$$**

350 Main St., Cambridge, 02142 **Tel** *(617) 577-1300, (866) 566-1300* **Fax** *(617) 577-1377* **Rooms** *77*

The memorabilia here celebrates this boutique hotel's former life as a century-old Queen Anne-style firehouse. Eleven of the guest rooms were once the firemen's dormitory. The rest of the spacious rooms occupy newer additions. It is convenient to Massachusetts Institute of Technology and the T's Red Line. **www.kendallhotel.com**

CAMBRIDGE Best Western Hotel Tria
P **$$$$**

220 Alewife Brook Pkwy., Cambridge, 02138 **Tel** *(617) 491-8000, (866) 333-8742* **Fax** *(617) 491-4932* **Rooms** *69*

Though outside the usual tourist districts, this small hotel is big on contemporary style and comfort. Guest-pleasing perks include inexpensive parking, continental breakfast, and an exercise room. Children under 18 stay free. There is a complimentary shuttle service to Alewife on the T's Red Line and to Harvard Square. **www.hoteltria.com**

CAMBRIDGE Hampton Inn
P **$$$$**

191 Monsignor O'Brien Highway, Cambridge, 02141 **Tel** *(617) 494-5300* **Fax** *(617) 494-6569* **Rooms** *114*

This hotel is a five-minute walk from the Lechmere terminus of the T's Green Line, which makes it reasonably convenient for the Museum of Science and TD Garden. Bonuses include free breakfast and parking, and loaner bicycles. **www.hamptoninn.com**

CAMBRIDGE Harvard Square Hotel
P **$$$$**

110 Mount Auburn St., Cambridge, 02138 **Tel** *(617) 864-5200, (800) 458-5886* **Fax** *(617) 864-2409* **Rooms** *73*

This four-story motor-inn boasts an excellent location in the midst of Harvard Square. There is a small lobby and basic but comfortable guest rooms featuring light wood furnishings and warm colors. Register for special deals offered only by e-mail. **www.harvardsquarehotel.com**

CAMBRIDGE Holiday Inn Express
P **$$$$**

250 Monsignor O'Brien Hwy., Cambridge, 02141 **Tel** *(617) 577-7600, (800) 972-3381* **Fax** *(617) 354-1313* **Rooms** *112*

This business hotel features rooms with luxurious bedding, deluxe continental breakfasts, a small business center, and limited onsite parking. It is close to the Museum of Science and only a short walk to Lechmere T-stop. **www.ichotelsgroup.com**

CAMBRIDGE Hyatt Regency Cambridge
P **$$$$**

575 Memorial Dr., Cambridge, 02138 **Tel** *(617) 492-1234, (800) 233-1234* **Fax** *(617) 491-6906* **Rooms** *415*

This pyramid-shaped hotel cuts a dramatic profile along the Charles River and is perfectly situated for sunset views from a number of the guest rooms. Take advantage of the Charles River pathways by renting a mountain bike from the hotel. A regular shuttle service is available. **www.cambridge.hyatt.com**

CAMBRIDGE Mary Prentiss Inn

`P` $$$$

6 Prentiss St., Cambridge, 02140 **Tel** *(617) 661-2929* **Fax** *(617) 661-5989* **Rooms** *20*

The strong architectural features of this 1843 Greek Revival mansion are accentuated by the bold wallpapers, period furniture, antiques, and rich fabrics. Some rooms have wood-burning fireplaces and whirlpool tubs. Breakfast is served in the parlor or on the outdoor terrace in summer. **www.maryprentissinn.com**

CAMBRIDGE Charles Hotel

$$$$$

1 Bennett St., Cambridge, 02138 **Tel** *(617) 864-1200, (800) 882-1818* **Fax** *(617) 864-5715* **Rooms** *294*

Handmade quilts on the beds add a cozy touch to the restrained modern décor. The hotel's location on the edge of Harvard Square is a plus. A top-notch jazz club, restaurant, and hip bar serve visitors and locals alike. The weekly farmers market and outdoor dining enliven the hotel's plaza in warm weather. **www.charleshotel.com**

CAMBRIDGE Hotel Marlowe

$$$$$

25 Edwin Land Blvd., Cambridge, 02141 **Tel** *(617) 868-8000, (800) 825-7140* **Fax** *(617) 868-8001* **Rooms** *236*

Next to the Cambridgeside Galleria, this sleek hotel has something for everyone: a fitness center, a complimentary wine reception each evening by the fireplace in the lobby, and special packages for pets. A short walk to the Charles River, Museum of Science, and the T's Green Line. **www.hotelmarlowe.com**

CAMBRIDGE Inn at Harvard

$$$$$

1201 Massachusetts Ave., Cambridge, 02138 **Tel** *(617) 491-2222* **Fax** *(617) 520-3711* **Rooms** *113* **Map** *2 E3*

The four-story atrium of this modern hotel was modeled on Isabella Stewart Gardner's Italian-style palazzo turned museum. Rooms are comfortably appointed and filled with period furniture. Access to the nearby Harvard Faculty Club and its dining room is extended to all guests. **www.theinnatharvard.com**

CAMBRIDGE Le Méridien Cambridge

$$$$$

20 Sidney St., Cambridge, 02139 **Tel** *(617) 577-0200, (800) 543-4300* **Fax** *(617) 474-8366* **Rooms** *210*

This high-tech hotel is an interface between investors and the biotech engineers, electronics visionaries, and professors at the adjacent Massachusetts Institute of Technology. Sleekly contemporary (it is one of Le Méridien's design hotels), it's also handy to the bars and ethnic restaurants of Cambridge's Central Square. **www.starwoodhotels.com**

CAMBRIDGE Royal Sonesta Hotel

$$$$$

5 Cambridge Parkway, Cambridge, 02142 **Tel** *(617) 806-4200, (800) 766-3782* **Fax** *(617) 806-4232* **Rooms** *400*

The Royal Sonesta boasts a prime location on the pathway along the Charles River. Many of the comfortable rooms have river views and public areas are noted for outstanding art works. It is within easy walking distance to the T's Green Line. Family packages often include bicycles. **www.sonesta.com/boston**

CAMBRIDGE Sheraton Commander

$$$$$

16 Garden St., Cambridge, 02138 **Tel** *(617) 547-4800, (800) 325-3535* **Fax** *(617) 234-1396* **Rooms** *175*

Harvard Square's original hotel, built in 1927, sits across from Cambridge Common and a short walk from Harvard Yard. Though the hallways are narrow and some rooms are small, consistent refurbishment maintains the hotel's comfortable style. The restaurant specializes in traditional New England fare. **www.sheraton.com/commander**

CHARLESTOWN Constitution Inn

$$$

150 Third Ave., Charlestown, 02129 **Tel** *(617) 241-8400, (800) 495-9622* **Fax** *(617) 241-2856* **Rooms** *147* **Map** *2 D1*

Convenient to the Freedom Trail (*see pp54–7*), this unique property offers the lowest rates to Armed Services personnel. However, it also welcomes casual visitors and its well-maintained rooms, fitness center, pool, and sauna are a good deal for all. The staff are especially welcoming. **www.constitutioninn.org**

DORCHESTER Comfort Inn-Boston

$$

900 Morrissey Blvd., 02122 **Tel** *(617) 287-9200* **Fax** *(617) 282-2365* **Rooms** *132*

Located well outside the city center near South Boston beaches and the John F. Kennedy Library, this comfortable hotel is a good outpost for making forays into downtown via the T's Red Line. As part of a convention and exhibition complex, it's close to a family entertainment center with bowling, billiards, and arcade games. **www.bostonhotel.com**

DORCHESTER Ramada Inn Boston

$$

800 Morrissey Blvd., Dorchester, 02122 **Tel** *(617) 287-9100* **Fax** *(617) 265-9287* **Rooms** *177*

The Ramada Inn is well located for making daytrips into the city. The hotel offers a free shuttle to Logan Airport, JFK/UMass stop on the T's Red Line, and the World Trade Center. It's a convenient spot for travelers also planning to go to Cape Cod. **www.bostonhotel.com**

EAST BOSTON Hyatt Harborside

$$$$$

101 Harborside Dr., 02128 **Tel** *(617) 568-1234, (800) 233-1234* **Fax** *(617) 567-8856* **Rooms** *270*

Located on the East Boston waterfront near Logan Airport, this modern hotel was designed to maximize harbor views from the lobby, restaurant, and indoor pool. Half the spacious guest rooms also offer a water view, while the rest overlook the airport. Soundproofed windows minimize noise. Water taxi to downtown docks nearby. **www.harborside.hyatt.com**

NORTH END AND THE WATERFRONT Golden Slipper B&B Afloat

`P` $$$$

Lewis Wharf, 02110 **Tel** *(781) 545-2845* **Rooms** *2* **Map** *2 E3*

For a different perspective on Boston, this vintage Chris Craft yacht tied up at Lewis Wharf sleeps two in a comfortable bedroom, and two more can sleep on the lounge's pull-out couch. Galley kitchen, full bathroom, TV, and air conditioning. Convenient location in historic district, close to Faneuil Hall. **www.bostonsbedandbreakfastafloat.com**

Key to Price Guide *see p306* **Key to Symbols** *see back cover flap*

NORTH END AND THE WATERFRONT Boston Harbor Hotel 🏨🍴🛁🏋️🅿️ $$$$$
70 Rowes Wharf, 02110 **Tel** *(617) 439-7000, (800) 752-7077* **Fax** *(617) 330-9450* **Rooms** *230* **Map** *2 E4*

Dramatic public spaces and large rooms (500 square feet or more) are trademarks of this classically elegant hotel. Specify harbor or city view when booking. Located in the heart of waterfront activity, hotel is known for fine dining, winter wine festival, and for summer series of outdoor films and concerts on outdoor decks. **www.bhh.com**

NORTH END AND THE WATERFRONT Marriott Long Wharf 🏨🍴🛁🏋️🅿️ $$$$$
296 State St., 02109 **Tel** *(617) 227-0800, (800) 228-9290* **Fax** *(617) 227-2867* **Rooms** *412* **Map** *2 E3*

This red-brick hotel stretches along Boston's original China Trade Wharf at the foot of State Street. Rooms feature harbor or city skyline views. The seasonal outdoor terrace is a favorite with locals on weekend afternoons. A good base for exploring the waterfront or taking a ferry to the Harbor Islands. **www.marriottlongwharf.com**

NORTH END AND THE WATERFRONT Seaport Hotel 🏨🍴🛁🏋️🅿️ $$$$$
1 Seaport Lane, 02210 **Tel** *(617) 385-4000, (877) 732-7678* **Fax** *(617) 385-4001* **Rooms** *426* **Map** *2 F5*

This modern business hotel is connected by walkway to the Seaport World Trade Center. Weekend specials often include good options for families. Complimentary bicycles available to explore the waterfront. Water taxi to Long Wharf, the North End and Charlestown Navy Yard is a fun way to tour the Freedom Trail. **www.seaportboston.com**

NORTH END AND THE WATERFRONT The Westin Boston Waterfront 🏨🍴🛁🏋️🅿️ $$$$$
425 Summer St., 02210 **Tel** *(617) 532-4600, (800) 937-8461* **Fax** *(617) 532-4630* **Rooms** *793* **Map** *2 E5*

This hotel is located in the historic Seaport district, just 3 miles (1.9 km) from Logan Airport and a short cab or T-ride from Back Bay, the Financial District, and Faneuil Hall. Spacious guestrooms and suites feature luxurious beds and baths. Sauciety Restaurant and full-service health club are added attractions. **www.westin.com/bostonwaterfront**

OLD BOSTON AND THE FINANCIAL DISTRICT Harborside Inn 🏨🅿️ $$$$
185 State St., 02109 **Tel** *(617) 723-7500, (888) 723-7565* **Fax** *(617) 670-6015* **Rooms** *54* **Map** *2 E3*

This modest boutique hotel in an 1858 granite spice warehouse building is located near Faneuil Hall Marketplace and the New England Aquarium. Small guest rooms don't skimp on style — with exposed brick walls, wooden floors, sleigh beds, and Oriental carpets. **www.harborsideinnboston.com**

OLD BOSTON AND THE FINANCIAL DISTRICT Hilton Boston Financial District 🏨🍴🅿️ $$$$$
89 Broad St., 02110 **Tel** *(617) 556-0006, (800) 996-3426* **Fax** *(617) 556-0053* **Rooms** *362* **Map** *2 E4*

This 1928 Art Deco building was Boston's first skyscraper built on the edge of the Financial District. A careful hotel conversion preserved the marble floors in the lobby and bathrooms and polished wood and brass details in the public areas. Business people favor the sedate library as a meeting place. **www.hilton.com**

OLD BOSTON AND THE FINANCIAL DISTRICT Intercontinental Hotel 🏨🍴🛁🏋️🅿️ $$$$$
510 Atlantic Ave., 02210 **Tel** *(617) 747-1000, (866) 493-6495* **Rooms** *424* **Map** *2 D5*

Clad in reflective glass and polished granite, the Intercontinental is its own mini-city on the still-developing South Boston Waterfront. Great harbor views and stylish rooms are aimed squarely at executives traveling on expense accounts. The high rack rates, however, are sometimes offset by excellent special deals. **www.intercontinentalboston.com**

OLD BOSTON AND THE FINANCIAL DISTRICT Langham Hotel Boston 🏨🍴🛁🏋️🅿️ $$$$$
250 Franklin St., 02110 **Tel** *(617) 451-1900, (800) 223-6800* **Fax** *(617) 423-2844* **Rooms** *325* **Map** *2 D4*

Old money doesn't get much older than at the Langham, which occupies the Renaissance Revival palace on Post Office Square originally constructed as the Federal Reserve Bank. Painted dome and gilded vaults of the foyer hint at comforts of 19th-century French décor in the rooms. Special family programs. **www.boston.langhamhotels.com**

OLD BOSTON AND THE FINANCIAL DISTRICT Millennium Bostonian 🏨🍴🏋️🅿️ $$$$$
26 North St., 02109 **Tel** *(617) 523-3600, (800) 343-0922* **Fax** *(617) 523-2454* **Rooms** *201* **Map** *2 D3*

This upscale hotel is housed in three former warehouse buildings. Rooms vary greatly in size, but all boast luxury linens and 42" LCD televisions. Some have balconies overlooking the historic Faneuil Hall Marketplace. The lobby features a gas-burning fireplace for cool evenings. **www.millenniumhotels.com**

OLD BOSTON AND THE FINANCIAL DISTRICT NINE ZERO 🏨🍴🏋️🅿️ $$$$$
90 Tremont St., 02108 **Tel** *(617) 772-5800, (866) 906-9090* **Fax** *(617) 772-5810* **Rooms** *190* **Map** *1 C4*

Spare and elegant as a stem of freesia, NINE ZERO prides itself on winning design awards from the hotel and travel industries. Frette linens, Italian marble, and plenty of stainless steel and glass conspire to create an airy atmosphere in one of the densest parts of town. Excellent location between Beacon Hill and Downtown Crossing. **www.ninezero.com**

OLD BOSTON AND THE FINANCIAL DISTRICT Omni Parker House 🏨🍴🏋️🅿️ $$$$$
60 School St., 02108 **Tel** *(617) 227-8600, (800) 843-6664* **Fax** *(617) 742-5729* **Rooms** *551* **Map** *2 D4*

Memorabilia on display in the ornate lobby emphasize Parker House's status as America's longest continuously operating hotel. Some rooms are compact. Boston cream pie was first served here and Parkers Restaurant and Parkers Bar are favorites with politicians. Located on the Freedom Trail. **www.omnihotels.com**

OLD BOSTON AND THE FINANCIAL DISTRICT XV Beacon 🏨🍴🏋️🅿️ $$$$$
15 Beacon St., 02108 **Tel** *(617) 670-1500, (877) 982-3226* **Fax** *(617) 670-2525* **Rooms** *60* **Map** *1 C4*

This 1903 Beaux-Arts office building is now a chic hotel. Furnishings by a local celebrity designer mix traditional and contemporary style. All rooms feature gas fireplaces, CD players and 27" television sets. Beacon Hill location is convenient for walking, but complimentary chauffeured car service is available for trips within the city. **www.xvbeacon.com**

MASSACHUSETTS

AMHERST Allen House Inn
`P` `$$`

599 Main St., 01002 **Tel** *(413) 253-5000* **Rooms** *6*

Handy to both the Emily Dickinson House and the Amherst College campus, this Victorian bed-and-breakfast features furniture and architectural details from both English and American branches of the Arts & Crafts Movement. Beds are topped with goose down comforters and pillows. Free high-speed Internet. **www.allenhouse.com**

CHARLEMONT Warfield House Inn
`P` `$$`

200 Warfield Rd., 01339 **Tel** *(413) 339-6600, (888) 339-8439* **Fax** *(413) 339-5754* **Rooms** *8*

The sweeping views from this mountaintop inn are especially dramatic during fall foliage season. Rooms are in two farm-estate guest houses, each with a hot tub and a large, wood-burning fireplace. Children can tour the farmyard and meet the animals. Breakfast included. **www.warfieldhouseinn.com**

CHATHAM Chatham Wayside Inn
`P` `$$$$`

512 Main St., 02633 **Tel** *(508) 945-5550, (800) 242-8426* **Fax** *(508) 945-3407* **Rooms** *56*

Open all year, this sprawling inn in the heart of Chatham at the elbow of Cape Cod includes both the original stagecoach inn and a modern wing with even more spacious rooms, half of which overlook a park (with summer band concerts). Some rooms have porches or patios overlooking the adjacent golf course. **www.waysideinn.com**

CONCORD North Bridge Inn
`P` `$$$`

21 Monument St., 01742 **Tel** *(978) 371-0014, (888) 530-0007* **Fax** *(978) 371-6460* **Rooms** *6*

A renovated 1885 home just off Monument Square in downtown Concord, the North Bridge Inn has six suites, named for local 19th-century authors. Each suite has either a galley or full kitchen. Rates include daily cooked breakfast. Premium charge and minimum stay required during height of foliage season. **www.northbridgeinn.com**

CONCORD Colonial Inn
`P` `$$$$`

48 Monument Sq., 01742 **Tel** *(978) 369-9200, (800) 370-9200* **Fax** *(508) 371-1533* **Rooms** *56*

This landmark structure was built in 1716 and has operated as an inn since 1889. The original inn has 15 rooms, while others are located in the newer wing and adjacent buildings. Colonial Revival furnishings contribute to the antiquarian air. The tavern is a key stop on the folk music circuit. **www.concordscolonialinn.com**

EDGARTOWN The Lightkeepers Inn
`P` `$$$$`

25 Simpson's Lane, Martha's Vineyard, 02539 **Tel** *(508) 627-4600* **Fax** *(508) 627-4611* **Rooms** *6*

Private cottage and five two-room suites (each with a bedroom, living room, and kitchen/dining area) sit adjacent to the lighthouse at Edgartown harbor on the island of Martha's Vineyard. Suites share patio or private deck. Gauzy window treatments and lacy bedrooms emphasize the soft light of the island. **www.thelightkeepersinn.com**

FALMOUTH Palmer House Inn
`P` `$$$`

81 Palmer Ave., 02540 **Tel** *(508) 548-1230, (800) 472-2632* **Fax** *(508) 540-1878* **Rooms** *17*

Set in Falmouth's Historic District, this Queen Anne style inn and adjacent guest house feature stained-glass windows, hardwood floors, antique furnishings, and all the romantic lace and pillows that characterize Victorian style. There is a private suite cottage in the grounds. Rate includes breakfast cooked to order. **www.palmerhouseinn.com**

GLOUCESTER Ocean View Inn and Resort
`P` `$$$$`

171 Atlantic Rd., 01930 **Tel** *(978) 283-6200, (800) 315-7557* **Rooms** *62*

Although the room décor is somewhat dated, this complex of Edwardian-style summer mansions and more modern motel rooms offers a variety of lodging choices. There are superb ocean views from the restaurant and from some guestrooms. Swimming beaches a short drive away. **www.oceanviewinnandresort.com**

GREAT BARRINGTON Monument Mountain Motel
`P` `$$$`

247 Stockbridge Rd., 01230 **Tel** *(413) 528-3272* **Fax** *(413) 528-3132* **Rooms** *17*

Ideally located for outdoor activities and summer arts, this well-kept older roadside motel features king-size beds and some connecting family units as well as basketball and tennis courts. Within walking distance of an inexpensive restaurant and near some of the area's striking hiking trails. Free wireless Internet access. **www.monumentmountainmotel.com**

HYANNIS Captain Gosnold Village
`P` `$$`

230 Gosnold St., 02601 **Tel** *(508) 775-9111* **Rooms** *30*

Close to beaches and a few minutes' stroll from Hyannis Harbor, this family-oriented resort consists largely of pink-shuttered cottage accommodations. Most units include decks, gas grills, and private lawns. Cribs are available if requested in advance. Air-conditioning units can be rented, but they are rarely needed. **www.captaingosnold.com**

IPSWICH Inn at Castle Hill
`P` `$$$`

280 Argilla Rd., 01938 **Tel** *(978) 412-2555* **Fax** *(978) 412-2556* **Rooms** *10*

Understated elegance and serenity characterize this tranquil inn on the Crane Estate, a land conservation preserve along the North Shore noted for its abundance of nesting shorebirds, migrating songbirds. It features an extraordinary beach backed by sand dunes and extensive hiking trails. Breakfast and afternoon tea included. **www.theinnatcastlehill.com**

LENOX Cranwell Resort and Golf Club 🖼🍴🏊🏋🚗🅿 $$$$$

55 Lee Rd., 01240 **Tel** *(413) 637-1364, (800) 272-6935* **Rooms** *114*

Occupying a Gilded Age country estate in the Berkshires, this resort has rooms in several types of buildings, including a poshly appointed hotel and more independent townhouses. All guests have use of the quite extensive spa facilities, including steam and sauna rooms, Olympic-size indoor pool, and 18-hole championship golf course. **www.cranwell.com**

NANTUCKET Century House 🅿 $$$$

10 Cliff Rd., 02554 **Tel** *(508) 228-0530* **Rooms** *16*

Open since 1833 as Nantucket's oldest family-operated inn, this grey-shingled guest house with wrap-around veranda sits a short walk from the center of town atop a breezy cliff. Modern amenities (including cable TV in every room) mesh nicely with a graceful 19th century ambience. Continental breakfast. **www.centuryhouse.com**

NANTUCKET Union Street Inn 🅿 $$$$

7 Union St., 02554 **Tel** *(508) 228-9222, (800) 225-5116* **Fax** *(508) 325-0848* **Rooms** *14*

C.1770 house exemplifying Nantucket's historic, cedar-shingle architecture sits in the midst of the island's main village, handy for walking to virtually all attractions. Wide-plank pine floors and fireplaces in several rooms are complemented by modern luxury linens and amenities. Full cooked breakfast served daily. Closed Jan–Mar. **www.unioninn.com**

NEW MARLBOROUGH Old Inn on the Green 🍴🏊🅿 $$$$

134 Hartsville-New Marlborough Rd., 01230 **Tel** *(413) 229-7924* **Fax** *(413) 229-7964* **Rooms** *11*

On the picturesque green of this Berkshires village, the c.1800 inn and adjacent Thayer House provide spacious rooms decorated with country antiques, quilts, and folk art. Some luxury suites are available. Midweek specials combine an overnight stay with meals at the highly acclaimed restaurant. Breakfast included. **www.oldinn.com**

NEWBURYPORT Clark Currier Inn 🅿 $$

45 Green St., 01950 **Tel** *(978) 465-8363* **Rooms** *9*

Constructed in 1803 for a shipbuilder, this classic example of a three-story "square house" in the Federal Style retains almost all of its original architectural details such as hard-carved moldings. Furnishings blend Federal antiques with Victorian pieces. Hearty breakfast included. Some rooms are in the adjacent carriage house. **www.clarkcurrierinn.com**

NORTH ADAMS Porches Inn 🖼🏊🏋🚗🅿 $$

231 River St., 01247 **Tel** *(413) 664-0400* **Fax** *(413) 664-0401* **Rooms** *47*

The complex of early 20th-century millworkers' houses converted into a hip luxury hotel is located next to the Massachusetts Museum of Contemporary Art, itself converted from a mill complex. Décor is recherché with extensive use of souvenir china, photos, and posters. Breakfast and high-speed Internet access included. **www.porches.com**

OAK BLUFFS The Nashua House Hotel 🅿 $$

30 Kennebec Ave., Martha's Vineyard, 02557 **Tel** *(508) 693-0043, (888) 343-0043* **Rooms** *16*

This Victorian house sits in the center of Oak Bluffs village on the island of Martha's Vineyard, within walking distance of the ferry docks and Flying Horses Carousel. Many bedrooms have ocean views. Fully air-conditioned and heated, it's one of the rare Oak Bluffs inns open all year. Rooms have no TV, and all share baths. **www.nashuahouse.com**

OAK BLUFFS The Island Inn 🏊🏋🅿 $$$

Beach Rd., Martha's Vineyard, 02557 **Tel** *(508) 693-2002, (800) 462-0269* **Fax** *(508) 693-7911* **Rooms** *51*

A large resort compound featuring a mix of cottages, suites, and studios, many in townhouse condominiums. Most have spectacular views and many lodgings have both working fireplaces and full kitchens. On-site laundry. Within walking distance of two swimming beaches and adjacent to a 18-hole golf course. **www.islandinn.com**

PLYMOUTH Pilgrim Sands Motel 🏊🅿 $$

150 Warren Ave., 02360 **Tel** *(508) 747-0900, (800) 729-7263* **Fax** *(508) 746-8066* **Rooms** *64*

Directly across street from Plimoth Plantation, this modern motel has spacious rooms, a whirlpool spa, indoor and outdoor heated pools, and its own private beach that adjoins Plymouth Long Beach. Two self-catering suites are also available. Continental breakfast in the coffee shop and wireless Internet access included. **www.pilgrimsands.com**

PLYMOUTH John Carver Inn 🖼🍴🏊🏋🅿 $$$

25 Summer St., 02360 **Tel** *(508) 746-7100, (800) 274-1620* **Fax** *(508) 746-8299* **Rooms** *80*

This popular lodging combines Colonial Revival style, right down to pub-chair seating in the dining room, with a Pilgrim-themed indoor pool featuring an 80-foot water slide. Located on a hill across from historic grist mill, the inn is a few minutes' walk from waterfront attractions. Popular with bus tours. **www.johncarverinn.com**

PROVINCETOWN Chateau Provincetown 🖼🏊🅿 $$$$

105 Bradford St., 02657 **Tel** *(508) 487-1286* **Fax** *(508) 487-3557* **Rooms** *54*

This hilltop compound overlooking Provincetown harbor features luxuriant gardens, a large heated pool, and several decks. It offers surprisingly quiet private accommodations in a resort destination known for a certain edgy rowdiness. Continental breakfast included. **www.chateauprovincetown.com**

ROWLEY Country Garden Inn and Motel 🏊🏋🅿 $$

101 Main St. (Rte 1A), 01969 **Tel** *(978) 948-7773, (800) 287-7773* **Fax** *(978) 948-7947* **Rooms** *24*

A range of accommodations is available including motel rooms, a country inn, townhouses, suites with fireplaces, and cottages with whirlpool tubs. Set in lush landscaped grounds complete with picnic area, hammocks, gazebo and spa offering massage, manicures, and pedicures, the inn is open all year. **www.countrygardenmotel.com**

SALEM Hawthorne Hotel

🛏️ 🍴 📺 🅿️ $$$

18 Washington Square West., 01970 **Tel** *(978) 744-4080, (800) 729-7829* **Fax** *(978) 745-9842* **Rooms** *93*

Built in 1925 in the Federal style of a century earlier, the Hawthorne is a civic and social center for Salem, hosting annual Halloween events, including a costume ball. The city's only full-service hotel, it is located near Salem Common, the Peabody Essex Museum and the pedestrian shopping district. Free wireless Internet access. **www.hawthornehotel.com**

SANDWICH Sandy Neck Motel

🛏️ 🚶 🅿️ $$

669 Route 6A, 02537 **Tel** *(508) 362-3992, (800) 564-3992* **Fax** *(508) 362-5170* **Rooms** *12*

Located at the entrance to the extensive sand bar of Sandy Neck Beach (and near the tidal marshes famous for birding), this relaxing and well-kept older motel features lovingly landscaped grounds with lounge chairs and barbecue stations. Air conditioning, fridge, and high-speed Internet access. Some self-catering units available. **www.sandyneck.com**

SOUTH WELLFLEET Wellfleet Motel & Lodge

🍴 🛏️ 🚶 🅿️ $$$

Route 6, 02663 **Tel** *(508) 349-3535, (800) 852-2900* **Fax** *(508) 349-1192* **Rooms** *65*

A variety of rooms and suites are available on this property made up of several buildings. Many rooms have private balconies or patios overlooking landscaped central courtyard. Located near the northern terminus of Cape Cod Rail Trail and the Audubon wildlife sanctuary, the lodge is a great base for active sports. **www.wellfleetmotel.com**

STOCKBRIDGE Red Lion Inn

🛏️ 🍴 🛏️ 🅿️ $$$$

30 Main St., 01262 **Tel** *(413) 298-5545* **Fax** *(413) 298-5130* **Rooms** *108*

The most famous lodging in the Berkshires, the Red Lion Inn has welcomed travelers since the late 18th century. The main inn building is a spacious Victorian structure with an iconic porch for sitting, rocking, and observing village life. The guest houses offer a more modern alternative and often have larger rooms. **www.redlioninn.com**

STURBRIDGE Comfort Inn & Suites

🛏️ 🍴 🛏️ 🚶 📺 🅿️ $

215 Charlton Rd. (Route 20), 01566 **Tel** *(508) 347-3306, (800) 228-5150* **Fax** *(508) 347-3514* **Rooms** *77*

This three-story modern motel with indoor and outdoor pools and business center is surrounded by immaculate grounds and beautiful landscaping at the convergence of major travel routes in Sturbridge. Less than 1 mile (1.6 km) from the entrance to Old Sturbridge Village. Free wireless Internet access. **www.sturbridgecomfortinn.com**

STURBRIDGE Publick House Historic Inn

🍴 🛏️ 🚶 🅿️ $$

Route 131, 01566 **Tel** *(508) 347-3313, (800) 782-5425* **Fax** *(508) 347-5073* **Rooms** *15*

Combining 21st-century creature comforts with an 18th-century ambience, this 1771 inn lies in the midst of the rolling central Massachusetts countryside. The large backyard has a patio, swimming pool, and playground. The least expensive rooms are located in the adjacent motorlodge. **www.publickhouse.com**

WEST DENNIS The Barnacle Motel

🛏️ 🛏️ 🅿️ $$$

221 Main St. (Rte 28), 02670 **Tel** *(508) 394-8472* **Rooms** *35*

Located on a major route one mile (1.6 km) from the powdery sands of Sandy Beach on Nantucket Sound, this two-story modern motel features spacious rooms, including some self-catering units with two bedrooms for families. There is a large outdoor pool. **www.barnaclemotel.com**

WILLIAMSTOWN The Guest House at Field Farm

🛏️ 🅿️ $$$

554 Sloan Rd., 01267 **Tel** *(413) 458-3135* **Fax** *(413) 458-3144* **Rooms** *6*

This Bauhaus-inspired Modernist masterpiece home is filled with modern art and furniture collected by the original owners, who left the property to the conservation group, Trustees of Reservations. Four miles of trails can be traversed on foot or cross-country skis. Full breakfast included. Open weekends only, Nov–Apr. **guesthouseatfieldfarm.thetrustees.org**

WILLIAMSTOWN The Williams Inn

🛏️ 🍴 🛏️ 🅿️ $$$

On the Green, 01267 **Tel** *(413) 458-9371, (800) 828-0133* **Fax** *(413) 458-2767* **Rooms** *125*

On the campus of Williams College just two blocks from the center of the village, this three-story inn combines early 20th-and early 21st-century wings for a blend of traditional and contemporary style. The heated indoor pool features a hot tub and saunas. The dining room serves breakfast, lunch and dinner. **www.williamsinn.com**

RHODE ISLAND

BLOCK ISLAND 1661 Inn and Hotel Manisses

🍴 🅿️ $$$

Spring St., 02807 **Tel** *(401) 466-2421, (800) 626-4773* **Fax** *(401) 466-3162* **Rooms** *38*

The 21-room inn is open all year and features the best appointed rooms, but the 17-room Victorian Hotel Manisses (closed mid-Oct–Mar) is a grand tradition on Block Island. There is no air conditioning, some rooms lack TVs, and some share baths. Hotel guest rooms are furnished in Victorian antiques. **www.blockislandresorts.com**

BLOCK ISLAND Rose Farm Inn

🅿️ $$$

Roslyn Rd., 02807 **Tel** *(401) 466-2034* **Fax** *(401) 466-2053* **Rooms** *19*

In a peaceful sea and country setting, this inn sits on a large expanse of farmland that is now home to marsh hawks, ring-neck pheasants, and white-tail deer. The inn has its own bicycle rental. There is no TV or air conditioning in the rooms; some share baths. Closed mid-Oct–mid-Apr. Children 12 and older welcome. **www.rosefarminn.com**

BRISTOL Bristol Harbor Inn

🖼 🍴 🅿 $$$

Thames St. Landing, 259 Thames St., 02809 **Tel** *(401) 254-1444* **Fax** *(401) 254-1333* **Rooms** *40*

This hotel reflects the nautical history of the Bristol waterfront in its buildings, which include a 1797 bank, a rum distillery, and a coal and lumber warehouse. The French Provincial style rooms are popular with yachtsmen moored in Bristol's harbor. Continental breakfast included. **www.bristolharborinn.com**

CHARLESTOWN General Stanton Inn

🍴 🅿 $$

4115 Old Post Rd. (Route 1A), 02813 **Tel** *(401) 364-8888, (800) 364-8011* **Fax** *(401) 364-3333* **Rooms** *18*

With a portion dating from 1667, the General Stanton claims to be one of the oldest continuously run hostelries in North America. Much of that atmosphere persists in the low ceilings, massive fireplaces, brick ovens, and exposed hand-hewn timbers. Site of popular weekend flea market in warm weather. **www.generalstantoninn.com**

MIDDLETOWN Newport Beach Hotel and Suites

🖼 🍴 🅿 $$$$

Memorial Blvd. & Ware Ave., 02840 **Tel** *(401) 846-0310, (800) 665-1778* **Fax** *(401) 847-2621* **Rooms** *76*

Free beach parking, which elsewhere costs $25 in summer, is included at this hotel across the street from Newport's best surfing beach. It's a long way from downtown but within walking distance of Cliff Walk. Two-bedroom suites and whirlpool tub rooms are available. Rates include breakfast. **www.newportbeachhotelandsuites.com**

NEWPORT Beech Tree Inn

🅿 $$$

34 Rhode Island Ave., 02840 **Tel** *(401) 847-9794, (800) 748-6565* **Rooms** *8*

Located in a residential area away from waterfront hubbub, this Victorian bed-and-breakfast (built in 1887) is noted for offering the "biggest breakfast in Newport". Some rooms have gas fireplaces and whirlpool tubs; all have air conditioning and TV. Older children are welcome. The common area has a kitchen for guests. **www.beechtreeinn.com**

NEWPORT Best Western Mainstay Inn

🖼 ♨ 🅿 $$$

151 Admiral Kalbfus Rd., 02840 **Tel** *(401) 849-9880* **Fax** *(401) 848-4391* **Rooms** *199*

Just across the street from the Newport Grand Casino, 1 mile (1.6 km) from downtown, this Best Western is favored by visitors to the Newport Naval Base and War College a few blocks away. Clean and comfortable rooms and a good swimming pool. Bargain rates often available in off-season. **www.bestwestern.com**

NEWPORT The Black Duck Inn

🅿 $$$$

29 Pelham St., 02840 **Tel** *(401) 841-5548, (800) 206-5215* **Fax** *(401) 846-4873* **Rooms** *9*

The Black Duck Inn is situated in the heart of downtown Newport, opposite Bowen's Wharf. Each room is distinctively decorated in rich, modern colors. Most rooms are fitted with queen-size beds, and some boast a Jacuzzi and fireplace. Full breakfast included. **www.blackduckinn.com**

NEWPORT Francis Malbone House

🅿 $$$$

392 Thames St., 02840 **Tel** *(401) 846-0392, (800) 846-0392* **Fax** *(401) 848-5956* **Rooms** *20*

This painstakingly restored 1760 sea captain's mansion has been tastefully expanded with a rear addition and annexation of a colonial house. While much of the inn is furnished like a museum of colonial antiques, guest rooms and public areas are comfortable and welcoming. Rates include a gourmet breakfast and afternoon tea. **www.malbone.com**

NEWPORT Hotel Viking

🖼 🍴 ♨ 🛎 🅿 $$$$

One Bellevue Ave., 02840 **Tel** *(401) 847-3300, (800) 556-7126* **Fax** *(401) 849-0749* **Rooms** *222*

Built in 1926 by prominent local businessmen to provide a venue for social occasions and lodging for visiting friends, the original Viking now includes a tower that enables it to handle large tour groups and conferences. Furnishings are Queen Anne and Chippendale styles, and deluxe bedding and amenities are provided. **www.hotelviking.com**

NEWPORT Newport Harbor Hotel and Marina

🖼 🍴 ♨ 🛎 🅿 $$$$

49 America's Cup Ave., 02840 **Tel** *(401) 847-9000, (800) 955-2558* **Fax** *(401) 849-6380* **Rooms** *133*

Often the first choice of visiting yachtsmen and their crews, this hotel stretches along its own marina like a string of pearls on one of the prettiest harbors in New England. Rooms are spacious and most have harbor views. There is a heated indoor pool with saunas, and bargain off-season packages are available. **www.newporthotel.com**

NEWPORT Castle Hill Inn and Resort

🖼 🍴 ♨ 🛎 🅿 $$$$$

590 Ocean Dr., 02840 **Tel** *(401) 849-3800, (888) 466-1355* **Fax** *(401) 849-3838* **Rooms** *25*

Perhaps the most exclusive of resorts in Newport, Castle Hill occupies a prime spot on the peninsula at the west end of Ocean Drive. The main mansion was built as a summer home for scientist/explorer Alexander Agassiz in 1874, and property has a history of celebrity guests. Additional rooms in the chalet and beach houses. **www.castlehillinn.com**

NORTH KINGSTON Hamilton Village Inn

🍴 🅿 $

642 Boston Neck Rd. (Rte. 1A), 02852 **Tel** *(401) 295-0700* **Fax** *(401) 294-9044* **Rooms** *56*

Just a mile (1.6 km) outside the quaint village of Wickford, Hamilton Village Inn is open year-round. Off-season, Newport is only a 15-minute drive away. The country location is good for drivers, but isolated for walkers. The restaurant serves breakfast and lunch daily, and dinner on weekends in summer. **www.hamiltonvillageinn.com**

PROVIDENCE Courtyard Providence Downtown

🖼 🍴 ♨ 🛗 🛎 🅿 $$$

32 Exchange Terrace, 02903 **Tel** *(401) 272-1191, (888) 887-7955* **Fax** *(401) 272-1416* **Rooms** *216*

This low-rise hotel is set in the heart of downtown, adjacent to WaterPlace Park and connected via a walkway to Providence Place shopping mall and the R.I. Convention Center. There are good views from all rooms, covered parking, fitness center, and wireless Internet access. **marriott.com/property/propertypage/PVDDT**

PROVIDENCE Hotel Dolce Villa   🖥 P $$$
63 De Pasquale Sq., 02903 **Tel** *(401) 383-7031* **Rooms** *14*

All of the one- and two-bedroom suites (with pullout sofas for extra guests) have en-suite kitchens. Smart contemporary design includes white leather sofas and chairs – a Milan fashion look that's appropriate to the city's Italian district. All baths feature whirlpool tubs. Larger units have working fireplaces. **www.dolcevillari.com**

PROVIDENCE Providence Biltmore   🖥 🍽 🛎 P $$$
11 Dorrance St., 02903 **Tel** *(401) 421-0700, (800) 294-7709* **Fax** *(401) 455-3050* **Rooms** *289*

Set in downtown near Amtrak station, this 1922 mini-skyscraper has some rooms that are on the small side, but all are smartly appointed in contemporary style with comfortable beds, heavy draperies, and deluxe linens. Junior suites are popular with business travelers. Free Internet access. **www.providencebiltmore.com**

PROVIDENCE The Westin   🖥 🍽 🎿 🏋 🛎 P $$$
One West Exchange St, 02903 **Tel** *(401) 598-8000, (800) WESTIN* **Fax** *(401) 598-8200* **Rooms** *564*

A massive convention hotel sandwiched between the R.I. Convention Center and Providence Place shopping mall in the heart of downtown manages to fit into the city's historic skyline with surprising aplomb. Top-of-the-line Westin appointments (bed, linens, toiletries) make business travelers feel at home. Excellent restaurant. **www.westinprovidence.com**

PROVIDENCE The Hotel Providence   🖥 🍽 🛎 P $$$$
311 Westminster St., 02903 **Tel** *(401) 861-8000, (800) 861-8990* **Fax** *(401) 861-8002* **Rooms** *80*

Among the first of a wave of boutique hotels in New England, Hotel Providence combines the modern design sensibilities of Rhode Island School of Design with an appreciation of classic formality. The resulting property is sophisticated and luxurious yet restrained. Ideal location in downtown. **www.thehotelprovidence.com**

WESTERLY Pleasant View Inn   🍽 🏋 🎿 P $$
65 Atlantic Ave., 02891 **Tel** *(401) 348-8200, (800) 782-3224* **Fax** *(401) 348-8919* **Rooms** *112*

Evolved from a c.1900 beachside inn, the Pleasant View stakes out a long private stretch of beach along 4-mile (6.4-km) Misquamicut Beach on the Watch Hill end of Westerly with predominantly modern motel accommodations. Private sauna and two on-site restaurants. Inquire about package rates with golfing. Closed Nov–Apr. **www.pvinn.com**

WESTERLY Sand Dollar Inn   P $$
171 Post Rd., 02891 **Tel** *(401) 322-2000, (800) 910-7263* **Fax** *(401) 322-1590* **Rooms** *33*

Set inland about 2 miles (3.2 km) from Misquamicut and Weekapaug beaches, Sand Dollar inn sits in a haven of flowers and ornamental shrubs. It has a single-level motel, a cottage with fully equipped kitchen that sleeps four, and an apartment for a family with up to three children. Continental breakfast included. **www.visitri.com/sanddollarinn**

WESTERLY Woody Hill Bed and Breakfast   🎿 P $$
149 South Woody Hill Rd., 02891 **Tel** *(401) 322-0452* **Rooms** *3*

Surrounded by woods and pasture about 2 miles (3.2 km) from beaches, Woody Hill is perfect as a retreat where guests rock on the porch swing or stroll through fragrant gardens. On winter weekends, owner Ellen Madison gives hearth cooking lessons using the inn's walk-in fireplace. Continental breakfast included. Open all year. **www.woodyhill.com**

WESTERLY Andrea Hotel   🏋 P $$$
89 Atlantic Ave., 02891 **Tel** *(401) 348-8788, (888) 318-5707* **Fax** *(401) 596-1790* **Rooms** *24*

A local landmark since it was rebuilt after the 1938 hurricane, the Andrea has its own 300 ft (91 m) private sandy shore at Misquamicut Beach. Rooms include fridge, air conditioning, and heating. Nightly entertainment is a big draw for locals, and there is a game room for youngsters. Restaurant open Apr–Oct. **www.andreahotel.com**

WESTERLY The Villa   🎿 P $$$$
190 Shore Rd., 02891 **Tel** *(401) 596-1054, (800) 722-9240* **Fax** *(401) 596-6268* **Rooms** *8*

This romantic hideaway of flower gardens, Italian porticos, and private terraces features an outdoor Jacuzzi and a Mediterranean designer pool. Each room has its own Italian decorative theme, but all feature microwaves, refrigerators, and Jacuzzis. Breakfast included. Open all year. No children. **www.thevillaatwesterly.com**

WOONSOCKET Pillsbury House B&B   P $
341 Prospect St., 02895 **Tel** *(401) 766-7983, (800) 205-4112* **Rooms** *4*

With Victorian style to match the architecture of this 1875 home, the inn sits in what was once the mill-owners' district in this former industrial town. It's an excellent base for exploring the Blackstone Valley (from Worcester, MA, to Pawtucket, RI). Cooked breakfast included. Kitchenette available for guests. **www.pillsburyhouse.com**

CONNECTICUT

BRIDGEPORT Holiday Inn   🖥 🍽 🏋 🛎 P $$
1070 Main St., 06604 **Tel** *(203) 334-1234* **Rooms** *226*

As Bridgeport's only large hotel, this Holiday Inn serves as the de facto meeting center for the city's professional and social groups. The rooms offer good value, especially at depressed winter prices. Covenient location, cheerful staff, inexpensive garage parking, and free high-speed wireless Internet help seal the deal. **www.ichotelsgroup.com**

Key to Price Guide *see p306* **Key to Symbols** *see back cover flap*

COVENTRY Special Joys B&B   🅿 Ⓢ
41 North River Rd., 06238 **Tel** *(860) 742-6359* **Rooms** *2*

The owners are devotees and avid collectors of antique dolls and toys, and their passion is reflected throughout the hotel, conservatory, and flower gardens. There is also an antique doll and toy shop on the premises. Some rooms share a bath and the owners speak both French and German.

COVENTRY Daniel Rust House   🅿 ⓈⓈⓈ
2011 Main St., 06238 **Tel** *(860) 742-0032* **Fax** *(860) 742-0032* **Rooms** *4*

This historic home has been operating as an inn since 1800. Common areas include the former tavern, with its open hearth fireplace, and the formal dining room. A secret closet in one of the rooms is thought to have hidden slaves on the Underground Railroad. Children over 13 welcome. **www.thedanielrusthouse.com**

EAST HADDAM Bishopsgate Inn   🅿 ⓈⓈⓈ
Goodspeed Landing, Rte. 82, 06423 **Tel** *(860) 873-1677* **Fax** *(860) 873-3898* **Rooms** *6*

This colonial style home was constructed by a shipbuilder in 1818 in a quiet setting in the middle of town. The four rooms have open fireplaces, while the suite features a sauna. This section of the Connecticut River is especially noted for fly-fishing. Ample breakfast included. **www.bishopsgate.com**

ESSEX The Griswold Inn   🍴 🅿 ⓈⓈⓈ
36 Main St., 06426 **Tel** *(860) 767-1776* **Fax** *(860) 767-0481* **Rooms** *30*

The "Gris" has been a fixture in Essex since at least 1801, and reflects the maritime history of this important Connecticut River port town, especially in the original Currier & Ives prints and oil paintings on the walls. Five dining rooms dominate the historic structure, leaving guests to use the common rooms at Hayden House next door. **www.griswoldinn.com**

FARMINGTON Farmington Inn   📺 🍴 🅿 ⓈⓈ
827 Farmington Ave., 06032 **Tel** *(800) 648-9804* **Fax** *(860) 677-8332* **Rooms** *72*

Located in the heart of Farmington village and within walking distance of historic homes and museums, this Colonial-style hostelry makes a good base for exploring the entire Hartford region. Décor includes original landscape paintings of the Farmington valley and period antiques. **www.farmingtoninn.com**

GREENWICH The Cos Cob Inn   🅿 ⓈⓈ
50 River Rd., 06807 **Tel** *(203) 661-5845, (877) 549-4063* **Rooms** *14*

This Federal-style inn was constructed in early 19th century in a historic section of Greenwich near Bush-Holley House, the summer outpost of American Impressionist painters. Its furnishings reflect American Federal style and the walls are covered with reproductions of American Impressionist paintings. Breakfast is included. **www.coscobinn.com**

GROTON Best Western Olympic Inn   📺 🍴 ♨ 🏊 🖥 🅿 ⓈⓈ
360 Route 12, 06340 **Tel** *(860) 445-8000, (800) 622-7766* **Fax** *(860) 449-9173* **Rooms** *140*

Spacious rooms and good amenities make this blocky roadside motel a good base for exploring both the seashore and interior of southeastern Connecticut: notably Mystic Seaport and the Foxwoods and Mohegan Sun casinos. Large suites are available for families, and there's a weekend shuttle service to Mohegan Sun. **www.bestwestern.com**

HARTFORD America's Best Value Inn   Ⓢ
100 Weston St., 06120 **Tel** *(860) 724-0222* **Fax** *(860) 724-0433* **Rooms** *109*

Located at Jennings Road exit off I-91, 3 miles (5.4 km) north of downtown Hartford, this modest chain motel in an incongruous hacienda style is a good stopover between New York and northern New England. Convenient to the Buckland Hills Mall, the premier shopping destination in central Connecticut. **www.americasbestvalueinn.com**

HARTFORD Crowne Plaza Hartford Downtown   📺 🍴 ♨ 🏊 🖥 🅿 ⓈⓈ
50 Morgan St., 06120 **Tel** *(860) 549-2400, (877) 227-6963* **Fax** *(860) 549-7844* **Rooms** *350*

This 18-story behemoth was built to serve the convention and lodging needs of Hartford's now-dwindling insurance industry. Rooms are reasonably priced. Hotel offers free shuttle within a 3 mile (5 km) radius. Walking distance to State House, Wadsworth Atheneum, and downtown arts and shopping. **www.lchotels.com**

KENT Constitution Oak Farm   🅿 Ⓢ
36 Beardsley Rd., 06757 **Tel** *(860) 354-6495* **Rooms** *4*

Rustic 1830s farmhouse on 100 acres (40 ha) of hill country. Rooms feature period furnishings and country quilts. Two rooms have a private bath, and two have TVs. Located south of the upscale village of Kent, which has good shopping and dining, and close to Lake Waramaug. The area is known for its waterfalls. **constitutionoak@hotmail.com**

KENT Fife 'N Drum   🍴 🅿 ⓈⓈ
53 North Main St., 06757 **Tel** *(860) 927-3509* **Fax** *(860) 927-4595* **Rooms** *11*

Eight rooms with vaulted ceilings are in the main inn next to the Fife 'N Drum restaurant, and three additional rooms are in the adjacent Victorian house. Its central location is a short stroll to the upscale boutiques, galleries, and crafts stores of Kent as well as to sample the wares of the local Belgian chocolatier. **www.fifendrum.com**

LAKEVILLE Wake Robin Inn   📺 🍴 🅿 ⓈⓈⓈ
106 Sharon Road (Rte. 41), 06039 **Tel** *(860) 435-2000, (800) 435-2000* **Fax** *(860) 435-6523* **Rooms** *38*

The main inn, with traditional decor, holds 23 of the rooms. A motel augments the number of lodgings in the summer months. A walking trail through the extensive property passes wild trilliums for which the inn is named. Breakfast included. **www.wakerobininn.com**

318 TRAVELERS' NEEDS

LEDYARD Stonecroft Country Inn　　🍴 P　　$$$
515 Pumpkin Hill Rd., 06339 **Tel** *(860) 572-0771, (800) 772-0774* **Fax** *(860) 572-9161* **Rooms** *10*

This inn consists of an 1807 Georgian colonial farmhouse, listed on the National Register of Historic Places, and a renovated barn. Nine of the rooms have fireplaces, some have TVs, and all are designed for an elegant country retreat. Older children are welcome. **www.stonecroft.com**

LITCHFIELD Litchfield Inn　　P　　$$$
432 Bantam Rd., 06759 **Tel** *(860) 567-4503, (800) 499-3444* **Fax** *(860) 567-5358* **Rooms** *32*

Colonial décor belies the 1982 founding of this inn, the largest hostelry in Litchfield and the epicenter of the country squire lifestyle of the Connecticut hills. The lobby's chandelier and dramatic but delicately carved staircase set the tone. Eight luxury rooms go all-out with styling. Continental breakfast included. **www.litchfieldinnct.com**

MADISON Madison Beach Hotel　　🍴 P　　$$
94 West Wharf Rd., 06443 **Tel** *(203) 245-1404* **Fax** *(203) 245-0410* **Rooms** *35*

The quintessential old-fashioned beach hotel, the Madison was rotated in 1904 so that all the rooms face the water. Little has changed since, right down to the matchstick wainscoting and chenille spreads on the beds. The restaurant is popular with locals, and bar scene can be noisy. Closed Dec–mid-Mar. **www.madisonbeachhotel.com**

MASHANTUCKET Foxwoods Resort Casino　　🍴 P　　$$
39 Norwich-Westerly Rd., 06338 **Tel** *(860) 312-3000, (800) 369-9663* **Rooms** *1,416*

With 6 casinos, 24 restaurants, and 3 hotels, Foxwoods is the most successful casino complex in North America. Above the gaming halls, Grand Pequot Tower rooms are deluxe while Great Cedars Hotel rooms are smaller and less sumptuous. Most economical, Two Trees Inn is about a half mile (1 km) away, with shuttle service supplied. **www.foxwoods.com**

MYSTIC Brigadoon Bed and Breakfast　　P　　$$
180 Cow Hill Rd., 06355 **Tel** *(860) 536-3033* **Rooms** *8*

This roomy New England country farmhouse, dating from 1750s, is located 1.3 miles (2 km) from downtown Mystic and about twice as far from Mystic Seaport. Rooms have king- or queen-size beds and several have fireplaces. The big country breakfast and generous afternoon tea are served in a dedicated tea room. **www.brigadoonofmystic.com**

MYSTIC Whaler's Inn　　P　　$$
20 East Main St., 06355 **Tel** *(860) 536-1506, (800) 243-2588* **Fax** *(860) 572-1250* **Rooms** *49*

Located on Mystic's main thoroughfare within walking distance of Mystic Seaport, the docks, schooner fleet, and boutique and gift shopping. Several restaurants are nearby, including the iconic Mystic Pizza. Minimum 2-night stay on weekends and holidays except in winter. **www.whalersinnmystic.com**

MYSTIC Hyatt Place　　P　　$$$
224 Greenmanville Ave., 06355 **Tel** *(860) 536-9997* **Fax** *(800) 876-6152* **Rooms** *80*

These spacious rooms just off the highway are a short stroll from Mystic Aquarium, Mystic Seaport, and Mystic Village, while a weekend shuttle bus is available to Foxwoods and Mohegan Sun casinos. The fitness center, guest kitchen, and business center are open around the clock. Hot breakfast included. **www.hyattplace.com**

MYSTIC Steamboat Inn　　P　　$$$$
73 Steamboat Wharf, 06355 **Tel** *(860) 536-8300* **Rooms** *11*

With each room named for a vessel from Mystic's sailing heyday, this inn beside the historic drawbridge is about as nautical as it gets. The architecture is quirky, rooms have odd angles and views are sometimes blocked by a yacht docked outside. Breakfast buffet served in the morning; sherry and cookies in the afternoon. **www.steamboatinnmystic.com**

NEW CANAAN Roger Sherman Inn　　🍴 P　　$$$
195 Oenoke Ridge (Rte. 124), 06840 **Tel** *(203) 966-4541* **Fax** *(203) 966-0503* **Rooms** *17*

Rooms are distributed between the 18th-century main house and 19th-century carriage house. Property includes a popular restaurant and bar that is the center of nightlife in this rural burg that serves as a country retreat for New Yorkers. Some rooms allow small pets. Breakfast included. Live entertainment on weekends. **www.rogershermaninn.com**

NEW HAVEN Historic Mansion Inn　　P　　$$$
600 Chapel St., 06511 **Tel** *(203) 865-8324, (888) 512-6278* **Rooms** *7*

This graceful 1842 Greek Revival home sits within a few blocks of Yale University's old campus. Replica Queen Anne furnishings (but queen-size beds) complement the soaring architecture and marble fireplaces in each guest room. The inn offers free high-speed Internet. Breakfast is served in the formal dining room. **www.thehistoricmansioninn.com**

NEW HAVEN Study at Yale　　P　　$$$
1157 Chapel St., 06511 **Tel** *(203) 503-3900* **Rooms** *124*

This sleek, contemporary hotel strikes a Modernist pose just across the street from the Yale School of Art amid the university's most interesting and vibrant architecture. Large flatscreen TVs and iPod docking stations are the tech distractions in luxurious rooms with desks large enough to design your own hotel on. **www.studyhotels.com**

NEW PRESTON Hopkins Inn　　🍴 P　　$$
22 Hopkins Rd., 06777 **Tel** *(860) 868-7295* **Fax** *(860) 868-7464* **Rooms** *13*

Since 1847 this country inn on a knoll overlooking the north shore of Lake Waramaug has been a popular destination for city folks. The inn is open all year, and winter cross-country skiing rivals the pleasures of summer lakeside idleness. Its acclaimed restaurant serves Viennese cuisine (closed Jan–late Mar). **www.thehopkinsinn.com**

Key to Price Guide *see p306* **Key to Symbols** *see back cover flap*

NORWALK Four Points by Sheraton   🖥 🍽 📺 🅿 $$$
*426 Main Ave. (Rte. 7), 06851 **Tel** (203) 849-9828 **Fax** (203) 846-6925 **Rooms** 127*

Part of a chain designed for the business traveler, this three-story highway-side motel has some unusual features,
including a 24-hour front desk, concierge service, and a good fitness center. Located in the midst of the Norwalk business
district, but close to the attractions of scenic South Norwalk and a chic dining scene. **www.fourpoints.com/norwalk**

NORWICH The Spa at Norwich Inn   🖥 🍽 📺 🅿 $$$$
*607 West Thames St., 06360 **Tel** (860) 886-2401, (800) 275-4772 **Rooms** 100*

Pampered elegance is the mission of this spa property, which has guestrooms, suites, and private villas on 42 acres (17.4 ha)
of manicured grounds. Décor is soothingly simple, and the overall experience is complemented by health-conscious
gourmet dining and a variety of spa and fitness regimens, all at additional cost. **www.thespaatnorwichinn.com**

OLD LYME Bee & Thistle Inn   🍽 🅿 $$$
*100 Lyme St., 06371 **Tel** (860) 434-1667, (800) 622-4946 **Fax** (860) 434-3402 **Rooms** 11*

Built in 1756, the Bee and Thistle sits along the Lieutenant River surrounded by stately trees, an English sunken garden,
and lawns. Inside, the carved staircases, canopy and four-poster beds, and Oriental carpets reflect gracious styling. The
romantic restaurant serves contemporary American cuisine. Breakfast included. **www.beeandthistleinn.com**

OLD SAYBROOK Saybrook Point Inn   🖥 🍽 ≋ 📺 🚹 🅿 $$$$
*2 Bridge St, 06475 **Tel** (860) 243-0212 **Fax** (860) 388-1504 **Rooms** 80*

Adjacent to the yacht marina on Long Island Sound, this luxurious spa hotel sits amid a shoreline landscape that inspired
American Impressionist painters more than a century ago. Many rooms feature outstanding water views and some
include balconies, whirlpool tubs, and working fireplaces. **www.saybrook.com**

SALISBURY White Hart Inn   🖥 🍽 🅿 $$$
*15 Undermountain Rd., 06068 **Tel** (860) 435-0030, (800) 832-0041 **Rooms** 26*

This 1806 tavern expanded over the 19th century into a rambling country inn with a fabulous long porch for sitting,
rocking, and musing. Some rooms are very snug, others more spacious. Popular with parents visiting offspring at
boarding schools. Excellent fare available either in the Tap Room or airy Garden Room. **www.whitehartinn.com**

SIMSBURY Iron Horse Inn   🍽 ≋ 🅿 $
*969 Hopmeadow St., 06070 **Tel** (860) 658-2216 **Fax** (860) 651-0822 **Rooms** 27*

Favored by the parents of pupils at the various exclusive boarding schools of the Litchfield Hills, this is a small former
stagecoach inn in the heart of Simsbury and close to a scenic walking path leading behind the old country estates.
Rooms have small refrigerators and microwave ovens. There's an outdoor pool. **www.ironhorseinnofsimsbury.com**

STONINGTON The Inn at Stonington   📺 🅿 $$$
*60 Water St., 06378 **Tel** (860) 535-2000 **Fax** (860) 535-8193 **Rooms** 18*

Constructed in traditional clapboard style, this inn sits at a 400-ft (121 m) pier for visiting yachtsmen close to
a small beach and the village shops. Most rooms have a fireplace and oversized luxury bath (most have whirlpool
tubs) and some have harbor views. Bar on premises. Continental breakfast included. **www.innatstonington.com**

WINDSOR Residence Inn by Mariott   🖥 🍽 📺 🅿 $$
*100 Dunfey Lane, 06095 **Tel** (860) 688-7474, (800) 331-3131 **Fax** (860) 375-1208 **Rooms** 96*

This all-suite hotel offers a complimentary evening reception as well as the usual daily breakfast. Suites have
kitchens, as well as movies and free wireless Internet access. Pets are welcome. Located near the airport and
15 minutes from Hartford. **www.marriott.com**

WOODBURY Curtis House Inn   🅿 $
*506 Main St. S., 06798 **Tel** (203) 263-2101 **Rooms** 18*

While Woodbury is definitely upscale, this genuinely antique lodging (mid-18th century) retains its old, quirky
style without benefit of a designer makeover. Some of the rooms on two floors share baths; some rooms are
small. Popular for budget weddings. Babysitting and child care can be arranged. Continental breakfast included.

WOODSTOCK Inn at Woodstock Hill   🍽 🅿 $$
*94 Plaine Hill Rd., 06281 **Tel** (860) 928-0528 **Fax** (860) 928-3236 **Rooms** 21*

The main house dates from 1816, with typical New England steeply pitched hip roof, multiple dormers, and white
clapboard siding. Some rooms are small, and three are in the adjacent cottage. It's popular for weddings, and the
colonial-décor restaurant with a Continental menu is especially busy for Sunday brunch. **www.woodstockhill.net**

VERMONT

ARLINGTON Inn on Covered Bridge Green   🅿 $$$
*3587 River Rd., 05250 **Tel** (802) 375-9489, (800) 726-9480 **Fax** (802) 375-1208 **Rooms** 8*

This 1792 farmhouse was once the home of illustrator Norman Rockwell. The property is beside Battenkill River, famous
for flyfishing but also good for canoeing and kayaking. Rockwell's former studio and a barn have been transformed into
fully equipped cottages. There's a 2–3-night minimum stay in foliage season. **www.coveredbridgegreen.com**

ARLINGTON Arlington's West Mountain Inn 🍴 [P] $$$$

River Rd., 05250 ***Tel*** *(802) 375-6516* ***Fax*** *(802) 375-6553* ***Rooms*** *22*

Rooms are distributed among the historic farmhouse, three-suite cottage, and converted mill. There is a mix of Federal, Victorian and Vermont country antiques in rooms and common areas. The 150 acre (60 ha) wooded property is laced with hiking trails and contains a bird sanctuary. Bounteous breakfast included. **www.westmountaininn.com**

BRATTLEBORO America's Best Inn, Brattleboro ♿ ❄ 🏊 [P] $

959 Putney Rd., 05301 ***Tel*** *(802) 254-4583, (800) 329-7466* ***Rooms*** *46*

Located at the north end of the business district, this modern and comfortable hotel features water and air purification in rooms. The fitness center has a tanning bed as well as a hot tub and workout machines. Generous continental breakfast included. High-speed Internet access in the lobby only. **www.americasbestinn.com**

BRATTLEBORO Latchis Hotel ♿ ❄ [P] $$

50 Main St., 05301 ***Tel*** *(802) 254-6300, (800) 798-6301* ***Rooms*** *30*

One of only two remaining Art Deco buildings in Vermont, the Latchis Hotel & Theatre features modern but modest rooms with free wireless Internet service, fridge, and coffeemaker. A three-screen movie theater shows art and independent films, and the auditorium often hosts lectures and live concerts. Continental breakfast included. **www.latchis.com**

BURLINGTON Willard Street Inn [P] $$

349 South Willard St., 05401 ***Tel*** *(802) 651-8710, (800) 577-8712* ***Fax*** *(802) 651-8714* ***Rooms*** *14*

This charming 19th century mansion of brick and white marble is filled with antique and reproduction Victorian furniture and wallpaper. Breakfast is served in a marble-floored solarium looking out on Lake Champlain. Within walking distance of the University of Vermont campus. Free in-room wireless Internet access. **www.willardstreetinn.com**

BURLINGTON Sheraton Burlington Hotel & Conference Center ♿ 🍴 ❄ 🏋 🏊 [P] $$$

870 Williston Rd., 05403 ***Tel*** *(802) 865-6600* ***Fax*** *(802) 865-6670* ***Rooms*** *309*

The largest hotel in the state of Vermont, the Sheraton is located next to the University of Vermont's campus, near downtown, Lake Champlain, and the Burlington International Airport. All rooms are tastefully appointed and offer modern features such as wireless Internet access. A restaurant and pub are on site. **www.sheratonburlington.com**

BURLINGTON Hilton Hotel ♿ 🍴 ❄ 🏋 🏊 [P] $$$$

60 Battery St., 05401 ***Tel*** *(802) 658-6500, (800) 9HILTON* ***Fax*** *(802) 658-4659* ***Rooms*** *258*

Location is everything for Burlington's most upscale hotel, which sits between the heart of downtown and the shore of Lake Champlain. The best rooms have stunning views of the lake with the Adirondack Mountains rising behind. It's set up for business travelers, with a good business center and work desks in rooms. **www.hilton.com/burlington**

CHITTENDEN Mountain Top Inn ♿ 🍴 🏋 [P] $$$$

195 Mountain Top Rd., 05737 ***Tel*** *(802) 483-2311 or (800) 445-2100* ***Rooms*** *44*

With 31 rooms in the lodge, 8 chalets, and 5 pet-friendly rustic cabins, Mountain Top has lodging for all tastes. The property's lake has boating and swimming in summer, skating in winter. There is an extensive trail system for hiking and cross-country skiing. The resort fee covers breakfast, trail passes, and most activities. **www.mountaintopinn.com**

CRAFTSBURY COMMON The Inn on the Common 🍴 ❄ [P] $$$

1162 North Craftsbury Rd., 05827 ***Tel*** *(802) 586-9619, (800) 521-2233* ***Fax*** *(802) 586-2249* ***Rooms*** *16*

Three restored Federal homes in an idyllic village setting feature elegantly decorated rooms, beautiful views, and outstanding cuisine. Right on the doorstep is some of Vermont's best cross-country skiing. Some rooms have a fireplace or wood-burning stove. Country breakfast included. Closed Nov, mid-Mar–Apr. **www.innonthecommon.com**

EAST BURKE The Inn at Mountain View Farm 🍴 [P] $$$

Darling Hill Rd., 05832 ***Tel*** *(802) 626-9924, (800) 572-4509* ***Rooms*** *14*

This 1883 farm on 440 acres (178 ha) features lodging in the farmhouse and an old creamery with its butter churn cupola. The farm is also an animal sanctuary with docile miniature donkeys, Holstein steers, and sheep. The property is part of a network of hiking, mountain biking, and ski trails. Open May–Oct. **www.innmtnview.com**

EAST MIDDLEBURY Waybury Inn 🍴 [P] $$

457 East Main St., 05740 ***Tel*** *(802) 388-4015, (800) 348-1810* ***Fax*** *(802) 388-1248* ***Rooms*** *15*

The line of rocking chairs on the front porch suggests the pace of life at this inn, where Robert Frost used to dine. The inn dates from 1810, but rooms are all updated with private baths and comfortable country furniture. The excellent restaurant is a major draw of the region. It's popular for weddings and breakfast is included. **www.wayburyinn.com**

GRAFTON The Old Tavern at Grafton 🍴 [P] $$$

Route 35, 05146 ***Tel*** *(800) 843-1801* ***Fax*** *(802) 843-2245* ***Rooms*** *45*

Built in 1801 as a stagecoach stop, the Old Tavern has 11 rooms in the main building and others in charming guest houses. Truly a place of peace and quiet, there are no TVs or phones in the rooms and only one suite is air-conditioned. Operated by same foundation as Grafton Cheese Company, the inn has a top-notch restaurant. **www.old-tavern.com**

KILLINGTON The Inn at Long Trail 🍴 [P] $$

709 Route 4 (Sherburne Pass), 05751 ***Tel*** *(802) 775-7181, (800) 325-2540* ***Fax*** *(802) 747-7034* ***Rooms*** *19*

This rustic lodge at the intersection of the Appalachian and Long trails in heart of the Green Mountains is legendary among hikers and skiers. The Irish pub on the premises serves hearty pub food. A separate building holds modern suites with gas fireplaces. Breakfast included. Closed Apr–mid-Jun. **www.innatlongtrail.com**

KILLINGTON Mountain Meadows Lodge
285 Thundering Brook Rd., 05751 **Tel** *(802) 775-1010, (800) 370-4567* **Rooms** *17*

Vermont's only mountain lodge set both on a glacial lake and on the Appalachian Trail, the lodge is a perfect base for outdoors enthusiasts in almost every season. Excellent fishing and boating in warm weather, top skiing in winter. Popular for family reunions and weddings. **www.mountainmeadowslodge.com**

MANCHESTER The Equinox Resort
3567 Main St. (Rte. 7A), 05254 **Tel** *(802) 362-4700, (800) 362-4747* **Fax** *(802) 362-4861* **Rooms** *183*

A historic 18th-century resort with stunning public spaces and spacious rooms. Situated between the Green and Taconic mountains, the vast property has sweeping views. Outdoor activities (most with extra charge) include boating, golf, falconry, flyfishing, shooting, as well as nearby snowmobiling and skiing. **www.equinoxresort.com**

MIDDLEBURY Swift House Inn
25 Stewart Lane, 05753 **Tel** *(802) 388-9925, (866) 388-9925* **Fax** *(802) 388-9927* **Rooms** *20*

Rooms are in a Federal-era main house, modernized carriage house, and small gate house at the foot of the property on a hill above the picturesque college town. Décor blends Colonial, Federal, and Victorian eras with comfortable effect. Some rooms have fireplaces and whirlpool tubs. Breakfast included. **www.swifthouseinn.com**

MIDDLEBURY The Middlebury Inn
14 Court House Sq., 05753 **Tel** *(802) 388-4961, (800) 842-4666* **Fax** *(802) 388-4563* **Rooms** *75*

The town's principal hostelry since 1827, this historic inn offers well-equipped rooms furnished in reproduction antiques of the Federal style. Most rooms have private baths and some have whirlpool tubs. Some two-room suites with shared bath are geared toward families. Some rooms are in the adjacent mansion. **www.middleburyinn.com**

MONTPELIER Economy Inn
101 Northfield St., 05602 **Tel** *(802) 223-5258* **Fax** *(802) 223-0716* **Rooms** *42*

Clean and basic motel located conveniently off exit 8 of I-89, less than 1 mile (1.6 km) from the bustling downtown of the nation's smallest state capital. Staff are friendly, and the good rate and location make the Economy Inn a good base for exploring central and northeast Vermont.

MONTPELIER The Inn at Montpelier
147 Main St., 05602 **Tel** *(802) 223-2727* **Fax** *(802) 223-0722* **Rooms** *27*

Two beautifully renovated Federal-era houses comprise the capital city's most stately lodgings. A large verandah – perfect for summer sitting and rocking – wraps around the brick Lamb-Langdon House. In winter, warm up in front of one of the wood-burning fires after a day out. Generous breakfast included. **www.innatmontpelier.com**

NORTH HERO North Hero House Inn & Restaurant
Route 2, 05474 **Tel** *(802) 372-4732, (888) 525-3644* **Fax** *(802) 372-3218* **Rooms** *26*

Situated on the Lake Champlain Islands north of Burlington, this inn was constructed in 1891, when guests arrived by steamship. Rooms are spread across four buildings, three directly on Lake Champlain, the fourth across the road. The main house has a library, pub, and restaurant. Closed Dec–Apr. **www.northherohouse.com**

RICHMOND The Richmond Victorian Inn
191 East Main St., 05477 **Tel** *(802) 434-4410, (888) 242-3362* **Fax** *(802) 434-4411* **Rooms** *5*

Located in the foothills of the Green Mountains just 12 miles (19.5 km) east of Lake Champlain, this modestly priced inn's guest rooms are furnished in a country Victorian style with antiques, quilts, and other homey touches. No air conditioning. TV in suite and sitting room only. Children 6 and older welcome. **www.richmondvictorianinn.com**

SHELBURNE Inn at Shelburne Farms
1611 Harbor Rd., 05482 **Tel** *(802) 985-8498* **Rooms** *24*

This late 19th-century mansion overlooking Lake Champlain is the centerpiece of a historic farm that makes cheese and offers garden and property tours. The grounds were designed by Frederick Law Olmsted, the father of US landscape architecture, while the English gardens were created by the owners. **www.shelburnefarms.org**

SOUTH WOODSTOCK Kedron Valley Inn
Route 106, 05071 **Tel** *(802) 457-1473, (800) 836-1193* **Fax** *(802) 457-4469* **Rooms** *37*

This mid-19th century inn and tavern is so picturesque that it often appears on calendars or as the set for TV commercials. Country décor throughout and most rooms have fireplaces or wood-burning stoves. It is very popular with riders at the nearby stables. Breakfast included. **www.kedronvalleyinn.com**

ST. JOHNSBURY Comfort Inn and Suites
703 Route 5 South, 05819 **Tel** *(802) 748-1500, (800) 228-3362* **Fax** *(802) 728-1243* **Rooms** *92*

This surprisingly deluxe hotel for the Comfort Inn chain makes a comfortable, even elegant base for exploring the Northeast Kingdom. The indoor heated pool and sauna are popular all year. Some "lifestyle" suites feature a king-size bed, and executive desk and chair. **www.vtcomfortinnsuites.com**

STOWE Alpenrose Motel
2619 Mountain Rd., 05672 **Tel** *(802) 253-7277, (802) 253-4707* **Rooms** *8*

Bargain lodging doesn't get much better than the Alpenrose, where spacious rooms are augmented, in most cases, by at least a rudimentary kitchen. Some two-room units sleep up to five people. Located halfway between village and ski slope, Alpenrose has outdoor storage lockers for skis and snowboards. **www.gostowe.com/alpenrose**

STOWE Green Mountain Inn ❄ 🍴 👪 🏋 [P] $$$

18 Main St., 05672 ***Tel*** *(802) 253-7301, (800) 253-7302* ***Fax*** *(802) 253-5096* ***Rooms*** *107*

This grand old brick hotel in early 20th-century Colonial Revival style has long served as civic center of this mountain community. The original hotel's cozy rooms are augmented by townhouses and suites in the attached modern buildings right in heart of the village. A health club offers massage services as well as sauna. **www.greenmountaininn.com**

STOWE Trapp Family Lodge ❄ 🍴 🏊 👪 🏋 [P] $$$$

700 Trapp Hill Rd., 05672 ***Tel*** *(802) 253-8511, (800) 826-7000* ***Fax*** *(802) 253-5740* ***Rooms*** *96*

This is the world-famous resort of the family that inspired *The Sound of Music*. Set within massive grounds, the 96-room property features a large Austrian-style main lodge, 100 guest houses, nightly entertainment, a range of recreational activities, and exquisite cuisine. Some rooms are air-conditioned. **www.trappfamily.com**

WATERBURY Best Western Waterbury-Stowe 🏊 🏋 [P] $$$

45 Blush Hill Rd., 05676 ***Tel*** *(802) 244-7822, (800) 621-7822* ***Fax*** *(802) 244-6395* ***Rooms*** *84*

Located just off extremely scenic Route 100, this comfortable modern motel is close to Ben & Jerry's Ice Cream Factory *(see p236)* and about 10 miles (16 km) from Stowe's ski slopes. Facilities include a glassed-in pool, sauna, hot tub and state-of-the-art fitness center as well as a playground for kids. Continental breakfast provided. **www.bestwestern.com**

WELLS RIVER Whipple Tree Bed & Breakfast [P] $$

487 Stevens Place, 05081 ***Tel*** *(802) 429-2076, (800) 466-4097* ***Fax*** *(802) 429-2858* ***Rooms*** *6*

This chalet-style lodge serves as a rustic getaway in the Green Mountains. The area offers spectacular cross-country skiing and sledding in winter, and hiking, fishing, and hot-air ballooning in summer. The outdoor hot tub appeals to stargazers. Breakfast included. **www.whipple-tree.com**

WESTON Inn at Weston 🍴 [P] $$$$

Route 100, 05161 ***Tel*** *(802) 824-6789* ***Fax*** *(802) 824-3073* ***Rooms*** *13*

A truly a romantic hideaway in a charming village surrounded by ski mountains. The inn often hosts small weddings and civil unions and has and outstanding restaurant. Orchids from innkeeper's greenhouse enhance the décor. The least expensive rooms are in the former farmhouse. **www.innweston.com**

WOODSTOCK Jackson House Inn 🍴 [P] $$$

114-3 Senior Lane, 05091 ***Tel*** *(802) 457-2065, (800) 448-1890* ***Fax*** *(802) 457-9290* ***Rooms*** *15*

The six suites and nine rooms of this 1890 Victorian mansion are all air-conditioned and decorated in French Provincial, Vermont country, or Victorian styles. Grounds are lush and expertly landscaped, and the restaurant and wine list are at the highest level. The inn is a short drive from downtown Woodstock. Breakfast included. **www.jacksonhouse.com**

WOODSTOCK The Woodstocker Inn Bed & Breakfast 🍴 [P] $$$$

61 River St., 05091 ***Tel*** *(802) 457-3896, (866) 662-1439* ***Fax*** *(802) 457-3897* ***Rooms*** *9*

Situated at the foot of Mount Tom *(see p208)*, this B&B uses organic and energy-efficient products to maintain its "green" status. A short walk over a covered bridge leads to the town's shops and eateries. The inn's gourmet breakfasts and plush robes enhance its welcoming atmosphere. **www.woodstockervt.com**

NEW HAMPSHIRE

ALBANY Darby Field Inn & Restaurant 🍴 🏊 [P] $$$

185 Chase Hill, 03818 ***Tel*** *(603) 447-2181, (800) 426-4147* ***Fax*** *(603) 447-5726* ***Rooms*** *14*

Located just a few hundred yards off the east end of the Kancamagus Highway, this modernized 1826 inn has spectacular fall foliage as well as excellent private trails for cross-country skiing. Adjacent to White Mountain National Forest hiking trails and just a 10-minute drive from the shopping bustle of North Conway. **www.darbyfield.com**

ALTON BAY Bay Side Inn on Lake Winnipesaukee [P] $$

Route 11D, 03810 ***Tel*** *(603) 875-5005* ***Rooms*** *23*

Open May to October, this family-operated inn on Lake Winnipesaukee offers a lakeside sundeck and a breathtaking view of the White Mountains. Many rooms have their own patios or decks overlooking the lake and there are some self-catering units. Powerboat, jet ski, sailboat, and kayak rentals are available. **www.bayside-inn.com**

BETHLEHEM Adair Country Inn 🍴 [P] $$$$

80 Guider Lane, 03574 ***Tel*** *(603) 444-2600, (888) 444-2600* ***Fax*** *(603) 444-4823* ***Rooms*** *9*

Built as a country retreat for a wealthy legal clan in 1927, Adair was landscaped by the Olmsted Brothers. Converted to a B&B in 1991, it remains a tranquil, woody hideaway in the White Mountains in an area well-known for its healthy air. The restaurant is closed during April and November. **www.adairinn.com**

BRETTON WOODS The Mount Washington Hotel & Resort ❄ 🍴 🏊 🏋 [P] $$$$$

Route 302, 03585 ***Tel*** *(603) 278-1000, (800) 314-1752* ***Fax*** *(603) 278-8838* ***Rooms*** *200*

Since 1902, this elegant hotel *(see p267)* has offered high-quality service in a beautiful natural setting. The mountain air keeps the rooms comfortable during the summer season. Rates include dinner at any of the resort's five restaurants and nightly entertainment. **www.mtwashington.com**

BRIDGEWATER Inn on Newfound Lake ⏹⏹ $$

*1030 Mayhew Turnpike, 03222 **Tel** (603) 744-9111, (800) 745-7990 **Fax** (603) 744-3894 **Rooms** 28*

This classic country stagecoach inn on the Boston-Montreal route has welcomed guests since 1840. The inn is now an upscale Victorian showpiece with one of the best restaurants and liveliest lounges for many miles around. The large front porch is lined with rocking chairs. **www.newfoundlake.com**

CONCORD The Centennial Inn ⏹⏹⏹ $$

*96 Pleasant St., 03301 **Tel** (603) 227-9000, (800) 360-4839 **Fax** (603) 225-5031 **Rooms** 32*

Housed in a restored 1892 Victorian brick mansion, this centrally located inn provides rooms and suites handsomely furnished in antiques and quality reproductions. Six of the suites occupy the inn's striking twin turrets. High-speed wireless Internet access throughout and there's a popular bar and bistro. **www.thecentennialinn.com**

DIXVILLE NOTCH The Balsams Grand Resort Hotel ⏹⏹⏹⏹⏹ $$$$

*1000 Cold Spring Rd., 03576 **Tel** (603) 255-3400, (877) 225-7267 **Rooms** 200*

This all-seasons resort on 15,000 acres (6,070 ha) of wilderness features some of best summer golf and winter alpine skiing in New England. It is also where the first votes in each presidential election are counted. Rates cover all meals and activities, including tennis, skating, and hiking trails but equipment rental is extra. **www.thebalsams.com**

EXETER The Inn and Conference Center of Exeter ⏹⏹⏹ $$$

*90 Front St., 03833 **Tel** (603) 772-5901, (800) 782-8444 **Fax** (603) 778-8757 **Rooms** 49*

The Georgian-style inn was built in 1932 next to Phillips Exeter, one of the nation's premier private secondary schools. It has a good restaurant and rooms feature antique and reproduction furnishings. It is popular for small conferences and business or office retreats. **www.theexeterinn.com**

FRANCONIA The Franconia Inn ⏹⏹⏹ $$$

*1300 Easton Rd., 03580 **Tel** (603) 823-5542 **Fax** (603) 823-8078 **Rooms** 34*

A cozy inn built in 1935 with striking views of the White Mountains rising directly behind the building. Outdoor enthusiasts will find a variety of sports activities in almost all seasons, from rock-climbing and trail hiking to skiing and snowshoeing. There's no air-conditioning, but it rarely gets hot. Closed Apr–mid-May. **www.franconiainn.com**

FRANCONIA Lovett's Inn ⏹⏹⏹⏹ $$$

*1474 Profile Rd., 03580 **Tel** (603) 823-7761, (800) 356-3802 **Fax** (603) 823-8802 **Rooms** 19*

For 70 years the distinctive hospitality of this former country estate has attracted such guests as movie star Bette Davis and members of the Kennedy clan. Some rooms have television and most have air-conditioning. Closed April. The inn's dining room is a special draw, featuring well-crafted cuisine and a good wine list. **www.lovettsinn.com**

GLEN Bernerhof Inn ⏹⏹ $$

*Route 302, 03838 **Tel** (603) 383-9132, (800) 548-8007 **Fax** (603) 383-0809 **Rooms** 9*

The once-small rooms of this former stagecoach inn have been combined and reconfigured to make spacious suites, most with a dual whirlpool tubs and/or saunas for easing aching muscles after a day of skiing or climbing in the Presidential mountains. Reserve ahead for dinner at the outstanding restaurant. **bernerhofinn.com**

HAMPTON Ashworth by the Sea ⏹⏹⏹⏹ $$$

*295 Ocean Blvd., 03842 **Tel** (603) 926-6762, (800) 345-6736 **Fax** (603) 926-2002 **Rooms** 105*

Possibly the classiest grande-dame, this year-round beachfront hotel on New Hampshire's most popular beach exudes an air of old-fashioned elegance. Most of the spacious rooms have ocean views, and the white-linen dining room is a welcome break from the sand-in-your-shoes casual dining found in most eateries in town. **www.ashworthhotel.com**

HANOVER Chieftain Motor Inn ⏹ $$

*Route 10 North, 03755 **Tel** (603) 643-2550 **Fax** (603) 643-5265 **Rooms** 22*

This two-story motel north of Dartmouth College has three room grades, depending on the view and furnishings. The riverfront setting is enhanced in deluxe rooms, but even economy guests get complimentary canoes, heated pool, and barbecue area, and share the long stretch of riverbank. Family rooms sleep up to six. **www.chieftaininn.com**

HANOVER Hanover Inn ⏹⏹⏹ $$$$

*2 South Main St., 03755 **Tel** (603) 643-4300, (800) 443-7024 **Fax** (603) 643-4433 **Rooms** 113*

Attentive service and excellent dining mark this elegant inn, which has been operating for more than 200 years. All guest rooms are decorated in Colonial-style. The hotel functions as a lodging adjunct for scholars, dignitaries, and well-heeled parents visiting Dartmouth College, and it anchors one side of the Dartmouth Green. **www.hanoverinn.com**

KEENE Carriage Barn Bed and Breakfast ⏹ $

*358 Main St., 03431 **Tel** (603) 357-3812 **Rooms** 4*

Cheerfully decorated with local country antiques, this former carriage house of a mid-19th-century village home offers four rooms (one is twin-bedded). The tranquil setting is in the heart of town across the street from the campus of Keene State College. Children over 5 welcome. **www.carriagebarn.com**

KEENE E.F. Lane Hotel ⏹⏹⏹⏹ $$$

*30 Main St., 03431 **Tel** (603) 357-7070, (888) 300-5056 **Fax** (603) 357-7075 **Rooms** 40*

A luxury hotel carved out of the city's erstwhile upscale department store building, the E.F. Lane offers urban sophistication and ambience in an essentially rural college town. Reproduction furnishings give the air of an older property, but high-speed Internet suggests otherwise. Casual dining at Chase Tavern. **www.eflane.com**

MANCHESTER The Highlander Inn   🖥 🍽 ♨ 🅿 $$

2 Highlander Way, 03103 **Tel** *(603) 625-6426, (800) 548-9248* **Fax** *(603) 625-6466* **Rooms** *87*

This former boarding house and 1930s inn were completely transformed into a modern conference hotel aimed at business travelers. The Highlander is also a popular venue for weddings and graduation events. The location is convenient to Manchester airport. **www.highlanderinn.com**

MEREDITH Meredith Inn B&B   🅿 $$

2 Wauwekan St., 03253 **Tel** *(603) 279-0000* **Fax** *(603) 279-4017* **Rooms** *8*

This restored Victorian home has been updated with modern amenities. It is handy to activities on Lake Winnipesaukee, and within walking distance to the beach on Lake Wauwekan. In another direction lie the artisans' shops and restaurants of downtown Meredith. Most rooms have air conditioning. Reduced rates Nov–Apr. **www.meredithinn.com**

NEW CASTLE Wentworth By The Sea   🖥 🍽 ♨ 🍽 🅿 $$$$$

588 Wentworth Rd., 03854 **Tel** *(603) 422-7322, (866) 240-6313* **Fax** *(603) 422-7329* **Rooms** *161*

Many rooms at this historic grand hotel look out on the Atlantic Ocean at the mouth of Portsmouth harbor. A landmark when the Treaty of Portsmouth was signed here in 1905 to end the Russo-Japanese war, the hotel was resurrected a century later as a luxury property operated by Marriott. **www.wentworth.com**

NEW LONDON The New London Inn   🍽 🅿 $$$

353 Main St., 03257 **Tel** *(603) 526-2791, (800) 526-2791* **Fax** *(603) 526-2749* **Rooms** *24*

The owners transformed this Federal-style 1792 inn into a chic retreat with remodeled, boldly artistic rooms. They wisely maintained the country hotel look in the public areas, including the double-decker long porch furnished with wicker chairs and rockers. Excellent restaurant serves imaginative New American cuisine. **www.newlondoninn.net**

NORTH CONWAY Junge's Motel   ♨ 🧍 🅿 $

1858 White Mountain Hwy., 03860 **Tel** *(603) 356-2886* **Rooms** *28*

Budget-priced resort motel bordering the Saco River about 1.5 miles (2.4km) south of North Conway village and within walking distance of factory outlet shopping as well as the brewpubs and restaurants of this quintessential ski town. Oriented for family stays, with playground equipment and lawn games. **www.jungesmotel.com**

PORTSMOUTH The Inn at Christian Shore   🅿 $$

335 Maplewood Ave., 03801 **Tel** *(603) 431-6770* **Fax** *(603) 373-8421* **Rooms** *5*

This well-preserved early Federal era home is furnished with a mix of antiques, African art, and contemporary paintings that accord with the taste of the Argentine owner. The neighborhood is a close walk to the historic city center and waterfront. Gourmet breakfasts included. No children allowed. **www.innatchristianshore.com**

PORTSMOUTH Sheraton Harborside Portsmouth   🖥 🍽 ♨ 🍽 🅿 $$$$

250 Market St., 03801 **Tel** *(603) 431-2300, (888) 627-7138* **Fax** *(603) 433-5649* **Rooms** *219*

Located just two blocks from Market Square and adjacent to the docks for whale watching and harbor cruises, this Sheraton is a modern business hotel equally suited for the leisure traveler. A Redwood sauna, extensive fitness room and large pool set it apart from other Portsmouth lodgings. **www.sheratonportsmouth.com**

ROCHESTER The Governor's Inn   🍽 🅿 $

78 Wakefield St., 03867 **Tel** *(603) 332-0107* **Fax** *(603) 335-1984* **Rooms** *20*

Three Georgian-Colonial style brick homes built in the 1920s have been transformed into an inn. Lace woodwork, French-pane windows, and marble fireplaces grace the interior. During summer, the courtyard serves as extra dining area and is the setting for pop music concerts. Continental breakfast included. **www.governorsinn.com**

SUGAR HILL Sunset Hill House   🖥 🍽 ♨ 🧍 🅿 $$$$

231 Sunset Hill Rd., 03586 **Tel** *(603) 823-5522, (800) 786-4455* **Fax** *(603) 823-5738* **Rooms** *29*

Set at the north end of Franconia Notch, Sunset Hill House has splendid views of the tallest White Mountains peaks. The roads surrounding this restored 19th-century inn (with some rooms in an adjoining farmhouse) are lined with sugar maples that blaze with color in the fall. Golf course and ski runs nearby. **www.sunsethillhouse.com**

TROY The Inn at East Hill Farm   🍽 ♨ 🅿 $$$

460 Monadnock St., 03465 **Tel** *(603) 242-6495, (800) 242-6495* **Fax** *(603) 242-7709* **Rooms** *30*

A large resort with farm activities for children and outdoor fun for adults, including horseback riding, water skiing, and cross-country skiing. Rates quoted are per night but weekly rates are much lower. All meals are included and some rooms have TV and air conditioning. **www.east-hill-farm.com**

WALPOLE Inn at Valley Farms   🅿 $$$

633 Wentworth Rd., 03608 **Tel** *(603) 756-2855, (877) 327-2855* **Fax** *(603) 756-2865* **Rooms** *5*

There are two rooms and one suite in this 1774 farmhouse that welcomes children over the age of 12. Two cottages and another farmhouse next door provide good lodgings for families. The property also operates as an organic farm. An apple orchard and Walpole village are located nearby. **www.innatvalleyfarms.com**

WEIRS BEACH Lake Winnipesaukee Motel   ♨ 🅿 $

350 Daniel Webster Highway, 03247 **Tel** *(603) 366-5502* **Fax** *(603) 366-2388* **Rooms** *18*

This small motel in the heart of the Weirs Beach community takes pride in its warm hospitality, peaceful surroundings beneath a grove of tall trees, and more than 45 years of experience. A private, two-bedroom house is also available for larger groups. Open in February for ice-fishing and snowmobiling, then May–Oct. **www.lakewinnipesaukeemotel.com**

Key to Price Guide *see p306* **Key to Symbols** *see back cover flap*

WHITFIELD Mountain View Grand Resort & Spa

Mountain View Rd., 03598 **Tel** *(800) 438-3017* **Fax** *(603) 837-8884* **Rooms** *145*

Built in 1865 but extensively modernized since then, this hotel lives up to its name with stunning views of the white-capped Presidential range and the serrated ridge of the Kilkenny Range. The location is ideal for hikers as well as alpine skiers. On-site restaurants are more casual than others in the resort. **www.mountainviewgrand.com**

WOLFEBORO The Wolfeboro Inn

90 North Main St., 03894 **Tel** *(603) 569-3016, (800) 451-2389* **Fax** *(603) 569-5375* **Rooms** *44*

This historic inn on the waterfront of America's oldest summer resort has its own private beach on small lake that connects to Lake Winnipesaukee. Tastefully decorated rooms lean toward the country squire style. The inn offers the area's most ceremonial fine dining. **www.wolfeboroinn.com**

MAINE

BANGOR Fairfield Inn

300 Odlin Rd., 04401 **Tel** *(207) 990-0001, (800) 228-2800* **Fax** *(207) 990-0917* **Rooms** *153*

A modern, fully equipped hotel conveniently located less than 1 mile (1.6 km) from downtown Bangor. Continental breakfast, juice, and coffee is available and there is a choice of one king-size or two double beds. Amenities include cable TV with HBO, indoor pool, hot tub, sauna, and a fitness room. **www.marriott.com**

BAR HARBOR Atlantic Eyrie Lodge

6 Norman Rd. (off Highbrook Rd.), 04609 **Tel** *(207) 288-9786 or (800) HABA-VUE* **Rooms** *58*

Located on a high hill at the edge of town, this motel is a good base for Bar Harbor, a ten minute walk away. Rooms are modern and spacious and some have full kitchens. All have balconies overlooking the ocean. The property has a heated pool and benefits from a seasonal shuttle bus service to various destinations. **www.atlanticeyrielodge.com**

BAR HARBOR Mira Monte Inn and Suites

69 Mount Desert St., 04609 **Tel** *(207) 288-4263, (800) 553-5109* **Fax** *(207) 288-3115* **Rooms** *17*

Constructed in 1864, this is one of the few B&Bs in town owned by Bar Harbor natives. It features two formal gardens and an inviting wrap-around porch for rocking and reading. The center of town is a five-minute walk away from this residential neighborhood. All rooms have a fireplace and/or balcony. Closed Nov–Apr. **www.miramonte.com**

BETHEL Bethel Inn and Country Club

On the Common, 04217 **Tel** *(207) 824-2175, (800) 654-0125* **Fax** *(207) 824-2333* **Rooms** *150*

A premier Maine resort, with four colonial-style buildings, this property has its own championship golf course, golf school, and tennis courts. Summer rates include golf and dinner, except for town-house guests. Winter rates include cross-country trail fees. Located close to Sunday River Ski Resort. Air conditioning in some rooms. **www.bethelinn.com**

BOOTHBAY HARBOR Fisherman's Wharf Inn

Pier 6, 22 Commercial St., 04538 **Tel** *(207) 633-5090, (800) 628-6872* **Rooms** *54*

Set directly on the water in Boothbay Harbor, all of the inn's rooms have balconies overlooking the water. Shops, cruises, sailing expeditions, and fishing excursions are all within steps of the hotel. The inn's bar and restaurant are the de facto social center for the boating community. **www.fishermanswharfinn.com**

CAMDEN Camden Mainestay Inn

22 High St., 04843 **Tel** *(207) 236-9636* **Fax** *(207) 236-0621* **Rooms** *8*

This grand 1801 house, barn, and carriage house complex is one of oldest structures in Camden. Fireplaces grace the two parlors and many rooms have original wide pine plank floors. Eclectic country furnishings give the inn a homey atmosphere. Some rooms and first-floor sitting room have TV. Wireless Internet access. **www.camdenmainestay.com**

CAPE ELIZABETH Inn by the Sea

40 Bowery Beach Rd., 04107 **Tel** *(207) 799-3134, (800) 888-4287* **Fax** *(207) 799-4779* **Rooms** *57*

The modern hotel perches above Crescent Beach, Maine's top swimming beach. Many rooms and suites have ocean views or fireplaces. The inn is a short drive south of Portland and just north of Prout's Neck, made famous by painter Winslow Homer. Fine formal dining in the Seaglass Restaurant. Pet-friendly. **www.innbythesea.com**

CARIBOU Caribou Inn and Convention Center

19 Main St., 04736 **Tel** *(207) 498-3733, (800) 235-0466* **Fax** *(207) 498-3149* **Rooms** *73*

With low rates and a wide range of facilities and in-room amenities, this inn offers great value. The busiest season is January and February, when long-distance snowmobilers stop off on trails between Quebec and New Brunswick. The Greenhouse Restaurant is known for the best and cheapest breakfasts in the area. Pet-friendly. **www.caribouinn.com**

CARRABASSETT VALLEY Sugarloaf/USA Resort

Route 27, 04947 **Tel** *(207) 237-2000, (800) THE-LOAF* **Fax** *(207) 237-2718* **Rooms** *162*

One of New England's most renowned ski resorts *(see p295)* also features a picturesque Robert Trent Jones-designed golf course and mountain trails for summer activities. Guests may use the health club and, for an extra charge, take ski or snowboard lessons. There is a choice of casual slopeside inn, full-service hotel, or condo units. **www.sugarloaf.com**

CASTINE Castine Inn　　　　　　　　　　　　　　P　　　$$$
41 Main St., 04421 **Tel** *(207) 326-4365* **Fax** *(207) 326-4570* **Rooms** *17*

Classic inn trimmed with a wrap-around porch providing comfortable, simple rooms on second and third floors. It's located just one block from a superb harbor that serves as the home port for the Maine Maritime Academy and scores of sailing and pleasure craft. Dining room serves a big breakfast. Closed mid-Oct–Apr. **www.castineinn.com**

EAST MACHIAS Riverside Inn and Restaurant　　　　　P　　　$$
Route 1, 04630 **Tel** *(207) 255-4134, (888) 255-4344* **Fax** *(207) 235-0577* **Rooms** *6*

On the East Machias River, this serene getaway began life as the home of two sea captains in the 19th and early 20th centuries. Rooms are decorated with antiques and the terraced perennial garden is a great place for evening strolls, as are the banks of the river. Limited winter restaurant hours. **www.riversideinn-maine.com**

FREEPORT Harraseeket Inn　　　　　　　　　　🛏 🍴 P　　$$$
162 Main St., 04032 **Tel** *(207) 865-9377, (800) 342-6423* **Fax** *(207) 865-1684* **Rooms** *84*

Located just two blocks north of the world-famous L.L. Bean outlet, in the heart of Freeport, the Harraseeket Inn povides determined shoppers with a high-end retreat. Guests enjoy the property's 23 fireplaces, multiple Jacuzzis and indoor pool, and a pair of acclaimed restaurants. **www.harraseeketinn.com**

FRYEBURG Oxford House Inn　　　　　　　　　　　🍴 P　　$$$
548 Main St., 04037 **Tel** *(207) 935-3442, (800) 261-7206* **Fax** *(207) 935-7046* **Rooms** *4*

A charming bed-and-breakfast located in the activity-filled White Mountains and Western Lakes region of Maine. It has four beautifully decorated rooms in a 1913 Mission-style residence designed by John Calvin Stevens. The restaurant features fresh Maine fish and produce prepared in an impressive New American style. **www.oxfordhouseinn.com**

GREENVILLE Kineo View Motor Lodge　　　　　　　　P　　　$
Route 15, 04441 **Tel** *(207) 695-4470, (800) 659-9439* **Rooms** *27*

This modest family-run three-story motel sits at top of long hill 3 miles (4.8 km) south of Moosehead Lake with views so spectacular that travelers often pull in just to take a picture. Rates include continental breakfast in summer and fall only. All rooms have balconies and trails crisscross the extensive property. **www.kineoview.com**

GREENVILLE Greenville Inn　　　　　　　　　　　🍴 P　　$$$
40 Norris St., 04441 **Tel** *(207) 695-2206, (888) 695-6000* **Fax** *(207) 695-2206* **Rooms** *14*

Along with the four rooms in the main building, this beautifully appointed Victorian inn has six cottages, all with porches or decks. Children over seven are welcome. The seasonal restaurant is noted for New American fare featuring fresh, organic and locally grown meats, fish, and produce. **www.greenvilleinn.com**

KENNEBUNKPORT Captain Jefferd's Inn　　　　　　🛏 P　　$$$$
5 Pearl St., 04046 **Tel** *(207) 967-2311, (800) 839-6844* **Rooms** *15*

This sea captain's mansion, built in 1804, retains its antique charm and has beautifully landscaped gardens. There is also a wood-burning fireplace in the living room and some rooms have gas fireplaces. Ten rooms are in main inn, five more in the carriage house. It's conveniently located, one block from the old Town Green. **www.captainjefferdsinn.com**

KENNEBUNKPORT The Colony Hotel　　　　　　🛏 🍴 🛏 P　$$$$
140 Ocean Ave., 04046 **Tel** *(207) 967-3331, (800) 552-2363* **Fax** *(207) 967-8738* **Rooms** *123*

A short walk from Kennebunkport, the majestic Colony Hotel is perched overlooking the ocean. This environmentally responsible resort offers a heated saltwater pool, private surf beach, and extensive gardens. The main building has no air conditioning and TV is limited to the common area and bar. Closed late Oct–mid-May. **www.thecolonyhotel.com**

KENNEBUNKPORT Old Fort Inn Bed and Breakfast　　🛏 P　$$$$
Old Fort Ave., 04046 **Tel** *(207) 967-5353, (800) 828-3678* **Fax** *(207) 967-4547* **Rooms** *16*

Only one block from the Atlantic Ocean and Kennebunkport's beaches, the Old Fort Inn enjoys an ideal location for those in search of a calming getaway. Downtown Kennebunkport's numerous shops and restaurants are nearby. Each guest room is filled with elegant, stately antiques and there's a tennis court and heated pool. **www.oldfortinn.com**

LINCOLNVILLE BEACH Spouter Inn　　　　　　　　　P　　　$$
2506 Rte. 1, 04849 **Tel** *(207) 789-5171, (800) 387-5171* **Rooms** *7*

This appealing blend of Maine farmhouse and nautical inn sits directly across the street from Lincolnville Beach, the Isleboro ferry dock, and an iconic lobster shack. The charming Victorian-style rooms feature all kinds of modern amenities. Front-porch rockers and a lawn hammock are conducive to seaside indolence. **www.spouterinn.com**

LUBEC Home Port Inn　　　　　　　　　　　　　　🍴 P　　　$
45 Main St., 04652 **Tel** *(207) 733-2077, (800) 457-2077* **Rooms** *7*

Constructed in 1880 as a sea captain's home, this residence on a quiet, tree-lined street became a B&B inn in 1982. Flanked by Cobscook Bay and the Bay of Fundy, the village is the easternmost spot in the US. The inn's restaurant is among the most ambitious in area, with outstanding local seafood and local berries. **www.homeportinn.com**

MILLINOCKET Best Value Heritage Motor Inn　　　🛏 📺 P　　$
935 Central St., 04462 **Tel** *(207) 723-9777, (866) 633-9777* **Fax** *(207) 723-9777* **Rooms** *48*

The only nationally affiliated lodging in the area near Mount Katahdin, this inn makes a good base for back-country hiking and canoeing expeditions. The property also connects to most cross-country and snowmobile trails heading into northern Maine and adjacent parts of Quebec. Indoor pool and hot tubs available. **www.heritageinnmaine.com**

Key to Price Guide *see p306* **Key to Symbols** *see back cover flap*

MONHEGAN ISLAND The Island Inn ⬛ P $$$$

Monhegan Harbor, 04852 Tel (207) 596-0371 Fax (207) 594-5517 Rooms 34

Built in 1816 and expanded in 1907 and 1910, this steamship of an inn perches on a bluff above the harbor. The adjacent ocean cools the air and, although there is no heating, the public room fireplaces and bedroom duvets take off the chill. Some rooms share baths. Closed early Oct–late May. **www.islandinnmonhegan.com**

NEW HARBOR Hotel Pemaquid 🗒 $

3098 Bristol Rd., 04554 Tel (207) 677-2312 Rooms 30

A classic Maine inn, decorated with antiques, this former farmhouse first welcomed guests in 1888. It's a short walk from the coast and near the Pemaquid Point lighthouse, although the inn itself does not have an ocean view. Some rooms have a shared bath. No air conditioning. Closed mid-Oct–mid-May. **www.hotelpemaquid.com**

NEWCASTLE Newcastle Inn ⬛ ≋ P $$$

River Rd., 04553 Tel (207) 563-5685, (800) 832-8669 Rooms 14

This country inn overlooking the Damariscotta River harbor is perfectly situated for exploring the peninsulas of midcoast Maine. Rooms are spread among the main inn, cottage, and former carriage house. The guests-only pub is a great spot for drinking and relaxing. **www.newcastleinn.com**

NEWRY Sunday River Inn ⬛ $

23 Skiway Rd., 04261 Tel (207) 824-2410 Fax (207) 824-3181 Rooms 20

A family-oriented inn located close to the downhill runs of the Sunday River ski resort. A cross-country ski center and skating and sliding areas are located at the inn. Both private and dorm-style rooms are available, but some share baths. No air conditioning. TV in common room only. Closed early Apr–late Nov. **www.sundayriverinn.com**

OGUNQUIT The Cliff House Resort & Spa ⬛ ⬛ ≋ ⬛ P $$$$

Shore Rd., 03907 Tel (207) 361-1000 Fax (207) 361-2122 Rooms 196

Iconic oceanside resort built in 1872 with a full floor devoted to recreation. All rooms have balconies. The resort also has a noted full-service spa. Cliff House trolley takes guests to spots of interest in the area in July and August, including Ogunquit's excellent swimming beaches. Closed mid-Dec–Mar. **www.cliffhousemaine.com**

PORTLAND Inn at St. John P $$

939 Congress, 04102 Tel (207) 773-6481, (800) 636-9127 Fax (207) 756-7629 Rooms 39

Built in 1897 to accommodate rail passengers, this venerable inn stands just minutes from Portland's Old Port, Waterfront, and Arts districts. Rooms are tastefully decorated, but some share baths. The telephone is free if calling locally. Inexpensive extended stays are available off-season. Dogs are welcomed. **www.innatstjohn.com**

PORTLAND Eastland Park Hotel ⬛ $$$

157 High St., 04101 Tel (207) 775-5411, (888) 671-8008 Fax (207) 755-2872 Rooms 202

Across the street from the Portland Museum of Art (*see p280*), and a short walk from the Old Port (*see pp282–3*), this hotel is a convenient base. Guest rooms have plush mattresses and Egyptian cotton sheets. The Top of the East rooftop lounge has city views, and the 157 Café & Bar serves all three meals. **www.eastlandparkhotel.com**

PORTLAND Portland Regency Hotel ⬛ ⬛ ⬛ P $$$$

20 Milk St., 04101 Tel (207) 774-4200, (800) 727-3436 Fax (207) 775-2150 Rooms 103

Situated in the heart of the Old Port (*see pp282–3*), this conversion of the city's former Armory is Portland's premiere full-service hotel. Colonial-style furnishings, flat-panel TVs, and wireless Internet access throughout. The fitness center is free for guests. A complimentary town car is available between hotel and transportation facilities. **www.theregency.com**

RANGELEY North Country Inn Bed and Breakfast P $

2541 Main St., 04970 Tel (207) 864-2440, (800) 295-4968 Rooms 4

This 19th century Colonial bed and breakfast has a huge porch that looks out onto Rangeley Lake and surrounding mountains. No air conditioning, as temperatures rarely top 75°F (24°C). It's a good base for the legendary trout and salmon fishing or for winter snowmobiling excursions. Children over six are welcome. **www.northcountrybb.com**

RANGELEY Rangeley Inn ⬛ P $

2443 Main St., 04970 Tel (207) 864-3341, (800) 666-3687 Fax (207) 864-3634 Rooms 51

Rooms are available in the Main Inn (a meticulously restored century-old country hotel), the Motor Lodge, as well as in two lakeside cabins. Located two blocks from the public beach for boating and swimming. It's also a popular winter destination for skiing at Saddleback. The restaurant serves both fine dining and tavern cuisine. **www.rangeleyinn.com**

ROCKLAND Limerock Inn P $$

96 Limerock St., 04841 Tel (207) 594-2257, (800) 546-3762 Rooms 8

This turreted Queen Anne-style mansion with a large porch and landscaped gardens sits on a quiet street in walking distance of the world-class Farnsworth Museum and downtown shopping and dining. Wireless Internet access throughout. Printer, scanner, and fax in communications office. **www.limerockinn.com**

TENANTS HARBOR East Wind Inn ⬛ P $$$

Mechanic St., 04860 Tel (207) 372-6366, (800) 241-8439 Fax (207) 372-6320 Rooms 22

With a perfect spot directly on a major lobster fishing harbor, East Wind sprawls across three buildings, though the original inn is the most charming. It's furnished with a mix of country furniture and local antiques. The restaurant specializes in seafood right off the boats anchored outside. Closed Nov–Apr. **www.eastwindinn.com**

WHERE TO EAT

To many outsiders, New England is synonymous with simple, hearty, somewhat boring fare. While it is true that a traditional meal of the past often consisted of cod or boiled beef and cabbage served with potatoes, the regional menu is substantially more varied and tempting. Local cheeses, fruits and vegetables from rural areas complement the exquisite seafood, often caught fresh the same day, that is found up and down the coast. In recent years, the New England dining experience has been expanded to include a host of ethnic

Sign for Primo *(see p355)* in Maine

flavors, thanks to a steady stream of immigrants into the large urban areas. Boston (Massachusetts), Portland (Maine), and Providence (Rhode Island) are the region's top dining destinations. Boston's restaurant scene is particularly vibrant. The city's top restaurants serve a medley of styles, such as French and Italian, often using other Mediterranean and Asian accents. Boston was once called "Bean Town" because of the popularity of its baked beans; now it has good Indian, Southeast Asian, Latin American, and Caribbean restaurants.

OPENING HOURS

Most restaurants serve breakfast from 6 or 7am until 11am or noon. Some establishments serve breakfast all day. The choice is varied, with some spots offering little more than a bagel and a coffee and others whipping up portions of eggs, bacon, and sausages hefty enough to keep you going almost all day.

Lunch can run anytime from 11:30am until 2:30pm, and is equally varied. In downtown areas, businesspeople can be seen gulping down a sandwich at the counter of a local deli or sitting down to enjoy a sumptuous restaurant meal. In many places, the lunch menu is the same as it is for dinner, with smaller portions and significantly lower prices.

Elegant dining room at Rialto, Cambridge *(see p338)*

Radio Room at the Good News Café *(see p348)* in Woodbury, Connecticut

Some restaurants close for a few hours between lunch and dinner, while smaller family-run places may stay open throughout the afternoon, making them a good bet for eating at more unusual times.

Traditionally, New Englanders tend to serve up large dinners. You can usually sit down between 5:30 and 10:30pm. Some Boston restaurants, notably those in Chinatown and Kenmore Square, stay open late, supported mostly by the ravenous crowds heading home from the dance clubs and bars.

As a general rule, urban areas will have a much higher percentage of dinner-only establishments, while finding a casual eating spot open after 3pm in the countryside can be challenging.

State and local laws vary on the hours during which alcohol may be served, but in most parts of New England bars begin to close at midnight, with a few staying open until 2am in Boston and Cambridge. Food service, even at bars, usually finishes by 10:30pm.

On Sundays, alcohol sales are generally prohibited before noon, although some Boston establishments, notably in the South End, are allowed to serve cocktails with their amazing Sunday brunches. Hotels are also exempt from the alcohol prohibition and often serve champagne cocktails with their Sunday brunches.

It is not uncommon for restaurants to close on Mondays, as well as during quiet afternoon periods. As always, you should check in advance.

Rustic charm of the Grist Mill Restaurant *(see p349)* in Killington, Vermont

RESERVATIONS

Finer restaurants often require a reservation, though in most cases (especially weeknights) these can be made at short notice. In rural areas and small cities, reservations are only an issue during peak season – July and August on the coast and the Berkshires, September and October in the mountains, and January and February in ski country.

PAYING AND TIPPING

Waiters are generally paid fairly low wages, meaning they earn the bulk of their income through tips. This means that all restaurants with table service expect some sort of gratuity at the end of the meal. Each state charges a different meal tax, but it is standard practice to leave between 15 and 20 percent of the pre-tax bill as the tip. If the service is good or bad, adjust the tip rate accordingly. If you are paying by credit card, you may include the tip in the charged amount on the space provided on the receipt. Some fast-food restaurants have optional tip-jars next to the cashier.

ALCOHOL AND SMOKING

The legal drinking age is 21, so underage travelers should be aware that they will be denied access to most bars. They will also not be allowed to order wine with dinner in restaurants. The majority of places are strict about this and will often require you to show photo-

graphic ID before you are served. Passports are generally the best form of identification, since many people are unfamiliar with driver's licenses from abroad.

The legal age to purchase cigarettes is 18; identification may be required. Smoking is banned in restaurants and bars throughout New England. However, it is permitted in Vermont bars with a cabaret (entertainment) license.

Bogart-themed Casablanca *(see p337)* in Cambridge, Massachusetts

DRESS CODES

New England is a relaxed place where people dress on the casual side when they are dining out. This is especially true along the coast, where the casual beach atmosphere carries over into restaurants. There, shorts and T-shirts are commonplace. However, some establishments do have strict dress codes. For the top dining rooms, a jacket and tie are required for gentlemen and the equivalent is expected for women. Formal evening wear is uncommon, but in some of the finest restaurants it will not appear out of place.

CHILDREN

Children are welcome in most mid-range restaurants, although restaurants in urban business areas are often less accustomed to them. Avoid restaurants that feature a large bar and young crowds, as they are less likely to permit under 21s on the premises.

DISABILITIES

Federal and state legislation has made most restaurants in New England at least partially accessible by wheelchair *(see pp142–9)*, and many more are accessible to people with other disabilities. Historic structures are sometimes exempted from the accessibility requirements. Entrances are generally ramped, doors may be fitted with an automatic opener, and rest rooms usually include the appropriate stalls and sinks.

NEW ENGLAND'S MAPLE SYRUP

During the spring thaw in late March and early April, New England farmers hammer spigots into the trunks of their sugar maple trees in order to collect the trees' clear, slightly sweet sap in buckets. Traditionally sap is then poured into vats back at the "sugarhouse" and boiled for hours. When most of the excess water has been evaporated, an amber-colored syrup is left – a highly concentrated, thoroughly delicious product that is distinctly New England. The finest quality syrup goes best on pancakes and waffles and over ice cream.

The Flavors of New England

The geography and history of New England have produced some fine and highly distinctive culinary traditions. The long coastline accounts for the region's abundance of superb seafood, while the ethnic make-up of the area has led to some gastronomic highlights. Native Americans enjoyed staples such as corn, maple syrup, and cranberries. Early settlers brought dishes from England and Ireland, including hearty stews (known as boiled dinners) and puddings that remain popular to this day. Thanks to several Italian communities, New England boasts some of the best and most authentic pizza in America, and recipes from Portuguese fishermen pepper many menus.

New England apples

Typical lobster dish served at a beachfront restaurant

GIFTS FROM THE SEA

Seafood is at the heart of New England cuisine. The cold waters along the coast yield a bounty of delicious fish such as scrod (young cod), haddock, and swordfish. Maine lobster is a coveted delicacy. Tanks of live lobsters are shipped to restaurants all around America, but nowhere are

they as succulent and sweet as they are in their home state. Lobster is at its best when eaten at one of the informal outdoor lobster pounds that are found all along the shoreline. Here, diners can choose their own freshly caught specimen from a tank and then sit back and enjoy the view, while it is being steamed or boiled. Lobster is usually served with melted butter in which to dip the meat, and cups of clear steaming seafood broth.

THE MIGHTY CLAM

No food is more ubiquitous in the region than clams. They are served in so many different ways: steamed, stuffed, baked, minced in fish cakes, or in the famous New England clam chowder. Fried clams, a dish said to have been invented in Essex, Massachusetts, are found on almost every seafood menu. The large hard-shelled quahog clam – a delicacy from Rhode Island – is used

Corn on the cob   Baked potato   Steamed clams   Melted butter   Boiled lobster

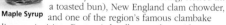

A typical New England clambake dinner

LOCAL DISHES AND SPECIALTIES

Like most Americans, New Englanders tend to have a light lunch and their main meal in the evening. Some New England dining experiences are too good to miss. Breakfasts are hearty, perhaps because of the cold winters, and at least one should include wild blueberry pancakes or muffins, and another an omelette made with tangy Vermont cheddar. Other musts are a lunch of lobster roll (chunks of sweet lobster meat in a mayonnaise-based dressing, stuffed into a toasted bun), New England clam chowder,

Maple Syrup

and one of the region's famous clambake dinners. A visit to Boston is hardly complete without sampling the superb local scrod and the rich classic cream pie, both found on menus all over the city along with Vermont's favorite ice cream, Ben and Jerry's.

Blueberry pancakes *Wild blueberries are stirred into batter to make a stack of these thick pancakes.*

Colorful display of pumpkins at a local farmers' market

to make stuffed clams known as "stuffies". There is also a distinctive Rhode Island-style chowder which is made with a clear broth, unlike the more usual chowder which is enriched with either milk or cream.

SWEET OFFERINGS

Sugar maples, which bring a dazzling display of color to the hillsides in fall, yield yet more riches in late winter, when the trees can be tapped and their sap boiled down to produce maple syrup. This is served on pancakes and made into sweets (candy) and sauces. New England also produces vast acres of wild blueberries, apples, and pumpkins that lend themselves to a variety of delectable desserts. Well into the 19th century,

molasses from the Caribbean was used as a sweetener, and is still added to many traditional sweet dishes, such as Indian pudding, a delicious slow-baked confection of spiced cornmeal, molasses, eggs, and milk.

Freshly picked wild blueberries, from the bumper summer harvest

DAIRY DELIGHTS

Vermont is home to over 1,500 dairy farms, where herds of well-fed cows produce the milk that goes into some of New England's famous dairy produce. This includes a selection of rich ice creams and the highly acclaimed Vermont cheddar cheese. Some of the best and most widely available cheeses are produced by the Cabot Creamery Cooperative, which is owned directly by a group of dairy farmers. The Vermont Cheese Council offers a map showing 39 dairies that make a variety of cheeses. Some welcome visitors.

WHAT TO DRINK

Poland Spring water This bottled water from Maine is the local favorite.

Frappé A New England-style milk shake made with ice cream and chocolate syrup.

Sakonnet Wines From Rhode Island, these are among the finest wines in the region.

Samuel Adams and Harpoon beers New England's best known brands are brewed in Boston.

Micro-brewery beers Some of the best are made by Thomas Hooker in Hartford, Connecticut; Smuttynose in Portsmouth, New Hampshire; and Magic Hat in Burlington, Vermont.

Baked scrod *Fillets of young cod (scrod) are rolled in breadcrumbs and baked, then served with tartare sauce.*

New England clam chowder *Fresh clams, either left whole or chopped, and chunks of potato fill this creamy soup.*

Boston cream pie *Layers of sponge cake, sandwiched with egg custard, are topped with chocolate icing.*

Choosing a Restaurant

Restaurants have been selected across a wide price range for their value, good food, atmosphere, and location. The chart below highlights some of the factors that may influence your choice of where to eat. Restaurants are listed by area, and within these areas by price. Map references for Boston restaurants refer to *pp122–7*.

PRICE CATEGORIES
The following price ranges are for a three-course meal for one, half a bottle of house wine and all unavoidable extra charges such as sales tax and service.
$ under $25
$$ $25–$40
$$$ $40–$50
$$$$ $50–$65
$$$$$ over $65

BOSTON

BACK BAY AND SOUTH END Mike's City Diner $
1714 Washington St., 02118 **Tel** *(617) 267-9393*   **Map** 3 C5

Show up early – very early. Mike's is open 6am–3pm every day, and there's usually a line out the door waiting for the luncheon specials rendered with just a little more care and finesse than you'll find on the Interstate. Political candidates always come by for a photo op during the quadrennial presidential nominating race. Breakfast and lunch daily.

BACK BAY AND SOUTH END Parish Cafe $
361 Boylston St., 02116 **Tel** *(617) 247-4777*   **Map** 3 B2

Think of this casual bar-restaurant as a sampler of Boston's most famous chefs. The owners convinced each to dream up a signature sandwich, and the results are most unusual. Landing one of the sidewalk tables can be hard, but it's more fun at the bar inside, watching the staff concoct their martinis. Lunch and dinner daily.

BACK BAY AND SOUTH END Steve's $
316 Newbury St., 02116 **Tel** *(617) 267-1817*   **Map** 3 A3

Possibly the cheapest place to eat well in Back Bay. Steve's is an old-fashioned Greek restaurant where spinach-feta pastries, eggplant dishes, and salads studded with dark olives are the standard fare. Steve's gets a deal on locally caught octopus, and aficionados rave about the lamb dishes. Breakfast, lunch, and dinner served daily.

BACK BAY AND SOUTH END Betty's Wok & Noodle $$
250 Huntington Ave., 02116 **Tel** *(617) 424-1950*   **Map** 3 A4

Offering tongue-in-cheek dining close to Huntington Theatre and Symphony Hall, Betty's is decorated in 1950s retro chic but the menu is all about modern choice. Pick a rice or noodle base, then a protein (shrimp, beef, chicken, tofu), then a sauce to create your own combo dish. Hefty American desserts round out the experience. Lunch and dinner daily.

BACK BAY AND SOUTH END Firefly American Bistro $$
130 Dartmouth St., 02116 **Tel** *(617) 262-4393*   **Map** 3 C3

Burgers, sandwiches, salads, and soups highlight the lunch menu at this fun spot across from Back Bay train station. Come night-fall, you might find such bistro fare as pan-seared tuna or grilled strip steak. The menu has many healthy options. Sunday brunch is very popular.

BACK BAY AND SOUTH END Orinoco $$
477 Shawmut Ave., 02118 **Tel** *(617) 369-7075*   **Map** 3 C5

This tiny dining room serves casual Venezuelan fare. Munch on *arepas* (meat-filled corn muffins) and plantain-stuffed *empanadas* (pastries) while sipping some lesser known wines of Argentina and Chile. Limited seating means no reservations. Delicious sauces and rubs available to take home. Lunch and dinner Tue–Sat, brunch Sun.

BACK BAY AND SOUTH END Pho République $$
1415 Washington St., 02118 **Tel** *(617) 262-0005*   **Map** 4 D4

Clubby and hip, this Vietnamese bistro is Southeast Asia with an edge that appeals to a young clientele. Many diners come in groups of four to six to pass around plates of tangy appetizers like sashimi tuna spring rolls while sipping lychee martinis. The kitchen is open until midnight.

BACK BAY AND SOUTH END B&G Oysters $$$
550 Tremont St., 02116 **Tel** *(617) 423-0550*   **Map** 4 D4

A side venture of the famed chef of No. 9 Park, this subterranean spot for mollusk lovers consists of a marble bar surrounded by stools and an open stainless steel kitchen that preps the raw bar offerings. At least a dozen varieties of oysters are available at any given time. There is also a broad selection of sparkling and mineral-rich white wines.

BACK BAY AND SOUTH END Brasserie Jo $$$
120 Huntington Ave., 02116 **Tel** *(617) 425-3240*   **Map** 3 B3

One distinct advantage of this solidly Alsatian restaurant in the Colonnade Hotel is that you can get a meal from dawn until after midnight. French beers are on tap, and the menu is replete with all the brasserie classics from *steak-frites* to *tarte tatin*. Popular as an after-work spot for a glass of kir and a plate of *pâté*. Breakfast, lunch, and dinner daily.

Key to Symbols *see back cover flap*

BACK BAY AND SOUTH END Ciao Bella

240 Newbury St. #A, 02116 **Tel** *(617) 536-2626*

Map *3 A3*

The outdoor tables on Newbury Street at Fairfield are a bigger draw than the retro Italian-American menu that runs from minestrone to chicken parmesan. Local sports figures and visiting minor celebrities often seem to end up eating here, so the paparazzi provide some good additional street entertainment.

BACK BAY AND SOUTH END Jasper White's Summer Shack

50 Dalton St., 02116 **Tel** *(617) 867-9955*

Map *3 A3*

The Back Bay venue of this chain of casual seafood restaurants, started by one of New England's best chefs, sits right above a bowling alley and within easy walking distance of Symphony Hall and Fenway Park. Look out for the daily wood-grilled fish specials, rich chowders, and excellent raw bar.

BACK BAY AND SOUTH END Masa

439 Tremont St., 02116 **Tel** *(617) 338-8884*

Map *4 D3*

A rarity in Boston, Masa draws inspiration from the new gourmet cuisine of the American Southwest. The chef is apt to serve mushrooms in a pumpkin seed mole sauce or grilled trout with a chili-pepper rub. This is not a salsa-and-chips tequila bar, but Masa does pour tasting flights of different styles of tequila. Dinner nightly, brunch Sat–Sun.

BACK BAY AND SOUTH END Petit Robert Bistro

468 Commonwealth Ave., 02215 **Tel** *(617) 375-0699*

Map *3 A2*

Once you've dined here, you'll wonder how any other restaurant in the neighborhood can stay in business. French bistro fare in French bistro portions by a French Master Chef at these prices is a steal. Simple, clean executions of the classics from *coquilles St-Jacques* to *steak frites* and *profiteroles*. Lunch and dinner daily.

BACK BAY AND SOUTH END Rocca

500 Harrison Ave., 02118 **Tel** *(617) 451-5151*

Map *1 C5*

Boston's only restaurant to focus on Ligurian cuisine – the herb-infused dishes of Genoa and the ocean-oriented food of the Italian Riviera – stands out by serving intensely flavored but light Italian food. The lively scene is fueled by an excellent cocktail bar and on-site parking (almost unheard of in the South End). Dinner nightly.

BACK BAY AND SOUTH END Sonsie

327 Newbury St., 02216 **Tel** *(617) 351-2500*

Map *3 A3*

Everybody loves the look of this upper-Newbury Street stalwart, especially when they swing open the glass doors in the summer and the outdoor tables fill up with patrons more interested in being seen than in eating the truly delicious food. Most dishes hail from the French and Italian rivieras, with the occasional Indochinese delight.

BACK BAY AND SOUTH END Stephanie's on Newbury

190 Newbury St., 02116 **Tel** *(617) 236-0990*

Map *3 B2*

Stephanie's has become an institution with its dinner salads and pasta dishes that are so big that diners routinely leave with "doggie bags" for the next meal. Signature plates include smoked salmon and sweet potato hash, and meatloaf layered with cheese and caramelized onions. The restaurant offers some of Back Bay's best outdoor tables.

BACK BAY AND SOUTH END Tapeo

266 Newbury St., 02116 **Tel** *(617) 267-4799*

Map *3 B2*

Authentically Spanish, this restaurant and *tapas* bar specializes in small plates that would be served with a glass of sherry in Spain. One of the few restaurants in Boston to serve true *jamón serrano* (the Spanish answer to Italian prosciutto), Tapeo also prepares exquisite bites like garlicky squid. Excellent sherry list. Lunch Sat–Sun, dinner nightly.

BACK BAY AND SOUTH END Toro

1704 Washington St., 02118 **Tel** *(617) 536-4300*

Map *3 C5*

The name is a bilingual pun of the Spanish for "bull" and Japanese for bluefin tuna belly sashimi – no surprise, given the erudite chef-owner's love of Spanish *tapas* and Japanese *sushi* and *sashimi* bars. The food is a hybrid of the two, united both by serving size and flavor intensity. Dinner nightly, lunch Mon–Fri, brunch Sun.

BACK BAY AND SOUTH END Azure

61 Exeter St., 02116 **Tel** *(617) 933-4800*

Map *3 B2*

While the chef is known for his bold treatments of grilled meats like lamb steak marinated in pomegranate juice, North Atlantic and Alaskan seafood dishes are the real stars. They are usually set off by an unusual fruit or vegetable, such as a mound of sweet and sour eggplant. The portions are large and Azure also serves a hearty breakfast.

BACK BAY AND SOUTH END Bouchée

159 Newbury St., 02116 **Tel** *(617) 450-4343*

Map *1 A5*

Boston's love affair with French food goes back at least to the American Revolution, and Bouchée delivers all the classics you'd look for in a Parisian brasserie, from *steak frites* and *coq au vin* to *bouillabaisse* and *cassoulet*. The excellent French wine list gets past the obvious to include many lesser-known appellations. Lunch and dinner daily.

BACK BAY AND SOUTH END Gaslight Brasserie du Coin

560 Harrison Ave., 02118 **Tel** *(617) 422-0224*

Map *1 C5*

This stylish, mid-priced dining option in the South End specializes in the casual cuisine of the French provinces, whether the *choucroute* of Alsace or the *pissaladière* of Provence. The *pommes frites* are crisp and golden, the hangar steak a nice shade of red in the center, and the pastries crumble beneath the fork. Dinner daily, brunch Sun.

BACK BAY AND SOUTH END Great Bay
                🖼 P $$$$

500 Commonwealth Ave., 02215 **Tel** *(617) 532-5300*   **Map** *3 A2*

Splashy seafood restaurant in Kenmore Square's Hotel Commonwealth treats regional and local catch with elegance and restraint, matching tarragon to lobster, or chorizo sausage to dayboat codfish. Diners interested in less formal plates can enjoy fish tacos, lobster, and crab rolls, or plates of *ceviche* at the bar. Dinner Mon–Sat.

BACK BAY AND SOUTH END Mistral
               🖼 $$$$$

223 Columbus Ave., 02116 **Tel** *(617) 867-9300*   **Map** *4 D3*

High style and Mediterranean warmth collude for a memorable dining experience. The chef-owner is no shrinking violet, and his bold food comes in large portions. Nominally a Provençal restaurant, the menu extends to dishes such as pan-roasted halibut or grilled Scottish salmon. Diners often share thin-crust pizzas as appetizers. Dinner nightly.

BACK BAY AND SOUTH END Les Zygomates
              🎵 P $$$$

129 South St., 02111 **Tel** *(617) 542-5108*   **Map** *4 F2*

The name refers to the facial muscles involved in smiling, which is what most diners do when they discover the relaxed French bistro fare, live jazz, and extensive selection of wines by the glass at this wine bar in the old Leather District close to South Station. Menu always includes a few vegetarian entrées. Lunch Mon–Fri, dinner Mon–Sat.

BACK BAY AND SOUTH END Sibling Rivalry
            🖼 🖼 P $$$$

525 Tremont St., 02116 **Tel** *(617) 338-5338*   **Map** *4 D4*

The name refers to the two vastly different menus by brothers who have achieved chef stardom elsewhere in the country. At this restaurant located on the ground level of a fashionably designed luxury condo complex, diners are the winners as the chefs try to outdo each other with imaginative dishes using local ingredients.

BACK BAY AND SOUTH END Tremont 647 & Sister Sorel
       🖼 🖼 P $$$$

647 Tremont St., 02118 **Tel** *(617) 266-4600*   **Map** *3 C4*

The extensively tattooed chef-owner is no shrinking violet, and his style of cooking favors big portions, bold flavors, and lots of smoke with the meat. South End trend-followers are always stopping in to determine what's *au courant*, whether it is high-alcohol caipirinhas or the weekend pajama brunches when diners show up in sleepwear.

BACK BAY AND SOUTH END Union Bar & Grille
           🖼 🧍 P $$$$

1357 Washington St., 02118 **Tel** *(617) 423-0555*   **Map** *4 D4*

An anchor for the rapidly gentrifying SoWa (south of Washington) neighborhood, this restaurant is popular with owners of the stylish loft conversions. A sleek restaurant serving unpretentious American food, its attentive service, sharp design, and deft bar make it a hit with those who love to dine out. Dinner nightly, brunch Sat–Sun.

BACK BAY AND SOUTH END Via Matta
            🖼 🖼 P $$$$

79 Park Plaza, 02116 **Tel** *(617) 422-0008*   **Map** *4 D2*

"Crazy Street" is as good a name as any for this hip bar-restaurant scene on the back side of Park Square. The food is solidly northern Italian – *risottos* and game from the Piedmont, tender veggie plates from Liguria, roasted meats of Tuscany, and heavenly sauces and cheeses from Emilia Romagna. The menu changes daily.

BACK BAY AND SOUTH END The Café at the Taj, Boston
      🖼 🧍 P $$$$$

15 Arlington St., 02116 **Tel** *(617) 598-5255*   **Map** *4 D2*

For more than half a century a Boston tradition for breakfast meetings, lively luncheons, and pre- or post-theater dining. Bright décor and windows overlooking fashionable Newbury Street. Seasonal menus spotlight signature dishes and local flavors. One of Boston's most attractive à la carte brunches. Breakfast, lunch, and dinner daily, brunch Sat–Sun.

BACK BAY AND SOUTH END Clio
                🖼 P $$$$$

370-A Commonwealth Ave., 02215 **Tel** *(617) 536-7200*   **Map** *3 A2*

Clio's chef-owner is widely celebrated as one of country's most inventive chefs. Small plates and appetizers often feature arcane Asian spices, dabs of various caviars, and decorative techniques worthy of an origami master. Entrées are simpler, with the emphasis on exquisite cuts of meat and fish treated to just one or two contrasting vegetable flavors.

BACK BAY AND SOUTH END Grill 23
            🖼 🍸 P $$$$$

161 Berkeley St., 02116 **Tel** *(617) 542-2255*   **Map** *4 D2*

Although many chain steakhouses have opened in Boston in recent years, Grill 23 has been the genuine article since 1983. Beef is certified hormone- and antibiotic-free and the bar serves exquisite martinis. There is a constantly evolving menu based on seasonal availability. The 900-plus label wine list ranks among the city's best. Dinner nightly.

BACK BAY AND THE SOUTH END Hamersley's Bistro
       🖼 🖼 P $$$$$

553 Tremont St., 02116 **Tel** *(617) 423-2700*   **Map** *4 D4*

A French country restaurant translated into an urban setting adjacent to the Boston Center for the Arts *(see p101)*. Chicken roasted with garlic, lemon, and parsley under the skin has been a signature dish for decades. The summertime tables on the plaza are some of the most sought-after in the city. Dinner nightly, brunch Sun.

BACK BAY AND SOUTH END Oak Room
      🖼 🍸 🎵 P $$$$$

138 St. James Ave., 02116 **Tel** *(617) 267-5300*   **Map** *3 C2*

The aromas that strike you when you walk in are seared beef and old money. The oak paneling helps preserve the men's club atmosphere in this venerable steak house where the meat comes big, bigger, and biggest, and vegetables are side orders well worth ordering. The Oak Bar is one of the city's most elegant. Lunch and dinner daily.

Key to Price Guide *see p332* **Key to Symbols** *see back cover flap*

BACK BAY AND SOUTH END Sorellina ♿ [T] [P] $$$$$

1 Huntington Ave., 02116 ***Tel*** *(617) 412-4600* **Map** 3 C2

A modern, airy dining space in which contemporary northern Italian cuisine is served. Sorellina (little sister) specializes in Tuscan-Piemontese dishes and choices range from pan-roasted red stag for the adventurous to herb-roasted chicken and grilled steaks for the less venturesome carnivores. Dinner nightly.

BEACON HILL AND THE THEATER DISTRICT Peach Farm $

4 Tyler St., 02111 ***Tel*** *(617) 482-1116* **Map** 4 F2

Hong Kong pop music welcomes diners to this series of interconnected underground rooms. Stop just inside the door to peruse the live tanks of glass shrimp before being seated. Hong Kong preparations of often locally caught seafood are the house specialty. Forget the menu and ask for what is fresh. Open late.

BEACON HILL AND THE THEATER DISTRICT Xinh Xinh $

7 Beach St., 02111 ***Tel*** *(617) 422-0501* **Map** 4 E2

A popular spot with many of Boston's Vietnamese residents, Xinh Xinh (pronounced Sin Sin) is a Saigon-style bistro serving such classics as lemongrass chicken with rice-paper wraps and smoky, tangy roasted whole quail. Other choices include the noodle soups that many Western diners associate with Vietnamese cuisine.

BEACON HILL AND THE THEATER DISTRICT Artú 👪 $$

89 Charles St., 02113 ***Tel*** *(617) 227-9023* **Map** 1 B2

The secret weapon of this trattoria is the ferociously hot oven, which produces sumptuous roast pork and lamb that mate perfectly with grilled Italian vegetables such as marinated eggplant. Prepare for a long wait at lunch, when office workers come here for the hearty sandwiches. Dinner is a quieter, more romantic affair. Lunch Tue–Sat, dinner nightly.

BEACON HILL AND THE THEATER DISTRICT Chau Chow City ♿ 👪 $$

83 Essex St., 02111 ***Tel*** *(617) 338-8158* **Map** 1 C5

Modern Hong Kong seafood dishes, such as honey-glazed jumbo shrimp and walnuts, top the menu on the lower two floors, while the third level is the reigning king of Boston's dim sum palaces. Shrimp dumpling is the benchmark of good *dim sum*, and this one is a perfect tender wrapper around sweet and crunchy shrimp.

BEACON HILL AND THE THEATER DISTRICT Figs ♿ 👪 $$

42 Charles St., 02114 ***Tel*** *(617) 742-3447* **Map** 1 B4

This small, casual eatery (a side operation of a local superchef) launched Boston's love for grilled pizzas. The signature pizza is topped with caramelized figs, prosciutto, and gorgonzola cheese, and the rich baked pastas are extremely popular too. The portions are so generous that virtually every entrée provides enough food to feed two people.

BEACON HILL AND THE THEATER DISTRICT Jacob Wirth Restaurant ♿ 👪 🍽 ♫ [P] $$

31 Stuart St., 02116 ***Tel*** *(617) 338-8586* **Map** 1 B5

This Boston landmark has been around since 1868, and is an old-fashioned restaurant best known for its bratwurst with sauerkraut and homemade potato salad. The sauerbraten may not be up to Munich standards, but the price is right and the evening piano bar can be a lot of fun. Lunch and dinner daily.

BEACON HILL AND THE THEATER DISTRICT Ma Soba ♿ 👪 [P] $$

156 Cambridge St., 02114 ***Tel*** *(617) 973-6680* **Map** 1 C3

Known for its prize-winning *sushis* and excellent noodle dishes, Ma Soba blends notes from different Asian cuisines to create a pan-Asian fusion. Korean dishes, such as the marinated *beef bolgogi* (grilled beef) also recommended. The *sushi* is quite possibly the most reasonably-priced in Boston. Lunch Mon–Fri, dinner nightly.

BEACON HILL AND THE THEATER DISTRICT Panificio ♿ 👪 $$

144 Charles St., 02114 ***Tel*** *(617) 227-4340* **Map** 1 B3

A popular bakery that specializes in rustic Italian breads and also structures light meals, served all day, from their baked goods. Piles of meat and heaps of vegetables fill the sandwiches, and soups are a big seller. Look out for fancy egg dishes such as frittatas, French toast, and different versions of eggs Benedict at the weekend brunches.

BEACON HILL AND THE THEATER DISTRICT Paramount Deli-Restaurant ♿ 👪 $$

44 Charles St., 02114 ***Tel*** *(617) 720-1152* **Map** 1 B4

This hangout has been a comfort-food destination since 1937. The busiest times are at breakfast and during the day when there is a cafeteria-style service. The evening table service emphasizes stir-fries and unfussy American bistro dishes, usually a grilled piece of meat atop a starch and graced with a light sauce. All the meals provide good value.

BEACON HILL AND THE THEATER DISTRICT Shabu-Zen $$

16 Tyler St., 02111 ***Tel*** *(617) 292-8828* **Map** 4 F2

"Shabu-shabu" means "swish-swish" – the sound chopsticks make as they swirl raw vegetables and slivers of meat and fish in hot broth. Season your broth with scallions, soy sauce, and hot pepper, settle on a meat or fish and a type of noodles, and assemble your own dinner.

BEACON HILL AND THE THEATER DISTRICT Taiwan Cafe 👪 $$

34 Oxford St, 02111 ***Tel*** *(617) 426-8181* **Map** 1 C5

Locals flock here for Taiwanese comfort food that makes few concessions to western tastes. If you are hunting for homestyle delicacies such as duck tongue, steamed taro, or meatballs in clay hot pots, this small second-story restaurant is the place. Luncheon specials (fish ball soup, for example) are a rare steal. This restaurant only accepts cash.

BEACON HILL AND THE THEATER DISTRICT Grotto
37 Bowdoin St., 02114 **Tel** *(617) 227-3434*

Map 1 C3

Visitors to Boston rarely find Grotto because it is tucked into a brownstone north of the State House. It is worth seeking out this fine northern Italian restaurant with spot-on service and a chef who emphasizes simple combinations of intensely flavored ingredients. Nightly fixed-price menu is good value.

BEACON HILL AND THE THEATER DISTRICT Lala Rokh
97 Mount Vernon St., 02114 **Tel** *(617) 720-5511*

Map 1 B4

North Africa's fine cuisine was born in Persia, and dining at Lala Rokh is like taking a gastronomic tour through the greatest hits of Persian cuisine. Dishes are redolent of herbs, citrus, and exotic spices, often featuring lamb and game birds. Most of the desserts are built around dates and nuts. Lunch Mon–Fri, dinner nightly.

BEACON HILL AND THE THEATER DISTRICT Legal Seafoods
26 Park Plaza **Tel** *(617) 426-4444*

Map 4 D2

This flagship restaurant is still a national leader in setting quality standards for fresh fish well prepared. Its amenities include an extensive wine cellar and a lounge popular for Back Bay business lunches and after-dinner drinks. Legal Seafoods offers an award-winning kids menu and a gluten-free menu for celiacs. Lunch and dinner daily.

BEACON HILL AND THE THEATER DISTRICT Avenue One
1 Avenue de Lafayette, 02111 **Tel** *(617) 422-5579*

Map 4 D2

Avenue One, at the Hyatt Regency Boston *(see p308)*, serves contemporary cuisine in a relaxed atmosphere. Conveniently located in the heart of downtown right in Downtown Crossing and the Theater District, and just steps to South Station, Avenue One is a great choice for power lunches, after-work drinks, and pre-theater meals.

BEACON HILL AND THE THEATER DISTRICT Beacon Hill Bistro
25 Charles St., 02114 **Tel** *(617) 723-7575*

Map 1 B4

Located in the Beacon Hill Hotel *(see p308)*, this intimate restaurant features American staples for breakfast and lunch but offers an American interpretation of French bistro cuisine at night. Steak-frites, for example, is made with New York strip steak, while local codfish gets a Mediterranean treatment with roasted tomatoes and Greek olives.

BEACON HILL AND THE THEATER DISTRICT Bin 26 Enoteca
26 Charles St., 02114 **Tel** *(617) 723-5939*

Map 4 D1

With about 50 wines by the glass and 200 by the bottle, this nominally Italian wine bar also serves such tasty pastas as cocoa-flavored tagliatelle with porcini mushroom ragout, and heartier choices such as lamb chops redolent of cardamom. Portions tend to be small, but sausages and cheeses are especially good. Lunch Mon–Sat, dinner nightly, brunch Sun.

BEACON HILL AND THE THEATER DISTRICT blu
4 Avery St., 02111 **Tel** *(617) 375-8550*

Map 4 E2

Fitting in very nicely with the chic sports club on the same level of the Ritz-Carlton Boston Common Hotel *(see p308)*, this Ladder District pioneer features light, fresh, delicately nuanced New American cuisine. The exuberantly post-modern architecture and artistic presentation create a dramatic sense of occasion for a big night out.

BEACON HILL AND THE THEATER DISTRICT Pigalle
75 Charles St. South, 02116 **Tel** *(617) 423-4944*

Map 4 E2

This intimate room with rich, deep colors and antique chandelier exudes the Parisian bistro look. It also has the food to match the decor. The Theater District location makes Pigalle bustle with a pre-show crowd, so reserve for 8pm or later to have the time to savor the crackling roast duck or the chunky *cassoulet* (stew). Dinner Tue–Sun.

BEACON HILL AND THE THEATER DISTRICT Teatro
177 Tremont St., 02111 **Tel** *(617) 778-6841*

Map 4 E2

The high-arched mosaic ceiling and open kitchen of this erstwhile synagogue-turned-restaurant creates a theatrical atmosphere worthy of the name. Reservations aren't required, but make one if you need to eat in time for a curtain opening. Teatro offers a light grill menu and broad selection of northern Italian seafood and veal dishes.

BEACON HILL AND THE THEATER DISTRICT Aujourd'hui
200 Boylston St., 02116 **Tel** *(617) 351-2037*

Map 4 D2

One of the city's best restaurants overlooks Public Garden from the Four Seasons Hotel *(see p308)*. Contemporary interpretations of French *haute cuisine* draw on local ingredients; the wine list is exceptional. Book ahead, especially for the elegant Sunday brunch. The three-course tasting menu is a bargain. Dinner Tue–Sat, brunch Sun.

BEACON HILL AND THE THEATER DISTRICT The Bristol Lounge
200 Boylston St., 02116 **Tel** *(617) 351-2037*

Map 4 D2

Upscale New England comfort food awaits the loyal movers and shakers who convene for breakfast, lunch, tea, dinner, or cocktails at this ground-level restaurant in the Four Seasons Hotel *(see p308)*. The Bristol lives up to its reputation as "Boston's living room" with flawless service and food. Favorite pre- and post-theater spot.

BEACON HILL AND THE THEATER DISTRICT Locke-Ober
3 Winter Place, 02108 **Tel** *(617) 542-1340*

Map 1 C4

The original 1890s decor has been lusciously restored in this bastion of fine dining in Old Boston. Locke-Ober did not permit women until the 1970s, but now its kitchen is run by a female chef-owner who fills the giant footsteps of Escoffier with modern interpretations of culinary classics. Dinner Mon–Sat; call for lunch hours.

Key to Price Guide see p332 **Key to Symbols** see back cover flap

BEACON HILL AND THE THEATER DISTRICT Mantra ♿ 🧒 🎵 👔 [P] $$$$$

52 Temple Pl., 02111 ***Tel*** *(617) 542-8111* ***Map*** *4 E1*

Mantra's atmosphere combines the stateliness of a turn-of-the-century bank with an interesting decor of drapery and leatherette upholstery, plus a 30-ft wood structure called the "Hookah Den." There's a delicate balance of traditional French cuisine combined with the fragrant Indian spices of the chef's homeland. Lunch Mon–Fri, dinner Mon–Sat.

BEACON HILL AND THE THEATER DISTRICT No. 9 Park ♿ [P] $$$$$

9 Park St., 02108 ***Tel*** *(617) 742-9991* ***Map*** *1 C4*

Sports stars, state politicians, and hard-charging business people frequent this upscale room near the State House for bold American bistro food accompanied by an imaginative list of unusual wines. The chef-owner has a magical touch with duck, so the duck special of the night is often worth trying. Lunch Mon–Fri, dinner Mon–Sat.

CAMBRIDGE Mr. Bartley's Burger and Salad Cottage 💳 🧒 ⛱ $

1246 Massachusetts Ave., Cambridge, 02138 ***Tel*** *(617) 354-6559*

Harvard Square's quintessential burger shop specializes in a whopping piece of meat the size of a big man's fist. Other sandwiches have the sophomoric names linked to a celebrity, but the prices are right, the food is fresh, and it fills you up. On weekends, it can take up to an hour to get in the door to order. Lunch and dinner daily.

CAMBRIDGE Forest Café ♿ $$

1682 Massachusetts Ave., Cambridge, 02138 ***Tel*** *(617) 661-7810*

The mother cuisine of Mexico comes from Oaxaca, and so do the dishes at Forest Café. Don't let the bikers and beery regulars at the bar dissuade you from sitting down in the cheerful Mexican cantina. Several classic mole sauces are on the menu, and the grilled fish and pork dishes are worth special attention. Dinner nightly, brunch Sun.

CAMBRIDGE Le's Vietnamese Restaurant ♿ 🧒 $$

36 Dunster St., Cambridge, 02138 ***Tel*** *(617) 864-4100*

This Harvard Square restaurant specializes in the Vietnamese soup known as *pho*, a comfort food for many Asian students at Harvard. It also happens to offer an inexpensive, healthy meal in congenial surroundings. Heap on the basil and slurp away. Lunch and dinner daily.

CAMBRIDGE Tanjore ♿ 🧒 [P] $$

18 Eliot St., Cambridge, 02138 ***Tel*** *(617) 868-1900*

Located on the river side of Harvard Square, Tanjore is the most eclectic (and perhaps didactic) of Indian restaurants owned by a local family. The menu carefully identifies the regions from which all the dishes come, from the mild *dosas* of the south to the coastal *vindaloos* to the *tandoori* dry roasts of the north. Indian desserts. Lunch and dinner daily.

CAMBRIDGE East Coast Grill ♿ 🧒 [P] $$$

1271 Cambridge St., Cambridge, 02139 ***Tel*** *(617) 491-6568*

One of the country's acknowledged masters of open-fire grilling (seven books and counting) runs this colorful, casual restaurant in a funky Cambridge neighborhood. Grilled fish with tropical salsas, pulled BBQ pork, and icy oysters are among the hits. The Bloody Mary bar inevitably draws an overflow crowd during Sun brunch. Dinner nightly, brunch Sun.

CAMBRIDGE Casablanca ♿ 🧒 [P] $$$$

40 Brattle St., Cambridge, 02138 ***Tel*** *(617) 876-0999*

Few Harvard alumni can return without a nostalgic meal at this Bogart-themed *boite*. As the name implies, Casablanca approaches Mediterranean cuisine from North Africa, so cumin and coriander figure prominently in the lamb meatballs, and spicy hummus is more likely than mashed potatoes as a side. Lunch Mon–Sat, dinner nightly, brunch Sun.

CAMBRIDGE Chez Henri ♿ $$$$

1 Shepard St., Cambridge, 02138 ***Tel*** *(617) 354-8980*

Too elegant in its decor to really qualify as a French bistro, Chez Henri brightens up the usual bistro formula with a Cuban accent. This translates into an extensive but judicious use of guava and mango on the menu, smoked pork sandwiches at the bar, and a good list of rums and tropical cocktails. Good-value *coq au vin*. Dinner nightly.

CAMBRIDGE Craigie on Main [P] $$$$

853 Main St., Cambridge, 02138 ***Tel*** *(617) 497-5511*

French-trained chef-owner creates new dishes each day as menu comes together based on the fish, meat, dairy and produce deliveries. House terrines, *pâtés* and preserved vegetables provide some constancy, but each night's featured dishes tend to be surprises. Bargain fixed-price meals available. Dinner Tue–Sun.

CAMBRIDGE Oleana ♿ ⛱ [P] $$$$

134 Hampshire St., Cambridge, 02139 ***Tel*** *(617) 661-0505*

The chef-owner is the winner of numerous national culinary accolades. Her Mediterranean dishes are informed by the cuisines of all sides of that sea, so she's as likely to wax Lebanese in one dish, Moroccan in the next, and Catalan in another. Aromatic spices and intense sauces. Vegetarian tasting menu offered nightly. Dinner nightly.

CAMBRIDGE Temple Bar ♿ ⛱ [P] $$$$

1688 Massachusetts Ave., Cambridge, 02138 ***Tel*** *(617) 547-5055*

Named for the Dublin neighborhood, this local hangout between Harvard and Porter Squares takes the kitchen as seriously as it does the busy bar. Burgers, sandwiches, and gourmet pizzas are always available, but evening entrees are more ambitious New American bistro fare presented with considerable panache. Dinner nightly, brunch Sat–Sun.

CAMBRIDGE Rialto   🅿 $$$$$
1 Bennett St., Cambridge, 02138 **Tel** *(617) 661-5050*

High-end, sophisticated décor makes this a special event restaurant: the place to propose, celebrate a birthday, toast a corporate merger. But Rialto is friendly and more relaxed than most *haute cuisine* temples. The chef takes a luscious approach to the classic Mediterranean cuisines, where rosemary and basil create magic. Dinner nightly.

CAMBRIDGE Sandrine's Bistro $$$$$
8 Holyoke St., Cambridge, 02138 **Tel** *(617) 497-5300*

It's hard to resist the *tarte flambee* dishes of Alsatian flatbread topped with farmer's cheese, spices, and bacon, mushrooms or asparagus – and those are just starters on this menu where *charcuterie* is king and cabbage isn't eaten until it's sauerkraut. Modestly priced daily menu, as well as pull-out-the-stops tasting menu. Lunch Mon–Sat, dinner nightly.

CHARLESTOWN Paolo's Trattoria $$$
251 Main St., Charlestown, 02129 **Tel** *(617) 242-7229*

The heart and soul of Paolo's is somewhere in the Adriatic, halfway between Greece and Italy. Ostensibly Italian, the menu makes extensive use of Kalamata olives, feta and local goat cheese, and both dried and fresh figs. Wood oven pizzas include chef's signature "Paolo's," with Kalamata olives, salami, tomato sauce, and cheese. Dinner nightly.

CHARLESTOWN Olives   🅿 $$$$
10 City Square, Charlestown, 02129 **Tel** *(617) 242-1999*
Map *1 C1*

Home base for superchef Todd English, Olives pioneered a style of rustic Italian/Mediterranean cooking in Boston. Bold baked pastas and giant roasts of meat and fish pour out of the kitchen with admirable consistency. The Charlestown location is near USS *Constitution* at the end of the Freedom Trail. Dinner nightly.

NORTH END AND THE WATERFRONT Ernesto's Pizzeria $
69 Salem St., 02113 **Tel** *(617) 523-1373*
Map *2 D2*

This simple pizza shop with plastic seating offers 24 different combinations of toppings and delivers to most Boston hotel rooms, beating the pizza chains at their own game. The signature *mala femina* pie is topped with artichoke hearts, fresh tomatoes, and blue cheese.

NORTH END AND THE WATERFRONT La Famiglia Giorgio's $$
112 Salem St., 02113 **Tel** *(617) 367-6711*
Map *2 D2*

Upbeat Italian meals with generous portions at a price that will not break the bank. Great for couples and families on a casual night out. The menu is simple: pizzas, pastas with a choice of sauces, and filling chicken or veal dishes. Unlike many North End restaurants, they do serve dessert and coffee. Lunch Mon–Fri, dinner nightly.

NORTH END AND THE WATERFRONT Pomodoro $$
319 Hanover St., 02113 **Tel** *(617) 367-4348*
Map *2 D2*

The tiny Pomodoro often has long lines of diners waiting for tables. The eponymous tomato sauce is one of the North End's best, and the kitchen shines with its vegetable dishes. Even dedicated meat-eaters will find pleasure in a meal of cold grilled vegetable antipasti, great bread, and a warming bowl of soup. Dinner nightly.

NORTH END AND THE WATERFRONT Antico Forno $$$
93 Salem St., 02113 **Tel** *(617) 723-6733*
Map *2 D2*

With its statue of San Rocco, its mural of Tuscany, and its beehive wood-fired brick oven, Antico is popular with North End residents who frequent this underground room for the Neapolitan pizzas. The oven also works wonders with roasted meats and baked pasta dishes. A wood grill supplies smoke and flavor to many fish dishes as well.

NORTH END AND THE WATERFRONT Barking Crab $$$
88 Sleeper St., 02110 **Tel** *(617) 426-CRAB*
Map *2 E5*

Although it is open all year, this Fort Point Channel restaurant is best in summer, when diners can sit outdoors at picnic tables and wield heavy stones to crush lobster and crab shells. Local cod, haddock, flounder, tuna, halibut, clams, and crab are available fried, steamed, or broiled. The Boston skyline views are an added bonus.

NORTH END AND THE WATERFRONT Carmen $$$
33 North Sq., 02113 **Tel** *(617) 742-6421*
Map *2 E2*

Practically next door to Paul Revere's House (*see p88*), this cozy *trattoria* specializes in small dishes for those who want a bite while sipping wine – a bowl of mussels or some oil-drizzled cheese. The fine pasta dishes with classic sauces show great finesse. Close quarters and below-street seating combine to give Carmen a romantic atmosphere.

NORTH END AND THE WATERFRONT Terramia $$$
98 Salem St., 02113 **Tel** *(617) 523-3112*
Map *2 D2*

This snug trattoria (the sister restaurant to Antico across the street) eschews the red-sauce neighborhood heritage in favor of Piedmontese roasted meats (including game), deeply savory dishes with dark mushrooms and caramelized onions, and bright Ligurian-style seafood lightly dressed with capers and lemon. There is sadly no coffee or dessert.

NORTH END AND THE WATERFRONT Bricco $$$$
241 Hanover St., 02113 **Tel** *(617) 248-6800*
Map *2 D2*

Bricco's kitchen keeps finding new twists on traditional Italian cooking, offering a gourmet range of antipasti, freshly handmade pasta dishes, and delicious entrées. They also offer a five-course tasting menu with a matching wine selection. A sophisticated late-night lounge serves wood-oven pizzas from 11pm to 2am Tue–Sat.

Key to Price Guide *see p332* **Key to Symbols** *see back cover flap*

NORTH END AND THE WATERFRONT Sel de la Terre ⬛⬛⬛⬛ $$$$

255 State St., 02109 **Tel** *(617) 720-1300* **Map** 2 E2

A study in contrasts, this casually elegant dining room near the Aquarium *(see pp90–91)* specializes in the hearty rustic dishes of Provence. Fish dishes make good use of whatever is sold at morning fish auction down at the harbor. Great breads and *charcuterie*. The *boulangerie* sells breads and sandwiches. Lunch Mon–Fri, dinner nightly, brunch Sat–Sun.

NORTH END AND THE WATERFRONT Mare Organic ⬛ $$$$

135 Richmond St., 02113 **Tel** *(617) 723-MARE* **Map** 2 E3

Acclaimed as one of the top 10 new restaurants in the US when it opened, Mare features classic Italian coastal cuisine, including rarities such as barbecued octopus. The chef uses deep-water fish, locally-farmed shellfish, and organic meats and vegetables. The chic contemporary design helps to create a gallery-like setting. Dinner nightly.

NORTH END AND THE WATERFRONT Meritage ⬛⬛⬛⬛ $$$$$

70 Rowes Wharf, 02110 **Tel** *(617) 439-3995* **Map** 2 E4

Exquisite regional and seasonal contemporary American dishes match choices from this hotel restaurant's wine list. Thus, the list leads with dishes for sparkling wines and light whites, proceeds through robust reds and ends with rich desserts or a platter of fine cheese matched to ports and Sauternes. Dinner daily, brunch Sun.

NORTH END AND THE WATERFRONT Prezza ⬛⬛⬛ $$$$$

24 Fleet St., 02113 **Tel** *(617) 227-1577* **Map** 2 E2

True to its name, Prezza bases its menus on the mountain and shore cuisine of Abruzzi, with delicate handmade pastas and chunky meat and fish dishes cooked on a wood-burning grill. Roughly four dozen Italian and New World wines by the glass complement the food. Unlike many neighboring restaurants, Prezza makes its own desserts.

OLD BOSTON AND THE FINANCIAL DISTRICT Durgin Park ⬛⬛⬛⬛ $$

340 Faneuil Hall Marketplace, 02109 **Tel** *(617) 227-2038* **Map** 2 D3

Legendary for its generous portions, Durgin Park began in 1826 as a lunch hall for produce and meat market workers. Family-style seating at long tables in the dining room makes for lively conversation. Traditional favorites include baked beans, Indian pudding, and grilled prime rib of beef big enough to hang over the edge of the plate.

OLD BOSTON AND THE FINANCIAL DISTRICT Times Irish Pub and Restaurant ⬛⬛ $$

112 Broad St., 02110 **Tel** *(617) 357-8463* **Map** 2 E4

While the taps mainly run Irish brews, the kitchen is far more eclectic. Office types throng the bar for sandwiches and burgers, but in the evening the menu also offers carefully prepared classics such as fish and chips, and old-fashioned stews. Of course, they all go well with a pint of stout.

OLD BOSTON AND THE FINANCIAL DISTRICT Union Oyster House ⬛⬛ $$$

41 Union St., 02110 **Tel** *(617) 227-2750* **Map** 2 D3

Some dishes probably haven't changed much since Daniel Webster was a regular in the 1830s, and people still point to the booth where John Kennedy used to have Sunday brunch and read the paper. Apart from Boston scrod, the best bet by far is the raw bar. Savor the differences in oysters from various waters of the world.

OLD BOSTON AND THE FINANCIAL DISTRICT Vinalia ⬛⬛ $$$

34 Summer St., 02110 **Tel** *(617) 737-1777* **Map** 4 F1

Wines by the glass from all over the world are the big draw here, with most diners picking a wine first and food second. Downtown workers often stop early for a glass of red and a small pizza or a dinner salad. Regulars return mid-evening for the wood-grilled meats and fish and the hefty desserts. Lunch Mon–Fri, dinner Mon–Sat.

OLD BOSTON AND THE FINANCIAL DISTRICT Café Fleuri ⬛⬛⬛ $$$$

250 Franklin St., 02110 **Tel** *(617) 451-1900* **Map** 2 D4

This brasserie-style restaurant in the Langham Boston Hotel claims a prize location beneath a six-story glass atrium. The menu uses fresh local ingredients in Mediterranean dishes, prepared in an open kitchen. Fleuri also offers a popular jazz buffet brunch on Sundays and a seasonal Saturday chocolate buffet. Breakfast and lunch daily, dinner Tue–Sat.

OLD BOSTON AND THE FINANCIAL DISTRICT Umbria ⬛⬛⬛ $$$$

295 Franklin St., 02110 **Tel** *(617) 338-1000* **Map** 2 E4

Umbria is known as "the green heart of Italy," and this fine-dining venue with attached nightclub remains strikingly true to the regional cuisine with such dishes as duck and chestnut filled pasta, wild game in a red wine sauce, and mixed seafood in savory broth. Many ingredients are imported directly from Italy. For a quiet meal, dine early.

OLD BOSTON AND THE FINANCIAL DISTRICT Oceanaire ⬛ $$$$$

40 Court St., 02108 **Tel** *(617) 742-2277* **Map** 2 D3

Part of a national chain of upmarket fish restaurants, Oceanaire retains the marble glamour of the bank that was once here, offering up a constantly changing menu of outstanding seafood. Unlike most Boston seafood restaurants, Oceanaire makes no bones about fish that is not available from local waters. Lunch Mon–Fri, dinner nightly.

OLD BOSTON AND THE FINANCIAL DISTRICT Radius ⬛⬛ $$$$$

8 High St., 02110 **Tel** *(617) 426-1234* **Map** 2 D5

This restaurant is often ranked as one of America's temples of trendy cuisine. The kitchen imbues dishes with explosive sensuality for those who can afford both the prices and the calories. Solo diners can join the convivial crowd at an elevated bar in one corner of the room. Lunch Mon–Fri, dinner Mon–Sat.

MASSACHUSETTS

AMHERST Amherst Chinese Food 🧒 $

62 Main St., 01002 ***Tel*** *(413) 253-7835*

Owner Tso-Cheng Chang grows much of his exotic produce on an organic farm in nearby Hadley (he also supplies other Chinese restaurants in New York and New England), guaranteeing super-fresh ingredients for stir-fries, steamed dishes, and other Cantonese and Szechuan, specialties. Most soups are vegetarian.

AMHERST Judie's 🧒 $$

51 N. Pleasant St., 01002 ***Tel*** *(413) 253-3491*

Giant popovers are a signature here, along with eclectic food served in a sunny greenhouse or quieter back room. Reflecting the community, the menu features such foodie favorites as lobster ravioli and gourmet vegetarian *risotto* cakes with black bean sauce. This is also a good spot for afternoon tea with homemade cake. Lunch and dinner daily.

CAPE COD Scargo Cafe ♿ 🧒 [P] $$$

799 Main St., Route 6A, Dennis, 02638 ***Tel*** *(508) 385-8200*

The welcoming ambience is matched by creative cuisine and excellent service. Main dishes range from lightly seared tuna with pickled ginger to tenderloin steak on mushrooms topped with soft goat's cheese. The handy location across from the Cape Playhouse *(see p158)* makes it a good bet for pre-matinée lunch or early dinner before the curtain rises.

CAPE COD Belfry Inne & Bistro ♿ 🧒 ⛱ ♫ [T] [P] $$$$

6-8 Jarves St., Sandwich, 02563 ***Tel*** *(508) 888-8550*

The kitchen draws inspiration from all corners of creation in this Genesis-inspired bistro in a de-sanctified church. Thus Thai peanut noodles appear next to lobster truffle *risotto* on a "world's greatest hits" menu that brings fusion harmony to dining through impeccable execution. A feast for the eye and palate. Dinner Tue–Sat (Nov–Apr: Wed–Sun).

CAPE COD Chillingsworth ♿ 🧒 ⛱ [T] [P] $$$$$

2449 Main St. (Route 6A), Brewster, 02631 ***Tel*** *(508) 896-3640*

For more than three decades, Chillingsworth has set the fine dining bar for Cape Cod with impeccable service and an elegant French *prix fixe* menu served in a 300-year-old house. More casual fare is served in the Bistro, whose menu is also available at the bar (known for its martinis). Lunch and dinner Tue–Sun, brunch Sun (closed Dec–mid-May).

CAPE COD Regatta of Cotuit at the Crocker House ♿ 🧒 [T] [P] $$$$$

4631 Falmouth Rd., Cotuit, 02635 ***Tel*** *(508) 428-5715*

Trophy dining rarely gets any better than this contemporary American menu with Italian and Asian accents. The chef takes luxury cuts of meat, hard-to-find ingredients, and the best fresh-market produce and fish and indulges in culinary alchemy. Romantic, expensive, and worth it. The cozy tap room offers a bargain menu.

CONCORD Walden Grille ♿ [P] $$

24 Walden St., 01742 ***Tel*** *(978) 371-2233*

This casual downtown spot is a favored gathering place for soccer moms at lunch and friends having after-work drinks and supper. The creative American fare is heavy on comfort food such as chicken pot pie, braised lamb shank, and apple cobbler. Open for Sunday brunch.

DEERFIELD INN Deerfield Inn ♿ 🧒 ⛱ [T] [P] $$$$$

81 Old Main St., 01342 ***Tel*** *(413) 774-5587*

Although the inn (with 23 guest rooms) dates from 1884, it reflects the Colonial style of the Historic Landmark village around it. Imagine how country squires c.1750 might have dined, and the nut-crusted rack of lamb and pan-roasted duck seem fitting. The menu uses produce grown in the Connecticut River valley. Breakfast daily, dinner Thu–Mon.

ESSEX Woodman's of Essex ♿ 🧒 ⛱ [P] $$

121 Main St., Route 133, 01929 ***Tel*** *(978) 768-6057*

This old summer favorite with families is known for its clam recipes, including clam bakes, and huge portions. Woodman's has the distinction of inventing the fried clam nearly a century ago, and the small hard-shelled clams from the flats of Essex and adjoining Ipswich are considered among the sweetest and most tender in New England.

GLOUCESTER Halibut Point 🧒 ⛱ [P] $

289 Main St., 01930 ***Tel*** *(978) 281-1900*

Join the fishermen, fishermen's wives and locals in the know at this working-class pub and grille for a grilled haddock and cheese sandwich and a pint of the locally brewed red ale, Fisherman's Brew. Spicy Italian fish chowder plays to the strengths of southern Italian family cooking at this gem in a legendary fishing port.

LENOX Bistro Zinc ♿ 🧒 [P] $$$$

56 Church St., 01240 ***Tel*** *(413) 637-8800*

With its long Parisian zinc bar, lemon-yellow walls, and tall windows, Zinc combines the styles of Paris bistro and Provençal country *boite*. The menu offers contemporary dishes such as roasted trout with Niçoise olives and cherry tomatoes, while holding up nicely with such classics as *steak frites* and *charcuterie*.

MARTHA'S VINEYARD Net Result 🍴

79 Beach Rd., Vineyard Haven, 02554 ***Tel*** *(508) 693-6071*

Fish really doesn't get any fresher than at this fish market café operated by Vineyard's largest seafood distributor. Choose your fish from the ice-packed cases and have it cooked, or enjoy sushi made from the local catch. Steamed lobster and clams are always available. Lunch and dinner daily.

MARTHA'S VINEYARD Sweet Life Café [T] $$$$$

63 Upper Circuit Ave., Oak Bluffs, 02557 ***Tel*** *(508) 696-0200*

Three intimate dining rooms and a garden terrace in an 1861 Victorian house serve as the stage for imaginative New American cooking. The cuisine shows the sure hand of an accomplished chef, with touches like balsamic-glazed red peppers as a balance to sweet corn chowder. Dinner Thu–Tue (closed Dec–May).

NANTUCKET 21 Federal ♿ 🍴 [T] $$$$$

21 Federal St., 02554 ***Tel*** *(508) 228-2121*

Four stylish minimalist dining rooms occupy an old house with wide wooden plank floors and big windows. Elegant New American fare with an emphasis on seafood, such as pan-seared swordfish with corn pudding, or halibut with lobster *risotto*. During slower season, there's also a lighter, less expensive bistro menu. Dinner Mon–Sat (closed mid-Dec–mid-May).

NANTUCKET Brant Point Grill ♿ 🍴 [T] [P] $$$$$

50 Easton St., 02554 ***Tel*** *(508) 228-2500*

The yachtsmen, politicians, and CEOs often gather at this swank restaurant at the White Elephant inn for a nice filet mignon, a gargantuan slab of grilled tuna or two-pound lobster, ideally preceded by exquisite martinis and accompanied by equally exquisite Burgundies. Pricey, but delivers. Closed early Dec–late Apr.

NEW MARLBOROUGH Old Inn on the Green 🍴 [P] $$$$$

134 Hartsville New Marlborough Rd., 01230 ***Tel*** *(413) 229-7924*

One of the region's top chefs left fancy resorts to run this historic lodging and cook to please himself – and his customers – with elegant and imaginative presentations of locally grown produce and meats. The midweek fixed-price menu covers three perfect courses at bargain price. The four dining rooms are lit by candlelight. Dinner nightly in season.

NORTH ADAMS Gramercy Bistro ♿ $$$

24 Marshall St., 01247 ***Tel*** *(413) 663-5300*

Located directly across the street from the entrance to the Massachusetts Museum of Contemporary Art, Gramercy performs artistry of its own with French-Italian contemporary cuisine that emphasizes the local products from farms in the Berkshires. Chicken with preserved lemons is a local favorite. Dinner Wed–Mon, brunch Sun.

NORTHAMPTON Eastside Grill ♿ 🚸 [P] $$

19 Strong Ave., 01060 ***Tel*** *(413) 586-3347*

An unprepossessing exterior belies the lively scene inside, as loyal fans tuck into the thick gumbos, oysters, popcorn shrimp, Cajun-spiced blackened pan-fried fish or steak, and other specialties of the American South. Rich desserts continue the theme with Key lime pie and and pecan- and coconut-studded New Orleans bread pudding.

NORTHAMPTON Northampton Brewery ♿ 🍴 $$

11 Brewster Court, 01060 ***Tel*** *(413) 584-9903*

The oldest brewpub in the Northeast (since 1987), this is a popular college-student hangout for such snacks as ale-battered shrimp and casual, somewhat messy meals, such as pulled pork plates. The brewing style leans toward the British Isles, with a concentration of bitters, stouts, and brown ales and there are usually a dozen brews on tap.

PLYMOUTH East Bay Grille ♿ 🚸 🍴 ♫ [P] $$

173 Water St., 02360 ***Tel*** *(508) 746-9751*

Traditional American fare is offered at this restaurant on historic Plymouth Harbor, although the menu puts a strong emphasis on seafood, offering many farmed species that are available all seasons. Relaxed environment with waterfront views and attentive service. Patio dining is first-come, first-served. Open for brunch on Sun.

PLYMOUTH Lobster Hut ♿ 🚸 🍴 [P] $$

25 Town Wharf, 02360 ***Tel*** *(508) 746-2270*

On the waterfront steps from the *Mayflower II*, this Plymouth institution has a classic fish shack menu and enough tables to serve the tourists hankering for baskets of fried clams or scallops, steamed or broiled lobster, or plates of fish and chips mounded high. Self-service, and food can be packed to take to the beach. Closed Jan.

PROVINCETOWN Ciro & Sal's ♿ $$$$

4 Kiley Court, 02657 ***Tel*** *(508) 487-6444*

A longtime Provincetown favorite for Northern Italian seafood, veal, and pastas, this atmospheric spot has a warren of small dining rooms downstairs as well as a larger, less historic upstairs room. The wine list is limited, and the best dishes are usually the specials. Dinner daily in season, Sat & Sun only off-season (closed Jan).

ROCKPORT Lobster Pool Restaurant ♿ 🚸 🍴 [P] $$

329 Granite St. (Route 127), 01966 ***Tel*** *(978) 546-7808*

This classic fish shack restaurant is known for its good prices and spectacular sunset views, including those from the "dog-friendly" picnic tables. Lobster is served in various forms along with fried and grilled seafoods. Home-made pies, zabiglione, bread pudding, and berry shortcakes are among the treats on offer. Closed Oct–Apr.

...ar & Grill   👤♫Ⓟ $$$
...0 Tel (978) 745-7665

...g, where Alexander Graham Bell made the first long-distance telephone call in 1877, you'll find
...f New American and grilled dishes. The elegant rooms have high ceilings and glass walls, and an
...mphasizes lesser-known California vineyards. Lunch Mon–Fri, dinner nightly, brunch Sun.

SANDWICH Marshland Restaurant and Bakery   👤Ⓟ $
109 Route 6A Tel (508) 888-9824

Classic Yankee cooking, such as a plate of fried fish with macaroni and cheese, all executed with special care. Locals covet the recipe for stuffed quahogs (hard-shelled clams). A few vegetarian dishes are available. Service is cheerful and friendly and the attached take-out bakery excels at muffins and bar cookies.

SAUGUS Hilltop Steakhouse   👤Ⓟ $$$
Route 1 South, 01906 Tel (781) 233-7700

The fiberglass cacti and mammoth steers out front have helped make this beef-lover's paradise an icon of roadside dining kitsch. Huge steaks, from the 12-oz (340-g) filet mignon to the 22-oz (625-g) porterhouse, are as red as you can stand them. Chicken, pasta, and seafood are also available. Serves brunch on Sun.

SPRINGFIELD Student Prince   👤Ⓟ $$$
8 Fort St., 01103 Tel (413) 788-6628

A Springfield institution, Student Prince is among the region's few old-time German restaurants, right down to the beer stein collection. Specialties include several veal dishes (in paprika or red wine sauce) as well as excellent German sausages and *Sauerbraten* (sour roast beef). Valet parking. Lunch Mon–Sat, dinner daily.

STURBRIDGE Publick House   👤Ⓟ $$$$
295 Main St., 01566 Tel (508) 347-3313

This roadside inn has greeted and fed weary travelers since 1771, and in keeping with the preservationist spirit of nearby Old Sturbridge Village, the inn maintains the open hearths and plain fare that the Founding Fathers would have sought. Favorites include lobster pie, roast prime rib of beef, and baked scrod.

SUDBURY Longfellow's Wayside Inn   👤Ⓟ $$$
72 Wayside Inn Rd., 01776 Tel (978) 443-1776

Historic surroundings of this Colonial-era stagecoach inn make the tap room a favorite for simple fare, such as prime rib and fresh seafood. The specialty drink in the Old Bar Room (the inn has run a bar since 1716) is the Coow Woow, an early American cocktail of two parts rum and one part ginger brandy.

SWAMPSCOTT Red Rock Bistro   👤 $$$
141 Humphrey St., 01907 Tel (781) 595-1414

Sitting on a point that defines the north end of Swampscott's long sand beach, Red Rock is set up so almost everyone has an ocean view (especially those dining outside). The menu favors simply prepared seafood. In summer, fried-fish shack fare is available from a take-out window. Serves a good Sunday brunch. Lunch and dinner daily.

WALTHAM Watch City Brewing Company   ♿ $$
256 Moody St., 02453 Tel (781) 647-4000

Once an old bank, this is a fun place for microbrewery beer aficionados. The brewmaster keeps a steady line of pale and red ales but excels in unusual seasonal choices, such as a barley wine and Belgian-style sour red. Good pub grub is served in a friendly ambience. Lunch and dinner nightly. Closed Sun in summer.

WALTHAM Tuscan Grill   👤 $$$
361 Moody St., 02453 Tel (781) 891-5486

One of the pioneers of serious modern cuisine in Boston created this stylish *trattoria* back in the 1980s and has now handed the toque over to his son, who continues the bold style. The open kitchen and wood-fired grill lend both drama and the searing heat necessary for Tuscan and Piedmont meat and game dishes.

WELLESLEY Blue Ginger   👤Ⓟ $$$$$
583 Washington St., 02482 Tel (781) 283-5790

Foodies consider this East-West bistro operated by TV celebrity superchef Ming Tsai unique in this part of the state for its blend of Asian and Western cuisines, extensive wine list, and blue-accented minimalist decor. It is worth a detour. Getting a table without a reservation is unlikely. Lunch Mon–Fri, dinner Mon–Sat.

WELLFLEET Catch of the Day Seafood Market & Grill   👤Ⓟ $$
975 Route 6, Wellfleet, 02667 Tel (508) 349-9090

Savor the famous bluepoint oysters of Wellfleet on the half shell as a starter before moving on to the serious business of selecting your favorite fish from the fresh market and specifying just how you'd like it cooked. Fisherman's stew stars local clams, mussels, squid, and shrimp in saffron broth. Closed mid-Oct–late May.

WESTPORT Back Eddy   👤Ⓟ $$$$
1 Bridge Rd., 02790 Tel (508) 636-6500

With a location near Horseneck Beach and a menu that emphasizes grilling over a hot wood fire, Back Eddy is bold, convivial, and at the cutting edge of casual cuisine. Most diners start with the raw bar of all-local shellfish before choosing between organic beefsteak, lamb, or the catch of the day. Closed Mon–Tue: Nov–May.

WEST STOCKBRIDGE Truc Orient Express   🖈🏠🎵🅿 $$

1 Harris St., 01266 **Tel** *(413) 232-4204*

Oriental decor and Vietnamese specialties like Shaking Beef and Happy Pancake are among the best choices on the pan-Asian menu. Truc is one of the least expensive spots in the southern Berkshires, and, true to is name, there's rarely a wait for a table or for the food. Lunch daily (Jul–Aug only); dinner nightly (except Tue: Dec–Apr).

WILLIAMSTOWN Gala   🖈🏠🎵🍴🅿 $$$

222 Adams Rd., 01267 **Tel** *(413) 458-9611*

Dinner at this upscale dining room inside the Orchards Hotel feels like a civilized meal at an English countryside inn that happens to have a talented kitchen staff from France and Italy. Since it's considered one of the most romantic spots in the northern Berkshires, reservations are essential. Breakfast Mon–Sat, lunch and dinner daily, brunch Sun.

WORCESTER Boulevard Diner   🖈🅿 $

155 Shrewsbury St., 01604 **Tel** *(508) 791-4535*

More than 650 diners were built in Worcester, including the lovingly restored 1936 Boulevard Diner (complete with glowing neon). This classic Italian-American eatery welcomes the weary, the hungry, and those who crave a plate of manicotti and Italian sausage after the bars close. Open 24 hours except Sun 5–10pm, when it closes for a cleanup.

RHODE ISLAND

BLOCK ISLAND Eli's   🖈🏠🅿 $$

456 Chapel St., 02807 **Tel** *(401) 466-5230*

A deceptively simple restaurant that began life as just another spaghetti house, Eli's features more imaginative fare than the knotty pine walls would suggest. Seafood medley over cappellini is as close as it gets to spaghetti these days. Arrive early or prepare to wait, as the room only seats 50 at a time. Closed mid-Nov–mid-Mar.

BLOCK ISLAND Finn's Seafood Restaurant   🖈🏠🎵🅿 $$

Water St., 02807 **Tel** *(401) 466-2473*

This restaurant sports a seafood market next door, a sure sign of fresh fish in these parts. Both fried and broiled fish are dependable, but species vary with the season and the luck of the fishing boats. Lobster, steamed mussels, clam rolls, and broiled swordfish are all tasty. The upstairs deck has great views. Closed mid-Oct–May.

BLOCK ISLAND Gatsby Room, Hotel Manisses   🖈🏠🅿 $$

Spring St., 02807 **Tel** *(401) 466-2421*

This bistro option at the grand old Hotel Manisses is for evenings when you don't want the formal four-course dinner in the main dining room. The *à la carte* menu here leans toward American bistro favorites such as grilled ribeye steak with *pommes frites*. Closed Nov–Apr.

BLOCK ISLAND Atlantic Inn   🖈🏠🍴🅿 $$$$

High St., 02807 **Tel** *(401) 466-5883*

A formal favorite of urbane locals for the spectacular ocean views and *prix fixe* menu with numerous sophisticated choices, such as braised monkfish with wild mushrooms. Late tables on the verandah are prized for sunset dining. Reservations required. Closed mid-Sep–Apr.

BRISTOL Lobster Pot, Inc.   🖈🏠🎵🅿 $$

199-121 Hope St., 02809 **Tel** *(401) 253-9100*

More a restaurant than a simple fish shack, the Lobster Pot prides itself on more sophisticated than usual preparations of extremely fresh local seafood, offering lobsters up to 3 lb (1.4 kg) and scallops baked with sherry and cheddar cheese. There are three dining rooms, a patio, and unsurpassed views of Bristol harbor. Closed Mon.

CHARLESTOWN Wilcox Tavern   🖈🏠🎵🅿 $$$

5153 Post Rd., Route 1, 02813 **Tel** *(401) 322-1829*

This gray-shingled tavern on one of New England's earliest roads dates from about 1730, and the menu which includes roast prime rib of beef and baked stuffed flounder wouldn't have surprised travelers of two centuries ago. Colonial décor adorns the dining room. Good value specials on Sunday.

GALILEE George's of Galilee   🖈🏠🎵🅿 $$

250 Sand Hill Cove Rd., 02882 **Tel** *(401) 783-2306*

As the very name suggests, the village of Galilee is one of New England's leading fishing ports, and it seems like George's always gets the pick of the catch. This bustling, wildly busy waterfront landmark is famous throughout southern Rhode Island for its seafood platters, chowder, and clam cakes. Closed Dec.

HARRISVILLE Wright's Farm Restaurant   🖈🅿 $

84 Inman Rd., 02830 **Tel** *(401) 769-2856*

The all-you-can-eat chicken dinner is a specialty of restaurants in northern Rhode Island. Wright's Farm seats more than 1,000 diners and is the king of the genre. Each week the restaurant serves over 14,000 lb (6,363 kg) of plain baked chicken accompanied by pasta, french fries, rolls, and salad. Dinner Thu–Sun, lunch Sat–Sun.

MIDDLETOWN Sea Shai 　　　　　　　　　　　　🚹🅿️　　$$

747 Aquidneck Ave., 02842 **Tel** *(401) 849-5180*

Sushi is ocean-fresh at this, one of the state's only Korean restaurants. Located just over the town line from Newport near the beach, this seafood spot is sister to the downtown hibachi grill by the same name. The menu has Korean grilled BBQ meats and seafood and Japanese specialties such as *shabu-shabu, sukiyaki*, and *tempura*.

MIDDLETOWN Atlantic Beach Club 　　　　　🚹🍴🎵🅿️　　$$$

55 Purgatory Rd., 02842 **Tel** *(401) 847-2750*

This restaurant offers casual daytime patio dining at the beach in warm weather and a more formal indoor dining room and banquet hall. Local clams are among the highlights, as well as grilled fish from New England waters. In the cooler months, roast duck and rack of lamb are popular menu items. Lunch and dinner daily. Closed Jan–Mar.

NARRAGANSETT Coast Guard House 　　　　🚹🍴🎵🅿️　　$$$

40 Ocean Rd., 02882 **Tel** *(401) 789-0700*

This renovated 1888 Coast Guard station has views of the beach, good swordfish, and prime rib and is known for its Sunday brunch. Plates are large, and some servings are novel for the area, such as veal and lobster sauteed together with mushrooms and red peppers. Jul–Aug: lunch and dinner daily; Sep–Dec & Feb–Jun: lunch and dinner Wed–Sun.

NEWPORT Fluke 　　　　　　　　　　　　　　　　　　　　　　$$$

41 Bowens Wharf, 02840 **Tel** *(401) 849-7778*

Light, contemporary American fare emphasizes tasty local produce and the catch of the local fishing fleet. Fluke also offers an extensive list of wines by the glass and specialty cocktails. Cheese and charcuterie are popular munchies while sipping drinks and watching the sun set over the harbor. Dinner Mon–Sat, brunch Sun. Closed Mon–Wed in winter.

NEWPORT Scales & Shells 　　　　　　　　　　　📋🚹　　$$$

527 Thames St., 02840 **Tel** *(401) 846-3474*

Combining Newport's two favorite foods – pasta and seafood – this casual room is a boisterous spot for slurping mollusks from the raw bar while drinking longnecks, or savoring fresh fish treated to a hot mesquite wood grill. Shrimp, scallops, and monkfish can be ordered with lemon caper sauce or garlic and lemon. Dinner only. Closed mid-Dec–mid-Jan.

NEWPORT Pronto 　　　　　　　　　　　　　　　　　　　$$$$

464 Lower Thames St., 02840 **Tel** *(401) 847-5251*

This Mediterranean/Italian bistro has visual panache with rich colors, soft lighting, and big windows. An open kitchen lets diners watch the chefs at work. Menu emphasizes fresh seafood, with handmade pastas and spicing that ranges from Moroccan to Ligurian. Several dishes reflect Rhode Island's Portuguese heritage. Desserts are made on the premises.

NEWPORT Puerini's 　　　　　　　　　　　　🚹🍴　　$$$$

24 Memorial Blvd. W., 02840 **Tel** *(401) 847-5506*

This family-run eatery strikes a casual note, but is serious about the food. The menu has 11 different preparations of veal alone, as well as numerous dishes featuring homemade pasta. Homemade polenta is served differently every day. The outdoor bar and garden dining are especially popular in warm weather.

NEWPORT Sardella's 　　　　　　　　　　🚹🍴🅿️　　$$$$

30 Memorial Blvd. W., 02840 **Tel** *(401) 849-6312*

Located between downtown Thames Street and historic Bellevue Avenue, this Italian eatery is popular with locals, whether for casual meals outdoors on the patio or for special occasions in the white linen dining room. Their veal dishes are the most popular, though pasta, fish and chicken are also well-represented on the menu.

NEWPORT The Black Pearl 　　　　　　　🚹🍴　　$$$$$

Bannister's Wharf, 02840 **Tel** *(401) 846-5264*

A rundown sail loft on Bannister's Wharf was transformed into one of Newport's most elegant dining spots. Famous for its clam chowder, this landmark blends classic French fare in the sedate Commodore Room with casual dining in the tavern and bar. Competition can be fierce for the best sunset tables. Closed Jan–mid-Feb.

NEWPORT White Horse Tavern 　　　　　🚹🅿️　　$$$$$

26 Marlborough St., 02840 **Tel** *(401) 849-3600*

The oldest operating tavern in America, with low-beamed ceilings, hearth fires, colonial bric-a-brac, and candlelit dining rooms. Good American food with modern touches. For a main dish treat, try the Beef Wellington topped with a pâte of *foie gras*. Lunch and dinner daily, brunch Sun.

PROVIDENCE Rick's Roadhouse 　　　　　🚹🎵　　$

370 Richmond St., 02903 **Tel** *(401) 272-7675*

The ideal place for diners who like their meat piled high and heavily spiced. The wood-fired grill is the mainstay of the kitchen, which turns out juicy steaks and burgers, as well as slow-roasted beef ribs, Texas-style brisket, and Carolina (vinegar-marinated) pulled pork. Wide selection of beer, bourbon, and sour mash whiskeys. Lunch and dinner daily.

PROVIDENCE Venda Ravioli 　　　　　　　　🚹　　$

265 Atwells Ave., 02903 **Tel** *(401) 421-9105*

Best known as an Italian gourmet shop with a huge selection of pastas, sausages, cheeses, and roasted and pickled vegetables, Venda Ravioli also serves bounteous Italian meals from late breakfast through early supper at tables lining the back of the store. Later diners can cross the square to sister Costantino's Ristorante. Open Mon–Sat.

Key to Price Guide *see p332* **Key to Symbols** *see back cover flap*

PROVIDENCE Don Jose Tequila's
351 Atwells Ave., 02903 **Tel** *(401) 454-8951*

Among the many Italian restaurants in the Federal Hill area, this Mexican spot stands out. Along with delicious traditional fare, you'll find some standouts such as camarones à la tequila and large shrimps served in a tequila-lime sauce. Sit outside, order a margarita and pretend you are in Mexico for a night. Lunch Thu–Sun, dinner nightly.

PROVIDENCE Pot au Feu
44 Custom House St., 02903 **Tel** *(401) 273-8953*

Something of a landmark in this city that takes dining very seriously, Pot au Feu offers classical Parisian cuisine (chicken breast in brandied tarragon cream) in an upstairs salon while casual bistro fare (onion soup and roast duck) is served in the brick-walled downstairs bistro. Lunch Mon–Fri, Bistro dinner Mon–Sat, salon dining room Thu–Sat.

PROVIDENCE Siena
238 Atwells Ave., 02903 **Tel** *(401) 521-3311*

Federal Hill has a century-long tradition as a southern Italian stronghold, but relative newcomer Siena owes more allegiance to Tuscany and Piedmont than to Naples and Sicily. Even wood-grilled pizzas smack of the north, with wild mushrooms and goat cheese on top. Free valet parking. Dinner nightly as well as late-night menu.

PROVIDENCE Viva!/Paragon
234 Thayer St., 02906 **Tel** *(401) 331-6200*

Located in a vintage building with big storefront windows on College Hill, Viva!/Paragon offers a casual setting for dining. The restaurant is quieter than the cafe, where you can choose from Mediterranean *mezzes*, soups, seafood, and steaks. Viva also has an extensive martini menu and the ambience to match. Lunch and dinner daily, brunch Sun.

PROVIDENCE Al Forno
577 South Main St., 02903 **Tel** *(401) 273-9760*

Wood-fire grilled meats, pizzas from stone-floor ovens, and baked pasta dishes are signatures of this popular, informal, place that has received top national reviews. The chef-owners keep inventing new and fabulous dishes that use fresh local ingredients and draw diners from as far away as Boston. Arrive early or prepare to wait. Dinner Tue–Sat.

PROVIDENCE Aspire
311 Westminster St., 02903 **Tel** *(401) 521-3333*

An upscale interpretation of Rhode Island cuisine is on the menu at sophisticated Aspire, in the Hotel Providence. There is an emphasis on local oysters and littleneck clams, and meats and vegetables are largely drawn from local farms. The fresh pasta dishes are particularly delicious. The wine list is extensive. Dinner nightly.

PROVIDENCE Capriccio
2 Pine St., 02903 **Tel** *(401) 421-1320*

Grand style classical Continental cuisine continues to hold forth in this grotto-like dining room with candlelit tables. It has livened up its menu and features light modern northern Italian dishes, such as scallops and pasta Bolognese. The wine list is impressive. Lunch Mon–Sat, dinner daily.

PROVIDENCE New Rivers
7 Steeple St., 02903 **Tel** *(401) 751-0350*

A pair of 1870s storefronts on the hill below Benefit Street form the intimate spaces for this treasure of New American dining, which divides between a 40-seat dining room and a cozy bar. Look for such treats as harissa-rubbed lamb rack or grilled salmon on lemon *risotto* cake. Bistro desserts include a cookie plate. Dinner Mon–Sat.

WARWICK Legal Sea Foods
2099 Post Rd., 02886 **Tel** *(401) 732-3663*

A welcome outpost of the famous Boston chain boasts a similar nautical theme décor and carries on the tradition of offering the freshest of fresh seafood, prepared in a variety of ways. There's a sizeable raw bar, but most diners go straight for the signature clam chowder, grilled swordfish, or the baked-stuffed lobster.

WATCH HILL Olympia Tea Room
74 Bay St., 02891 **Tel** *(401) 348-8211*

This octogenarian restaurant, near the famous Flying Horses carousel, has had a facelift in recent years, and now features an eclectic menu that roams the globe, with American regional dishes, Spanish, Asian, and others. During the warmer months there can be a long wait for one of the outdoor tables. Closed Nov–Mar.

WESTERLY Up River Café
37 Main St., 02891 **Tel** *(401) 348-9700*

For serious diners, this elegant and genteel place is worth the detour for artistically presented creative food. Set on the banks of the Pawcatuck River, it has an outdoor patio for summer dining. The American bistro menu changes seasonally and always includes a daily fish special based on the fresh catch of the day.

WOONSOCKET Chan's Fine Oriental Dining
267 Main St., 02895 **Tel** *(401) 765-1900*

This Chinese restaurant does double duty as a popular jazz club. Start off with a pu pu platter, then move on to the chef's recommended medley of scallops, ham, chicken, broccoli, baby corn, straw mushrooms, water chestnuts and carrots surrounded by fried jumbo shrimp. Finish up with a cool serving of jazz.

CONNECTICUT

DARIEN Coromandel   [&][⚥][P] $$$
25-11 Old Kings Hwy. N., 06820 **Tel** *(203) 662-1213*

This may be the state's best Indian restaurant, with South Indian specialties from Tamil Nadu and Andrha Pradesh served amiably in a limited, well-decorated space. Better known Goan and northern dishes are also available, but surprisingly few vegetarian main dishes are offered. Lunch and dinner daily, brunch Sun.

FARMINGTON Apricots   [&][⚥][▦][♫][P] $$$$
1593 Farmington Ave., 06032 **Tel** *(860) 673-5405*

An airy two-story restored trolley barn overlooks a sequence of rapids on the river and sets the stage for the creative New American cooking presented here. The restaurant wins consistent plaudits for its wine list. The informal downstairs pub is a popular after-work watering hole. Lunch and dinner daily.

GREENWICH Penang Grill   [&][⚥] $$
55 Lewis St. **Tel** *(203) 861-1988*

This stylish but casual spot is known for speedy service and for its extensive and tasty Malay-Chinese menu. Check out the seasonings in such offerings as grilled lemongrass shrimp, basil beef, or grilled salmon in black bean sauce, but inquire about the level of spiciness before ordering.

GREENWICH Restaurant Jean-Louis   [&][T][P] $$$$$
61 Lewis St., 06830 **Tel** *(203) 622-8450*

In this nationally acclaimed, chef-owned French restaurant (named best chef in the Northeast in 2006), you may dine *à la carte* or on the *menu degustation*. Chef knows his way around American sources, daringly offering strictly American caviar selections and slow-braised American bison. Lunch Mon–Fri, dinner Mon–Sat.

GUILFORD Whitfield's on Guilford Green   [&][P] $$$
25 Whitfield St., 06437 **Tel** *(203) 458-1300*

Bright artwork lends a sense of style to this contemporary café located in a late 18th-century home on pretty Guilford Green. House-made pastas might include lobster and salmon ravioli or black pepper fettuccini with vegetables. Lunch Mon–Sat, dinner daily, brunch Sun.

HARTFORD Peppercorn's Grill   [&][⚥][T][P] $$$
357 Main St. **Tel** *(860) 547-1714*

Translating a successful *trattoria* near the Trevi Fountain in Rome to urban Hartford seems improbable, but the Cialfi family has proved a hit with this stylish, two-level dining room that serves a prinicipally northern Italian menu where most fish and meat dishes get a loving kiss from the wood grill. Lunch Mon–Fri, dinner Mon–Sat.

HARTFORD Max Downtown   [&][⚥] $$$$
City Place, 185 Asylum St., 06103 **Tel** *(860) 522-2530*

Smart, modern, bustling, this favorite-with-locals downtown spot features excellent modern American dishes, including a selection of chophouse specials that range from a petite steak *au poivre* to a gigantic porterhouse that hangs off the plate. It is the flagship of the local group of Max restaurants here and in the suburbs. Lunch Mon–Fri, dinner nightly.

KENT Fife 'n Drum   [&][⚥][♫][P] $$$
53 North Main St., 06757 **Tel** *(860) 927-3509*

Traditional fine dining features French, Italian and American dishes, such as roasted rack of lamb or a *filet mignon* version of steak *au poivre*. More casual chicken and pasta dishes are also available. An outstanding wine selection complements the cuisine. The concert pianist owner provides music six nights a week. Lunch and dinner daily.

LEDYARD Paragon   [&][♫][T][P] $$$$$
Grand Pequot Tower, Mashantucket Pequot Reservation, Foxwoods, Rte 2, 06339 **Tel** *(860) FOXWOODS*

Elegant continental cuisine is only one of the attractions of Paragon, which boasts sweeping vistas of the Connecticut countryside. Menus change seasonally but always feature oysters flown in from around the globe, dry-aged Kansas City sirloin, and Maine lobster. Excellent wine selection. Dinner Thu–Sun.

LITCHFIELD West Street Grill   [&][⚥][▦][P] $$$$
43 West St. **Tel** *(860) 567-3885*

The area's most popular gathering place for big-name New Yorkers who weekend in the Litchfield Hills offers pace-setting food in a comfortably casual setting. Serves a relatively casual lunch (including burgers) and a more formal new American style. In summer and fall, there can be extended waits for a table. Closed Mon–Tue in winter.

MANCHESTER Cavey's   [&][⚥][♫][T][P] $$$$$
45 East Center St., 06040 **Tel** *(860) 643-2751*

This restaurant has two separate kitchens for two very different rooms. Upstairs offers casual Northern Italian fare, while downstairs is the signature formal French version of Cavey's where the best bet is usually the *prix fixe* dinner, which changes weekly. Downstairs suggests a jacket for men. Both are terrific. Lunch (upstairs only) and dinner Tue–Sat.

Key to Price Guide *see p332* **Key to Symbols** *see back cover flap*

MYSTIC Mystic Pizza ♿ 🧒 [P] $

56 West Main St., 06355 ***Tel*** *(860) 536-3700*

This pizza-and-pasta parlor in downtown Mystic gained national attention in the Julia Roberts' movie, but is more famous to diners for its "secret recipe" sauce. Order a house special pizza slathered with the sauce and smothered with pepperoni, meatballs, sausage, green peppers, onions, and mushrooms.

MYSTIC Flood Tide Restaurant ♿ ⛱ 🧒 [P] $$$$

3 Williams Ave., 06355 ***Tel*** *(860) 536-9604*

Local lobster, clams, and scallops always figure prominently on the Flood Tide's menu – steamed or baked into hearty casseroles in the brick oven. Meat choices are limited but invariably include superb steaks, pork loin, and herb-roasted chicken. Children's menu available. Lunch & dinner daily in summer, reduced hours off-season.

NEW BRITAIN Fatherland ♿ 🧒 [P] $

450 South Main St., 06051 ***Tel*** *(860) 224-3345*

With the largest Polish population of any city in Connecticut, it's not surprising that New Britain's Fatherland serves heaping portions of *sauerkraut*, steamed red cabbage, *pierogies* and other stalwarts of hearty, home-style Polish cooking. Daily soup specials sell out early.

NEW HAVEN Frank Pepe's Pizzeria ♿ 🧒 [P] $

157 Wooster St., 06511 ***Tel*** *(203) 865-5762*

Opened in 1925, Frank Pepe's thin-crust pizzas have an almost cult following among Yale students and other locals. The white clam pizza is the most popular, though sausage, salami, and pepperoni are available for traditionalists, or spinach and broccoli for vegetarians. No frills here; it's all about the food. Lunch Mon–Fri, dinner nightly.

NEW HAVEN Bentara ♿ 🧒 [P] $$

76 Orange St., 06510 ***Tel*** *(203) 562-2511*

Malay cooking is said to be the mother cuisine of Southeast Asia from which all others evolved. Bentara serves real Malaysian food in spacious, high-ceilinged rooms decorated with Asian artifacts. Most dishes blend sweet, pungent, spicy and salty notes. Exceptional wine and beer lists. Lunch and dinner daily; closed lunch Sat–Sun in summer.

NEW HAVEN Ibiza ♿ 🧒 $$$$

39 High St., 06510 ***Tel*** *(203) 865-1933*

A cheerful spot, well suited to eating Spanish-style at the bar from the extensive *tapas* menu or in the dining room on the upscale menu that accurately recalls the Balaeric island namesake. The tasting menu (Mon–Thu) is a good way to sample the offerings. Paella is available on Tuesdays. Lunch Fri, dinner Mon–Sat.

NEW HAVEN Zinc ♿ [P] $$$$

964 Chapel St., 06510 ***Tel*** *(203) 624-0507*

Stunning minimalist decor suits the vibrant food, a stylish blend of New American with liberal touches of Southeast Asian influences, such as the *tamari* marinade for the grilled tuna. Situated directly on New Haven Green. The menu draws extensively on local green markets and organic growers. Lunch Tue–Fri, dinner nightly.

NEW HAVEN Union League Café ♿ 🧒 👔 [P] $$$$$

1032 Chapel St., 06510 ***Tel*** *(203) 562-4299*

An historic building plays second fiddle to superb French food, impeccably prepared and served on formal tables with white linens. This is the real deal, with such treats as braised veal cheeks, wild bass steamed with fennel, and a casserole of vegetables enriched with truffle butter. Lunch Mon–Fri, dinner Mon–Sat.

NEW PRESTON Boulders Inn ♿ ⛱ [P] $$$$

East Shore Rd., Route 45, 06777 ***Tel*** *(860) 868-0541*

Boulders Inn serves highly praised New American cuisine in the glass-enclosed Lake Room or (in warm weather) on an outdoor terrace overlooking Lake Waramaug. There is a top-notch wine list. Think south of France – but in western Connecticut. Dinner Wed–Sun in summer; dinner Thu–Sat & brunch Sun in winter.

NOANK Abbott's Lobster in the Rough ♿ 🧒 ⛱ [P] $$

117 Pearl St., 06340 ***Tel*** *(860) 536-7719*

Fresh lobster, clam rolls, and other seafood are served at plain picnic-style tables facing the harbor on Mystic River. Abbott's does not have an alcoholic beverage license, but patrons may bring their own beer and wine. Lunch and dinner daily (weekends only Sep–mid-Oct). Closed mid-Oct–mid-May.

NORWALK The Restaurant at Rowayton Seafood ♿ 🧒 ⛱ [P] $$$$

89 Rowayton Ave., 06853 ***Tel*** *(203) 866-4488*

This small house with an even smaller outdoor dining porch overlooks Cavanaugh's Marina and the fishing fleet that docks in Five Mile River. The stupendous raw bar of local clams and oysters draws locals. Lunch tends toward fried and grilled dishes, while dinner can get fancier, with treats like scallops in a wonton wrapper purse.

OLD LYME The Bee & Thistle Inn ♿ ♫ 👔 [P] $$$$$

100 Lyme St., 06371 ***Tel*** *(860) 434-1667*

This dining room in a 1756 house-turned-inn is often voted the most romantic place to eat in the state. It's easy to enjoy the experience while sampling the four-course tasting menu that might include dishes such as crab Napoleon with roasted tomatoes or grilled beef tenderloin with wild mushrooms. Dinner Wed–Sat.

OLD SAYBROOK Al Forno   🛇 🚶 🅿 $$$$
1654 Boston Post Rd., 06475 **Tel** *(860) 399-2346*

New Haven diners are fussy about pizza, so this Al Forno (no relation to the Providence, RI, institution by the same name) takes three days to craft its dense and chewy dough for Florentine-style pizza and bread. The massive brick ovens also produce a delectable line of roast meat and fish dishes as well as baked pastas. Lunch and dinner daily.

OLD SAYBROOK Terra Mar Restaurant   🛇 🚶 🅿 $$$$
Saybrook Point Inn, 2 Bridge St., 06475 **Tel** *(860) 388-1111*

Serene marina views where the Connecticut River meets Long Island Sound compete with a menu of New American dishes with a Mediterranean accent. Roasted salmon, for example, is usually accompanied by an asparagus-prosciutto salad. The Sunday brunch buffet is extremely popular. Breakfast Mon–Sat, lunch and dinner daily.

PLAINVILLE (FARMINGTON) Confetti   🛇 🚶 🖼 🅿 $$$
393 Farmington Ave., 06062 **Tel** *(860) 793-8809*

In an area where good restaurants are hard to find, this is an oasis of hearty, well-prepared Italian food in an inviting setting. Known for seafood dishes, such as mussels *ailoi* or shrimp scampi over linguine, it also offers four different preparations of calamari. There's a good-value Sunday brunch. Lunch and dinner Tue–Sat.

PLAINVILLE Cottage Restaurant & Cafe   🛇 🚶 $$$
427 Farmington Ave., 06062 **Tel** *(860) 793-8888*

It's worth making a detour for this friendly, family-run restaurant. The chef is known for her generous plates of food with robust flavors and seasonings, such as braised pork shank with carrot and ginger risotto. Her brother makes a mean mixed drink. Lunch Tue–Fri, dinner Tue–Sat.

SIMSBURY Métro Bis   🛇 🚶 🅿 $$$
928 Hopmeadow St., 06070 **Tel** *(860) 651-1908*

This lively bistro presents bold American bistro food with Mediterranean and Asian accents and an intriguing selection of mostly New World wines. Chef's desserts include a heavenly maple and white chocolate bread pudding. The nightly tasting menu is selected by the chef's cookbook-author wife. Lunch and dinner Mon–Sat.

SOUTH NORWALK SoNo Seaport Seafood   🚶 🖼 🅿 $$$
100 Water St., 06854 **Tel** *(203) 854-9483*

There's something reassuring about peering out the windows of a seafood restaurant and seeing working commercial fishing vessels at anchor. This casual dining spot evolved from the adjacent fish market. Most plates are deep-fried, though large fish, such as swordfish, are grilled.

SOUTH NORWALK Match   🛇 $$$$$
98 Washington St., 06854 **Tel** *(203) 852-1088*

Expert gourmet pizzas and lovingly crafted baked pastas emanate from the kitchen's open-fire brick hearth at this ultra-hip restaurant. The killer martini menu is favored by those who prefer to stand at the bar. Very busy in the late hours, when an abbreviated menu is offered along with drinks.

SOUTH NORWALK Ocean Drive   🛇 🚶 🖼 🎵 $$$$$
128 Washington St., 06854 **Tel** *(203) 855-1665*

A cool South Beach Miami look combined with inventive seafood dishes makes this a fashionable scene. A large cluster of diners stand three deep at the stunning raw bar, balancing small plates and large drinks, while others hunker down in their designer best in the dining room under the gargantuan Dale Chihuly glass sculpture dangling from the ceiling.

STONINGTON Noah's   🅿 $$$
113 Water St., 06378 **Tel** *(860) 535-3925*

Bargain prices on fresh local seafood and a lively bar scene are the big draws at Noah's, a fixture in Stonington Village for nearly three decades. Multiple daily specials reflect both the catch of the day and the chef's whim, which often leans toward Portuguese cuisine. Excellent home-made breads and desserts. Open lunch and dinner Tue–Sun.

WESTBROOK Boom   🛇 🚶 🅿 $$$
Pilot's Point Marina, 06498 **Tel** *(860) 399-2322*

Innovative American cuisine is served in this restaurant overlooking the yacht moorings on beautiful Westbrook harbor. Try barbecued duck *quesadillas*, grilled hangar steak with *gorgonzola*, or pan-roasted *halibut*. The luncheon plate of fried oysters is always a hit. Lunch and dinner Tue–Sun (closed Nov–May).

WESTPORT Tavern on Main $$$$
146 Main St., 06880 **Tel** *(203) 221-7222*

This neighborhood favorite for smart New American dining doesn't miss a beat. The chef makes superb use of seasonal ingredients such as morels and ramps in spring, other wild mushrooms and winter squashes in fall. Enjoy the friendly bar and cozy, fire-lit dining area.

WOODBURY Good News Cafe   🛇 🚶 🖼 🅿 $$$$
694 Main St. South, 06798 **Tel** *(203) 266-4663*

Good News lives up to its name and is consistently voted one of the top restaurants in the state by readers of Connecticut Magazine. The chef is attuned to the seasons and uses fresh and organic products from local farmers to create an adventurous menu. For diners in a rush, there's even a "To Go" menu. Lunch and dinner Wed–Mon.

Key to Price Guide *see p332* **Key to Symbols** *see back cover flap*

VERMONT

BURLINGTON Penny Cluse Café ♿ 🧒 $
169 Cherry St., 05401 ***Tel*** *(802) 651-8834*

There's often a wait for tables on weekends in this friendly spot that is equally popular with locals and visitors. The menu offers something for every taste – from gingerbread pancakes to scrambled tofu to *huevos rancheros* for breakfast. Or try chicken and biscuits or fish tacos for lunch. Breakfast and lunch daily.

BURLINGTON India House Restaurant ♿ 🧒 [P] $$
207 Colchester Ave., 05401 ***Tel*** *(802) 862-7800*

A stalwart among the Burlington area's college students, this spot specializes in traditional North Indian food, with both vegetarian and non-vegetarian choices. Authentic *tandoori* cooking includes *reshimi kabob* and pork chunks seared in the clay oven's dry heat. There's a good choice of beers, including Kingfisher in large cans.

BURLINGTON Leunig's Bistro ♿ ⛱ $$$
115 Church St., 05401 ***Tel*** *(802) 863-3759*

Located in a 1920s Art Deco building in the middle of downtown, this award-winning Mediterranean grill and bistro serves fresh pasta, grilled fish and meat, and substantial vegetarian dishes. The crab cakes are great while the signature cocktail is a French champagne over ice, with muddled sugar, lemon, and a shot of cognac. Brunch served Sat & Sun.

BURLINGTON Trattoria Delia ♿ 🧒 [T] $$$$
152 St. Paul St., 05401 ***Tel*** *(802) 864-5253*

This family-run restaurant emphasizes an Old World ambience and stately formality in a city that mostly features casual dining. Good regional Italian specialties including homemade pasta are served amid stone walls, exposed beams, and fireplace. The restaurant received an award of excellence from *Wine Spectator*, hence the need to book ahead.

COLCHESTER Libby's Blue Line Diner 💳 🧒 [P] $
1 Roosevelt Hwy., 05446 ***Tel*** *(802) 655-0343*

From the unbroken yolks of the eggs over easy at breakfast to the homemade chocolate cream pie for a luncheon dessert, Libby's has never lost the 1950s vibe of a proper roadside diner. This is largely thanks to the impeccable cleanliness and unusually fresh food served here. There are always lines of people out the door at Sunday brunch.

CRAFTSBURY Trellis ⛱ [T] [P] $$$$
1165 North Craftsbury Rd., 05826 ***Tel*** *(802) 586-9619*

When skiers want to dress up, they head for this famed restaurant in a charming Federal inn. Cuisine is contemporary American, drawing on products from local farms and orchards. The *prix fixe* menu changes daily and might include baked cherry planked salmon or sautéed breast of duck. Excellent wine list. Book ahead. Dinner Fri–Sat for non-inn guests.

ESSEX JUNCTION Butler's Restaurant ♿ 🧒 [T] [P] $$$$
70 Essex Way., 05454 ***Tel*** *(802) 764-1413*

Part of the New England Culinary Institute, Butler's provides future chefs with the opportunity to work under the watch of dedicated chef instructors. Upscale seasonal menus feature items such as pan-roasted quail, house-made charcuterie, braised short rib and butter-poached lobster. Open Mon-Sat; brunch Sun (dinner Sun May–Dec).

GRAFTON Old Tavern at Grafton ♿ 🧒 ♫ [T] [P] $$$$
92 Main St., 05146 ***Tel*** *(802) 843-2231*

Housed in an 1801 inn, this restaurant departs from the Olde New England model by offering gourmet cooking with seasonal changes and influences from the Mediterranean, Malaysia, and Korea. Fresh produce includes herbs from the inn's garden, and local meat and dairy products. Reservations required. Closed mid-Mar–May.

JAMAICA Asta's Swiss Restaurant 💳 ♿ 🧒 [P] $$$
3894 Main St., Route 30, 05343 ***Tel*** *(802) 874-8000*

Talk about cross-cultural influences. This tiny Vermont village boasts a charming Swiss restaurant. The chef specializes in Swiss/German cuisine such as *sauerbraten* or grilled lamb chops with Swiss herbs and puts local apples to good use in apple *strudel*. Diners on the enclosed sunporch have a soothing view of a babbling brook. Dinner Wed–Sun.

KILLINGTON Inn at Long Trail 🧒 ♫ $$
709 Route 4, Sherburne Pass, 05751 ***Tel*** *(802) 775-7181*

A little taste of Ireland in the Green Mountains. The dining room was built around boulders too big to move and the menu features such specialties as Guinness beef stew, Irish bangers, and a rich and satisfying soda bread pudding with Irish whiskey cream sauce. The adjacent McGrath's Irish pub claims to have the state's largest array of whiskey.

KILLINGTON The Grist Mill Restaurant ♿ 🧒 ⛱ ♫ [P] $$$
Killington Rd., 05751 ***Tel*** *(802) 422-3970*

Designed to look like an old mill, this award-winning building has a dining room and separate entertainment lounge. The menu offers a wide range of New England-style food in hearty portions. Smoking is allowed in the lounge, which features live music and a signature cocktail called the "Goombay Smash." Lunch Fri–Sat, dinner daily, brunch Sun.

LOWER WATERFORD The Rabbit Hill Inn ♿ ♫ [T] [P] $$$$$

48 Lower Waterford Rd., 05848 ***Tel*** *(802) 748-5168*

New American cuisine served in a tranquil and romantic 1795 country inn near St. Johnsbury. The *Prix fixe* dinner varies from three to five courses, depending on season, but always features local specialties. An à la carte menu is also available. It is cited by many as the most exclusive dining in Vermont so reservations are required. Children 13 and over only.

MANCHESTER CENTER Little Rooster Cafe 🥗 ♿ 👪 $

Route 7A S., 05255 ***Tel*** *(802) 362-3496*

This is the spot to prepare for a day of outlet shopping with a breakfast of Belgian waffles, pancakes with maple syrup, or an omelet special. Prompt coffee refills will guarantee the necessary buzz. Or take a break for a hearty sandwich – roast beef or crab cakes, for example – for lunch. Breakfast and lunch Thu–Tue.

MANCHESTER CENTER Up for Breakfast 👪 $

4935 Main St., 05255 ***Tel*** *(802) 362-4204*

Delicious, nutritious breakfasts, with many varieties of eggs, pancakes, French toast, waffles, fruit plates, and tofu "eggs vegetarian" that will keep you going until dinner time. There's a good choice of coffees, including a maple latté, freshly squeezed grapefruit juice, or a champagne-and-orange juice mimosa. A full champagne menu is also available.

MIDDLEBURY American Flatbread ♿ 👪 [P] $$

137 Maples St., Suite 29F, 05753 ***Tel*** *(802) 388-3300*

Principally known as a pizza factory that supplies healthy frozen pizzas to organic food stores, American Flatbread turns the production floor into a casual pizzeria for dinner on Friday and Saturday evenings. One large pizza easily feeds two, and toppings vary with seasonal vegetables and meats available from local organic growers.

MONTPELIER La Brioche ♿ 👪 🍴 $

89 Main St., 05602 ***Tel*** *(802) 229-0443*

The pastry chefs of tomorrow train at this bakery-café operated by the New England Culinary Institute. Everyone in town, from manual workers to state representatives, comes here for soups, salads, and sandwiches at lunch. Delicious cookies, scones, and muffins draw the crowds the rest of the time. Breakfast, lunch, and snacks daily.

MONTPELIER Main Street Grill & Bar ♿ $$

118 Main St., 05602 ***Tel*** *(802) 223-3188*

Students of the New England Culinary Institute staff this smart-looking spot just down the street from the school. The menu features quality contemporary American food with French touches and an emphasis on fresh, local ingredients. You never know – your waiter may be the next star chef. Lunch and dinner Tue–Sun, breakfast Sat, and brunch Sun.

NORTH HERO North Hero House Inn and Restaurant ♿ 👪 ♫ [P] $$$

3643 US Route 2, 05474 ***Tel*** *(802) 372-4732*

An 1891 inn in the picturesque Champlain Islands. Chefs serve up a wide range of American food, from herb-roasted chicken with sautéed apples, raisins, cranberries, and maple syrup to rainbow trout stuffed with crabmeat. There is a Friday-night lobster buffet in summer. A glassed- or screened-in porch overlooks the lake.

QUECHEE The Farmer's Diner ♿ 👪 [P] $

5573 Woodstock Rd., 05058 ***Tel*** *(802) 295-4600*

This chef-owned old-fashioned roadside diner buys from local farmers to make tasty breakfast and lunch dishes – available all day. Huge variety of food on offer, from pancakes and scrambled eggs to hush puppies and roast chicken wraps. No alcohol, but the diner does sell chocolate milk. Breakfast and lunch daily, dinner Thu–Mon.

QUECHEE Simon Pearce Restaurant [P] $$$$

1760 Quechee Main St., 05059 ***Tel*** *(802) 295-1470*

Located in a restored mill overlooking the Ottauquechee River, Simon Pearce enjoys a scenic location. After checking out the namesake glass-blowing studio, where the glassware and pottery used by the restaurant are produced, guests fill the romantic dining room to enjoy fresh, modern American cuisine and an award-winning wine list.

SHELBURNE Restaurant at the Inn at Shelburne Farms ♿ 👪 🍴 [T] [P] $$$$$

1611 Harbor Rd., 05482 ***Tel*** *(802) 985-8686*

Creative regional cuisine in an historic mansion overlooking Lake Champlain. Some produce comes from the estate's market garden, and the farms produce cheese and bread for the restaurant as well. Free-range chicken, lamb, beef, fish, and seafood feature on a changing menu. Reservations required. Closed mid-Oct–mid-May.

STOWE Pie in the Sky ♿ 👪 🍴 [P] $

492 Mountain Rd. ***Tel*** *(802) 253-5100*

If you're planning to put in a long day on the ski slopes or out mountain biking, this is the place to fill up on hearty baked pastas, calzones, giant *strombolis*, and pizzas with a multitude of topping options. The weekday "all-you-can-eat" lunch buffet of soup, salad, and pizza is a good bargain.

STOWE The Shed ♿ 👪 $$

1859 Mountain Rd., 05672 ***Tel*** *(802) 253-4364*

This ski country favorite focuses on American comfort food for customers with hearty appetites and ales brewed for drinkers with a powerful thirst. Burgers are large and beefy, barbecued ribs are sweet and spicy. The sedate dining room and boisterous pub offer the same menu. Lunch and dinner daily.

Key to Price Guide *see p332* **Key to Symbols** *see back cover flap*

STOWE Norma's at Topnotch Resort and Spa
$$$

4000 Mountain Rd., 05672 **Tel** *(802) 253-8585*

The primary dining option at the Topnotch Resort, Norma's serves creative, contemporary fare in a casual environment. This all-purpose bistro has an open kitchen, serving meals with an emphasis on locally grown organic ingredients. Terrace tables afford scenic views of Mount Mansfield *(see p231)*, Vermont's highest peak.

STRATTON Verdé
$$$$$

Landmark Building, Stratton Mountain, 05155 **Tel** *(802) 297-9200*

The chef here champions locally grown produce and meats in an upscale contemporary bistro at this mountain resort. Enjoy pork osso bucco after a day on the ski slopes, or savor a rib-eye steak from grass-fed Vermont beef. A bargain menu is offered on week nights. Closed May & Nov.

WOODSTOCK Bentley's Restaurant
$$

3 Elm St. **Tel** *(802) 457-3232*

Visitors rub elbows with locals who stop to catch sports events on the TV in the bar, participate in trivia contests, or catch occasional live music. Deep couches add to the welcoming atmosphere. The burgers and steak sandwiches are popular, but the menu also features pasta, chicken, pork, and seafood. Lunch Mon–Sat, dinner nightly, brunch Sun.

NEW HAMPSHIRE

BEDFORD Bedford Village Inn
$$$$$

2 Olde Bedford Way, 03110. **Tel** *(603) 472-2001*

The Bedford Village Inn serves upscale regional cuisine in eight unique dining rooms. Typical menu items include seared duck brushed with a glaze of rum, vanilla beans, molasses and brown sugar, or sautéed, double-breaded goat cheese, stuffed with sweet apricots and pine nuts. Connoisseurs will delight in the epic wine list.

CANTERBURY Shaker Table
$$$$

288 Shaker Rd. **Tel** *(603) 783-4238*

The dining room at Canterbury Shaker Village serves the hearty fare favored by country folk used to a hard day of work, such as roast turkey with crabapple chestnut stuffing, and chicken pot pie. Many dishes have been updated including the meatloaf sandwich served on red pepper foccacia. Mid-May–Oct: lunch daily, dinner Fri–Sat, brunch Sun.

CENTER SANDWICH Corner House Inn
$$$

22 Main St., 03227 **Tel** *(603) 284-6219*

Local residents have been dining at this country inn for more than a century. Traditional American country cuisine with a few Italian dishes (principally pastas) is served in four cozy rooms. House specialty breads and salads with buttermilk dill dressing accompany entrées. Lunch and dinner daily, brunch Sun (closed Nov–May).

CONCORD The Common Man
$$

25 Water St., 03301 **Tel** *(603) 228-3463*

American comfort food such as meatloaf, roast prime rib, and baked macaroni and cheese makes this New Hampshire institution a local favorite. Choose between the spacious downstairs dining room or the upstairs pub where cozy couches, parlor games, and free cheese and crackers beckon. Lunch and dinner daily.

DANBURY Alphorn Bistro, The Inn at Danbury
$$$

67 Route 104, 03230 **Tel** *(603) 768-3318*

The servers in *lederhosen* signal that this cheerful restaurant specializes in German, Swiss, and Austrian cuisine. Try the tasty *wiener schnitzel* the German way (with red cabbage and *spaetzle*), or Austrian style (with warm potato salad and cranberry sauce), or a combination plate of *schnitzel* with *wurst*. Lunch Fri–Sat (summer), dinner Wed–Sat.

DURHAM The Three Chimneys Inn
$$$$$

17 Newmarket Rd., 03824 **Tel** *(603) 868-7800*

Evoking a French country inn with a Michelin-starred restaurant, the menu offers fine American and European cuisine such as New England *bouillabaise* and duck *confit*, in a beautiful 1649 mansion dining room. The same menu is available in the historic pub on the lower level, and vegetarian dishes are prepared upon request. Lunch Tue–Sat, dinner nightly.

EXETER Epoch Restaurant and Bar
$$$$$

90 Front St., 03833 **Tel** *(603) 772-5901*

The restaurant of this elegant inn offers an equally elegant (and delicious) dining experience. The creative chef offers dishes such as fennel-seared sea bass or scallop and lobster *papardelle*. The dining room can become crowded with conference guests, so be sure to reserve a table. Brunch is available on Sundays.

GLEN Bernerhof
$$$

Route 302 **Tel** *(603) 383-9680*

The most romantic item on the Dining Room menu may be the cheese fondue for two, but many diners can't resist the *wiener schnitzel* served with *spaetzle* and braised red cabbage. More casual fare is available in the Black Bear Pub, including burgers and a venison steak sandwich. Dinner Thu–Mon in summer and winter; dinner Fri–Mon in spring and fall.

HAMPTON Bonta

287 Exeter Rd., 003842 **Tel** *(603) 929-7972*

Located a few miles from Hampton Beach, Bonta serves an assortment of Mediterranean and New American specialties, from seafood to prime steaks and chops. The polished mahogany bar hosts live music on select weekend nights. Dinner Mon–Sat. Closed Mon in winter.

HANOVER Lou's

30 South Main St., 03755 **Tel** *(603) 643-3321*

At least four generations of Dartmouth College students have found comfort and hearty food in this quintessential college town hangout. The pastry cases at the entry are full of temptations, but be sure to sample the breakfast and lunch fare first. Many offerings seem inspired by Mexican cuisine.

HANOVER Zins Wine Bistro

Main St., 03755 **Tel** *(603) 643-4300*

The Hanover Inn's stylish restaurant is a town and gown favorite. The menu makes the most of local ingredients for such dishes as free range chicken breast with farm-fresh vegetables or grilled beef tenderloin with wild mushroom ragout. Thirty-five wines are available by the glass, as well as many regional micro-brews. Dinner Tue–Sat.

KEENE Elm City Brewing Company

222 West St., 03431 **Tel** *(603) 355-3335*

This renovated 19th-century woolen mill turned restaurant/brewery offers eight handcrafted beers on tap and well-chosen pub standards, including burgers, sandwiches, and grilled sausages with potato pancakes. Larger full dinners include several pasta dishes. The atmosphere is generally boisterous in the college town hangout.

KEENE Luca's Mediterranean Café

10 Central Square., 03431 **Tel** *(603) 358-3335*

Born in Turin, chef/owner Gianluca Paris offers an eclectic approach to the cuisines bordering the Mediterranean, with primary focus on flavors of Italy, France, and Spain with occasional forays to North Africa, Greece, and Turkey. Look for pistachio-crusted roast fish or ravioli with artichoke hearts. Lunch Mon–Fri, dinner nightly (Apr–Dec).

LITTLETON Miller's Cafe & Bakery

16 Mill St., 03561 **Tel** *(603) 444-2146*

Former mill building has found new life as congenial café with two-story deck that provides sweeping views of the Ammonoosuc River. In bad weather, diners can sit indoors and watch the staff prepare muffins, scones, brownies, and pies, as well as grilled sandwiches, soups, salads, and quiche. Lunch only. Closed Sun and Mon: Nov–May.

MANCHESTER Cotton

75 Arms St., 03101 **Tel** *(603) 622-5488*

Cotton serves updated comfort food in a casual bistro-style environment. Expect such tried-and-true fare as meatloaf, fried chicken, wood-grilled pork chops, or lamb sirloin and warm spinach salad. The bar is known for its martinis and its delectable crabcakes. Lunch Mon–Fri, dinner nightly.

MEREDITH Hart's Turkey Farm Restaurant

Route 3 & Junction 104, 03253 **Tel** *(603) 279-6212*

The country-style turkey dinner is a staple of New England dining. This family business specializes in Thanksgiving every day, but also offers turkey pot pie, turkey livers, and even turkey tempura. A huge selection of non-turkey dishes is also available, such as prime rib and a full line of seafood.

NASHUA Michael Timothy's Urban Bistro

212 Main St., 03060 **Tel** *(603) 595-9334*

Michael Timothy's is a sophisticated spot, with exposed brick wall, white linen tablecloths, and a chic jazz bar. The menu updates bistro classics with dishes such as scallops with sundried tomato polenta or seared duck breast and confit leg with *fôie gras risotto*. Wood-grilled pizzas are also popular. Dinner nightly, brunch Sun.

NEW CASTLE Wentworth Dining Room

140 Main St., 03257 **Tel** *(603) 422-7322*

The Wentworth by the Sea's dining room serves upscale regional cuisine, with a heavy reliance on fresh local ingredients including Maine lobster, locally harvested scallops, and Atlantic cod. With a scenic harbor view and a fireplace, the restaurant has a romantic atmosphere, making it a favorite for celebrating special occasions.

NEW LONDON Rockwell's at the Inn

353 Main St., 03257 **Tel** *(603) 526-2791*

The dining room is decorated with the owner's collection of art glass and food posters. The talented young chef mixes French and Asian influences in dishes such as seared sea scallops with thyme *beurre blanc* or roasted duck with jasmine rice and mango sauce. Dinner Tue–Sun (nightly in summer), brunch Sun (summer only).

NORTH CONWAY Moat Mountain Smoke House & Brewing Co.

3378 White Mountain Highway, Route 16, 03860 **Tel** *(603) 356-6381*

This brewpub offers seven of its own handcrafted ales to complement a full menu of barbecued meats slow-cooked in smokers. Carolina-style pulled pork, dry-rubbed beef ribs, and Texas-style beef brisket are among the favorites. For lighter fare, try the wood-grilled pizzas. Lunch and dinner daily (summer and ski season), weekends rest of year.

PORTSMOUTH The Blue Mermaid Island Grill

409 The Hill, 03801 **Tel** *(603) 427-2583*

A wonderful selection of internationally flavored dishes that includes spiced pork, marinated lamb, and a great choice of Caribbean-spiced seafoods prepared on a wood burning grill. Grazers will find the long list of small plates appealing. The beverage list has nine margaritas, tropical coolers, martinis, and a selection of wine and draft beer.

PORTSMOUTH Café Mirabelle

64 Bridge St., 03801 **Tel** *(603) 430-9301*

Creatively country-style French cuisine prepared by a classically trained chef from Paris is served in an elegant yet casual environment. A perfect opener is a *crepe* of smoked salmon and sundried tomatoes, while the house specialty is sautéed chicken and lobster with asparagus and prosciutto. Try the superb cakes and *creme brulee* for dessert. Book in advance.

PORTSMOUTH Portsmouth Gas Light Co.

64 Market St. **Tel** *(603) 431-9122*

Table-service dining at the Gaslight focuses on casual southern Italian pastas and American grill menu. Pizzas and some of the pastas are available downstairs at the more casual Downtown Pizza. The third floor has a bar-nightclub, with some food available late evening. Lunch and dinner daily; breakfast at Gaslight on Sat–Sun.

PORTSMOUTH The Dunaway Restaurant at Strawbery Banke

66 Marcy St., 03801 **Tel** *(603) 373-6112*

In a Colonial home on the grounds of Strawbery Banke, the restaurant features fresh seafood, local produce, and vegetables from the museum's gardens. The seafood chowder, with scallops, shrimp, clams, and bacon-leek cream, is a menu favorite. Diners at the Chef's Food Bar can watch the kitchen at work.

PORTSMOUTH The Oar House

55 Ceres St., 03801 **Tel** *(603) 436-4025*

Located in a restored 1803 warehouse literally steps from the harbor, the décor reflect's Portsmouth's maritime heritage. But the menu is thoroughly up to date, featuring an excellent *bouillabaisse* and an apricot-glazed roast chicken. The wood-fire grill enriches the flavor of fish and beef steaks. Reservations recommended. Brunch available on Sun.

PORTSMOUTH Pesce Blue Italian Seafood Grille

103 Congress St., 03801 **Tel** *(603) 430-7766*

Meat lovers will find a number of good options, but the menu emphasizes seafood, and the freshness of the fish and the Italian-inspired preparations may convert meat and potato lovers. The kitchen is equally adept at simple grilled swordfish or a robust bowl of fettuccini with mussels, shrimp, lobster, tomatoes, chilli, and garlic.

SUGAR HILL Sunset Hill House – A Grand Inn

231 Sunset Hill Rd., 03585 **Tel** *(603) 823-5522*

Combine a talented chef with the phenomenal effect of sunset reflected on the White Mountains to the east and the result is a memorable dining experience. The menu is contemporary French, and there is lighter, more casual fare available in the tavern. Breakfast is served to guests only. Dinner Fri–Sun year-round; extended days in summer.

WEST LEBANON Three Tomatoes Trattoria

1 Court St., 03766 **Tel** *(603) 448-1711*

This is a popular spot for authentic Italian food in a relaxed environment across from the Lebanon Green. Sit-down service, beer and wine, and a full dessert menu set this friendly spot apart. Thin-crust pizzas from the wood-fire oven are local favorites with families and college students alike.

MAINE

BANGOR Thistles Restaurant

175 Exchange St., 04401 **Tel** *(207) 945-5480*

Ambitious fine dining with a Spanish accent and many other Mediterranean dishes makes Thistles the most avant garde dining room in Bangor. Some of best dishes are steamed local mussels and pan-fried local crab cakes with a garlic *aioli*. The lobster pie of meaty chunks in a sherry-cream sauce is a Maine fine-dining classic.

BAR HARBOR Lompoc Cafe and Brewpub

36 Rodick St., 04609 **Tel** *(207) 288-9392*

Named for a bar in the WC Field movie *Bank Dick*, the Lompoc is an intimate café and bar that has a heated outdoor dining room and a *bocce* garden where locals socialize over a pint of the pub's own microbrews and an eclectic mix of Middle Eastern and Mexican dishes, or veggie-laden pizzas. Closed mid-Nov–mid-May.

BAR HARBOR West Street Café

76 West St. **Tel** *(207) 288-5242*

The menu boasts a full array of seafood choices (as well as steak and pasta), but many diners simply opt for the perennially popular "Downeast Special," which features a steamed lobster, clam chowder, french fries, and blueberry pie. Located near the waterfront in downtown Bar Harbor. Closed Dec–Mar.

BATH Mae's Café & Bakery
160 Centre St., 04530 **Tel** *(207) 442-8577*

The outstanding bakery is the heart of this bright restaurant in an old house that serves breakfast and lunch daily, a hearty Sunday brunch, and good snacks. Some customers stop by just for the cookies. Signature lunch dishes include a classic quiche Lorraine and lobster *quesadillas*, best followed by fresh blueberry or raspberry pie.

BELFAST Chase's Daily
96 Main St., 04915 **Tel** *(207) 338-0555*

This is a combination bakery, restaurant, and fresh market in one. The creative all-vegetarian fare including many vegan dishes is supplemented with a small but excellent wine and beer selection. In season, most vegetables on the menu and for sale at market are from the family's organic farm in nearby Freedom. Lunch Tue–Sat, dinner Fri, brunch Sun.

BETHEL Bethel Inn and Country Club
Broad St., 04217 **Tel** *(207) 824-2175*

New England gourmet cuisine with an emphasis on roast beef, rack of lamb, and, of course, steamed lobster is dished up in lovely surroundings. A glassed-in verandah allows for year-round views. Table service is by candlelight, with a pianist tinkling away at the Steinway. Closed mid-Oct–mid-Dec & mid-Mar–mid-May.

BOOTHBAY HARBOR Brown's Wharf Restaurant
121 Atlantic Ave., 04538 **Tel** *(207) 633-5440*

Brown's Wharf is not just the middle of the harbor. It's the middle of town, where everyone from the fishermen in gum boots to the yachtsmen in striped sweaters gather for simply cooked fish, mixed drinks, and copious quantities of beer. Breakfast daily, dinner Wed–Mon (closed mid-Oct–mid-May).

CARIBOU Greenhouse Restaurant
19 Main St., 04736 **Tel** *(207) 498-3733*

Located in the Caribou Inn, this restaurant offers good home cooking at reasonable prices in a region with a paucity of full-service restaurants. Known for its inexpensive breakfast menu and for the full turkey dinners served every Sunday. Popular in winter with touring snowmobilers tired of campstove cuisine. Breakfast, lunch, and dinner daily.

GEORGETOWN Five Islands Lobster Co.
1447 Five Islands Rd., 04548 **Tel** *(207) 371-2990*

Five Islands is the name of a harbor village at the tip of the Georgetown peninsula. It's also the name of the truly most picturesque lobster shack on the entire coast. You might actually see your meal delivered on side of the dock before it's steamed and handed to you on a plate. Lunch and dinner daily in summer, weekends only Sep–mid-Oct.

GEORGETOWN Robinhood Free Meetinghouse
210 Robinhood Rd., 04548 **Tel** *(207) 371-2188*

Yachtsmen who put in at Robinhood Marina and foodies who will go to the ends of the earth for a great meal are the main clientele here. Chef Michael Gagné combines his French technique with Maine seafood and the occasional Thai seasoning to create meals to remember. Dinner nightly mid-Jun–mid-Oct.

GREENVILLE The Greenville Inn
40 Norris St., 04441 **Tel** *(207) 695-2206*

Housed in an 1895 mansion, the Greenville Inn is a gourmet restaurant hidden away in remote northern Maine. Both the large round dining room and smaller Victorian room have sweeping views. The chef serves rack of lamb, venison, fresh fish, and roast duckling, but will cater to vegetarian and other special requests. Dinner Mon–Sat late Jun–mid-Oct.

KENNEBUNKPORT The Clam Shack
2 Western St., 04046 **Tel** *(207) 967-3321*

This take-out stand is the quintessential seaside experience of hot mollusks and crustaceans next to cool surf. The menu consists of some of the best fast seafood you'll find, including fried and steamed clams, scallops, and a truly memorable lobster roll. It's known for its fresh-cut onion rings. Closed mid-Oct–mid-May.

KENNEBUNKPORT Grissini Italian Bistro
27 Western Ave., 04043 **Tel** *(207) 967-2211*

Upscale in culinary ambition but comfortably casual, Grissini employs a wood grill and wood-fire oven for the dishes on its largely Tuscan menu. Notable for offering several gourmet vegetarian options each night along with simple pizzas, pastas tossed with vegetables, and grilled meats and fish.

KENNEBUNKPORT Stripers at Breakwater Inn & Spa
131 Ocean Ave., 04046 **Tel** *(207) 967-5333*

The Breakwater Inn & Spa's in-house restaurant, Stripers, is an upscale yet casual spot for waterside dining. The restaurant is popular with locals and visitors alike for its raw bar lounge, breezy outdoor patio, and sunset views of the river and ocean. Lunch and dinner daily (closed Thu–Sun off-season).

LINCOLNVILLE BEACH Lobster Pound
Route 1, 04849 **Tel** *(207) 789-5550*

This classic seafood restaurant sits at the edge of the beach, with the best views from the enclosed patio at the rear. Not hungry enough for a boiled lobster dinner? Try a lobster or crabmeat roll, light on mayonnaise so as to not overwhelm the flavor of the fish. Limited but good choices for non-fish eaters. Closed mid-Oct–mid-May.

OGUNQUIT Barnacle Billy's

Perkins Cove Rd., 03907 **Tel** *(207) 646-5575*

This is a classic, bare-bones Maine lobster house with a basic seafood menu, a casual atmosphere, and seaside surroundings. Set directly on the waterfront in Ogunquit, it is quite a bargain in an often pricey resort town. The more expensive but full-service Barnacle Billy's Etc. is right next door. Closed Nov–Apr.

OGUNQUIT Arrows Restaurant

Berwick Rd., 03907 **Tel** *(207) 361-1100*

One of the most ostentatious restaurants in Maine, with a showcase country setting, Arrows serves innovative American cuisine with produce taken from the vegetable garden and presented with great fanfare. Also has very good caviar and a trophy wine list. Reservations required.

PORTLAND Cinque Terre

36 Wharf St., 04101 **Tel** *(207) 347-6154*

Named for the legendary cliffside villages of Liguria, this gem celebrates both the boldness and finesse of northern Italian cuisine. Much of the produce is raised organically by the owners. Pasta dishes are offered in both first course and entrée sizes and there's a fabulous wine selection. The best bet is the six-course chef's tasting menu – an all-evening affair.

PORTLAND Hugo's

88 Middle St., 04101 **Tel** *(207) 774-8538*

Specializing in inventive modern fare, such as chilled melon soup with prosciutto, veal sweetbread ravioli, or caramelized lamb shoulder, this acclaimed restaurant serves only *prix-fixe* and tasting menus in its dining room. Those looking for a quicker, less expensive experience can sit in the bar, where an *à la carte* menu is offered. Dinner Tue–Sat.

PORTLAND Back Bay Grill

65 Portland St., 04101 **Tel** *(207) 772-8833*

The Back Bay Grill has a seasonal menu and offers elegant New American food in a modern setting that makes it Portland's most popular fine-dining restaurant. A *Wine Spectator Award of Excellence* winner, this restaurant has an enormous selection of wine and is also known for its superb desserts. Dinner Mon–Sat.

PORTLAND Katahdin

106 High St., 04101 **Tel** *(207) 774-1740*

The Katahdin features an brightly painted yet relaxed setting matched by a mouth-watering New American bistro menu that features the likes of roasted duck breast with cranberries and pan-roasted oysters. An excellent selection of wines by the glass makes it a popular choice for after-work drinks. No reservations, so get here early. Dinner Tue–Sat.

RANGELEY Club House Restaurant

2809 Main St., 04970 **Tel** *(207) 864-9955*

Family dining in a casual environment evokes the outdoors nature of the region with dinner entrées suggested by "the rod club" (fish) and the "gun club" (meat). Stupendously rich desserts cater to the north country sweet tooth. On Saturdays, the lounge offers music and a lively dance floor.

ROCKLAND Primo Restaurant

2 South Main St., 04841 **Tel** *(207) 596-0770*

This stage for a talented chef who went back to the land where she could raise her own produce (and pigs) wins steady national accolades for the innovative market cuisine and the kitchen's utter respect for great local seafood and vegetables just pulled from the ground. Dinner daily mid-June–mid-Oct, Thu–Sun in spring and fall, weekends only in winter.

TENANTS HARBOR Cod End Cookhouse

Commercial St., 04860 **Tel** *(207) 372-6782*

Essentially the town restaurant in a small community where the folks who don't sell real estate to the tourists work as commercial fishermen. Simple Maine cooking, with a killer grilled cheese sandwich along with lobster stew, rolls, or dinners. Fish and chips use the local catch. Lunch and dinner daily (closed Oct–late May).

WALDOBORO Moody's Diner

Route 1, 04572 **Tel** *(207) 832-7785*

Moody's Diner is a Maine institution, where locals, vacationing families, and long-haul truck drivers all grab a seat for hearty diner fare prepared with care. Family-owned and operated for three generations providing a friendly service and good food. Don't miss the blueberry muffins and walnut pie.

WELLS Billy's Chowderhouse

216 Mile Rd., 04090 **Tel** *(207) 646-7558*

While many travelers opt for seafood shacks on the beach, Billy's has one of the most striking locations in Maine amid the waving green grasses and rich flats of the marshes behind the Wells barrier beach. It's ideal for whiling away an afternoon drinking beer and snacking on wine-steamed mussels. Closed early Dec–mid-Jan.

YORK BEACH Blue Sky on York Beach

2 Beach St., 03910 **Tel** *(207) 363-0050*

From the lamb pizza to deep-fried short ribs with goat cheese, the fresh market cuisine of Blue Sky never fails to surprise. Appropriately enough for the location, the menu has an entire section devoted to lobster dishes. Maine potatoes also get special treatments. Dinner nightly, brunch Sun.

SHOPPING IN NEW ENGLAND

New England offers a wide and ever-growing variety of high-quality stores and merchandise. For gifts with regional flavor, maple syrup and maple sugar candy, especially plentiful in the northern states of Vermont, New Hampshire, and Maine, fit the bill. Many coastal souvenir shops carry beautiful replicas of whalebone scrimshaw carvings. Regional arts and crafts can be found everywhere.

Red Sox baseball cap

Some of New England's best-known shopping is in factory outlet stores in Freeport and Kittery, Maine and North Conway, New Hampshire, where brand-name goods are sold at a discount. The region's best and most varied shopping is found in Boston. Long known as an excellent center for antiques, books, and quality clothing, the shopping options have evolved to become vibrant and eclectic.

Large glass atrium of the busy Shops at Prudential Center in Boston

SALES

There are two major sale seasons in New England. In July, summer clothes go on sale to make room for fall fashions, and in January, winter clothing and merchandise is cleared after the holidays. Most stores also have a sale section or clearance rack throughout the year.

PAYMENT AND TAXES

Major credit cards and traveler's checks with identification are accepted at most stores. Sales tax in the New England states ranges from 5 to 7 percent. In some states, clothing items may be exempt. New Hampshire is unique in that it has no sales tax.

OPENING HOURS

Most stores open at 10am and close at 6pm from Monday to Saturday, and from noon to 5 or 6pm on Sunday. Many stores stay open later on Thursday nights, and major department stores often stay open until 9pm during the week. Weekday mornings are the best times to shop. Saturdays, lunch hours and evenings can be very busy.

SHOPPING MALLS IN BOSTON

Shopping malls – clusters of stores, restaurants, and food courts all within one complex – have become top destinations for shopping, offering variety, dining, and entertainment. With long winters and a fair share of bad weather, New Englanders flock to malls to shop, eat, and, in the case of teenagers, simply hang out.

Copley Place, with its elegant restaurants and more than 100 stores over two levels, is based around a dazzling 60-ft (18-m) atrium and waterfall. Across a pedestrian overpass, **Shops at Prudential Center** encompasses Saks Fifth Avenue department store, a huge food court, and a multitude of smaller specialty stores. The city's most upscale mall, **Heritage on the Garden** looks out over Boston's Public Garden, and features the boutiques of top European designers, fine jewelers, and stores selling other luxury goods.

Outside the center of town, across the Charles River, **Cambridgeside Galleria** has over 100 stores and a pondside food court. For last-minute purchases, **Boston Landing** at Logan Airport Terminal C has stores, restaurants, banking, and Internet access.

DEPARTMENT STORES IN BOSTON

Boston's major department stores offer a large and varied selection of clothing, accessories, cosmetics, housewares, and gifts. Some also have restaurants and beauty salons, and provide a variety of personal services. For those wanting to shop at several stores, **Concierge of Boston** provides a shopping service

An elegant display of contemporary fashion at Barney's New York

in metropolitan Boston. At Downtown Crossing (see p70), a bustling shopping district between Boston Common and the Financial District, generations of Bostonians once shopped at Filene's, now closed. The department store's cut-price offspring, **Filene's Basement**, pioneered the "automatic markdown," in which goods are discounted more deeply as days pass, creating a risk-and-wait game for bargain-hunters. The original Basement should reopen when renovation work is complete.

Across the street, **Macy's**, the legendary New York emporium, offers an impressive array of fashions, cosmetics, housewares, and furnishings.

Heading uptown, through Boston Common and Public Garden to Boylston Street, you can spot the Prudential Tower, centerpiece of a once nondescript but recently revitalized complex of stores, offices, and restaurants. It includes the venerable **Saks Fifth Avenue**, which caters to its upscale clientele with renowned service, a luxurious ambience, and strikingly stylish displays. For the ultimate high fashion, high profile shopping experience, stop by **Neiman Marcus** (NM) in Copley Place, which specializes in haute couture,

precious jewelry, furs, and gifts. The store is well known for its Christmas catalog, with gift suggestions that have included authentic Egyptian mummies, vintage airplanes, a pair of $2-million diamonds, and robots to help out around the house. Contrasting Manhattan chic against NM's Texas cheekiness is **Barney's New York**, the first new large-scale outlet of the premier New York retailer in decades. Not only can shoppers sample exotic perfumes inside "smelling columns," they can rely on the in-store concierge to book their theater tickets and make dinner reservations. Next door is **Lord & Taylor**, well known for its classic American designer labels, juniors' and children's departments, and menswear. The store also carries a range of crystal, china, and gifts.

Boutiques of genteel Newbury Street

Sign for Brattle Book Shop

SPECIALTY DISTRICTS IN BOSTON

From the fashionable boutiques to the many stores selling cosmopolitan home furnishings or ethnic treasures, to the varied art and crafts galleries, Boston has evolved to cater to every shopping need. Charles Street has been one of the nation's leading centers of fine antiques for generations, while Newbury Street is known for couture and art galleries. A younger and more trendy gallery scene has emerged in recent years in the SoWa (south of Washington Street) section of the South End.

Home decor stores also tend to cluster in the South End, especially along the 1300 block of Washington Street. Shoppers seeking contemporary designer furniture find a treasure trove on the 1000 block of Massachusetts Avenue in Cambridge. Despite the inroads made by online book dealers, Harvard Square retains one of the greatest concentrations of bookstores in the United States. See Specialty Dealers (pp358–9).

DIRECTORY

SHOPPING MALLS

Boston Landing
Terminal C Logan
International Airport,
East Boston.
www.massport.com

Cambridgeside Galleria
100 Cambridgeside Pl.,
Cambridge.
Tel (617) 621-8666

Copley Place
100 Huntington Ave. **Map**
3 C3. **Tel** (617) 369-5000.
www.simon.com

Heritage on the Garden
300 Boylston St. **Map** 4
D2. **Tel** (617) 426-9500.

Shops at Prudential Center
800 Boylston St. **Map** 3
B3. **Tel** (800) 746-7778.
www.prudentialcenter
.com

DEPARTMENT STORES

Barney's New York
5 Copley Place,
100 Huntington Ave. **Map**
3 C3. **Tel** (617) 385-3300.

Concierge of Boston
165 Newbury St.
Map 3 C2.
Tel (617) 266-6611.
www.concierge.org

Filene's Basement
426 Washington St.
Map 4 F1.
Tel (617) 542-2011.
Closed for renovation.

Lord & Taylor
760 Boylston St.
Map 3 B3.
Tel (617) 262-6000.

Macy's
450 Washington St.
Map 4 F1.
Tel (617) 357-3000.

Neiman Marcus
5 Copley Place,
100 Huntington Ave.
Map 3 C3.
Tel (617) 536-3660.

Saks Fifth Avenue
Prudential Center.
Map 3 B3.
Tel (617) 262-8500.

Boston Fashion and Antiques

Bostonians have always preferred their traditions reinvigorated with an edge, making both clothing and decorative arts distinct from other parts of the country. While the top national names in apparel are well represented, so are virtual unknowns with fresh ideas. The city is also a major international center for fine arts in craft media as well as home to the region's top purveyors of antiques – some of which were made right here in Boston.

MEN'S FASHION

Gentlemen seeking the quintessential New England look should head to **Brooks Brothers** on Newbury Street, longtime purveyors of traditional, high-quality menswear. America's foremost fashion house, **Polo/Ralph Lauren** offers top-quality and high-priced sporting and formal attire, while **Jos. A. Bank Clothiers** sells private label merchandise as well as major brands at discounted prices. Professors and students alike patronize the venerable **Andover Shop** and **J. Press** in Cambridge for top-quality Ivy-League essentials.

WOMEN'S FASHION

No woman need leave Boston empty-handed, whether her taste is for the haute couture of **Chanel** or the earthy ethnic clothing at **Nomad**. Newbury Street's high-fashion boutiques include **Kate Spade**, **Betsy Jenney**, and **Max Mara**. Local retailer **Life is Good** offers affordable casual clothes with optimistic mottoes. On Boylston Street, **Ann Taylor** is the first choice for modern career clothes, while **Talbots**, a Boston institution, features enduring classics.

Other Cambridge shops include **A Taste of Culture**, which sells beautiful woolens from Peru; **Settebello**, with its elegant European apparel and accessories; and **Clothware**, which emphasizes natural fiber clothing by local designers.

DISCOUNT AND VINTAGE CLOTHES

First among discount chains is **Marshall's**, promising "brand names for less" and offering bargains on clothing, shoes,

and accessories. Trendsetters head to **H&M**, the popular Swedish retailer, for the latest fashions for adults and kids.

Vintage aficionados love the vast collections at **Bobby from Boston**, a longtime costume source for Hollywood and top fashion designers. **Keezer's** has provided generations of Harvard students with used tuxedos and tweed sports jackets. **Second Time Around**, with locations in both Boston and Cambridge, offers a select array of top-quality, gently worn contemporary women's clothing.

SHOES AND ACCESSORIES

Many Boston stores specialize in accessories. **Helen's Leather** is known for jackets, briefcases, purses, and shoes, as well as Western boots. At Downtown Crossing, **Foot Paths** carries a range of shoes from major manufacturers. Stylish Spanish shoes and bags are the specialty at **Stuart Weitzman** at Copley Place, while the adventurous will find more unusual shoes at **Berk's** and **The Tannery** in Cambridge.

For sports gear, **Niketown** shows video re-runs of sports events while shoppers peruse the latest designs in clothing and footwear. Visitors don't mind going out of the way for huge discounts on athletic and street shoes and apparel at the **New Balance Factory Outlet** store.

ANTIQUES

There are several multi-dealer antiques emporiums in town. **Boston Antiques Cooperative I and II** has everything from quilts, candlesticks, and wicker to chandeliers and

furniture. In Cambridge, **Cambridge Antique Market** encompasses more than 100 dealers, offering antiques, collectibles, furniture, jewelry and more.

Charles Street, Boston's antiques mecca, also features specialty shops for those with specific tastes. Collectors of fine Asian antiques should not miss **Alberts-Langdon, Inc.** and **Judith Dowling Asian Art**, for everything from screens and scrolls to lacquer-ware, ceramics, and paintings.

Antique jewelry is a specialty at **Marika's Antiques Shop**, along with paintings, porcelain, glass, and silver. **Twentieth Century Ltd.** excels in glittery costume jewelry from top designers.

Danish Country carries Scandinavian furniture, while **JMW Gallery**, near South Station, specializes in 19th- and early 20th-century American objects associated with the Arts and Crafts Movement.

FINE CRAFTS

Collectors with a more contemporary bent will find several distinguished galleries with a wide variety of American crafts. **Mobilia** in Cambridge has a national reputation for its jewelry, ceramics, and other objects. The **Society of Arts and Crafts**, established in 1897, has a shop and gallery, with exhibits from the 350 artists it represents. The **Cambridge Artists' Cooperative**, owned and run by over 250 artists, offers an eclectic collection ranging from hand-painted silk jackets to ornaments and jewelry. **The Artful Hand Gallery** also has a range of fine items, crafted primarily by American artists.

SPECIALTY DEALERS

There are shops specializing in everything from posters to rare books, early maps to tribal rugs. Top-brand and vintage watches are a specialty at **European Watch Co.**, while the **Bromfield Pen Shop** has been the purveyor of new, antique, and limited edition pens for over 50 years. For vintage posters from the

19th and 20th centuries, try **International Poster Gallery** on Newbury Street. **Brattle Book Shop** has a huge selection of used, out-of-print and rare books, magazines and vintage photographs. **Eugene Galleries** features antiquarian maps, prints,

and etchings, as well as a comprehensive selection of books. Harvard Square is one of the best places in the United States for bookstores. Specialists abound, including the legendary **Grolier Poetry Book Shop**, and the children's literature specialist,

Curious George Books and Toys. The **Harvard Coop Bookstore** has a nearly encyclopedic selection of new books, while **Harvard Bookstore** offers used and remaindered books in addition to a wide range of carefully chosen new titles.

DIRECTORY

MEN'S FASHION

Andover Shop
22 Holyoke St, Cambridge.
Tel (617) 876-4900.

Brooks Brothers
46 Newbury St. **Map** 4 D2.
Tel (617) 267-2600.

Jos. A. Bank Clothiers
399 Boylston St. **Map** 4 D2. *Tel (617) 536-5050.*

J. Press
82 Mount Auburn St, Cambridge.
Tel (617) 547-9886.

Polo/Ralph Lauren
93/95 Newbury St. **Map** 3 C2. *Tel (617) 424-1124.*

WOMEN'S FASHION

Ann Taylor
800 Boylston St. **Map** 3 B3. *Tel (617) 421-9097.*

A Taste of Culture
1160 Massachusetts Ave, Cambridge.
Tel (617) 868-0389.

Betsy Jenney
114 Newbury St. **Map** 3 C2. *Tel (617) 536-2610*

Chanel
5 Newbury St. **Map** 4 D2.
Tel (617) 859-0055.

Clothware
52 Brattle St, Cambridge.
Tel (617) 661-6441.

Kate Spade
117 Newbury St. **Map** 3 C2. *Tel (617) 262-2632.*

Life is Good
285 Newbury St. **Map** 3 B2. *Tel (617) 262-5068.*

Max Mara
69 Newbury St. **Map** 3 C2. *Tel (617) 267-9775.*

Nomad
1741 Massachusetts Ave, Cambridge.
Tel (617) 497-6677.

Settebello
52 Brattle St, Cambridge.
Tel (617) 864-2440.

Talbots
500 Boylston St. **Map** 3 C2. *Tel (617) 262-2981.*

DISCOUNT AND VINTAGE CLOTHES

Bobby from Boston
19 Thayer St. **Map** 4 E4. *Tel (617) 423-9299.*

H&M
350 Washington St. **Map** 4 F1. *Tel (617) 482-7081.*
100 Newbury St. **Map** 3 C2. *Tel (617) 859-3192.*

Keezer's
140 River St, Cambridge.
Tel (617) 547-2455.

Marshall's
500 Boylston St. **Map** 3 C2. *Tel (617) 262-6066.*

Second Time Around
176 Newbury St.
Map 3 B2.
Tel (617) 247-3504.
8 Eliot St, Cambridge.
Tel (617) 491-7185.

SHOES AND ACCESSORIES

Berk's
50 John F. Kennedy St, Cambridge.
Tel (617) 492-9511.

Foot Paths
489 Washington St.
Map 4 F1.
Tel (617) 338-6008.

Helen's Leather
110 Charles St.
Map 1 B3.
Tel (617) 742-2077.

New Balance Factory Outlet
40 Life St, Brighton.
Tel (877) 623-7867.

Niketown
200 Newbury St. **Map** 3 B2. *Tel (617) 267-3400*

Stuart Weitzman
Copley Place. **Map** 3 C3. *Tel (617) 266-8699.*

The Tannery
39 Brattle St, Cambridge.
Tel (617) 491-1811.

ANTIQUES

Alberts-Langdon, Inc.
135 Charles St. **Map** 1 B3. *Tel (617) 523-5954.*

Boston Antiques Cooperative I and II
119 Charles St. **Map** 1 B3. *Tel (617) 227-9810.*

Cambridge Antique Market
201 Msgr. O'Brien Hwy, Cambridge.
Tel (617) 868-9655.

Danish Country
138 Charles St. **Map** 1 B3. *Tel (617) 227-1804.*

JMW Gallery
144 Lincoln St. **Map** 4 F2. *Tel (617) 338-9097.*

Judith Dowling Asian Art
133 Charles St. **Map** 1 B3. *Tel (617) 523-5211.*

Marika's Antiques Shop
130 Charles St. **Map** 1 B3. *Tel (617) 523-4520.*

Twentieth Century Ltd.
73 Charles St. **Map** 1 B4. *Tel (617) 742-1031.*

FINE CRAFTS

The Artful Hand Gallery

Copley Place. **Map** 3 C3.
Tel (617) 262-9601.

Cambridge Artists' Cooperative
59a Church St, Cambridge.
Tel (617) 868-4434.

Mobilia
358 Huron Ave, Cambridge.
Tel (617) 876-2109.

Society of Arts and Crafts
175 Newbury St. **Map** 3 B2. *Tel (617) 266-1810.*

SPECIALTY DEALERS

Brattle Book Shop
9 West St. **Map** 1 C4. *Tel (617) 542-0210.*

Bromfield Pen Shop
5 Bromfield St. **Map** 1 C4. *Tel (617) 482-9053.*

Curious George Books and Toys
1 JFK St, Cambridge.
Tel (617) 498-0062.

Eugene Galleries
76 Charles St. **Map** 1 B4. *Tel (617) 227-3062.*

European Watch Co.
232 Newbury St. **Map** 3 B2. *Tel (617) 262-9798.*

Grolier Poetry Book Shop
6 Plympton St, Cambridge.
Tel (617) 547-4648.

Harvard Bookstore
1256 Massachusetts Ave, Cambridge.
Tel (617) 661-1515.

Harvard Coop Bookstore
1400 Massachusetts Ave, Cambridge.
Tel (617) 499-2000.

International Poster Gallery
205 Newbury St. **Map** 3 B2. *Tel (617) 375-0076.*

Shopping in New England

Although New England does not immediately conjure up images of unrestrained shopping, in reality there are bargains to be had on a huge variety of consumer goods as well as regional specialties. With a few notable exceptions including Boston *(see pp356-9)*, the greatest concentration of stores generally occurs outside the downtown area, usually along the highways at the outskirts of town. Some of New England's best-known shopping experiences occur at the factory outlet stores in Freeport and Kittery in Maine, and North Conway in New Hampshire, where brand-name clothing and other goods are offered at discount prices.

SHOPPING MALLS

With free parking and a wide range of stores gathered under one roof, malls are popular throughout the region. Here you can find fashions for the whole family, home furnishings, electronic goods, books, toys, music, beauty products, jewelry, sporting goods, food courts, and virtually anything else you could need.

Large department stores are increasingly serving as anchor stores to mall complexes. These "magnet" stores include upscale retailers such as Seattle-based Nordstrom, Lord & Taylor, and branches of Manhattan retail giant Macy's. For widest appeal, these pricey emporiums often share mall space with popular discount chains such as J.C. Penney, Kohl's, big-box electronics retailer Best Buy, and Sears.

The **Arcade** in Providence, Rhode Island, is considered the first indoor marketplace in America; it is currently closed for renovation. **Providence Place**, a 13-acre (5.3-ha) shopping complex in the heart of the city, has more than 170 stores. Highlights include one of New England's two Nordstrom department stores, an IMAX theater and Dave & Buster's, a combination restaurant and amusement arcade.

Downtown Hartford, Connecticut, has been overshadowed by nearby malls. Only 7 miles (11.2 km) southwest, **Westfarms Mall** boasts 160 shops, including the first Nordstrom in New England as well as Lord &

Taylor for those with deep pockets. Twelve miles (19 km) east of Hartford, **The Shoppes at Buckland Hills**, one of the state's biggest and most successful malls, caters to families by offering a play area for children and a carousel in the large food court. The success of the mall has attracted many other retailers to the surrounding area. In an ironic nod to the past, **Evergreen Walk** is a recreation of a typical main street, lined with housewares shops such as Country Curtains and Williams Sonoma; fashion retailers such as The Gap, J. Jill, and Talbots; and restaurants and ice cream shops. For a different kind of experience, **Olde Mistick Village** in Mystic, Connecticut is designed to resemble a colonial village, with more than 60 shops and restaurants set among duck ponds and gardens. Along with clothing and household items, merchandise ranges from scrimshaw carvings to Christmas ornaments, from Irish imports to folk art.

In New Hampshire, options include the **Mall of New Hampshire** in Manchester with about 125 specialty stores as well as J.C. Penney, Sears and Best Buy anchor shops and the somewhat smaller **Steeplegate Mall** in Concord with about 75 shops. New Hampshire is the only state in New England that does not have a sales tax, making savings on shopping purchases even greater. The **Maine Mall**, only 6 miles (10 km) south of Portland, has not reduced the lively

boutique shopping scene at the Old Port. Nonetheless, it attracts a large crowd to its 140 stores, anchored by Macy's, Best Buy, and The Sports Authority, the country's largest full-line sporting goods dealer. The mall also boasts about 20 eateries.

In bucolic Vermont, the largest mall is **University Mall** in South Burlington, with about 70 shops. When it's time for a break, shoppers can stick to local purveyors: Green Mountain Coffee Roasters or Ben & Jerry's Ice Cream.

Travelers looking for a unique shopping environment should visit **Thornes Marketplace** in Northampton, Massachusetts. A Victorian-era department store building was converted into a five-story mall with retailers offering something for everyone: upscale home accessories and clothing, trendy merchandise for college students, ethnic imports, crafts items, and organic foods.

DISCOUNT AND OUTLET SHOPPING

Dedicated bargain hunters will want to pay a visit to some of New England's famed outlet centers, where many top designers and major brand manufacturers offer late-season and over-stocked clothing and goods at big discounts. Generally sold at 20 to 30 percent less than retail prices, some items can be found reduced by as much as 75 percent. In addition to clothing, outlets are good places to find bargains on kitchen goods, linens, china, glassware, leather goods, luggage and sporting goods.

In Wrentham, Massachusetts, 33 miles (53 km) southwest of Boston, are the **Wrentham Village Premium Outlets**. The stores here sell designer clothing, housewares, and accessories from many leading manufacturers. Serving the upscale Long Island Sound community, the **Tanger Factory Outlet Center** in Westbrook, Connecticut, emphasizes fashion and style in its mix of about 60 shops. **Kittery** (*see p278*), Maine, is an even larger outlet destination, with about 120 shops lining a 1-mile (1.6-km) stretch of busy Route 1. Merchants offer everything from footwear and designer clothes to sports equipment, perfume, books, china, glass, and gifts. There are also numerous restaurants. Many shoppers prefer **Freeport**, farther up the coast, about a 20-minute drive north of Portland. Outlets, individual shops, and eateries mingle along the streets of the historic village, making it easy to park the car and stroll from Anne Klein to Brooks Brothers or to check out leather goods and luggage at Dooney & Bourke or Hartmann Factory Store.

The **Manchester Designer Outlets** in Manchester, Vermont, focus on some of the top names in the fashion world, such as Michael Kors, Escada, Giorgio Armani, and

BCBG Max Azria, in addition to Jones New York, Polo/ Ralph Lauren and Tse for soft, luxurious cashmere. The latest designers to look out for include Kenneth Cole and Kate Spade New York.

North Conway, New Hampshire, was one of the first major outlet centers in the region. The 3-mile (5 km) stretch along Route 16 is lined with factory outlets selling fashion, furniture, and outdoor gear.

OUTDOORS OUTFITTERS

With mountains to climb, streams to fish, woods to hike, and lakes and oceans to paddle, New England has an abundance of outdoors outfitters who offer everything from custom flyrods to specialized rock-climbing gear. They also sell "outdoors chic" casual clothing for those more interested in looking the part than breaking a sweat. The regional leader in outdoor

sporting equipment (especially hunting and fishing gear) is **L.L. Bean**, which has its flagship store in Freeport, Maine. The hunting and fishing section is open daily around the clock. The 23,000 sq ft (2137 sq m) flagship store of **Orvis** in Manchester, Vermont, sits on the company's extensive campus, where visitors can tour the adjacent signature flyrod factory or practice flycasting in company trout ponds. Fans of Bogner winter sports apparel will find the **Bogner Haus Outlet Store** in Newport, Vermont, once a Bogner manufacturing center. **Eastern Mountain Sports** focuses on climbing, trekking, mountain biking, and kayaking. Its flagship store is located in Peterborough, New Hampshire. Outdoor stores at the North Conway Factory Outlets include Eddie Bauer, Norm Thompson, and Chuck Roast who sell warm and durable winter outerwear.

DIRECTORY

SHOPPING MALLS

The Arcade
65 Weybosset Street,
Providence, RI.
Tel (401) 598-1199.

Evergreen Walk
501 Evergreen Way
South Windsor, CT.
Tel (860) 432-3398.
www.theshopsatevergree
nwalk.com

Maine Mall
364 Maine Mall Road
South, Portland, ME.
Tel (207) 774-0303.
www.mainemall.com

**Mall of New
Hampshire**
1500 S. Willow Street,
Manchester, NH.
Tel (603) 669-0433.
www.simon.com

Olde Mistick Village
I-95, exit 90, CT.
Tel (860) 536-4941.
www.oldmysticvillage.com

Providence Place
1 Providence Place
Providence, RI.
Tel (401) 270-1000.

**The Shoppes at
Buckland Hills**
194 Buckland Hills Drive,
Manchester, CT.
Tel (860) 644-6369.
www.theshoppesat
bucklandhills.com

Steeplegate Mall
270 Loudon Road,
Concord, NH.
Tel (603) 224-1523.
www.steeplegatemall.com

**Thornes
Marketplace**
150 Main Street,
Northampton, MA.
www.
thornesmarketplace.com

University Mall
Dorset Street at Williston
Rd, South Burlington, VT.
Tel (800) 863-1066.
www.umallvt.com

Westfarms Mall
500 Westfarms Mall Road,
Farmington, CT.
Tel (860) 561-3024.
www.shopwestfarms.com

DISCOUNT AND
OUTLET SHOPPING

**Freeport Merchants
Association**
Freeport, ME.
Tel (800) 865-1994.
www.freeportusa.com

Kittery Outlets
Kittery, ME.
Tel (888) 548-8379.
www.thekitteryoutlets.com

**Manchester
Designer Outlets**
Manchester, VT.
Tel (802) 362-3736.
www.manchesterdesigner
outlets.com

**North Conway
Factory Outlets**
North Conway, NH.
Tel (888) 667-9636.

**Tanger Factory
Outlet Center**
314 Flat Rock Place
Westbrook, CT.
Tel (860) 399-8656.
www.tangeroutlet.com

**Wrentham Village
Premium Outlets**
Wrentham, MA.
Tel (508) 384-0600.
www.premiumoutlets.
com

OUTDOOR
OUTFITTERS

**Bogner Haus Outlet
Store**
172 Bogner Drive, Newport,
VT. *Tel (802) 334-0135.*

**Eastern
Mountain Sports**
1 Vose Farm Road,
Peterborough, NH.
Tel (603) 924-7231.
www.ems.com

L.L. Bean
95 Main Street, Freeport,
ME. *Tel (800) 441-5713.*
www.llbean.com

Orvis Headquarters
4200 Route 7A,
Manchester, VT.
Tel (802) 362-3750.
www.orvis.com

Antiques, Crafts, Books, and Country Stores in New England

While the highway-side shopping centers are the focus of mercantile New England, the goods closely associated with the region are more likely to be found in shops along the byways or in the villages. Visitors looking for gifts with a regional flavor might consider maple syrup, found widely in Vermont and New Hampshire. Coastal shops often have excellent reproductions of scrimshaw whalebone carvings. The nostalgia-oriented country stores often sell the most typical goods of the region, from freshly ground cornmeal to carved wooden toys.

ANTIQUES AND FLEA MARKETS

Perhaps the region's most famous antiquing event is the thrice-yearly Brimfield Antique Show *(see p161)* in Brimfield, Massachusetts. On Cape Cod, scenic Route 6 is peppered with antique shops, especially the charming towns of Dennis and Brewster. Up to 300 dealers fill the parking lot of the **Wellfleet Drive-In Theater** for the flea market on weekends from mid-April through October. The towns of the southern Berkshires are also known for antiquing. **Hill House Antiques** and **The Emporium Antique Center** cover a broad range of Americana. You can't beat the ambience of **Buggy Whip Antiques** in Southfield, where 100 dealers display their wares.

Shops continue as Route 7 crosses the border to Vermont. This state's largest antiques emporia is **Vermont Antique Mall** at Quechee Gorge Village, with more than 450 booths.

Connecticut's Litchfield Hills is another antiques hotbed. The town of Woodbury has dozens of high-quality shops, including **Country Loft Antiques**, which sells many wine implements. A cheaper option is the **Woodbury Flea Market**, which operates on Saturdays all year selling a wide range of new and collectible merchandise. The former mill town of Putnam has reinvented itself as an antiques center. Chief among the shops is **Antiques Marketplace**.

In Rhode Island, go to Spring Street and lower Thames Street in Newport for a variety of shops with select, upmarket merchandise. One of the state's largest flea markets is held on weekends from April through October at Charlestown's **General Stanton Inn**. Up to 200 dealers offer a wide range of antiques and collectibles.

In Maine, Route 1 between Kittery and Scarborough is lined with antiques shops and one of the largest is **Arundel Antiques** with more than 200 dealers. The seafaring town of Searsport has a mix of multi-dealer shops and weekend flea markets. **Hobby Horse Flea Market** features indoor and outdoor stalls. For nautical antiques, quilts and old tools, visit **Pumpkin Patch Antiques Center**.

New Hampshire's antiquing areas include Route 4 between Concord and Durham, Route 101A in Milford, and Route 119 in Fitzwilliam. The highly regarded **Northeast Auctions** conducts five major auctions a year in Manchester and Portsmouth, as well as smaller estate sales. The **Londonderry Flea Market** operates on weekends from mid-April through October.

CRAFTS GALLERIES

New Hampshire has the region's best-established program to support local craftspeople. The **League of New Hampshire Craftsmen** was founded in 1932 and its annual fair in early August is one of the most important in the region. The League also operates seven crafts galleries throughout the state.

The **Frog Hollow Vermont State Craft Center** began modestly in 1971 by offering pottery classes for children. Now it offers a wide array of programs and operates a gallery that displays traditional and contemporary work by about 250 Vermont artisans.

In Connecticut, the **Brookfield Craft Center** was founded in 1954. It offers classes, and showcases the work of American crafts-people through its exhibitions and gallery.

Fifteen Maine potters have formed a collective to market their work through the **Maine Potters Market** in Portland. The functional and decorative pieces represent a wide range of styles and colors. Nearby **Abacus American Craft Gallery** displays the work of American artists, including many from New England.

The Berkshire hills of Massachusetts are home to many crafts artists, including ceramist Thomas Hoadley. His work and that of other local and national artists is displayed in the **Hoadley Gallery**.

BOOK DEALERS

Specialists in antiquarian and used books abound in New England, but few stores have the variety of out-of-print volumes – especially of cookbooks and culinary titles – as **New England Mobile Book Fair**. For sheer volume of used books, check out **Old Number Six Book Depot** in Henniker, New Hampshire, or **Big Chicken Barn Books** in Ellsworth, Maine. Illustrated books and Vermontiana are specialties of **Monroe Street Books** in Middlebury, Vermont, while **Harbor Books** in Old Saybrook, Connecticut, has a broad range of new and used nautical books. **Tyson's Old & Rare Books** in East Providence, Rhode Island, specializes in American history, nautical themes, and Native American literature.

COUNTRY STORES

New England's country stores offer an old-fashioned atmosphere and specialize in local foods: honey, maple syrup, cheese, mustards, and jams.

At **Brown & Hopkins Country Store** in Chepachet, Rhode Island, well-worn pine planks line the floors and a glass case of penny candy sits by the door. **The Store at Five Corners** in Williamstown, Massachusetts, claims to be the country's oldest continuously operating business, having served as a tavern, stagecoach stop, gas station, tea room and general store. In Vermont, the **Weston Village Store** has a pressed tin ceiling and scuffed wooden floors. Sturdy pottery, weathervanes and wooden bowls supplement the wide selection of cheese and fudge. The **Vermont Country Store** sells outdoor clothing, quirky but useful gadgets, and local foodstuffs. In Sugar Hill, New Hampshire, **Harman's Cheese & Country Store** and is known for its aged white cheddar. **The Old Country Store and Museum** in Moultonborough also offers cheddar cheese, along with cast iron cookware.

DIRECTORY

ANTIQUES AND FLEA MARKETS

Antiques Marketplace
109 Main Street, Putnam, CT. *Tel (860) 928-0442.* www.putnamantiques.com

Arundel Antiques
Route 1, Arundel, ME. *Tel (207) 985-7965.*

Buggy Whip Antiques
Route 272, Norfolk Road, Southfield, MA. *Tel (413) 229-3576.*

Country Loft Antiques
557 Main Street South, Woodbury, CT. *Tel (203) 266-4500.*

The Emporium Antique Center
319 Main Street, Great Barrington, MA. *Tel (413) 528-1660.*

General Stanton Inn Flea Market
4115 Old Post Road, Charlestown, RI. *Tel (800) 364-8011.* www.generalstantoninn.com

Hill House Antiques
276 S. Undermountain Road, Sheffield, MA. *Tel (413) 229-2374.*

Hobby Horse Flea Market
383 Main Street, Searsport, ME. *Tel (207) 548-2981.*

Londonderry Flea Market
RR 102 Londonderry, NH. *Tel (603) 883-4196.*

Northeast Auctions
www.northeastauctions.com

Pumpkin Patch Antiques Center
15 West Main Street, Searsport, ME. *Tel (207) 548-6047.*

Vermont Antique Mall
Route 4, Quechee, VT. *Tel (802) 295-1550.*

Wellfleet Drive-In Theater Flea Market
Route 6, Wellfleet, MA. *Tel (508) 349-0541.* www.wellfleetdrivein.com

Woodbury Flea Market
40 Sherman Hill, Woodbury, CT. *Tel (203) 217-8449.*

CRAFTS GALLERIES

Abacus American Craft Gallery
44 Exchange Street, Portland, ME. *Tel (207) 772-4880.*

Brookfield Craft Center
286 Whisconier Road, Brookfield, CT. *Tel (203) 775-4526.*

Frog Hollow Vermont State Craft Center
85 Church Street, Burlington, VT. *Tel (802) 863-6458.* www.froghollow.org

Hoadley Gallery
21 Church Street, Lenox, MA. *Tel (413) 637-2814.* www.hoadleygallery.com

League of New Hampshire Craftsmen
32 Main Street, Center Sandwich, NH. *Tel (603) 284-6831.* www.nhcrafts.org
36 North Main Street, Concord, NH. *Tel (603) 228-8171.*
13 Lebanon Street, Hanover, NH. *Tel (603) 643-5050.*
81 Main Street, Littleton, NH. *Tel (603) 444-1099.*
279 Daniel Webster Highway, Meredith, NH. *Tel (603) 279-7920.*
2526 White Mountains Highway/Route 16. North Conway, NH. *Tel (603) 356-2441.*
15 North Main Street, Wolfeboro, NH. *Tel (603) 569-3309.*

Maine Potters Market
376 Fore Street, Portland, ME. *Tel (207) 774-1633.* www.mainepottersmarket.com

BOOK DEALERS

Big Chicken Barn Books
1768 Bucksport Road, Ellsworth, ME. *Tel (207) 667-7308.*

Harbor Books
146 Main Street, Old Saybrook, CT. *Tel (860) 388-6850.*

Monroe Street Books
70 Monroe Street (Route 7 N.), Middlebury, VT. *Tel (802) 398-2200.*

New England Mobile Book Fair
82–84 Needham Street, Newton Highlands, MA. *Tel (617) 964-7440.*

Old Number Six Book Depot
166 Depot Hill Road, Henniker, NH. *Tel (603) 428-3334.*

Tyson's Old & Rare Books
178 Taunton Avenue, East Providence, RI. *Tel (401) 431-2111.*

COUNTRY STORES

Brown & Hopkins Country Store
1179 Putnam Pike, Chepachet, RI. *Tel (401) 568-4830.*

Harman's Cheese & Country Store
1400 Route 117, Sugar Hill, NH. *Tel (603) 823-8000.*

The Old Country Store and Museum
1011 Whittier Highway, Moultonborough, NH. *Tel (603) 476-5750.*

The Store at Five Corners
Routes 7 and 43, Williamstown, MA. *Tel (413) 458-3176.*

Vermont Country Store
Route 100, Weston, VT. *Tel (802) 824-3184.*

Weston Village Store
Route 100, Weston, VT. *Tel (802) 824-5477.*

ENTERTAINMENT IN BOSTON

From avant-garde performance art to serious drama, and from popular dance music to live classical performances, Boston offers an outstanding array of entertainment options, with something to appeal to every taste: the Theater District offers many excellent plays and musicals; the Wang Theatre hosts many touring productions; and

Quincy Market entertainer

Symphony Hall is home of the renowned Boston Symphony Orchestra. Boston is also well acquainted with jazz, folk, and blues as well as being a center for more contemporary music, played in big city nightclubs. In summer, entertainment often heads outdoors, with many open-air plays and concerts, such as the famous Boston Pops at the Hatch Shell.

PRACTICAL INFORMATION

The best sources for information on current films, concerts, theater, dance, and exhibitions include the Thursday and Friday "G" section of the *Boston Globe* and the Friday entertainment weekly, the *Boston Phoenix*. Even more up-to-date listings can be found on the Internet at the following sites: www.bostoncity search.com; www. boston.com; www.bostonphoenix.com.

Boston entertainment listings magazines

BOOKING TICKETS

Tickets to popular musicals, theatrical productions, and touring shows often sell out far in advance, although theaters sometimes have a few returns or restricted-view

tickets available. You can either get tickets in person at theater box offices, or use one of the ticket agencies in Boston. For advance tickets these are **Ticketmaster** and **Live Nation Tickets**. Tickets can be purchased from both of these agencies over the telephone, in person, or online. Half-price tickets to the majority of non-commercial arts events as well as to some commercial productions are available from 11am on the day of the performance at **BosTix** booths. Purchases must be made in person and only cash is accepted. BosTix also sells advance full-price tickets. Special Boston entertainment discount vouchers, available from hotel lobbies and tourist offices, may also give a saving on some shows.

Tchaikovsky's *Nutcracker*, danced by the Boston Ballet *(see p366)*

DISTRICTS AND VENUES

Musicals, plays, comedies, and dance are generally performed at venues in the Theater District, although larger non-commercial theater companies are distributed throughout the region, many being associated with colleges and universities.

The area around the intersection of Massachusetts and Huntington Avenues hosts a concentration of outstanding concert venues, including Symphony Hall, Berklee Performance Center at Berklee College of Music, and Jordan Hall at the New England Conservatory of Music.

Many nightclub and dance venues are on Lansdowne and nearby streets by Fenway Park and around Boylston Place in the Theater District. The busiest areas for bars and small clubs offering live jazz and rock music are Central and Harvard Squares in Cambridge, Davis Square in Somerville, and Allston. The principal gay scene in Boston is found in the South End, with many of the older bars and clubs in neighboring Bay Village.

Boston's Symphony Orchestra performing at Symphony Hall *(see p366)*

OPEN-AIR AND FREE ENTERTAINMENT

The best free outdoor summer entertainment in Boston is found at the Hatch Shell *(see p92)* on the Charles River Esplanade. The Boston Pops *(see p366)* performs here frequently during the week around July 4, and all through July and August jazz, pop, rock, and classical music is played. On Friday evenings from late June to the week before Labor Day, the Hatch Shell also shows free big-screen family films.

Music is also performed during the summer months at the **Bank of America Pavilion** on the waterfront, which holds live jazz, pop, and country music concerts. City Hall Plaza and Copley Plaza have free concerts at lunchtimes and in the evenings, and the Museum of Fine Arts *(see pp106–9)*

Free open-air music concert outside New City Hall *(see p80)*

operates a summer musical concert series in its courtyard. Most of the annual concerts and recitals of the New England Conservatory of Music *(see p366)* are free, although some require advance booking.

Other open-air entertainment includes a series of free productions of Shakespeare, sponsored by **Citi Performing Arts Center** in July and August, and ticketed performances of various plays by the **Publick Theater** at Christian Herter Park on the Charles River.

An area that has more unusual open-air entertainment is Harvard Square, famous for its nightly and weekend scene of street performers. Many recording art-

ists paid their dues here, and other hopefuls still flock to the square in the vain hope of being discovered – or at least of earning the cost of dinner.

Details of all free entertainment happening in the city are listed in the "G" section of Thursday's and Friday's *Boston Globe*.

DISABLED ACCESS

Many entertainment venues in Boston are wheelchair accessible. **Very Special Arts Massachusetts** offers a full Boston arts access guide. Some places, such as **Jordan Hall**, the **Cutler Majestic Theater**, and the **Wheelock Family Theater**, have listening aids for the hearing impaired, while the latter also has signed and described performances.

Entrance to the Shubert Theatre *(see p71)*

DIRECTORY

BOOKING TICKETS

BosTix
Faneuil Hall Marketplace.
Map 2 D3.
Copley Square.
Map 3 C2.
Tel *(617) 482-2849.*
www.bostix.org

Live Nation Tickets
Downtown Crossing.
Map 1 C4.
Various outlets.
Tel *(800) 431-3462.*
www.livenation.com

Ticketmaster
Various outlets.
Tel *(800) 745-3000.*
www.ticketmaster.com

OPEN-AIR/FREE ENTERTAINMENT

Bank of America Pavilion
290 Northern Ave.,
South Boston.
Map 2 F5.
Tel *(617) 728-1600.*
www.bankofamerica
pavilion.com

Citi Performing Arts Center
Parkman Bandstand,
Boston Common.
Map 1 C4.
Tel *(617) 482-9393.*
www.citicenter.org

New England Conservatory of Music
290 Huntington Ave.
Tel *(617) 585-1260.*
www.newengland
conservatory.edu

Publick Theater
Christian A. Herter Park,
1175 Soldiers Field Rd.,
Brighton.
Tel *(617) 454-1444.*
www.publick
theater.com

DISABLED ACCESS

Cutler Majestic Theater
219 Tremont St.

Map 4 E2.
Tel *(617) 824-8000.*
www.maj.org

Jordan Hall
30 Gainsborough St.
Tel *(617) 585-1260.*

Very Special Arts Massachusetts
89 South St.
Map 4 F2.
Tel *(617) 350-7713;*
TTY *(617) 350-6535.*
www.vsamass.org

Wheelock Family Theater
200 Riverway, Brookline.
Tel *(617) 879-2300.*
TTY *(617) 879-2150.*
www.wheelock.edu/wft

The Arts in Boston

Although some theaters are closed on Mondays, there is rarely a night in Boston without performing arts. For classical music lovers, the season revolves around the Boston Symphony Orchestra, with many Brahmins *(see p63)* occupying their grandparents' seats at Symphony Hall. Bostonians are also avid theatergoers, opting for touring musical productions in historic theaters as well as ambitious contemporary drama at repertory theaters. (Occasionally shows preview in Boston before debuting on Broadway.) The prestigious Boston Ballet performs at the Opera House and other smaller venues. With huge student and expat populations, the city also enjoys a healthy cinema scene, with annual film festivals and a number of art-house theaters.

CLASSICAL MUSIC AND OPERA

Two cherished Boston institutions, the **Boston Symphony Orchestra** and its popular-music equivalent, the Boston Pops, have a long history of being led by some of America's finest conductors. The BSO performs a full schedule of concerts at Symphony Hall from October through April. The Boston Pops takes over for May and June, performing at the Charles River Esplanade *(see p96)* for Fourth of July festivities that are the highlight of the summer season.

The students and faculty of the **New England Conservatory of Music** present more than 450 free classical and jazz performances each year, many in Jordan Hall *(see p365)*. **Boston Lyric Opera** has assumed the task of reestablishing opera in Boston, through small-cast and light opera at venues around the city.

Boston's oldest musical organization is the **Handel & Haydn Society** (H&H), founded in 1815. As the first American producer of such landmark works as Handel's *Messiah* (performed annually since 1818), Bach's *B-Minor Mass* and *St. Matthew Passion*, and Verdi's *Requiem*, H&H is one of the country's musical treasures. Since 1986, the society has focused on performing and recording Baroque and Classical works using the period instruments for which the composers

wrote. H&H gives regular performances in Boston at Symphony Hall, Jordan Hall, and other venues.

Classical music is ubiquitous in Boston. **Emmanuel Music**, for example, performs the entire Bach cantata cycle at regular services at Emmanuel Church on Newbury Street. The Isabella Stewart Gardner Museum *(see p105)* hosts a series of chamber music concerts, continuing a 19th-century tradition of professional "music room" chamber concerts in the homes of the social elite.

The **Celebrity Series of Boston** brings world-famous orchestras, soloists, and dance companies to Boston, often to perform at Jordan Hall and other venues.

THEATER

Though much diminished from its heyday in the 1920s, when more than 40 theaters were in operation throughout Boston, today the city's Theater District *(see pp58–71)* still contains a collection of some of the most architecturally eminent, and commercially productive, early theaters in the United States. Furthermore, during the 1990s, many of the theaters that are currently in use underwent major programs of restoration to bring them back to their original grandeur, and visitors today are bound to be impressed as they catch a glimpse of these theaters' past glory.

The main, commercially run theaters of Boston – the **Colonial**, **Wilbur**, and Shubert *(see p71)* theaters, and the **Opera House** and the Wang Theatre *(see p71)* – often present Broadway productions that have already premiered in New York and are touring the country. They also present Broadway "tryouts" and local productions.

In stark contrast to some of the mainstream shows on offer in Boston, the most avant-garde contemporary theater in the city is performed at the **American Repertory Theater** (ART), an independent, non-commercial company associated with Harvard University *(see pp112–13)*. ART often premieres new plays, particularly on its second stage, but is best known for its often radical interpretations of traditional and modern classics. By further contrast, the **Huntington Theatre**, allied with Boston University, is widely praised for its traditional direction and interpretation. For example, the Huntington was the co-developer of Pulitzer-Prize winning plays detailing 20th-century African American life, by the late August Wilson, an important chronicler of American race relations.

Several smaller companies, including **Lyric Stage**, devote their energies to showcasing local actors and directors and often premiere the work of Boston-area playwrights. Many of the most adventurous companies perform on one of the four stages at the **Boston Center for the Arts**.

DANCE

The city's largest and most popular resident dance company, the **Boston Ballet** performs an ambitious season of classics and new choreography between October and May at the opulent Opera House and other venues. The annual performances of the *Nutcracker* during the Christmas season are a Boston tradition.

The somewhat more modest **José Mateo's Ballet Theater** has developed a strong and impressive body of repertory choreography. The company performs in the neo-Gothic Old Cambridge Baptist Church, which is situated near Harvard Square. Modern dance in Boston is represented by many small companies, collectives, and independent choreographers, who often perform in the **Dance Complex** and **Green Street Studios** in Cambridge. Boston also hosts many other visiting dance companies, who often put on performances at the **Cutler Majestic Theater**.

CINEMA

Situated in Harvard Square *(see p110)* close to Harvard Yard, the **Brattle Theater**, one of the very last repertory movie houses in the Greater Boston area, primarily shows classic films on a big screen. For example, the Brattle was instrumental in reviving moviegoers' interest in the Humphrey Bogart, black-and-white classic *Casablanca*. Something of a Harvard institution, the Brattle has long served as a popular "first date" destination.

Serious students of classic and international cinema patronize the screening programs of the **Harvard Film Archive**, for its range of foreign, art, and historical films. The **Kendall Square Cinema** multiplex is the city's chief venue for non-English language films, art films and documentaries. Multiplex theaters showing mainstream, first-run Hollywood movies are found throughout the Boston area. Some of the most popular are **Loews Theaters**, located at Boston Common, and the **Regal Fenway 13** in the suburb of Brookline.

Tickets for every kind of movie in Boston are often discounted for first shows of the day on weekends and all weekday shows before 5pm.

DIRECTORY

CLASSICAL MUSIC AND OPERA

Boston Lyric Opera
various venues.
Tel (617) 542-6772.
www.blo.org

Boston Symphony Orchestra
Symphony Hall, 301 Massachusetts Ave. **Map** 3 A4. *Tel (617) 266-1200, (617) 266-1492.*
www.bso.org

Celebrity Series of Boston
various venues.
Tel (617) 482-6661.
www.celebrityseries.org

Emmanuel Music
Emmanuel Church, 15 Newbury St. **Map** 4 D2. *Tel (617) 536-3356.*
www.emmanuelmusic.org

Handel & Haydn Society
various venues.
Tel (617) 266-3605.
www.handelandhaydn.org

New England Conservatory of Music
Jordan Hall, 30 Gainsborough St. **Map** 3 A4. *Tel (617) 585-1260.*
www.newenglandconservatory.edu

THEATER

American Repertory Theater
Loeb Drama Center, 64 Brattle St., Cambridge.
Tel (617) 547-8300.
www.amrep.org

Boston Center for the Arts
539 Tremont St.
Map 4 D3.
Tel (617) 933-8600.
www.bostontheaterscene.com

Colonial Theater
106 Boylston St.
Map 4 E2.
Tel (617) 426-9366.
www.broadwayacrossamerica.com

Huntington Theatre
264 Huntington Ave.
Map 3 B4.
Tel (617) 266-0800.
www.huntingtontheatre.org

Lyric Stage
140 Clarendon St.
Map 3 C3.
Tel (617) 585-5678.
www.lyricstage.com

Opera House
539 Washington St.
Map 4 E1.
Tel (800) 982-2787.
www.broadwayacrossamerica.com

Wilbur Theater
246 Tremont St. **Map** 4 E2. *Tel (617) 931-2000.*

DANCE

Boston Ballet
various venues.
Tel (617) 695-6955.
www.bostonballet.org

Cutler Majestic Theater
219 Tremont St. **Map** 4 E2.
Tel (617) 824-8000.
www.maj.org

Dance Complex
536 Massachusetts Ave, Cambridge.
Tel (617) 547-9363.
www.dancecomplex.org

Green Street Studios
185 Green St, Cambridge.
Tel (617) 864-3191.
www.greenstreetstudios.org

José Mateo's Ballet Theater
400 Harvard St, Cambridge.
Tel (617) 354-7467.
www.ballettheatre.org

CINEMA

Brattle Theater
40 Brattle St, Cambridge.
Tel (617) 876-6837.

Harvard Film Archive
24 Quincy St, Cambridge.
Tel (617) 495-4700.
hcl.harvard.edu/hfa

Kendall Square Cinema
1 Kendall Square, Cambridge.
Tel (617) 499-1996.

Loews Theaters
Boston Common.
Map 4 E2.
Tel (617) 423-5801.

Regal Fenway 13
201 Brookline Ave.
Tel (617) 424-6266.

Music Venues in Boston

Boston's mix of young professionals and tens of thousands of college students produces a lively nightlife scene, focused on live music, clubs, and bars. Since the 1920s, Boston has been especially hospitable to jazz, and it still has an interesting jazz scene, with the world-renowned Berklee College of Music playing an important part. Cambridge is an epicenter of folk and acoustic music revivals and alt-rock, while Lansdowne Street (behind Fenway Park) is the main district for rock clubs. Virtually every neighborhood has a selection of friendly bars, many with live music. The city's audiences, considered to be among the country's most eager and receptive, make Boston a must-stop destination for national touring acts.

ROCK MUSIC

Two famous dance clubs – Avalon and Axis – closed in 2008 with the sale of the complex at 13–15 Lansdowne Street to the **House of Blues**. This was a move that spelled the end of an era for late-night dancing and the beginning of another for year-round indoor rock and blues concerts. The successful House of Blues chain originated in Harvard Square but expanded to other cities because Greater Boston did not have structures large enough to host its concerts. After extensive renovation to establish a concert facility, the House of Blues opened in 2009.

Roxy, Boston's "other" mega-club, offers the occasional big-time concert with international performers including Prince and Ziggy Marley, but it makes its name by hosting some of the city's most raucous club nights, with world-famous DJs and hordes of scantily clad clubbers.

Located on the edge of Boston University's campus, the **Paradise Rock Club** has long been a local institution (the likes of U2, Coldplay, and the Police have all graced the stage). The front lounge offers a relaxed spot for an inexpensive pre-show meal and hosts smaller acts on most nights.

In a city that's chock full of historical sites, the **Orpheum Theater** stands out as the oldest concert venue. The original home of the New England Conservatory of Music (see pp366–7) dates back to 1852 and serves as Boston's premier venue for acts that are too big for the clubs but can't quite fill an arena. While the sightlines are above-average, the venue loses major points for having a no food or beverage policy in the stands (concert-goers are forced to enjoy their overpriced beers in the stuffy lobby).

Arena-level acts head to the 18,000-seat **TD BankNorth Garden**, home of the Boston Bruins (NHL) and Celtics (NBA), or Boston University's **Agannis Arena**, which is roughly half the size of the Garden. Come summertime, those same acts head outdoors to play the massive **Comcast Center for the Performing Arts** – located 30 miles (48 km) southwest of Boston – and smaller **Bank of America Pavilion** (see p365), which enjoys scenic skyline views from its South Boston waterfront home.

At the other end of the size spectrum are places like the **Green Dragon Tavern** near Quincy Market, known for its Irish and cover bands; **Bill's Bar** on Lansdowne Street, a rock and reggae venue; and **An Tua Nua**, a Boston University hangout with cover bands and salsa dancing.

Middle East, Cambridge's premier all-purpose club, offers three distinct stages in which to enjoy everything from local folk collectives and belly dancing to national rock acts. The eponymous restaurant provides a relaxed spot for a pre- or post-show drink or snack.

For anyone who's always wanted to be close enough to taste a rock star's sweat, **TT the Bear's** is the place. This diminutive club, located just behind the Middle East, puts fans right in the middle of the action, with nothing separating those at the front from the low stage.

Also located in Cambridge are the **Lizard Lounge** and **All-Asia Café**, tiny clubs that host wildly eclectic schedules, and **Plough & Stars** and **Toad**, both of which are popular with local singer-songwriters.

Away from the city center, up-and-coming Somerville is home to **P.A.'s Lounge** and **Sally O'Brien's**, a pair of dive bars that are good for cheap drinks and local rock acts.

JAZZ AND BLUES

As one would expect from one of the nation's most respected music schools, **Berklee Performance Center** houses perhaps the best acoustics and sightlines in Boston. The auditorium hosts everything from jazz legends and big band revues to contemporary acts. The only drawback is that no food or drink is allowed in the seats.

On a nondescript stretch of Massachusetts Avenue resides **Wally's Cafe**, one of the city's hidden gems. This atmospheric jazz club hosts live music 365 days a year, with bebop, swing and Afro-Cuban Latin jazz. Now and then professionals pop up, but most lineups comprise students and amateurs. On weekends, there's usually a line.

The majority of national jazz touring acts stick to one of three clubs: **Regattabar** (in Harvard Square's swish Charles Hotel), **Ryles Jazz Club** (in Cambridge's Inman Square) and **Scullers Jazz Club** (in the Doubletree Hotel, on the Brighton-Cambridge border).

Those looking to avoid paying steep cover charges stick to lower-key spots like Central Square's **Cantab Lounge**, Allston's **Wonder Bar** and **Les Zygomates**, a stylish French bistro in Boston's gentrifying Leather District that hosts free live jazz most nights.

FOLK AND WORLD MUSIC

Since 1958, Harvard Square has been home to **Club Passim**, one of the country's seminal folk clubs. The small venue held the Northeast's first hootenanny, and has seen eveyone from Bob Dylan to Joan Baez play here.

Johnny D's Uptown Restaurant & Music Club in Somerville's Davis Square is one of the area's most diverse music clubs, where you might stumble upon a hillbilly jam or Latin funk artist. There's a live jazz brunch and blues jam on Sunday's. The **Somerville Theatre** is a stuffy venue that's popular with world music acts,

while just down the street is **The Burren**, an Irish pub that hosts lively sessions and Celtic acts. The Museum of Fine Arts' **Remis Auditorium** has wonderful acoustics for world music gigs. International acts ranging from Afro-pop to ska play at large venues across Boston in a concert series presented by promoters **World Music**.

DIRECTORY

ROCK MUSIC

Agganis Arena
925 Commonwealth Ave., Boston.
Tel (617) 931-2000.
www.agganisarena.com

All-Asia Cafe
334 Massachusetts Ave., Cambridge.
Tel (617) 497-1544
www.allasiabar.com

An Tua Nua
835 Beacon St.
Tel (617) 262-2121.

Bank of America Pavilion
290 Northern Ave.
Tel (617) 728-1600
www.bankofamerica pavilion.com

Bill's Bar
5 Lansdowne St.
Tel 617-421-9678.
www.billsbar.com

Comcast Center for the Performing Arts
885 S Main St, Mansfield, MA.
Tel (508) 339-2331.
www.livenation.com

Green Dragon Tavern
11 Marshall St.
Tel (617) 367-0055.

House of Blues
13–15 Lansdowne St.
Tel (888) 693-2583.
www.houseofblues.com

Lizard Lounge
1667 Massachusetts Ave., Cambridge, MA.
Tel (617) 547-0759.

Middle East
472/480 Massachusetts Ave., Cambridge. *Tel (617) 864-3278 ext 221.*
www.mideastclub.com

Orpheum Theater
1 Hamilton Place.
Map 1C4.
Tel (617) 482-0106.

P.A.'s Lounge
345 Somerville Ave., Somerville.
Tel (617) 776-1557.
www.paslounge.com

Paradise Rock Club
969 Commonwealth Ave.
Tel (617) 562-8800.
www.thedise.com

Plough & Stars
912 Massachusetts Ave., Cambridge.
Tel (617) 576-0032.
www.ploughandstars.com

Roxy
279 Tremont St.
Tel (617) 338-7699.

Sally O'Brien's
335 Somerville Ave, Somerville, MA.
Tel (617) 440-7690.

TD Garden
1 Causeway St.
Map 1C2.
Tel (617) 624-1000.
www.tdbanknorth garden.com

Toad
1912 Massachusetts Ave., Cambridge.
Tel (617) 497-4950.
www.toadcambridge.com

TT The Bear's
10 Brookline St. (Central Square), Cambridge.
Tel 617-492-BEAR (2327).
www.ttthebears.com

JAZZ AND BLUES

Berklee Performance Center
Berklee College of Music, 136 Massachusetts Ave.
Map 3 A3.
Tel (617) 266-7455.
www.berkleebpc.com

Cantab Lounge
738 Massachusetts Ave., Cambridge.
Tel (617) 354-2685.
www.cantab-lounge.com

Les Zygomates
129 South St.
Tel (617) 542-5108.
www.winebar.com/

Regattabar
Charles Hotel, 1 Bennett St., Cambridge.
Tel (617) 395-7757.
www.regattabarjazz.com

Ryles Jazz Club
212 Hampshire St., Cambridge.
Tel (617) 876-9330.
www.rylesjazz.com

Scullers Jazz Club
Doubletree Guest Suites, 400 Soldiers Field Rd., Brighton.
Tel (617) 562-4111.
www.scullersjazz.com

Wally's Cafe
427 Massachusetts Ave.
Tel (617) 424-1408.
www.wallyscafe.com

Wonder Bar
186 Harvard Ave. Allston, MA.
Tel (617) 351-2665.
www.wonderbar boston.com

FOLK AND WORLD MUSIC

The Burren
247 Elm St., Somerville, MA.
Tel (617) 776-6896.
www.burren.com

Club Passim
47 Palmer St., Cambridge.
Tel (617) 492-7679.
www.clubpassim.org

Johnny D's Uptown Restaurant & Music Club
17 Holland St., Somerville.
Tel (617) 776-2004.
www.johnnyds.com

Remis Auditorium, Museum of Fine Arts
465 Huntington Ave.
Tel (617) 267-9300.
www.mfa.org

Somerville Theatre
55 Davis Square Somerville, MA.
Tel (617) 625-5700.
www.somervilletheatre online.com

World Music
various venues.
Tel (617) 876-4275.
www.worldmusic.org

Pubs, Clubs and Sports Bars

While large-scale events and concerts abound, the regular nightlife of Boston revolves primarily around drinking establishments. The legal drinking age here is 21, and you may be asked to show proof of identification *(see p383)* if you appear to be under 35. Not all bars and clubs are clearly marked, but they can usually be identified by their address and the cluster of smokers puffing away near the entrance in all weather. (Smoking is not permitted in clubs and bars in New England.) Ironically, the window for nightlife is short, as most venues don't liven up until 10pm, and Boston's drinking laws shut off alcohol service at 1 or 2am, depending on the neighborhood.

SPORTS BARS

Bostonians love sports, and while most bars have at least one game on the television over the bar, hard-core fans want more, and the city's dozens of sports bars oblige with multiple channel offerings. The **Cask 'N' Flagon**, adjacent to Fenway Park (to the west of Back Bay), is perfect for celebrating victory or softening the pain of defeat, while **Jillian's Boston** is just up the street, drawing a mixed-gender crowd for billiards and sports-watching. At **Kings**, big-screen sports televisions vie with bowling lanes, while the **Sports Depot** in the college-student enclave of Allston is mammoth, with a giant television placed every few feet. The area near North Station is filled with bars catering to Boston Celtics and Boston Bruins fans. One of the most notable is **The Fours**, where the sandwiches are named for sports legends and the memorabilia extends beyond basketball and hockey to boxing and baseball. One of the friendliest neighborhood sports bars of South Boston is the **Boston Beer Garden**, where locals refer to the city's hockey team as the "Broonz."

PUBS & BREWPUBS

With the largest per capita population of Irish descendants in the US, it's not surprising that Boston has many Irish pubs, which offer a convivial setting for good hearty food, pints of Guinness and live music. Among these are **Kinsale**, near Government Center, where

the entire bar was transported brick by brick from Ireland; the **Phoenix Landing Bar and Restaurant**, a mock Irish pub in Cambridge's Central Square lined with mahogany and screening English football on cable TV on weekend nights; **The Burren**, which has some of the finest musicians in the city; and the smaller **Druid**, where as the evening wears on, crowds of young professionals give way to recent Irish immigrants. **The Independent** in Somerville's Union Square is a good place to catch Irish bands, as well as unplugged rock. Darts and stout are the main draws at **The Field**, which is reputed to serve more Guinness on draft than any other bar in the US. The **Plough and Stars** ranks as one of the city's most seriously literary bars. It also features English League football on weekends.

Boston was in the forefront of the national brewpub craze in the 1980s, but of that first wave of artisanal brewers, only **John Harvard's Brew House** in Harvard Square and **Cambridge Brewing Company** in Kendall Square continue to flourish. Successful newcomer **Boston Beer Works** has a built-in clientele by virtue of its location next to Fenway Park and Boston University. No serious drinker or student of Boston history should miss **Doyle's Café**, famous for its continuing role in Boston political campaigns and a flagship bar for nearby Boston Beer Co., which debuts its seasonal Sam Adams brews here.

GAY CLUBS & BARS

Boston's gay scene comes into sharpest focus in the South End and Bay Village, but bars and clubs are found throughout the city that hold gay nights. These events are often a staple of otherwise straight nightclubs. **Club Café Bar & Lounge** runs separate front and back dance rooms with different themes every night. Girls take over the club for women's T-dance on Sunday nights. The perpetually packed **Fritz Lounge** is a stalwart South End bar. Boston's longest-running gay club, **Jacques**, features rock acts Friday through Monday and female impersonator cabaret the rest of the week. The leather and denim set are drawn to the sociable, mellow Ladder District bar, **The Alley**, and to Boston's largest gay cruise bar, **Ramrod** in the Fenway. A suave lesbian (and, to a lesser extent, gay) scene goes on nightly at **209**, where Back Bay and South End meet. The weekly *Bay Windows* newspaper provides more information, as do other listings.

NIGHTCLUBS

Boston has a club for almost every type of dance music. Like club scenes everywhere, little happens until at least 11pm. **Parris**, beneath the Quincy Market rotunda, offers the cutting edge for martini-bar dancing on its hardwood floor. The **Grand Canal** near North Station spins techno and house music for a youthful clientele. Located in the rear of a stylish restaurant, the **Gypsy Bar** has a Latin night as well as house and techno music. Chandeliers and full-length mirrors add drama at cavernous **The Estate** on Piano Row. **Precinct** in Somerville's Union Square has lively music every night, ranging from Irish rockers to local singer-songwriters to good-times, old-fashioned rock-n-roll. More middle-of-the-road is the **Roxy** in the Theater District, with classy touches like doormen instead of bouncers, marble walls, and a vast dance floor.

COMEDY CLUBS

Many clubs and bars program occasional evenings of standup comedy, and several specialize in it. The **Comedy Connection** at Wilbur Theatre presents an impressive line-up of comedians, who are familiar from their work on national TV. **Nick's Comedy Stop**, on the other hand, tends to focus on homegrown talent, grooming performers who often go on to the "big time." Located in Cambridge's nightlife-busy Central Square, **Improv Boston** mixes audience-participation cabaret, skit comedy, revues, the occasional hootenanny, and even serious theater. The very name of **Improv Asylum** explains it all: lunatic comedy based on audience suggestions. Local comedian Dick Doherty hosts the shenanigans (including open mike nights) at **Dick's Beantown Comedy Vault**. Somewhat edgier laughs from newcomers and television comedy writers can be had at **The Comedy Studio**.

DIRECTORY

SPORTS BARS

Boston Beer Garden
732 East Broadway,
South Boston.
Tel (617) 269-0990.
www.bostonbeer
garden.com

Cask 'N' Flagon
62 Brookline Avenue.
Tel (617) 536-4840.
www.casknflagon.com

The Fours
166 Canal Street.
Map 1 C2.
Tel (617) 720-4455.
www.thefours.com

Jillian's Boston
145 Ipswich St.
Tel (617) 437-0300.
www.jilliansboston.com

Kings
50 Dalton Street.
Map 3 A3.
Tel (617) 266-2695.

Sports Depot
353 Cambridge Street,
Allston.
Tel (617) 783-2300.
www.sportsdepotboston.
com

PUBS AND BREWPUBS

Boston Beer Works
61 Brookline Avenue.
Tel (617) 536-2337.
www.beerworks.net

The Burren
247 Elm Street, Somerville.
Tel (617) 776-6896.
www.burren.com

Cambridge Brewing Company
1 Kendall Square, Building
100. *Tel (617) 494-1994.*
www.cambrew.com

Doyle's Cafe
3484 Washington Street,
Jamaica Plain.
Tel (617) 524-2345.

Druid
1357 Cambridge Street,
Cambridge.
Tel (617) 497-0965.
www.druidpub.com

The Field
20 Prospect Street
(Central Sq.), Cambridge.
Tel (617) 354-7345.

The Independent
75 Union Square,
Somerville. *Tel (617) 440-6022.* www.theindo.com

John Harvard's Brew House
33 Dunster Street,
Cambridge.
Tel (617) 868-3585.
www.johnharvards.com

Kinsale Irish Pub & Restaurant
2 Center Plaza. **Map** 1 C3.
Tel (617) 742-5577.
www.classicirish.com

Phoenix Landing Bar and Restaurant
512 Massachusetts
Avenue, Cambridge.
Tel (617) 576-6260.

Plough and Stars
912 Massachusetts
Avenue, Cambridge.
Tel (617) 576-0032.
www.ploughandstars.com

GAY CLUBS AND BARS

209
209 Columbus Avenue.
Map 4 D3.
Tel (617) 536-0972.

The Alley
14 Pi Alley. **Map** 4 F4.
Tel (617) 263-1449.

Club Café Bar & Lounge
209 Columbus Ave.
Map 4 D3.
Tel (617) 536-0966.

Fritz Lounge
25 Chandler Street.
Map 4 D3.
Tel (617) 482-4428.

Jacques
79 Broadway.
Map 4 F4.
Tel (617) 426-8902.

Ramrod
1254 Boylston Street.
Tel (617) 266-2986.

NIGHTCLUBS

The Estate
1 Boylston Pl.
Map 4 E2.
Tel (617) 251-7000.

Grand Canal
57 Canal Street.
Map 2 D2.
Tel (617) 523-1112.

Gypsy Bar
116 Boylston Street.
Tel (617) 482-7799.

Parris
2nd Floor, Quincy Market.
Tel (617) 248-9900.

Precinct
70 Union Square,
Somerville.
Tel (617) 623-9211.
www.precinctbar.com

Roxy
279 Tremont Street.
Map 4 E2.
Tel (617) 338-7699.

COMEDY CLUBS

Comedy Connection
Wilbur Theatre, 246
Tremont St. **Map** 4 E2.
Tel (617) 931-2000.
www.thewilburtheatre.
com

The Comedy Studio
Hong Kong Restaurant,
3rd Floor,
1236 Massachusetts
Avenue, Cambridge.
Tel (617) 661-6507.
www.thecomedystudio.
com

Dick's Beantown Comedy Vault
124 Boylston Street.
Map 1 B5.
Tel (800) 401-2221.
www.dickdoherty.com

Improv Asylum
216 Hanover Street.
Map 2 D3.
Tel (617) 263-6887.
www.improvasylum.com

Improv Boston
40 Prospect Street,
Cambridge.
Tel (617) 576-1253.

Nick's Comedy Stop
100 Warrenton Street.
Tel (617) 423-2900.
www.nickscomedy
stop.com

OUTDOOR ACTIVITIES

Squeezed within New England's relatively compact borders there is a wealth of outdoor activities. Mountain ranges, forests, rivers, and miles of coastline have been preserved as natural playgrounds for outdoor enthusiasts ranging from people just looking for a quiet afternoon in the sun to serious backcountry trekkers.

Striped bass, Woods Hole, Massachusetts

While the majority of unspoiled, rugged wilderness is found in the northern states of New Hampshire, Vermont, and Maine, there are still plenty of outdoor adventures to be had in the much more densely populated south. Visitors will find plenty to do on sea and land throughout Massachusetts, Rhode Island, and Connecticut.

CAMPING

Always a popular activity in New England, camping can also save you money on accommodations – depending on how much you are willing to rough it. While there are designated primitive camping areas in

Camping in White Mountain National Forest, New Hampshire

the backcountry of selected national forests, the more established campgrounds make up the majority of sites. Standard campgrounds, usually found in state and national forests, are equipped with facilities such as toilets, garbage disposal, and often facilities for hot showers. The tent sites at such places are usually spaced well apart and cost between $12 and $20 a night. For the hardcore camper, primitive campsites found in national forests offer only the bare minimum: rudimentary cooking areas, pit toilets, and cold running

water. These sites are perfect for the frugal outdoor enthusiast, usually costing around $10 a night.

On the opposite end of the spectrum, private campgrounds are models of luxury. Most cater to large recreational vehicles (RVs) and motor homes, with running water and electrical hookups. Hot showers and sewage hookups are often provided as well. Many upscale campgrounds have a host of recreational facilities that range from swimming to miniature golf courses. These sites are somewhat more expensive, costing $20 to $40 dollars or so a night.

Government-run campgrounds usually follow the summer season from the end of May through to early October. For the most part, private campgrounds have a much longer season, with some staying open year-round. Regardless of the type of camping that will be done, it is always a good idea to reserve a campsite early, especially during the busy summer months. Contact the **National Park Service** or the **National Recreation Reservation Service** for campground information and reservations. As a safety

Friendly welcome sign typical of campsites in New England

Boston's Swan Boats offering gentle cruises (see pp64–5)

measure, always remember to notify someone of your itinerary and your approximate time of arrival at your destination should you decide to camp or hike by yourself.

HIKING

Hiking trails crisscross almost all of New England, with the two most popular being the New England section of the Appalachian Trail (see pp22–3) and Vermont's 265-mile (426-km) Long Trail. Both trails can be quite challenging in spots, with extremely steep mountain climbs to stunning vistas. Maine's Baxter State Park (see p298) and New Hampshire's White Mountain National Forest (see p265) are both well known for their extensive networks of demanding trails.

Not all nature walks need be difficult, however. Acadia National Park (see pp288–9) in Maine has an excellent system of easier hiking trails that lead past some of the most breathtaking coastal scenery. The **Rails-to-Trails Conservancy** provides information and maps on 1,359 trails along abandoned railroad tracks that have been converted into convenient and accessible paths for cyclists and pedestrians alike. These paths stretch across a vast portion of New England. Companies such as **New England Hiking Holidays** organize excursions that last between two and five days, so that you can choose an itinerary to suit your fitness and experience level.

Easy biking amid New England wildflowers

Hiking at Center Sandwich, New Hampshire

BIKING

In addition to the more formal bike paths, the region possesses hundreds of miles of quiet back roads that are a cyclist's paradise. The pastoral scenery is beautiful, but the distances between towns are rarely so great that you will feel isolated. Cape Cod (see pp154–9) is famous for its wonderful bike paths, as is Nantucket (see p153) with its network of easy trails leading to pristine beaches. Many people believe that the best way to see Martha's Vineyard (see pp152–3), Block Island (see pp192–3), and the Litchfield Hills (see pp208–9) is by bike. Various outfitters such as **VBT** offer organized bike tours for some of New England's most scenic regions, supplying everything from bicycles and protective gear to maps and accommodations.

Mountain bikers also have plenty to choose from. Some ski areas let bikers use their lifts and slopes in the summer, and many of the region's forests are open to biking. Acadia National Park, Mount Desert Island (see pp288–9), and the White (see p265) and Green (see p244) mountains all have excellent facilities. To avoid damaging the surrounding environment, mountain bikers should stick to the marked trails. Cyclists should wear helmets and other protective gear.

DIRECTORY

CANOEING AND RAFTING

Maine Island Trail Association
58 Fore St, Portland, ME 04101.
Tel (207) 761-8225.
www.mita.org

Raft Maine
PO Box 78, West Farms, ME 04985.
Tel (800) 723-8633.
www.raftmaine.com

HIKING AND BIKING

Appalachian Trail Conservancy
799 Washington St,
PO Box 807, Harpers Ferry,
WV 25425-0807.
Tel (304) 535-6331.
www.appalachiantrail.org

Green Mountain Club
4711 Waterbury-Stowe Rd,
Waterbury Center, VT 05677.
Tel (802) 244-7037.
www.greenmountainclub.org

New England Hiking Holidays
PO Box 1648, North Conway,
NH 03860. *Tel (603) 356-9696*
or *(800) 869-0949.*
www.nehikingholidays.com

Rails-to-Trails Conservancy
2121 Ward Ct NW,
Washington, DC 20037.
Tel (202) 331-9696.
www.railtrails.org

VBT
614 Monkton Rd, Bristol, VT 05443.
Tel (802) 453-4811
or *(800) 245-3868.*
www.vbt.com

TECHNICAL OR ROCK CLIMBING

Acadia Mountain Guides Climbing School
92 Main St, Orono, ME 04473
or 198 Main St, Bar Harbor,
ME 04609 (summer only).
Tel (888) 232-9559 or
(207) 288-8186.
www.acadiamountain guides.com

New England Climbing
www.neclimbs.com

Rhinoceros Mountain Guides
55 Mountain View Rd,
Campton, NH 03223.
Tel (603) 726-3030.
www.rhinoguides.com

FISHING

If you like to fish, you will love New England. Deep-sea fishing is best at Point Judith in Rhode Island, where you can rent boats through the **Rhode Island Party and Charterboat Association**. Farther up the coast at Cape Cod, surfcasters test the waters for striped bass and bluefish, which are most plentiful between July and October. Brook trout, walleye, and bass are plentiful in the inland streams and lakes, especially in Maine. Contact the **Maine Sporting Camp Association** for information regarding the state's top fishing camps and lodges. Fly-fishermen seeking to hone their skills can do so in one of the highly regarded programs run by **Orvis** in Manchester, Vermont. Fresh-water fishing licenses are mandatory throughout New England and can be obtained at fishing supply stores.

Turbulent rapids in one of New England's mountain rivers

CANOEING, KAYAKING, AND WHITE-WATER RAFTING

Maine is the premier destination for paddlers, beginning with sea kayakers who flock here each summer to ply the waters along the 3,500-mile (5,630-km) coast. One of the state's most popular excursions is the 350-mile (563-km) Maine Island Trail, which goes from Portland to Machias.

Maine's latticework of rivers is ideal for canoeing, with its most famous trek being down the challenging Allagash Wilderness Waterway *(see p299)*. New Hampshire's

Whale-watching on a regional cruise ship

Androscoggin River is another demanding waterway best tested by experienced paddlers. Canoeists looking for a more leisurely ride can skim across the calm waters of northern New England's lakes and ponds.

White-water rafting is the paddler's roller-coaster ride and, once again, Maine is the region's best theme park. The state's three major rivers, the Penobscot, Kennebec, and Dead, offer gut-wrenching tests of rafters' skills. **Raft Maine** will put you in touch with the proper outfitter. New Hampshire's Saco River is another favorite among the white-water set.

BOATING

New England's reputation as one of the world's great cruising areas is well deserved. The thousands of miles of shoreline are dotted with hundreds of anchorages. Penobscot Bay, Maine, and Newport, Rhode Island, are both considered sailing meccas. For those who want something a little calmer than the Atlantic Ocean, New England has countless lakes, large and small, including popular cruising destinations such as Sebago Lake, Lake Champlain, and Lake Winnipesaukee.

Boat rentals are available at many seaside and lakeside resorts in New England. A few outlets will rent a large sailboat for a day or night. These so-called "bareboat charters" are only for experienced sailors, particularly in Maine, where water and weather conditions can be treacherous.

Hinckley Yacht Charters in Southwest Harbor, Maine, is one of New England's larger companies, with 25 crafts available. This company will also provide fully crewed yacht charters.

Top-notch wind-surfing sites and windsurfing equipment rentals are also available at many locations up and down the New England coast.

CRUISES

Whale-watching cruises have become one of the region's most popular activities, with more and more coastal towns trying to cash in. Not quite an exact science, a successful whale-watching trip relies both on the experience of the ship's captain and on the guidance offered by high-tech sounding gear to find these majestic mammals. Most companies will offer a rain check if no whales are sighted.

Plan whale-watching trips carefully. Choose a calm day. Choppy water causes most people to become seasick. If you fear you will get sick, buy some ginger capsules at a health food store and take the recommended dose just before boarding.

Sightseeing and nature cruises are also available throughout New England. For a different view of the city, **Boston Harbor Cruises** offers sunset tours throughout the summer. River cruises are available on several New England waterways, including both the Charles

Group rafting run on the Cold River at Charlemont, Massachusetts

DIRECTORY

BIRD-WATCHING

Audubon Society of New Hampshire
84 Silk Farm Rd,
Concord, NH 03301.
Tel (603) 224-9909.
www.nhaudubon.org

Audubon Society of Rhode Island
12 Sanderson Rd,
Smithfield, RI 02917-2600.
Tel (401) 949-5454.
www.asri.org

Audubon Vermont
255 Sherman Hollow Rd,
Huntington, VT 05462.
Tel (802) 434-3068.
www.audubon.org/chapter/vt/

Connecticut Audubon Society
2325 Burr St,
Fairfield, CT 06430.
Tel (203) 259-6305 or
(800) 996-8747.
www.ctaudubon.org

Maine Audubon Society
20 Gilsland Farm Rd,
Falmouth, ME 04105.
Tel (207) 781-2330.
www.maineaudubon.org

Massachusetts Audubon Society
208 S Great Rd, Lincoln, MA 01773.
Tel (781) 259-9500 or
(800) 283-8266.
www.massaudubon.org

United States Fish and Wildlife Service
Regional Office,
300 Westgate Center Dr,
Hadley, MA 01035-9589.
Tel (413) 253-8200.
www.fws.gov/northeast

BOATING

Hinckley Yacht Charters
Great Harbor Marina,
PO Box 950,
Southwest Harbor, ME 04679.
Tel (800) HYC-SAIL or
(207) 244-5008.
www.hinckleycharters.com

CAMPING

Connecticut Campground Owners Association
14 Rumford St,
West Hartford, CT 06107.
Tel (860) 521-4704.
www.campconn.com

Department of Environmental Protection
79 Elm St, Hartford, CT 06106.
Tel (860) 424-3000.
www.dep.state.ct.us/rec/

Maine Campground Owners Association
10 Falcon Rd, Suite 1,
Lewiston, ME 04240.
Tel (207) 782-5874.
www.campmaine.com

Maine Department of Conservation
18 Elkins Lane,
Augusta, ME 04333.
Tel (207) 287-3821.
www.state.me.us/doc/parks

Massachusetts Parks
251 Causeway St, Suite 600,
Boston, MA 02114.
Tel (617) 626-1250.
www.state.ma.us/dcr/

National Park Service Northeast Region
Custom House, 200 Chestnut St,
Philadelphia, PA 19106.
Tel (800) 365-2267 or
(215) 597-7013.
www.nps.gov/nero

National Recreation Reservation Service
Tel (518) 885-3639 or *(877) 444-6777.* www.recreation.gov

New Hampshire Campground Owners Association
PO Box 1074,
Epsom, NH 03234.
Tel (800) 832-6764.
www.ucampnh.com

New Hampshire Division of Parks and Recreation
PO Box 1856,
Concord, NH 03302.
Tel (603) 271-3556.
www.nhparks.state.nh.us

Rhode Island Department of Parks and Recreation
2321 Hartford Ave, Johnston,
RI 02919-1719.
Tel (401) 222-2632.
www.riparks.com

Vermont Department of Forests, Parks and Recreation
103 S Main St,
Waterbury, VT 05671.
Tel (802) 241-3655.
www.vtstateparks.com

CRUISES

Bar Harbor Whale Watch Company
1 West St,
Bar Harbor, ME, 04609.
Tel (207) 288-2386 or
(800) WHALES-4.
www.whalesrus.com

Boston Harbor Cruises
One Long Wharf, Boston, MA
02110. *Tel (617) 227-4320*
or *(877) 733-9425.*
www.bostonharborcruises.com

FISHING AND HUNTING

Maine Sporting Camp Association
119 Millinocket, ME 04462.
www.mainesportingcamps.com

Rhode Island Party and Charterboat Association
PO Box 3198,
Narragansett, RI 02882.
Tel (401) 737-5812.
www.rifishing.com

Orvis
Rte 7A, Manchester, VT 05254.
Tel (802) 362-3750 or
(888) 235-9763.
www.orvis.com

HANG GLIDING AND PARAGLIDING

Morningside Flight Park
357 Morningside Lane,
Charlestown, NH 03603.
Tel (603) 542-4416.
www.flymorningside.com

Vermont Hang Gliding Association
www.vhga.org

Boats at pier in Edgartown Harbor, Martha's Vineyard

and the Connecticut rivers in Massachusetts and Connecticut's Mystic River.

Windjammer cruises are also popular in Massachusetts, Rhode Island, and Maine.

BIRD-WATCHING

With its diverse habitats, ranging from mountains to coastal marshes and sand flats to conifer and mixed hardwood forests, New England offers some of the most interesting birding in the U.S.

Massachusetts, home to the first Audubon Society in America, is famous for several areas, most notably the northeast coast at Newburyport, Cape Cod, and around the Berkshires. At Machias Seal Island, Maine, birders have a good opportunity to sight nesting colonies of Atlantic puffins. Special boat excursions to the island are offered by local charters.

National parks along with national wildlife refuges and protection areas are often the best places to bird since they are protected and unspoiled. **The US Fish and Wildlife Service** can provide information on the location of refuges and the birding opportunities at each. Every state's **Audubon Society** will provide information on birding in the state as well as on Audubon field trips to various hotspots.

GOLF

New England has more than its share of outstanding golf courses – in all price ranges and at all levels of difficulty. Dedicated golf vacationers have a choice between some stunning coastal and mountain resorts. Of the former, Samoset Resort, located in Rockport, Maine, stands out above all the rest.

With ocean views on 14 holes, Samoset has been called the most visually appealing course in New England. Two other terrific coastal links, the Seaside course at New Seabury and the Ocean Edge Resort and Golf Club, are located on Cape Cod.

For a full-fledged mountain golf holiday, consider the Equinox resort in Manchester, Vermont. It features a championship 1927 Walter J. Travis design surrounded by the Green Mountains.

Some famous ski destinations offer great golf as well. In western Maine, Sugarloaf/USA Golf Club presents a memorable Robert Trent Jones, Jr. layout that *Golf Digest* has

ranked among the top ten for both memorability and aesthetics. Mount Snow is ranked as one of Vermont's top five courses. Both courses also offer summer golf schools, as does Quechee in Vermont. Other worthwhile mountain courses include The Balsams in northeastern New Hampshire and Cranwell Resort and Golf Club in the Berkshires.

TECHNICAL OR ROCK CLIMBING

With New England's Green Mountains and White Mountains, it's little surprise

The signature of New England: a beautiful, well-kept golf course

that this part of the country offers some great climbing.

In Maine the vast majority of cliff climbing falls along its rugged south coast, with high-quality routes in a setting that is truly stunning. Acadia National Park is the most popular destination. Alpine climbers will also find a worthy test in Maine. Mount Katahdin, the state's highest peak, has some of the longest routes in New England.

New England's best climbing, however, is found in New Hampshire, where Cannon Cliff, Cathedral Ledge, and Whitehorse Ledge make up a triumvirate of diverse, challenging peaks. New Hampshire also offers bouldering and sport climbing at several sites, the best of which is Rumney in the center part of the state.

Connecticut and Rhode Island are not especially famed for their climbing, but both offer several quite good bouldering sites, most notably at Lincoln Woods, Rhode Island.

Climbing in Massachusetts is varied, with the central area of the state offering longer scenic routes and Boston providing some of the country's best urban cragging.

Vermont has few developed sites, though the treacherous sport of ice climbing is practiced at Smuggler's Notch and Lake Willoughby.

HUNTING

With its wide range of game spread across its diverse woodlands, New England offers something for every hunter. Among the big game are white tail deer, bear and moose, while small game includes rabbit, hare, and squirrel. For those interested in bird hunting, turkey, duck, goose, pheasant, quail and grouse can be found. The hunting seasons are concentrated in the late summer and fall, with limited exceptions. Hunters in all six states require licenses.

Climber in bold ascent of New Hampshire's White Mountains

Ruffed grouse

In most cases, the fees are significantly higher for out-of-state hunters. Guns must be kept unloaded during transport in all states, and in some of them, a secure transport case is mandatory. There are also regulations that govern transport of game out-of-state. For specific information on regulations in each state, contact the government department responsible for wildlife management in that state.

HANG GLIDING AND PARAGLIDING

Good hang gliding and paragliding sites abound in New England. That's no surprise, considering the large number of accessible places throughout the Green Mountains and the White Mountains. The best place to start is Morningside Flight Park in Charlestown, New Hampshire. It is the only full-time flight school and flying center in New England, and it has a 450-ft (137-m) summit launch site on the premises. Not far away in Vermont, Mount Ascutney is known as the premier cross-country hang-gliding site in New England, with flights having reached the Atlantic coast.

Southern New England is not without its advantages, however. Two of the best sand cliff launches are located in Cape Cod, Massachusetts, and Block Island, Rhode Island. Training is essential before attempting these sports. It is important to check local regulations before making any flight. You will find that many sites require memberships or have strict guidelines about landing areas. At state sites in Vermont, gliders must sign a waiver before making any flight. Contact the state association or a local club before making any jump.

Daring way to view the Berkshires at North Adams, Massachusetts

Winter Activities

Snowmobile

Far from lamenting the end of the stunning fall foliage season, New Englanders instead begin readying themselves for winter activities. Skis and snowboards are pulled out and dusted off, snowmobiles are tuned up, and skates are sharpened in anticipation of cold weather and the slate of outdoor fun it brings. In New England top-notch ski hills and cross-country ski and snowmobiling trails are never far away. This is especially true in the region's northernmost reaches, where the annual blanket of snow is thickest and, for outdoor enthusiasts, most inviting.

Sleigh ride through Hancock Shaker Village in Pittsfield, Massachusetts

SKIING

People have been downhill skiing on New England's rounded peaks for more than a century. While the region does not have the elevation of the Rockies, it does offer many large hills, some with a vertical rise of more than 2,000 ft (610 m). The best skiing and snowboarding is concentrated in the three northern states. Vermont has the most high-quality peaks, with **Killington** offering the most trails at 191. But it is **Stowe** that can claim the title of New England's ski capital. A world-famous resort set in the quaint village of the same name, Stowe has the state's highest peak and offers excellent trails for skiers of all levels. For the experienced skier, **Mad River Glen** near Waitsfield provides a stern test in one of the most pristine settings in the world. It also forbids snowboarding.

The White Mountains in New Hampshire have a plethora of good ski hills; downhill, alpine, and cross-country trails are arguably the best in the Northeast. In Maine, **Sugarloaf/USA** and **Sunday River** are considered to be the best hills in the state.

Downhill ski trails in New England are accurately rated following a standard code: Easier = green circle; More Difficult = blue square; Most Difficult = black diamond; and Expert = double diamond. Rental equipment is available at all resorts, as are skiing and snowboarding lessons for all levels. Where price is concerned, in general, the larger, more famous resorts charge more for lift tickets. If you have time, look for off-site sellers. They typically offer reduced prices. Also ask about package deals and senior or child discounts.

Cross-country ski trails are also plentiful in New England. Towns such as Craftsbury Common, Vermont, and **Jackson, New Hampshire** have miles of groomed trails. State parks also often provide good trails. These are good areas for other winter activities such as sliding and snowshoeing. **Catamount Trail**, set aside for skiers and snowshoers, runs 300 miles (482 km) down the length of Vermont. Many renowned downhill resorts also offer cross-country trails. The trails at the **Trapp Family Lodge Ski Center** in Stowe are considered among the best in New England.

Low in the turn at Vermont's majestic Stowe resort

SNOWMOBILING

Snowmobiling is extremely popular all across New England, but Maine is truly the mecca for this activity. The state is interconnected by 12,500 miles (20,000 km) of trails and has more than 85,000 registered snowmobiles using them. Resorts such as **Northern Outdoors** in The Forks and the **New England Outdoor Center** in Millinocket will rent snowmobiles and accommodations, and supply guides for excursions. Most agencies require that renters have a valid driver's license.

SKATING

In winter, New England has plenty of frozen lakes and rivers for skating. Always check with local authorities to be sure the ice is safe.

Winter also brings droves of bundled-up skaters to the Boston Common Frog Pond in Boston. Rentals are available in the warm-up shed or alternatively at the **Beacon Hall Skate Shop**. The **Department of Conservation and Recreation** runs numerous indoor rinks in Boston, Cambridge, and the surrounding communities.

Freestyle skiing, common at New England ski resorts

DIRECTORY

SKIING

Attitash Bear Peak
PO Box 508, Rte 302,
Bartlett, NH 03812.
Tel (877) 677-7669 or
(603) 374-2368.
www.attitash.com

Bretton Woods Mountain Resort
Rte 302, Bretton Woods, NH 03575.
Tel (800) 314-1752 or
(603) 278-1000.
www.brettonwoods.com

Catamount Trail Association
1 Main St, Suite 350,
Burlington, VT 05401.
Tel 802-864-5794.
www.catamounttrail.org

Jackson Ski Touring Foundation
PO Box 216, 153 Main St,
Jackson, NH 03846.
Tel (800) 927-6697 or
(603) 383-9355.
www.jacksonxc.org

Killington
4763 Killington Rd,
Rutland, VT 05751.
Tel (800) 621-MTNS or
(802) 422-3261.
www.killington.com

Mad River Glen
Rte 17, Fayston, VT 05673.
Tel (802) 496-3551.
www.madriverglen.com

Ski Maine Association
Box 7566, Portland, ME 04112.
Tel (207) 773-7669.
www.skimaine.com

Ski New Hampshire
PO Box 528,
North Woodstock, NH 03262.
Tel (603) 745-9396 or
(800) 887-5464.
www.skinh.com

Ski Vermont
26 State St, PO Box 368,
Montpelier, VT 05601.
Tel (802) 223-2439.
www.skivermont.com

Stowe Mountain Resort
5781 Mountain Rd, Stowe, VT
05672. *Tel* (800) 253-4754 or
(802) 253-3000.
www.stowe.com

Sugarloaf/USA
5092 Access Rd,
Carrabassett Valley, ME 04947.
Tel (800) THE-LOAF or
(207) 237-2000.
www.sugarloaf.com

Sunday River Ski Resort
Sunday River access road,
Newry, ME 04261.
Tel (800) 543-2SKI or
(207) 824-3000.
www.sundayriver.com

Trapp Family Lodge Ski Center
700 Trapp Hill Rd,
Stowe, VT 05672.
Tel (800) 826-7000 or
(802) 253-8511.
www.trappfamily.com

SNOWMOBILING

Maine Snowmobile Association
PO Box 80,
Augusta, ME 04332.
Tel (207) 622-6983.
www.mesnow.com

New England Outdoor Center
PO Box 669, Millinocket, ME 04462.
Tel (800) 766-7238.
www.neoc.com

New Hampshire Snowmobile Association
614 Laconia Rd, Tilton, NH 03276.
Tel (603) 273-0220.
www.nhsa.com

Northern Outdoors
PO Box 100, 1771 Route 201,
The Forks, ME 04985.
Tel (800) 765-7238.
www.northernoutdoors.com

Snowmobile Association of Massachusetts
PO Box 386, Conway, MA 01341.
Tel (413) 369-8092.
www.sledmass.com

SKATING

Beacon Hill Skate Shop
135 South Charles St,
Boston, MA 02116.
Tel (617) 482-7400.

Department of Conservation and Recreation
251 Causeway St, Boston, MA
02114. *Tel* (617) 626-1250.
www.mass.gov/dcr/parks

SURVIVAL
GUIDE

PRACTICAL INFORMATION

New England offers a wide variety of recreational activities within a relatively small area. Vacationers can hike the White Mountains of New Hampshire in the morning, swim at Maine's Ogunquit Beach in the afternoon, and take in the Boston Symphony Orchestra at night. Because tourism is such an important part of the regional economy, visitors will find numerous agencies and facilities geared toward making their stay an enjoyable one. Accommodations and restaurants (see

Acadia welcome sign

pp302–55) come in all price ranges, allowing you to sleep and eat in comfort while staying on budget. For people without cars, transportation is readily available in Boston and throughout the six states (see pp391–5). The following pages offer some practical advice for people traveling in the New England states. Personal Security and Health (see pp386–7) outlines some general guidelines, while Banking/Currency and Communications (see pp388–9) answers some basic financial and media queries.

WHEN TO GO

New England is a four-season vacation destination but is particularly popular in the summer and fall. Generally speaking, the peak tourist period is from mid-June, when schools let out, through October. During this time accommodations and restaurant reservations can be hard to come by, especially in the busy resort towns along the coast. There is another rush during fall-foliage season (see pp20–21), which lasts from sometime in mid-September to late October. During this month-long stretch the hotels and B&Bs farther inland near the woods are booked solid. The length of the ski season depends entirely on the weather. It is not unheard of for New England winters to run from late November right

Enough signs to keep visitors busy in Center Sandwich, New Hampshire

through March, during which time New Hampshire and Vermont, which possess the bulk of New England's ski centers (see pp378–9), are busiest. If you are planning a backwoods vacation, it is prudent to avoid wooded areas in April and May, when the ground can be extremely muddy and swarms of hungry black flies fill the air. Don't be fooled by their small size; they have a big bite.

ENTRY REQUIREMENTS

All travelers to New England and the US, including Canadians and returning Americans, should have a machine-readable biometric passport valid for six months longer than their intended period of stay. Holders of a valid EU, Australian or New Zealand passport and a return ticket do not need visas if staying 90 days or fewer on vacation or

business in the US. However, visitors must apply for entry in advance via the Electronic System for Authorization. Applications must be made at least 72 hours before travel at https://esta.cbp.dhs.gov. Sometimes foreign visitors must prove they carry sufficient funds. Ask your travel agent or contact the US Embassy for current requirements.

CUSTOMS ALLOWANCES

Visitors over the age of 21 are permitted to enter the US with two pints (1 l) of alcohol, 200 cigarettes, 50 cigars or 4 lbs (2 kg) of smoking tobaccos, and gifts worth up to $100. Prohibited items include meat products, cheese, and all fresh fruit. Travelers entering the country with more than $10,000 in cash or in traveler's checks must declare the money to customs officials upon entry.

Snowboarding, popular with the young, daring, and fit

◁ Boston Skyline

TAXES IN NEW ENGLAND			
State	**Lodging**	**Meal**	**Sales**
Connecticut	12%	6%	6%
Maine	7%	7%	5%
Massachusetts	12.5%	6.25%	6.25%
New Hampshire	8%	8%	–
Rhode Island	13%	7%	7%
Vermont	9%	9%	6%

TOURIST INFORMATION

State tourism offices are excellent sources of information and are happy to send road maps, brochures, and listings of accommodations, seasonal events, and attractions free of charge. Some offices also carry discount vouchers for lodging, restaurants, and admission fees. Tourist information booths or welcome centers are equipped with toilets and rest areas are usually found upon entering states on major highways. Many towns maintain a visitors' bureau that dispenses information on local activities, lodgings, and restaurants.

OPENING HOURS

Offices are generally open from 9am to 5pm Monday to Friday and do not close for lunch. Most stores keep hours from 9 or 10am to 6pm Monday to Saturday, although they often stay open until 9 or 10pm on Thursday and Friday. More and more stores are opening on Sunday. Most New England banks are open from 9am to 3 or 4pm Monday to Friday. Many banks are open on Saturday mornings from 9am to noon or 1pm. The larger museums are usually open 10am to 5pm Tuesday through Sunday, but

Making the most of summer weather at outdoor cafés

check with the hours listed in this guide. Smaller museums may have seasonal hours and often shut down during the winter. An increasing number of gas stations and convenience stores now stay open 24 hours a day.

ALCOHOL AND CIGARETTES

The legal drinking age throughout New England is 21, and most young people will be asked to produce a photo ID as proof of age in order to buy alcohol or enter a bar. Your passport is usually your best bet. Drinking in public spaces is against the law, and the

penalties for driving under the influence of alcohol are severe, including the loss of your driver's license.

Cigarettes can be sold only to people 18 years of age or older. It is against the law to smoke in public buildings, such as hospitals, and on public conveyances, including subways and buses. A few restaurants still permit smoking in designated sections, although more and more are completely "smoke-free."

ELECTRICITY

Electricity flows at the standard US 110-120 volts AC (alternating current). Foreign-made electrical appliances may require a US-style plug adapter and a voltage converter.

TAXES

Taxes vary on a state-by-state basis. There is no federal sales tax, but all New England states, with the exception of New Hampshire, levy their own sales tax. All states charge taxes on hotel rooms and restaurant meals and some cities have additional taxes. Many accommodations tack on additional surcharges such as housekeeping and parking fees to bills that can increase the total by up to 15 percent. To avoid unpleasant surprises at the end of a stay, visitors should inquire about extra service charges before they check in.

TIPPING

Although there are no set guidelines for tipping, a gratuity is usually given for most services. Travelers should give waiters 15 to 20 percent of the bill, bartenders 50¢ to $1 per drink, barbers 15 percent of the bill, and taxi drivers between 12 and 18 percent of the fare. Porters usually get $1 per piece of luggage and hotel maids at least $1 per night. Tipping is not usually required at fast-food restaurants, although there is sometimes a jar by the cash register for tips that will be shared by employees.

Mopeds, a popular form of transportation for visitors on the go

HOLIDAYS

While each state may have its own set of holidays, some major public holidays are celebrated throughout the US. Visitors should keep in mind that on these days schools, banks, and government offices are closed. Museums and transportation services operate on limited schedules, but many retail stores and restaurants maintain regular business hours.

New Year's Day
Jan 1.
Martin Luther King, Jr. Day
3rd Mon in Jan.
President's Day
3rd Mon in Feb.
Memorial Day
Last Mon in May.
Independence Day
Jul 4.
Labor Day
1st Mon in Sep.
Columbus Day
2nd Mon in Oct.
Veterans' Day
Nov 11.
Thanksgiving
4th Thu in Nov.
Christmas Day
Dec 25.

Patriotic decorations for Independence Day

Youngsters taking a break from sightseeing on a New England wharf

TRAVELING WITH CHILDREN

New England is a fairly child-friendly place. Many museums, zoos, and aquariums offer hands-on and interactive exhibits that encourage younger participants. The multitude of state parks and forests and public beaches give children lots of space to burn excess energy.

Many establishments and services cater to families by having children's menus and reduced admission rates. Most hotels and motels will charge $10 to $20 per cot so that children can stay in the same room as their parents. The same is generally not true for inns and bed and breakfasts (B&Bs), some of which will not take children under a certain age.

STUDENT TRAVELERS

Students from abroad should buy an **International Student Identification Card** (ISIC) before traveling to New England. Numerous discounts are available to cardholders at such places as hostels, museums, and theaters. This is especially true in Boston. The **Student Advantage Card** is a similar card and is available to all American university students. It is advisable for young travelers to carry their passports or driver's license for entry into bars or to buy alcohol in restaurants.

SENIOR CITIZENS

Seniors are eligible for a myriad of discounts ranging from car rentals and lodgings to national parks and museums. Depending on the place, the minimum qualifying age for seniors can be as low as 50. Visitors should contact the **American**

Easy bird-watching at Claremont Hotel, Southwest Harbor, Maine

Association of Retired Persons (AARP) for more information. Also, travelers should try the Boston-based, international senior travel organization **Elderhostel**. The organization offers discount lodgings, educational programs, and field trips throughout New England and the US for travelers over the age of 55.

DISABLED TRAVELERS

While US federal law requires that businesses are accessible to the disabled, some historic buildings have limited access for wheelchairs. Most hotels and restaurants are equipped for people with special needs, and more and more small inns are retrofitting some of their rooms. Many outdoor recreation areas, including all national parks, now provide rest rooms and facilities for the disabled, including tour buses and wheelchair-friendly trails. The best advice for disabled travelers is to call ahead or to contact organizations such as the **Society for Accessible Travel and Hospitality** or Mobility International. Both groups provide information and comprehensive guides on the issues of accessibility for the disabled.

Celebration of the first same-sex civil union in Vermont

GAY AND LESBIAN TRAVELERS

New England has a number of vibrant gay communities, including Provincetown *(see pp156–7)* on northernmost Cape Cod, Ogunquit *(see pp278–9)*, Maine, Northampton *(see p163)*, Massachusetts, and Boston's South End. In addition, gay marriage is legal in all New England states except Rhode Island. *Bay Windows*, New England's largest gay and lesbian weekly, includes arts and cultural listings for all six states. For on-line information covering the entire region, check the *New England Blade* at www.innewsweekly.com.

DIRECTORY

TOURIST INFORMATION

Connecticut Commission on Culture and Tourism
One Constitution Plaza,
Hartford, CT 06103.
Tel (860) 256-2800 or
(888) 288-4748.
www.ctvisit.com

Greater Boston Convention and Visitors Bureau
2 Copley Place, Suite 105,
Boston, MA 02116.
Tel (888) 733-2678 or
(617) 536-4100.
www.bostonusa.com

Maine Office of Tourism
59 State House Station,
Augusta, ME 04333-0059.
Tel (207) 287-5711 or
(888) 624-6345.
www.visitmaine.com

Massachusetts Office of Travel & Tourism
10 Park Plaza, Suite 4510,
Boston, MA 02116.
Tel (617) 973-8500 or
(800) 227-6277.
www.massvacation.com

New Hampshire Division of Travel & Tourism Development
172 Pembroke Rd, PO Box 1856,
Concord, NH 03302.
Tel (603) 271-2665 or
(800) 386-4664.
www.visitnh.gov

Rhode Island Tourism Division
315 Iron Horse Way, Suite 101,
Providence, RI 02908.
Tel (800) 250-7384.
www.visitrhodeisland.com

Vermont Department of Tourism and Marketing
National Life Building, 6th Floor,
Drawer 20, Montpelier, VT 05260.
Tel (800) VERMONT.
www.1-800-vermont.com

STUDENTS

STA Travel
Tel (800) 781-4040.
www.statravel.com

Student Advantage Card
280 Summer St,
Boston, MA 02210.
Tel (617) 912-2011 or
(800) 333-2920.
www.studentadvantage.com

SENIOR CITIZENS

American Association of Retired Persons (AARP)
601 E St NW,
Washington, DC 20049.
Tel (888) 687-2277.
www.aarp.org

Elderhostel
11 Ave de Lafayette, Boston,
MA 02111. *Tel (800) 454-5768.*
www.elderhostel.org

GAY AND LESBIAN

Bay Windows
46 Plympton St,
Boston, MA 02118.
Tel (617) 266-6670.
www.baywindows.com

New England Blade
www.innewsweekly.com

DISABLED VISITORS

Society for Accessible Travel and Hospitality
347 Fifth Ave, Suite 605,
New York City,
NY 10016.
Tel (212) 447-7284.
www.sath.org

USEFUL WEBSITES

Boston Citysearch
www.boston.citysearch.com

Boston Globe Online
www.boston.com

NewEngland.com
www.newengland.com

Visit New England.com
www.visitnewengland.com

Personal Security and Health

Park Ranger

New England's comparatively low crime rate makes it a safe vacation destination. Even its largest metropolitan area, Boston, has seen crime on a steady decrease since the early 1990s. Nonetheless, it is always a good idea for travelers to take a few simple precautions to make sure that their trip is a safe one. This same rule of thumb applies to the wilderness areas. Almost free of crime, these areas possess a number of natural hazards that can be minimized.

Motorized police patrol on Surfside Beach, Nantucket, Massachusetts

LAW ENFORCEMENT

Three agencies share law enforcement duties: city police, sheriffs (who patrol county areas), and the state Highway Patrol, which deals with traffic accidents and offenses outside city boundaries. New England law enforcement officials are friendly and helpful.

EMERGENCIES

Should you require emergency medical, police, or fire services, call 911. The call is free from public phones. Emergency phone boxes are located along major highways. **The Travelers' Aid Society** specializes in providing assistance for those travelers who find themselves stranded.

LEGAL ASSISTANCE

Travelers from outside the US who are in need of legal assistance should immediately contact their nearest consulate or their embassy in Washington, D.C. Should you be arrested you have the right to remain silent and are given the right to make one phone call. The police will provide you with the embassy and consulate telephone numbers upon request.

GUIDELINES ON SAFETY

As with all large urban centers, New England's major cities, including Boston, Burlington, Worcester, Springfield, New Haven, Hartford, Providence, and Portland, have pockets of crime. Generally speaking, the main tourist areas are safe as most of the problems occur in neighborhoods not usually frequented by travelers. While the numbers of street people or "panhandlers" in cities is on the rise, they are almost always harmless.

It is a good policy to avoid wandering into city neighborhoods that are off the beaten track. Pickpockets are sometimes at work in the busy centers and will target anyone who looks like a tourist. Your best defense is common sense. Avoid wearing expensive jewelry and carry cameras and camcorders securely. As well, you should carry only small amounts of cash. Credit cards and traveler's checks are the most secure options. Money belts or pouches worn under clothing provide maximum security against pickpockets, especially in crowded areas such as buses and malls. While theft in hotels is not common, it is prudent to store valuables in the safe when you are out.

Always lock your car when you leave it and store bags and valuables in the trunk. Valuables left in the open in unattended cars are easy targets for smash-and-grab thieves. In major urban areas it is best to avoid walking through parks or strange neighborhoods at night. Always use automatic teller machines (ATM) on busier, well-lit streets.

Before you leave home, make a photocopy of important documents, including your passport and visa, and keep them with you, but separate from the originals. Also make a note of the numbers of your traveler's checks and credit cards, in the event they are stolen.

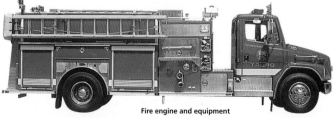

Fire engine and equipment

LOST AND STOLEN PROPERTY

Although the chances of retrieving lost or stolen property are very slim, report all missing items to the police and make sure you get a copy of the police report for your insurance claim. In the event of a loss or a theft, it is useful to have a record of your valuables' serial numbers and receipts as proof of possession. If you have misplaced something, retracing your steps can also help: try to remember the taxi companies and bus or train routes you were using when the item went missing. Most taxi and transport companies have Lost and Found departments which can be reached by phoning the general access phone number.

PASSPORT

A stolen passport should be reported immediately to your country's embassy or consulate. Most credit card companies have toll-free numbers to report a lost or stolen card, as do Thomas Cook and American Express for lost traveler's checks *(see right)*, which can often be replaced within a few hours.

TRAVEL INSURANCE

The US does not have a national health program and, as a result, emergency medical and dental care, though excellent, can be very expensive. Medical travel insurance is highly recommended in order to defer some costs related to an unscheduled stop in a US hospital. Even with medical coverage you may have to pay for services when you receive

Passports, easily stolen from careless visitors

them, then claim reimbursement from your insurance company later. Make sure the insurance policy you choose covers trip cancellation and baggage or document loss, emergency medical care, and accidental death.

OUTDOOR SAFETY

New England offers a wide variety of outdoor recreational activities, some of which entail certain risks. Helmets and other protective items are essential, and often mandatory, for such activities as white-water rafting and mountain biking, as are life jackets for all types of boating. Hikers should always stay on marked trails; those who are hiking or camping alone should notify someone of their destination and estimated time of arrival. Campers should never feed animals and should suspend food from a tree branch to avoid visits from bears. If you see a bear in the distance, yell and wave your arms so as not to surprise it, then back away. If the bear is close, don't look it in the eyes. Back away slowly, while talking softly. Do not run.

Hiking trail marker

DIRECTORY

EMERGENCIES

Police, Fire, Medical (all emergencies)
Tel Call 911 (toll-free, or dial 0 for the operator.)

Area Hospitals
Tel Call 411 for directory assistance

Travelers' Aid Society
17 East St,
Boston, MA 02111.
Tel (617) 542-7286.
(For branches in other cities in Massachusetts, Connecticut, or Rhode Island, look in the Yellow Pages or dial 411 for directory assistance).
www.travelersaid.org

LOST OR STOLEN CREDIT CARDS AND TRAVELER'S CHECKS

American Express
Tel (800) 528-4800 (cards).
Tel (800) 221-7282 (checks).

Diners Club
Tel (800) 234-6377.

Discover
Tel (800) DISCOVER.

MasterCard
Tel (800) 826-2181.

Thomas Cook
Tel (800) 223-7373 (checks).

Visa
Tel (800) 336-8472.

Campfires should be carefully extinguished with water. Mountain hikers and rock climbers should always be prepared for sudden changes in the weather. Ocean swimmers are advised to use beaches with lifeguards and should ask about undertows. Wear a hat and apply sun block in summer. Hikers would be smart to wear bright-colored clothes and avoid forests and fields during hunting season. To avoid any risk of catching Lyme Disease from ticks, always cover up well when walking through woods and fields.

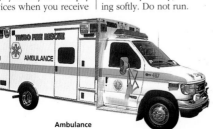

Ambulance

Banking/Currency and Communications

Because many New England banks outside of Boston do not exchange foreign currency, travelers from abroad should plan to use their credit cards, US-dollar traveler's checks, or, most conveniently, Automatic Teller Machine (cash machine) cards. Never carry all your money and credit cards with you at the same time, and keep in mind that most banks and foreign currency exchanges are closed on Sundays.

A dollar bill ($1), a quarter (25¢), pennies (1¢), and a nickel (5¢)

BANKING

Most New England banks are open from 9am to 3 or 4pm Monday to Friday. Many banks are open on Saturday mornings from 9am to noon or 1pm. All banks are closed on Sunday and public holidays.

Traveler's checks can usually be cashed at banks with a recognized photo ID, such as a passport. Main branches of national banks are located in the large urban areas and will exchange foreign currency for a small fee. It is always a good idea to ask about hidden service charges or commissions before you make a transaction. In general, you will get the best rates at big city banks or private exchange bureaus in larger centers.

The most commonly accepted credit cards in New England

AUTOMATIC TELLER MACHINES

Automatic teller machines (ATMs) are found throughout New England, even in tiny country villages. Look for them in bank foyers or just outside the entrances. ATMs are also found in airports, train stations, shopping malls, supermarkets, large gas stations, and along streets of most major cities. Widely found bank-card networks include Cirrus, Plus, NYCE, and Interlink. The machines also will dispense money to credit cards such as VISA or MasterCard. Before leaving home, ask your bank if your card can be used in New England. Bank cards can also be used to pay at many hotels, restaurants, retail stores, and gas stations.

CREDIT CARDS

The most commonly accepted credit cards in New England are MasterCard, VISA, and American Express, although Diner's Club and the Discover Card are gaining popularity. Credit cards can be used at restaurants, shops, and hotels, as well as to reserve tickets on the phone or to book a rental car. The biggest benefit of credit cards is that they offer you much more security than having to carry around large sums of cash, and they can be very useful in emergency situations.

TRAVELER'S CHECKS

The major advantage offered by traveler's checks is that, unlike cash, they can be refunded if they are lost or stolen. American Express and Thomas Cook traveler's checks are accepted in many US shops, restaurants, and hotels, especially in the major tourist centers. It is often easier to pay directly with US-dollar traveler's checks than cashing them in advance, and you will get your change in cash.

Banks and exchange bureaus will exchange your US-dollar traveler's checks directly into cash. Traveler's checks in foreign currency can be cashed at a bank or with a cashier at some major hotels. Exchange rates and commission charges are always posted and sometimes a little shopping around will save you some money. Personal checks drawn on overseas banks are rarely accepted in the US.

FOREIGN EXCHANGE

Once you are outside the major cities, you may find it difficult to exchange your foreign currency. Most foreign exchange offices are open from 9am to 5pm weekdays. Among the best-known agencies are **American**

DIRECTORY

FOREIGN EXCHANGE BUREAUS

American Express Interactive Travel
Tel (800) 221-7282.

Travelex Currency Services
Tel (800) 287-7362 (for branch locations).

Imaginative country mailboxes near Grafton, Vermont

Express Travel Agency and
Travelex Currency Services.
For the best rates, avoid
exchanging your money at
airports or train or bus stations. Banks will usually give
you the most favorable rates.

TELEPHONES

While all New England pay
phones accept coins (5¢,
10¢, and 25¢), more and
more are being retooled to
take phone and credit cards
as well, especially in the
major urban areas. Local
calls cost between 50¢ and
$1 for three minutes from
pay phones, while long-
distance rates vary and
include both a fixed call
charge and a per-minute
charge. The easiest way to
find out the ever-
changing rates is to
dial **0** and ask the
operator. Do not get
the operator to put the
call through, however,
as calling direct is sub-
stantially cheaper. Of
course, dialing direct
from your hotel room
can carry hefty sur-
charges, meaning it is
usually cheaper to place
the call yourself using
the pay phone in the
lobby. Generally speak-
ing, the least expensive
times to make long-distance
calls are between 11pm and
8am on weekdays and on
weekends (except 5pm to
11pm on Sunday). During
these periods, you can benefit from a discount of up to
60 percent.

All numbers with a **1-800,
1-888, 1-866,** or **1-877** prefix
are free of charge, as is

**Public pay
phone**

directory assistance from a pay
phone (dial **411** for local, **00**
for international), and emergency services (**911**). Operator
assistance (**0** for local, **01** for
international) has a charge.

Mobile phones can be
rented in many New England
centers. Visitors from abroad
who wish to bring their
mobile phones with them
should check with their
providers before leaving
home. Some plans do have
international plans that cover
the US, but it may be easier
to rent a mobile phone once
you are in the US.

POSTAL SERVICE

Post offices are open
weekdays from 9am to
5pm, with some branches
offering service on
Saturday. All are
closed on Sunday and
federal holidays.
Letters and small
parcels (less than 16
ounces) with the
proper postage can
be placed in any blue
mailbox. Domestic
mail takes one to five
days for delivery –
longer if you forget
the zip code. You can
speed up delivery by
several days by pay-
ing for **Priority Mail** or
Express Mail's next-day
delivery for domestic mail. It
is faster to send overseas mail
via airmail.

COMMUNICATIONS
AND MEDIA

The most popular US
newspaper in terms of
circulation is the *Wall Street*

Journal, followed by *USA
Today, The New York Times,*
and the *Los Angeles Times.*
They can be found in virtually all major cities. The
Boston Globe is the most
well-respected and widely
read newspaper coming out
of New England. The *Boston
Herald* is a popular tabloid-
style daily. The region has
many fine local newspapers.

Reality shows, soaps, sit-
coms, and talk shows dominate the US television
airwaves. Cable channels
offer 24-hour access to sports,
movies, music videos, and
news. Public station PBS
offers a more highbrow diet
of documentaries, concerts,
and classic films. Hotels
usually have access to the
major networks such as CBS,
NBC, and ABC, as well as
the more popular cable channels such as ESPN (specializing in sports) and CNN (the
top news station).

In general, radio stations
follow a specific program-
ming format. Those stations
on FM frequencies tend to
stick to a particular type of
music, be it rock, jazz, Top
40, or country western. AM
stations are usually geared
toward talk-radio shows in
which listeners call in to dis-
cuss the issues of the day.

Surfing the Internet is fairly
easy. Many New England
libraries are plugged into the
Internet and have terminals,
although you may have to
pay at some locations. Cyber
cafés have declined in popularity, even in the larger cities.
More and more hotels also
offer Internet access.

**Some of New England's many fine
local newspapers**

Getting to New England

While the most common ways to get to New England are by plane or by car, train and bus services also provide decent access to many regions, particularly the southern New England states. Many people like to begin their vacation in Boston because the city's Logan International Airport handles international flights. Boston is also the hub for rail and bus services coming in from all over the US and parts of Canada.

Bird's-eye view of Camden Harbor in Maine

ARRIVING BY AIR

Boston's **Logan International Airport** (BOS) is the region's busiest, although some domestic and international carriers use **Manchester Airport** (MHT), in New Hampshire, **T.F. Green Airport** (PVD) in Warwick, Rhode Island, which serves Providence, and **Bradley International Airport** (BDL) in Windsor Locks, Connecticut, which serves Hartford. A few major commercial airlines also fly into Bangor (BGR) and Portland (PWM), Maine; and Burlington (BTV), Vermont. Other gateways to New England include Montreal, Quebec, and, of course, New York City's three major airports.

Smaller domestic airlines cover specific geographical regions while also offering a few national flights. Although they have fewer flights than the major carriers, they often have substantially reduced fares. A number of regional commuter airlines shuttle passengers around New England, with small, single-prop planes flying to such destinations as Cape Cod and the various islands off the coast.

International travelers will be given a customs and immigration form during their flight and will be required to hand in the completed form to customs officials in the airport. At the immigration area there are two lines, one for US citizens and another for non-US citizens. If you are entering the country via New York's busy JFK, be forewarned that the immigration lines are often long and the process can be a time-consuming ordeal.

AIRFARES

It is always best to plan your vacation early and to shop around for the best airfares; a little research can go a long way in terms of securing a substantial discount. For inexpensive consolidated tickets, contact **Expedia.com** online or **IAATC** online. **CheapTickets.com** gives you instant access to the best published prices on the web. Keep in mind that even with the small fees they may charge, travel agents are often your best allies in your search for savings.

The busiest times of year for travel to New England are June through October, as well as the major holidays of Christmas, Easter, Labor Day, and most especially Thanksgiving. Book flights during these periods well in advance. In general, you will get the lowest airfares if you plan to travel during non-peak periods of the year – for instance, prices drop substantially following Labor Day. It is almost always cheaper to fly in and out of New England on weekdays rather than on weekends.

Passenger jet in flight

AIRPORT	INFORMATION	DISTANCE FROM CITY
Logan International (Boston, MA)	(617) 561-1800	3 miles (4.8 km) from Downtown Boston
Manchester Airport (Manchester, NH)	(603) 624-6556	6 miles (9.5 km) from Downtown Manchester
T.F. Green Airport (Warwick, RI))	(401) 737-8222	10 miles (16 km) from Downtown Providence
Bradley Intl. (Windsor Locks, CT)	(860) 292-2000	12 miles (19 km) from Downtown Hartford

ARRIVING BY TRAIN

The major american railroad is **Amtrak**. One of Amtrak's busiest routes services southern and central New England up to Boston. Amtrak recently unveiled its high-speed *Acela Regional* train service between New York and Boston, which has cut 90-minutes off regular travel time of about 6 hours. While it is available at a premium price, it is still less expensive than most airfares and has the added convenience of taking you from downtown to downtown without the added expense of taxis or shuttle buses. In November 2001, a rail service between Boston and Portland, Maine was inaugurated. During the summer, there is a stop at Old Orchard Beach in Maine.

Train station in North Conway, New Hampshire

ARRIVING BY CAR

Getting to New England by car is relatively easy, and you have several options. Beginning in Florida, I-95, also known as Route 128 in the Boston area, is one of the most popular drives for travelers coming from the South. This major interstate highway sticks close to the coast as it passes through Connecticut and Providence, Rhode Island, en route to the outskirts of Boston. Circumventing the city, the highway continues up through New Hampshire and Maine before crossing the border into Canada. Drivers should note that truck traffic along I-95 can be particularly heavy, especially when the route approaches Boston.

Wheeled luggage

The two major gateways into New England from the north are I-89 and I-91. The latter crosses from Canada into Vermont at Derby Line and then follows a relatively straight line south along the Vermont/New Hampshire border, through both central Massachusetts and Connecticut all the way down to New Haven. I-89 starts in Vermont's northwest-ernmost corner and then from Burlington cuts diagonally to Concord, New Hampshire where it links up with I-93 into Boston. The major western points of entry into New England are I-84 and I-90 from New York state.

ARRIVING BY BUS

As it stands, you can get just about anywhere in New England via bus, so long as you are not in a hurry. Many of the bus companies serve particular sections of New England. **Concord Trailways** has routes in Maine and New Hampshire. **Peter Pan** has stops in Connecticut and western Massachusetts. Other parts of Massachusetts, most notably Cape Cod and the South Shore, are served by **Plymouth & Brockton.** **Greyhound Lines** is a nationwide carrier and has stops throughout New England. Greyhound

works in conjunction with Vermont Transit, and Peter Pan lines. Most major bus lines offer discount rates for students and seniors (with proper ID), and offer unlimited travel during a set period.

A Greyhound bus

Getting Around Boston

Public transportation in Boston and Cambridge is very good. In fact it is considerably easier to get around by public transportation than by driving, with the added benefit of not having to find a parking space. All major attractions in the city are accessible on the subway, by bus, or by taxi. The central sections of the city are also extremely easy to navigate on foot.

MBTA commuter bus, with distinctive yellow paint

FINDING YOUR WAY IN BOSTON

The more planning you do before your trip, the easier it will be to locate sights and find your way around the city. The **Greater Boston Convention and Visitors Bureau** *(see p385)* will be a helpful contact point, and your hotel is also likely to be able to offer advice. To find out about any upcoming cultural events, check websites for **Boston City-search** and the **Boston Globe** *(see p385).*

Most of Boston is laid out "organically" rather than in the sort of strict grid found in most American cities. When trying to orient yourself, you'll find that it helps if you think of Boston as enclaves – of neighborhoods around a few central squares. In general, uphill from Boston Common is Beacon Hill, downhill is Downtown, while Back Bay begins west of Arlington Street. The North End sticks out from the north side of Boston, while the Waterfront is literally that, where Boston meets the sea.

MBTA SUBWAY AND TROLLEY BUSES

Boston's subway system is the oldest in North America, but it has been vastly expanded and modernized since the first cars rolled

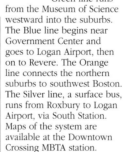

"Charlie" card, valid on all MBTA services

between Park Street and Boylston Street on September 1, 1897. The street trolley system began in 1846 with trolleys drawn along tracks by horses. The system was electrified in 1889. The combined subway and trolley lines are generally known as the "T." The T operates 5am to 12:45am Monday through Saturday and 6am to 12:45am Sunday. Weekday service is every 3 to 15 minutes, on weekends less frequently. There are five lines. The Red line runs from south of the city to Cambridge. The Green line runs from the Museum of Science westward into the suburbs. The Blue line begins near Government Center and goes to Logan Airport, then on to Revere. The Orange line connects the northern suburbs to southwest Boston. The Silver line, a surface bus, runs from Roxbury to Logan Airport, via South Station. Maps of the system are available at the Downtown Crossing MBTA station.

Admission to subway stations is via turnstiles into which you insert a paper "Charlie" ticket ($2) or plastic "Charlie" card ($1.70). Day or week Link passes for unlimited travel can be purchased at Downtown Crossing, South Station, Back Bay, Government Center, and North Station subway stops.

MBTA BUSES

The bus system enlarges the entire transit network to cover more than 1,000 miles (1,600 km). However, buses are often crowded, and schedules can be hard to obtain. Two useful sightseeing routes are Haymarket-Charlestown (from near Quincy Market to Bunker Hill) and Harvard-Dudley (from Harvard Sq via Massachusetts Ave through Back Bay and the South End to Dudley Sq in Roxbury). Cash or a paper "Charlie" ticket ($1.50) or plastic "Charlie" card ($1.25) is required for the fare.

TAXIS

Finding a taxi in Boston and Cambridge is rarely difficult except when it is raining. Taxis can be found at stands in tourist areas and can be hailed on the street. Taxis may pick up fares only in the city for which they are licensed – Cambridge taxis only in Cambridge, Boston taxis only in Boston. If you need to be somewhere on time, it is advisable to call a taxi company and arrange a definite pickup time and place.

Rates are calculated by both mileage and time, beginning with a $2.25 "pick-up" fee when the meter starts running. In general, the taxis in Boston and Cambridge are more expensive than those in other US cities, except New York. Taxis to Logan Airport are required to charge an airport

Boston taxis waiting for fares at one of the city's many taxi stands

use fee ($3); those coming from the airport charge for the harbor tunnel toll ($6). Additional surcharges may apply late at night. A full schedule of fares should be posted inside the vehicle.

The driver's photograph and permit and the taxi's permit number will also be posted inside all legitimate taxicabs, along with directions for reporting complaints.

Boston parkland, ideal for walking

WALKING IN BOSTON

Boston is a great walking city: it is compact and virtually all streets are flanked by sidewalks. It is nonetheless essential to wear comfortable walking shoes with adequate cushioning and good support.

Because Boston is mainly a city of neighborhoods, it is often best to use public transportation to get to a particular neighborhood, and then walk around to soak up the atmosphere. Walking also allows you to see parts of the city that are impractical to explore by car because streets are too narrow; for example, Beacon Hill, parts of the North End, and Harvard Square.

DIRECTORY

SUBWAY AND BUSES

MBTA
(Route and schedule information)
10 Park Plaza.
Tel (617) 222-3200.
www.mbta.com

TAXIS

Boston Cab Dispatch, Inc.
Tel (617) 262-2227.

Checker Cab of Cambridge
(Cambridge)
Tel (617) 497-9000.

Boston Town Taxi
Tel (617) 536-5000.

Yellow Cab
(Cambridge)
Tel (617) 547-3000.

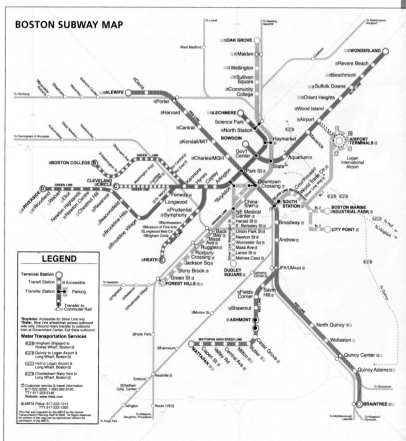

BOSTON SUBWAY MAP

Driving in New England

Important road sign

While flying is the fastest and most efficient way to get to New England, driving is by far the best way to explore the region. In fact, much of New England's charm is found along scenic jaunts down the coast and driving tours during fall-foliage season. It is important to remember that large areas of the region are essentially wild, so you should always be prepared for any eventuality, such as a breakdown. This is doubly true in the winter, when sudden blizzards and white-outs caused by blowing snow can leave motorists stranded. Boston's public transit system makes it possible to do without a car *(see pp392–3)*, but once outside the city you will need a vehicle to do your best exploring.

Country roads beckoning drivers to leave the crowds behind

A rented convertible, perfect for exploring in good weather

CAR RENTAL

The major car rental chains have outlets in most of New England's major cities and larger airports. These national chains include **Avis, Budget, Enterprise, Hertz, National, Rent-A-Wreck**, and **Thrifty**. While their rates are somewhat higher than smaller local companies, they usually offer extremely efficient service.

In order to rent a car, you must be 21 and possess a valid driver's license. People under 25 will sometimes have to pay a surcharge. A major credit card is usually required as well, unless you are prepared to put down a hefty cash deposit. Credit cards sometimes provide coverage against damage or theft of the vehicle, but it is wise to check what the terms are with your credit card company. Regardless, make sure that your car

rental agreement includes Collision Damage Waiver (CDW) – also known as Loss Damage Waiver (LDW) – or else you will be liable for any damage to the car, even if it was not your fault. This supplemental insurance can cost between $10 and $20 extra a day.

Sightseeing by car, stopping where and when you want

SPEED LIMITS

It is important to pay attention to the signs, as speed limits can vary from one place to the next depending on your proximity to a town or city. In general, the maximum speed on an interstate highway varies from 55 to 65 mph (88–105 km/h). On smaller highways, it can range between 30 and 55 mph (50–88 km/h). Cities and towns set speed limits between 20 and 35 mph (32–56 km/h), drastically lower around hospitals and schools. Police often pick strategic points along highways – often right after a sign for lower speed – to set up their radar equipment in order to catch drivers who are going too fast. Do not try to pay tickets or fines directly to the police officer who pulled you over; this can be interpreted as attempted bribery and can land you deeper in hot water.

DRIVING TOURS

There are a number of books on the market listing the best driving tours of the region. Some magazines, such as *Yankee* might, include a complete itinerary of recommended routes, historic stops, and the best places to eat and stay. Tours vary from a single day to an entire week and take in everything from dramatic coastal scenery and tiny fishing villages to mountainous terrain and country towns.

Of course, the favorite season for drivers is in the fall, when the rural roads are flanked by the brilliant colors of leaves *(see pp20–21).*

State tourism offices *(see p385)* can give you the contact information for organizations that plan foliage tours. Each state also has a hotline

number that gives frequently updated foliage reports. Remember, though, that traffic on New England's roads peaks in the fall.

SAFETY TIPS

If you are planning on spending a lot of time in your car, you should follow these simple procedures to ensure your safety and that of your passengers. The **National Highway Traffic Safety Administration** offers news on everything from school bus safety to road rage and operates an Auto Safety Hotline.

- Passengers should wear their seat belts at all times. Infants and young children should be secured in a car seat in the back seat. Follow child seat instruction manuals precisely. A rear-facing child seat should NEVER be placed in the front seat of a vehicle equipped with an air bag.
- Never leave children unattended in your car.
- Clean your windshield and adjust your mirrors for optimum visibility.
- Check your oil, radiator reservoir, brake fluids, and your fan belt before setting off on a long drive.
- Make sure all your lights and turn signals are working properly.
- Check your tires for undue tread wear and make sure that the air pressure is correct. Also see that your spare tire is roadworthy.
- Be sure that you have a working jack and road flares or reflective triangles in the trunk. Pack extra windshield wipers, and in winter stock salt, a snow brush and an ice scraper, and small shovel.
- Also keep a small medical kit in your trunk, along with a blanket and an emergency flashlight. In winter, make sure you have extra gloves, boots, and warm clothes.
- If you do get stuck in winter in an out-of-the-way place, stay inside your car. Keep the motor running for warmth, but open your window slightly to guard against carbon monoxide buildup. Make sure your exhaust pipe is clear of snow.
- Check road conditions on the radio, especially in winter. Heavy snowfalls can leave many areas impassable. Individual state transportation departments often have hotlines dispensing up-to-date information on road conditions and closures.
- Be wary of deer and moose that may run onto the road. Hitting a moose poses more of a threat to you than it does to the animal.

Sign on a Vermont highway warning drivers to watch for moose

DIRECTORY

CAR RENTALS

Avis
Tel (800) 831-2847.
www.avis.com

Budget
Tel (800) 527-7000.
www.budget.com

Enterprise
Tel (800) 736-8222.
www.enterprise.com

Hertz
Tel (800) 654-3131.
www.hertz.com

National
Tel (800) 227-7368.
www.nationalcar.com

Rent-A-Wreck
Tel (800) 944-7501.
www.rentawreck.com

Thrifty
Tel (800) 847-4389.
www.thrifty.com

DRIVING TOURS

Yankee **magazine**
www.newengland.com

FOLIAGE HOTLINES

Connecticut
Tel (888) 288-4748.

Maine
Tel (800) 777-0317.

Massachusetts
Tel (800) 227-6277.

New Hampshire
Tel (800) 258-3608.

Rhode Island
Tel (800) 556-2484.

Vermont
Tel (800) 837-6668.

HIGHWAY MANAGEMENT

National Highway Traffic Safety Administration
Tel (888) 327-4236.
www.NHTSA.gov

General Index

Acknowledgments

Dorling Kindersley would like to thank the following people whose contributions and assistance have made the preparation of this book possible.

Main Contributors

Eleanor Berman is an award-winning travel writer and author of 11 travel guides, including *Away for the Weekend: New England* and *Recommended Bed and Breakfasts: New England*. She was the principal contributor to the *Eyewitness Guide to New York*.

Patricia Brooks, a longtime freelance travel and food writer, has lived in Connecticut since 1956. She has authored or co-authored 16 books and writes frequently for national US magazines. Since 1977 she has been the food critic for *The New York Times*' Connecticut Weekly section and writes its weekly Dining Out column of restaurant reviews.

Helga Loverseed's work has taken her to 165 destinations in her 23 years as a travel journalist and photographer. She has won awards both for her photography and her writing, has contributed to six travel guides, and is a travel columnist for several leading newspapers and magazines.

Pierre Home-Douglas has worked as a travel writer and book editor since the late 1980s. His articles on subjects ranging from bicycling through Vermont to sailing up the Nile have appeared in many newspapers and magazines. He has also written for *Great Railway Journeys of the World* and *Explore America*.

For Dorling Kindersley

Senior Publishing Manager Louise Bostock Lang
Publishing Managers Kate Poole, Helen Townsend, Jane Ewart
Project Editor Marcus Hardy
Art Editor Nicola Rodway
Editor Simon Hall
Designers Elly King, Nikala Sim
Map Co-ordinators Dave Pugh, Casper Morris
DTP Maite Lantaron, Jason Little, Conrad van Dyk.
Picture Researcher Brigitte Arora
Production Michelle Thomas, Marie Ingledew
Design & Editorial Assistance Sam Borland, Katherine Mesquita, Lynne Robinson
U.S Editor Mary Sutherland
Researcher Timothy Kennard
Revisions Emma Anacootee, Brigitte Arora, Claire Baranowski, Tessa Bindloss, Sherry Collins, Anna Freiberger, Rhiannon Furbear, Jo Gardner, Eric Grossman, Vinod Harish, Mohammad Hassan, Vincent Kurian, Esther Labi, Kim Foley Mackinnon, Carly Madden, Nicola Malone, Martha E. Mayne, Sam Merrell, Catherine Palmi, Helen Partington, Amir Reuveni, Ellen Root, Sands Publishing Solutions, Azeem A. Siddiqui, Susana Smith, Brett Steel, Rachel Symons, Helen Townsend, Ros Walford, Hugo Wilkinson
Contributors Tom Bross, Brett Cook, Patricia Harris, Carolyn Heller, David Lyon, Juliette Rogers, Kem Sawyer
Photographers Demetrio Carrasco, Linda Whitwam (Additional photography: Peter Anderson, David Lyons, Ian O'Leary, Angus Oborn, Clive Streeter)
Illustrators Stephen Conlin, Gary Cross, Richard Draper, Chris Orr & Associates, Robbie Polley, John Woodcock
Maps Ben Bowles, Rob Clynes, Sam Johnston, James Macdonald (Colourmap Scanning Ltd)

Thanks To

Philippe Arnoldi, Danny-Pierre Auger, Rosemary Barron, Lorraine Doré, Joey Fraser, Dominique Gagné, Pascale Hueber, Solange Laberge, Rob Lutes, Edward Renaud, Odette Sévigny.

Special Assistance

Sam Ankerson, Shelburne Museum; Amy Bassett, New Hampshire Parks and Recreation Division; Janel Blood, Concord Chamber of Commerce; Don Boccaccio, The Quality Group; Nancy E. Boone, State of Vermont Division for Historic Preservation; Becky Bovill, R.I. Tourism Division; David Bush, Karen Miller, The Mark Twain House; Andrea Carneiro, Melissa Fanny, Preservation Society of Newport County; Heidi Clarke, South County Tourism Council; Katherine Fox, Destination Salem; Hope Jordan, Currier Gallery of Art; Margaret Joyce, New Hampshire Office of Travel and Tourism Development; Lauren Kedski, Providence Warwick Convention and Visitors Bureau; Valerie Kidney, New Brunswick Tourism; Sharon Kotok, Strawbery Banke; Linda Levin, Connecticut Dept. of Environmental Protection-Parks Division; Pierre L'Heureux, Dawson College; Renny Loisel, Greater New Haven Convention & Visitors Bureau; Amanda C. Lowe, Massachusetts Office of Travel & Tourism; Caroline Marshall, Greater Portsmouth Chamber of Commerce; Brenda Milkofsky, Wethersfield Historical Society; Wanda Moran, NPS-Acadia National Park; Mike Morand, New Haven and State Affairs Department of Yale University; Sue Moynahan, Marianne McCaffery - NPS - Cape Cod National Seashore; Dr. Virginia Nixon, Liberal Arts College, Concordia University; Amy O'Brien, Greater Boston Convention and Visitors Bureau; Michele Pecoraro, Plimoth Plantation; Greg Gerdel, Vermont Department of Tourism and Marketing; Janice Putnam, Susanna Bonta, Old Sturbridge Village; Jessica Roy, Maine Office of Tourism; Janet L. Serra, Litchfield Hills Visitors Bureau; Tim Shea, Burlington Chamber of Commerce; Sherry Smardon, Greater Hartford Tourism District; Evan Smith, Jan Hagerstrom, Newport County Convention and Visitors Bureau; James R. Spencer, Connecticut Department of Transportation; Amy Strack, Massachusetts Office of Travel and Tourism; Paulette Weaver, Lakes Region Association; Katrina White, North of Boston Convention and Visitors Bureau; Leah Wiedmann, Portland Convention and Visitors Bureau; Tricia Wood, Sarah Fisher, Mystic Seaport Museum; Mary Woods, The Coastal Fairfield County Convention & Visitor Bureau; Janie Young, Canterbury Shaker Village.

Photography Permissions

Dorling Kindersley would like to thank all those who gave assistance and permission to photograph at their churches, museums, hotels, restaurants, shops, galleries, and other sights too numerous to list individually.

Picture Credits

t = top; tl = top left; tlc = top left centre; tc = top centre; tr = top right; cla = centre left above; ca = centre above; cra = centre right above; cl = centre left; c = centre; cr = centre right; clb = centre left below; cb = centre below; crb = centre right below; bl = bottom left; b = bottom; bc = bottom centre; bcl = bottom centre left; br = bottom right; d = detail.

Every effort has been made to trace the copyright holders and we apologize in advance for any unintentional omissions. We would be pleased to insert the appropriate acknowledgments in any subsequent edition of this publication.

Works of art have been reproduced with the permission of the following copyright holders:
Arts of the West Thomas Hart Benton © T.H Benton and R.P Benton Testamentary Trusts/DACS, London/VAGA, New York 2006 202cr; *Stegosaurus* Alexander Calder © ARS, NY and DACS, London 198cr. Courtesy of FLORENCE GRISWOLD MUSEUM: *The Harpist, A Portrait of Miss Florence Griswold*, Alphonse Jongers, 1903 216tl.

ADVANCED DIGITAL PHOTOGRAPHY.COM: John W. Hession/ Christopher P. Williams Architects 260clb; ALAMY IMAGES: Mary Liz Austin 10cra; Clair Dunn 258bl; Dynamic Graphics Group / Creatas 11tr; EcoPhotography.com / Jerry and Marcy Monkman 374tc; Glow Images 10bl; Andre Jenny 331tl; AROOSTOOK STATE PARK/Bruce Farnham: 299tl; BARNEY'S NEW YORK: Curtis Liscotti 356br; BOSTON BALLET: Farnsworth / Blalock Photography 364cr; BOSTON POPS ORCHESTRA: Michael Lutch 350bc.
ROBERT CHARTIER: 388bl; BRUCE COLEMAN INC., NEW YORK: Mark Newman 4bl; Gene Ahrens 1, 226, 300/301; John M.

Burnley 249; Jeff Foott 268/269; Carolyn Schaefer 380/381; CORBIS: John L. Amos 29c; Archivo Iconografico S.A.: 35 tr; Bettmann: 29tl, 28cl, 28c, 28br, 30c, 30br, 37t, 38t, 42bl, 43cl, 44cr, 44br, 45bc, 47bl, 48 bl, 48br, 71br, 120b, 128/129, 142b, 253t; Burstein Collection: 39br; Steve Jay Crise 41br, 47bl; Edifice, Philippa Lewis 56c; Kevin Fleming 28tr, 352tl, 364bl; 384cr; George Hall 390b; Historical Picture Archive: 36; Anne Hodalio 29 br; Robert Holmes 31t, 102; 330cla; Hulton-Deutsch Collection: 29bl, 47t, 48tr, 267c; Todd Gipstein 30tr, 47br; Farrell Grehan 30bl; Kelly-Mooney Photography: 32bc; Lake County Museum: 38b; Magma: 25t, 28bl, 29cl, 37b, 45tl, 46cr, 47c; John-Marshall Mantel 31br; Francis G. Mayer 40-41c; Gail Mooney 357tl; David Muench 40tr, 273cb; Greg Nikas 351tl; Reuters Newsmedia Inc.:120t, 352b, 352b, 385; Bill Ross 387t; Bob Rowan/Progressive Image: 28cb; Alan Schein Photography 11bl; Phil Shermeister 34t, 394; Joseph Sohm 40bl, 43bc; Paul A. Souders 41cr; Ted Spiegel 35br, 350cl; Peter Turnley 29tr; CONNECTICUT STATE PARKS DIVISION: 219tl, 219br.

MARY EVANS PICTURE LIBRARY: 8/9, 9c, 31c, 38c, 39t, 39cl, 39bc, 40tl, 41t, 42tl, 42c, 43tc, 43cr, 44t, 44cl, 45cr, 46t, 47tr, 48c, 129c, 301c, 381c.

FOXWOODS RESORT CASINO: 302c; GETTY IMAGES: Photonica/ Doug Plummer 331c; GOOD NEWS CAFE: Charles Heyman 328cr; GRANGER COLLECTION, NEW YORK: 51 (inset); 81b.

HARVARD UNIVERSITY ART MUSEUMS: © President and Fellows of Harvard College, courtesy of Fogg Art Museum, Alpheus Hyatt Purchasing and Friends of the Fogg Art Museum Funds Kneeling Angel Gian Lorenzo Bernini, c.1674-1675 – 114cr; courtesy of the Busch-Reisinger Museum, Gift of Sibyl Moholy-Nagy, © DACS, London 2006 Light-Space Modulator, Laszlo Moholy-Nagy, 1930 – 114b; courtesy of Fogg Art Museum, The Hervey E. Wetzel Bequest Fund Christ on the Cross between the Virgin and Cardinal Torquemada and St. John the Evangelist Fra Angelico, c.1446 – 115b; courtesy Fogg Art Museum, Bequest: Collection of Maurice Wertheim Skating, Edouard Manet, 1877 - 115cl; HISTORIC DEERFIELD, INC./Amanda Merullo: 163b; DAVE G. HOUSER: 130tr, 178/179; HULTON GETTY COLLECTION: 76b.
INSTITUTE OF CONTEMPORARY ART, BOSTON: Iwan Baan 82;

PHILIP C. JACKSON: 131br, 169, 171b, 180cl, 182tr, 182tl, 182c, 183tl, 184tl, 184tr, 184cr, 184br, 185tl, 185c, 185br, 186tr, 187tr, 187cr; KILLINGTON, VERMONT: 382bl; KORTENHAUS COMMUNICATIONS: 328bl; LANGHAM HOTELS: 81tr; JAMES LEMASS: 70br, 72, 95crb; DAVID LYON: 303bl.

MAINE OFFICE OF TOURISM: 21bl, 23tr; Gary Pearl 23c, 131tr, 295b, 303br; THE MARK TWAIN HOUSE: 130bl, 200bl, 201tl; MARTIN PHOTOGRAPHY: 148b; MASSACHUSETTS OFFICE OF TRAVEL AND TOURISM/Kindra Clineff: 20tr, 32t, 356tr, 373cr, 374br, 376b, 377b, 378c; MUSEUM OF FINE ARTS, BOSTON: HU-MFA Expedition Shawabtis of Taharka 52b, 106t; Bequest of Mrs. Beatrice Constance (Turner) Maynard in Memory of Winthrop Sargent Revere Silver Teapot 106ca; Egypt Exploration Fund Inner Coffin of Nes-mut-aat-neru 106cb; Picture Fund Dance at Bougival Pierre-Auguste Renoir,

1883 – 107t; Ruth and Carl J. Shapiro Colonnade and Vault John Singer Sargent Murals 107c; Francis Bartlett Donation of 1900 Head of Aphrodite, Greek Late Classical or Early Hellenistic period –107b; Tompkins Collection 36.270 Where Do We Come From? What Are We? Where Are We Going? (1897-1898) Paul Gauguin 108br; George Nixon Black Fund Ewer and basin 108t; M. and M. Karolik Collection of American Paintings, 1815-1865, by exchange, Boston Harbor Fitz Hugh Lane 108c; Maria Antoinette Evans Fund Babylonia: Nebuchadnezzar II 109t; Gift by Contribution Horse, early 8th century, China 109c; Richard Norton Memorial Fund Fragment of fresco from villa at Contrada Bottaro 109b; MUSEUM OF NEW HAMPSHIRE HISTORY/ Bill Finney: 259t. NANTUCKET ISLAND CHAMBER OF COMMERCE/ Michael Glavin: 32cl. NEW ENGLAND AQUARIUM: 91 cra; Bob Kramer 90t/b, 91t. DAVID NOBLE: 50–51

OLD NORTH CHURCH:, BOSTON: 87cl; OLD STURBRIDGE VILLAGE/Thomas Neill: 130cl; OMNI PARKER HOUSE: 74clb.

LAURENCE PARENT PHOTOGRAPHY, INC: 2/3, 146/147, 274; PEABODY MUSEUM OF ARCHAEOLOGY AND ETHNOLOGY/ HARVARD UNIVERSITY: © President and Fellows of Harvard College 1976. All Rights Reserved. Photos Hillel Burger 116c/b. PHOTO RESEARCHERS INC.: WORLDSAT INTERNATIONAL INC. 12br; THE PRESERVATION SOCIETY OF NEWPORT COUNTY: 186c, 186b, 187tl, 187b; PRIMO RESTAURANT: 328tc; PROVIDENCE WARWICK CONVENTION & VISITOR'S BUREAU: Marianne Groszko 176cra; 383t.

RED LION INN: Kristian Septimius Krogh 303br; RIALTO RESTAURANT: Peter Vanderwarker 328bl; ROCKLAND-THOMASTON AREA CHAMBER OF COMMERCE/Richard V. Procopio: 33tr; ROSE FARM INC: Robert M. Downie 302b;

SALEM WITCH MUSEUM, SALEM, MASSACHUSETTS: Photo courtesy of Tina Jordan 137tl; SEAPORT HOTEL/PETER VANDERWALKER: 304b; SPRINGFIELD SCIENCE MUSEUM, SPRINGFIELD, MA./DINOSAUR HALL: 162tr; STATE OF NEW HAMPSHIRE DIVISION OF TRAVEL AND TOURISM DEVELOPMENT: 378tl; David Brownell 372cl; Nancy G. Horton 329c; Craig Alness 373bl; Jeffery E. Blackman 374cl, 377t; STOWE MOUNTAIN RESORT/CHUCK WASKUCH: 378b; Don Landwehrle 379tr; STRAWEBERY BANKE MUSEUM: 254tr; 255tl.

JACQUES DE TONNACOURT: 181cr; TOPHAM PICTUREPOINT: 53tr; THE UNION-NEWS AND SUNDAY REPUBLICAN/David Molnar: 161br; USFWS PHOTO: 19tr. VERMONT DEPARTMENT OF TRAVEL AND TOURISM: 49cr, 237b; VICTORIA MANSION, Portland, Maine: Photo by J. David Bohl - Dining Room Victoria Mansion (1858-1860), Original furnishings by Gustave Herter, New York, 1860 280bl. YALE CENTER FOR BRITISH ART/Richard Caspole: 223t; YALE UNIVERSITY OFFICE OF PUBLIC AFFAIRS: 222t.
FRONT ENDPAPER: All commissioned photography with the exception of BRUCE COLEMAN INC: Gene Ahrens tl; LAURENCE PARENT PHOTOGRAPHY, INC: tr.
JACKET
Front – CORBIS: Bob Krist; main image; DK IMAGES: David Lyons clb.; Back – ALAMY IMAGES: Chad Ehlers tl; Andre Jenny, cla; clb, bl. Spine CORBIS: Bob Krist t; DK IMAGES: b.

All other images © Dorling Kindersley.
See www.dkimages.com for further information.

SPECIAL EDITIONS OF DK TRAVEL GUIDES

DK Travel Guides can be purchased in bulk quantities at discounted prices for use in promotions or as premiums. We are also able to offer special editions and personalized jackets, corporate imprints, and excerpts from all of our books, tailored specifically to meet your own needs.

To find out more, please contact:
(in the United States) SpecialSales@dk.com
(in the UK) TravelSpecialSales@uk.dk.com
(in Canada) DK Special Sales at
general@tourmaline.ca
(in Australia)
business.development@pearson.com.au